The Best of SPORT 1946–1971

THE BEST OF **SPORT**

1946 - 1971

EDITED BY AL SILVERMAN

NEW YORK · THE VIKING PRESS

First published in 1971 by The Viking Press, Inc.
625 Madison Avenue, New York, N.Y. 10022

Published simultaneously in Canada by
The Macmillan Company of Canada Limited

SBN 670-15907-7

Library of Congress catalog card number: 74-162659

Printed in U.S.A.

Acknowledgments: MYRON COPE: "Alex Karras: 'Right or Wrong, I Say What I Think'" by Myron Cope, copyright © 1966, Myron Cope. "Boxing's Artful Brothers" by Myron Cope, copyright © 1963, Myron Cope. CURTIS BROWN LTD.: "Lineup for Yesterday," by Ogden Nash, copyright © 1949, Ogden Nash; reprinted by permission of Curtis Brown Ltd. TOM DOWLING: "The Lesson of Syracuse" by Tom Dowling, copyright © 1971 by Tom Dowling. BILL FURLONG: "The Price of Fame for Bobby Hull" by Bill Furlong, copyright © 1966 by William Barry Furlong. PAUL HEMPHILL: "How Jacksonville Earned Its Credit Card" by Paul Hemphill, copyright © 1970 by Paul Hemphill. ROGER KAHN: "The Ten Years of Jackie Robinson" by Roger Kahn, copyright © 1955 by Roger Kahn. "The Crucial Part Fear Plays in Sports" by Roger Kahn, copyright © 1959 by Roger Kahn. "Willie Mays, Yesterday and Today" by Roger Kahn, copyright © 1969 by Roger Kahn. "Lew Alcindor's Life as a Pro" by Roger Kahn, copyright © 1970 by Roger Kahn. THE STERLING LORD AGENCY: "Are You All Right, Smoke?" by Al Hirshberg, copyright © 1967 by Al Hirshberg. "Tom Landry, God, Family, and Football" by Gary Cartwright, copyright © 1971 by Gary Cartwright. "Pro Football's Dropouts" by Roger Rapoport, copyright © 1971 by Roger Rapoport. "Muhammed Ali Then and Now" by Dick Schaap, copyright © 1971 by Dick Schaap. All reprinted by permission of the Sterling Lord Agency.

"Without heroes, we are all plain people
and don't know how far we can go."
—Bernard Malamud, *The Natural*

An anthology of this nature is the product of the interest, cooperation, and enthusiasm of a large number of people. Among the many who helped me through twenty-five years of *Sport,* I would particularly like to thank Cork Smith of The Viking Press for his patience, inspiration, and understanding. I would also like to thank Francine Boren, Sandra Forman, and Lydia Paglio for helping me amass the material. And I owe special thanks to the authors and agents who graciously granted permission to reprint the selections that constitute this book.

Contents

Illustrations

Introduction

In June of 1946, another great war having wound down some nine months earlier, I was standing by the side of a dusty road in rural Arkansas composing a song to myself. *This is the night for music, this is the night the moon is full. This is the night I fell in love . . . but where, where are you?* Although the lyrics were powerful, the music was truly beautiful. One of the many regrets of my life was that I failed to pass this song on to Julie Styne or Sammy Fain or Harold Arlen or Frank Sinatra. I think it might have gone all the way.

I had been discharged a few hours earlier in Texas and had made it through Texarkana into Arkansas with little difficulty. I was wearing my Navy blues and hoping that someone with sufficient patriotism and gratitude would stop for me and carry me a few more paces north. But now I had been thumb-tripping in the same spot for hours and all there was by the side of the road was sand and scrub and a near-empty pre–World War II highway—and me and my duffel bag and my music.

The song was developing splendidly when a car pulled up. There were two Marines inside, and the driver said, "We're going to Lawrence, Mass., kid." Thrilling words, since I came from Lynn, Massachusetts. But I had this girl in New York. I said I would ride with them, if it was okay, to New York City.

They let me off two days later in the middle of 42nd Street, facing the East River. I hustled out of the car, jumped over to a Bond's clothing store, and bought a brown tweed suit for thirty dollars because my girl had never seen me in civilian clothes and I wanted to surprise her and show her that I was essentially the tweedy type.

Destiny was awash that day. In an office building a few doors down from where I had been let loose into the free world, a nest of scientists was huddled over drawing boards, plotting out a new magazine, which would be called *Sport*. The founders felt that postwar America was ready for such a magazine. In the first issue they enunciated "ten planks cut from its editorial platform." The chief plank stated that "*Sport* will stress the human interest side of people in athletics. . . . it will concentrate, when it can, on human drama."

I didn't see that pioneering issue until many years later. In the fall of 1946 I was too busy trying to adjust to civilian life. I enrolled in Boston University. A couple of months later, messing through a magazine rack, I chanced upon a copy of *Sport,* the first time I had seen the magazine. Tom Harmon was on the cover. He was standing by the stands in his Los Angeles Ram uniform, holding hands with his pretty wife, the actress Elyse Knox. The Harmon story was titled "The Truth about Tommy Harmon." (Much later the editors found out from Harmon himself that he absolutely detested being called "Tommy.") The cover didn't grab me but I was very interested in learning the truth about Tommy Harmon. So I bought the magazine. And a connection was made.

Another connection came about a year later when I submitted a short item to *Sport* for its front-of-the-book potpourri column called "Sport Talk." A few days later I received a check for ten dollars. My first sale as a writer!

At that time of course I had no idea my destiny would be intertwined with that of *Sport* magazine. I knew I wanted to be a journalist of some kind—but sports?

As a boy I had loved sports—I loved to play sports, and I envied my contemporaries who were the sports heroes of our town. Also, I rooted desperately for the local teams, who were then mostly losers. I followed the Boston Braves, for instance, with the hopeless passion of a Cyrano.

But never in my most rococo dreams did it occur to me that I might someday make a living from sports. My father, after all, was a tailor. He had never had time to play at sports, let alone earn money from sports (except on those infrequent occasions when he scored a "hit" on the numbers or at the racetrack). Besides, I had literary pretensions. As a boy I had been set afire by Thomas Wolfe, that hungry Gulliver who stomped out of North Carolina determined to swallow up all experience whole. Wolfe in those days was a sorcerer to young men; he turned them on far out of proportion to his rank as a novelist today. In this McLuhanesque age, the cool prevails. Thomas Wolfe, apostle of heat, is dead.

But then—in the thirties and forties—he drove the young onward, to seek Wolfe's stone, his leaf, his unfound door.

And so it was that I found myself in New York City looking for a job in journalism. I would take anything. I just wanted a start. Besides times, in 1950, were tough. The job I finally found was with *Sport* magazine. All of a sudden I was working on 42nd Street, hard by that Bond's clothing store, working in a field that had consumed me as a boy. But now I was an adult, who saved all copies of the *Saturday Review* and the *Partisan Review*. Was this the fulfillment of the American dream? I was embarrassed.

I got over that embarrassment long ago as I came to make discoveries about sports and the relationship of sports to our society, as I began to understand that sports and what is called the American Way parallel each other endlessly, that sports, like art, also imitates life.

As much as sentiment might move me to include "The Truth about Tommy Harmon," it will not be found in this volume. Rereading the story recently, I saw, with some sorrow, not only stylistic lapses but truth imperfectly served. My aim here, seizing the perspective of twenty-five years, is to offer stories that contain truths about the subject and stories that also help illuminate the age in which they were written. Roger Kahn, one of the keenest observers of sports in America (his four contributions within are testaments to his perceptions), has written, "Clearly, sports is significant. . . . It is a theater of truth and it holds up a mirror to society and humanity."

Great things have taken place in our country in the last twenty-five years. And monstrous things, too. Prosperity spreads, but so do the poor. Population swells, but wisdom declines. Government rules, but with enfeebled power. Our leaders cry peace, but wage barbaric war. Technology in the last twenty-five years has run amok, leaving behind in its awesome advance reeling institutions. And sports, suffering, at the very least, humanity's sympathy pains, has run alongside, holding up a mirror to reflect that theater of truth in all its dimensions.

The fact is, sports in the last twenty-five years has run very competitively against rampant technology. Our athletes of today are bigger and stronger and faster and richer and, on the whole, more heroic than the athletes of any other era. The golden age of sports they called the 1920s, the years of Jack Dempsey and Babe Ruth and Bill Tilden and Red Grange and Bobby Jones. Fine athletes all, fine gentlemen, too. But fall back, baby, before Rocky Marciano and Muhammad Ali, Ted Williams and Willie Mays, Pancho Gonzales and Rod Laver, John Unitas and Jim Brown, Arnold Palmer and Jack Nicklaus. The golden age of sports is laid on us now.

What helped perpetuate the mythology of sports in the 1920s were the sportswriters of that time. Paul Gallico, who was once one of them, called them the "Gee-whizzers." They were the suckers, he said, "for the theology of the good guys and the bad guys." There is a sample or two in this volume. Grantland Rice was perhaps the most eminent gee-whizzer of his time. ("Outlined under a blue gray October sky, the Four Horsemen rode again." That sentence, written in 1925 to describe the Notre Dame backfield, is easily the most famous sports lead ever written.) In *Sport*'s early days, Grantland Rice was the Bernard Baruch of the magazine, an elder statesmen who kept to his own vision of sports and who lent dignity and prestige to the new magazine. Rice's "My Greatest Thrill in Sports" is a fair example of the gee-whiz genre, evocative of a past age, but not far from the sentiments of the immediate post–World War II period.

But now we are in the midst of the *new journalism.* A few years ago the new journalists in sports came to be known as "chipmunks." The nickname is of uncertain derivation, but it came about from a group of then young New York sportswriters who began to look at sports as fun and games and not necessarily life and death. The most representative chipmunk-type repartee that we can think of came the day the New York Yankees were celebrating their 1962 World Series triumph over the San Francisco Giants. It is the custom of *Sport* magazine to award a new automobile to the Most Valuable Player of the World Series. In 1962 that man was Ralph Terry, who pitched the decisive victory. In the locker room after that game, as he was being informed of his prize, Terry was called to the phone. It was his wife, who had to tell him how happy she was for him and also that their new baby was coming along fine.

As soon as he hung up, a reporter asked, "What's your wife doing?"

"Feeding the baby," said Terry.

"Breast or bottle?" asked a chipmunk, at the ready.

What is the new journalism? Jack Newfield, an enthusiastic practitioner, explains it as "advocacy, complex detail, personal feeling." Writing in the *Dutton Review,* Newfield allowed that the new journalists "have exploded the old, impersonal, objective journalism school formulas, to get closer to the human core of reality . . . to be more than 'clerks of fact.' " Newfield mentioned W. C. Heinz as one of the pioneers of the new journalism and cited Bill Heinz's story on Rocky Graziano in *Sport,* written in 1952, which you will find here and which does indeed typify the new journalism at its earliest and also at its very best.

So this book has gee-whizzers and new journalists and also writers who resist classification. If there is any sense of unity at all in these pages it comes from the way the magazine, the writers, and the athletes themselves changed with the times. And unity perhaps from one other element—heroism.

We have divided the book into four parts to coincide with the epochs of the last twenty-five years. The postwar years, 1946 to 1950, were the years of recovery. In the very first issue of the magazine, what more appropriate cover subject than the postwar Joe DiMaggio (peering out of that cover with four-year-old Joe, Jr., beside him) struggling to regain his baseball legs and bring order to his private life?

If there was one other major sports movement in this period, it was the boom in college football. The jocks were returning to college in vast numbers, undergraduates who should have been well into their professional careers. It made for lusty competition and no team competed with more lust than the Notre Dame of Frank Leahy, Johnny Lujack, and a squadron of All-Americas.

The euphoria of postwar America all came to an end with the dawn of the Holy Television Empire. It is only logical to suggest that television's course may have been set way back then, when two of its most highly rated sports turned out to be wrestling and the roller derby.

Part Two concerns a different type of euphoria, that of the 1950s, the Eisenhower years, the quiet decade, a very good breeding period for sports. Only in such a time could there have been created the ultimate college hero. His name was Doak Walker and he became a mythic figure in Texas and a Jack Armstrong everywhere else. Because of changing circumstances it would be impossible to conceive of a Doak Walker coming to flower today. He was our last All-American American.

But it wasn't entirely a sleepwalking period. In 1954 the Supreme Court delivered a historic decision that, in theory at least, opened up white schools to black children. In the 1950s sports opened up to the Negro athlete. These were the years of Jackie Robinson and, near the end, the years of Floyd Patterson and Oscar Robertson.

The era came to a perfect show-stopping finale the day Ted Williams played his last game, which was a little over a month before the election of John F. Kennedy. Williams had been a prewar hero, a postwar hero, a cosmic hero of the 1950s (after all, not only had he interrupted his career to fly in World War II but he flew once again in Korea). And now he was to go out with a flourish, by hitting a home run in his last time at bat. He was also to go out in character, by refusing to tip his cap as he rounded the bases. Our man, Ed Linn, approached Williams in the locker room afterward and asked him quite innocently, "Didn't you have any feeling that it might be nice to go out with a show of good feeling?"

"I felt nothing," Williams said.

"No sentimentality? No gratitude? No sadness?" Linn asked.

"I said *nothing*," Ted said. "Nothing, nothing, nothing!"

So much for the 1950s.

And, suddenly, life began to speed up. Part Three spans only 1961 through 1965, because too much was happening too fast, too much in life, too much in sports. The New Frontier came in and our vision of ourselves expanded, and sports expanded too, and there was excitement and hope and energy and some love, and there was direction at the top. Why, the President himself not only looked like an athlete but even spoke and acted like an athlete. Arnold Hano quotes John F. Kennedy as saying, "I can't hold back the stops. I have to go flat out, all out." And he did, until it ended with the assassin's bullet in the back of the neck. A cover we ran in March 1964 neatly signified the closing of Camelot and the opening of Armageddon: One cover line read, "John F. Kennedy: His Legacy to Sports"; the face on that cover was that of Cassius Clay.

Well, life *is* transient as well as unfair. The last story in this volume concerns Muhammad Ali, formerly Cassius Clay, about to become the former heavyweight champion of the world. Ali is a remarkably fitting symbol of the last tumultuous five years in sports because he epitomized the emancipated athlete. And in these five years, when Ali was at the center of things even when he wasn't allowed to fight, others were being emancipated—the white athlete, the Spanish-American athlete, the black athlete, the hippie athlete, the free-thinking athlete. There was even a breakthrough in sex as it came to be known that athletes as a whole liked sex, a fact of life that had been repressed by the gee-whiz-zers and others over the years.

Many stories in Part Four reflect this fight for independence, ex-pressed perhaps best in the title of the Alex Karras story: "Right or Wrong, I Say What I Think." And the athlete's lib movement continues under maximum thrust into the 1970s.

Maximum thrust. That is what it is all about in sports. What is John F. Kennedy's "I have to go flat out, all out," but the cry of the athlete testing his manhood (remember that not only one's livelihood is con- stantly at stake in sports but also one's manhood)? The athlete must try to remain true to himself. And that truth, as we have said, is encom-passed in the word called heroism. In the end, big-time sports is the act of heroism constantly repeating itself, and the effects of heroism on the heroes. So this book is essentially about heroes. It is about past heroes, present heroes, failed heroes.

Since sports does so slavishly imitate life, we do, alas, come upon failed heroes. Hank Thompson, a member of the New York Giants baseball team from 1949 through 1956, described in his 1965 article for *Sport* what he would like to do when he got out of jail after serving his ten-year sentence for armed robbery. He said he would move to Fresno, where his mother, a missionary in the Church of God in Christ, lives, and he would help her with her calling. Thompson left jail in 1968 and died less than a year later at forty-three, a victim of failed dreams.

The hero in sports often becomes the victim but the beauty of sports, for the spectator surely, is that the hero is replenishable. Especially now. We are living in an age when heroes and heroic acts are accelerat-ing in sports. Heroes abound everywhere. The next twenty-five years in sports, assuming civilization survives, will celebrate the achievements of a Bobby Orr in hockey, a Lew Alcindor in basketball, a Johnny Bench in baseball, a George Foreman in boxing, a Jim Plunkett in football— and others who are yet nameless but who are pushing up from the ground like the first flowers of spring. Heroes abound. Let us hope that Menander was exaggerating when he said that "barren countries pro-duce the most heroes."

Certainly there *is* a barrenness in sports today. There is still too much intolerance, too much greed, too much self-indulgence, too much meanness, too much cruelty. But there is rich promise, too. We live in the most dangerous age ever for mankind, but our awareness of the danger offers us the most opportunity. There is still the chance for the greening of the land.

The paradox holds in sports. Recently, one of the contributors to this volume, Murray Kempton, wrote an essay in *The New York Review* on "jock-sniffers." Reviewing certain sports books, Kempton used the occasion to emphasize the brutishness and inhumanity involved in sports, especially football. But Kempton ended up, like all of us, as a fan. "Still," he wrote in his last paragraph, "how to dismiss that joy of the game . . . ?" How, indeed? Sports, whatever its shortcomings, still has the magic to enrich for us that landscape which bears such a close resemblance to the life we all live.

AL SILVERMAN

Part One | 1946–1950

The Story of Big and Little Joe DiMaggio

Tom Meany | **1 9 4 6**

This is the story of the DiMaggios, of Big Joe and Little Joe. It is the story of a father and his son, but it's a little different from the average father-and-son story. You have to understand Big Joe first, before you can understand the relationship. And understanding Big Joe takes some doing, because Joe isn't one for talking much about his troubles.

You have to go back a bit to get the full story, back to the summer of 1942, when the Yankee Clipper, visibly unstrung by rumors that all was not well between him and his wife, was vehemently denying all reports. It was evident, however, that Jolting Joe was himself being jolted. This was a new experience for DiMaggio. Until the summer of 1942, he had sailed serenely through baseball, playing it as though the game had been invented for his benefit. Pennants and world's championships fell to his lot, as did batting titles and home-run crowns. The rifts between Joe and the former Dorothy Arnold, whom he met when both were cast in the movie *Manhattan Merry-Go-Round,* were patched up, but each time the rifts grew longer and the periods of amity, shorter. Then, too, there was the matter of a world war on Joe's mind. Life, which once had been simple and pleasant for Joe, was rapidly growing more complicated.

Despite the general belief that DiMaggio's chronic ulcers would exempt him, Joe didn't wait for his draft board. He enlisted in the Army. While DiMaggio was discovering that army life, even in the U.S.A., was vastly different from life as the Yankee Clipper, he and his wife were divorced.

DiMaggio must have done a lot of thinking, deep thinking, during his three years in the Air Forces. He missed his baseball and, no doubt, his baseball pay, but most of all he missed his wife and his son.

DiMaggio came out of the service a chastened and more mature man. Back in New York last winter, Joe made one more desperate effort to bring back the life he had known before. He spent as much time with Dorothy and Little Joe as he could arrange, and there were many who anticipated an early re-marriage. When it didn't come off, Big Joe turned all his affection on Little Joe, visiting him at the nursery school when he could, having him over to Yankee Stadium when ever possible.

Little Joe became a familiar figure around the Yankee bench, almost from the time the season opened. Many fans began to look for Joe's kid regularly. They liked to see this tiny four-year-old out in front of the dugout, playing catch with himself, tossing a ball a few feet into the air and then making vain attempts to catch it.

One day this spring Little Joe was outdoing himself, catching the ball perhaps one time in four, although the fielder's glove he wore was as big as his navy-blue sweater. In addition, he had on a regulation baseball cap and a man-sized catcher's mask. DiMaggio knelt on the top step of the dugout and watched the youngster's efforts with affectionate amusement. Joe McCarthy, who was then still the Yankee manager, came out of the tunnel from the dressing room and paused for a moment beside DiMaggio.

"Get that mask off him and give him a bat, Joe," advised the skipper. "No DiMaggio looks right unless he has a bat in his hands."

"That's right, Joe," chimed in Bill Dickey, the manager-to-be, who was seated nearby strapping on his shin-guards. "Tell the kid to shed those 'tools of ignorance.' It's a mistake to ever put 'em on—I know." DiMaggio grinned widely. Sensing, as kids will, that he was the subject of the conversation, Little Joe turned and surveyed the bench. "You don't know me," he declared in an insistent, childish treble. "I'm not Little Joe—I'm a ballplayer!"

Joe beckoned his son to toss the ball to him, but before his fond parent could toss it back, Little Joe had dropped his mask, cap, and glove and, after tugging at the bat rack, produced a bat some inches taller than himself. Brandishing the bat as best he could, Little Joe called, "Throw, Daddy, throw!" Nick Etten, Yankee first baseman, grinned and said, "Now the kid looks natural."

Little Joe, on such days as he visits the Stadium, is a great favorite with the Yankees. And, it may be remarked, so is his old man. The Yankees have a deep, but rarely evinced, liking and admiration for Big Joe whom they unqualifiedly consider the best ballplayer of his generation. DiMaggio often has been pictured as taciturn and reserved, sometimes even as sullen. He has been called a dead-pan from one end of the American League to the other. But if you ever saw him cast a doting eye on Little Joe, you'd never again think of Big Joe as a dead-pan.

Joe's obvious affection for his offspring has more than once been a topic of conversation on the Yankee bench. One teammate put it this way: "Joe loves Little Joe more than he does his base hits!"

Coming from a ballplayer, that really means something. Base hits, in case you don't already know, are the bread and butter of a ballplayer's existence. A ballplayer who isn't getting his quota of base hits is quite likely to growl at his wife and snarl at his best friends. Some ballplayers won't admit they're in love with their base hits, others make no bones about it.

Joe Medwick, the former Cardinal slugger, never hid his affection for his base hits, sometimes making public demonstrations of indignation when the official scorer had called an error on a ball that he thought should have been declared a base hit.

Mike Gonzales, veteran Cardinal coach, used to kid Medwick about his passion for base hits. "Who your best friend is, Joe?" Mike would ask in his own peculiarly fractured English which has resisted more than three decades of baseball in this country. "Base hits," Medwick would reply unhesitatingly. And he wasn't kidding. Thus, when a teammate speaks of DiMaggio having a deeper affection for Little Joe than he has for his own base hits, it is intended as a compliment. And received as such.

Joe's affection for his son is, I believe, accentuated by the fact that the path of true love hasn't run smoothly. It has run, in fact, up hill and down dale and, occasionally, around corners. Joe has been denied the privilege of a normal father-son relationship with Little Joe. During game trips, weeks, sometimes months, will pass without Joe seeing his offspring. Later, father and son will be together almost daily until the Yankees take to the road again.

These conditions undoubtedly have magnified Joe's affection for his son, an affection which is equally strong in the grandparents of Little Joe. Pop and Mom DiMaggio, who live in San Francisco, attach a characteristically Old World importance to their male grandchild, the successor to the DiMaggio dynasty. Big Joe has come out of his troubles a stronger man. Nobody, save one who has been through it, can appreciate the mental turmoil of domestic strife. Today he centers his love upon his son.

One of Joe's favorite stories about the boy concerns a day last September when, on final leave from the Army, he brought Dorothy and Little Joe to a game at Yankee Stadium. As Joe, in his sergeant's uniform, made his way to a box behind the Yankee dugout, he was preceded by Mrs. DiMaggio and Little Joe. The fans, of course, recognized the Clipper immediately, and he was greeted on all sides with shouts of "Hello, Joe," "Welcome home, Joe," "Wotta ya' know, Joe," etc. Little Joe, of course, heard all these salutations, and he turned to his pop with amazing gravity and complacency, for one a month short of his fourth birthday, and remarked, "See, Daddy? Everybody knows me!" Right then and there, DiMaggio was convinced that he was the sire of a potential star on the Quiz Kid program or maybe, even, Information Please.

Outside of his obvious devotion to his son, DiMaggio keeps his emotions well under control. He is neither communicative nor articulate, and sportswriters found him a tough nut to crack when he first showed up at a Yankee camp ten years ago. First impressions were unfavorable. His unwillingness to talk was put down as stubbornness or sullenness, with a touch of swollen ego.

Actually, Joe is neither stubborn, sullen, nor swell-headed, but he is shy. Even after all these years of stardom, he has a hesitancy about committing himself to newspaper quotes. He has an absolute horror of being taken for a pop-off and, stoically, is willing to be known as a dead-pan instead.

Among friends, Joe can let the bars down and be entertaining. His fellow Yankees swear by him, not only as a great ballplayer, but as a friend and companion. The fact that Joe is a target for flashlight bulbs at every stop the Yanks make rouses sympathy, rather than jealousy, among his fellow players who can understand the trials of stardom.

Like Bob Feller, Ted Williams, Pete Reiser and the other name players who went into service, it is hard to estimate DiMaggio's true worth merely by comparing it with the records of older stars of the game. Records no longer are a reliable yardstick when measured against years of uninterrupted ballplaying on one hand, and, on the other, against records which show a three-year gap at the very time when they might have been the most productive.

The Yankees, as a team, believe that DiMaggio is the greatest ball-player they have ever seen. Even when his playing falls off as it did this year due to his being tired as a result of a grueling pre-season exhibition series in the sweltering heat of the Canal Zone, they still rate him as great. Veteran sportswriters who traveled in the days of Babe Ruth and Ty Cobb are swinging to that opinion, too. Even among the old guard there is a breakdown, noticeable when one of the old-timers, in picking an all-time, all-star team, breaks up the ancient outfield trinity of Ruth, Cobb and Speaker and drops Joe into Speaker's place.

Despite his batting slump, DiMaggio was named to play in this year's All-Star game. But he sprained a knee, which put him on the shelf, not only for that tilt, but for most of the Yankees' mid-season home-stand. This injury came at a tough time, just when the old Clipper was starting to belt the horsehide as of old.

To give any athlete the absolute superlative is to invite a storm of criticism. Ted Williams is a greater batsman than DiMaggio, just as Babe Ruth was undoubtedly a greater home-run hitter and Ty Cobb a more dynamic player. Joe's trick is that he can do all things well and all things easily. The fact that he goes about his duties with such an air of nonchalance is, in the eyes of other ballplayers, the final testimony to his greatness, yet, for the layman, Joe's effortless grace serves often to blanket his true worth.

For an idea of DiMaggio's place among the ballplayers of today, you have only to listen in on their shop talk once in a while to discover that Joe is being used as the standard. For example, when the Pasquel brothers from Mexico were dangling their pesos before Pete Reiser of the Dodgers, the newspapers proclaimed it an attempt to snare "the Di-Maggio of the National League."

One of the Yankees' war-time acquisitions, who was seeing Di-Maggio for the first time last spring in the Canal Zone, decided that Joe must have the magnifying eyes of a horse to be able to follow a pitched ball so well and to hit it so solidly. "The ball must look like a grapefruit to Joe," this player remarked. "There is no other explanation for his being able to get so much of his bat on every pitch."

Prior to entering the Army, DiMaggio played seven seasons with the Yankees and they won six American League pennants and five world championships. They might have won these pennants without Di-Maggio, of course, but they didn't suffer any from having him on the ball club. In 1940, the only season the Yankees didn't win the pennant, Joe led the American League in hitting.

In his last year with the Yankees, 1942, before entering service, Joe had what was for him an off season. He batted "only" .305, a figure which some players spend a lifetime in baseball trying to achieve. Yet, so great is the respect in which DiMaggio is held by his mates that they made apologies for him that season. "Most of that season, Joe wasn't carrying a bat up to the plate," explained one of the Yankee vets. "He was carrying a torch."

The reference, of course, was to the still-tangled marital status of the DiMaggios. Little Joe was not yet a year old, and already there were rumors of divorce. Joe protested that everything was serene. The impending divorce didn't come off. Joe and his wife patched things up in September with the result that the Yankee Clipper played brilliantly all during the World Series, even though the Cardinal speed-boys ran away with the ball games.

Whether Little Joe ever will be a professional baseball player, let alone a great star like his daddy, remains to be seen. Joseph Paul, Jr., achieves the ripe old age of five this October 21, and even Branch Rickey isn't signing 'em that young.

Few if any youngsters, however, ever shared the close association with big-league baseball that Little Joe has now. Under the terms of the divorce, each parent was supposed to have the custody of the child for six months. But Joe, who was in the Army when the decree became final, waived his rights, insisting that, as long as he and Dorothy were friends, the mother should bring up the child, provided he could visit the boy whenever he felt like it.

Judging by the repeated appearances of Little Joe at the stadium, and Big Joe's visits to the nursery school, he wants to see his son every day, for which he can't be blamed. Sons of big leaguers now following in their father's footsteps are few, Jim Bagby with the Red Sox, Charley Gilbert with the Cubs, and Dick Sisler of the Cardinals, being the only big leaguers today pursuing their fathers' profession. Yet it never would do to sell the DiMaggio brothers short when it comes to playing base-ball.

There are, in the major leagues, only sixteen center fielders and two of them are named DiMaggio, brother Dom being with the Red Sox. A third brother, Vince, was with the Giants until mid-season. That's a pretty fair family representation.

Physically, Little Joe is a dead ringer for his pappy, the same searching brown eyes, the same profile. The one exception is the youngster's hair, fairer than Joe's and a sort of reddish brown, a concession to the blondness of his mother. Students of heredity would be quite interested if they could see Little Joe struggling with a bat at Yankee Stadium some afternoon. If any DiMaggio is worried about his game, it's not the little fellow. He looks natural, assured of himself, and perfectly at home.

My Greatest Thrill in Sports

Grantland Rice | **1947**

When you have looked at some ten thousand contests and competitions for over forty-six years, selecting your leading thrill or thrills is not easy.

In my case, these contests and competitions include baseball, football, racing, boxing, golf, polo, tennis, track and field, rowing, basketball, swimming, diving, billiards, field hockey, soccer, and hunting and fishing—to mention only a few. From this extended list, I would say that baseball, football, racing, boxing, and golf have provided the largest share of pulse-lifters.

All games have their thrills. I can still recall the excitement I felt when Little Bill Johnston and Big Bill Tilden were meeting at Forest Hills. Their series of championship tennis matches, between 1920 and 1925, have never been surpassed for skill and thrill combined.

When one looks back down the long years that gave us Babe Ruth, Ty Cobb, Shoeless Joe Jackson, Tris Speaker, Walter Johnson, Grover Cleveland Alexander, Cy Young, Nap Lajoie, Frank Frisch, Rogers Hornsby, Christy Mathewson, Mike Donlin, Honus Wagner, Hal Chase, Addie Joss and so many others, it is easy enough to see how many unforgettable thrills must have come from the ball field.

My two leading baseball thrills were provided by Walter Johnson and Babe Ruth, with the Big Train from Washington slightly in the lead.

I was sitting in the press box that day in Chicago during the World Series of 1932 when the overpowering Babe called his famous home run off Charlie Root. The crowd was riding the Babe, and the Babe was riding both the crowd and the Chicago Cubs.

There were two strikes called on the Babe that afternoon, with the big crowd roaring, when Ruth suddenly stepped to the plate and pointed to the pole in center field. On the next pitch, the crack of bat meeting ball sounded like an explosion of nitroglycerine. The drive, not too high, kept its course until the ball disappeared from sight beyond the wall. It was the most dramatic hit in baseball history.

But I had an even more extended thrill that day in Washington, in 1924, when Walter Johnson (Old Barney) finally got his revenge. Bucky Harris' Senators were playing John McGraw's Giants that afternoon in the seventh game of the World Series. Johnson, who had never drawn a World Series chance in his prime, had been beaten twice in that series. He had been the big flop instead of the leading star.

The Senators seemed to be beaten until they tied it up in the eighth inning and I'll never forget the tidal wave of human voices that greeted the Big Train as he slouched to the box to face the McGrawmen in the ninth inning. He was to have another chance. It was in this inning that the great Frank Frisch struck a triple off Johnson with only one out. But Old Barney rallied, struck out Kelly, and went on to retire the side.

For three more innings, the greatest pitcher of them all, now well over the hill, held the Giants in check. He struck out four men in these three innings and repulsed every Giant bid. As the last of the twelfth came along, the darkening shadows indicated that the game would soon have to be called. But destiny, in the shape of a loose catcher's mask tangled with Hank Gowdy's feet, made Hank miss a high foul from Muddy Ruel, now manager of the Browns.

After that, Ruel doubled and came home on a hit by Earl McNeely to give Johnson his first World Series victory in a series of thrills that lasted for over an hour. The king had mounted his throne at last.

Then I recall the day at Pimlico when Seabiscuit was matched against War Admiral in the Pimlico Special, November 1, 1938, run off at Baltimore, Maryland.

This was my greatest racing thrill. As the two famous rivals passed the big crowd on their way to the starting line, War Admiral carried all the looks and dash. Head up and prancing, War Admiral was the perfect picture of a sure winner. Seabiscuit looked bedraggled. And the odds on the big tote board indicated War Admiral was the odds-on favorite at 1 to 4.

As the two horses broke, the crowd got its first shock. It wasn't War Admiral who rushed to the front. It was Seabiscuit, by a good two lengths. The crowd was stunned. But War Admiral soon drew alongside and once again the noisy gathering saw Seabiscuit's certain defeat.

The two might have been one horse outlined against an autumn skyline as they traveled the backstretch together. Nose and nose, then inches apart, they came into the head of the stretch.

It was here that the gallant Seabiscuit, probably the most romantic horse of all time, began to pull away. Charlie Kurtsinger called on War Admiral for all he had to give. But the veteran Biscuit went on to win in a killing finishing rush with something to spare.

Turning to the gridiron, it is only natural that some five hundred football games, going way back to the late 1890s, should have given me enough thrills to last several lifetimes.

From Los Angeles to Boston, from Minneapolis to New Orleans, from New Haven to Texas, they have been packed with palpitating, spine-tingling episodes.

From the long list I can't recall a greater thrill than the famous contest between Notre Dame and Ohio State back in 1935 at Columbus.

Ohio State, with a great team that fall, was leading 13 to 0 at the end of the first half. The showdown came in the final period when Notre Dame, led by the spectacular play of halfback Andy Pilney, finally struck. Notre Dame, as I recall, was trailing 13 to 6 with only three minutes left. On a spectacular eighty-yard march, Notre Dame scored again, with Pilney running wild and the Irish passes clicking.

But once again Notre Dame failed to kick the extra point, so Ohio State held the lead at 13 to 12 with less than a minute left. There were just forty seconds on the clock. Ohio State had possession of the ball at midfield. The odds at this point against the South Bend gridders were at least 1000 to 1. All Ohio State had to do was run four line plays and the game would be over.

But once again destiny stepped in. Ohio State fumbled her first running play. Notre Dame recovered. There was time enough for just three more plays. It was the kind of situation that you think is phony when you see it in the movies.

Bill Shakespeare hurled a long desperate pass to his tall teammate, end Wayne Milner. There wasn't a chance in the world that Milner could catch it—but miraculously he did. And that turned the trick, in one of the greatest surprise thrillers in football history. Final score— Notre Dame 18, Ohio State 13.

Golf has given me many thrills, especially in the days of Bobby Jones, Walter Hagen, and Gene Sarazen. Of all the high-spots, I'll pick the 1922 PGA championship, which brought Sarazen and Hagen together in the final round at Pelham, New York.

These two great golfers had battled on even terms for thirty-seven holes. Coming to the second extra hole, the thirty-eighth, a short dogleg affair, Hagen's great drive stopped just off the green, over three hundred yards away. Sarazen's hooked drive crashed into a tree bordering the out-of-bounds limit. It barely fell in bounds, over a fence, but the ball was in a young wheat field.

I was standing with Hagen at the time, only thirty feet from the cup with a shallow trap intervening. The odds in his favor then were 50 to 1. But from that waist-high grass, Sarazen's pitch hit the green and stopped only two feet from the cup. This unexpected recovery was a knife in Hagen's heart, and no golfer I ever saw had a bigger or a stouter one. He flubbed his short pitch into the sand and then almost holed his shot from there. Sarazen really earned that victory.

But if I had to pick out one occasion that gave me, and some eighty thousand spectators, the biggest thrill of all time, it would have to be the Dempsey-Firpo fight in 1923 at the Polo Grounds.

Firpo, nicknamed by the late Damon Runyon "The Wild Bull of the Pampas," looked outclassed. He was big, slow, crude, without even the semblance of boxing skill and a left hand that was like a feather duster.

Firpo was as clumsy as a man with two left feet. But he did have two worthwhile qualities in the ring—a stout heart and a long, rubber right arm with a stunning fist attached. As Bill Brennan said: "He throws rocks at you."

Dempsey took one good look at the shaggy-looking brute, over six feet, weighing 220 pounds, and decided that the quicker he could end this party, the better it would be for him.

I was sitting in the first row, at the middle of my section, exactly where Dempsey came through later on. The ring had been raised for the benefit of the crowd, making any fall from it much more dangerous. Just before the fight started, I moved a few feet over to be nearer my wire.

The first ten seconds of this fight packed more thrills than most fights

ever produce in a far longer period. Dempsey came out in a hurry and
threw a left hook at Firpo's body. If it had landed, it would have been a
one-punch knockout. But it missed by a fraction, and in return, Firpo
nailed Dempsey on the chin with that paralyzing right.

Dempsey went almost to his knees. He admits that he remembers little after that punch.

Jack was badly dazed, but he still was guided by one of the greatest
fighting instincts the ring ever saw. Coming out of his half-stupor,
Dempsey tore into Firpo and knocked him down. As Firpo got halfway
up, Dempsey knocked him down again. "I wasn't fighting for the championship of the world, or a million dollars," he told me later. "I was
trying to keep from being killed. I have only a vague idea what happened after that first punch."

Dempsey knocked Firpo down repeatedly. Twice Firpo went down
without taking a punch as Dempsey's left hook barely grazed his hairy
stomach. The crowd, already in a wild uproar, was looking for the kill
any second. But an even greater thrill was just ahead. Swinging his long
right again, half punch and half shove, Firpo sent Dempsey spinning
through the ropes. Jack came through head down, and only self-pro-
tecting (and, possibly, Dempsey-protecting) hands saved him from a
stunning jolt and a certain knockout.

The crowd of eighty thousand saw the champion of the world dangling head down through the ropes. But only a few actually saw all that
happened, for the big mob, standing up, began fighting, shoving, and
pushing for a better view. The crowd, even those close to the ring, was a
milling mass of people gone completely mad. One well-padded spectator near the front had an apoplectic stroke, collapsed, and rolled into
the aisle. Another spectator jumped on his prostrate body to get a better view. The police couldn't control them.

Dempsey was still hanging, head down, through the ropes.

Even today, no one can say definitely how long the old Manassa
Mauler was out of the ring. Possibly seven or eight seconds. Possibly
ten or twelve.

Half shoved and half scrambling, Dempsey finally got back inside
the ropes. But he was still too dazed to start any attack. His legs wob-
bled.

He leaned against the ropes, swaying from side to side as Firpo threw
wild punches at his head and chin. None of these landed, and the first
round ended.

It is impossible to recapture in words the wild, three-minute thrill
that began with Firpo's first jolting punch and ended with his last wild

swing. The swift drama of each moment made this first round the most famous spot in all of boxing's annals.

I was sitting next to Bob Edgren, a famous ring expert and a veteran writer and observer. Even Edgren could not follow the swift and varied action that left us all confused. Dempsey himself can tell you little about it. I talked with Jack only a few months ago. "It was all a blur to me," he said. "And it is still a blur. All I know is that I wouldn't want to be back in that ring again through that first round."

The second round was short, sharp, and decisive with Dempsey in complete command. No one ever recovered as quickly as the Mauler from Manassa. He could take as well as give.

You may understand from this round-up why I pick the Dempsey-Firpo meeting as the greatest thrill I've known in almost a half-century of looking at competitive action in the sports arena.

For here was a mixture of action, drama, turmoil, and caveman savagery, with the heavyweight championship of the world, and at least a million dollars, hanging on every second of the 180 seconds that completed the surprising story of what came close to being the most spectacular upset in sport history.

Lujack, Leahy, and Notre Dame

Jack Sher | **1947**

Last November, in the gray light of an early morning, a heavily loaded New York Central train moved eastward through Indiana. It carried among its passengers a football team from the University of Notre Dame. As the train slowed down, moving through a small town, one of the players suddenly sat up straight in his seat and said, "Hey, look!"

"Well, look at that," another added, softly.

Clustered on the station platform and strung out along the track were groups of school kids. Here and there among them were nuns. The kids ranged in age from seven to sixteen. It was not yet seven in the morning. It was cold.

The kids held up two paper banners. One of them read BEAT ARMY; the other, in irregular letters, spelled out VICTORY FOR NOTRE DAME. One of the smaller kids was crying, whether from discomfort, or a rebuke, or emotion, the players would never know. The others were waving and shouting, but their sounds could not be heard over the powerful noise of the train. And then they were gone from sight.

In dozens of small towns all the way from South Bend, through Indiana, Ohio, Pennsylvania, and New York, similar scenes were repeated.

The incident is told to show the emotional tie, the fervent feeling and love that youngsters of Catholic faith have for Notre Dame. It is this phenomenon, more than anything else, that explains how a small, Mid-western school with a normal enrollment of some 3400 students, could become such a colossus on the national sport scene.

For more than two decades, the colorful, victory-laden campaigns of the Notre Dame football team have been splashed across the sports pages of the nation's newspapers. The movies have cashed in on the school's spirit, glamour, and fame. Almost everyone knows the tune and words of the Victory March, has heard about the Golden Dome, can recite the seemingly endless list of the great players who have worn the Blue and Gold. It starts with Rockne and Dorais, goes to George Gipp, the Four Horsemen, Miller, Layden, Crowley, and Stuhldreher, and the stars of more recent years, Frank Carideo, Marchy Schwartz, Jumpin' Joe Savoldi, Moon Mullins, Angelo Bertelli, up to today's sen-sational T-formation quarterback, Johnny Lujack, and the team's famed hard-driving coach, Frank Leahy.

Long before the plane on which I was riding revealed the dazzling sight of the Golden Dome beneath its wings, there were many questions crowding my mind about Notre Dame. Questions that had grown through the years, that went back to street-corner arguments, heated controversies, rumors, and opinions. And questions of the present, the condition of the team, the reputation of the coach, Frank Leahy, the stories about players, Lujack, Connor, Strohmeyer.

If I've ever seen a loaded team, this 1947 Notre Dame squad is it. They are virtually the same bunch that won eight games last year, lost none, and battled the West Point Cadets to a scoreless tie. Opening against Pitt on October 4, they should win in a breeze and go on to take them all, including their toughest opponents, Southern Cal, Army, Iowa, and the Navy.

At left tackle the All-American, George Connor, will still be standing like a rock. So will the bruising, buoyant center, George Strohmeyer. On the flanks will be two sophomore ends who are rated among the best defensive men in college football, Leon Hart and Jim Martin. At left guard is the All-American play-stopper, Bill Fischer. On the other side of the line is his rugged mate, Joe Signaigo. The only position in the first-string line that's still open is right tackle, and it can be filled by any one of a half-dozen veterans, including Ziggy Czarobski, Johnny Fallon, Ralph McGehee, and Wilmer Russell.

That's the line Doctor Blanchard tried last year and diagnosed as the toughest he had ever faced. "Mr. Outside," Glenn Davis, voted the same ticket after trying unsuccessfully to leg it around the ends—and ending up on his.

In the backfield, the Connellsville Comet, Johnny Lujack, should reach new heights handing 'em off from the T-quarterback position. There was talk last spring of switching him to halfback, in order to allow him to lug the ball. Spectators at spring practice were surprised to see Lujack working out in the running position. Up to this year, he's done little ball-carrying, winning his All-American laurels on his masterminding of the team, his beautiful ball-handling, his passing, and his superb defensive play. But Johnny can also run with a ball, and would like to prove it.

If Lujack does any half-backing, Frank Tripucka and Pete Ashbaugh are Grade A quarterbacks. The other halfbacks are tried and proven men. All of them showed more stuff last spring on Cartier Field than they did in the stadiums a year ago. Big Bob Livingstone should go strong, and Terry Brennan, Larry Coutre, Fred Earley, Emil Sitko, and if his knee gets back into shape, Ernie Zalejski, are all threats.

Then there is a small, five-foot-nine-inch Texan who scales some 165 pounds, who may become the surprise of the year—a twenty-year-old phantom named Coy McGee. At fullback, John (Pep) Panelli is a powerhouse, and he's backed up by the equally fine rookie, Floyd Simmons.

These are the names you'll be hearing on the air and seeing in the stadiums all this month and next. These are the boys who are out to sweep the field for Notre Dame. It doesn't seem possible that any collection of eleven men in the country, short of the pro ranks, can possibly stop them. It is the strongest Notre Dame team since the 1941 champions, a team on a par with the Rockne-coached unbeatables of 1924, 1929, and 1930.

One of the reasons why it's such a hot team is the twenty-two-year-old, six-foot, 180-pound Lujack. The kid who wears the number 32 on his broad back has already earned a place among Notre Dame's all-time greats.

As a sophomore, eighteen years old, Lujack won varsity monograms in four major sports—football, basketball, track, and baseball. That has been done only twice before at Notre Dame, by Rupert Mills and Dutch Bergman.

Although most of Johnny's fame has been gained by his stunts in a football uniform, he is as good, if not better, on a baseball diamond. Even as a high-school player, he showed enough class to get an offer from the Pittsburgh Pirates. At the end of his first football season at Notre Dame, Lujack became a first-string guard on the basketball team. Spring came around and he by-passed baseball to go out for track.

When the Notre Dame nine dropped five in a row, coach Jake Kline persuaded Johnny to join the team as right-fielder in a game against Western Michigan. What Johnny did that day will be long remembered at Notre Dame. He belted three hits, and led the ball club to a 3 1 victory. Between innings, still in his baseball uniform, Lujack trotted to an adjacent field and won the javelin throw in a track meet against De Pauw. He might have won the high jump, one of his specialties, but his baggy baseball jeans knocked off the bar at five feet ten inches.

The things about Johnny Lujack that have made him a great quarterback are his defensive play, his sharp passing skill, his feeling for the tempo of an offensive, the speed with which he can run plays, and the intelligence he shows in picking them. Against Iowa Pre-Flight, in 1943, he sent his team through thirteen plays in four minutes and thirty seconds, shooting a back at the Iowa team once every twenty seconds. In his first three games as a first-string quarterback, he completed eighteen out of thirty-nine passes for a total of 287 yards.

Nobody has ever tried to count the number of crucial tackles Lujack has made during his football career at Notre Dame. Those who saw the Army game last year will never forget the spectacular shoe-string tackle he laid on Doc Blanchard in the closing moments of the game. Those on the field, knowing Johnny, never doubted he would make it.

A Lujack pass was intercepted on the Army fifteen by Tucker, who ran it back to the thirty-seven. All afternoon, Blanchard had been trying to break through the Notre Dame line and, on the first play after the interception, he did. Big Doc broke around end and headed down the sideline, completely in the clear. Lujack, with his usual deadly instinct, had seen the play coming. He cut across the field, the only man who had any chance at all of waylaying a back who was almost never stopped in the open. Blanchard thundered down the sidelines, while seventy thousand spectators held their breath, and Lujack closed in. Johnny hit him like something shot out of a rifle, right at the ankles. Doc went down on the Irish thirty-seven-yard line, and he went down hard.

An endless amount of copy has been written about Johnny Lujack's phenomenal feats on the football field. It is unusual, almost fantastic, that so little has been revealed about his background, his kid days in a rugged, hilly, small, railroad town in the Western Allegheny mountains —days that went into molding, in mind and body, an athlete of tremendous skill and heart. It is strange that this part of Lujack's life has been touched on so lightly. It is a story filled with warmth and drama, American earthiness and color.

In essence it is the story of a hard-working, struggling Polish family, their love and their dreams for their youngest son, Johnny. Most of it was told to me by Johnny himself, and part by his life-long friend, Henry Brown, who grew up just around the corner from where the Lujack family lives in Connellsville, Pennsylvania, population seventeen thousand.

Let's begin with meeting Lujack in the lobby of a Chicago hotel one day last summer. He and Brown were on their way to spend a few weeks in Evanston, Illinois, where Brown now lives. Johnny had come East from Connellsville, where he had spent the early part of the summer, home with his family, helping his father, John, Sr., repaint their house.

It is usually a fairly simple thing, even for an untrained eye, to pick out a football player among a group of average citizens. Their size, the way they walk, something in their manner, makes both pro and college players easy to spot. But you wouldn't pick Lujack as one. You might spot him as an athlete, because of the fine build, broad shoulders, and the athlete's walk, the bouncy step. But he doesn't look like a football player.

Lujack is an unusually handsome young man, a fact which photographs seldom reveal. He has dark, wavy, brown hair, a strong, sensitive face, light-brown eyes, a mild, friendly smile. He is extremely well-poised, talks easily and intelligently, and has, as his teammates, teachers, and student friends will tell you, a quick sense of humor.

Coach Frank Leahy mentioned Lujack's sense of humor in telling a story about a conversation on the train coming home from the '46 Army game. During the game Arnold Tucker, the Army quarterback, had intercepted three of Lujack's passes. Leahy, remarking about this, said, "Tell me, John, why did you throw so many passes to Tucker?"

"Coach," Lujack grinned, "he was the only man open."

There have been rumors, as there always will be about star performers, that Lujack has a king-sized head, swollen from the ever-increasing fan mail he gets (some fifty letters a day, many from girls) and his loaded scrapbooks. It doesn't seem to be true. There is nothing of the big-time-operator in his manner. The boys who play with him ridicule the idea, all of them pronouncing him a regular guy.

"Johnny," an Irish guard said, "has a lot of confidence, but not a swelled head. We have the same confidence in him. He always knows what he's doing out there."

One of the Notre Dame players did admit he thought Lujack made a bad mistake during the Army game last year, a decision that might well have cost them the ball game. It was Notre Dame's only chance to score, after a long, pounding series of drives down the field.

Jerry Cowhig started the march by picking up six yards on two tries. Then Lujack sneaked around right end for five yards and a first down. Cowhig, Gompers, and Panelli cracked through for another first down on the Notre Dame thirty-four-yard line. Johnny then tossed a beautiful twenty-five-yard pass to Skoglund that put the ball on the Army forty one.

Gompers shot through guard for another nine yards. Cowhig took a shovel pass from Lujack and drove down to the twelve-yard line. The fans were roaring. On the next play, it was Cowhig again, for another two yards. Then Gompers cracked the Cadets for six more, bringing the ball to Army's four-yard line as the Notre Dame partisans began going crazy.

It was third down coming up. Lujack decided to switch strategy. He called a quarterback sneak. The entire Army line rose up and smothered him cold. Then Johnny called Gompers wide around right end, but big Hank Foldberg chased him out of bounds on the three-yard line, ending Notre Dame's only real chance to score. It was implied at the time, by some sportswriters, that Lujack called that quarterback sneak to grab the glory of scoring. It's true it was not a particularly wise choice, but nobody on the team really felt Johnny was trying to become the afternoon's hero.

"I was sore at the time," the Notre Dame player who criticized him said. "But it wasn't because I figured Johnny was trying to be a star and win the game by himself. If the play had worked, it would have been swell. I just thought, and still think, it was a bad choice. But the guy was in a spot and it's awfully easy to second-guess. He's a right guy, he plays for the team, and he's got a wonderful record for calling 'em right."

Lujack, in the tradition of most Notre Dame field generals, is a quarterback who believes in taking chances. He took a big one in the opening period of the Pittsburgh game last year. Some have said it was because Johnny's temper got the better of him, but those in the game said Lujack just decided to pull a surprise.

The way it happened, Johnny was penalized fifteen yards for clipping, a judgment he thought was completely unfair. The ball rested on the Notre Dame one-yard line. Lujack dropped back, ostensibly (and reasonably) to kick. Instead, he suddenly threw a long pass. It was completed. Three straight passes later, all thrown by Lujack, Notre Dame went over the Pittsburgh goal-line.

Johnny's brother, Val Lujack, saw that game. He saw six out of the ten games his kid brother played last year. Val Lujack is a steelworker. In order to earn the extra money to make the trips to see Johnny play, he worked four hours a night overtime, lugging cement sacks.

Seeing Johnny heave those passes means a lot to the three older Lujack brothers—Val, Allie, and Stan. They taught him how to throw his first ones in the stony backyards and vacant lots of Connellsville. They were all fine athletes. Val, thirty-two, the oldest, starred in baseball and basketball at Connellsville High. Stan was a good enough first-baseman to play minor-league ball, and Allie played left end at Georgetown a few years ago. But, in the youngest of the Lujack family, the "kid brother" Johnny, the older boys knew they had something special.

"I got all the breaks," Johnny will tell you. "My brothers brought me along, taught me all they knew, spent hours training me. Any one of them is really better than I am. It's just that by the time I came along, Dad was in a little better way financially. I was able to spend all my time on sports."

Johnny Lujack, like so many of the great athletes of our country, is the son of a workingman. The Lujacks are of Polish descent. John Lujack, Sr., is a quiet, sturdy, well-liked man who has been a boiler-maker on the Pittsburgh–Lake Erie Railroad for thirty years.

When Johnny was born, on January 4, 1925, there were five other children ahead of him, the three brothers and two girls, Vicky and Dolores. The family was not poor, but life was not easy, either. Every dollar meant a good deal. By 1936, chipping in, the Lujacks were able to buy their first automobile. They still have it. Johnny remembers the year they bought the car. He was eleven and his older brothers used to stack the car full of football players on Saturday and ride to nearby towns to play games. Johnny would hide in the trunk so he could watch Val, Allie, and Stan in action.

"They knew when I hid back there," Johnny grinned, "but they pretended they didn't see me, because Mom would bawl them out for taking me so far away from home."

As Johnny grew older, his brother Al, who was the football star of the crowd, began to teach him how to pass, how to let go long ones, how to shoot bullet passes, how to throw on the run. It got so that the combination of the pint-sized Johnny throwing and Al receiving could make any touch-football game a shoo-in for the Lujacks.

Brown remembered a game in which Johnny threw his brother a pass that Al really had to stretch to nab. Allie came back to the huddle glaring. "What's the matter with you?" he yelled. "You're getting careless."

Johnny looked hurt. Brown edged up to Al and told him to take it easy on the kid.

"I can't," Al said. "I have to talk to him that way. It will make him a better passer."

The work the older brothers put in on the kid paid off. Long before the youngest Lujack went to Notre Dame he was touted around Connellsville as the greatest athlete the town had ever turned out. It began when he was thirteen, playing for Cameron Junior High School. He weighed only 120 pounds but he kicked, passed, and ran circles around kids twenty and thirty pounds heavier. In his spare time he practiced the high jump in a pit his brothers helped him dig in the yard.

At Connellsville High, in 1939, he began a three-year career that made him the most talked-about kid in town. His fame began to spread throughout the state. Connellsville used the Pitt single wing, which stresses power plays and cuts down on passing. But when a game was in the fire it was halfback Johnny Lujack's passing arm that pulled it out. In one game, with two minutes to play, he completed six passes in succession, advancing the ball some ninety yards. He ran back two successive punts against Mt. Pleasant High one afternoon, each jaunt going seventy yards.

In Connellsville they used to say Johnny Lujack had four coaches— the one on the field and his three large brothers, who roamed the sidelines. In the classroom, Johnny was an honor student for two years. He was elected president of the senior class. He wound up his career for his home-town school as captain, guard, and high-scorer on the basketball team, and played a good enough shortstop in the city league to get that bid from the Pirates we mentioned earlier.

The year Lujack graduated from Connellsville High, he had offers of scholarships from thirteen big-time colleges. The Congressman in his district, without telling Johnny, got him an appointment to the United States Military Academy. The people of Connellsville were happy. He'd be the first from their town to attain that honor, their first West Pointer.

At the graduation exercises, the Congressman rose and made the announcement that John Lujack, Jr., had received an appointment to

West Point. When the cheering died down, the eighteen-year-old kid got to his feet, walked to the center of the platform, and made a simple, honest speech the people of Connellsville will never forget.

Here's what Johnny said: "I'm very thankful for the honor you have bestowed upon me, but my heart is at Notre Dame. I wish to complete my education there and, if I can, play football on that team."

Leahy remembers Johnny Lujack's first appearance on Cartier Field. "It seemed," he said, "as though one kid on the freshman team was making all the tackles." Playing in the backfield on the "milk squad," he made life miserable for the varsity. Leahy, who had seen them all— Carideo, Schwartz, Mullins—knew he had a star. The football world didn't know it until one day early in November 1943. Until that time, all eyes were spotlighted on Angelo Bertelli, "the Springfield Rifle," the first Notre Dame T-formation quarterback, and one of the school's greatest passers.

After Bertelli had led the Irish to a 33–6 victory against Navy, in late October of '43, he hung up his football shoes and went into the Marines. The opinion among sportswriters was that his "kid understudy," Johnny Lujack, was a good football player, but that he could never fill Bertelli's shoes. In the dressing room after the Navy game, a veteran writer asked Bertelli what he thought Notre Dame's chances would be after he left.

"Johnny will take over," Bertelli smiled. "And don't worry— Johnny's all right."

Lujack really did fill Bertelli's shoes, not figuratively, but literally. He was still growing, and the day before his debut against Army he complained to the trainer that his shoes were too small. The trainer opened Bertelli's locker, handed Johnny his predecessor's shoes, and said, "Try these on for size." Johnny put them on, trotted around the locker room in them, and said they felt fine. "Keep 'em," the trainer said, tersely.

There is a good deal of drama in an eighteen-year-old boy taking over a powerful team against its traditional rival. It was heightened by the fact that here was a youngster who had only been introduced to the T for one year, and was going to run that complicated system against one of the most rugged teams Army had ever produced. And yet the Notre Dame players didn't have the slightest worry about Lujack. They knew him from Cartier Field.

The day after the Army game, Johnny Lujack's name was spread out all over the sports pages of the nation. The kid from Connellsville had carried the game in the palm of his hand for almost sixty full minutes. He led an inspired Notre Dame team to a 26–0 win, handled the ball with the coolness of a pro, made split-second decisions that hadn't missed, completed eight of fifteen passes, two for TD's. It was in this game that Army learned about Lujack's ability to size up a defense. They also learned about his tackling.

In the last half, Glenn Davis, Army speed merchant, intercepted one of Lujack's passes. He started downfield with two blockers ahead of him. Lujack knocked all three of them down to prevent a score. That day his defensive play alone would have been enough to elevate Lujack to the ranks of great football stars.

One of the things that makes Lujack a great player is that he adheres religiously to the Leahy theory that unless a player improves with every game, he might as well turn in his uniform. To help Lujack's game, Leahy had Sid Luckman coach him all during spring practice this year. Luckman and Lujack are close friends. It's possible that Johnny may be the one who steps into the Bears' quarterback position when Sid leaves. Draft rights to Lujack are held by the Bears in the National League and the Chicago Rockets in the AAC.

"You never stop learning when you're quarterbacking the T," Johnny said. "It's tough to carry out the fakes. I'm always tempted to watch the man who is carrying the ball, see who tackles him, find out what happened. But if a T-quarterback doesn't carry out his fakes, the deceptive quality of the play is often ruined."

At home, Johnny's mother still worries about his getting hurt. The first year he went to Notre Dame, during his second scrimmage at Cartier Field, he got four of his front teeth knocked out tackling halfback Bill Earley, now one of his backfield coaches. Johnny had a fine bridge made, and kept the mishap a secret from his parents all during the war.

The first game his parents saw him play for Notre Dame was the 1943 Michigan game. In the third quarter Johnny was making a hand-off to the Notre Dame fullback. The player temporarily lost his balance and banged his shoulder against Lujack's jaw as he went around him. As soon as the play ended, Johnny dropped down on one knee and called time. The Notre Dame trainer, Scrap Iron Young, rushed out to him.

"What's the matter, Johnny?" he asked, anxiously. "You hurt?"

"Naw," Johnny mumbled. "My bridge just got knocked out. Tell the guys to crowd around me. My folks are up there in the stands and I don't want them to see me putting it back in. They don't know about me losing my teeth."

Once a law student, Lujack will be graduated from Notre Dame this year with a Political Science major. He is one of the best contract-bridge players in the school, a game he learned to play as an Ensign in the Navy. He served eleven months on a sub chaser in the Atlantic, and played service ball at Fort Pierce. Three of his teammates on the Connellsville High team were killed in the war, as was one of his closest friends, Bud Henry.

Bud went to the University of West Virginia, where he was an outstanding athlete. Last summer Johnny met his father on the main street of Connellsville. Lujack didn't know what to say. He remembered how Bud's father had often listened to their boyhood conversations, heard them talking about their dreams of some day becoming college football stars, big-time baseball players. Lujack said he will always remember what Bud Henry's father said to him just before he walked on down the street.

"Johnny," he said, "it's too bad that old Bud can't be here to enjoy your success."

Lujack considers that the most unselfish comment he ever heard.

This year's Notre Dame team, Johnny believes, should be the best on which he has ever played. He thinks that among the standout players will be Pep Panelli, the fullback, Jim Martin, end, and Bill Fischer, guard. He has high praise for three youngsters who have several more years to play at Notre Dame, halfback Ernie Zalejski, end Leon Hart, and a smart fireball of a ball-carrier named Terry Brennan.

To Leahy, Johnny Lujack gives the lion's share of the credit for the great playing years he has had at Notre Dame. He doesn't think anyone in the country, including himself, loves football as much as Leahy, or knows as much about it. Very often, when the going is rough, Leahy will call Lujack aside and ask him if he thinks he's driving the team too hard.

"Well, coach," Johnny said once, "the boys are certainly squawking."

"If they don't squawk," Leahy smiled, "they aren't working hard enough."

But the thing that has sold Lujack on Frank Leahy is his genuine concern for the welfare of the men who play for him, not only on the football field, but in all phases of their college careers and future lives. During the daily meetings from 12:30 to 1:00 p.m., Leahy often asks one of the boys to stand up and give an informal talk to the squad, a speech on something other than sports.

"In later life," Leahy tells them, "you lads are going to be called upon to speak in public. If you learn how to talk here, it will be of great help to you after you leave Notre Dame."

Frank Leahy, of course, is a central figure in any story of Notre Dame football.

"We can have any kind of a team our players want to have. If they decide to rest on their laurels, we can lose four games. But if we work hard and give a little blood, we ought to do all right."

When he said that to me, Frank Leahy was making probably the most optimistic statement he has ever made since becoming a football coach.

Just over his desk, in a small office in the athletic building, was a large photograph of the late Knute Rockne. On Rockne's face was the wide, floppy, friendly grin so characteristic of him. It is Leahy's favorite portrait of the man who taught him most of the fine points of football, the beloved figure under whom Leahy played at Notre Dame.

If you could pick one man to typify Notre Dame football, it would probably be most sensible and honest to choose Frank Leahy. In a sense, he is more representative of the average Notre Dame man than the revered Rockne. For Rockne created the glory and tradition of Notre Dame football. Leahy, like so many other great stars after Rockne, had to live up to the standards, the ideals and the playing savvy and spirit that the Rock established. He has not only had to live up to them as a player, but carry on the Rockne tradition as a coach.

If anything, what Rockne did was easier. He was the Master. He made Notre Dame football. All Leahy has had to do is walk in the gigantic footsteps of what was, undoubtedly, the greatest coaching genius of our time. If he has not done it, he has come closer to it than anyone else.

It is unavoidable to compare the two men. Physically, there is no resemblance at all. Knute Rockne at Leahy's age was a squat barrel of a man, bald-headed, round-faced, with a flattened nose and small, twinkling eyes. Not one of God's most beautiful creatures, a plain-spoken man, as stubborn as the hard Norwegian soil from which he came, he was at times as good-humored as a spring wind.

Leahy, at thirty-nine, is a large, handsome man, well-groomed, as poised and scholarly as Rockne was earthy and simple. He has intelligent, deep-set blue eyes, a strong jaw, a smile that is friendly and completely charming, but does not twist and flop around the way the Rock's did. His voice is soft, well-modulated. His command of language is studied and impressive.

The first impression of Frank Leahy—one that many reporters have —is that nobody could be so charming and gentlemanly without putting on an act. He is, actually, a very sincere man in everything he says and does. His sociability off the playing field is honest. He likes people and wants them to like him. But on a football field his personality changes. He becomes grim, driving, serious, and sarcastic.

Any boy contemplating a football career at Notre Dame should be warned that for every minute of glory he may enjoy, he will pay for it with hours of sweat, grind, and tears. Every player will tell you that the most rugged bodily punishment they take is not during the games on Saturday afternoon, but in the practice sessions on Cartier Field.

"What's the toughest line you ever faced?" I asked a large Notre Dame tackle.

"The second-string line in practice," he answered, without hesitation.

From a perch in a tower just off the practice field, Leahy watches the players below him with hawklike eyes. It's impossible to loaf. Leahy can spot the slightest flaw in a play, and his voice booms out over a loudspeaker, sharp and cutting. "Did everyone see how that boy made that tackle? I don't want anyone to ever make a tackle like that again!" Or, as a back stumbles going through the line, "Well, well, what did you trip over—a chalk-line?"

As the last minutes of the two hours of pounding scrimmage approach, as the legs get heavy and the bodies ache, it is doubtful whether Leahy would win a popularity poll taken among his players. He does not tolerate swearing or dirty play, and he shows not the slightest favoritism toward any of his men. He almost always addresses his players as "Gentlemen"—but no gentleman ever worked as hard as a Notre Dame football player does under Leahy.

The way a GI still remembers his serial number, Notre Dame players probably never will forget Leahy's favorite expression during practice. "Nothing," he reiterates, "is as important as that good, solid thump, thump, thump." And he wants to hear that sound when a tackle is made or a man throws a block.

The language he uses is often amusing to the players. It's a form of the King's English that would be acceptable to even the most pedantic professor. "Gentlemen," he will say, "we will attempt to obliterate our deficiencies." In a pre-game pep talk, when he wants his men to soften up a rugged, unruly opponent, he will remark, quietly, "You will find an enemy there. Please give him a little treatment."

Coaches have left Notre Dame because they couldn't stand the unceasing drive that Leahy demands of them. He expects more of them than he does of his players, often keeping them up until the early hours of the morning, going over plays, talking about opponents, devising methods to improve the team offensively and defensively. Nothing is as important to him as football, Notre Dame football.

During the football season, the last light extinguished on the Notre Dame campus is the one in Frank Leahy's office. Twice during his career at the school, he has worked himself into complete physical and mental exhaustion. Many nights he doesn't even go to his home in Michigan City, fifteen miles away. He curls up on a couch in his office, or walks wearily to the firehouse on the campus, where he stretches out on a cot to snatch a few hours of sleep before morning.

So far, under Leahy, Notre Dame teams have spent very satisfying Saturday afternoons. Losing football games has become almost a novelty for the South Bend school. Leahy's own record of victories can't be matched by any man now coaching. His complete six-year record, including two years at Boston College where he won twenty out of twenty-two games, shows fifty-two wins, only five losses, and four ties.

Even more than a win, Leahy enjoys watching a perfectly executed play. His love for football goes so deep he can even appreciate it when a rival team pulls off a beautifully worked out play. He hates to lose, but if he has to drop one, he likes to feel the loss was justified.

In 1943, Notre Dame tangled with the Navy's Great Lakes outfit, one of the best squads playing service football. It was the last game of the season. Notre Dame had gone undefeated. The game was rugged, dazzling, with both teams playing all-out to win. In the fourth quarter, with only thirty-five seconds to play, Notre Dame led by one point. Then Steve Lach of Great Lakes pulled a quick fake, dropped back, and tossed a beautiful pass to Paul Anderson, who went over to win the game for Navy 19 to 14.

The Notre Dame squad huddled dejectedly in the dressing room. The play had spoiled what would have been another undefeated season for Notre Dame and Leahy. The coach came into the room and looked around. Then he said, "You can feel proud of the way you played. You happened to be beaten by one of the most splendidly executed plays I've ever seen. I have no criticism to make of you for this game."

It has often been said that Leahy's respect for opponents sometimes reaches the ridiculous. He has a reputation for being the most pessimistic coach in the country. Father Cavanaugh, head of the school, has an amusing story he tells about Leahy's cautious comments and dire warnings.

At the close of a successful season, with a powerful team returning in the fall, Father Cavanaugh visited Leahy's office. He entered the room, closed the doors, and with his characteristic sense of humor, made sure all the windows were locked.

"Now, Frank," he said, "nobody can possibly hear us. Tell me, what are our chances for next year?"

"Well, Father," Leahy said, "they are all going to be tough. We can lose any of them. But I will say this: I believe we'll beat Pittsburgh and Illinois."

Father Cavanaugh couldn't, in spite of prodding, get Leahy to admit the possibility of any more than these two victories. When the season opened, the Pittsburgh team held a tough opponent scoreless in the first half. That night Leahy telephoned the priest and said, "Father, do you remember what I said about my believing we will beat Pittsburgh?" The priest said he did. "Well, Father," Leahy said gloomily, "you hadn't better count on that."

The final score was Notre Dame 41, Pittsburgh 0.

Actually, Leahy is not a pessimist. It is impossible for a perfectionist, such as he is, to be a down-in-the-mouther. What he really is, by his own admission, is a worrier. It is not what his own team will do that worries Leahy, it is what the other team might do—the unexpected breaks that can happen on any football field.

Leahy's pre-game fears were undoubtedly inherited from years of association with Knute Rockne. It was not a Rockne policy to be gleefully optimistic before any game.

The pessimistic attitude was probably just one of Rock's many tricks. If so, it is one that Leahy has borrowed, used effectively, and will go on using. A Leahy-coached team never goes into any game brimming with over-confidence. If they were playing his home-town high school in Winner, South Dakota, Leahy would probably warn his men to expect trouble.

Today, walking the campus at Notre Dame, you still feel Rockne. There has been a memorial built to him, a thing of steel and stone, but that is not what has kept him so alive in the hearts of those at Notre Dame. The stories about him are legion, and the men who played for him still carry and pass on the inspiration he gave them. But that is not entirely it either. The thing that keeps Rockne so beloved by youngsters coming up, by those who never even knew him, is their knowledge of his love for the school, for Notre Dame. They know how much it meant to him, and that's what gets them.

The closeness of Leahy and Rockne has not been exaggerated. In many ways, they had much in common. Both came from poor families. Rockne had to work four years in a post office in Chicago to earn enough to attend Notre Dame. Leahy arrived at the school under much the same conditions. He had to work his way through college.

The son of a homesteader who had moved his large family westward to Winner, South Dakota, young Leahy grew up on the barren plains of a then half-settled state. At the age of six, he rode a hayrake in the field around Winner for a dollar a day. He hauled freight by wagon, clerked in stores, rode herd, sweated in the fields as a day laborer.

Leahy did not arrive at Notre Dame with any great build-up, although he had won three letters at Winner High in football, basketball, and baseball. When the family moved to Omaha, he played for Central High of that city, being switched from halfback to tackle. He was good, a strong man in the line, but not sensational.

Like most Catholic kids, young Leahy knew all about Notre Dame and Rockne. By 1926 the Rockne legend was well-established. It had been growing through the years, since 1913 when a small, unknown school, scheduled as a breather for Army, had swamped the West Pointers 35 to 13. That was the year a couple of brash youngsters, Knute Rockne and Gus Dorais, unleashed a "perfected" forward pass that kept the heads of the Cadets up in the air all afternoon and cut the ground from under them.

That Army-Notre Dame game might have gone down in the sport history books as a fluke. But Rockne wouldn't let it. By the time Leahy reached Notre Dame, it had the best-known football team of any school in the country. Leahy arrived on the South Bend campus one year after hearing Rockne speak at a dinner to which he had been invited by Earl Walsh, an ex-Notre Dame player and his coach at Winner High.

Leahy came to Notre Dame at a time when making the team was as tough as it is today. He made it because he was a plugger, working harder physically than he had ever worked in his life. In 1928 Rockne put him into three games as a center. In '29, the coach shifted him to tackle, where Leahy played a fine, solid game, earning a first-string slot on a team that became national champions. He once even fooled Rockne into allowing him to play with a dislocated elbow, showing the then bed-ridden coach his good arm instead of the bad one.

Injuries dogged Leahy all through his playing career. But it was an injury, a cracked-up knee in the pre-season training of 1930, that gave him the greatest break in his life. Rockne allowed him to help with the

line coaching, and showed him the fine points of training ends and
backfield men. In that one year, Leahy picked up information that few
players at Notre Dame have ever been able to garner. At the close of
the season, Rockne went to the Mayo Clinic for treatment of a leg ailment that had nearly cost him his life. He asked Leahy to go along with
him.

"You might as well get that knee operated on," he said. "And, besides, I'll need company."

What Rockne meant by company was someone with whom to talk
football. All through the long afternoons, while Leahy awaited his operation, he listened to Rockne, in the bed beside him, talk about the game
he knew so well. Leahy asked innumerable questions. Rockne asked
Leahy almost as many, and gave freely of the information he had gathered in his years at Notre Dame.

When Fritz Crisler, then head coach at Minnesota, dropped in to see
him, Rockne introduced Crisler to Leahy. As Crisler was leaving,
Rockne said to him, "Fritz, that boy lying there on the bed is going to
make a great coach some day."

While Leahy was still hobbling around the Notre Dame campus on a
cane, on March 31, 1931, the plane in which Knute Rockne was riding
crashed into a pasture in Kansas. And ten years later, the last boy he
ever coached, the kid who had lain in the bed next to him at the Mayo
Clinic, became the head coach of the Notre Dame football team.

For Leahy, the lowest periods of his life were the months following
Rockne's death, and the first few weeks of his second season as head
coach and athletic director of Notre Dame. After his brilliant beginning
in 1941, in which the team went undefeated, they began the 1942 season
with a tie and loss. It was a sad beginning for what is now the famed
Notre Dame T-formation.

The story of the T at Notre Dame really began at a football game in
1941 between the Chicago Bears and the All-Stars. From the stands in
Soldier Feld, Leahy watched the magic hands of quarterback Sid Luckman explode plays which even Leahy himself could not follow. The
College All-Stars, among the greatest in the country, dived for handfuls
of nothing. In the final twelve minutes of play, Luckman and Company
ran up three TD's in breathtaking style.

"What did you think of the T-formation the Bears were using?"
Leahy asked Father John Cavanaugh, then vice-president of the school,
as they rode back toward Notre Dame.

"It looked mighty good to me," Father Cavanaugh said.

"I'm convinced we should use it at Notre Dame, Father," Leahy said. "With your permission and that of Father O'Donnell, I'd like to put it into effect next year."

Leahy obtained the permission and set out to learn the mystery of the T. All through the pro football season, he haunted Wrigley Field, watching the dazzling performances of the Bears and the razzle-dazzle of Luckman. But the T is complicated. There are too many facets to it to learn much about it from a stadium seat.

In February of '42, three men gathered in Room 455 of the Commodore Hotel in New York. They pushed all the furniture back against the wall and dismissed the bellboy, who thought they were either stewed or screwy. They were neither. One of them was Frank Leahy, who doesn't drink. The second was one of his assistant coaches, Joe McArdle. The third man in the room, holding a football lightly in his hands, was Sid Luckman. Leahy stood a little to one side as McArdle straddled the ball Luckman had tossed to him. He passed it to Sid and the lessons began.

For almost five hours, Luckman whirled through the various pivots that make up the T, the mousetrap, the crossover, the reverse, the counter-pivot, the forward pass. And as he went through the motions he explained, or answered the innumerable questions in Leahy's mind. The lessons didn't end in the hotel room. Leahy rented an empty office on Sixth Avenue, and Luckman went through more drills. It was the beginning of a deep friendship that still exists between the two men.

"Sid was wonderful to me," Leahy said. "He's one of the finest and most intelligent men I've ever known. He was the first to instruct me in the fundamentals of the T, and I don't see how anyone could have done a better job."

From Luckman, the Notre Dame coach journeyed west again to see George Halas, owner-coach of the Bears. Halas gave him more instructions on the basic principles of the T and sent him on to the Bear line coach, the former Notre Dame star, Hunk Anderson. In a Detroit hotel room, Anderson and Leahy spent days on the T in relation to line play. Leahy's last jaunt, just before spring drills in 1942, took him to Maryland, where he indulged in hour after hour of skull sessions with the thin, graying master of the T, Clark Shaughnessy.

"I'm deeply indebted to all these men," Leahy will tell you emphatically. "They gave me all the time and advice I asked. Their help was invaluable."

When Leahy announced that the T was to be used at Notre Dame, it was met with the same reception as an announcement that the Blarney Stone would be removed from Ireland. The tried-and-true Notre Dame shift was as respected and loved as the man who perfected it, Knute Rockne. Leahy knew he was going out on the well-known limb. He expected to be accused of being a fool, an ingrate, an upstart, gambling on an untried system that could lead only to disaster. He was accused of even more than that.

The only answer Leahy gave at the time was to work himself into a physical wreck to get the T down as pat as possible before the opening game. His coaching staff gathered at 5:15 every morning to study diagrams and movies. The quarterbacks, Bertelli and his young understudy, Johnny Lujack, spent long hours in Leahy's office poring over chalkmarks on a blackboard. Leahy worked fourteen hours, then eighteen hours a day. His health began to fail. He got severe pains in the back of his head and neck. He was suffering from spinal arthritis caused, more than anything else, by tension and overwork.

Notre Dame opened against Wisconsin and Leahy's critics gathered to watch the fiasco. Four of the first-string men suffered injuries just before the game. Bertelli took the wrong train in the Chicago Union Station and arrived a scant few minutes before the kick-off, completely unnerved.

The game was not quite a fiasco. It ended in a 7–7 tie, but Notre Dame was such a superior team to Wisconsin that it should have swamped the Badgers by at least three touchdowns. The T is a formation which requires split-second ball handling, speed, and confidence which the green, over-anxious kids completely lacked. They fumbled and stumbled and failed to get under way. The following week, against a stronger Georgia Tech team, they were belted down 13 to 6. The harassers of Leahy and his T-formation had a field day. A loud cry went up for a return to the Notre Dame shift.

Leahy never saw the first successful results of the year he had spent trying to master the T-formation. He was ordered to the hospital by the heads of the school, backed up by his wife, Floss, and his first lieutenant, Ed McKeever. On a bed in the Mayo Clinic, not far from where he had once shared a room with Rockne, he heard a radio announcer describe the clicking of the T as the Fighting Irish ran down Stanford 27 to 0. Leahy began to get well in a hurry. Two victories later, after Notre Dame blanked the Iowa Seahawks 28 to 0, and licked a strong Illinois 21 to 14, Leahy was back.

Navy went down 9 to 0; the Army got whipped 13 to 0. Leahy's T was accepted by even the most die-hard followers of the Rockne system.

The boys who play football at South Bend are an unusual aggregation of young men. They believe, almost to a man, that nothing is as wonderful as playing football for Notre Dame. Most of them have been believing that for a long time, for many years before they enrolled at the school. It is not so much the rah-rah attitude which you find at some schools, as it is a mission and an honor, as though winning a game were something of a crusade.

Any grade-school kid knows the inducements that many big colleges offer to get promising material. Notre Dame does not have to compete in this market. Its recruiting is done gratis, not only by alumni, but by parish priests in small towns and big cities, by loyal followers everywhere, through the simple medium of impressing upon youngsters, particularly those of the Catholic faith, that few things in life are more glorious than playing for Notre Dame.

In talking to the players, the answers you get as to why they came to Notre Dame are strikingly similar. Benny Sheridan, one of the great stars of a few years back, now a salesman in South Bend for a large radio concern, said, "Ninety percent of all the players want to come to Notre Dame for the same reasons I did. My mother and father wanted me to go to the school. The priest in my home town, Havana, Illinois, talked to me a great deal about it, even taking me to see Notre Dame games. From the time I first began to lug a football, I wanted to come to the school."

George Strohmeyer's father was a close friend of Moon Mullins, a great backfield star during Leahy's playing days. When Mullins coached Strohmeyer at Iowa Pre-Flight during the war, he also propagandized for Notre Dame.

Pep Panelli came to Notre Dame in spite of the fact that the headmaster of his prep school in Connecticut urged him to go to Yale, and the mayor suggested Cornell. "Too many other people, closer to me, wanted me to go to Notre Dame," Pep said. "Nothing the headmaster or the mayor said could make me change my mind about playing for a school I had loved since I was a kid."

A good deal of bitter criticism was tossed at the school and George Connor when that All-American tackle, after two years of brilliant play at Holy Cross, suddenly appeared on the Notre Dame roster. It looked like a pressure job, but it wasn't. Connor, influenced greatly by his uncle, enrolled at Holy Cross. During the war Connor was assigned to Notre Dame as a V-7, earning his Navy commission on the South Bend campus. He became so engrossed in the activities of the school, so taken with that intangible quality that is called Notre Dame spirit, that he decided, entirely on his own, to switch to Notre Dame after the war. He knew it would arouse a protest from followers of Holy Cross, but after talking it over with his family, he decided to make the difficult choice.

Almost all of the present Notre Dame players are veterans. Vetville, a collection of pre-fabricated houses just across from the campus, houses 117 families. Returning vets have swollen the enrollment at Notre Dame to some 4600. Students from all the forty-eight states now swarm the crowded campus, gather at the Huddle for malteds, work out in the Rockne Memorial Field House, or play softball at night on Badgin Bog between the dorms, moving over the green field that once felt the feet of George Gipp, Red Miller, Elmer Layden, Johnny Niemiec, and other Notre Dame immortals. Sorin Hall, the oldest building on the campus, the dorm that sheltered so many great players of the past, is still very much in use today, housing young men who a few short years ago were flying B-29s, slogging through Italy, or hunching in foxholes in the Pacific.

Bob Livingstone, a tall, handsome kid who spent three years in the infantry in the ETO, said he noticed a difference in the players when they returned from the war. They all felt an even closer tie to each other, and they were more mature.

From Livingstone himself, the Notre Dame coaches are expecting some great ball-carrying this year. A whirlwind his first year, the three years of pounding his legs took in the infantry slowed him down during the '46 season. It has taken a whole year to get them back into shape, but in practice sessions they finally loosened up and he's beginning to run with the same speed, the same break-away dash that once gave so much trouble to opposing tacklers.

Probably every football team has a character, an unorthodox personality. At Notre Dame it's a barrel-chested, outspoken, cocky but likable Texan named George Strohmeyer. Before any football game, Strohmeyer bounces around assuring everyone within hearing distance that Notre Dame is certain to win by at least five or six touchdowns.

On the way to the Illinois game last year, Strohmeyer was sharing a seat in the Pullman with Father John H. Murphy, vice-president of the university. Just in back of them sat Leahy, worrying, as usual, about the outcome of the game. At one point, he leaned over, tapped Strohmeyer on the shoulder and began warning him about the trouble he should expect from Buddy Young.

"Don't worry about him, coach," the big center boomed. "We'll stop him cold. Why that guy only gets into his pants one leg at a time like all the rest of us."

Father Murphy and the other players burst into laughter as Leahy threw up his hands in despair. But Strohmeyer gets away with his slap-happy boasting because he has always backed up what he says he will do on a football field. In the Army game the huge, beefy center squashed play after play, dumping the thundering Blanchard especially hard. Hurt in the final quarter of the game, Strohmeyer refused to quit, staying in the line, cracking down the Army plungers. On the offensive, Strohmeyer pulls out of the line like a fire-truck and is a top-notch leader of interference.

At Iowa Pre-Flight George started as a fullback, put up a kick when the coach wanted to switch him to center. The Navy mentor listened to Strohmeyer's beef, then said, "Okay, you can stay at fullback and play thirty minutes of the game. If you'll try center, I'll let you play sixty."

"Coach," Strohmeyer said. "You just got yourself a center."

At the end of the season, he was nominated as All Service center and he has played that position ever since.

One of the things the other Notre Dame players like about Strohmeyer is his all-out love of competition and his plain, unadulterated guts. Coach Bill Earley tells about a practice session in which he observed Strohmeyer coming across the field headed for the locker room. Because George is always out there plugging, Earley strolled over to see what was the matter. Strohmeyer took his hand away from his face, at the coach's request.

"Be right back," he mumbled. "Just a little bloody nose."

A piece of bone stuck out through the skin on the bridge of Strohmeyer's nose. Of course, it was broken.

From a dramatic standpoint, nothing touched the story I picked up about the half-pint halfback, Coy McGee.

Coy is a soft-spoken, quiet boy who looks as though he might be a sophomore in high school. Hailing from Longview, Texas, McGee spent the war years in the Air Force, and came to Notre Dame in 1945. He came for two reasons—to go to Notre Dame's famed aeronautical school, and to play football.

"It's a funny thing," he said. "I didn't even know Notre Dame was a Catholic school until two weeks before I enrolled. It wouldn't have made any difference, but some of the fellows sure got a kick out of it when I told it to them. One thing I did know. I knew they had one of the best aeronautical engineering schools in the country.

McGee worked hard on the playing field, but his first year at Notre Dame, the best he could do was make the B squad. Coach Hughie Devore, who had taken over while Leahy was in the Navy, took McGee to the Iowa game. He was injured after a short spell on the field. In the Northwestern tiff, so many of the Notre Dame boys were hurt that the fourth-string McGee was sent into the game again. He carried seven times, averaging six and a half yards every time he lugged the ball.

But in '46, when Leahy came back, McGee was still plugging along on the B squad, being considered too small for duty among the first-stringers. Along came the Army game, and McGee wasn't even taken on the trip. It was a big disappointment to swallow, but when the guys came back from the Army battle, Coy was still in uniform, going through the ordeal of every practice.

Then, one day late in the season, Leahy was treated to the sight of a small, wriggling, hunk of football flesh squirming and dodging its way through the entire first team. The tiny player went seventy yards for a touchdown. All that afternoon Coy McGee ran back punts against the first team, sliding out of the hands of the sharp, tough Notre Dame first-stringers. His performance on Cartier Field that afternoon opened Leahy's eyes, but wide.

The Tulane game was coming up, and McGee wanted to make that trip to New Orleans. The coach of the Tulane team, Henry Frnka, had been the head coach at Tulsa University, where he had sympathetically but firmly told an eighteen-year-old youngster named Coy McGee that he was too small for the team. Leahy took McGee to New Orleans and turned him loose in the pastures guarded by Frnka's big line. The coach who had told McGee he was too small watched the twenty-year-old kid, same height, same weight, romp through his team for a touchdown.

The story doesn't end there. A week later, in the second period of the last game of the season, Coy McGee trotted onto the field again. The score was tied 0 to 0. The ball went to McGee on a shovel pass and the tiny speedster took off like a rocket. The downfield blocking was good and Coy raced forty-nine yards before stumbling trying to avoid one of his own men on the seventeen-yard line.

The Irish fumbled on the next play. Southern Cal recovered. The Trojans quick-kicked eighty-two yards, the ball rolling over the Notre

Dame goal line for a touchback. It was Notre Dame's first down on their own twenty-yard line. One play netted three yards. Then the players began to chatter in the huddle.

"Let's give it to McGee again."

"This time we won't get in his way."

"Yeah, let's shake Coy loose. Same play—shovel pass to the right."

Southern Cal saw the play coming. As McGee trotted in motion to his right, the Trojan secondary began to point at him. A tackle moved out of the line, the halfback shifted over. But the way McGee ran that afternoon, nothing could have stopped him. He went seventy-seven yards for a touchdown and it paved the way for Notre Dame's 26–6 victory. That afternoon the tiny halfback gained 146 yards in only six carries.

Coy is a Baptist but that hasn't made the slightest difference to the Catholic boys on the team. He goes to a Baptist church every Sunday in South Bend, but lately has also taken to attending early mass with some of the Catholic players. Almost every Notre Dame football squad, since the earliest days, has had several players on the team not of the Catholic faith.

What few people know is that some of Notre Dame's greatest stars have been Protestant and Jewish boys. Rockne, himself, as many do know, did not become a Catholic until 1925, after he had been connected with the school as a player and coach for over thirteen years. It didn't matter to Rockne what a boy's religion was. If he liked to play football, and he believed Notre Dame was the best school in the country, that was all Rockne asked.

One of the greatest games Notre Dame ever played, the game that has been called one of the most thrilling football contests in the history of the sport, was won on a pass from a Protestant boy, Bill Shakespeare, to a lanky end of Jewish faith, Wayne Milner. That was the classic Notre Dame–Ohio State game of 1935, won by the Irish in the last minute of play 18 to 13.

There are few colleges in the country whose teams have come from behind so many times to win ball games as Notre Dame's. They have always been one of the great last-ditch football teams. Notre Dame alumni are still talking about the 1926 Southern Cal game. The Irish led all the way until the Trojans scored in the last five minutes to go on top 12 to 7. That would have taken the heart out of most ball clubs, but Notre Dame's great southpaw passer, Art Parisien, tossed two long ones into the hands of Johnny Niemiec, who galloped over with the second one to win the game 13 to 12.

This year, at South Bend, Notre Dame will play what may be its last game against the Army. It will end—at least for a while—a series that for color, thrills, and great football, will probably never be equaled. The termination of the annual meeting of these two traditional rivals has caused bitterness, sadness, and no small amount of speculation.

A joint statement was issued by Father Cavanaugh and Major General Maxwell D. Taylor, which said: "It was the conviction of the authorities of both schools that the game had grown to such proportions that it had come to be played under conditions escaping the control of the two colleges, some of which were not conducive to wholesome intercollegiate sport."

This pedantic statement only hints at the real reasons for the calling off of the series. Gambling has been given as one reason, but it is only one. It was estimated that over five million dollars was bet on the 1946 game. Ticket speculation is another. Last year, fifty-yard-line seats at the Yankee Stadium were going for as high as four hundred dollars, inducing many of the youngsters of both schools to give up their seats.

The ticket problem became a colossal migraine to the authorities of both schools. Notre Dame alone returned over four hundred thousand dollars from loyal followers of the Irish who could not be supplied with ducats, causing tremendous hard feeling. Alumni of both schools who didn't get their money up in time to get their promised seats were heartbroken and bitter. Fans traveled many thousands of miles only to be turned away at the gate.

Scandal dogged the game. Seats in the press sections were said to have been given to high-ranking Army officers and their wives. The seats given to Notre Dame students were in such a bad position, low on the playing field, that they had difficulty seeing the game. Scalping reached an all-time high, and ushers were reported to have sneaked in some five thousand fans at five bucks a head.

Some wise sportswriters give still another reason. They say Army wanted to call the series off because Notre Dame is entirely too strong for them, and they are weary of taking it on the chin. The record shows the Cadets have been doing just that. In thirty-three games since 1913, the Irish have won twenty-two, and lost only seven to the Army. Four games have been tied. After their 1931 victory, Army didn't win a game from the rugged Blue and Gold teams until 1944.

So the Army series has been called off, perhaps never to be resumed again and critics of Notre Dame say the Irish are playing themselves out of suitable opponents.

Last year, as happens almost every year, cries went up about "de-emphasizing" the schools which consistently have winning football teams. In a biting speech, delivered January 13, 1946, at a Notre Dame football banquet, Father Cavanaugh, president of the school, said, in part: "Reform will never be brought about by innuendo and insinuation, nor by the constant juxtaposition of the two words 'winning' and 'de-emphasis,' as if winning had to be de-emphasized rather than dishonesty and real abuses that are supposed to exist in some quarters connected with football.

"We at Notre Dame make no apologies about wanting winners," he went on. "We shall always want Notre Dame men to play to win, so long as there is a Notre Dame. But with even more emphasis, we want Notre Dame to win cleanly and according to the rules, and because Notre Dame men are reared on this campus in this spirit and because they exemplify this spirit all over the world, they are the envy of the nation."

You never hear even the noisiest, most cynical critics of college football aiming salvos of indignation at Notre Dame. You'll hear plenty this fall about the staggering sums of spending money slipped to this grid hero or that grid hero, but you won't hear it about Notre Dame. Johnny Lujack, the kingpin of the Fighting Irish, has no classy Cadillac convertible, no lavish apartment off the campus, no open expense account at a swank hotel, no bundle of cash in his hip pocket. This is not to say all Notre Dame football players must either have private means or sell magazines to put themselves through college. Athletic scholarships are available, of course, but in this day and age of blatant semiprofessionalism in college football, that's unassailable purity.

A priest in a small town in the South once asked a visiting Notre Dame football player how many members of the squad were actually candidates for degrees. He was surprised to hear that all of them are. And they are. Not only that, but although 70 is a passing mark at Notre Dame, in order to participate in athletics a player must have a 77 average. There is no hedging on the point. It would be embarrassing to mention their names, but several of the men on the present squad were attending summer school this year to boost their average in order to be able to play. One of them had to boost it less than one point. He had a 76.6 average but it wasn't enough.

Most of the players on the '47 team are working for degrees in the tough colleges of Science, Engineering, Law, and Commerce. Only 7 percent of the players on the football squad are taking the Physical Education course, probably the easiest.

There are many things about Notre Dame that are certain to surprise anyone who visits the school for the first time. You might not like the discipline. It's strict, probably exceeded only by that of West Point and Annapolis. No favoritism is shown, as football stars who have been dropped from the school know. But making up for the many rules, and the rigid discipline, there exists at Notre Dame something most Americans prize highly. That is a genuine, realistic democracy. It is the most striking thing any investigator discovers about the school.

It begins with finding out about the treatment of the non-Catholic boys who attend the school. About 10 percent of Notre Dame's students always have been young men of Protestant, Jewish, or no particular faith at all. Their beliefs are respected. The present faculty consists of 74 priests, 4 teaching brothers and 301 laymen, including many Protestants and Jews.

Most of the students at Notre Dame live on the campus, with the exception of those who are married. It is considered bad taste to discuss the financial background or the family standing of any student. When a boy enters Notre Dame he is told he is beginning a new life. It doesn't make any difference whether his father is a millionaire or a truck driver. All this may be difficult to believe, but to one who has seen this democracy-in-action, it is a memorable thing.

What surprises you is that few of the players know anything about the family or financial background of even such well-known stars as Connor, Lujack, Panelli, or Strohmeyer. They didn't know, nor were they interested in knowing.

At Notre Dame the students eat, sleep, study, play, and pray together. The traditional ritual of praying before every game always has been observed and always will be. The prayer is simple. They pray, as any player will tell you, to win for Notre Dame, or to lose like good sports. They add a prayer that no player on either team will be hurt.

Unlike most schools, any boy can go out for any sport at Notre Dame and stay out as long as he likes. Nobody is cut off the football squad, no matter how inept a player he is. They aren't always given the best of equipment by custodian John McAllister, but they get complete uniforms and are allowed to participate fully. The practice sessions at Notre Dame are, as has been mentioned, so rugged that the frail or inexperienced players soon weed themselves out of competition.

Scholars, teachers, and scientists at Notre Dame have been struggling for years to offset the general impression that Notre Dame is built around a football field. The tremendous engineering and scientific and cultural things that have been accomplished at Notre Dame have been overshadowed by the exploits of the fleet-footed, hard-charging young-sters who have made Notre Dame the top football team of the country.

Few of the wild-eyed, cheering fans who root for or against Notre Dame on the gridiron know anything at all about the hard work, sac-rifice, and energy that have gone into building the school. If they visit the campus today they look for the familiar faces of football stars, see a beautiful 1700-acre campus studded with buildings, trees, lawns, ath-letic fields. There are forty-five buildings now standing at Notre Dame. There is the famed Grotto, replica of Our Lady of Lourdes, there are thirteen residence halls, two lakes, an eighteen-hole golf course.

It is a beautiful campus. It did not begin as one. It began as a ten-acre wooded tract of land with nothing standing on it but a rough log chapel. The University of Notre Dame was started on a total capital of four hundred dollars by six brothers of the Congregation of Holy Cross, led by a courageous priest named Father Sorin.

The tireless workers in laboratories, for which Notre Dame is noted among scientists, have kept up an unceasing fight against disease, worked miracles in metallurgy and electronics, have toiled in the stub-born struggle of man against nature. The first wireless message trans-mitted successfully in this country was sent by Dr. Jerome Greene of the Notre Dame faculty from the campus in May 1899. Father Julius A. Nieuwland, CSC, one of Notre Dame's most brilliant scientists, is cred-ited with having discovered synthetic rubber in 1920, after years of re-search. Pioneer aeronautical experiments were conducted by Dr. Albert Zahm, former Notre Dame professor. You can go on and on, ad in-finitum.

One of the things all Notre Dame players have been taught, ever since Rockne, is that football at its best is a fleeting, transitory thing in a man's life—as any glory always is. The reputation and fame of Notre Dame football has not been kept such a bright and living thing by any one man—not even Knute Rockne, or the Gipper, or the Four Horse-men, or any of the Irish stars of the past or present. It has been kept alive by the performances of its teams from year to year, by kids who come up out of railroad towns, from cities and farms, with a dream of playing for Notre Dame.

Nine games from now, one of these kids who came up from nowhere, Johnny Lujack, will join the ranks of the passing great who have played for Notre Dame. It will be a pretty good heritage to have. It will link him with men who have, with skill and courage, written some of the most inspiring passages in American sport history.

It also ties him to the future, to the kids who will play for his school in the years to come, to some now unknown youngster to whom the names of Lujack, Connor, Fischer and Strohmeyer weave a special kind of magic, because they play for Notre Dame.

Lineup for Yesterday

Ogden Nash | **1 9 4 9**

A is for Alex.
  The great Alexander;
More goose eggs he pitched
Than a popular gander.

B is for Bresnahan
  Back of the plate;
The Cards were his love,
And McGraw was his hate.

C is for Cobb,
  Who grew spikes and not corn.
And made all the basemen
Wish they weren't born.

D is for Dean.
     The grammatical Diz,
When they asked, "Who's the tops?"
Said correctly, "I is."

E is for Evers,
     His jaw in advance;
Never afraid
To Tinker with Chance.

F is for Fordham
     And Frankie and Frisch;
I wish he was back
With the Giants, I wish.*

G is for Gehrig,
     The Pride of the Stadium;
His record pure gold,
His courage, pure radium.

H is for Hornsby;
     When pitching to Rog,
The pitcher would pitch,
Then the pitcher would dodge.

I is for Me,
     Not a hard-hitting man,
But an outstanding all-time
Incurable fan.

*P. S.—
Thanks to Durocher,
Now everything's Kosher.

J is for Johnson.
    The Big Train in his prime
Was so fast he could throw
Three strikes at a time.

K is for Keeler,
    As fresh as green paint,
The fastest and mostest
To hit where they ain't.

L is Lajoie,
    Who Clevelanders love,
Napoleon himself,
With glue in his glove.

M is for Matty,
    Who carried a charm
In the form of an extra
Brain in his arm.

N is for Newsom,
    Bobo's favorite kin.
If you ask how he's here,
He talked himself in.

 is for Ott
    Of the restless right foot.
When he leaned on the pellet,
The pellet stayed put.

P is for Plank,
    The Arm of the A's;

When he tangled with Matty
Games lasted for days.

Q is Don Quixote
Cornelius Mack;
Neither Yankees nor Years
Can halt his attack.

R is for Ruth.
To tell you the truth,
There's no more to be said,
Just R is for Ruth.

S is for Speaker,
Swift center-field tender;
When the ball saw him coming,
It yelled, "I surrender."

T is for Terry,
The Giant from Memphis,
Whose 400 average
You can't over-emphis.

U would be 'Ubbell
If Carl were a Cockney;
We say Hubbell and baseball
Like football and Rockne.

V is for Vance,
The Dodgers' own Dazzy;
None of his rivals
Could throw as fast as he.

W Wagner,
    The bowlegged beauty;
Short was closed to all traffic
With Honus on duty.

X is the first
    Of two x's in Foxx,
Who was right behind Ruth
With his powerful soxx.

Y is for Young
    The magnificent Cy;
People batted against him,
But I never knew why.

Z is for Zenith,
    The summit of fame.
These men are up there,
These men are the game.

The Strange Case of Carnera

Jack Sher | **1948**

The title of this tale is pitifully inadequate. No single phrase or sentence can possibly capsule into a few words the incredible career of that giant-sized figure, part hoax and part hero, who stumbled blindly into the world sport scene in the year of our Lord 1928 and who, curiously enough, is still part of that scene.

The story of Primo Carnera, the uncommon, outlandish giant of the twentieth century, will be a difficult one for future generations to believe. Even now, well over a decade since the most brutal episodes took place, a reporter delving into Primo's past needs a strong stomach not to be sickened by the facts he uncovers—the filth, the greed, the depravity. This is not, in essence, a sport story, but the tale of a gargantuan, simple, and yes, courageous man who was preyed upon by all the known varieties of human lice.

Those in the fight game who have read Budd Schulberg's best-seller *The Harder They Fall,* recognize it as a thinly disguised novel of Carnera's life. It etches a sharp and sordid picture of conditions in Cauliflower Alley in the thirties. It throws a harsh light on the thugs who, through violence and skullduggery, made this helpless giant the heavyweight champion of the world. It shows how they then cheated, befouled, and degraded him, and left him at the last a battered, paralyzed wreck, friendless and without hope.

Everyone connected with the ring knows the shameful details. No one knows them better than Primo.

"That book, yes, I have read it," he said, nodding his huge head. "It is all true." Then he spread his tremendous, ham-like hands. "But I wish he had come to me. I would tell him so much more."

Carnera could. For, although the novel tells what happened to Carnera on the American scene, although it exposes the gangsters, gamblers, politicians, bankers, bums, fighters, trainers, and petty crooks who infected his career, it does not tell the complete story. It could not tell it completely, because the story has not yet ended. It is still being lived by Primo Carnera. And it will not end, as the novel did, on a note of despair. The story, in its entirety, is not only one of man's inhumanity to man, but one that reveals the dignity of the human spirit, and shows the courage of a pitiful creature who refused to stay down.

Nobody in the fight game likes to talk about Carnera's ring career. Even those who were in no way responsible for it give their information grudgingly. They say it would be best if it were forgotten. The only one who will talk about it honestly, completely, is Primo Carnera himself, the one man who has nothing to hide, the one man who has done nothing of which to be ashamed. Of the dozens of people, the decent and the dirty, who contributed to this document, none gave so much or so freely and fairly as Carnera. At times the simple dignity of his words gave you a choked-up feeling in the throat. His lack of bitterness, where bitterness should have been, created an anger in the listener.

Primo Carnera told his story from the beginning. It is the only way it should be told. It is the only way the events which took place can be wholly understood, seen in their proper light against the confusing, chaotic, shifting background of treachery and rapaciousness. It is impossible to understand the forces that act upon a man, unless you know what he is, what conditioned him, how he became a thing that could be shaped, twisted, deceived, and tortured.

This is the story, from birth to now.

A birth is a most commonplace occurrence on this spinning earth, but it is always a thing of wonder. No man is a replica of another, nor will he ever be repeated. And so, perhaps, the wonder of birth is that into the world comes not only flesh and blood, another to take its place among the billions of shapes, but something new and different.

The child born on October 26, 1906, in the village of Sequals, in the North of Italy, weighed twenty-two pounds at birth. It was a most uncommon weight. But the mother, Giovanna, was not aware of that when she spoke to her husband, a stone-cutter named Sante Carnera, saying, "Since he is our first child, I shall call him Primo." The word

Primo in Italian means *first,* and the out-sized baby with the strange name was to be the first in the world in many ways—first and set apart from others, looked upon as a freak because of his tremendous proportions.

Carnera's parents were of average weight and height, as were the two brothers who followed him into the world. The family was extremely poor. They lived in a hutlike shelter in the foothills of the towering Alps. Sequals is a place of some three thousand people and Primo's father, Sante, eked out his existence in the manner of most men of the village, fashioning intricate mosaics in stone. The artistry of the craftsmen of Sequals, though poorly paid, earned them a reputation throughout Europe.

Primo and his brothers were taught stone-cutting almost as soon as they could stand. The brothers are still practising that time-honored craft, one in Newark, New Jersey, the other in London. It would have been much happier for Primo if he had been allowed to stay at it. But the extraordinary man, the giant, has little chance of living an ordinary life. He is singled out, gawked at, prodded, exhibited, and forced along paths not of his choosing.

This pattern began early for the boy who was as large as a man, the mountainous Primo. His parents went to Germany to seek work, and the six-year-old boy was left with his grandmother. At eight, he was man-sized and apprenticed to a cabinet-maker to learn that trade. He became quite skillful at this work, attended school spasmodically, and proved to be of average intelligence.

"My childhood was miserable, very miserable." It is an adjective Primo uses quite often. "We were always hungry. I worked very hard, extremely hard. At school I was not happy, I was too large to be accepted. Miserable. It was miserable." He smiled. "I did not take part in the sports then. I was too large and clumsy. It was a bad time for me, this childhood time."

This is the way Carnera spoke. Anyone who sits down with him for extended periods of time, who gets him over his initial shyness, is usually amazed by his manner of speech. Once you become accustomed to the booming, deep-toned voice, it is easy to follow what he is saying. His vocabulary is extensive, his choice of words intelligent.

During the time Primo was touring tank-towns in America, belting over set-ups, the sportswriters had a field day ridiculing this guileless, friendly foreign giant. Stories were circulated that he was as stupid as he was large. At the time, his unfamiliarity with the English language was offered as proof of his mental backwardness.

"What do you think of Hollywood?" a reporter was supposed to have asked him.

"I knock him out in the second round," Primo was reported as saying.

It is possible that he did say it. An American not familiar with the Italian language might easily have made just as ridiculous an answer. It is a fact that Primo learned English very rapidly and, besides his native tongue, he also speaks French and Spanish fluently. The endless stories told to humiliate him did not go unnoticed, as many believed. They hurt, but Carnera took them without complaining, never losing his temper, always conducting himself with dignity.

Harry Markson, the press agent for the Twentieth Century Sporting Club, who sees more than the muscular surface of fighters, said:

"Primo was a nice guy and a very sensitive guy. I remember," he went on, "how he came in to Jimmy Johnston's office one day. He took Murray Levin the sportswriter aside and said, 'Please, Mr. Levin, call me anything you want, but do not call me Satchel Feet any more.' He was very sweet about it and there was something pathetic about it, too."

In talking about his childhood, Carnera did not try to play on sympathy, or exaggerate it. It would be hard to exaggerate. His parents, who had gone to Germany, were interned when the First World War broke out, and were placed in a forced labor battalion. They returned to Italy in 1918, when Primo was eleven years old. The war had had the usual devastating effect, and for a year the family was close to starvation. Carnera's father finally set off for Cairo, where he had the promise of a job. When he began sending money back home, Primo decided it was time to get out on his own.

He was now twelve years old. He was around six feet tall. He looked like a man and people took him for a man. Carnera said that he had a miserable childhood. Actually, he had no childhood at all. At twelve, almost penniless, he hoboed into France. For the next five years, the boy with the giant frame worked at everything he could to keep alive.

"I worked very hard," he said, "so hard I was often weak and food was scarce. I did laborer's work. I carried cement bags, I laid bricks. I worked for a time at my father's profession, the stone-cutting. I did all sorts of work. I could not go back. What for? There was nothing at home for me. The years were bad. I was an innocent," he smiled. "How do you say it, an ingenuous child."

At seventeen, the ingenuous child stood six feet, five and three-quarter inches tall, had a fifty-inch chest, arms and legs like tree trunks. He weighed 250 pounds and was stalking through the streets of Paris hungry, with no job prospect in sight. In desperation, he appealed to the manager of a traveling circus. Here is a body, the boy said; do what you will with it, put it up for people to stare at, make jokes about it, exhibit it for the world to see, do this to me, but food is necessary if I am to stay alive—and I wish to live.

The circus man did not need a sharp eye to see money in the form of the huge boy. He was the first to wring profits from the giant from Sequals, to play upon his freakishness of size, to realize that a trick nature had played could bring francs into his pocket. It was the circus that started Primo on the career that would eventually rob him of pride and self-respect and place his body on the rack.

The curious, jostling throngs that crowded around the booth where Primo was on display were treated to all sorts of wild theories, mystical explanations of Carnera's size. It was not discovered until many years later, long after Primo had been in the ring, that he was afflicted by acromegaly, a tropic disease that makes giants.

Primo hated the circus life. "It was no good," he said. "It is no life to live. I feel foolish and I am very lonely most of the time. I am paid very little, which I do not realize at the time, and the work is hard and the conditions bad. I get very homesick many times, when I am with the circus, more than when I was a laborer."

Under a variety of names, Carnera was billed first as a freak, then as a strong man, finally as a wrestler. He could, at seventeen, snatch a 350-pound weight into the air and hold it over his head. He often wrestled as many as ten or twelve men a day, taking on all comers. In the beginning he was a poor wrestler, but it was good business for the circus when one of the town locals could best the giant.

When circus business was slow, the manager would stage a special wrestling match. He'd paste posters around the town announcing that "The Terrible Giovanni, Champion of Spain," would be seen in an exhibition match. As Giovanni, Primo would perform against experienced mat men. He often made miserable showings, but his size pleased the crowd. He stayed with the circus three years and, toward the end, actually became a fairly competent wrestler.

Eighteen years later, in 1946, it was the things he learned about wrestling in that small-time circus that were to save him, bring him out of obscurity, give him back the self-respect and the fortune that had been denied him as a fighter.

The circus, after traveling all over Europe, wound up in Paris in 1928 and disbanded. A second-rate heavyweight pug named Paul Journée, walking through a park one day, came upon Primo sprawled disconsolately on a bench. Journée marveled at his size. He sat down and began to talk to him. It was this simple action that started Primo Carnera on his fabulous ring career. Here began the blood, sweat, frame, and fix that, in six short years, were to see him crowned heavyweight champion of the world.

"If I had not been broke that day," Carnera said, "if I had not been so miserable, I do not think I would have gone with Journée to talk to this fight manager, Leon See."

The fight game has had few characters of such clashing temperament as Leon See. He was a strange mixture of a man—at once sentimental and shrewd, tough and learned, a diminutive, kindly charlatan; who had earned a degree at Oxford, been a fighter, promoter, gambler, and referee, a hanger-out in the subterranean dives of Paris, rich one day and poor the next. From the first time he laid eyes on the shuffling giant, the tiny, energetic man had an enormous affection for him.

Carnera has nothing bad to say about Leon See. "He was shrewd, you have no idea how shrewd," Primo said, "but we were friends. He was always my friend, even though he did wrong many times. His son is here in America now. I do not know where Leon is now. I talked to his son. It is strange," he went on, "we meet here in the lobby of the hotel and we talk about old times. He is a fine boy."

The bustling Frenchman, who enjoyed posing for pictures standing under Carnera's outstretched arms, was delighted with his new charge. He believed him to be the strongest man in the world, and promptly arranged a fight for him. It was the first of many sad mistakes. The twenty-one-year-old Primo knew nothing about boxing. He had over-developed muscles, and was slow and clumsy. Yet, within two weeks after See signed him, he was matched against Leon Sebilo, a Parisian pug of doubtful reputation. Even See, who loved Da Preem, could not resist the opportunity of making quick money.

Primo kayoed Sebilo in two rounds. Whether the fight was on the level, only See knows, and he has never told.

From the moment he took Carnera into his heart, and his training camp, Leon See became a frenzied, driven man. It did not take him long to discover Primo's weakness, which was the fact that a slight tap on the chin by a man a hundred pounds lighter would send Carnera reeling. Carnera had courage. He could take blows to the body all day long, but the giant had a glass jaw and the wily Leon was quick to find that out.

The little manager worked long and frantically to teach Primo the rudiments of defense. At the same time, undoubtedly motivated by a desire to cash in, he tossed the huge Italian into the ring at every opportunity, rushing him through thirteen fights in less than a year. Primo won most of them by quick knockouts, fighting in Paris, Milan, Leipzig, and Berlin.

Whether these waltzes were on the level is highly debatable, but See was wise enough never to allow his big boy to think he was anything but invincible. Some of the fights might have been square, because some of the so-called fighters who went up against Carnera couldn't have lasted a round with any American tank-town bum. Names like Luigi Ruggirello, Islas Epifanio, Constant Barrick, Ernst Roseman, Jack Humbeek, Marcel Nilles, to name a few, were patted over by Carnera in quick order, or as cynical French and English boxing writers put it, "to order."

The reputation of Leon See was far from spotless. His connections among the lower depths of Parisian life were solid and extensive. In fact, in those days, there was something of an international underworld linked to the fight game. It was not long before a coterie of mobsters from New York, U.S.A., took a trip abroad to have a look-see at this large-type character who might make them a fast buck. In less than a year's time, the unknowing Primo was being "cut into pieces," parts of him being sold to sharpsters who frequented the shadowy sections of America.

"It is well known," a prominent booker of fights and wrestling matches told me, "that Leon See sold over 100 percent of Carnera before they ever left France."

The noted sportswriter, Paul Gallico, was the first to uncover the machinations of the underworld types who were preparing to use Primo to bamboozle the public into parting with their money. Some six months after Primo started fighting, Gallico happened to wander into a smoky fight club in Paris, mildly curious about the word-of-mouth publicity that had been passing around about the giant. The place was called Salle Wagram and Primo was matched against a 174-pound powderpuff puncher named Moïse Bouquillon.

One of the first mobsters to buy into Primo was also there that night. He did a slow burn when he heard about the presence of Mr. Gallico. Later he said to the sportswriter, "Boy, was that a lousy break for us that you come walking into Salle Wagram that night and see that the big guy can't punch! Just that night you hadda be there. We could have got away with a lot more if you don't walk in there and write stories about how he can't punch."

Primo won that fight, taking a ten-round decision. He went on pushing down the pushovers. The only fighter of any reputation he fought before coming to America was Young Stribling. Strib was no world-beater, but he was a fair enough boy with his dukes. The fights, one in London and one in Paris, both ended in fouls. Carnera won the first, Stribling took the second after being struck a low blow. The English scribes were rather indelicate in their descriptions of the contest, implying that both fights were as rehearsed as a Shakespearean play.

Through all of this, Carnera was kept completely in the dark. This may be hard to believe, but Leon See was with him night and day, censoring what he read and thought. Leon's magic tongue worked triple-time, his words convincing Primo that his strength was as the strength of ten and his punch devastating. Leon even arranged to have Gene Tunney, then visiting abroad, pose for newsreel pictures with Primo, "Europe's challenger for the title." As sincerely as Leon liked Primo, he couldn't ever pass up an angle.

"Tunney was very friendly to me," Primo said. "I was just a novice then and he was very nice. I feel he was pulling for me. He said he hoped he would see me in America soon and wished me luck."

If ever a man worked hard and sincerely to become a fighter, it was Primo Carnera. The huge, simple, gullible giant believed with all his heart and soul that he had the makings of a great champion. He believed no man alive could hurt him. He believed that his punch was dynamite and that he had mastered the rudiments of *la boxe,* as Leon See called it.

"I dreamed of going to America," he said. "It was with me all the time, this wish, this dream. I work very hard and I was sure that I would someday soon be the champion of the world."

Those last few days in Paris, preparing to sail forth on his conquest of the new land, were very happy ones for Primo. The twenty-three-year-old mountain-sized boy was led across the ocean to his eventual triumphs and cruel slaughter in the spirit of the knight on the white charger. Gene Tunney just happened to be down on the dock when the boat, groaning under the weight of the huge Italian, docked. Again he wished Primo luck. The big fellow was all smiles, filled with sweetness and love toward his fellow men and his newly chosen profession.

It is no credit to us, as Americans, that we can be duped and ballyhooed into believing anything. The very people, even the sportswise, who later sneered and smeared the giant Carnera for his simple-mindedness, for allowing himself to be so blatantly tricked and cheated, were among those who created the legend of his fistic prowess. It was late in 1929, the stock market had crashed, the world was confused and churning, when Carnera came to the United States. He was immediately hailed as "a mighty killer," a "Neanderthal type with a tremendous punch," "a new, giant menace on the American boxing scene."

The lying, shameless, vicious men who pulled a gunny-sack over the eyes of the giant and the public did a masterful job of it. They were quite a collection of tawdry and dangerous individuals. There were Broadway Bill Duffy and Owney Madden, both of whom had spent time behind bars for anti-social acts of a violent nature. There were, in minor capacities, such cute characters as Mad Dog Vincent Coll (later rubbed out), Big Frenchy DeMange, Boo Boo Hoff, and other parties of odious repute. It is still considered not altogether healthy for anyone to poke his nose too deeply into some of the "deals" these charming chaps cooked up while interested in cashing in on Carnera.

The fraud started in Madison Square Garden on the night of January 24, 1930, when Primo Carnera was sent into the ring against a built-up, fourth-rate heavy named Big Boy Peterson. The evil faces crowding around Carnera's corner at ringside were a bit anxious about the affair, knowing that if the spectators failed to swallow the hoax, their plans would be knocked into a cocked hat. Not having anything to offer in the way of a fight, they had wisely decided to give the onlookers a "show." It was some show.

Anyone who has ever seen Primo Carnera cannot help but be amazed by his awesome size. The powerful effect of that tremendous figure of a man, as he lumbers toward a ring, is enough to send shudders through even the most hardened fight fan who revels in bloody slaughter. Primo Carnera, coming down the aisle that night, looked like nothing human. This was a deliberate piece of staging. Followed by the tiny Leon See and other carefully picked midget-sized men, Carnera did not wear the usual fighter's bathrobe. Instead, he was dressed in a hideous green vest, a weird, visor-type cap, and black trunks on which was embroidered the head of a wild boar.

The humorous mutterings of the press, which had implied before the fight that it was to be a phony, were disregarded and forgotten by those who witnessed the spectacle in the Garden that night. The massive figure of Carnera, the lumbering tower of might and muscle that pawed at Peterson, somehow pleased the collected gathering. The men behind the scenes knew that they were "in" and could put the show on the road.

It was a fight that deserves little attention. Peterson managed to get his jaw in front of a glove containing Primo's pumpkin-sized hand and fell to the floor. He was counted out in the first round, undoubtedly resting comfortably on the canvas and contemplating the steaks he would be eating for the next several months. Back in the dressing room, Monsieur See was jubilantly bouncing about the room telling one and all about his fighter's glorious future. Primo sat on the table, surrounded by the tough guys, his large, kindly brown eyes dreamy and filled with wonder. That night he proudly sent a cablegram to his parents in Sequals, telling of his triumph.

"It was the first cable ever received by anyone in my town," he said. "It was very impressive."

The gang bundled up their giant and began a cross-country tour, moving from state to state and leaving behind them a trail of fixed fights, intimidated and coerced pugs and managers. Working with gangsters and gamblers, and using threats and violence, they cold-bloodedly staged one outrageous swindle after another. In one year, Carnera watched twenty-two victims go down under his playful pushes, more frightened by what they saw outside the ring than by the big, helpless man they faced.

In Chicago, the Illinois Athletic Commission proved somewhat more determined than the New York hierarchy. After Primo cuffed Elziar Rioux to the canvas in forty-seven seconds of the first round, the yowls of the press were so long and loud that the fighter's purse was held up. But the gang pulled strings and Primo was given the green light, Rioux taking the blame for a poor showing.

What Rioux knew was that it was better to do poorly and live than to tag Carnera and die. The men behind the giant were intent on cleaning up and that they did, gathering unto themselves over $700,000 on the tour. If an opponent refused to take the dive, to "talk business," he was shoved about a little by the muscle-men. If that didn't work, he often found himself, just before a fight, staring into the tiny, round opening of a .38-caliber weapon. Does it sound unbelievable? It happens to be the absolute truth. . . .

In Philadelphia, a Negro heavyweight named Ace Clark walloped hell out of Carnera through the first five rounds. Just before the bell called him out for the sixth, a small, icy-faced man slid up against the ropes near his corner and said, "Look down here, Ace." The fighter looked, saw something gleaming and metallic beneath a coat, and performed an extremely believable dive in the next thirty seconds. A Newark pug was visited in his dressing room and treated right roughly when word reached the "crowd" that he might double cross them and put up a fight. He too melted in the first round.

Out in Oakland, California, a large, classy puncher named Bombo Chevalier was having a lot of fun belting the amazed Primo around the ring. He might have ended the string of faked victories then and there, but midway through the fight he suddenly discovered something had gone wrong with his eyes. One of his own handlers had been bought, during the course of the fight, and had rubbed his orbs with some sort of inflammatory substance. That incident smelled so foully that an investigation followed, but the gang weasled out of it and went on to the next swindle.

Some of the fighters Carnera bowled over were not bums, but they were all made to see the light. George Godfrey, a large, fast-moving, and skillful puncher, had a terrible time losing to Primo. It was almost impossible for this boy to fight badly enough for the huge Italian even to hit him! He finally solved the dilemma by fouling Primo in the fifth round.

After the fight, several suspicious reporters came into Godfrey's dressing room and began to ask him how hard Primo could hit. "Hit?" the large Negro grinned, "That fellow couldn't hurt my baby sister." The reporters began to laugh and then into the room walked several of the gentlefolk who were handling Carnera. Godfrey's face changed. "That white boy sure has some punch," Big George said quickly. "I thought the house had fallen on me a couple of times there."

It was that raw. Long before Primo Carnera became champion of the world, the Duffy crowd had given the heave-ho to Leon See. As sharp as the little Frenchman was, even he could not stomach the conniving that was part and parcel of the Carnera buildup. He could visualize the end. He knew that the "fix" could not go on forever, that someone would tag the vulnerable chin of the giant and the inevitable decline would begin.

Leon did not always play square with Primo in the matter of money. But he did try to teach him to defend himself, and he did his best to keep the big fellow from suffering physical harm. After he was ousted by the gang, See took to writing a syndicated column, exposing the fights Carnera had. He stated outright that on the few occasions when opponents could not be threatened by guns and brass knuckles, then Primo lost.

While Leon See was at Primo's side, life was bearable for Carnera.

"He was the one friend I had in America," Primo said. "He did not always do right. He was reckless and foolish in handling my money, but he was my friend."

Carnera saw very little of the juicy sums collected for the eighty-odd fights he participated in before winning the title. In California, Leon took a chunk of Carnera's dough and invested it in real estate, buying two homes. In Oklahoma, he sank a potful of cash in an oil well that was dry as dust.

"I didn't know what he was doing," Carnera said, shaking his head. "The banks notified me that the homes he had bought for me were no longer mine. I did not pay something or other. The mortgage, that was it. Leon bought many things for me, but I believe he was cheated."

While Leon was with him, Primo at least had someone with whom he could talk, someone to kill the hours of loneliness. See treated him like a son, babied him, became maudlin and sentimental over the giant he knew was going to be taken away from him by the wolves. Carnera idolized the little manager. If he went out to a movie alone at night, he would scrawl a note to Leon telling him at what time he would return. Then he would rush back to the hotel to tell him all about the picture he had seen.

Shortly after Leon See was forced out of the picture, the dazed and unhappy giant was asked how he felt a manager should treat a fighter. By that time, Primo knew (or suspected) that all was not well, that he was not quite as invincible as he had been led to believe. "He who goes slow, goes surely," he said. "He who wants to travel far, is kind to his horse."

It was after the fight against Jack Sharkey on October 12, 1931, that Primo Carnera knew that he had been tricked and deceived, that he was not the one-punch killer that he had been led to believe since the days in Paris. It was a terrible, humiliating, cruel fact for him to face. It was much harder to take than the beating the Boston gob gave him.

No one who saw that fight in New York will ever forget the look of pain and wonder on big Primo's face as he went down under Sharkey's blow. It was a sharp left hook to the jaw and it dumped Carnera to the canvas with a thud that could be heard in Times Square. He sat there dumbfounded, his eyes glazed. He finally got up on his feet, but when he saw the scowling Sharkey advancing on him, he dropped to his knees, a pitiful, abject, and stunned creature.

Those who crucified him as being cowardly, who taunted him with boos and derisive cries, did not know what was going on inside the huge man. As later fights proved, he was courageous beyond belief. He could take merciless punishment. That night, it was not Sharkey from whom he was cowering. He was hiding from himself, from the realization that he was nothing but a gigantic fraud in the hands of hoodlums, that he had nothing, neither a punch nor a defense.

Sharkey almost lost that fight. When Primo sank to his knees without being hit, the sailor started to jump out of the ring, thinking the fight was finished. It would have disqualified him, but his handlers managed to restrain him. He went on to pound, jab, poke, and cut up the giant for nine more rounds. Primo took it, then tottered down the aisle, his head hanging.

After that fight, Carnera wanted to quit. He was broke, lonely, sick-at-heart. "It was too late, then," he said. "They had me by the throat. They would not let me quit. Every fight was to be my last one, but it never was. I had no friends in the game, nobody I could talk to even, or ask advice. Everyone cared for the money, that's all. I knew it, and this is a very lonely thing."

The gang had an answer for everything. After he beat King Levinsky and Vittorio Campolo, they hustled Carnera out of the country until the stench of the upset would blow over. They pushed him into fights in London, Paris, Berlin, Milan. There was quick and easy money to be made in these places. Carnera's string of knockouts in America could be made to look very impressive and the Sharkey thing could always be explained as a fluke.

"After Leon left," Carnera revealed, "they did not even care whether I trained or not. I did the best I could by myself. They did not care whether I was in condition, or what I did. They just made the matches and took the money and that was all."

Eight months in Europe and then the gang led Carnera back to the States again, arranged another tour, and lined up a bevy of such hand-me-down old-timers as Les Kennedy, Jose Santa, K. O. Christner, Jack Spence, Jim Merriott and even Big Boy Peterson again! By this time, even the public was wise to the set-ups, so the mob used a convenient ruse to ride Carnera into the fight for the title against Jack Sharkey.

On February 10, 1933, Primo kayoed Ernie Schaaf in the thirteenth round of a fight at Madison Square Garden. Shortly after the fight, Schaaf died. The ugly fact is that Ernie Schaaf was a sick man before he entered the ring that night. A few months before, in Chicago, he had been terribly battered by Max Baer. He should have been in a hospital bed that night instead of a ring. It was not Primo's ineffectual jolts that killed him, but a lax Boxing Commission.

The death of Ernie Schaaf was just the sort of thing that the men who had the giant in chains could use to boot him into a fight for the heavy-weight title. It was just the gimmick they needed. They passed the word around that Primo's mighty punch was responsible for Schaaf's demise.

The incident still has painful memories for Carnera. "It was not me who did this to him," he said. "Everyone knows now that it was not my fault. I would not do such a thing. When it happened I felt sick. I told everyone that it was not my fault."

But the mob made use of the tragic accident—their boy was a mighty man again—and they signed him to meet Jack Sharkey for the title on June 29, 1933, at the Long Island Garden Bowl.

The Boxing Commission closed their eyes and allowed the fight to take place. There were some very queer strings being pulled in high political circles. It was not the first time that top national figures had been reached to pull the mob behind Carnera out of the fire. The zippy, dark-haired, fast-talking Jimmy Johnston had intervened a few months before to square Carnera with the New York Athletic Commission, going all the way up the ladder to make a pitch to Jim Farley.

The behind-the-scenes knavery was so obvious that when you study the reports of that heavyweight title fight, you sense the shame of the newsmen who were sent to cover it. Few of them came right out and called it a fake and a swindle, but all of them either felt it or knew it. Nat Fleischer, the most renowned ring expert in the country, stated in plain English that he couldn't understand how Primo won. When I talked to him about it recently, he said, "Sharkey should have knocked him out. Carnera won that fight with an invisible punch. I don't hold Carnera responsible though," he went on. "He was built up by set-ups. He was a nice guy and never meant anyone any harm. He just wasn't made to be a fighter."

And Gallico, who had been keeping close tabs on Carnera's ring activities ever since that night in Paris, was another who announced in clear and ringing words that nothing would ever convince him that it was an honest prizefight, contested on its merits. Paul was still feeling hot under the collar about it as late as 1938, when he wrote his *Farewell to Sport.*

"Sharkey's reputation and the reputation of Fat John Buckley, his manager, were both bad," Gallico wrote. "Both had been involved in some curious ring encounters. The reputation of the Carnera entourage, by the time the Sharkey fight had come along in 1933, was notorious, and the training camps of both gladiators were simply festering with mobsters and tough guys. Duffy, Madden, et Cie., were spread out all over Carnera's training quarters at Dr. Bier's Health Farm at Pompton

Lakes, New Jersey. A traveling chapter of Detroit's famous Purple Gang hung out at Gus Wilson's for a while during Sharkey's rehearsals. Part of their business there was to muscle in on the concession of the fight pictures."

Primo climbed through the ropes that night looking very unlike a confident, keyed-up challenger rarin' to slug his way to the heavyweight championship. He looked miserable, ill-at-ease, soggy, and listless. Sharkey scowled convincingly from his corner, but the beefy John Buckley seemed uncomfortable, as though someone had been following him all day.

For five weary rounds Sharkey scored point after point, bouncing light left hooks off the huge target that floundered around in front of him. Jack was always an in-and-outer, but at his worst, he should have been able to put Primo away in four heats. He had, some eighteen months before, hardly worked up a sweat belting Carnera unmercifully for fifteen rounds. On this June night, however, his punches had about as much kick to them as a wet sock swung by a ten-year-old. In the sixth round, after a mild exchange of blows, Sharkey went down as though he had been hit by a Dempsey.

He was counted out. Manager Buckley, making pantomimic gestures, rushed to Carnera's corner and demanded to inspect Primo's gloves implying that they must have contained horseshoes or other such implements of iron. The amazed Carnera stood helplessly in his corner while this farce was being enacted. The entire scene was fragrant with an unmentionable type of odor.

It must have been a sweet night for the gamblers. The odds were in favor of Sharkey, 5 to 4. Everyone cleaned up. By this time, the vultures who had been cleaning the big bird through 79 fights had cut themselves in on grosses that amounted to over two million dollars. And Carnera? The day after he won the Championship of the World, he had just $360 to his name.

A month after the fight, the bewildered giant filed a bankruptcy suit. He was also being hailed into the courts on a breach of promise case involving a waitress, who claimed the champ had promised her a ring and a trip down the aisle. Primo escaped to Italy for a few months of peace and attempted, among his own people in the tiny village of Sequals, to collect his wits.

In Rome, the Fascisti hailed the giant as they would a conquering hero returning from ancient wars. A match was arranged against Paolino Uzcudun, a tired old warhorse who submitted to Primo's clumsy clouts for fifteen rounds. Mussolini stuck his jaw out an inch or so further, pounded his chest, dressed Carnera in military uniform, and sent pictures to the far corners of the earth showing Primo executing the Fascist salute.

It is not to Carnera's credit that he played ball with the Fascist hoods. But he was politically unaware and, by this time, conditioned to take orders from anyone who held the whip-hand. The element he had been dealing with in America had not been a whit more scrupulous or less brutal than the dictatorship to which he returned.

Primo did disobey Mussolini once. It is not very well known, but the massive man had an inordinate love for automobile racing. He would cram his huge frame into a tiny racing car and, with utter fearlessness, give it the gun. The belligerent Benito forbade him to race, but Primo, on the sly, entered the annual thousand-mile Italian auto race. He didn't have the moola for a car of his own, so he drove for the Alfa Romeo auto company and placed third.

"When the boss heard about it," Primo said, smiling, "he called me to Rome to see him and he gave me hell."

When Carnera returned from Italy to America, he brought with him a little Italian banker named Luigi Soresi. How Soresi was able to chisel into a "cut" on Carnera, why the mob allowed him a share of their boy, is something that Primo, to this day, does not know. Soresi conned Carnera into believing that he would protect him. The way it turned out, he was even more ruthless than the others.

Some of the statements Primo gave out to the press in those days were lulus. In Miami, preparing for a defense of the title against Tommy Loughran, in 1934, Carnera told reporters: "I don't pay any attention to money and such things. I am crazy about boxing. The rest I don't give a damn about!"

And the shifty-eyed, sharply dressed group who hovered around him managed to keep a straight face. They were having the time of their lives in Miami nightclubs, spending C notes in huge quantities, tossing lavish parties, and carrying on in a style that was imitative of Capone in his heyday. They paid absolutely no attention to their fighter's training or condition. They set him up in miserable quarters on one of the backlots of the town and never even bothered to see him. Primo tried to get in shape for a week or so, then gave up and sat brooding, lonely and filled with despair. He came into the ring against Loughran some twenty pounds overweight.

Carnera is proud of the fact that he won a decision against Loughran. In a sense, he has a right to be. It was one of the few fights he is certain was on the level. Actually, the Carnera crowd knew that they were taking few chances sending their boy in against Tommy Loughran. They knew Loughran was completely honest and could not be fixed, but he was an aging, washed-up fighter. He was thirty-two years old, had been fighting for fifteen years, and had always been a powder-puff puncher. Most of Tommy's reputation had been made as a clever light-heavyweight. Carnera outweighed him that night by a mere 105 pounds!

Actually, the gang desperately needed one honest fight to hold up in front of the public, no matter how uneven the match. Writers like Quentin Reynolds were putting the finger on them in national magazines, stating, "Carnera is directed by very rough characters, who hover about his corner and sometimes the corner of his opponent." The boys did not consider this a very nice way to talk about them. It hurt them right where they lived, in their pocketbooks.

So Primo leaned against Tommy Loughran for fifteen rounds in Miami. He was little better as a boxer than when he had started, but Loughran was unable to hurt him, or he Loughran, and he was awarded the decision. That same year, such whirlwind pugs as Walter Neusel, Johnny Risko, and Jose Caratoli also punched out a decision over the tired Tommy. At that, Loughran managed to whack Primo a couple of times in such a manner as to make his legs wobble. Carnera landed on Tommy's button time after time with righthand uppercuts that had more steam than the one that floored Sharkey and won him a title. Loughran barely blinked.

The characters behind Carnera might have gone on forever lining their pockets with championship gates, but law and order finally stepped in and took charge. The Roosevelt Administration had outlawed the speakeasies, and G-men were putting the chase on Public Enemies. Mister Duffy took a trip to the jailhouse for evasion of income tax. Others in the select circle who had a piece of Carnera did not consider it quite safe to be seen in daylight and things, in Runyonesque lingo, had become very deplorable, indeed.

Max Baer was clamoring for a crack at the title. The public was fed up with poor Primo, and the unhappy giant was badly in need of money. He agreed to meet Baer.

The thing that took place on the night of June 14, 1934, in Madison Square Garden Bowl, was not a fair fight either. It was a slaughter, an indecent and pitiful thing to watch. Max Baer could hit. He made a bloody mess of the monstrous, defenseless, reeling ex-circus freak and strong man.

"I never liked Carnera before," a rival fight manager told me. "To me, he was nothing but a big, stupid bum. But, by God, I loved and pitied the big, blind ox that night, because I never seen so much guts."

Baer knocked Carnera down three times in the first round. He gave him a worse beating than Joe Louis later gave Max, but the giant got up and kept on taking it. At the end of the tenth frame, his face a grotesque, bruised, and bloody mask, after being knocked down in every round for a total of thirteen times, Primo was still in there taking it. Baer never did beat him into unconsciousness. It would have been much more humane if he had been able to do so. The referee stopped the fight in the eleventh, to the relief of everyone but Carnera. Primo was too numbed by that time to feel much of anything.

Did the gang relinquish their hold on Carnera then? They did not. There was still the possibility of wringing more blood-money out of the peaceful Italian. There were still sadistic fans who would shell out to see what they considered a monstrosity being hammered into a pulp by a mere, ordinary man. Soresi and company patched Carnera up and carted him off to South America to paw some pesos out of our unsuspecting friends south of the border. For six months Primo wallowed around rings in Argentina, Uruguay and Brazil, earning his backers still more dough.

Citizen Duffy was released from prison, and one of his first acts was to bring Primo back from South America. The boys had arranged an interesting and remunerative little fracas for their sorely battered fighter. They were throwing him into the same ring with a harmless young heavyweight out of Detroit, a certain Joe Louis. After all, the Bomber couldn't kill the big lug, although it is doubtful if that would have made the slightest difference to the men in Primo's corner on that memorable night.

In the first few seconds of the fight, one of Joe's jolts completely smashed in Carnera's mouth. Who among those who saw the fight and knew the story behind Carnera will ever forget the sight of Duffy and the boys shouting angrily into the ears of the bloody giant, shoving him out round after round to what looked like certain death?

The time was 2:32 in the sixth round when the ghastly affair was halted. What a wretched thing was dragged from the ring that night, what a mess of a man! Thus had fate dealt with the uncommon offspring of Giovanna Carnera, who had once said, softly, "Since he is our first child, I shall call him Primo."

Here on a night in June 1935 was the apparent end of a career that had started because a miserable giant-boy of twelve had wandered hungrily into France in search of any work that would keep him alive, and had once listened to the words of an old prizefighter who had found him on a park bench.

If ever a man should have been through with the ring, it was Primo Carnera after the Louis debacle. But the jackals who still had him in tow never asked themselves such a humane question as, "How much is enough?" His name would still draw the suckers.

Carnera kept fighting through 1935 and into 1936. A third-rate Negro heavyweight named Leroy Haynes finally administered the *coup de grâce*. He kayoed Carnera in three rounds at Philadelphia. The fight drew a fairly good crowd, so it was repeated just eleven days later in Brooklyn. Haynes hammered, cut, and chopped Primo for nine rounds, beating him so fiercely that one of the giant's legs became paralyzed and he could no longer stand up to take his punishment. He was hustled from the ring to a hospital.

His tormentors then released him.

Listen to Carnera's words. "I lay in the hospital bed for five months. My whole left side was paralyzed. I was in much pain. During all this time, not one of them came to see me. Nobody came to see me. I had no friend in all the world."

When Primo was released from the hospital, he was still limping. He hobbled up a gangplank and took a boat back to Europe. In Paris he stopped long enough to pick up a meager purse in a fight against someone called Tony Duneglio, which he lost in ten rounds.

A week before Christmas in 1937, on a snowy night in Budapest, Primo Carnera, the former heavyweight champion of the world, was knocked out in two rounds by an unknown Hungarian heavyweight named Josef Zupan.

It was his last fight. The New York newspapers devoted a couple of lines to it.

The world of sport had written the giant off the books. It looked as though that was the way it was going to be.

Primo went back to Sequals, to the village where he was born. His parents had died, but the people of the small town still had great affection for their giant, and he for them. He built himself a house, lived simply, devoted himself to farming. He was married, in 1939, to a girl who worked in the post office in a nearby town.

After they were married, Primo and Pina planned to settle down to a peaceful life in Sequals. They had two children, a handsome, sensitive-faced boy named Umberto, now seven, and a girl, Joanna Maria, now five years old.

But Carnera's peace was short-lived. The war began, and the Nazis moved into Italy. Primo and Pina buried most of their household furnishings in the ground. The Germans put Carnera to work with a pick and shovel at twenty cents a day. On Carnera's back is a deep, indented scar, fully five inches long, a wound suffered at the hands of the Germans during this time. At night he would scavenge around the countryside, trying to find food for his children.

One day a plane came in low over Primo's house in Sequals and the family hustled to the cellar in terror. When it had gone, Primo went out into the yard and found a huge box had been dropped. "I approach it very carefully," he said. "I poked it with a stick. I thought it might blow up. It was from you—from the Americans. It was food, all kinds, and canned milk and cigarettes and beer and almost everything. I knew then that it would soon be over."

The GIs finally trudged into Sequals. They shook hands with Primo, stayed in his house, took pictures of him, talked about fights and America. When the war was over, Carnera was broke, but he was no longer a lonely or hopeless man. The world had hit him with everything, but he was still standing upright and thinking of the future. There came offers from the United States. He was not completely forgotten. . . .

At random, Primo chose the offer of a smalltime Los Angeles promoter named Harry Harris. He wrote agreeing to come to America and work for him, providing Harris would send him enough money to make the trip. Harris called the Olympic Auditorium, owned by the matchmakers Babe McCoy, Cal Eaton, and Johnny Doyle. He got McCoy on the telephone and said, "I've got Primo Carnera. Are you interested?"

"Yeah?" There was a pause. "Where is he?"

"In Italy," Harris said. "Would you put up the money to bring him over and get him started?"

McCoy talked it over with his partners. They decided they could use Primo as a referee at fights and wrestling matches, signed a deal with Harris, and sent Primo the money to come to Los Angeles.

On the 1st of July 1946, ten years after he had left the United States a crippled and broken man, Primo was back again. He was forty years old, but even under the careful scrutiny of the matchmakers of the Olympic, the giant looked as powerful and in as good condition as he had been before the sluggers had gone to work on him. They took him to a gym and watched in amazement as he wrestled playfully but skillfully with some of the grunt-and-groan boys.

"What the hell," they said, in effect, "we don't have to use this guy as ref. He wrestles better than most of the beefs we're booking."

A month after Primo's arrival, in August 1946, he was matched against Tommy O'Toole in the main event at the Olympic Auditorium in L.A. McCoy and Harris had not the slightest idea how Carnera would fare as a draw or as a grappler. The fact that he had looked good in a gym could mean nothing.

The night of the match, the one cheerful, confident figure was the old Preem himself. Wrestling was something he knew about. He felt he was right for it, fashioned by nature for it and would not look freakish at it, the way he had always looked with those big, padded mittens on his fists.

The giant was right. The match was a sell-out. Primo won handily against the burly O'Toole. The crowd loved him.

This was the beginning of one of the most amazing and ironic comebacks in the annals of sport. In one year's time, Primo Carnera, who fell harder than any prizefighter in ring history, has climbed to the very top of the wrestling business. From the Hudson Bay Territory to New Orleans, from New York to California, the Italian giant is now the biggest drawing card in professional wrestling. The grosses on Primo's matches have gone over the million-dollar mark.

Those who come to see Carnera wrestle generally come back for his return engagements. They may come, the first time, because they expect to see a freak, or to stare at a man who was a former heavyweight boxing champion. But they discover that Carnera has more to offer than the memory of a pitiful past.

It is a wonderful sight to see Primo Carnera striding toward the ring, whether you see him in an impressive auditorium in a large city, or in a smelly, smoky, barnlike structure in some of the tank-towns where wrestling is staged. Once the enormous red-and-blue bathrobe is unfurled, the huge body is still an awesome thing to behold. But now, in contrast to the flabby opponents he faces, you are struck by the beautiful proportions of the giant. The skyscraper height, the massive shoulders and chest and legs, the powerful arms send a thrill rather than a shudder through the crowds who watch him.

But what is most impressive of all is the new-found dignity of the huge man. You know he understands what it is all about now. You know he feels he has found where he belongs, a place and a profession where he is no longer regarded as a freak.

In the seamy by-ways and smoke-filled auditoriums of wrestling, where a turbaned "Hindu," a self-styled "Champion of Greece," a bearded Tyrolean Terror or Man Mountain is commonplace, Carnera gives you the feeling that he is playing his new role as straight as his curious profession will allow.

He studiously refrains from the elaborate play-acting, the contortions, the grunts and groans and burps that are as standard with most grapplers as are the mannerisms of the burlesque "stripper."

In the ring, Primo wears a self-deprecating smile that seems to say to his fans: "You and I know what this is all about. But what the hell— you're having fun, and so am I, so what's the difference?"

Against Tony Galento one night in Newark, New Jersey, Carnera put on a performance that would have been ludicrous in lesser hands. Towering over his opponent, he looked as though he could pick him up with one hand and throw him into Market Street.

Instead, he crouched and stalked and clenched his huge-fingered hands and went through an elaborate ritual of holds and spills and falls that at times looked almost convincing.

The crowd booed without restraint, but the jeers were friendly:

"Don't worry, Primo! If you lose this one, you'll win next week in Pittsburgh!"

The "contest" ended in a draw. The crowd applauded and whistled and stamped and yelled, but their faces were smiling, and they seemed well pleased. They had got what they paid for—a spectacle—a monster of a man rolling on the mat like a big, good-natured bear in a sideshow.

As a private citizen, Carnera is looked upon today as a decent and honorable man.

When you walk with him through the lobby of a New York hotel, people turn and wave at him. They call "Hi, Primo!" They are not just struck by his size; in their faces are the friendliness and respect that he has needed for so many years. For Primo is one of God's most warm and likable creatures, a man who has a deep and genuine affection for people, and who needs the same treatment in return.

With the exception of one month of vacation, Carnera has been wrestling four to six nights a week for the past year and a half. He has traveled over a million miles by air and wrestled some three hundred opponents. He's lost just one match—in Montreal, when a large, rough boy named Ivan Rober punched him in the jaw. Primo whacked him back, and Ivan went down and out. Carnera was disqualified.

"Carnera is a wonderful trouper," Al Mayer, who books him in the

East, said. "He always shows up for his matches. He never disappoints a promoter. The fans love him."

Mayer opened the books and pointed to some of the black figures that indicated how Primo had been drawing. In four appearances in New York, the gross was over $100,000; in Montreal, $64,000 for three dates; in Cleveland, Los Angeles, and Philadelphia, his single-shot dates gathered $18,000 in each city; in Detroit, $17,000 for a night; in Chicago, $16,000; and in Miami $12,000. And so it goes.

And Primo now gets his check every week, on the line. He gets a large and fair percentage of the take, and he handles the money himself. He has bought himself a $30,000 home in the fancy Westwood section of Los Angeles. It is clear this time, no mortgages.

The men now connected with Carnera are a different breed of cats from his associates in pugilism. His personal manager and closest companion is Joe (Toots) Mondt, a former heavyweight wrestling champion. The bulky, genial Toots has the face of a benign Santa Claus. His reputation in wrestling circles is spotless and his devotion for Primo is completely and wholly genuine.

"I've been traveling with Primo for over a year now," Toots smiled, "and I'll tell you that anyone who can't get along with him must have a hole in his head. He's become one of the best friends I've ever had in this world. He is a clean-living guy, an honest man, and I couldn't ask for anyone better to handle."

Mondt gave up a flourishing business as a promoter around Washington and Oregon to handle Primo. Toots was so impressed by Carnera, who appeared in a match Mondt promoted, that he accepted Babe McCoy's offer to train and handle Primo. Toots is making quite a performer out of Da Preem. And Mondt is the man who can do it. He has met them all—Stanley Zybysko, John Friedberg, Jim Londos, Big Munn, and the renowned Strangler Lewis.

"When I took Primo on a year ago," Mondt said, "I never dreamed he would do so well. After all, he was forty years old. But age doesn't seem to mean anything in Primo's case. He seems to get better as he goes along."

In an easy-going, effortless, and unphony way, Toots Mondt can sit all day long and spin yarns about his friend, Primo Carnera. He likes to tell you about the giant's tiny appetite; how Primo, who actually eats very little, is always embarrassed by the huge portions he is served everywhere he goes.

"We have a terrible time at parties and dinners," Mondt chuckled.

"The host or hostess always gets upset because Primo does not eat much. They think he does not like their food and they never believe it when I tell them that the only time he eats a fairly average meal is at breakfast."

"It is true," Primo chimed in, smiling, "I do not eat much."

It is constantly amazing to Mondt how easily Carnera makes friends and how many of them he now has. As a fighter, he was undoubtedly the loneliest figure in ring history. As a wrestler, Primo is constantly surrounded by admirers and friends. He gets innumerable invitations to parties and affairs in every city in which he appears.

"He likes people," Mondt explained. "I never knew a man who liked to be among people so much. I can't understand it when he tells me he was once afraid of them and lonely. Now, he is happiest when he is among people. In towns where he has not appeared before, he will strike up friendships with people in the lobby of the hotel, even with strangers he meets on the street, and invite them to our room.

"Milwaukee!" Mondt exclaimed, throwing up his hands. "He is always after me to get a match for him in Milwaukee. There are two men in the contracting business there, Andre and Bruno Bertin. Primo knew them in Sequals. They were boyhood friends of his. He gets into Milwaukee and he practically lives with those Bertin guys and their families. It is hard to get him out of the town."

Even the fighters who slugged Carnera insensible are now included among his friends. He is like a man trying to embrace, with a bearlike hug, the whole world. Max Baer, who took the heavyweight championship away from him, who pounded him so unmercifully, is now counted as one of his pals. In Detroit a few months ago, Baer bought front-row seats to watch Primo wrestle Joe Dusek.

"O ho!" Primo bellowed happily, "Max was very excited that night. When Dusek took a slug at me with fists, Max jumped up and screamed at him and took off his coat and was going to get into the ring to help me." Carnera looked wise. "Maybe it was a joke, maybe he was only clowning, but it shows he is for me, he likes me. Afterwards, he invited me to the nightclub where he is playing and I am in the show with him and we make jokes together. I like Max Baer. He's a good guy."

And old Jack Sharkey, the surly gob, another of the sluggers who pasted Primo to the deck in their first fight, has now benefited by the giant's affection. Sharkey was hired to referee one of Primo's matches, a tangle with Jules Strongbow. It was a very different night, financially, from the one when they met for the second time and the Boston gob got the heavy dough in losing the title while Primo wound up with a pocketful of stones. For the wrestling match, Carnera got 40 percent of an $18,500 gate, while Sharkey got $300 for overseeing Primo's victory.

Everything has changed for the giant from Sequals. The odds which were once so heavily stacked against him have switched. A world that had no place for him has suddenly opened up what must seem like limitless horizons. At this writing, Primo has left for Mexico, to be re-admitted to the United States under a quota and be allowed to take out the first papers that will eventually make him an American citizen.

Pina, Umberto, and Joanna Maria Carnera are on their way across the ocean, hoping to live permanently in their father's big house in Westwood, California. "This," Carnera said, almost reverently, "will make everything completely happy for me."

But Toots Mondt has still another dream for the giant. He wants to make Primo Carnera the Heavyweight Wrestling Champion of the World. This is what he's been shooting at during all the months he has been touring with Carnera back and forth across the country.

The business of being proclaimed the World's Champion Wrestler, as Toots Mondt explained it, is a complicated set-up. There are about half a dozen men, in as many states and subject to as many rules, who claim to be the Champions of the World. Toots wants Carnera to settle it once and for all, by beating all of them. Primo will therefore have to whip Frank Sexton, whom some recognize as the champion. He will have to beat Louie Thez, the St. Louis boy who holds the National Wrestling Association title. He will also have to pin to the mat such heavies as Bill Longston, Whipper Watson of Toronto, Jim Londos, Orville Brown, Bronko Nagurski, and Roughie Silverstein, former Big Ten Champion from Illinois.

"It is my opinion that Primo can beat every one of these men," Toots said, with a completely straight face. "If the officials are fair and honest, Primo will win all these matches. I mean to see that they *are* honest," Toots concluded, "because I intend that Primo Carnera shall be the next Heavyweight Wrestling Champion of the World."

If this happens, Carnera will be the only man in sport history who has held both titles, the championship of the world in boxing and wrestling. How much or how little the grappling title means, it is still quite a prospect for the once hopeless and crippled, bruised and life-battered giant who hobbled up a gangplank in 1936 headed for oblivion.

Not even those idealistic weavers of words who created ancient tales designed solely to point out a moral could improve the true-life ending of this story. For what has happened to the ruthless, shameless, cruel, and greedy handful of men who tricked and humiliated and bled the giant? Almost to a man, life has repaid them. Three of them are now penniless, two are in ill health, and one frequents the grimy alleys of crime, fearful for his life.

A few months ago, in a large Eastern city, one of them provided us with a thing that is rare in this modern world, a moment of poetic justice. One of these men who had held the giant in bondage for so many years, one of the elite of the once high-riding mob, approached Primo Carnera after a wrestling match and, in our own graceless, work-a-day language, he put the bite on him.

"He looked very bad," Primo said, "but I could not find it in myself to give him money. Instead, I bought him a meal."

What About the Roller Derby?

John Lardner | **1949**

It develops that there are certain parts of this country in which the thing called the Roller Derby is still unknown. The people in such places live in the same state of uneasy innocence as the Indians did before the white man came among them, bringing civilization, uncut whisky, glass beads for all hands, and two or three new variations of hoof-and-mouth disease.

It's a matter of record that the Indians could not get this kind of civilization fast enough, once they had a look at it, and the same thing is true of the Roller Derby. Those in America who have not yet seen the Derby are sending out loud, clear calls to know what it is all about. The more advanced tribes, who have tasted the Derby by television, or been exposed to it in person, are clamoring and stampeding for more—or so we are told by Mr. Leo A. Seltzer, who sells the stuff to the natives.

Of course, Mr. Seltzer's definition of a stampede is flexible. Back in 1935 B.T. (before television), when he tried his first Roller Derby on the public for size, Mr. Seltzer was satisfied with a stampede of three or four hundred people, at any wide place in the road. He did not care how many of them wore shoes. Today, in the age of so-called video, he measures his clients by the million. The incidence of shoes among them is getting higher. Some even wear neckties. In short, Mr. Seltzer feels he has finally got hold of the *bon ton*, and got them where it hurts.

The Roller Derby, mark you, is a sport. Its backers will stand up and raise their right hands and swear it is. And they are right. Defenestration is also a sport, for those who like it (defenestration is pushing people out of windows). So is extravasation (extravasation is blood-letting, with a license). So is lapidation (lapidation is stoning people to death, or near there). So is the grand old game of suttee, which consists of barbecuing live widows over a charcoal fire.

So, for that matter, is wrestling—and here we are getting close to the meat of the matter. For wrestling is the thing that the Roller Derby threatens to replace, in certain ways. When the television business started to warm up, after the war, it was found that many set-owners took a morbid interest in the actions of wrestlers like Primo Carnera and Gorgeous George. The more grotesque, the better. Then televised wrestling began to seem a little cold and stately. That was the spot into which the Roller Derby stepped.

Mr. Seltzer and his staff of calculators estimate that of the more than a million new addicts who paid to see his skaters in the last year, 91 percent were won and brought over by the telecasts of noted television broadcasters like Joe Hasel, of WJZ-TV, in New York City, where the Roller Derby broke into Madison Square Garden this year and took its place in Garden history with the Democratic Convention of 1924 (also a sport). That is a pretty solid estimate, that 91 percent, for Mr. Seltzer did not just pull it out of the air, like a butterfly. He went around to the customers in person, feeling their pulses and asking them, "What in the world brings you to my place, friend?" Most of them said television, which is good enough for Mr. Seltzer. He now feels that, after thirteen lean years or so, the tide has turned, that the nation is his oyster, that America is about to break out with Roller Derby teams and leagues at every pore.

Your correspondent set out the other day to learn the details of the sport, in behalf of those tribes which have not yet put their wampum on the line to see it. It was a most interesting visit. As I knocked at the door, they were just pulling six inches of light, seasoned timber out of the flank of a Miss Marjorie Clair Brashun, daughter of a plumber from St. Paul, Minnesota. Miss Brashun, known to the trade, for what seems to be satisfactory reasons, as Toughie, is one of the leading female skaters of the Roller Derby troupe. Since she likes to wear wood next to her skin, she had gone on skating for some time before the house doctors learned that she had bumped into the guard rail of the track and acquired a piece of it internally.

The sight of Miss Brashun being de-frosted caused a slight argument among the Roller Derby people as to whether she is four feet eleven or four feet ten in height. Personally, I think it might be one or the other. I have never gone close enough to a live rattlesnake to put a tape-measure on it, and, in the same way, I am willing to be an inch or two wrong about Miss Brashun.

"The girls in this sport are tougher than the boys," said Mr. Seltzer.

"That's right," snarled Miss Brashun.

"If the girls have a fight on the track," said Mr. Seltzer, "they go right on fighting after the match, maybe for two or three years. In their spare time, they spit in each other's teacups. But the girls have a weakness. They are tender in the coccyx."

The coccyx, it should be said, is a vestigial bone at the southern end of the spine. Women skaters wear a special strip of sponge-rubber over this area, since they are always falling upon it and making it ring like a bell. In fact, their uniforms are padded all over, and so are the men's—with hip pads, shoulder pads, and thigh pads, topped off by a helmet borrowed partly from football and partly from Marshal Rommel's Afrika Korps. There is lots of padding, but not enough.

A Mr. Billy Reynolds went to the hospital recently with six breaks in one leg. A Miss Margie Anderson (out of Miami) had twenty-four stitches taken in her shapely Gothic torso. A Miss Virginia Rushing broke her pelvic bone in a warm debate, but went on skating for several weeks before she noticed it. Your correspondent would estimate that the number of stitches embroidered in Mr. Seltzer's troupe each week is about the same as Betsy Ross took in making the first flag.

Before establishing the fact that the Roller Derby is, like cutting throats, a sport, let us glance at its history for a moment. Mr. Seltzer, who operates out of Chicago, is an old dance-marathon man. You can tell by the way he stands erect and looks at the world through clear eyes that he got out of that business long ago. At the peak of the depression, he rounded up a few roller-skaters and went on the road with the first Derby. For a while, like Virginia Rushing with her pelvic bone, nobody noticed. Things were tough and slow. Once, among the Southern hills, twenty-two of the skaters were killed in a bus accident. It may be, in view of the way they made their living, that this was an easy and merciful death, but probably not, for the skaters seem to enjoy the work.

Today, old-timers come up to the Derby's doors, in each town it plays, and introduce themselves as former members of the troupe. Recently a deaf-mute pants-presser approached the Seltzer staff and opened conversation with the following written message: "I'm an old

Roller Derby ace." He was, at that, and the sight of him reminded Mr. Seltzer that the man was probably responsible for the fact that the Derby today enjoys a strong deaf-mute following wherever it plays.

Now that the show—beg pardon, sport—has struck gold, it plays mostly the big towns, in the television belt. It carries a squad of anywhere from thirty skaters up (there were sixty-five at Madison Square Garden), half of them men, half women, and a portable Masonite track which is eighteen laps, or two quarts of blood, to the mile. It also packs a staff of referees, medical men, and penalty boxes. The referees put the skaters into the penalty boxes, if the medical men have not previously put them into local hospitals.

There are certain laws of God and man the violation of which, I am told, will get a skater thrown out of the match for the night, but I hesitate to imagine what those could be. The penalty boxes take care of the rest, as in hockey. As in football, blocking is encouraged. As in six-day bike racing, you can jam and sprint at will. As in osteopathy, you can probe for new bones in your fellow man. As in wrestling—well, I was especially interested in the work of a Mr. Silver Rich, who has developed a two-handed kidney punch from behind which puts me strongly in mind of the technique of the five wrestling Duseks from Omaha. It is extremely legal, by Roller Derby rules.

The squad is divided into separate teams of boys and girls, the boys playing the boys for fifteen minutes, then the girls playing the girls for fifteen minutes, and so on alternately, while Mr. Seltzer counts the house. In a wholesome, high-spirited way, Mr. Seltzer calls the teams by the names of towns, such as Brooklyn, New York, Philadelphia, and Cleveland. A player like Miss Toughie Brashun (but there are, I am glad to say, no other players like Miss Brashun) will represent Brooklyn in the same way that Mr. Luis Olmo, the Dodger from South America, represents Brooklyn—that is, she wears a Brooklyn shirt.

There is a further similarity, and Happy Chandler can sue me if he likes, between baseball and the skating dodge. The skaters do not like new equipment. They hone, grind, cut, gouge, and chew on their skates and shoes as ballplayers hone their bats, break in their gloves, and cut their shirtsleeves. They sometimes get friends to break in their shoes, and they file down their wooden skate wheels so close that Mr. Seltzer has to supply them with three or four new sets of wheels apiece per evening. The wheels are wooden because metal wheels set up such a vibration that Miss Brashun, for instance, could not hear herself thinking up a plan to murder Miss Gerry Murray, her deadliest rival, in cold blood, if she wore them.

As in bike-racing, the fastest skaters on each team sprint for points—one point for passing one rival within two minutes, two points for three, and five points for passing the whole enemy team of five. The other skaters form packs to deter hostile sprinters from passing. At the end of the match, the winning and losing teams split a percentage of the gate on a 60–40 basis, and walk, or are carried, home to supper. In their spare time, roller-skaters often get married, to each other. Miss Brashun is the bride of a skater named Ken Monte, while Miss Murray is Mrs. Gene Gammon in private life. Like other people, skaters have children, and these, Mr. Seltzer hopes, will grow up to be skaters too. The supply is short, and he cannot afford to miss a bet.

That raises the question of where Roller Derby skaters come from. Some of them used to be bike-riders, some of them used to be ice-skaters, some of them used to be ballplayers, and some of them used to be home girls. A Miss Peggy Smalley was a home girl on a high hill in Tennessee when the Roller Derby suddenly surrounded her. The skate shoes they gave her were the first shoes she had ever seen. If it weren't for the skates, she would throw them away. It is claimed that one of the boys in the troupe deserted the St. Louis Cardinal chain for the Derby because he could make more money that way. That may be a gratuitous sneer at baseball, but, on the other hand, thinking about the Cardinals, it may be true. Mr. Billy Bogash, recognized as the Ty Cobb of roller-skating, makes consistently better than $10,000 a year, and when a good girl skater and a good boy skater have the presence of mind to marry each other, the pair can knock down from $15,000 to $20,000 per annum, as well as everything that gets in their way.

Pending the arrival of the next generation, Mr. Seltzer has got to dig up and train new skaters to keep the market supplied. Toward this end, he runs a skating school in Chicago, where prospects are polished at the house's expense. It takes about a year of training to get a skater ready for the "pack," and three years to make a top, point-sprinting performer. Like piano teachers, who dislike to take on pupils who have learned to play "Yankee Doodle" with one finger, Mr. Seltzer prefers absolutely fresh recruits, with no fixed skating tricks and no bad habits. A bad habit in a roller-skater, for instance, would be kindness. Those things have got to be pruned out of the subject while he is young.

The new Roller Derby helmets, which were put on view for the first time at Madison Square Garden, are not entirely popular with skaters, especially the ladies (I use the word in a general sense) among them. Neither are all the pads. There is a certain vanity among girl skaters, when they are not too busy tattooing their initials on the shins of the next girl, and they point out that Mr. Seltzer's scheme of padding, while technically useful on the track, does not coincide with nature's scheme. They prefer nature's. As for the helmets, there are two things against them. The ladies like to have their hair float behind them in the breeze when they skate. It looks better. Also, the helmet protects the hair of their victims. A lady skater who cannot sink her hands, wrist-deep, into the coiffure of an enemy, take a good hold, and pull off the scalp at the roots, feels frustrated. She feels that her individual liberties have been violated. She wonders what to do with herself.

"Have a heart," said Miss Toughie Brashun to Mr. Seltzer the other day. "I have my eye on a hair-do that I want to rip open from here to Texas."

"Nothing doing," said the chief sternly. "Helmets will be worn. Safety first. Players desiring concussions must obtain them on their own time. Security and dignity are the rule of the sport."

"That's what you think," muttered Miss Brashun, baring her fangs. The final issue remains in doubt. As we go to press, history awaits the outcome.

Part Two | 1951–1960

Good-bye, Graziano

W. C. Heinz | **1 9 5 2**

We were sitting in the living room of a hotel suite in Chicago, and it was about nine o'clock at night. Rocky Graziano was sitting in an easy chair, with his legs over one of the arms. He had on slacks and a T-shirt, and he was sucking on a dry pipe and trying to spit small, almost-dry spit into a wastebasket over by the near wall.

There were a couple of sparring partners on the sofa, and Whitey Bimstein and Irving Cohen were sitting with a card table between them and Irving was counting through a batch of tickets. There was a small radio on the window sill and the Cubs' game was on. The only noise in the room was the noise of the announcer.

I was watching the Rock. I was watching him sit there, sucking on the pipe and spitting and then staring straight ahead, and I had it all figured out for myself.

This is a guy, I was thinking to myself, who is not listening to a ball game. This is a guy who is twenty-five hours away, a guy in a ring fighting Tony Zale for the middleweight title for the second time and remembering the first time in Yankee Stadium when he had Zale down and beaten and Zale came out the next round, his legs wobbling, and pumped that right hand into the body so it brought this guy's right knee up and then followed it with the hook to the chin that knocked this guy out.

(85

"It's a single over short going into left center field," the announcer said, his voice rising. *"The runners on third and second will score, and here they come. . . ."*

"You see?" the Rock said suddenly, swinging his feet around onto the floor and taking the pipe out of his mouth and pointing it at us. "If they make that double play they get out of the inning and no runs score. You see?"

I am thinking of this now because on February 20 the Rock is going back into that same ring in Chicago, this time against Sugar Ray Robinson for that same middleweight title. This is just a guy out for the big pay night now, but when he had it he was the most exciting fighter of our time. Now they say this is where he gets off and that this will probably be the last magazine piece anybody will write about him for a long time.

"All right," Whitey said after a while. "You better get up to bed now, Rock. It's time you were in."

He got up from the chair and he stretched and he started out the door. Whitey motioned over his shoulder with his head and I followed them out.

We went down the hall and took the stairway up to the next floor. It was a two-room suite with three cots in one room for the sparring partners and two beds in the other room, one for Whitey and the other for the Rock.

"You better try those trunks on," Whitey said.

The Rock got undressed. He had been training for months and he was in great shape, and he tried on the two pairs of trunks, black with the red stripes, squatting down and standing up.

"The first ones are too tight," he said. "These are best."

He got, naked, into one of the beds then and he pulled the covers up. He put two pillows under his head, so he was half sitting up, and Whitey walked into the other room.

"So, I'll go now, Rock," I said.

"Okay," he said.

"You have to lick this guy, Rock," I said suddenly, bending over the bed. "If you ever had to win a fight, you have to win this one."

He knew what I meant. In New York they had revoked his license for failing to report the offer of a bribe he had never accepted for a fight that had never been fought. There were those of us who had gone day after day to the hearings, who had been able to see through this to the politics behind it, and we had been appalled that such a thing could happen in this country.

"I despise them for what they did to you," I said, "and you hate them, and there's only one way you can get even. If you lose tomorrow night, you're done, not only in New York but everywhere. You have to win. Rock."

"I know," he said.

"You have to stick it," I said. "You have to win the title, because when you win the title it's yours and they can't take it away from you outside the ring. You win it and they need it and they'll come crawling back, begging you on their hands and knees."

"I know," he said, lying there in the bed and looking right at me. "If I have to, I'll die in there, tryin'."

We shook hands and he snapped off the light over the bed and I left. I felt bad for having made a speech like that, because they make few better guys than Tony Zale and they make them no tougher inside the ropes, and where do you get off telling another guy he has to take those Sunday shots in the belly and on the chin while you sit at ringside feeling a lot but taking nothing and just looking up?

It was 120 degrees at ringside inside the Chicago Stadium that July night. They drew $422,918 for a new indoor record and had them hanging from the rafters. Suddenly the hot, wet, sweat-smelling air was still and the organ started "East Side, West Side" and a roar went up in the back and down the aisle came the Rock. He had the white satin robe with the green trim over his shoulders and Whitey and Irving and Frank Percoco were behind him. The noise was all over the place now and Whitey was rubbing his back under the white robe as they came and then, two steps from the stairs, he broke from Whitey and took the three stairs in one step and vaulted through the ropes, throwing his arms so the robe slid off.

"Yes," I said to myself, "he'll stick it all right."

He stuck it, and there were times when it looked like he'd have to die doing it. Over his right eye the brow swelled and came down and shut the eye, and when Zale cut the left eye the blood flowed into it so he was stumbling around blind or seeing only through a red haze. Zale pitched all his big stuff at him and he took it all. There were times in the third round when I said to myself that if this were just a fight, and not bigger than a fight, he would go down. I said to myself that he couldn't win it but at least he showed them he had guts. Then a funny thing happened.

Between the fourth and fifth rounds, Frank Percoco took the hard edge of a quarter and, pressing with it between his fingers, broke the skin of the swelling over the right eye. When the blood came out the swelling came down enough for the lid to pull up, and Rocky could see okay. For two bits they won the middleweight title and made maybe $250,000 and nobody else ever knew it and I never wrote it.

He had Zale helpless on the ropes in the sixth round. Zale, collapsing, had his back to him and, in that frenzy that made him what only he and Dempsey were, Rocky climbed all over him, hitting him wherever he could find a place to hit him. Then the referee stopped it. And now he was standing in the shower stall, the right eye shut again, a clip holding the other cut closed, only a fireman in uniform with us, standing guard.

"Well," I said to him, "the world is a big place, and how does it feel to be the middleweight champion of it?"

"I don't know," he said, hurt and leaning back and resting one arm on the shower handles, trying to think and to talk. "I don't know. I mean . . . I mean as a kid I . . . I mean I was no good . . . I mean nobody ever . . . You know what I mean?"

He was standing, naked and cut and swollen in this basement and holding his hands out to us. It was quiet but for the drip of the shut-off shower.

"I know what you mean, Rocky," the fireman said, out of nowhere. "You're giving a talk on democracy."

"I mean I never . . ." the Rock said, and then he turned to the fireman and he said: "You're a good guy. You're all right. You know what I mean?"

They came through the door then, a half dozen newspaper men from the mob in the dressing room. They got him in a corner, all of them with their pencils and paper out.

"But how did you feel in there?" one of them shouted at him.

"I wanted to kill him," he said. "I got nothing against him. He's a nice guy. I like him, but I wanted to kill him."

That is the kind of a fighter he was, a special kind. I remember the night he fought Marty Servo in the Garden. Marty had just knocked out Red Cochrane for the welterweight title, and now Graziano had him against the ropes, holding Marty's head up with his open left glove, clubbing him with his right. He'd have killed Marty if he had had a knife in there that night, and he would have been guilty of only one thing. He would have been guilty of giving himself over completely to that which they send two men out to do when they face one another in a ring.

Don't you know, too, that the Rock liked Marty and Marty liked the Rock? Marty was never a fighter again after that beating. He had to give up his welterweight title without ever defending it, and by that beating he lost the money he had counted on to give him security the rest of his life. I remember a night a couple of years later. The Rock was walking ahead of us and we were going out to eat.

"Where are we going?" I said.

"We're going to that place where Marty Servo tends bar," Irving Cohen said. "Rocky likes him and he always tries to bring business into the place."

We went into the place and Marty, in a white jacket, was standing behind the bar, leaning against the rack that holds the glasses in front of the mirror. When he saw us his face brightened and he leaned over the bar and shook hands. When he shook hands with the Rock, he smiled and faked as if to hook with his left. The Rock, leaning over the bar, stuck his left under Marty's chin as he had that night and faked to throw the right, and then the two of them dropped their hands and laughed.

"I'll be glad when that Graziano stops fighting," a guy said once in Stillman's, "it's gettin' so you can't even move in here."

When the Rock trained, they would stand packed, all the way back to the wall. They would be packed on the stairs and they would be packed in the balcony, too. In his dressing room, there was always a mob. There was one little guy there named Barney who always wore a dirty cap and who played the harmonica. He didn't play it by blowing on it with his mouth. He played it by blowing on it through his nostrils.

"Ain't he a good musician?" the Rock would say, sitting back in his robe and listening. "Did you ever see anybody do that before? I'd like to get this poor guy a job."

The guy would smile and then he'd play some more. He had three numbers. He'd play "Beer Barrel Polka," "Darktown Strutters' Ball," and "Bugle Call Rag." All the time he was playing "Bugle Call Rag," blowing on the harmonica through his nostrils, he'd salute with his left hand.

"Ain't that great?" the Rock would say, and he would mean it. "Why can't I get this guy a job?"

The guy was satisfied. The Rock staked him. He staked a lot of them. One day I saw him give a guy the shirt he was wearing. The Christmas of the first year he made any money he bought a secondhand 1940 Cadillac and filled it with $1500 worth of toys. He drove it down to his old neighborhood on the East Side and unloaded the toys on the kids and another $1500 on their parents. He never mentioned it. It came out because a trainer from the gym who lives in the neighborhood saw it.

"Look, Rocky," Irving Cohen said to him. "It's nice to do things like that, but you haven't got that kind of money and you've got to save money. You won't be fighting forever."

"Sure, Irving," the Rock said, "but those are poor people. They're good people. They never done no wrong. They never hurt nobody. They just never got a break."

One day in Stillman's, the Rock walked up to Irving. He asked him for a touch.

"I've got fifty bucks," Irving said.

"Give it to me," the Rock said, "and hustle up another fifty for me."

Irving circulated and borrowed fifty and gave that to the Rock. The Rock walked away and Irving, who is a little, round guy, sidled after him.

As you come into Stillman's there are rows of chairs facing the ring. In one of the chairs there was a former fighter sitting. This one is still a young man, but he is blind. The Rock sat down next to him and talked with him for a while. Irving sidled up behind them, and then the Rock leaned over and slipped the rolled-up bills into the lapel pocket of the fighter's jacket.

"There's something in your pocket," he said, and he got up.

It is a shame we lied to a guy like this when we told him that, if he won the title that night in Chicago, he would be all right because they could never take it away from him outside the ring. We didn't tell it as a lie. It just came out a lie. It came out a lie because when he won the title he became big in people's minds. He was a name, and now they got it out of Washington that he had gone AWOL in the Army, had put in seven months in Leavenworth, and had a dishonorable discharge. They wanted to bar him from the ring.

I remember the night after he ran out on a fight in California. His disappearance made headlines, and finally he walked through the door into a suite at the Capitol Hotel across Eighth Avenue from the Garden. He had on a beautiful camel's hair polo coat, but there was the growth of several days' beard on his face and under the coat he wore an old woolen shirt and dirty slacks and there were heavy running shoes on his feet.

"I'm with my friends," he said, and he held his hands out.

They were New York sportswriters called there on the promise that he would show up. Only some of them were his friends, but they all stood up when he came in and when he said that you could hear every breath.

"It's like I got a scar on my face," he said, staring through them and bringing his right hand up slowly to his right cheek. "Why don't they leave me alone or put me in jail?"

Of course, they took his title away outside the ring. They let him defend it against Zale in Newark on June 10, 1948, and they paid him for it, but he was no fighter then. The things they had done to him had taken out of him that which had made him the fighter he had been. He walked toward Zale as he was to walk toward those others in that hotel room another time, and Zale measured him and for two rounds gave him a terrible beating and in the third round knocked him out.

It is an odd thing, but once Rocky Graziano would have fought Ray Robinson for the fun of it. That would be four or five years ago, and he made Irving Cohen's life miserable with it.

"Get me Robinson, will you, Irving?" he would say, over and over again. "Believe me, Irving, I'll knock him out."

"Sure, Rocky," Irving would say. "Sure you will. But wait."

There were just those two things, you see, that the Rock had that made him what he was. He could take your head off your shoulders with that right-hand punch, and he fought with that animal fury that is the pure, primitive expression of the essence of combat.

He has not put those two things together in a ring since the night he won the title from Zale in Chicago and they pulled the Army on him. There is no evidence that they are any longer a part of him, and if that is so then this is the end of the road, the last big pay night, the final chapter of a memorable book—and I can't find the one big sentence with which to end it.

The Adventures of Doak Walker

Jack Newcombe | **1 9 5 2**

It seems only natural that the sovereign State of Texas, which has given us the wide-brimmed hat, Linda Darnell, Judge Roy Bean, and air-conditioned Cadillacs, should also produce one of the most fabulous football players of our time. In many ways, he is *the* most fabulous. Yet unlike most things for which Texas has become famous, he is neither very big nor very flamboyant.

His name is Doak Walker and Texans have long since regarded him as one of the natural wonders of their republic. At Southern Methodist University in Dallas, where he was an All-American three seasons in a row, he became the most heavily publicized football player of our time. His face, an exceedingly photogenic one, framed in the familiar red helmet, was on the covers of dozens of publications, big and small. In the fall of 1948, it was impossible to approach a newsstand anywhere in America without seeing him. In the post-war sports frenzy, he was all college football heroes rolled into one—a handsome, striking athlete of magnificent skills who seemed to rise to breathless heights in game after game.

In fact, Doak had accomplished so much on the football field and had become so well known by the end of his junior year that some people felt he was too much the paragon and that he could go nowhere but down from then on. When, in his senior year, playing for a weaker team and bending under the heavy pressures, he became ill and injured, there was reason to believe this was true. Hadn't he made all-everything, won all the trophies available, starred in two bowl games, scored better than a touchdown-per-game for four seasons and received such attention from the public as comes to few people in a lifetime? Doak could have stopped there. The legend already was secure in the hands of countless hero-worshiping Texans.

But Doak chose to go into pro football, the one field left for him to conquer. When he did, even his most fanatical believers feared that, despite his remarkable talents and poise, his lack of size (he weighed less than 160 pounds after his senior season) might prove an insurmountable handicap. His detractors, and there were a number among the rooters for other Southwest Conference teams, believed the pros would lay bare the Doak Walker myth. Even Doak himself was unsure of his chances.

In 1950, his rookie season with the Detroit Lions, he led the National Football League in scoring with 128 points, ten less than the all-time pro record set by Don Hutson eight years before. He was unanimously picked as an all-pro halfback. Last fall, he was third on the scoring list, again an all-star selection who amazed more and more people with his versatility. Doak raced for big-gainers through the line, caught passes, kicked field goals and extra points, did some of the punting, and handled kickoff and punt returns. He did everything that made him a three-time All-American in college except throw passes and play defense. T-quarterback Bobby Layne, Doak's high-school pal, takes care of the former very nicely and the Lions pay other more expendable players to handle the latter.

The story of Doak Walker could begin and end with his football playing and there would be more than enough raw drama to sustain a plot. But it would not be the whole story. Closer still to the realm of fiction is the character of the hero himself. He is, in a way, more amazing than any of the heroics he has pulled off on the football field. In a world that is not without its cheats, phonies and tinsel heroes (and where don't they exist?) Doak emerges as one of those rare persons who stands up in every way as a gentleman and a celebrity. Sportswriters spend their time creating heroes for their readers; rarely, if ever, do they completely believe in them. But Doak Walker has made a believer of many. I'm one of them.

If you're in the market for an individual example of the good that can come from big-time college football, Walker is the perfect choice. Although it cannot be said that football alone enabled him to get a college education, because he came from a middle-class family that would have made certain he attended college, it did open the door to some unusual post-graduate business opportunities in his hometown. But Walker is the shining product of big-scale, emphasized football because, throughout the fantastic whirl of publicity to which he has been subjected in recent years, he has remained the thoroughly decent, natural human being he was before it all began. Unconsciously, he is the model athlete, the very ideal his father, a former high-school football coach, had in mind when he first acquainted him with the game's fundamentals in the backyard of their Dallas home.

Without being priggish—or in any way a hypocrite—Doak could stand before the fourth, fifth and sixth grades of the Bradfield School in Highland Park, as he did not long ago, and tell the youngsters they should eat green vegetables, drink gallons of milk, and keep regular sleeping hours if they wanted to grow up to be athletes. That is exactly what he does. No one laughs or wisecracks about Doak's Golden Rule sermon, which he delivers to dozens of young audiences during the year, because they know he practices what he preaches. Effectively but unintentionally, Doak makes fools of the cynics.

Admiration and respect for Doak run deep in Dallas. It is hard to get some of the citizens to speak rationally of him. They feel he is not only the doggondest football player who ever lived, but the finest young ambassador Texas could have. Better than anyone, or anything, else he proves to the outside world that there is more to the state than sagebrush, big-talking oilmen and cattle.

When, five days before Christmas in 1949, and a few weeks after Doak's final college game, "a group of anonymous admirers" presented him a yellow convertible and a small wardrobe of clothes as tokens of appreciation for all he had done in the past four years, the home folks thought it was neither irregular nor enough. Someone suggested he be given a lifetime pass to the Cotton Bowl, since he, more than any other individual, had been responsible for its expansion from 45,000 seats to 75,000.

The impact Doak Walker has made on the booming city of Dallas, with its half-million population, is hard to understand unless (1) you know Doak Walker and (2) you are aware of the grip football has on the natives. In a football sense, Dallas is an overgrown Massillon, Ohio.

On the sports desk of the Dallas *Morning News,* Doak is described as "the patron saint," and the paper has faithfully chronicled his every move from the time he was a teen-age whirlwind for the Highland Park High School team.

Young Dallas boys and girls have grown up the last four or five years with the belief, shared by many of their elders, that Doak Walker is the first citizen of this country. Students of Stephan J. Hay School, in Dallas, a couple of years ago, made Doak a class study project, much in the manner other pupils in other schools were studying George Washington, Abe Lincoln and, maybe, Sam Houston. A group of seventh-graders did a Walker mural, which was proudly hung in the corridor; others felt the lack of a comprehensive Doak Walker biography and started to compile one.

Doak's mailbox was stuffed with an average of a hundred letters a week and he and his girl friend, Norma Peterson, were kept busy mailing out requested photographs during his junior and senior years at Southern Methodist. Fans sent him four-leaf clovers and "good luck" telegrams before every game. His football number—37—attained magic proportions. It appeared everywhere—in store windows, cars, on signboards and on the backs of hundreds of young Texans. Dallas sporting goods salesmen reported that they unloaded more than a thousand jerseys with number 37 on them in the Christmas rush of 1949. One dealer, who had been cleaned out of 432 of them, said, "We got Kyle Rotes and Gil Johnsons and others but everybody has to have a Walker." It looked as if every football-minded moppet in Dallas was running up and down vacant lots and playgrounds wearing the numeral 37 on a red jersey. Schoolboys who drew uniform 37 were treated with envy and respect.

As a pro with the Detroit Lions, Doak is neither out of sight nor out of mind. Last year, before Dallas had its franchise in the National Football League, films of the Detroit games were shown each week over a local TV station. The newspapers kept the folks posted on Doak's accomplishments. A column appeared under his byline regularly in the Dallas *Times-Herald.* His first local appearance in an exhibition game against the New York Giants (and ex-teammate Kyle Rote) drew 56,000 to the Cotton Bowl in August 1951. Doak rose to the occasion, just as he had so many previous times on the same field, and scored eighteen points, including a field goal and two touchdowns, one of which was a ninety-five-yard run with a kickoff return. The game was enough to convince any doubting Texans that even in pro competition he was the same old Doaker.

I first met Doak Walker when in January 1949 he came to New York to accept *Sport*'s Top Performer award in college football. It was one of the many major banquet appearances he made following the 1949 season at SMU. (A month before, he had received the John W. Heisman trophy as the nation's outstanding football player at the Downtown Athletic Club in New York.) He was accompanied by his father and coach Matty Bell, and he was almost painfully polite and reserved. But apparently he enjoyed himself, despite the uncomfortable amount of attention focused on him, and he still talks of the wonderful time he had meeting the other sports celebrities. He attended the Top Performer dinner the next year, too, and an indication that he felt more at home this time came the first night when he and Kyle Rote, also a guest, sneaked into the hotel room of a Dallas newspaper columnist, short-sheeted his bed and filled the room with a freezing amount of January air by throwing the windows wide open.

The next time I saw Doak he was whittling on a stick while walking barefooted across the campus of St. John's Military Academy in the small summer resort town of Delafield, Wisconsin, where the 1950 College All-Stars were training. He was in his favorite atmosphere—a pleasant blend of football and camp life. When an SMU alumnus from Chicago buttonholed him and requested he address a group in that city, Doak politely agreed to the plans, even though it required a long trip after practice in the evening. I knew he much preferred to stay at camp. Many of the All-Stars took advantage of off-duty hours to seek out the nearest glass of Milwaukee beer but Doak, usually in the company of Charlie Justice and Eddie LeBaron, headed for the local ice cream emporium where they lapped up milk-and-ice-cream drinks at an unbelievable pace and joked about the rumors they had heard of the vast extent of their financial resources.

This past summer I visited Doak at his home in Dallas just before he left for Michigan and the Lions' pre-season training base. His house is in a new residential section that is expanding on a treeless slope about nine miles north of the center of Dallas. It is a long, low ranch-style home with a two-car garage occupied by Doak's Oldsmobile and his wife's Ford. When I arrived, the hot Texas sun was beating down on unshaded roofs and lawns. A sprinkler in the front yard was scattering water on the struggling grass. Doak opened the door and I stepped into an air-conditioned hallway. It was the first thing I mentioned. Doak said they had moved in on May 15, 1951, and after a summer without it, had decided to install an air-conditioning unit. The house was built by Paul Page, a backfield mate of Doak's at SMU and one of his close friends. The interior, which combines Early American and modern design, looks as if it had been lifted right out of the pages of *Better Homes*

& Gardens. Both the living room and huge den have oak-paneled walls and beamed ceilings. The kitchen is completely electrically equipped. A massive fireplace of Colorado ledge stone stretches for approximately fourteen feet across the front of the living room. On the mantel, the 1948 Heisman football trophy is flanked by the two *Sport* Top Performer trophies Doak won as a college and pro player.

"The fireplace is my doing," Doak said. "It's the only thing I can take credit for. The rest is Norma's."

Because I had not seen him since he entered the National Football League, I first asked some familiar questions about pro and college ball. Doak made it plain that he liked his job with the Lions.

"And I think there's more spirit with the pros," he said. "I'm not sure how to explain it except to say that in pro ball you know you're the cream of the crop. You've reached a peak and take more pride in your work. There's a certain lack of confidence in what you and your teammates will do in college. It's the trial-and-error period.

"Yes, there's less pressure for me, of course. My last two years in college I *had* to come through. For three years I played both offense and defense. With the Lions I'm a halfback on the T and a flanker right and left. I don't have as much to do. I guess I passed all of five times last year. I got a kick out of those stories in the papers that said I'd injured my passing arm." (Doak received a deep cut above his right elbow while attempting to move a car in the parking lot at the National Open golf tournament in Dallas last June.)

Another reason Doak thinks it's more fun to play pro is that he is able to keep his mind on football throughout the week, yet he averages only an hour and a half of actual on-the-field practice each day. "At school we spent more time than that and you had to worry about classwork after you got through," he said.

I asked Doak if he had had a team preference when he decided to play pro football. He was originally assigned to Ted Collins' nomadic Yanks in the National Football League but rights to deal with him were shifted to Detroit in exchange for T-quarterback Johnny Rauch. Cleveland held first claim to him in the All-America Conference but the dissolution of that league resulted in Detroit being Doak's one and only choice.

"No," he said, "we didn't know much about the pro leagues down here. It didn't matter which team got me. I was glad to go with Detroit after I learned Bobby [Layne] was there. It's funny, but when we were in high school we talked of playing together in college. When we got out of the service, I went to SMU and he went to Texas and we said maybe we'd get together later on. You might say it was a teen-age dream come true when we finally did."

Doak paused and rubbed his wounded elbow. "I was really skeptical about making it in pro at first. When I joined the Lions after the All-Star game, I still didn't know how I'd go. Everybody looked so big, I felt even smaller."

Old pros in the National Football League, who habitually cast jaundiced eyes at hotshot All-Americans trying to break into the ranks, viewed Walker doubtfully. He looked too small to most of them, too.

But a few weeks after he joined the Lions, there wasn't a skeptic in sight. His teammates had hardly had a chance to get acquainted with him when he scored all the points for them as Detroit beat the Packers 24 to 21. Bobby Layne knew him and knew what he could do. He threw passes, Doak caught them and Green Bay fell victim to a typical Walker finish. After booting a field goal, he caught an eight-yard touchdown pass in the last two minutes of play.

Doak has an excruciatingly hard time supplying the details of the big games he has played, as if in the recounting of them he might find something that would embarrass him. Nearly all of the game-action description here comes from sources other than the Doaker. He is hard pressed to supply even the scores.

When Doak signed a contract with the late Bo McMillin of the Lions, there was some heavy (and largely erroneous) guesswork about the terms. The generally accepted estimate was $60,000 for three seasons. Doak admits to the three-year agreement, which expires at the end of this season, and to receiving a bonus for signing, but he says the reported figures are badly out of shape. His annual salary would be more accurately estimated at $13,000. "Pro salaries are greatly exaggerated," Doak commented. "I would say the better halfbacks in the league were now getting between $8,000 and $12,000. Your top quarterbacks get more, of course. Things changed fast after the other league broke up."

Largely because of business reasons, Doak thinks this will be his last season in pro football. It will take a handsome new contract offer from the Lions to get him out of Dallas next summer. "I know I'll have to quit sometime and I have such fine offers here I can't afford to postpone them much longer," he said.

Along with the largesse Doak received in his senior year at SMU came a number of attractive business opportunities from Dallas firms. He found it hard to turn them down. Although Doak was brought up in a middle-income family (his father is assistant superintendent of schools in Dallas) and he was on a full scholarship at SMU, he never had money to throw around. When the alumni gifts to him were made public in the winter of 1949, Doak was quoted by the campus newspaper as saying, "I'm very happy with them. I'm tired of being poor."

There is slim chance of Doak becoming poor again. His present financial interests in Dallas include a half share in Doak Walker Sport Center, Inc., which sells children's toys, clothes, and sports equipment, and a February-through-May assignment on the sales staff of Triangle Motors, the local Oldsmobile dealer. His string of endorsements lists Wheaties, Dr. Pepper, Gillette and Wilson Bros., with whom he has a contract for signatured football equipment. In his last semester at Southern Methodist, Doak blossomed out as a minor capitalist by acquiring a gas station in Highland Park. He has since sold it. The station raised a few eyebrows (outside Texas) but actually Doak put up some of his savings and the bonus he received from the Lions to purchase it.

While we talked, Doak's wife, Norma, came into the living room, carrying their four-month-old daughter, Laurel Lea. Norma is the same lovely, brown-haired girl who appeared with him on magazine covers and in newspaper photos everywhere in 1948 and '49. As Norma Peterson, a coed at SMU, she was picked Cotton Bowl Queen and Drake Relays Queen. They conducted one of the best-recorded, non-Hollywood romances in the country, through no fault of their own. He was the All-American football hero and she was the All-American girl—not the girl next door exactly, but she lived in the same end of town and they attended the same high school. The romance came to a perfect cinematic climax on March 17, 1950, when they were married at Highland Park Presbyterian Church. Doak's father was best man and Kyle Rote and Bobby Layne were among the groomsmen. A wedding trip to Canada in a twin-engine Beechcraft with Coach and Mrs. Rusty Russell and Mr. and Mrs. W. H. Davison, president of Core Laboratories, owner of the plane, was interrupted but not seriously marred when the craft groundlooped at the Denver airport.

They may have been the most famous college couple in the country a few years ago but, at the time, Doak and Norma worried only about seeing each other between classes—and football games.

"He was always in that athletic dorm, or if he wasn't there he was at football practice," Norma said. "We were both PE majors so we had some classes together."

I asked her when they first started going together and she suggested Doak tell me.

"Well, it was some time in 1945," Doak began.

"It was Thanksgiving Day 1945," Norma said.

Doak gave his wife a sheepish grin and continued. "Norma was dating an end on the team. Not all the time but pretty regularly. He introduced me to her and we had a sandwich date. I went out a couple times with them, then we double-dated, and pretty soon he was going out with us. Then I took over."

Two years after their marriage, on March 10, 1952, Laurel Lea was born. "We had an awful time naming her," Norma said. "I went into the hospital with a list of fifty girls' names. We couldn't agree on one of them. She was nameless for three days. There were so many people around all the time, the only way Doak and I could talk about it was to have him call me on the phone."

The baby has enabled them to slide into a living routine they both enjoy. In Dallas, Doak's schedule starts at six in the morning. "I get up, put the bottle in the warmer, go out and fix the lawn hose, come in and change the baby, give her the bottle, read the paper, and then I wake up Pedro." (His nickname for Norma comes from an abbreviation of Peterson, her maiden name.) They find it easy to leave Laurel Lea with either grandparents when they go to a swimming party at the Brook Hollow Country Club or get together with college friends. Doak has a weakness for Western films on television and admits he spends hours watching them, even though Norma says she can't understand why anyone will sit and watch something for so long when he knows how it will turn out. Doak doesn't mind if the scenery and plot never change.

They are active church members and attend the Highland Park Presbyterian Church in Dallas. The only book I saw in their living room was a Bible inscribed "Norma and Doak, May 17, 1950." Doak long has been a steady church-goer. At the end of the 1948 season, when the SMU team was asked to pick a date to vote on a choice for a Cotton Bowl opponent, the Sunday morning following the last game was suggested. Doak said he was sorry but he couldn't be there because he would be attending Sunday school and church services then. The meeting was set for the afternoon. Among the many citations he received in 1949 was one in *The Presbyterian Outlook,* which pointed him out as one of the "notable Presbyterians of the year."

The Walkers enjoy going to Detroit at the end of the summer even though it means a major packing job and looking for a place to live over again. "Still, it's kind of a vacation for us," Norma said. "We look forward to it. We live near many other players and their families and we see a lot of each other."

I wanted to know what she thought of pro ball and of Doak's playing.

"I like it," she said emphatically. "And I'm glad he's playing. When he's under a big pile I suppose I worry some."

"You do?" Doak said in mock astonishment.

"Sure I do. Especially at first when they all seemed so big and you were so small."

Doak looked a little embarrassed. He didn't say anything.

Later, Norma had an appointment in town and Doak drew the baby-sitting assignment. He sprawled on the living-room sofa and Laurel Lea sat facing him in the "Baby Butler," taking occasional swipes at the attached rattles and listening to her old man tell how he decided to go to Southern Methodist.

"Bobby and I were in the Maritime Service together," he said. "We took our basic at St. Petersburg and then we went to New York to radio school. We were in New Orleans planning to ship out as radio officers when we found out they had a long waiting list of unassigned officers. We were down toward the bottom. When they gave us our choice of waiting a couple of months—with no pay—or taking a discharge, we got out.

"I really wanted to go to the University [of Texas] with Bobby, who was already enrolled there. While we were in New Orleans for our discharge, we saw SMU play Tulane. They [SMU] lost and then I was sure I would go to the University. It was the sorriest performance I'd ever seen. You know the story about Bobby and I going to the hotel to see Blair Cherry, the Texas coach. We just missed him. But this is how we missed him. In the lobby, we ran into Henry Spraggins, a great SMU rooter who carried the sideline chains for years at games. We asked him if he had seen Cherry and he said yes, he went that way. He sent us in the wrong direction. I guess Henry got a big kick out of that later on.

"I went home after my discharge and when I walked in on the folks I told them I wanted to go to the University. I knew they were anxious I stay home. Daddy asked me if I wanted to live and work in Dallas after I graduated and I said yes, I suppose I did. He pointed out the advantages I'd have if I went to SMU. He was right, of course. In the meantime, coach Rusty Russell, who had been my high-school coach and was then assistant to coach Bell at SMU, came over to the house and spent all day Sunday there. The next day I went over and enrolled. Rusty clinched it by being there."

One week after Layne and Walker sat in Tulane Stadium in New Orleans and talked about playing together at Texas, they faced each other in a game. This surprising circumstance was made possible by the war-time curriculums in existence at both schools at the time. Bobby, a sophomore, stepped right into his old job as quarterback of the Long-horns, and Doak, eligible through the freshman rule and completely fa-miliar with the Russell-designed offense used by the Mustangs, became the regular tailback after three days' practice. The two friends put on quite a show. Doak ran thirty-seven yards for a first-half touchdown, Bobby passed to two scores, and the Longhorns won 12 to 7. Neutral observers called the Layne-Walker duel a standoff.

The Methodists, who won two of six games before Doak arrived, went on to take three of four Southwest Conference battles. Freshman Walker was such a sensation he was picked as the second-best back in the conference. Layne was first choice. He was invited to the East-West Shrine game and pitched a touchdown pass that tied the score 6 to 6.

SMU rooters were understandably grieved when the Doaker was drafted into the Army, February 28, 1946.

"I went in a private and came out a private," Doak said. "I guess I wasn't very enthusiastic about it, having been in the Maritime Service. I wasn't much of a soldier. I used to stay in bed until the last possible moment and then race out for rollcall. I had it timed to the second. After basic training at Fort Lewis, Washington, I was assigned to Brooke Medical Center and I spent the next fall playing left-halfback in the T. I really had it pretty good, playing football all the time."

Doak asked me if I'd like something to drink. "How about a Dr. Pep-per?" he said, making a small joke of it. We drank Dr. Pepper.

One subject Doak will talk freely about, without much encourage-ment, is the aid he got as a football star at Southern Methodist. I first heard him discuss it in a bull-session with teammates at the 1950 All-Star football training camp. He spoke then as if he were trying to dis-prove rumors he was sure were being circulated. When I asked him to spell out the provisions of his scholarship, he said, "It was the regular football scholarship—board, room, books, tuition and four dollars a month for laundry. Later on the laundry money was pushed up to ten dollars. If you had spent yours, you could go out and help someone else spend theirs. We were always rich with the ten bucks.

"If they were handing anything else out to the boys, I should have known about it. I know that at one time a few fellows on the team took advantage of some alumni. They'd borrow their cars for a weekend and they maybe hit them up for expenses or clothes. But Matty moved in when he heard about it and put a stop to it. We worked according to conference regulations. During the track season, the football team helped out running the meets and vice versa. I didn't do much work because I played both football and baseball. Everything was above the table. That's the way it should be."

If you are familiar with Doak Walker's background and boyhood, you know there was neither the need nor the urge for a handout when he became a college football player. It has been written that his father, Ewell Doak Walker, Sr., a Tennessean who played football as an undergraduate at Austin College in Sherman, Texas, and later coached the game at North Dallas High, brought Doak up to be an All-American. Whether or not he consciously set such a lofty goal for Doak after his birth on January 1, 1927, he and Emma, his wife, reared their son well. Doak can't remember when he first started playing football. He always had a regulation-size ball to play with and his father spent hours tossing it to him or sticking it in his belly, in the manner of a T-quarterback, as he ran by.

The boy who was to grow up to become a hero to millions of young Americans had his own idol in those days. He was Harry Shuford, who was an All-Conference fullback at Southern Methodist in 1935. Doak first met him at a summer camp in Ward, Colorado, where he accompanied his father, a counselor. Shuford wore number 37 on his jersey. It would make a nice story to say that Doak would have no other number from then on but, he confesses, he wore 84 in high school. Anyway, Shuford was his hero and he often asked his father to take him over to the SMU practice field to watch him. Doak once put his sentiments about Harry on paper. The title of a composition he wrote in a fourth-grade writing class was "The Great Fullback Named Harry Shuford."

Six years later, Doak was running from tailback on the Highland Park High School team and drawing worshipful glances from fourth-grade boys along the sidelines. As a high-school athlete, Doak won twelve letters—three each in football, basketball and swimming, two in baseball and one in track. First and foremost he was a football star.

Had you been one of the 19,000 people seated in Ownby Stadium on the Southern Methodist campus, December 23, 1944, you would have seen an amazing action preview of Doak Walker, All-American. Highland Park High, equipped with the same plays that Walker and others were later to use with such success at SMU, played San Angelo High in the semi-finals of the state football championship that Christmas weekend, and Doak gave a performance that he was to copy many times on the same field and, later, in the Cotton Bowl.

Although today Doak can't tell you what he did in the game, he does remember how much he and his teammates pointed for San Angelo, who had knocked them out of championship play the year before. Doak was then a lean, 158-pound triple-threat, on his own completely now that his former Highland Park sidekick, Bobby Layne, was playing his first season at Texas. Doak scored 121 points that fall, and when anybody in the state talked high-school football, they talked of Doak Walker at Highland Park.

The San Angelo game was Doak's last schoolboy appearance before a Dallas crowd (he was to graduate at mid-term), and he made it a spectacular one. Highland Park rolled to a 39–6 victory and Doak's chief contributions, in chronological order, were: a five-yard dash for a touchdown; a pass to Bill Moxley for a second; three touchdown passes to Harold Clark; a lateral to Moxley that enabled him to scamper fifty-nine yards to a score. Doak got one drive under way by taking a punt off his shoetops and sprinting twenty-six yards with it. His pass interception set up another. Three of his six placement attempts were good.

In a somewhat anti-climactic title game at Austin, Doak and his teammates lost 20 to 7 to a superior Port Arthur club. Doak's last high-school scoring act was a twenty-three-yard pass for Highland Park's one touchdown.

Small wonder then that coach Rusty Russell, after becoming an assistant to Matty Bell at SMU, camped in the Walkers' living room that Sunday until he was sure he would see more of his ace. Rusty knew his immediate future looked brighter with Doak along.

In September 1947, Russell was one of many people at Southern Methodist who were happily relieved to see Walker pull on a red jersey again and do battle for the Mustangs. Not yet nineteen, Doak already had had one short varsity season under his belt and a term in the Army, where his chief duties were scoring touchdowns for dear old Brooke Medical Center. Football optimism in Dallas, always high as a kite, soared even higher before the season started. Matty Bell had what looked like a first-class backfield. There was the smacking fullback, Dick McKissack, and the fleet wingback, Paul Page, who skimmed low to the ground and was difficult to upend. There was the bullseye passer with the balding pate, Gil Johnson, and there was Walker. It was a backfield to be compared to the Ponies' history-making 1935 Rose Bowl quartet, which included Harry Shuford and the redoubtable Bobby Wilson, the greatest back Southern Methodist had had.

It wasn't many weeks before Wilson was being compared to Walker.

The Mustangs, driven by their remarkable tailback, who ran and passed and called plays and stood at safety on defense, rode over Santa

Clara, Missouri, Oklahoma A&M, Rice, and UCLA. Their November 1
date with Texas, always a violent enemy, suddenly assumed the proportions of a showdown battle for the Southwest Conference title. The
Longhorns had stampeded six opponents with an attack that had averaged four touchdowns a game. Behind the scoring barrage was Doak's
towheaded pal, Bobby Layne.

Once more Bobby and Doak squared off, this time under the most
dramatic circumstances possible.

A packed house in the Cotton Bowl shrieked itself hoarse as SMU
went into an early lead right at the kickoff. Then, in the second period,
Doak floated out of his halfback post and sped downfield under a high,
arching pass thrown by Gil Johnson. Forty-five yards from the line of
scrimmage, on the Texas twenty-yard line, he twisted into the air and
gathered the ball in. Longhorn defenders moved in on him but he
slipped away and darted for the corner of the end zone. He came within
an eyelash of making it but was knocked out of bounds on the one.
Dick McKissack took care of the short yardage remaining, bulling
through the line for the touchdown. Doak kicked his second extra
point. It was the difference in the two teams because Texas, behind
Layne's tireless passing, scored twice and missed one conversion.

It was the last game in which Bobby and Doak played against each
other.

After the victory over Texas, the Mustangs—and Walker—were everybody's target. But Texas A&M, Arkansas and Baylor couldn't bring
them down. Only Texas Christian, the oldest and most traditional foe
of SMU, stood between them and a perfect season and, of course, clear
title to the conference championship.

The 1947 SMU-TCU game will be recounted, with a steadily dimin-
ishing amount of accuracy, for years to come around the lobbies of the
Baker and Adolphus hotels in Dallas and on Fort Worth street corners,
or wherever fans will congregate on the eves of future TCU-SMU
games. It is one of the events that has added fuel to the belief that in no
other section of the country do they play such spectacular, all-out, hell-
for-leather football as they do in the Southwest. It is also one of the
games which added an incredible chapter to the already preposterous
Doak Walker biography.

Part of it, at least, should be replayed here: One not necessarily reliable eyewitness reported that ninety seconds remained in the game when
the purple-and-white-jerseyed TCU team, trailing 12 to 13, broke out of
the huddle on its own twenty-yard line, third down and twenty to go.
The Horned Frogs went into one of their characteristic widespread for-

mations with Lindy Berry back. He took the center pass, danced back a few steps and then fired the ball thirty-five yards to the speeding Morris Bailey who took it in stride and bolted for the Southern Methodist goal line. As he did so, both McKissack and Walker laid sure hands on him and would have stopped the play on the spot had not Bailey shoveled the ball to Charlie Jackson who happened by. Whether it came by accident or design, the lateral sprung Jackson downfield and he hit the SMU eight-yard line when Bobby Folsom finally caught him and rolled him over. On the first play from that point, Berry lit out for the right side, stopped short in face of the Mustangs' pressing defense and flung a lateral that tumbled around unclaimed near the ten-yard line. Fullback Pete Stout got his hands on it and he pushed through the disorganized SMU line for a touchdown. Suddenly, SMU found itself trailing 19 to 13.

The following kickoff went to Walker, much to TCU's distress, standing on the three-yard line. The Doaker started toward the right sidelines with a gait that suggested he might be contemplating a reverse. But he kept the ball, and as his blockers formed, picked up speed. At midfield, he was flying down the sidelines and no one could stop him until he had reached the Frogs' thirty-five. At that point the Mustangs took time and rushed in Gil Johnson, who had been waiting at coach Bell's elbow. Matty himself says that Walker let out a shout for Johnson as he roared by the bench on his sixty-two-yard kickoff return. Doak's call for Johnson was no stroke of genius but it was delivered under unusually pressing circumstances.

Gil came in, cranked up his arm and let fly, as everyone expected. Twice he overthrew on pass plays to Walker and Sid Halliday in the end zone. On third down he shot one to Doak who made what witnesses describe as a miraculous catch in the neighborhood of the ten-yard line. Doak had done everything else that day; a diving, glue-fingered grab of a tough pass was not too much to ask. The clock raced toward "0" as Johnson dropped back for the fourth time. Everyone in TCU Stadium, who was still on his feet and could see, followed number 37 as he darted into the end zone. So did most of the desperate Texas Christian defense, because Johnson rifled a pass to captain Sid Halliday, crouched on his knees, over the goal line. As Sid squeezed the ball to his belly, pandemonium broke out that shook houses half the way to Dallas. In the broadcasting booth, high above the stadium, the hysteria-choked voice of Bill Stern told a breathless audience across the country: "SMU goes ahead, 19–19!"

Bill was one kick ahead of the story. Doak had the conversion to

make if SMU was to pull this fantastic game out and conclude an un-
beaten, untied season. But at this point, as thousands screamed, the
Doaker became a flesh-and-blood human being again. He missed.

For those who had seen what he had done that day, it might have
been too much to accept if his kick had been true. After all, they had already watched him break away on twisting, weaving runs of eighty,
sixty-one and fifty-six yards. They had seen him throw fourteen passes,
ten of which gained 136 yards for the Mustangs. They had seen him average fifty-four yards on three kickoff returns. They had seen him score
two touchdowns and outwit and outmaneuver the hopped-up Horned
Frogs, who were bent on stopping him and destroying the only perfect
record in the Southwest. They had seen him do as much as any player
ever had done in a game at TCU Stadium. There was a limit—even for
the Doaker.

The tie did not prevent Southern Methodist from becoming conference champion and sectional representative in the Cotton Bowl for the
first time since the series of post-season games was started in the Dallas
stadium in 1937. Selected to oppose the Mustangs was Penn State's undefeated and seldom scored-upon eleven. The Nittany Lions, who had
scored seventy-five points on Fordham and had had but three touchdowns registered against them all fall, were considered tough company
for anyone.

They didn't discourage Walker, however. Traps were set for him all
over the floor of the Cotton Bowl that New Year's Day. State prevented
him from running away with the ball game only after (1) he had arched
a high, fifty-three-yard pass to Paul Page who caught it on the dead run
on the visitors' thirteen and raced for the score and (2) he had bucked
the final three yards for a second touchdown. The two rivals ended in a
dead-heat, 13 to 13.

For Doak and his teammates, the game ended a grueling four-month
season that had grown in tension and strain as the weeks went by. They
were kings of the Southwest and, in a fashion, co-champs of the East
with Penn State. Doak made dozens of All-America teams. He was
hailed as the college player of the year. He found it more and more
difficult to retreat to normal campus life. There were constant requests
for luncheon and banquet appearances in and around Dallas. He was
invited to Philadelphia to receive the Maxwell Club football award
from commissioner Bert Bell of the National League.

He was happily relieved when winter passed and the invitations
slowed down. In the spring, there was more time for his studies (he took
a summer course at North Texas State to help catch up), for dates with

Norma, bull-sessions at the Phi Delta house and baseball. Doak won three letters in baseball at SMU. He still likes to play, and before his arm was injured last summer, he was an outfielder for the Bell Roofers in a Dallas semi-pro league. When I asked Doak what he was hitting, he thought for a moment and then said: "Oh I guess I hit about one-third."

The spontaneous flow of publicity for Doak, which had thinned down to a trickle in the spring, burst wide open in the late summer of 1948. Lester Jordan, the director of sports publicity at Southern Methodist, did not have to lift a hand to his typewriter. Newspapers, football magazines and national weeklies clamored for his picture. Doak posed in football uniform, at home with his family, on the campus with Norma, etc. Probably no college boy ever got so much publicity and was so little swayed by it.

In the wake of this pre-season publicity blast aimed at their star tailback, the Mustangs won their first two games in a way that hinted they would be tough to beat again. Added to the all-star backfield was sophomore Kyle Rote who, some people thought, might be better than Walker.

A surprising Missouri team caught SMU with its offense sputtering and whipped the Texans 20 to 14. Many scouts and sportswriters, who saw the upset at Columbia, believe Walker showed more stripes of an All-American that day than in any other single game.

His pass-catching was breath-taking but, then, Doak has left many other audiences breathless with his catches. He took one pass for a touchdown and another of his circus grabs lined up the second, which he made on a run. But what everyone talked about after the game was the incredible one-man defense he played. The greatest offensive star in college football had the big pro-Missouri crowd roaring at his shoe-string tackles and perfectly timed pass interceptions. He plucked two Tiger passes out of the air at the brink of the SMU end zone and twice spilled ball-carriers as they broke into the open field with touchdown gleams in their eyes. As few players have been before or since, Doak was a 100-percent All-American that day.

On October 30, 1948, the University of Texas had further cause to rue the day Doak decided to go to SMU. Before 68,750 people, the largest football gathering in Southwest Conference history up to the time, Doak had another field day against the Longhorns. SMU won by a substantial 21–6 margin and Walker had a hand—or foot—in all of the winning points. For the first score, he faked a pass and then stepped sixty-seven yards through the scattered Texans. He went over again on a point-blank dive into the line. The third Mustang touchdown came on a play, originating on the Texas eighteen-yard line, which saw the Doaker leap up and flip a short pass to Ralcigh Blakely, who in turn lateraled to Kyle Rote. Doak's three placements were all true.

Another tie with Texas Christian, this one also achieved on a last-minute pass by Gil Johnson, was the only irregularity on the Mustangs' 1948 conference record. Again they won the right to play in the Cotton Bowl on New Year's Day.

The University of Oregon provided the opposition and Doak, celebrating his twenty-second birthday, and Kyle Rote provided the fireworks. SMU won 21 to 13. Doak completed six of ten passes, quick-kicked eighty yards and threw a few blocks that rattled typewriters in the press box. One of them sent Rote shooting all the way to the two-yard line from where Doak carried it across on the next play.

Reporters surrounded Oregon coach Jim Aiken in the dressing room after the game and asked him what the Northwest thought of the Southwest's pride and joy. Jim was munching soberly on a chunk of fruit cake. Between bites he said, "What can you say? He was the works . . . the greatest I've ever seen."

Jim didn't know it, but the last statement put him in an exclusive league with one hundred other college coaches, all of whom have publicly stated at one time or another that Doak is positively the greatest they have ever seen.

Football coaches have been quoted as saying many things about Walker. Yet they all come to the same general conclusion. They have remarked he is not fast. (The last time anyone held a stopwatch on him —his junior year in high school—he was timed at 10.2 for one hundred yards.) They say he is not very big (which is true). They describe him as a fairly good passer—but no great marksman. (In college, he completed 139 of 239 passes for 1786 yards.) They describe him as an adequate but not unusual punter. (He averaged 39.6 yards with the eighty-five kicks he made at SMU.) They rate him as a fair blocker. (The Chattanooga *Times* picked him on its twelfth annual All-American blocking team for 1949.) But they admit they never have seen anyone quite like him on a football field.

The fantastic merry-go-round of public appearances, award presentations and radio-television requests whirled even faster that winter of 1948–49. Doak was at Love Field, the Dallas airport, so often he looked like a commuter. On the trip to New York to accept the Heisman award, he was accompanied by his mother and father, his sister Pat, and Norma.

After three punishing seasons, during which he had been the first target of every team on SMU's schedule, nature—and the opposition—caught up with Doak in his senior year. It was no secret that teams had informally conspired to "get" him in the past. Rumors that arch-rivals had put a price on his head floated around the Southern Methodist campus before many big games.

Not until the third game of the 1949 season did an opponent succeed in knocking Doak out of commission. It happened while Rice was in the process of inflicting the first beating the Mustangs had taken in conference competition since 1946. Gerald Weatherly of Rice tackled him out of bounds, dumping him against a wheelchair on the sidelines. The blow knocked him out. Doak was lugged to the dressing room but he was back on the field during the second half.

Whatever Doak thought about it at the time, he wanted the public—and Weatherly—to believe he considered it an accident. He walked into the Rice dressing room after the game and congratulated the Owls on their 41 to 27 victory. The following summer, when Doak met the former Rice center, Joe Watson, at the All-Star training camp in Wisconsin, he said to him: "Just how much was that pot you had up for me last fall?" Joe smiled and said he wasn't sure there was one. Doak gave him a grin and said, "Well, I was curious to know how much you guys figured I was worth."

The injury in the Rice game was the first of a string of misfortunes Doak encountered that fall. When Kentucky came to Dallas to play the Mustangs the following Saturday, Doak was in bed with a virus condition and dysentery. SMU won 20 to 7, and the boys went to the infirmary afterward and gave Doak the ball.

Against Texas the following weekend, Doak made six brief appearances. On the last one, he calmly booted the extra point that won the game, 7 to 6, even though teammate Billy Weatherford juggled the low pass from center.

Before the Texas A&M game at College Station, Doak's weight went below 150 pounds. (His first year at SMU he weighed 175; his normal playing weight with the Lions is 170.) Because of a weak stomach he could swallow nothing but a half bottle of ginger ale before game-time. But the Aggies, who chased his flying heels over the goal line twice and saw him kick three extra points in the 27–27 deadlock, could work up no sympathy for his condition. Neither could an Arkansas team which yielded three touchdowns to him, plus a scoring pass, the next weekend.

On paper, at least, the Doaker was his normal devastating self again. The Mustangs lost to Baylor 35 to 26, despite his three touchdowns. He scored one of them by stabbing a pass from Fred Benners while lying flat on his back in the end zone.

But Doak wasn't up to par, despite outward appearances. His weight was still down and he had an aggravating charley horse in his leg. In the next-to-last game on the schedule, a losing effort to TCU, he kept his team in contention with some gallant passing and running until he re-injured his leg in the second half. The crowd at TCU Stadium, many of whom had seen him perform the miracle of 1947 on the same field, stood up and cheered his limping exit. They didn't know they were applauding Doak's last appearance in a Southern Methodist uniform.

The Hollywood scenario writer would have had the Doaker bowing out under more dramatic conditions. At the least, he would have had Kyle Rote, who staged an historic one-man riot against Notre Dame the following Saturday, diving over the Irish line for the third time and saying, "There's one for the old Doaker." Unfortunately, there is no evidence that Kyle was of such romantic turn of mind.

It was later suggested to Doak, by a somewhat romantic sportswriter, that he might have inspired that tremendous effort against Notre Dame. "Wasn't there," the reporter said hopefully, "some mention of winning the game for you in the huddle before the kickoff?"

Doak's smile burst into laughter. "Well, that's *one* I never heard before," he said.

After his signing with Detroit became public knowledge, many of Doak's friends worried out loud over his future. They knew he would weigh forty or fifty pounds less than most of the linemen and linebackers who would be taking professional cracks at him. They knew he had taken a weary battering from some of the best college players in the country for four seasons.

One football fan in Dallas, a misplaced Baylor rooter, said to me, "There were people in Texas who hoped he wouldn't make it, too. It's not easy to understand because Walker is such a high-type fellow, but school ties are so strong down here some of the University and TCU crowd resented his publicity and attention. Maybe they had been beaten by him too many times. I know those folks hoped he'd go up to Detroit and get his ears pinned back."

It is a matter of record that he didn't. No matter how highly you judged him as a college player, Doak had an astonishing first season in pro ball. With his 170 pounds—and all that goes with them—he scored 128 points. Against the college boys, Doak scored 303 points in four years. Included in that total were forty touchdowns, sixty conversions and a lone field goal. The Lions were hard up for a dependable field-goal kicker when he arrived, so Doak put in some extra practice and booted eight of them as a rookie.

He did a lot of other things people didn't think he could get away with as a pro. He averaged nearly five yards whenever he carried the ball. He caught thirty-five passes for an average gain of 15.3 yards. He punted thirty-two times and ranked ninth in the league with an average of a fraction under forty yards. As described earlier, he scored all twenty-four points when the Lions beat the Packers that fall. He embarrassed the New York Yanks by averaging 11.5 yards every time he carried the ball against them.

Last year, his running and pass-receiving (his two chief offensive assignments in the Lions' T-offense) gained 777 yards. He scored ninety-seven points, third best in the league.

Doak has a lot more help as a pro than he did in college. He doesn't have to go around saving games with last-ditch tackles or non-stop, goal-to-goal runs very often. But there were times last year when the Lions needed Doak's magic hand to bail them out.

One of them came in the Los Angeles Coliseum last December 8 where 67,892 fans had gathered to see the Rams and Lions in a duel for the lead of the National Conference. Doak had scored once on a neat double reverse but Bob Waterfield had kicked five field goals for Los Angeles, which held a 22–17 lead as the game swung into the final three minutes. The Lions started a drive that picked up momentum but the clock threatened to kill it. A pass play by the old Highland Park High combination, Layne to Walker, covered twenty yards. On a quarterback keep-it, Bobby poked his way through the left side of the Rams' line and raced twenty-five yards before he was stopped on the twenty-two. The next play started in the same direction but Layne palmed the ball to Doak, running from left-halfback, who took off toward the right flank. The Rams' end, tackle and linebacker on the right side swarmed in on him. Suddenly, he stopped and pitched a perfect pass to Leon Hart over the goal line. The Lions won 24 to 22. Shades of Doak running them dizzy in the fading seconds of a Southwest Conference battle!

On the last afternoon of my visit with Doak, we drove the short distance from his home to the SMU campus where he was taking daily workouts. Because he knew I had not seen much of the school and its grounds, he drove up and down the streets between the impressive brick colonial buildings which cover the 133 acres of high ground in University Park. He pointed out some of the more prominent halls and dormitories. A group of boisterous coeds exploded through the doors of one building as we passed. "They're going to cheerleading school," Doak said matter-of-factly.

I asked him if he had any yearning to return to Southern Methodist as a coach. Apparently a job is open to him for the asking. "I'm not so sure," he said. "There are times when I think I would like to stay in football as a coach . . . and then I remember how little security there is in it."

Doak stopped the car behind Ownby Stadium, which is located at one corner of the campus. Before the Mustangs started playing their games in the Cotton Bowl, the large concrete-and-wooden stands served as their home field. Now it is used for practice. Doak put on a pair of shorts and football shoes and got a football from the janitor on duty. I followed him through the dim tunnel and out into the bright sunlight on the field. Fred Benners and Pat Knight, two recently graduated SMU football stars who had signed pro contracts, were throwing passes to each other. Doak greeted them and then started limbering up, jogging up and down the field.

I climbed up high in the empty stands so that by craning my neck I could see the brick-red and green campus beyond the stadium wall and, to the south, the Dallas skyline hazy in the late-afternoon heat. On the field below, Doak assumed the approximate proportions he might if you were watching him from a stadium seat during a game. He looked even smaller, of course, without his uniform. He was running and jumping up and throwing left-handed passes that went thirty or thirty-five yards. As I watched him, I remembered a conversation I had had with a man from Dallas in the hotel that morning. He was a local businessman. The polished, pointed toes of his cowboy boots and a faint drawl betrayed his origin. Our talk about football got around to the recent epidemic of de-emphasis which has swept a few athletic conferences. It was obvious he considered it pretty silly business. He said that Texans liked their football just the way it was. "Anyway," he added, "who in hell would want to de-emphasize Doak Walker?"

Who would?

The Ten Years of
Jackie Robinson

Roger Kahn | **1 9 5 5**

When the Brooklyn Dodgers are at home, Jackie Robinson may visit the United Nations on a Monday afternoon and discuss sociology with a delegate. "There is still a little prejudice in baseball," he will remark, "but we have reached the point where any Negro with major-league ability can play in the major leagues." That Monday night, Robinson may travel to Ebbets Field and discuss beanballs with an opposing pitcher. "Listen, you gutless obscenity," he is apt to suggest, "throw that obscene baseball at my head again and I'm gonna cut your obscene legs in half." If Jackie Robinson is an enigma, the reason may be here. He can converse with Eleanor Roosevelt and curse at Sal Maglie with equal intensity and skill.

As Robinson approaches the end of his tenth and possibly final season in organized baseball, he is known in many ways by many people.

Because in the beginning, Robinson endured outrage and vituperation with an almost magic mixture of humility and pride, there are those who know him as a saint.

Because today, Robinson fights mudslinging with mudslinging, and sometimes even slings mud first, there are those who know him as a troublemaker.

Because Robinson destroyed baseball's shameful racial barrier, there are those who know him as a hero.

Because in the ten seasons Robinson has turned not one shade lighter in color, there are those who know him as a villain.

Although Jackie Robinson is, perhaps, no longer baseball's most exciting player, he is still its most controversial one. The world of baseball is essentially simple. The men in the light uniforms—the home team—are the good guys. They may beat little old ladies for sport, they may turn down requests to visit children in hospitals, but on the field, just so long as their uniforms are white, they are the good guys. The fellows in the dark uniforms are bad. They may defend the little old ladies and spend half their time with the sick, but as soon as they put on gray traveling uniforms, they become the bad guys.

The one modern player who does not fit the traditional pattern is Robinson. He has been booed while wearing his white uniform at Ebbets Field. He has been cheered as a visiting player in Crosley Field, Cincinnati, or Busch Stadium, St. Louis. Robinson is not "of the Dodgers," in the sense that the description fits Pee Wee Reese or Duke Snider. First, Jackie is the Negro who opened the major leagues to his race. Second—but only second—he has been one of the Dodgers' most spectacularly effective stars.

As a ballplayer, Robinson has created one overwhelming impression. "He comes to win," Leo Durocher sums it up. "He beats you."

It is not as a Dodger star but rather as a man that Jackie arouses controversy. Ask one hundred people about Robinson as an individual, and you are likely to get one hundred different impressions.

"They told me when I went to Brooklyn that Robinson would be tough to handle," said Chuck Dressen, who managed the Dodgers from 1951 through 1953. "I don't know. There never was an easier guy for me to manage and there never was nothing I asked that he didn't do. Hit-and-run. Bunt. Anything. He was the greatest player I ever managed."

Walter O'Malley, who replaced Branch Rickey as Dodger president in 1951 but did not replace Rickey as Robinson's personal hero, has a different view. "Robinson," he insisted in an off-guard moment last May, "is always conscious of publicity and is always seeking publicity. Maybe it's a speech he's about to make, or a sale at his store, but when Robinson gets his name in the headlines, you can be sure there's a reason. Why, that business with Walter Alston in spring training, it was ridiculous. It was just another case of Robinson's publicity-seeking."

"I'll say this for Jack," Duke Snider declared. "When he believes something is right, he'll fight for it hard as anybody I ever saw."

"I'm just about fed up with Robinson fights and Robinson incidents and Robinson explanations," admitted a widely syndicated columnist.

"He's boring. I'm going to heave a great big sigh of relief when he gets out of baseball. Then I won't have to bother with him any more."

"When I first came up, I was pretty scared by the big leagues," Carl Erskine recalled. "I remember how friendly Jackie was. I was just a kid. It's something you appreciate a whole lot."

"He's the loudest man around," an umpire said. "No, maybe Durocher is just as bad. But Robinson's gotta second guess every call and keep his big mouth going all the time."

"I've got to admire him," Ralph Kiner said. "He had a tough time when he was younger and he was a pretty rough character. That's no secret out on the Coast. But he's gotten over that now. You have to hand it to Robinson. He has come a long way and he's taken a hell of a lot but he's never stopped coming."

On the 1955 Brooklyn Dodgers, Jackie holds a peculiar position. In point of years he is an elder statesman, and in point of spirit he is a club leader. Yet he has no truly close friends among either white or Negro Dodgers.

Jackie is an inveterate card player and when the Dodgers travel, this passion seems to bring him near players with whom he cannot have much else in common. Frequently he plays with Billy Loes, a pitcher who walked out of the blackboard jungle and into the major leagues. Loes is interested in girls and, to a lesser degree, in baseball; he is interested in little else. Jackie's conversations with him occasionally run two sentences long.

"Boy, am I havin' lousy luck," Loes may offer.

"Your deal, Billy," is a typical Robinson reply.

Jackie rooms with Jim Gilliam, the young second-baseman who usually has less to say than any other Dodger. Even when he might have roomed with Joe Black who, like himself, is a fluent and fairly sophisticated college man, he roomed with Gilliam. Robinson and Gilliam, in a sense, are business associates rather than friends, but Gilliam, during a recent burst of conversation, was able to cast a great deal of light on Robinson's relationship with other Negroes both in and out of baseball. "Some of my friends, when they hear I room with Jack, they say 'Boy, you room with him? Ain't he stuck up?' " Gilliam reported. "I tell them the truth. He's been wonderful to me. He told me about the pitchers and stuff like that, and how much I should tip and where I should eat and all that. He ain't been stuck up at all."

Inside the Brooklyn clubhouse, Robinson's position is more of what one would expect. He is a dominant figure. His locker is next to that of Gil Hodges. Next to Hodges' locker is a space occupied by a small gas heater, and on the other side of that sits Pee Wee Reese. As captain, Reese is assigned the only locker in the entire clubhouse that has a door.

Duke Snider is nearby and Reese's locker is one of the gathering points in the clubhouse. (The television set is another and that isn't far from Robinson's locker, either.) During clubhouse conversations, Jackie, like Reese and Erskine, is a club leader.

In many ways Jackie, after ten years, is the natural captain of the Dodgers. He is the team's most aggressive ballplayer and it has been suggested that had Robinson been white he would be captain now. Reese is the most respected of all Brooklyn players, but he doesn't have Robinson's fire.

To this day, a few Dodgers make occasional remarks about color. "Don't you think they're gonna take over baseball in ten years?" a player challenged a newspaperman earlier this year after a long and obviously fruitless conversation. "They can run faster; they'll run us white guys right out of the game." The player spoke sincerely. He has been happy to have Robinson on his side, but he is afraid that Robinson represents a threat. This ambivalent feeling is not uncommon on the Dodgers.

"The players were the easiest part of all," Jackie himself insisted once when reviewing his struggle. "The press and fans made things a whole lot tougher." Robinson tends to say what he wishes were true and offer his wish as truth. The resentment of players obviously was among the most difficult obstacles he had to surmount. Robinson's introduction into the major leagues prompted Dixie Walker to ask that he be traded, and brought the St. Louis Cardinals to the verge of a player strike. A great deal of player resentment still remains, and in some cases Jackie's success has made it even stronger. Naturally, players who resent Robinson do not tell him so. Public proclamations of bigotry have virtually ended in baseball. Yet Jackie's subconscious awareness of resentment, plus the fact that resentment remains, are significant parts of any evaluation of his place on the Dodgers today. There has been integration. It has not been complete.

Jackie Roosevelt Robinson today is grayer, fatter, richer, and far more assured than he was ten years ago. He has built a handsome home set among three acres of rolling Connecticut woodland, but he has developed a nervous stomach. He has acquired considerable presence before a microphone; he is a good speaker.

We talked most recently one morning on a bumpy bus that carried the Dodgers from the Chase Hotel in St. Louis to the city's airport.

Robinson is permitted to stay at the Chase and has been for the last two years. It is interesting to note that when the hotel management first suggested to the club that it was time the Negro players checked in at the Chase along with the rest of the Dodgers, certain qualifications were laid down. "They'll have to eat in their rooms," the hotel official said, "and they'll have to agree not to hang around the lobbies and the other public rooms." Told about the offer, Roy Campanella said he would pass it up. Roy wasn't going to stay anywhere he wasn't wanted. Don Newcombe, Jim Gilliam, and Joe Black agreed. But Jackie Robinson said he guessed the terms were all right with him, he would stay at the Chase. It was a wedge, anyway. So he did, and within an amazingly short time the hotel lifted all the bars and quietly passed the word that Jackie should consider himself just another guest and go where he pleased in the hotel and eat where everybody else ate. So now, because Jackie, eight years after he hit the big leagues, long after the "pioneering" days were supposed to be ended, was still willing to humble himself in order to advance the larger cause, all Negro ballplayers are welcome at the Chase—and another barrier has come down. Wherever Jackie goes, he encounters reminders of barriers that no longer exist because of himself.

"We feel," he began, "that . . ."

"Who is we?"

"Rachel and me," Robinson explained. Rachel, his wife, has played a tremendous role in the ten years of Jackie Robinson.

"Anyway," he said, "we feel that those barriers haven't been knocked down because of just us. We've had help. It isn't even right to say *I* broke a color line. Mr. Rickey did. I played ball. Mr. Rickey made it possible for me to play."

Of all the men Robinson has met in baseball, he considers Rickey "the finest, in a class by himself." Before the 1952 World Series, Jackie made a point of specifying that he wanted to win the Series for two people: "Rae and Mr. Rickey." Rickey was then general manager of the Pittsburgh Pirates and O'Malley had succeeded him as Dodger president. "But I wanted to let Mr. Rickey know where he stood in my book," Jackie explained.

"Aside from Mr. Rickey I haven't made any what you call real close friends in baseball," Jackie said. "I mean, I got a lot of respect for fellows. Pee Wee Reese."

I was taking notes on a bouncy bus. "Shall I write Durocher's name here, too?" I asked.

"No," Robinson said. "Don't write down Durocher. But I mean fellows like Gil Hodges. One of my biggest kicks was when I heard Ben Wade talking about me being a team man. It indicated to me a lot of guys have that feeling. I felt pretty happy about it."

"Are you pretty happy about most things?"

Robinson was carrying two large packages on his lap, juggling them as the bus swayed. "I don't think I can be any more contented than I am now," he said. "I've been awfully lucky. I think we've been blessed." He nodded toward the packages. "These are for Rae. Presents. We're very close. Probably it's because of the importance of what I've had to do. We've just gotten closer and closer. A problem comes up for me, I ask Rae. A problem for her, she asks me."

"What does she say about all the fights you get into?"

Jackie grinned. This had come up before. "Whenever I get in a real bad argument, I don't care about O'Malley or anything like that. I'm kinda worried about coming home. What's Rae gonna say? My real judge of anything is my family relations. That's the most important. The house, you know, it wasn't so important to me. Rae, it's something she always wanted for the kids. It's no real mansion. I mean there's only four bedrooms."

"Do *you* think you get involved in too many incidents?"

"If I stayed in a shell," Robinson said, "personally I could be maybe 50 percent better off in the minds of the little people. You know, the people that feel I should mind my place. But people that I know who aren't little, you know, people who are big in their minds, I've lost nothing by being aggressive. I mean that's the way I am, and am I supposed to try to act different because I'm Negro? I've lost nothing being myself. Here in St. Louis, you know how much progress in human relations we've made? Aggressiveness hasn't hurt."

"Suppose, Jack, you were to start in again. Would you be less aggressive? Would you act differently?"

Around Robinson on the bus, his teammates chattered among themselves. None bothered to eavesdrop. "I'll tell you one thing that would be different," Jackie said. "I sort of had a chip in the beginning. I was looking for things. Maybe in the early years I kept to myself more than I should have because of that chip. I think maybe I'd be more—what's the word?—outgoing. Yeah, I know that. I'd try and make friends quicker."

Jackie looked at his shoes, then glanced out the bus window. It was a factory neighborhood. The airport was still twenty minutes away. "I wouldn't be different about aggressiveness if I was doing it over again," he said. "I guess I'm an aggressive guy." Robinson stopped as if he were waiting for a refutation. "Funny thing," he said when none was offered, "about this whole business. A lot of times you meet white fellows from the South who never had a chance to mix. You find them more friendly than a lot of Northerners. It's the Northerners sometimes who make the fuss about aggressiveness."

Over the years, Jackie has been asked about retirement frequently. In 1952 he said difficulty with umpires was making him think of quitting. Since then he has repeatedly mentioned the thought of retirement from baseball, but only recently has he secured a high-paying job which is to start when his playing career ends. Robinson says he is now financially independent of baseball. He is playing only because he feels he owes the game a debt which he must repay by remaining in it as long as he can play well.

"I don't know about next year," he said. "It depends on the ball club; how much I can help the ball club. I'll be able to tell easy how much I can help, soon as I see the contract they offer me."

The bus pulled onto a concrete highway and, quite suddenly, the bouncing stopped. The sun had risen higher and heat was beginning to settle on St. Louis. It was going to be good to escape. There was only one other question I wanted to ask Jackie. His answer was not really satisfactory.

"The toughest stretch since I came into baseball?" he said. "I guess it was that Williams thing. I ran into Davey Williams at first base and there I was right in the middle of a big obscene mess again and I figured when I get home Rachel's gonna be sore and what the hell am I doing this for? I don't need it. I don't need the money. What for?" Jackie sometimes gets excited when he recalls something that is important to him and he seemed about to get angry all over again. Sal Maglie had thrown at a few Brooklyn hitters one game in May, and Robinson bunted to get Maglie within spiking distance. Maglie stayed at the mound and, instead, Davey Williams covered first after Whitey Lockman fielded the bunt. Jackie was out easily but he bowled over Williams as he crossed the base. Thereafter Maglie threw no more beanballs, and the Dodgers won the game, but Robinson, praised by some and damned by others, was a storm center again. As he thought of it, his anger rose.

"Wasn't it tougher in the early years?" I asked quickly.

"No," Jackie said. "In the early years I never thought of quitting. There was too much to fight for. With that Williams thing, I was fighting for nothing except to win. That was the toughest stretch I ever had to go through. I mean it."

If Robinson's evaluation of the Williams affair was valid, then he is the recipient of a lot of misplaced credit. Actually, his evaluation was wrong. The hardest thing Robinson ever had to do in baseball was the first thing he had to do—just to be the first Negro in modern history to play organized ball. Almost willingly, he seems to have forgotten a great deal of his difficult past. Rarely now is there talk in baseball of the enormously courageous thing which Jackie accomplished.

On a train between Milwaukee and Chicago, Rube Walker, a reserve Dodger catcher from Lenoir, North Carolina, was talking about bean-balls. "I don't like 'em nohow," he said.

"But what we see isn't so bad," said Dixie Howell, the Dodgers' number-three catcher, who lives in Louisville. "I was at Montreal when Robinson first broke in. Man, you never saw nothin' like that. Ev-y time he come up, he'd go down. Man, did they throw at him."

"Worst you ever saw?" asked Walker.

"By a long shot," Howell said.

Ballplayers are not demonstrative and Walker did not react further. This was in a dining car and his next words were merely "pass the salt, please." But he and Howell felt a matter-of-fact professional admiration for one of Jackie Robinson's many talents—his ability to get up from a knockdown pitch unfrightened.

To make a major point of a North Carolinian and a Kentuckian sharing admiration for a Negro would be wrong. After Jackie Robinson's ten years, Walker and Howell are not unique. The point is that after the ten years, Howell still regards the beanballs directed at Robinson by International League pitchers during the 1946 season as the most vicious he has ever seen. Jackie himself never mentions this. He cannot have forgotten it, nor is it likely that he has thrust the memory into his subconscious. But he would like to forget it.

It is no small part of the ten years of Jackie Robinson that nobody any longer bothers to count the number of Negro players who appear on the field in a big-league game. There once was much discussion of what John Lardner called "the 50-percent color line." Branch Rickey described it as "the saturation point." When a major-league club first attempted to field a team of five Negroes and four white players, it was whispered, there would be trouble. There seemed to be an enormous risk in attempting to topple white numerical supremacy on a major-league diamond. Today the Dodgers can start Don Newcombe, Roy Campanella, Sandy Amoros, Jim Gilliam and Robinson without so much as a passing comment.

In October 1945, William O'Dwyer was mayor of New York City, and Harry Truman was a rookie President. Dwight D. Eisenhower was wondering what new field he should try, because World War II had been over for two months. On the 23rd of the month, Branch Rickey announced that the Brooklyn Dodgers had signed a twenty-six-year-old Negro named Jackie Robinson and had assigned him to play for their Montreal farm team.

On the 24th of October, the late William G. Bramham, commissioner of minor-league baseball, had a statement to make. "Father Divine will have to look to his laurels," Bramham told a reporter, "for we can expect Rickey Temple to be in the course of construction in Harlem soon." Exercising iron self-control, Bramham called Rickey no name worse than a carpetbagger. "Nothing to the contrary appearing in the rules that I know of," Bramham said with open anger, "Robinson's contract must be promulgated just as any other."

The day he announced the signing, Rickey arranged for Jackie to meet the press. "Just be yourself," he told him. "Simply say that you are going to do the best you can and let it go at that." Since more than twenty-five newspapermen flocked to the press conference, Robinson could not let it go at that.

"He answered a dozen questions," wrote Al Parsley in the Montreal *Herald,* "with easy confidence but no cocksureness. His was no easy chore . . . he was a lone black man entering a room where the gathering, if not frankly hostile, was at least belligerently indifferent." Robinson handled his chore splendidly; press reaction was generally favorable, although frank hostility was evident throughout much of baseball and in some newspaper columns.

Alvin Garner, the president of the Texas League, announced: "I'm positive you'll never see any Negro players on any teams in the South as long as the Jim Crow laws are in force."

Happy Chandler, commissioner of baseball, refused to comment.

Clark Griffith, president of the Washington Senators, who had long ignored clamor urging him to hire a Negro, suddenly accused Rickey of attempting to become "dictator of Negroes in baseball!"

Jimmy Powers, sports editor of the New York *Daily News,* a tabloid with the largest circulation of any newspaper in America, predicted: "Robinson will not make the grade in the big league this year or next . . . Robinson is a 1000–1 shot."

Red Smith, writing in the now dead Philadelphia *Record,* summarized: "It has become apparent that not everybody who prattles of tolerance and racial equality has precisely the same understanding of the terms."

There was precious little prattling about tolerance in Florida that winter. In late February, Robinson flew from his California home to Daytona Beach, where the Montreal Royals were to train after a week of early drills at Sanford, a smaller town twenty miles distant. Jackie was cheerfully received by newspapermen, Dodger officials, and Clay Hopper, the Mississippi-born manager of the Royals, but he was received in the established Southern tradition by the white citizens of Sanford. After two days of practice at Sanford, Robinson was forced to return to Daytona Beach. Before running him out of town, Sanford civic groups explained: "We don't want no *Nigras* mixing with no whites here."

At Daytona Beach, Jackie lived with a Negro family and encountered only isolated resistance. When the Royals traveled to Deland for an exhibition game with Indianapolis some weeks later, he was given another taste of democracy as it was practiced in Florida during mid-March of 1946. As Robinson slid across home plate in the first inning of the game, a local policeman bolted onto the field.

"Get off the field right now," he ordered Robinson, "or I'm putting you in jail!"

Robinson claims that his first reaction was to laugh, so ludicrous did the situation seem. But he did not laugh. Then, as always in the South, Robinson had attracted a huge crowd, and as he faced the policeman, the crowd rose to its feet. The Indianapolis players, in the field, stood stark still, watching. Then Jackie turned and walked toward the dugout, and Clay Hopper emerged from it.

"What's wrong?" Hopper asked.

"We ain't havin' *Nigras* mix with white boys in this town," the policeman said. "You can't change our way of livin'. *Nigras* and white, they can't sit together and they can't play together and you know damn well they can't get married together."

Hopper did not answer.

"Tell that Nigra I said to git," the policeman said. And Jackie left.

Spring training ended on April 14, and when it did, the burden of living in the South was lifted from Jackie's shoulders. He had made the team, and when the 1946 International League season began, his job was pretty much limited to the field. Jackie had played shortstop for the Kansas City Monarchs when Clyde Sukeforth scouted him for Rickey in 1945, and he had tried out for the Royals as a shortstop. But the Royals owned a capable shortstop named Stan Breard and that, coupled with some questions about the strength of Robinson's arm, prompted a switch. As the 1946 season opened, Jackie Robinson was a second-baseman.

This was the season of the beanballs Dixie Howell remembers. It was the season in which a Syracuse player held up a black cat and shouted: "Hey, Robinson! Here's one of your relatives!" It was the season in which Baltimore players greeted Jackie with vile names and profanity.

But it was also the season in which beanballs so affected Robinson that he batted .349. And rather than answer the Syracuse player with words, Robinson replied with a double that enabled him to score the winning run. Rather than match names with the Baltimore players, he stole home one night and drew an ovation from the Baltimore fans. Probably 1946 was baseball's finest year, for in 1946 it was proved that democracy can work in baseball when it is given a chance.

At times during the 1946 season, Branch Rickey would travel from Brooklyn to Montreal for talks with Robinson. "Always," Rickey once said, "for as long as you are in baseball, you must conduct yourself as you are doing now. Always you will be on trial. That is the cross you must bear."

"I remember the meeting when Rickey said that," a man in the Dodger organization said. "Jackie agreed, too." The man chuckled. "I guess Jack's sort of changed his mind over the years." But it wasn't until the place of Negroes in baseball was assured that Robinson's conduct changed.

Late in the 1946 season, the Dodgers found themselves involved in a close race with the St. Louis Cardinals, and there was pressure applied to Rickey to promote Robinson in August and September. For a while Rickey held his peace, but finally he announced: "Robinson is the property of Montreal and that is where he will stay. Montreal is going to be involved in a playoff and we owe it to our Montreal fans to keep Robinson there." Montreal, with Robinson, won the Little World Series. The Dodgers, without him, lost a pennant playoff to the Cardinals in two consecutive games.

There was little connection between the reason Rickey gave for not promoting Robinson and the reasons that actually existed. As far as he could, Rickey wanted to make Robinson's task easy. To do that he needed time. All through the winter of 1946–47, Rickey met with leaders of the American Negro community. Just as Robinson would be on trial as a major-leaguer, he explained, so would Negroes be as major-league fans. Working directly with Negro groups and indirectly through Negro leaders, Rickey worked to make sure there would be as little friction in the grandstand as possible. While barring Negroes from play, owners had not refused to allow them to buy tickets, of course, and the idea of Negroes in big-league stadiums was nothing new. Yet, with Robinson on the Dodgers, a whole new set of circumstances applied to the old idea. Rickey's caution was rewarded in 1947 and in Robinson's first major-league season there was not one grandstand incident worthy of note.

In another foresighted move, Rickey shifted the Dodger and Montreal training camps to Havana, where the air was free of the fierce racial tensions that throbbed in America's South. Finally, Rickey did not place Robinson on the Dodger roster before spring training started. He wanted the Dodgers first to see Jackie and to recognize what a fine ballplayer he was. Then, Rickey hoped, there would be a sort of mass demand from Dodger players: "Promote Robinson." This just was not to be. Leo Durocher, who was then managing the Dodgers, is a man totally devoid of racial prejudice, but some of Durocher's athletes thought differently.

Dixie Walker wanted to be traded and wanted other Dodgers to join with him in protest against Robinson. Eddie Stanky wasn't sure. Happily, Walker found few recruits, and his evil influence was countered by that of Pee Wee Reese, a Kentucky gentleman. "The first time I heard Robinson had been signed," Reese said, "I thought, what position does he play? Then I found out he was a shortstop and I figured, damn it, there are nine positions on the field and this guy has got to be a shortstop like me. Then I figured some more. Maybe there'd be room for both of us on the team. What then? What would the people down around home say about me playing with a colored boy? I figured maybe they wouldn't like it, and then I figured something else. The hell with anyone that didn't like it. I didn't know Robinson, but I knew he deserved a chance, same as anybody else. It just didn't make any difference what anybody else had to say. He deserved a chance."

While the Dodgers trained in the city of Havana, Montreal drilled at Havana Military Academy, fifteen miles away. The team was quartered at the school dormitory, but Robinson, who had been accompanied by a Negro pitcher named John Wright during 1946 and now was one of four Negroes in the Brooklyn organization, was booked into a Havana hotel. This meant thirty miles of travel daily and Robinson, unable to understand the reason for a Jim Crow pattern in Cuba, asked Rickey about it. "I can't afford to take a chance and have a single incident occur," Rickey answered. "This training session must be perfectly smooth."

For two weeks Montreal played exhibitions with a Dodger "B"

squad and then the Royals and the Dodger regulars flew to Panama for
a series of exhibitions. Shortly before the trip, Mel Jones, then business
manager of the Royals, handed Robinson a first-baseman's mitt. "Listen," Robinson said, "I want to play second base. Didn't I do all right
there last year?" Jones said he was sorry. "Just passing an order down
from the boss," he said. "Mr. Rickey wants you at first base." Robinson
did not do badly at first base in the Panama series, and in the seven
games he batted .625 and stole seven bases. This was the demonstration
Rickey had awaited. Unprejudiced Dodgers said they were impressed.
Prejudiced Dodgers insisted that they were not. "I've seen hot-hittin'
bushers before," one said. After the series the teams flew back to Cuba,
and late one night Rickey passed along word to Robinson that on April
10 he was to become a Dodger. Eddie Stanky was the Dodger second-
baseman. Robinson would have to play first.

Happy Chandler's suspension of Leo Durocher had taken the spotlight away from Robinson by the time April 10 arrived, and in retrospect Jackie insists he was just as glad to have a respite from publicity.
The Dodgers had not asked for his promotion and as a whole their reception was cool. Robinson in turn remained aloof.

Jack has dark memories of 1947. He was reading in the club car of a
train once while several other Dodgers played poker. Hugh Casey, the
pitcher, was having a hard time winning a pot, and finally he got up
from the table and walked over to Robinson. Without a word Casey
rubbed Robinson's head, then turned and went back to his card game.

In 1947, Burt Shotton, who replaced Durocher, put Robinson second
in the Brooklyn batting order. On several occasions Dixie Walker hit
home runs with Robinson on base, but at no time did Jackie follow
baseball custom and shake Walker's hand at home plate. "I wasn't sure
if he'd take my hand," Robinson said, "and I didn't want to provoke
anything."

In 1947 the Philadelphia Phillies, under Ben Chapman, rode Robinson so hard that Commissioner Chandler interceded.

But there are other memories of 1947 for Robinson; more pleasant
ones. Jeep Handley, a Philadelphia infielder, apologized for Chapman's
name-calling. Clyde Sukeforth, a coach under Shotton, never once left
Robinson's corner. Hank Greenberg told him: "Let's have a talk. There
are a few things I've learned down through the years that can help
make it easier for you."

One player on the Chicago Cubs attempted to organize a strike
against Robinson, but was unsuccessful. The situation on the St. Louis
Cardinals was more serious. Only splendid work by Stanley Wood-

ward, a magnificent newspaperman who at the time was sports editor of the New York *Herald-Tribune,* brought the story to light. Only forthright work by Ford Frick, the president of the National League who has since become baseball commissioner, killed the Cardinal strike aborning.

The original Cardinal plan, as exposed by Woodward, called for a strike on May 6, date of the team's first game against the Dodgers. "Subsequently," Woodward wrote, "the St. Louis players conceived the idea of a general strike within the National League on a certain date." An uncompromising mandate from Frick to the players who were threatening to strike went like this: "If you do this, you will be suspended from the league. You will find that the friends you think you have in the press box will not support you, that you will be outcasts. I do not care if half the league strikes. All will be suspended. . . . This is the United States of America and one citizen has as much right to play as any other."

If, in all the ten years of Jackie Robinson, there was a single moment when the success of his mission became assured, then it was the instant Frick issued this directive. It is impossible to order people to be tolerant, but once the price of intolerance becomes too high, the ranks of the bigots tend to grow slim.

For Robinson, 1947 was very much like 1946. He never argued with an umpire. When Lenny Merullo, a Chicago infielder, kneed him, Jackie checked the punch he wanted to throw. When Ewell Blackwell stopped pitching long enough to call him a long series of names, Robinson said only: "Come on. Throw the ball." Then he singled.

But gradually the web of tension in which Robinson performed began to loosen. In the spring of 1948, the Ku Klux Klan futilely warned him not to play in Atlanta. But by the summer of '48, Robinson had relaxed enough to argue with an umpire. This was in Pittsburgh, and he was joined by Clyde Sukeforth. The two argued so violently that they were ejected.

Robinson became a major-league second-baseman in 1948, but, except for an appearance before the House Committee on Un-American Activities, it was not a notable year for him. Called to Congress to refute Paul Robeson's statement that American Negroes would never fight against the Soviet Union, Robinson delivered an eloquent speech. Rickey and Lester Granger, head of the Urban League, a national Negro organization, helped him write it and applause came from all sides. On the field, however, Robinson slumped. He had grown fat over the winter and not until 1949 was Robinson to regain top form.

The Dodgers finished third in 1948 but in 1949, when Robinson won the batting championship and a Most Valuable Player award, they won the pennant. By '49 Robinson felt free to criticize umpires whenever the spirit moved him; by '50 he was feuding with umpires and Leo Durocher and by '51 he was just about as controversial as he is today.

Currently Robinson will call a newspaperman down when he feels the reporter has been biased or inaccurate. Two seasons ago he had his most interesting argument with a reporter. Dick Young, of the *Daily News,* had written somewhat sharply about Robinson and then made a customary visit to the dugout before a Dodger game in Philadelphia. A few minutes before game-time nearly all the Dodgers were seated in the dugout and Young was standing nearby talking. "If you can't write the truth, you shouldn't write," Robinson shouted quite suddenly from his seat.

Unaware that Robinson was shouting at him, Young continued talking. "Yeah, you, Young," Robinson hollered. "You didn't write the truth."

George Shuba, the Dodger sitting next to Robinson, was studying the floor. Other Dodgers were staring at left field. None was saying anything.

"Ever since you went to Washington, Robinson," Young screamed as he attempted to seize the offensive, "your head has been too big."

"If the shoe fits," Robinson shouted, "wear it."

"Your head is big," Young screamed.

"If the shoe fits wear it," Robinson shouted.

The screaming and shouting continued until game-time, when Young left for the press box and Robinson devoted his attention to his job. "I couldn't let him get away with yelling at me in front of the whole team," Young said later. Relations between the two were cool for a while but time has healed the rift.

This season Robinson called down Francis Stann, a Washington columnist, before an exhibition game in Griffith Stadium. Stann had quoted an anonymous third party as saying that Robinson was about through and Robinson lashed him mercilessly and profanely.

"What good can that possibly do?" someone asked Robinson. "You'll only make an enemy."

"I can't help it," Robinson said. "I get so mad I don't know what I'm saying."

Why get so angry at newspapermen, who as a class are not more bigoted or biased than lawyers, congressmen or physicians? Well, newspapermen have hurt Robinson and in his lifetime Robinson has been hurt more than any man should be.

When a Dodger kicked in the door to the umpires' dressing room at Braves Field late in 1951, a Boston reporter blamed Robinson for the kicking. "I'm sorry, Jackie," the reporter said when he was told the truth. "It was right on the deadline and I didn't have time to check."

Another newspaperman once stole Robinson's name to use as a by-line on a story consisting of lies and opinions with which Robinson did not agree. This was during a period of racial tension on the Dodgers and the reporter's piracy put Robinson in the position of lying about the most important cause in his life. No one could take this in stride, of course, but Robinson took it particularly badly.

The rantings at reporters are well-known in the newspaper business and possibly because they have made him a formidable target for all but the most bull-voiced of critics, Robinson has almost reveled in his notoriety. But he gets along with most reporters most of the time and he occasionally makes an effort to help one.

Three springs ago during the period when Robinson was associated with a magazine, he fell to chatting in Miami with a newspaperman whose newspaper had just died. They talked vaguely of baseball for ten minutes before the newspaperman without portfolio ambled off in the general direction of a martini.

"He didn't take any notes," Robinson mused aloud. "I guess I didn't give him a story."

A bystander pointed out that the man's paper had folded. "Well, what's he doing down here?" Robinson asked.

"Looking for a job in baseball, maybe."

"Is he in a bad way?" Robinson said bluntly.

"He's not in a good way."

"Well, look," Robinson said. "He can write, can't he?"

"Sure."

"Well, look," Robinson repeated. "Tell him to go see the fellows at the magazine when he's in New York. I'll let them know he's coming and they'll give him some stories to write."

Robinson and the unemployed newspaperman had never been close. When a different sort of misfortune befell a sportswriter with whom he had been friendly, Robinson's reaction was even more direct and more swift. Telephoning about a luncheon, Robinson asked how things were and the sportswriter mentioned the death of a child.

"Oh, no," Robinson exclaimed. Instantly, he added: "How is your wife?"

"Not too bad."

"Is she home now?" Robinson asked.

"Yes."

"I'm going to call her," Robinson said and, without another word, he hung up.

Later, the sportswriter's wife was explaining how much the call had moved her. "It wasn't just that Jackie called," she said. "It was the way he called. The first thing he said was: 'I hope my bringing this up doesn't upset you, but I just want you to know that I'm sorry.' That was a particularly sensitive thing to say. It was a lovely way to say something that I know must have been very hard for him to say at all."

There are assorted targets for Robinson's current wrath. He is a harsh bench-jockey, and his needling is sharper than it ought to be. Even when he is not angry, he is so intent upon speaking his mind, regardless of whom he may hurt, that he is often indiscreet.

Jackie Robinson will speak his mind. This American Negro born in Georgia, bred in California, loved and hated everywhere, will not sit in the back of a bus or call all white men "Mister." He does not drawl his words and he isn't afraid of ghosts and he isn't ashamed of his skin and he never ever says: "Yowsah, boss." This American Negro, this dark symbol of enlightenment, is proud and educated and sensitive and indiscreet and hot-tempered and warm-hearted.

Those who do not know Robinson will call him "troublemaker." Those who do not understand him will call him "pop-off guy." Perhaps both terms are right. Robinson has made trouble for bigots, more trouble than they could handle.

Branch Rickey, who supposedly is the finest scout in baseball history, chose Robinson with wisdom, that borders upon clairvoyance, to right a single wrong. Robinson had the playing ability to become a superstar, plus the intelligence to understand the significance of his role. He had the fighting temperament to wring the most from his ability and he had the self-control to keep his temper in check. Why has he let himself go?

One excuse might be that he has been called "nigger" a thousand times in ten baseball seasons; another is that he was scarred in his crusade. But, really, Jackie Robinson doesn't need any excuse. If the man rugged enough to break baseball's color line turns out to be a thoroughly rugged man, no one has any license to be surprised.

What Price Olympic Peace?

John Lardner | **1 9 5 6**

Unofficial statistics show that good will prevails over bad will in the Olympic Games by a ratio of about nine to one, which is why the Games are still in business and a fine thing, too. Nonetheless, in memory and in history, it is the bad will that sticks out, like Sandy Saddler's thumb. The mind of man (a trouble-loving organ, at best) turns back with relish to such dates as these:

A.D. 400—Somebody stole the statue of Zeus from the Olympic Stadium in Greece.

1948—Somebody stole the Olympic flag from the stadium at St. Moritz.

1904—The first man home in the marathon turned out to have traveled twelve miles of the distance by automobile. He was excused from marathon-running for life.

1908—The American tug-of-war team resigned because the English team's shoes were too big. The British tuggers were, of course, cops.

1928—The French Olympic team was barred at the gate by a Dutch gatekeeper.

1932—On returning home to Argentina from the Games, the Olympic heavyweight boxing champion was put in jail for fighting.

1936—Avery Brundage threw a lady off the American Olympic team for drinking champagne with sportswriters.

1948—A young male member of the American team heard that Avery Brundage was planning to make a test run down the bob-sled course. "I hope he breaks his leg," said the young man, for publication.

1952—A maiden in a white nightgown floated around the arena, promoting peace. She was run off the premises.

1956—A man in a white flannel nightshirt floated round the arena, promoting peace. He was run off the premises.

Apart from the man in the nightshirt, alleged to be a Communist, the Olympics of 1956 have been mild, to date. American girl figure skaters were reprimanded, though not fined, for intramural cattiness. A male skater from Minnesota told the press that America should stop giving its money away, and save it to spend on amateur skaters, as the Russians do. This is pretty quiet stuff; the indications are that major rhubarbs will not break out this year until November, in Melbourne, Australia, which can take a hint, is said to be insuring everything in the country that is not nailed down, and to be putting a double guard over the museum which houses the nation's proudest possession, the heart of the racehorse Phar Lap. It is every Australian's belief that Phar Lap was poisoned in the U.S.A. What is to keep some foreign hop-step-and-jumper from stealing what is left of the big fellow?

At its best, however, the 1956 Olympics does not figure to produce a ruction to match the one in 1904, when Fred Lorz tried to revolutionize marathon-running. With most connoisseurs, this is the favorite Olympic rhubarb. Boiled down, it appears that Lorz, representing the Mohawk A.C. and America in the Games at St. Louis, developed cramps while he was still seventeen miles from the finish. The motor-car had just been invented. A motor-car was going Lorz's way. He climbed aboard, and soon out-distanced the field, to which he waved as he passed it. Five miles from home, the car took a tip from Lorz and broke down. Fred did the last five miles on foot, breezing. He breezed into the stadium, and was about to accept his prize from the President's daughter, Alice Roosevelt, when word got out that he owed his long lead to the internal-combustion engine.

Lorz was not lynched by the crowd. However, he was barred for life by the AAU, and became as popular in amateur sports as Benedict Arnold is with history students. There seems to be no doubt that Lorz was joking. There seems to be no doubt, either, that he had the narrowest escape from death of any Olympic counterfeiter since Pisidorus' mother.

Pisidorus was a runner in the ancient Greek games at Olympia. His mother was also his trainer. Women were barred from the stands in those days. The mother of Pisidorus disguised herself as a man, took a seat, saw her boy win, and expressed her satisfaction with tribal yells. It was this that tipped off the law. "That fellow is getting quite a bang out of the race," said one badger to another. (Badgers, or badge-wearers, or officials, are as old as Olympic history.) "True," said the other badger, looking closely at the noisy fan, "and the reason is that she is a dame." The boys studied the rules, and found that the penalty was death. Eventually, however, this was commuted to a handshake and a season's pass to the Games, for the public was on the lady's side, and the heat was removed from Pisidorus' mother by another rhubarb, when a boxer named Eupolus was convicted of bribing three of his Olympic opponents to take it easy. They fined the stuffing out of him.

Centuries passed, the old Olympics died, the modern Olympics were born, and we find the badgers still at work. Prince George of Greece, who stood six feet five inches tall, was officiating in the 1500-meter walk at Athens. Wilkinson, of England, was a great walker, as walkers go—but few walkers go very far without cheating. Like trotting horses, they tend to "break" into a run. The Prince noticed that Wilkinson had begun to run like a cheap silk stocking. He stepped out on the track and waved the Englishman off. "You are all through," he said, except that he said it in Greek. Wilkinson went right on going, but, as he came around on the next lap, Prince George struck a blow for badgers everywhere by throwing a block on him and tossing him off the track.

"Why didn't you stop the first time?" Wilkinson was asked later.

"I don't speak Greek. I thought he wanted my autograph," said Wilkinson, as cool a walker as ever broke into a gallop.

At London, in 1908, British and American athletes declared war on each other, and Italy challenged the winner. Trouble began with the tug-of-war—a gentle event on the face of it. The American team came out full of confidence, but stopped dead at the sight of the British team's shoes. Each boot was a city block long, and covered with cleats. "I didn't know the fleet was in town," the American captain said. "You have to use shoes, not gunboats." The shoes were normal, however, for cops' shoes—the British team being made up of Liverpool policemen, whose feet are bigger than Pinkertons' feet. So the tug began. The Americans surrendered just in time to avoid being pulled into the English Channel. They refused to try any further tugs.

A second U.S. rebellion occurred in the 800-meter run. As the leaders hit the stretch, Carpenter and Robbins of America were ahead of Halswelle, the famous English half-miler. Suddenly, someone off the track shouted "Foul!" A British badger, roused from a sound sleep, reached out and cut the tape, which was then passed by Carpenter, Robbins and Halswelle in that order. The race was ordered re-run. Halswelle re-ran it alone, in a walkover, and was called the winner. The U.S. runners sat out the event in their hotel rooms, re-fighting the American Revolution. They might never have come out again, except for meals, which are indispensable to amateur athletes, if the marathon race, run on the last day of the Games, had not made everybody forget every battle but the last one.

This was the marathon in which Dorando Pietri of Italy, the favorite, reeled into the stadium ahead of the rest of the field, looked wistfully around him and fell on his face, through for the day. He was hauled the rest of the way to the finish line by loving arms—in British sleeves, to hear the American press tell it. With Dorando still unconscious, or thereabouts, there came into view a New York ribbon clerk named Johnny Hayes, just running out his race. Hayes crossed the line and became the startled winner of the 1908 Olympic marathon. Dorando was disqualified for starting the race alone but finishing as a group. "Robbery!" yelled the headlines in Italy. The howling continued until Thanksgiving night of the same year, when someone thought to sell tickets to a Hayes-Dorando re-match in Madison Square Garden.

Every Irish-American and Italian-American in New York bought a seat in the Garden, or tried to break down the doors. Bands played, and the customers beat time to the music on one another's jaws. Dorando— and his fans—went home early. Not even all the Irishmen in the house waited for Johnny Hayes to finish that night, since they had breakfast to eat. But Johnny, a loser by the distance from Marathon to Pittsburgh, had the consolation of his Olympic medal, which was more than Jim Thorpe was to have four years later.

Thorpe's case was *the* rhubarb, and the only rhubarb, of the 1912 Games in Stockholm. The big Indian won the decathlon and the pentathlon, and got his medals all the way home before Francis Albertanti, a New York sports editor, revealed that Jim had once or twice played baseball for money, under the cunning alias of Jim Thorpe. The King of Sweden got the medals back, the world went to war with guns, and it was eight years before the war in short pants was resumed. En route to Antwerp, in 1920, the American Olympic team mutinied against its keepers because—the boys said—the beds aboard the transport *Princess Matoika* were for horses, and the meals were for dogs. "All right, so go home," said the Olympic committee. The boys looked around at the Atlantic Ocean, and saw that this was not the place for it. The mutiny was adjourned to Antwerp, where the team lived in barracks. The committee fired a hop-step-and-jumper named Dan Ahearn for decamping to a hotel, an unheard-of move for a hop-step-and-jumper. The whole team struck. Ahearn was reinstated, and finished sixth in the hop-step-and-jump.

By 1928, the Winter Olympics had begun to prove that snow is just as hard on the nerves as sunshine. Irving Jaffee of the U.S. got through his clocking in the 10,000-meter skating event at St. Moritz in what seemed to be unbeatable time. But the home committee noticed that the ice was defrosting fast, and called off proceedings with four finalists still waiting to skate their turns. The race was ruled no contest. The International Olympic Committee protested; Jaffee protested; the Swiss team, coming to see Irving off on the train for home, carried banners reading "JAFFEE, WINNER OF THE 10,000-METER RACE! LONG LIVE AMERICA!" But the records still say it was no race, and Jaffee had to wait for 1932 and Lake Placid to show he was the world's best. Meanwhile, the summer Games of 1928 set a new high in defensive play, at Amsterdam. The French team marched up to the gate on opening day, but a gatekeeper stopped them. France protested. Holland apologized. Next day, the French came up to the gate again, and again the keeper turned them back. France protested. Holland apologized. It was one of the greatest one-man stands since Horatius at the bridge—but the Dutch finally removed their star gatekeeper and France got into the Games in time to win the marathon on closing day.

To lure competitors to the summer Games of 1932, the town of Los Angeles invented a new event by suppressing a weather report. Some Europeans feared that Los Angeles was too hot. To prove it wasn't, the Chamber of Commerce took thermometer readings in 1931 for the dates corresponding to the Olympic dates. The worst heat wave in the city's history ensued. The chamber studied the readings and threw them into an ashcan. As a result of this shrewd move, everyone came to Los Angeles the next year—including, against great odds, the Brazilians and the Argentinians.

The Brazilian team had no money, so its government put the boys on a ship with fifty thousand sacks of coffee and told them to beat their way north by selling the stuff en route. Coffee sales were so poor that when the athletes docked in California, forty-five of them couldn't afford the one-dollar landing charge. The rest went ashore, and the ragged forty-five sailed up and down the West Coast peddling coffee until the Games were over. Argentina was racked by civil dissension in 1932. At Los Angeles, the Argentine team got its coach fired by cable, and the new ruling faction then produced the heavyweight boxing winner in Alberto Lovell, later a good pro. On the voyage home, civil dissension was resumed, with fist and gun. The ship's captain radioed ahead to Buenos Aires and the police met the boat and put Senor Lovell and his medal in jail.

All the world knows how, in 1936, on the ocean voyage to Berlin, Eleanor Holm, the backstroke swimmer, wet her lovely whistle with a champagne cocktail or two, and was detached from the team by Mr. Avery Brundage, the noblest badger of them all. "The athletes rode in the steerage, dry," reports Miss Holm. "The sportswriters rode first class, which was wet. The sportswriters invited me up, and I went." Miss Holm adds that, dry or fueled, she could have won her event with one hand.

The world also knows how, in Berlin, when U.S. Negroes began knocking over medals like bowling pins, the late Adolf Hitler was accused of congratulating no winners except white winners, and it became an international hassle. A more obscure, but actually livelier, issue developed that year on the soccer field, when Peru was penalized for flaws in etiquette and was instructed to replay a game it had won from Austria. The Peruvian delegation withdrew from the Games in a body.

It's a matter of Olympic record that soccer and hockey, in which mayhem is committed by hand and by club, respectively, are the leading sports in the production of international ill will. In the 1948 winter Games, hockey came close to wrecking the entire Olympic system before a stick was drawn. America sent two teams to St. Moritz, on opposite sides of the ship—one backed by the American Hockey Association and the *Ligue Internationale de Hockey sur Glace,* the other by the AAU and the IOC. The first team was thought to be more professional—as amateur hockey teams go—than the second. Yet the Swiss host committee loved the "outlaw" AHA team on sight, and the outlaws went right to work playing the schedule on behalf of America, while the AAU-Olympic team watched and booed.

Every day for a week, Brundage and the Swiss committee wrestled two falls out of three in a hotel room. Daily, the fate of the Games hung in the balance. Hockey was wiped off the books, then reinstated (when the outlaw team finished fourth). In the end, the *Ligue Internationale* was suspended by the IOC.

In the heat of the battle, it was not much noticed that the Canadian hockey team was thrown off the ice one day for roughness. Or that fiends in human form got to the U.S. bobsleds by night, and loosened the steering screws. Or that America's badgers—covering the team's retreat from Switzerland, when the Games had ended—lost the international combined bookkeeping-and-room-service event to the Swiss hotel-keepers. This is a quiet, savage contest that takes place in every Olympic year. Usually, the public does not hear of it, but in 1948 the blood of the U.S. management boiled over on two counts:

1. By adding special charges for milk and hot baths, the hotel-keepers billed the U.S. finance committee bowlegged, and broke its budget in two places.

2. The U.S. complained that there would have been more money to pay the tabs with if the Swiss gatekeepers at the Games had not passed in so many relatives and other free-loaders.

The following summer, in London, British-American war broke out again, on a small scale. The U.S. 400-meter relay team of Barney Ewell, Lorenzo Wright, Harrison Dillard, and Mel Patton won clearly from the British team in the final. But the judges ruled that England had won, because the Americans had committed a foul in passing the baton outside the legal zone. The winning medals went to the British runners. Then someone thought of consulting J. Arthur Rank's motion pictures of the race. The films showed that America's baton-passing had been as clean as a baby's mind—and the medals were pried loose from the British just in time to save the English-speaking Union.

There is a moral in this: Films can prevent rhubarbs, and restore peace to the Olympic Games. That leaves the question, who gets the film rights? As 1956 began, they were having a rhubarb about it.

Sunday's Gladiator

Irv Goodman | **1957**

When the alarm tinkled at 6:15 a.m. on Sunday morning, Alan Ameche stumbled across the room, clapped his large hand over the small clock, gave a grunt of satisfaction, and staggered back to bed. He moved so quickly through the chill of the blue-gray morning that his wife, Yvonne, heard nothing and slept on. It took half a day for the Ameche household to catch up with itself after that.

There was an important reason why the alarm had been set for 6:15. Sunday is the day Alan plays football, and in this well-ordered family Yvonne goes to early Mass on that day, before any of their three children—the oldest is not yet four years old—wake up, and without having to disturb Alan. She is always back before the children are up, prepares their breakfast, and is ready on the firing line when they come pouring out of bed like so many hungry little bears. Under this system, Alan gets to sleep until nine, or even later, enjoys a peaceful breakfast without the kids under foot, goes to ten-o'clock Mass, lounges around the house a while reading the Sunday papers, and then drives out to the park about noon. It is the thoughtful act of a young and conscientious wife that makes it all possible.

But on this Sunday morning, because sleepy Alan forgot why the alarm was sounding, thoughtfulness and orderliness went out the window—and sound and fury reigned. Yvonne didn't wake up until after eight o'clock, when the mother's master alarm clock—children rising—jarred her into wakefulness. The kids, Brian, three and a half, Alan, Jr., just two, and Kathy, eight months old, were up and hollering for breakfast. Yvonne rushed to the kitchen and got the pots to brewing, but she knew, with all her speed and determination, that this was a battle lost. She would fight it most of the day, but there would be no catching up.

Alan, undaunted, jammed the pillow over his head and slept on. It was no small accomplishment. Kids wake up like four-engined turbojet airliners turning over their motors. They don't lounge in semi-wakefulness, they don't seek the pleasure of a warm bed before bouncing out. Either they're asleep or they're awake, with no halfway measures. And when they are awake, it is never a secret. The turmoil that racked the Ameches' two-story, semi-detached, rented home did not abate. But Alan was stubborn; he refused to surrender. For half an hour, that is.

Then he, too, climbed down the stairs and into the battle. The boys by now were playing with large glasses of orange juice, and little Kathy was squirming in her playpen. Alan picked her up while Yvonne prepared her breakfast cereal and milk bottle. Then, while Yvonne fed the hungry little girl, Al helped the boys with their cereal. That is, he kept bowls from falling, spoons from flying and milk from splashing. He did his job well; nothing broke.

When the boys wanted cookies with their milk, Yvonne called in from the dining room, where she was feeding the baby, that they could have only one cracker each. (For some unknown reason, mothers always ration in units of one.)

"But they're only chocolate grahams," Alan said in the reasonable tones of the male animal. "They're good for the kids."

Yvonne shrugged. "Since when?" she said, and let it drop. Al left a half dozen or so more crackers on the table and went upstairs to get dressed. There was no time for him to have breakfast now. He would eat after church. Maybe order would return by then.

It was 10:10 before he got out of the house, and just to prove that there was no changing the kind of morning it was, at church he got caught in a double collection, the usual Sunday contribution and a second one to help pay for the new church. The same thing had happened to him earlier in the year in Madison, Wisconsin—he had gone back to Wisconsin for the few points he needed for graduation—where he also attended a new church.

While Alan was at church, Yvonne remained on the treadmill.

Things wouldn't get done. There were the breakfast dishes in the sink, lunch to be made for the kids, then the lunch dishes to do, the living room to be dusted, getting dressed, picking up the baby-sitter and trying to make time through what would surely be heavy traffic to the stadium for the game. What to do first? How to get finished? Yvonne didn't know, so she sat down and smoked a cigarette.

At about 10:30, the telephone rang. It was Mrs. Joe Campanella, whose husband is a middle guard for the Baltimore Colts and a close friend of Alan's. "I don't know what to do," Yvonne said over the phone. "I'll never be ready in time to pick up the baby-sitter. I think I better tell her to take a cab over."

Little Alan, hanging on the bannister, heard his mother talking. "Where's Mommy going?" he wanted to know.

"No place," Yvonne told him, finishing her phone talk and attacking the sink full of dishes. It was no use; her plans would have to be changed. She called the babysitter. "Would you mind taking a cab over? I'm worried about the traffic. And I think I'll let you give the children lunch. I won't have time. We'll forget about the meat loaf. Just broil some hamburgers. The meat's all ready. Or I have some chicken legs, if you want. . . . Okay, then. You'll be here about 12:30? Fine."

That was as much as she could hope for with three young children and a new babysitter. It was a calculated risk, but what could she do? They had had a regular baby-sitter last year, but her husband got a job out of town. Yvonne had been trying to find another suitable regular sitter for several weeks now, but with no luck. The babysitter they had the week before must have been seventy years old, Yvonne said, and she came all dressed in white. "I don't know what she expected," Yvonne said. "Two of our children are still in diapers, and white's no color to use while taking care of them. When we got back that evening, she complained because I had left sandwiches for her lunch instead of having a chicken dinner ready, which she told me she prefers on Sunday. 'All I have to say, Mrs. Ameche,' she told me when she left, 'is that your children were terrible.' Now I wonder what this one will have to say."

Al was back by eleven, had breakfast—two eggs, four sausages and instant coffee—and sat down in the living room and read the Saturday afternoon football scores in the morning paper. There was some yelling in the street, and he went out on his lawn to see what the kids were doing. By the time he got there, the kids—including Brian—were friends again. Alan stood out there for a while watching them play. "Somehow I can't get used to these houses all so close together," he said as he looked down the street of identical homes. "Back home you've got some ground around your house."

"Back home." He wasn't sure what that was going to mean any more. It had been a rough year for Yvonne and him. Both his father and her mother had passed away early in the year. And next February, Alan is going into the Army under the new six-month training program. Where would home be now? Kenosha, where he and Yvonne were raised? Madison, where they lived so pleasantly in a big house for four years? Or Baltimore, where, more and more, they were making friends and getting used to big-city life? As of now, Yvonne favored Madison. "It's a nice town for bringing up children." Alan still liked Kenosha. "It's our home town. All my friends live there. And it's an industrial city. I'd have a chance to get established in some sort of business."

Al waved to a neighbor across the street and went back in the house. It was time to go. He picked up his play book, a critical part of the Colt system. The play book must be carried at all times, to practices and to the game. To fail to deliver the book to the dressing room on Sunday means an automatic two-hundred-dollar fine. The penalty is so severe because, supposedly, the total fund of Baltimore football wisdom is transcribed therein. No Colt has been fined yet for failure to produce the book. Al kissed his wife on the cheek, said he would see her later and drove over to pick up Joe Campanella, who lives nearby.

Hearing Alan honk the horn, Joe came trotting out of his house and down the street, his play book under his arm. Joe, a good-sized fellow with a pleasant face, didn't look like the 250-pound, aggressive linebacker that he is. He settled beside Alan in the car and asked, "Did you sleep okay, Hoss?" Alan nodded.

A little later, Joe said solemnly, "Old Weeb (coach Weeb Ewbank) won't have to make any speeches today." They were playing the Chicago Bears this day, and for several reasons the Colts wanted this one badly. The Bears were the top choice to win the National Football League championship; they had defeated the Colts 38 to 10 the last time they met; and owner-coach George Halas, now only owner, said afterward that the Colts didn't cause his boys "too much trouble." This after the Colts had whipped the Bears 23 to 17 earlier last season.

"Looks like we're going to be on time for once," Ameche said.

"We'll shock people," Campy said with satisfaction.

"Maybe Weeb'll notice what a good influence I've become for that troublemaker Campanella," Alan said.

They drove down The Alameda, through a pleasant residential section and up to the new steel-and-brick Municipal Stadium. "Do you know the 'special'?" Alan asked, pointing to the attendant at the gate to the parking lot.

"Yeah, sure," Campy said.

The "special" waved them down and stuck his head in the window. "You fellows supposed to be parkin' here?" he started. Then, raising his voice, he said, "Hey, that's the Horse, ain't it?"

"That's him," Campy said. "Show him, Hoss."

And Alan, climbing out of the car, neighed mightily and then snorted. The "special" slapped him on the back heartily. "That's a good one," he chuckled.

On the way to the players' entrance, a crowd of youngsters jumped Ameche. "You the Horse? Sign here, Horse, whadaya say, sign here. Attaboy!"

Campy walked on ahead as Ameche signed the scraps of paper and fancy notebooks and bubble gum cards. "That's Joe Campanella," Alan said in a stage whisper. "Whyn't you get him to sign?"

Joe overheard it, as he was supposed to. "That Ameche," he said to another, "always giving me the business with the kids. Make believe we don't hear." And Joe stepped up his stride; the kids followed hesitantly, not sure that it really was Joe Campanella. They both laughed when Alan caught up to Campy in the tunnel leading to the Colt dressing room.

Most of the team was already there. A line was waiting outside the trainer's room to get taped. Like almost everything else about the Colts, pre-game taping has a precise system of execution. A taping schedule is issued to every player. The rookies begin coming in at 11:00, linemen at 11:30, offensive backs, who get taped last, after 12:00. Each man has an appointment time, with five-minute intervals between appointments. But, no matter how late a player's taping date is for, all men must be in the clubhouse at noon, two hours before game time. Alan's appointment was for 12:20. He stripped down to his shorts and went into trainer Ed Block's tiny rubbing room. Somewhere the schedule had broken down; Alan wasn't taken until 12:30. In a matter of minutes, Block had his ankles taped and was waving him off the table. Like most offensive backs, Alan required no fancy adhesive work. A few, though, like rookie Lenny Moore from Penn State, go in for complicated tapings. Moore gets taped *after* he has put on his low-cut running shoes. He has a habit of running out of his shoes when he turns, so he has the shoes taped to his feet. Of course, Moore gets a razzing because of his peculiar request; with the tape wrapped under and over his shoes and then around his ankles, he looks like the only football player in the world who wears spats.

Linemen who ask for special tapings, however, are seeking needed protection against the frequent kicks in the shins they receive in the line. Regular shin guards are too unyielding, so most of them have magazines or cardboard taped to their legs. Art Donovan, the big defensive tackle, wears used adhesive tape containers against his shins, but he does his own taping to avoid the jeers of the other huskies on the club.

"That Block, he's an artist with the tape," Alan said as he walked stiff-legged back to his locker and began dressing.

L. G. (Long Gone) Dupre, the fast little halfback from Baylor, was sitting on a stool alongside Ameche. Dupre reached into the bottom of his locker where equipment man Fred Schubach, Jr. had laid out all the gear and fresh clothing they would be wearing, and gave out with a shriek. "New socks!" he yelled. "Freddie's gone mad!"

Al put on a new pair of socks, then put on an old pair over them. He spread out his equipment; it was quite a collection of leather and canvas. The pro football player is issued gear that would do an infantryman proud. He has a warmup jacket, bench coat, belt, several pairs of pants, high stockings, both heavy and light sweat socks, a helmet, jerseys, shoulder pads, kidney pads, hip pads, thigh pads, knee pads, speed shoes, high shoes, sneakers (in case the field is frozen), cotton gloves (for very cold weather) and hand warmers.

The room was unusually quiet and relaxed as the men dressed. "The coach doesn't want any screwing around before the game," Alan explained. "Anyway, we've got plenty of time so everybody moves nice and easy." Ewbank, a short, squat man who must have been what football people call a watch-charm guard in his playing days, kept moving crisply around the room. He carried a sheet of paper covered from edge to edge with notes scribbled in a tiny handwriting. He moved from man to man, giving each the word after checking what he had written on his sheet. When he got to Ameche, he read from the sheet, "Get that start, keep thinking about it. When you flank, move out there and keep checking if they're following you." Then Ewbank moved on to his next *tête-à-tête*, and Ameche put on his pants. "I must be losing weight," he said loudly and proudly. "These things are getting looser and looser."

It was a happy note for Al since he had spent part of the pre-season training period at the Fat Boys' Table. A big fellow with an admirable appetite, he had gone up to 235 during the off-season. In another example of the exhausting thoroughness that Ewbank applies to his coach-

ing, a list of fifteen calisthenic exercises had been sent out in the spring
to every player expected to be invited to the training camp at Western
Maryland College. It included the usual pushups, toe-touching and
sprinting, and such interesting items as backward running (for the legs)
and cross-over running (to strengthen groin muscles). Alan did his daily
dozen dutifully, and reported in at 217 pounds, his playing weight. But
after a couple of weeks of hard work and harder eating, he went up to
225.

Voluntarily, Al put himself with the Fat Boys. One of his table mates
was Gerald Peterson, a tackle from Texas who checked in at 310
pounds. Gerald was on lettuce leaves and fruit salad with cottage
cheese until he came down to 265. It wasn't that bad for Alan. He had
his steaks and lean beef and plenty of vegetables, but no dressing on his
salads, no potatoes or bread or fats or sugar, and a drastic cutdown on
starch intake of any kind. Al wasn't particularly happy about his diet,
but he didn't go hungry and he did go down to 217 again. This time he
stayed there.

"Ten minutes," Ewbank yelled. By now, the players were all dressed
except for their shoulder pads and jerseys. They waited for the last moment to put these on because the room was warm. Defensive halfbacks
tossed a football back and forth. A few of the boys moved some
benches to the center of the room and lined them in rows facing a
blackboard.

"Five," Weeb called, and the players helped each other put on the
shoulder pads, tightening the laces in the back, and the tight jerseys. All
dentures were removed; this, too, is a club rule. Chewing gum was
tossed away. Gum or false teeth might be jammed in the throat during
the game. All rings except wedding bands had to be taken off; another
rule. Alan removed his wedding ring. "I once saw a fellow get his hand
stepped on. It cracked his ring and drove it into his hand."

Play books were brought forward and placed into small trunks with
slots marked for each book. When all the books were in—and this is
checked carefully—the trunks were locked and sealed in the equipment
room. The books are returned to the players on Tuesday morning, before the team's first workout of the new week.

These play books are the heart of the method employed by coach
Ewbank, a man with as many slogans as a political party in an election
year. One of them—the one that explains the play books—is that "a
team plays the game the way it practices it." And practice to Ewbank
means study plans, written exams, report cards and training films more
than it does scrimmaging. On Tuesday, the Colts hold a light workout,

on Wednesday they work on offense, on Thursday on defense, on Friday they put the two together, and on Saturday they hold another light workout, just enough to "break a sweat." But every day, before every workout, the team goes to class. The play book, which has been filled with play assignments, scouting reports, routines for warming up, and even assignments for pregame calisthenics, is studied in these classes. Scouting reports on *every* man on the team coming up on Sunday are copied into the books. General observations about the opposition are delivered by the coaches. For example, for that week's game against the Bears, one of the items put into the notebooks was that the Bears liked to "blitz," that is, send the inner linemen and linebackers charging into the backfield in an attempt to break up a play before it can get going. The Colts' answer to this, copied into the book and practiced on the field, was to use a quick count on the snap of the ball. This, in theory, would cause the Bears to lose the momentum they were trying to build up.

Ewbank, of course, lectures from a play book of his own, a volume two inches thick which he has been collecting and collating for twenty years. Weeb goes all the way by his book because "I want my men to know what we're trying to get done that day, or even that week, on the field before I send them out to work." To Weeb, there is no such thing as too much repetition; he likes to stay with a point down to the end.

He stood before the blackboard in the dressing room, his sheet of notes in his hand, and announced: "We'll be introduced at two." It was now 1:15. Quietly, the players took seats on the benches and waited.

"Time," Weeb called, and as a reflex action, equipment man Schubach walked through the room, quietly asking all visitors to leave. The door was left open because the room was very warm by now, but a uniformed guard, standing spread-eagled at the door, blotted out the outside world.

There was no need for Ewbank to call his class to order. The players were ready. The building of "victory pressure" (Ewbank's phrase) was beginning. So was the cram session. It looked like a briefing at some remote air base. Weeb checked out the "ready list," those twenty or so plays from their library of over three hundred that would be used this day. These are the plays the coaches have decided should work best against the personnel and defensive patterns of the opposition. Then Ewbank checked off the specialty teams for punting, kicking off and receiving, and as he called off each team, players stood and Weeb counted heads to make sure there were eleven, and the correct eleven, men standing. He went over defensive signals and gave instructions for the pre-game warmup, and as he went along he dropped key "victory pressure" words into his talk. Like "dig in there" and "smack when you go" and "move 'em out!"

At 1:22, someone yelled past the uniformed guard that the Bears were on the field. Ewbank stayed with his sheet of scribbled notes. To Ameche, he mentioned that he (Alan) must listen to quarterback George Shaw bark out the defensive alignment when he starts his signal calling. "Remember, that'll tell you how far to flare (flank out), and watch the linebacker. Maybe he's assigned to move with you. We want to know it."

At 1:30, on the button, Ewbank folded his sheet of paper and said with a snort, "Let's go." The Colts rumbled down the passageway and out into the bright sunlight, where they were welcomed by a loud, sudden cheer. It is not difficult to understand why players in all competitive sports like to play at home—after you hear such a reception. A cheer sounds different on the field than it does in the stands. That first shock wave of enthusiasm and encouragement as the home team comes into view is warm and exciting. The players can feel the throb of the cheer. To yells like "Go get 'em!" they must be tempted to answer back, "Damn right."

For ten minutes the Colts went through a quick but thorough warmup. They did all the exercises and drills, and at doubletime. Ameche's assignment, after the deep-knee bends and arm-waving, was to return kickoffs and catch passes while quarterback Shaw warmed up his arm. In pro ball, the quarterback is the cock of the walk whether he likes it or not. At 1:40 they trotted back to the dressing room for the pep talk. This time the door was closed.

It is questionable if Ewbank's "victory pressure" has much effect on his players. Pro football players, it would seem, don't need artificial stimulants at the last minute. They have worked all week at getting ready; they have had very little else to do. While Weeb made his speech about "This is the one that belongs to us and they're not going to take it away from us because we won't let 'em," more than a few Colts seemed not to be listening. Ameche sat through the talk with his head down. He may have been listening; he may have been praying; or he may have been trying to remember all the things that had been told to him in the past hour.

On the field, before forty-six thousand people, the honorary water boy for the game was being introduced. He had won a contest to give a nickname to rookie Lenny Moore. His winning entry was "The Bolt." Next the honorary girl cheerleader for the day was introduced. She, too, had won in the contest, with "The Whippet." Both youngsters got a boisterous reception. Then the Colt's mascot, a white saddle pony, was introduced, but the horse was not permitted on the playing field, the announcer explained, because the turf was a little wet. (Good enough for football players, but not for a horse?)

Suddenly there was a blare of trumpets. The Colt Marching Band, loud and brassy, was quick-stepping across the gridiron. It was just like a big college game, with the band, the leggy cheerleaders and the waving chrysanthemums.

Up in the stands, people began calling for Cheerleader Charley. "Come on, Charley," they yelled. "Let's have a C!" And Charley, a rotund, moon-faced fellow, stood up in his seat high up in the stands and hollered in his frog's voice: "Okay then, gimme a C!"

And the crowd responded clear and crisp: "C!"

"Now gimme an O!"

"O" was roared back at him.

"Yeah, now let me hear an L!"

"L" it was.

"Then gimme a T!"

"T" came clear and loud.

"An' what say an S!"

"S-S-S!"

By now, Charley's arms were raised high. He paused, ecstatic, for a moment, then swept the stands with a defiant roar: "Put 'em all together an' whadaya got?"

"COLTS!" cascaded down from thousands of seats. It was a spectacle of sight and sound to challenge the wildest cheers at USC.

The roars went up again when the Colts were introduced just before the kickoff. The talking was over now, for a while. The Bears kicked off, the ball was downed in the end zone, and play began. On the first play from scrimmage, the Bears lined up in a 5-3-3 defense with the ends tight, a pattern designed to protect against inside running and outside passing. The first game these two teams had played the year before had featured a different Bear defense. Then they defended against rookie Shaw, who had rolled out of the T-formation slot frequently and effectively at Oregon. The ends were wide and the center was relatively open. On that day, the Bears were not defending against rookie Ameche, and on the second play of the game, the first time he had carried the ball as a pro, Alan went seventy-nine yards for a touchdown. It was the longest run from scrimmage for him or any other Colt that season. On a handoff from Shaw, he had gone through the line at left tackle, turned evenly into the middle of the field and exploded. Once he cleared the line of scrimmage, not a Bear touched him. For the remainder of the game, Alan kept hitting the middle of the Bear line effectively; he gained 194 yards in twenty-one carries for a new Baltimore single-game rushing record.

It was quite different the first time he carried the ball in this game. It didn't happen until after the Colts gave up the ball and the Bears marched to a quick touchdown. Then Shaw gave him the ball on a quick handoff over left guard, and Al got two yards. (After the game, he was asked if he had thought, on this play, about that other first carry against Chicago, and Alan laughed. "I didn't think of that once all day. Quite a difference between those two runs, wasn't there?")

The Colts couldn't get going in the first quarter. From the sidelines Ewbank kept yelling, "Get some life in there! Move that ball! Where the hell's the blocking?" Shaw kept decoying with Ameche and throwing his halfbacks, Moore, Dupre, and Royce Womble, outside, but the Bear secondary, playing up because they believed Shaw could not throw long passes effectively, were able to come up fast to hit them as they turned the ends. Just before the end of the quarter, Shaw tried Ameche up the middle. Again there was no hole, and as he hit the line, Alan was turned sideways and his helmet was knocked off. He came out of the pileup with a scratch on the bridge of his prominent nose.

During the time out that followed, he got his face wiped clean with a damp towel. The Colts, like the Cleveland Browns, have no drinking water on the field during a game; they aren't allowed any even during practice sessions. On warm days there are ice bags on the bench, and a fellow can cop a chunk of ice to suck on, but that's all.

In the second quarter Shaw began hitting with passes, both short and long. Finally the ball was at the Bears' three-yard line, and it was Alan's turn. He bolted straight ahead on a power play, but the Bears piled him up for only a one-yard gain. Shaw sent him in again, this time on a fake. Then Shaw rolled out and lobbed a pass to Moore for the touchdown. Bert Rechichar's kick tied the score.

Late in the quarter the Colts got a break. The Bears tried for a first down on fourth at midfield, and the Ferocious Five, the famous Colt inner defense of Gino Marchetti and Don Joyce at the ends, Art Donovan and Gene Lipscomb (sitting in for the injured Tom Finnin) at the tackles and Campanella at middle guard, stopped them. Four Shaw passes in a row clicked, Womble catching the last one over his head and falling into the end zone. On each of the pass plays, Ameche stayed with Shaw, blocking out the hard-rushing ends. When the placement team came in, Alan trotted back to the bench. For the first time since the game had started there was a smile on his face. It lasted for only a moment. Then he slouched down on the wooden bench and put an ice bag on his neck. He hadn't carried the ball once on the touchdown drive, but he was tired.

Just before the end of the half, with the ball on the Colts' twenty, Ameche went up the middle to kill the clock. But as he struck the line, ramming in with his shoulder, something gave and Alan reached daylight. He cut sharply to the right, moved around the outside linebacker, who had moved in fast to catch him coming up the middle, and started downfield. He was running almost straight up now, the way he always had in college, and moving with good speed. One halfback came to him but couldn't hold him. No blockers had been able to form in front of him, and as Alan slowed up to shake off the halfback, the safety reached him with a slashing tackle from the side. He had gained twelve yards. The clock ran out before another play could be run.

That had been his first chance to display his peculiar running style— something of an upright galloping stride with knees pumping, arms flailing and nothing but moving muscle to grab. With his head up and his back straight, he looked as if he would be easy to hit. In fact, one pro scout watching him run at Wisconsin, said, "He'd get killed if he ever tried that with the pros."

It hasn't happened because, strong and unexpectedly quick, Alan can cut away, move in hard, change direction and take punishment. Style has nothing to do with any of this. Alan's running reminds many football people of Frankie Sinkwich. Al has that same duck-walk running motion, that wide-braced footing that keeps him from getting knocked over easily. And he can "run up," that is, gather himself at the last moment before crunching into the line or jarring against a linebacker. Where most fullbacks barrel into a defense head first, Alan puts his body behind one of his good-sized shoulders and rams. In slow motion, it looks like a fellow pushing against a jammed door.

"There were some things we might have changed about Ameche," Ewbank has explained often, "but because he seemed to be able to handle himself anyway, we decided to leave him alone." What probably bothered Ewbank more than anything else about Ameche's running was his footwork. The Colt T-formation is quick and precise. Every step of a play is pre-determined and clocked. But Alan, with his big feet, would over-step in his moves toward the line. Going off tackle, for example, where the fullback is supposed to make his cut with his rear foot and then, in three steps, be at the line, Alan would cut with his front foot (that's the way he always did it) and get to the line in four steps. "We weren't too fussy about it," Ewbank said. "Instead of forcing him to cut with that rear foot, we just lined him up a step closer to the line. That way, we were able to maintain our close timing and Alan was able to keep his peculiar running habit."

During the halftime break, the Colts sat on the benches in the dressing room, sucking on oranges and listening to Ewbank and his assistants. The press box spotters gave succinct reports on what they had seen. They said the Bears had deployed against fullback running during most of the first half but tended to spread a bit toward the end. They still were defending against the short pass instead of the long one. Down the middle looked good for running and for long passes. Then Weeb gave a chalk talk on the first half and checked out some new plays for the second half. One thing he pointed out was that the "pluggers" (the linebackers) were staying outside the ends. He told Shaw to call plays that would send the halfbacks behind Ameche on wide runs. If Ameche blocked the linebackers wide, the halfbacks could cut in. Otherwise, they were to sweep while Ameche drove the linebacker inside.

When the Colts got the ball for the first time in the second half, Shaw handed off to Alan three times in a row, for five, four and two yards. Then he threw a pass long down the middle to end Jim Mutscheller, who was downed on the Bears' one-yard line. While the Colts huddled for the next play, a chant started in the stands. "Amech!" they called. "Amech!" And Amech it was, going in low and being stopped cold. The Bears, however, had been offside and the ball was moved to the half-yard line. Again Shaw called Ameche's play. As he crouched low, waiting for the snap, Alan decided how he was going to do it. The Bears had submarined on that last play, and now, with a nine-man line, they would probably dig in low again. On the snap, he drove low, his body bent at the hip. Shaw rammed the ball into his stomach, Alan took one driving stride, then leaped high—and through. He landed four feet inside the end zone. The Bear line, hanging in on all fours, looking to grab him low, where it is easy to topple a man, and throw him back, could not rise up quickly enough to reach his hurtling body.

Going back to the bench this time, Al felt real good. His talk was more aggressive. He was excited and satisfied with himself. "Move 'em out!" he yelled to the Colt defense. "They'll give!"

The Bears scored a touchdown midway in the quarter, and the Colts led now 21 to 14. But Shaw was still able to move through the air. Dropping back for a third-down pass, he was cornered and turned wide to the left to break away. The left end had him hemmed in, however, and Shaw had no room to move, when Ameche, delaying his block deliberately, came across and hit the end at the shins. Shaw went for a first down.

More passes brought the ball close to the Bear goal line, and the chant for "Amech! Amech!" began again. It was second down on the three, and Ameche charged in. It looked as if he was going to get through when tackle M. L. Brackett grabbed him by the metal face mask (an illegal hold, by the way) and pulled him sideways. It had the effect of a rodeo cowboy successfully bulldogging a steer by twisting his horns. Alan's body had to follow the twist of the head, and he was stopped on the one, his body lying parallel to the goal line. He tried again and was stopped, but the Bears had been offside. So once again the ball was on the half-yard line.

No one doubted that Al would carry again. This was where he did his best work—grounding out the vital inches and feet to pay dirt. The Bears were in a nine-man line, dug in shoulder to shoulder. Shaw, standing over the center, barked his signals slowly: "Set. One hup, two hup, three hup. . . ." On "six" the ball was snapped and Ameche was moving. He took the handoff cleanly, never looking at the ball, and crashed into the line, his shoulder driving forward like a shield of steel. At the line he was hit in the stomach by a shoulder pad. The grunt that came gasping from his insides was heard clearly on the sidelines. His forward motion stopped for an instant, his head rocked back, and he looked dead. But his legs never stopped driving. There was no hole in the wall, but his relentless power actually forced the wall back, inch by inch, until the ball, nestled deep against his ribs, was pushed over that last chalk line. It was there just by inches and just for a moment; then the defensive wall pushed Ameche back until he was toppled backward on the three-yard line. But the score had been made. When Alan held the ball over the line, the referee's hands shot up.

"Mule!" the Baltimore bench shouted admiringly as Alan trotted toward them. "Mule, you old son of a gun!" His face was dirty, his shoulders sagged, he was exhausted and dizzy. Too tired to remove his helmet, he sank down on the bench. An assistant trainer rushed over with the smelling salts. His helmet was taken off and an ice bag was applied to his head and neck. Ewbank, nervous and excited, came over. "Keep goin'," he said and began to move away. Then he realized he had forgotten something. He walked back and leaned over. "You okay?" he asked. Alan nodded. Satisfied, Weeb turned back to the game, yelling "We gotta get another!"

A heavy sponge of water was squeezed over Al's head. It was cold and it felt good. He shook his head like a puppy and let the cool water trickle down his face.

By the time he looked up at the game, the fourth quarter had started and the Bears had moved to two first downs. But the Colts stopped them, and Ameche, feeling good again, went in. Neither team was able to move the ball until, after nine minutes of the quarter, Al socked up the middle for nine yards. On the next play he went over right guard for three yards and a first down. Again he carried, over left guard for another nine. He was running low now, that shoulder bulging out, his legs pumping fiercely. He was falling forward for that extra yard.

With third and twenty-seven, after Shaw had been thrown for a loss, the quarterback sent Dupre on a sweep with Ameche as a close blocker. Alan, stirred up now and unable to untrack, threw his block at the end too soon and missed. Lying on the ground, he tried to reach out with his arm to stop the end. Again he missed. The officials didn't spot the illegal hand block, probably because it hadn't worked.

The Bears took over and went for a touchdown. Now the Colts led 28 to 21 with two minutes left to play. After the kickoff, Ameche's understudy, Dick Young, an aggressive kid from Chattanooga, went in. It was the first offensive play, other than punt situations, that Alan had missed. But the time off didn't last. On the first play Young went up the middle for one, and Ewbank got mad. "No, no!" he yelled. "Kill time! I want those men running wide. Go in, Al. I want that clock moving."

The clock kept moving; first Moore, then Dupre, then Moore again ran the ends, with Ameche blocking. The Bears took over with only seconds left, and their one play, an attempted pass, was smothered.

When the gun went off, the gang on the Colt bench ran out on the field, congratulating teammates and meeting friends among the Bears. Alan walked to the Bear bench to say hello to a couple of old Wisconsin teammates, Harlan Carl and Jim Haluska. The cut on his nose was bleeding again, but how was he feeling? "Man, I'm feeling great." On the way in, youngsters slapped his shoulder pads and Al smiled down at them. Lenny Moore trotted by, and Al said, to no one in particular, "He's a cat."

Steam was pouring out of the dressing room by the time Al got there. "Some game," everybody was saying. Carroll Rosenbloom, the owner of the club and a popular man with his players, came in. "Pretty sweet one, huh?"

"Oh buddy, yeah!" someone standing naked in the middle of the room yelled back at him.

General manager Don Kellett came over to Ameche. "Feels good, huh?" he said.

Alan could only grin and answer, "Oh, boy." He sat down and took off his dirty gear. "It's great to be on a winner," he said. "Nothing like it. When you lose, it's different, I'll tell you."

He went into the shower. Yelling and singing and friendly cussing came pouring out. After a minute or two of just standing under the nozzle and soaking in the hot water, Ameche washed up and came out. "Hey, where's some towels?" he called, standing wet and naked. Big Lipscomb threw a soggy towel at him. "Watch that, Big Daddy," Al said to him, grinning. Finally he found a dry one and wiped himself. There was still something he couldn't forget. "It's not like this when you lose," he said. "Then you cuss everything. You don't ask for a towel. You say, where's that miserable towel."

The players didn't linger in the dressing room too long. There were crowds outside to greet them. When Alan came out, Yvonne was waiting for him along with a bunch of fans. He had to sign autographs as he made his way through them to his wife and gave her a kiss. "Nice," she said.

The Campanellas were waiting for Al, too. The four of them soon got out of the crowd and to Ameche's car. They drove to the Hillendale Country Club, where they had been invited for dinner and a dance. Alan and Joe had huge slabs of roast beef. They ate quietly and slowly, the boys talking over the game, the girls joining in for little notes. Mostly, though, the wives let their husbands unwind.

After dancing for a while, they went to a party. (On Sunday night, the Ewbank System is suspended; all rules are off.) The four bachelors on the Baltimore squad—Gino Marchetti, Doug Eggers, Don Shula and Bill Pennington—share an apartment, and were giving a victory party that night, everyone invited. When the Ameches and Campanellas showed up, the place was a mess. There could be no mistaking that a party had taken place. But nobody was there any more. The crowd had moved on to another spot.

It was almost eleven now, so the two couples headed home. On the way, the boys talked about the game again, mostly how they thought they would be graded. This, too, was part of the Ewbank method. Every player is graded on every play—receiving points from one to five on each. A one is no good, a bust. A two is acceptable. Three is good; it means the man did his assigned job. Fours and fives are bonuses, for a second effort or perfect execution. Fours are not infrequent. Fives are rare.

Ewbank brings his coaches to his home on Monday where they spend the day studying the movies, which are run over and over. A single player is watched and rated by a coach through an entire showing. His progression in each play is studied—did he carry out every part of his particular assignment, did he start right, was his approach correct, did he do his blocking, did he get to his assigned man, was his man then out of play? Nothing is omitted. On Tuesday the players are given their grades and watch the movies to check their grades.

Another part of the grading system is the batting average. On what percentage of his plays did a man carry out his assignment satisfactorily? Or "get his man?" If a player did his job well on seven of ten plays, he has a 70 percent batting average. The way Ewbank teaches the game, if each man can register 82 percent "got men," they'll win the ball game.

Alan didn't learn until Tuesday that the game against the Bears was rated the best he had played for Baltimore. He was given a grade of 96 percent. He was in on sixty-seven plays, fifty-seven of them gradable. And he was credited for "got men," or satisfactory jobs, on 96 percent of those plays.

His blocking, the one trouble spot the coaches worked on during training, was rated excellent. When Al made Rookie of the Year the season before and was named to the All-Pro team, the only rookie to make it, some critics thought he was being over-rated because he didn't block well. And he didn't. The fact that he led the league in rushing with 961 yards for a 4.5 average perhaps meant only that he was a workhorse. To Ewbank, it meant much more. His 4.5 average was the best the Colts had ever had from a fullback. "And it's good enough for me," Weeb said. The Colts, of course, wanted his blocking to improve, and they worked hard on it. Now they are satisfied he can do it.

On his report card for the Bear game were the following notations: "Faking very good. Hit in on short yardage situations. When a first down was needed, moved with excellent power. Carried sixteen times for a 3.5 average. But four attempts were at the goal line, which necessarily reduces overall average. Disregard these four attempts, and average for day was five yards. Had no chance to break into open because situations never progressed that fully on his running plays. In grades, received one four, no fives, two ones, rest all threes." (The four was on his excellent fake into the line when Shaw rolled out and passed, while Ameche was being tackled in the line. His ones were on breakdowns in pass protection when he failed to get his man.)

It was a good report card, and further confirmed the Colts' faith in the twenty-two-year-old fullback. They had taken a gamble when they originally drafted him. A scouting report from the Big Ten, still in the Colt files, reads as follows: "Power runner with good speed. Fair linebacker only. Does not blast line too well but is bruising in open field. Will go in pros but is not a [Tank] Younger."

The Colts' own scout report on him was more hopeful: "Great pro prospect. Has good speed and power. Can run to outside. Picks his holes well. Good linebacker. Has been approached by Canada. [Alan refused to consider the Canadian offers, just as he turned down a proposition to become a professional wrestler for a $50,000 guarantee.] Salary may have to be high if drafted. [It was—a reported $12,000 per year on a two-year contract, which, by the way, Al is sorry he insisted on after his good rookie year.] Should be easily coached."

Back to the drive home—the Ameches got to the house at about 11:30, and Alan drove the babysitter home. She had put in eleven hours, which is quite a dent in the pocketbook, but she didn't complain about the kids and, apparently, the kids had no complaints about her.

When Alan drove up to his home later, he found Yvonne was next door at a neighbor's. They had asked her in for coffee, and they insisted that Alan stay, too. He was tired, but he agreed. They sat there for over an hour, reliving the game again. But what the heck, Al figured. It's fun to talk about a victory, and Monday is his off day—even if he did get up to give the boys breakfast, and mix the baby foods for Kathy. He does that every day anyway—except Sunday. On Sunday he plays football.

The Crucial Part
Fear Plays in Sports

Roger Kahn | **1959**

A theory that fear is something experienced only by the intelligent has spread almost as fast as strontium 90 during the past ten years. I suspect that the theory was devised by a smart coward in search of prestige, but its precise origin remains unknown and somehow people accept it as tradition and even apply it to such innocent fields as sports.

Do you know why Ralph Branca is now selling insurance near New York City instead of pitching every fourth day for the Los Angeles Dodgers? "It's because he's bright and went to NYU," one NYU man suggests, modestly. "If Ralph were dumber, Bobby Thomson's homer wouldn't have preyed on his mind, because he wouldn't have had the sense to worry. Hell, a dumb Branca would win twenty games every year."

Do you know why Joe Louis was a great champion? "Because he was too slow-witted to be afraid," insists a quick-witted club fighter, who quit just in time to preserve his brain pan. "Joe wasn't sharp enough to know how much he could be hurt. A smarter Louis would have dropped that second fight to Schmeling."

Perhaps two dozen other examples come to mind, but by now I imagine the concept has come clear. Sports is the one area in which stupidity counts. Smart guys finish last. The good rockhead always beats the good egghead. The trouble with each of these statements is also the trouble with the theory that lies behind them. They withstand everything except analysis.

A few hours after the Dodgers had turned the harvest moon blue by winning the 1955 World Series from the New York Yankees, Pee Wee Reese was idling at the bar in an aged Brooklyn hotel which was the site of the official victory party. Reese had thrown out the final batter on a routine ground ball to shortstop.

"Hey, Pee Wee," said a nearby semi-drunk, "what was you thinking with two outs in the ninth?"

Reese smiled benignly. "I was just hoping the next man wouldn't hit the ball to me," he said.

"Shmerf?" said the drunk, in surprise, as his beer asserted itself.

Well, there it was. Honest, intelligent Pee Wee Reese had given an honest, intelligent answer, and anyone within hearing distance could now report that a great professional had known the cold hand of fear in the clutch. But had the drunk asked the same question of a duller ballplayer, had he picked on a triumphant rockhead, things might well have been reversed. Pinned against a stein of beer, the rockhead probably would have been the man to say, *"Shmerf?"*

The quick conclusion, which is that the dull athlete was not touched by fright, is careless and probably incorrect. A dull athlete might have felt far more fear than Reese did, but he could not have put the feeling into intelligible English. Emotion, not words, is the issue, and it's ridiculous to assert that you have to be smart to be afraid. I know a six-year-old shortstop, not especially precocious, who feels exactly as Reese did, every time he sees his pitcher throw the ball.

One day last spring, I was driving down a flat, narrow Florida highway to cover a sports car race at Sebring. It had been raining and water lay in dull, black puddles near the palmettos along the side of the road. The car jerked and hissed through the water as I kept it at 60 miles an hour and I remember thinking that the men who were trying to do 120 at Sebring must be having a difficult time.

It was night when I reached the race course, and Phil Hill, a slim Californian who is accepted as the best American driver, was pacing near the pits, his driving done, his team's victory all but assured. Hill is a sensitive-looking man, just over thirty, who reads a great deal and whose musical taste runs to Beethoven.

"How was it out there?" I said.

"What kind of a question is that?" Hill said, intensely. "Can't you imagine what it was like?"

I had to admit I'd never driven a Ferrari.

"A bloody nightmare," Hill said, his face going pale. "Some courses drain. This one doesn't. Trying to control the car out there for me was like it would be for you trying to drive on ice. I was moving. There must have been five, six, a dozen times, when I thought I was dead. I'd hit a puddle and the car would start to go and I'd be skidding toward somebody and I'd figure this was it. It wasn't, but don't ask me how. Lord, don't ask me how I'm still alive." Hill's hands were shaking. They continued to shake and for a time he was so wound up in tension that he was unable to stop talking.

Two years ago, before the start of an equally dangerous auto race, a reporter asked Juan Manuel Fangio, the former world champion driver, if he was thinking about death.

"Death?" Fangio said. "I only give it a quick, glancing thought."

Fangio is a phlegmatic man who once drove a bus in Argentina and who seems far less imaginative than Hill. Again the outward signs indicate that the egghead, Hill, was frightened, and the duller man, Fangio, was not. But last year, still in his prime and still a champion, Fangio quietly retired from Grand Prix racing. Despite his stolid disposition, he was afraid that matters might turn around, that Death might now give quick, glancing thoughts to Juan Manuel Fangio.

Fear strikes athletes without regard to race, creed or intelligence. It also strikes them without regard to the actual peril in their work. For the fear athletes feel is composed of two distinct things. First, there is the fear of physical pain. Here we have auto racers afraid of auto wrecks, jockeys afraid of horses' hooves, halfbacks afraid of linebackers, batters afraid of beanballs and swimmers afraid of the water. Then there is the fear, psychological but still real, of performing badly in front of an audience. Thus we have pitchers afraid to throw changeups, quarterbacks afraid to call their own plays, golfers afraid of the first tee, and girl tennis players afraid that their gold panties won't catch the summer sunlight.

Sometimes an athlete feels such physical fear that he cannot so much as move his head out of the way of an inside pitch. Sometimes he feels such psychological fear he cannot pick up the sort of grounder he has handled ten thousand times before. Sometimes an athlete's fear is a combination of the physical and psychological. But at different times and in different ways, all athletes learn what it is to be afraid.

During the 1952 Olympics, Ingemar Johansson, the Swedish Tiger, was matched against the late Ed Sanders in a heavyweight bout. After a few moments of preliminary sparring, Johansson sized up his opponent and ran. He didn't actually run out of the ring, because the ropes were in the way, but he fled as best he could inside the ring, obviously terrified, until kindly Olympic officials intervened and awarded the fight to Sanders.

"INGEMAR, FOR SHAME!" one Swedish newspaper headlined, unkindly. "He's worse than the British heavies," an American sportswriter said. "They always get knocked out, but at least they take a couple of punches first."

Johansson himself had no comment. Sanders outweighed him by more than twenty pounds and possessed a fierce scowl, but no losing fighter ever pleads fright. The difference between Johansson then and Johansson now is partly craft, but it is also that he has learned to control the fear all fighters feel. When Johansson is frightened these days, he punches or back-pedals or clinches or covers up. He no longer does what comes naturally, which is to run.

A jockey, to be successful, must be willing to urge his horse into potentially fatal positions. He must move up between a rival horse and the rail even though the outside horse may lug in at any time, closing the gap. He must move between two other horses, although either may veer and cause an accident.

Some years ago, in spots of this sort, Eddie Arcaro had four spills in ten days. Each time, as he lay in the dirt, horses thundered past, their hooves knifing up clods of dirt and drumming like a charge of cavalry. "For around two weeks," Arcaro said, "I couldn't get to sleep without seeing those hooves around my head." Gradually, the fear waned. "I wouldn't say I'm ever afraid of a horse now," Arcaro insisted recently. "I'm nervous about some, sure, but if I was actually afraid of one, what the hell, I just wouldn't ride him, and that hasn't happened."

Some riders become so involved with fear that they stop taking chances. In the tack room, their colleagues say simply, "He's riding like a married jock." There is no quicker way for a jockey to go out of business. He must either find a way to live with his fear or quit.

Ten days before the Army-Navy football game last fall, Red Blaik, the cool, analytical man who coached Army football for almost two decades, was holding forth on halfbacks he had known. Traditionally, Army halfbacks run with a difference; knees high, head up, driving over, around or through the opposition. "Speed," Blaik was saying, "and feinting and intelligence." He was walking across a practice field where Pete Dawkins and Bob Anderson were running against a scrub line. "Watch them," Blaik said.

The backs ran hard, and after they were hit, they sprang up instantly, as if unwilling to give their tacklers any more than the bare minimum of satisfaction. Another Army back was hit and limped slightly.

"All right," Blaik said, "no limping. If you have to limp, don't scrimmage. If you want to scrimmage, don't limp."

The limp disappeared in a hurry.

"Over here," Blaik said, indicating another part of the field, "is a boy with as much physically as Anderson or Dawkins. Maybe he even has more."

A jayvee halfback was plunging, but not in the accepted Army style. He ran well, but just before he was hit, there was a slight but noticeable change in frame. The body tightened, stiffened, tensed, and it was clear that the back was bracing for a fall even before the lineman touched him. When a tackler missed, the back, ready to be tackled, lost a step before regaining full speed.

"Something you have to understand," Blaik said, "is that this isn't a question of courage, pure and simple. The boy could turn out to be a war hero. It's just that he doesn't like body contact. I've seen this hundreds of times and you can nearly always tell from the beginning. Some of them do and some of them don't. A boy who doesn't like contact shouldn't play football, because he isn't going to change."

If fighters change and jockeys change and learn to live with fear, why not college halfbacks? The answer ultimately comes down to time. Johannson was young enough to be a college student when he ran and Arcaro, in his sleepless days, was only slightly older. A college halfback is through at twenty-two.

Dealing with physical fear is a question of gradually accepting hazards, day after day, week after week, until suddenly they no longer seem dangerous. Humans are adaptable, but the adaptations require patience. One simply does not march into a battle area the first time as calmly as one does the second or third. A fighter of twenty-two is likely to be more frightened than he will be three years, or thirty bouts, later.

But there is a point where things turn around, where too many years of living with fear break down human drive. Fangio reached that point before he quit. Jersey Joe Walcott fought superbly against Rocky Marciano once, but the second time he sat down promptly after a punch of indeterminate power. Walcott knew Marciano could hit. He took his second purse without a review lesson.

The path of physical fear varies with the athlete, of course, but a general pattern does exist. First, the athlete encounters fear. This may come when he is a child, or when he is older, or only after he has been hurt. Then, for a time, he is at war with himself. Is the fun of the game and the pleasure of victory worth the risk of pain? The good athlete always answers yes, and sets about controlling his fear. Finally, after enough years in sports, it all gets to be too much trouble and he quits. He either sits down in the ring or he retires.

The other fear in sports, fear of failure, is less predictable, more common, less understood, more discussed, and runs into the science of psychiatry. To me it has seemed clearest in terms of poker.

Consider the frightened poker player who is dealt three kings. He blinks, his stomach talks, and he raises like a man who has been dealt a pair of deuces. It isn't purely money, for he plays with the same outrageous caution, regardless of stakes. It's chiefly that fear drives common sense out of his head.

He looks at his three kings and he considers. The man at his right is due for a straight. (No one is ever due for anything in cards. Each deal is independent of the others.) The next man seems confident. Maybe he has a full house. The dealer is smiling. He probably loaded the deck. So it goes and eventually the man with three kings gets about half of what he would have won if he had kept his head.

The non-frightened poker player knows that three kings will probably be good enough. He bids accordingly and if he loses, he goes ahead and the next time he has three kings he plays exactly the same way. At its worst, fear paralyzes, but rarely in sports does fright assume such proportions. What psychological fear does most frequently is block the normal reasoning process.

When Early Wynn pitches against the Yankees, he glares and knocks hitters down precisely as he would against any other team. But it is not quite the same operation. "Sometimes," he says, "when I get behind to a hitter, I figure I got to do something because here is Mantle coming up and maybe Berra and Skowron. I get behind and I figure I can't walk this guy and I can just feel that fear."

Wynn's solution, arrived at over the years, is to inhale mightily. "After I take that deep breath," he says, "I feel okay." The deep breath doesn't throw strikes, but it enables Wynn to forget what might happen and concentrate on the business at hand.

The best clutch ballplayer I remember was a man who suffered a nervous collapse during World War II, who jumped a team because he was homesick and who absolutely refused to travel by airplane. His name is Billy Cox, and although there have been many better ball-players, I can't think of anyone whose game improved so much under pressure.

Cox was a third-baseman, a small, wiry man with big bony wrists, who subdued ground balls with a little scooping motion and was one of the finest fielders of his time. Before ordinary games, Cox often busied himself thinking up excuses for not playing, but whenever the Brooklyn Dodgers were faced with an important series, he was almost eager to go to work.

In the big ones, he was everywhere. He guarded the line, cut in front of the shortstop, and charged topped balls with such agility that Casey Stengel once complained during a World Series, "He ain't a third-base-man. He's an unprintable acrobat." Cox was never a great hitter, but he was far better swinging in a clutch than he was when it didn't matter.

"I can't explain it," Cox once said. "My wife says I have 'fearless nerves.' Anyway, before the big ones, I feel my nerves all tightening up, sort of getting ready. You know what I mean?"

"But what about the homesickness?"

Cox's lean face was grim. He did not usually have much to say. "I be-lieve that everybody has some kind of problem," he said. "No matter how good a ballplayer is, there's something that bothers him. My prob-lem was that I got lonesome on the road. It takes nerve to lick your problem, but you got to have it."

"Well, doesn't it take nerve to play in clutch games?"

"They never bothered me," Cox said. "I never got scared. The thing that bothered me was that I wanted to go home."

Stan Musial insists that no one can be afraid and play baseball well. "If you're worried about what happens when you go bad," Musial says, "you shouldn't even get in the business." Musial is calling this as he sees it, but he forgets his own outlook when he left Donora, Pennsylva-nia, for the great world of baseball, with his wife, whose father owned a grocery.

"I'm not scared," he told a friend, "because if the baseball doesn't work out, I can always get a job in the store."

In the theater, stagefright, a single word, sums up all fear of failure. But in sports, which cover so large an area and employ so varied a jar-gon, there are a dozen words for what is roughly the same thing. "Choke" is currently most popular.

"When I get out on the field before the opening kickoff I feel it," Randy Duncan, Iowa's great quarterback last season, has remarked. "I can't eat breakfast that day, and when I see the crowd, I guess you could say I'm choked up. Then, on the kickoff, I have to belt someone. As soon as I block a guy hard, the fear disappears. Just body contact once, and I stop choking."

Tennis player Gussie Moran, in her greatest days, found a less taxing solution. "On the pro tour," she says, "I'd get so worried I wouldn't make a good showing, I started taking a slug of Canadian Club before each match. I got so I couldn't play at all without the slug."

The only tie between Phil Hill, trembling after an auto race, and Gussie, downing a shot before the first serve, is the fact of fear, and this drives to the root of the crucial role fear plays in sports. It doesn't matter what there is to be afraid of, whether it's death, or failure, or disgrace, or a double fault. The point is that there is something to cause fear in every avenue of sport, and whatever exists is sufficient. To the athlete, fear is a condition of the job.

Sometimes, after much research, a man announces that fighters or bull fighters, or pitchers who have learned to beat the Yankees are the bravest men in sports. But no one knows the fear someone else feels and so no one can prepare a valid yardstick of athletes' bravery. Only this much is sure: They are all afraid of different things in different ways at different times. It is never possible to conquer fear, but it can be subdued for a time. Watch the great athlete work at his craft and you see someone who has known fear before and who will know fear again but who goes about his job fearlessly. This is the courage of an athlete and it is towering to behold.

The Mixed Emotions of "The Big O"

Dick Schaap | **1 9 6 0**

Once upon a time, there were two little rabbits, a white one who was born in Kentucky and a black one who was born in Tennessee. As they grew up, the two little rabbits became two tall rabbits and everyone who knew them liked them, because they could run and jump and play better than all their friends.

Then, not so long ago, the white rabbit and the black rabbit both decided to go to a big school, which was collecting rabbits of all colors who could run and jump and play. At the school, the white rabbit and the black rabbit met each other and liked each other and, before long, they became good friends.

One day, the white rabbits back home in Kentucky heard that their old friend was spending a lot of time with a black rabbit. This disturbed them, because they had been taught that white rabbits and black rabbits should be kept apart. Pretty soon, the white rabbits started whispering.

"Going around with a black rabbit?" said one white rabbit. "No good'll come of that. They ain't like us at all."

"Next thing you know," said another white rabbit, "he'll be bringing this black rabbit home with him."

—A Fairy Tale

The grin that had creased the angular face of Ralph Davis, co-captain of the University of Cincinnati basketball team, was gone now, replaced by a frown. "There's been some talk back home," Davis, a native Kentuckian said, quietly. "I haven't heard it directly. But people talk. You know what they say. They say lousy things."

Davis leaned on a table in the main lounge of French Dorm at UC and, mechanically, opened and shut a textbook on how to write polite business letters. Normally, he is an ebullient young man, relaxed and outgoing, the epitome of the popular campus hero. But now, as he stared through a huge picture window facing the Cincinnati fieldhouse, Davis was not ebullient. He was intense and serious.

"They'd better not say anything to my face," he said. "Oscar's a good guy. He's as good a guy as anybody I ever met." Davis clenched his fist, whitening the knuckles. "They'd better not say anything to my face," he repeated. "Oscar's like a brother to me."

Oscar, of course, is Oscar Robertson, born in Tennessee and raised in Indiana. In the three years since he entered Cincinnati, Oscar has been called "The Big O," "The Wonderful O," "the greatest sophomore basketball player ever" and "the greatest junior basketball player ever." He has also been called "redcap," "porter," and other ugly, humorless labels.

It would be pleasant if the story of Oscar Robertson could be told on only one level, the level of his athletic skill. This would be a cheerful story, the account of a young man who blends strength and coordination and speed so perfectly that he is, in a sense, a physical miracle, a million-to-one shot. Oscar Robertson is more than a brilliant basketball player. He is a brilliant athlete. If he had grown up somewhere other than Indiana, where basketball is the state religion, he would have been a star in whatever game he chose. Suppose Robertson had come out of the western Pennsylvania coal country. Then he would have been a football player, most likely an end. "If he had gone out for football last year," says Roland Shadd, a member of the Cincinnati football squad, "Oscar could have been first string immediately. He's so fast, so strong, so shifty, and his hands are unbelievable. I've seen him catch passes that no one else possibly could have caught."

If Robertson had matured in northern California, an area which specializes in producing baseball players, he would have become a major-leaguer. On an intramural team at Cincinnati, Robertson, second base, and Ralph Davis, shortstop, form a slick double-play combination. Robertson, with his quick hands, is a sure fielder. At bat, his combination of magnificent eyes and coordination is unbeatable. He is a slugger, the hitter who led his team to the college championship.

Baseball, football, basketball, track and field, tennis, golf, fencing, polo—you name the sport and I'll bet that Oscar Robertson could excel at it. But he came out of Indiana, so Robertson chose basketball. Watch him in action. He is the complete player. He moves beautifully, six feet five inches tall and 200 pounds, sliding across the court with seemingly effortless grace. The other team shoots. Suddenly, Robertson slips under the basket. He times his leap perfectly, goes up and, stretching those long (size 37) arms of his, picks off the rebound the way a seagull plucks a fish out of water. In one fluid motion, he lands, spins and starts downcourt, his feet scarcely touching the ground, the ball magnetically coordinated with his hand. There may be three men between him and the basket. The path is blocked, closed, dead end, but somehow Robertson slithers through the defenders, reaches the scoring zone, jumps, and with a touch so delicate it belongs in ballet, lofts the ball through the basket.

Field goal by Robertson. This is what The Big O does better than anything else. But he also passes—crisp, precise passes that leave his hands so swiftly his teammates are sometimes caught off balance. He rebounds, he sets up plays, he does everything. Some people accuse him of being weak on defense. "If he's weak on defense," says Sandy Pomerantz, a Cincinnati sophomore who plays opposite Robertson in practice, "I'd hate to meet anyone who's strong. Oscar steals passes, deflects passes, blocks shots and doesn't let you get around him. His hands seem to be everywhere."

Robertson's accomplishments are without precedent. He led his Crispus Attucks (Indianapolis) High School team to the first undefeated season in the history of Indiana scholastic basketball. He averaged 33 points a game as a Cincinnati freshman (a school record), 35.1 as a sophomore (a national record) and 32.6 as a junior (a two-year national record). Opposing teams double-teamed him, triple-teamed him, zoned him, harassed him and fouled him, but still he scored. "The only way to stop him," Lou Rossini, the New York University coach, has suggested, "is to put four men on him and have your fifth man guard the other Cincinnati players. Maybe even that won't work."

Now team co-captain for the second straight year, Robertson is the reason the Cincinnati fieldhouse is jammed for every game. He is the reason all the cars parked on Calhoun Street and Clifton Avenue near the Cincinnati campus boast Bearcat stickers. He is the reason the University of Cincinnati is no longer simply a trolley-car college.

This, then, is Oscar Robertson, the basketball player. This is the athletic success story of a poor boy from a poor family, and it is the kind of American story that the U.S. State Department would love to spread around the world.

But the story of Oscar Robertson doesn't end on the basketball court. It should. It should be sufficient that a man excels at whatever activity he pursues. But it isn't. You can't say Oscar Robertson is a great basketball player and leave it at that, any more than you can say simply that Ralph Bunche is a great diplomat, Sidney Poitier a great actor or Thurgood Marshall a great lawyer. They are all distinguished Americans, each proficient in his own field. But they are also Negroes, and the fact that they are Negroes cannot be ignored. Perhaps the day will come when the color of a man's skin is incidental, like the size of his shoes or the tone of his voice. But, right now, whether you like it or Oscar Robertson likes it, color is not incidental. There are White Citizens Councils and NAACP chapters, Orval Faubuses and Branch Rickeys, and, running among them, there is a color line, broken and unbroken. The second story of Oscar Robertson, the one that isn't so pleasant, is the story of the color line. It is not the sort of story the State Department relishes.

Athletes, like other people, are of widely varying personalities and characters. Some of them will be warm, decent men; others might be disillusioning. Oscar Robertson falls among the warm and the decent. Meet Oscar Robertson and you will be impressed.

It is difficult to analyze exactly what it is about Robertson, the man, that makes him impressive. He is no intellectual giant, who can regard his game as a scientific art. Nor is he a glib, polished speaker. Among strangers, he talks seldom, and his statements are usually confined to a single word or, at most, a single sentence. His extracurricular tastes, revolving around rock and roll music and Western movies, do not distinguish him from other athletes.

Yet there is something about Robertson that sets him apart. Away from the basketball court, his boyish face and his easy smile create a favorable first impression. But first impressions, like surface characteristics, can be deceiving. The appeal of Oscar Robertson lies deeper within him. He has marked sincerity, friendliness, unaffected honesty. Meeting Oscar as he lay on his bed in a New York hotel room two years ago, listening to rock and roll music on the radio, you were struck by his genuine modesty. Only a sophomore, he seemed positively embarrassed that anyone should be interested in him. When he was compared with Wilt Chamberlain and Elgin Baylor, he twisted uncomfortably. Only when he talked about Crispus Attucks High School did he appear at ease. The next evening, at Madison Square Garden, he scored fifty-six points, but afterward, he was equally unaffected. He was just a nice kid, a quiet kid, who couldn't understand all the fuss that was being made about him.

Oscar has changed in two years. He is more confident now. He is not cocky, not a braggart, but he is sure of himself. He relaxes more readily and the sight of reporters no longer frightens him. He is still not verbose, but he will answer questions, and he answers them with a candor unusual among athletes. His innate intelligence shows through. He is sensitive and aware and, once his curtain of silence is pierced, his feelings flow out.

Shortly before the current season opened, I visited Oscar in his room, number 222, at French Dormitory. It is a small room, cluttered like most college dormitory rooms, a few phonograph records and sweat shirts strewn on the floor. On one side, there is an extra-long, double-decker bed. Oscar sleeps in the upper berth; a six-foot, ten-inch Negro sophomore, Paul Hogue, occupies the lower. Oscar apparently doesn't know or doesn't care that stars generally appropriate the lowers. A portable television set, resting on his desk top, gives some indication of Oscar's attitude toward school work.

"On the campus," he said, as he sat by his desk, "people come up to me. They say they want to say hello. They say they want my autograph. They say they just want to talk to me."

Robertson shook his head. "They want to talk to me because I'm a basketball player," he said, without raising his voice. "Suppose I was a ditch digger. Would they want to talk to me then? They like me because I'm a basketball player. Why don't they like me just because I'm Oscar Robertson? But people don't act that way. They wouldn't want to talk to Oscar Robertson, the ditch digger."

Robertson rolled a piece of paper into a tiny ball. As he talked, he lofted soft, one-handed shots—using the wad of paper—toward the ceiling. "People are phony," he said. "This town is phony. This campus is phony. People are phony."

His voice still soft and even, Robertson smiled slightly. "Don't get me wrong," he said. "I've got nothing against Cincinnati, the town or the college. It's no different here than anywhere else. New York. Boston. It's all the same. People are the same everywhere. Phony."

Oscar Robertson's words were bitter, but his tone and expression were not. He doesn't often discuss what bothers him and, when he does, he dismisses his complaints with a shrug or a grin. "Not serious," he implies. "Not serious. Doesn't mean a thing."

But, inwardly, the emotions that Robertson won't bring to the surface bubble furiously. He is not an automaton, a mechanical basket-scoring device. He is an individual, a sensitive human being, and he has feelings. He may genuinely dislike accepting trophies and making speeches, but when someone says he is a great basketball player, Oscar Robertson is proud. Similarly, when someone says or does something that slights him or other Negroes, Oscar Robertson is hurt. He may conceal his hurt, but this makes it no less real. "Oscar doesn't show it," says Jack Sherman, a Negro student at Cincinnati, "because that's not his nature. He doesn't get ruffled on the outside. But, inside, I'm sure he's concerned."

When Sherman says that it is not Robertson's nature to show his emotions, he reaches the core of the matter. Off the basketball court, Oscar almost never gets upset, at least not so upset that other people can see it. "I'm not a crusader," he says. "I can't change the world."

But the fact that he can't change the world doesn't mean that he wouldn't like to see it changed. When we talked in Cincinnati about two extremes of Negro personality—the militant, change-things-now Negro, who is willing to fight and suffer for what he believes is right, and the don't-rock-the-boat Negro, who accepts the white man's world as an inevitable, though evil, condition—Oscar indicated strongly that he preferred the first type. "I'd like to be the way Jackie Robinson is," he said. "I respect him for the way he stands up. That's the right way to act."

But Oscar himself, admittedly, does not act the way Robinson does. "It's just not my way," he said, in his dormitory room. "I don't get excited. I don't always like the way things are, and sometimes I say so. But if I was going to change the world, where would I start? There are too many things I'd like to see different."

Oscar Robertson has seen prejudice and he knows what it means to be a Negro. When he was a sophomore at Cincinnati, the Bearcats were scheduled to play in Houston one night. After their plane landed in Texas, the Cincinnati squad hurried to the plush Shamrock Hotel and began checking in. A clerk came up to Robertson as he stood with his teammates. "You can't stay here," the clerk said.

Robertson did not say, "Why?" He knew full well why. So The Big O, the star of the team, stayed by himself, away from the rest. "I didn't know it was going to happen," Oscar says now. "I had no idea. All of a sudden, there it was. I guess the school didn't know, either. They should have known, but I guess they didn't."

Since the Houston incident, whenever the Bearcats have played in Texas (the home state of two members of the Missouri Valley Conference, Cincinnati's league), the team has stayed together, usually in campus dormitories. The same procedure has been followed on other excursions into the South.

Last season, over Christmas vacation, Cincinnati competed in Raleigh, North Carolina, at the Dixie Classic, a tournament whose name alone should have been a warning to Robertson. The visiting teams which did not have Negroes on their rosters stayed in a fashionable Raleigh hotel. The teams which did have Negroes stayed at North Carolina State fraternity houses. Facilities were separate—and not quite equal.

At least Oscar was able to room with his teammates, but they couldn't help what happened when he stepped on the court at NC State's William Neal Reynolds Coliseum before capacity crowds. "It was terrible," co-captain Ralph Davis says. "They called him all kinds of names. Porter. Redcap. Things like that. It made me sick. I walked over to Oscar and talked with him and tried to help him forget it. The crowd was terrible." (This season, Cincinnati did not take a holiday excursion to the warm—and frigid—South. The team instead played in New York's Holiday Festival over Christmas.)

As bad as the insults were that Robertson heard in North Carolina, he was hardened against them by one fact. He was a visiting player, a talented visiting player, so he expected partisan fans to ride him. If he had been white, they probably would have yelled "heaver" or "gunner." The words would have been prettier, but the intent would have been the same: Get the opposition rattled.

For Oscar, there are worse things than being insulted in North Carolina. Unfortunately, he can't escape prejudice even when he returns to Cincinnati. The city itself is as much Southern as it is Northern. It's not a "Cracker" town, but it isn't "Yankee" territory, either. Geographically, Cincinnati is as far south as a Northern city can be. Step across the bridge and you're in Kentucky. Many of the inhabitants of Cincinnati are transplanted Kentuckians, and there is one section called the "hillbilly" district.

The Negro in Cincinnati walks a tightrope, surrounded by theoretical integration and emotional segregation. He may not be barred at public places, but he is made to feel uncomfortable, unwanted. Sure, come right in, step right up to the bar, but be prepared to wait for your drink to be served. Curiously, if the Cincinnati Negro seeks real integration in a night club, he must go across the bridge to Newport, Kentucky. There, the Negro night clubs, such as the Copa club, attract the finest entertainment, so whites swallow their bigotry and flock to listen to the name bands. The Copa has loud music, rock and roll music, and sometimes Oscar Robertson goes there to relax and hear the wild rhythms.

When Robertson was a freshman, he and Roland Shadd, a Negro football player from Pittsburgh, once went to a movie theater near the UC campus. "When I got to the window to buy the tickets," Shadd, an intelligent, well-spoken young man, recalls, "the man said the theater was closed. As soon as I stepped out of the line, he sold a ticket to the next person. I didn't have to be a mind-reader to figure that out." The policy has changed now at this particular theater, but the bad taste lingers. Still, some movie houses and coffee shops close to the Cincinnati campus discourage Negro patronage.

Probably the man best qualified to discuss the life of a Negro citizen in Cincinnati is Ted Berry, a Negro lawyer who was the city's vice-mayor in 1956 and 1957. "The first Negro vice-mayor," Berry says, "and probably the last."

As vice-mayor in 1956, Berry was one of the men responsible for convincing Robertson he ought to attend the University of Cincinnati. "I'm an alumnus," Berry said, "and I was asked to help recruit Robertson. He stayed at my house. I introduced him to people and told him that I hoped he'd choose Cincinnati."

Berry paused. "Actually, my contact with Oscar has been quite superficial," he said. "I thought I could be helpful in breaking the ice for him. I offered to help him if he ever had any problems. He never took me up on it. You can't probe Oscar. When you do, he withdraws into his shell."

"Suppose you had had the same opportunity that Oscar had?" I asked Berry. "Suppose you could have had an athletic scholarship to almost any college you wanted in the North. Would you have made Cincinnati your choice?"

Berry, a native Cincinnatian, is a truthful man. He considered the question carefully. "No," he said, finally. "If I had it to do over again, I would go somewhere else. I'd probably go to Michigan."

But Oscar Robertson chose Cincinnati. What does he mean to the University of Cincinnati? For comparison, consider another brilliant athlete. Some people say that Pete Dawkins, the Army football player, stands a chance of becoming the most famous graduate in West Point history. All he has to do is become a general, win a war, run for President and be elected. Oscar Robertson has a chance to become the most famous graduate in Cincinnati history. All he has to do is graduate.

It is regrettable that the Cincinnati campus doesn't mean as much to Robertson as he means to it. Perhaps, if conditions were ideal on the campus, he would be able to ignore the insults he endures in the South and in the city of Cincinnati. But even his own college is no haven for Oscar Robertson.

This doesn't mean that the UC student body is a militant enemy camp. It isn't. Overt discrimination doesn't exist on the campus. No one burns crosses or wears white hoods. No one shouts, "Black boy, go home." But, in less blatant ways, the Negro student is made to feel he is an outsider, a visitor in on a pass. "So far as I know," says Marvin Youkelis, the president of the UC Student Council, "there has never been a Negro on the Student Council."

A year ago, a graduate law student at Cincinnati wrote vitriolic letters to the *News Record,* the student newspaper, attacking the Negro as an inferior social being. The Board of Publications, a faculty-student advisory group, quickly ordered the newspaper to stop printing the letters, but the damage, as you can see, had already been done.

Next to the Student Council and the *News Record,* one of the most influential groups on the campus is the Interfraternity Council, composed of representatives of the various social fraternities on campus. Cincinnati has three Negro fraternities. None is a member of the Interfraternity Council. "They say we've got to get a certain number of members," Jack Sherman, one of the leaders of Kappa Alpha Psi, points out. "We're getting close now. Then we'll see what happens at Cincinnati."

This school year, Robertson joined Kappa Alpha Psi. He had been invited previous years, but until now, he had refused. "The Negro fraternities figured that if I joined," Robertson says, "they'd have a better chance to get campus recognition. That's fine. I'm all for it. But I think they ought to get it on their own. If they get it through me, it wouldn't mean as much."

Why did he join in his senior year? Robertson shrugs. "My friends were joining," he says. "I wanted to stick with them."

Robertson could have joined a "white" fraternity, but this is not such a strong move toward integration as it sounds. The white fraternities which extended bids to The Big O were primarily after his name. They didn't have to worry about him moving into their fraternity houses. Like all other full scholarship students at UC, Robertson is required to live in the dormitory.

"Oscar means a lot to the Negro students on campus," says Shirley Billings, a sophomore from Cincinnati, who is majoring in math. "He's helped us indirectly. Other students are more careful of their actions toward Negroes because they don't want to insult Oscar. It's a false attitude, in a way. They don't really care about Negroes. They just care about the way Oscar plays basketball. That's all."

"Oscar and I were the first Negro scholarship students to live in the dorms," Roland Shadd says. "Now there are more, and I guess things are improving. But there's still not much of a life for us on campus. Neither Oscar nor I has ever attended a campus social function. I don't think we ever will."

"Why should I?" Robertson asks. "If I go with a date, people are just going to stare at us. And I'm sure not going to find a stag Negro girl at a campus dance."

On the UC campus, where Oscar Robertson is the king of basketball, he is also an outcast. He is not a member of the student body who happens to play basketball. He is a basketball player who happens to attend classes. Other students, except for some fellow athletes and a few men who live near him in the dorm, have never come to know Oscar Robertson. They know his scoring average and his shooting percentage, but they don't know what he is like. Even Norm Aitken, the student sports editor of the *News Record,* who must base many of his stories on Oscar, doesn't know him. "I've taken a couple of trips with the team," Aitken says, "but I don't know Oscar well. I can't interview him unless either George Smith (the coach) or Tom Eicher (the publicity man) is present."

Apparently, Smith and Eicher want to protect Oscar from saying the wrong thing at the wrong time. This is a noble idea, but it fails to give enough credit to Robertson's own intelligence and honesty. He is a college senior who has been around the country, and he is capable of taking care of himself. Smith is an able coach, who has never hesitated to give Oscar proper credit, and Eicher is an able publicity man, who has never hesitated to give Oscar proper ballyhoo, but they might both be better off studying the segregation policies of Texas hotels instead of shielding Oscar from the press.

In light of all the problems he faces, it is surprising that Robertson returned to Cincinnati this year for his final season. Double-teamed and triple-teamed, he is learning nothing in basketball that will ever help him when he becomes a professional. "I got this far," Oscar explains, "and now all I want to do is get it over with. In June, it'll be finished. I can hardly wait."

This, then, is Oscar Robertson, the Negro. This is the story of The Big O and the big barrier. Fortunately, the skills that Robertson himself created outweigh the obstacles he never built. What will be remembered about him, long after he has left the basketball spotlight, is his talent, his ability to pour basketballs through a round hoop. This is what the public will remember in years to come. Oscar Robertson's own memories may not be half so pleasant.

The Floyd Patterson
His Friends Know

W. C. Heinz │ **1 9 6 0**

The strange thing about Floyd Patterson is that he wasn't cut
out to be a fighter. This sounds ridiculous, I guess, for here is a man
who brings immense natural skill and complete dedication to his craft.
He was the youngest heavyweight champion of all time; he is the only
one ever to regain the championship. He must go down in the history of
his sport as one who belonged to it as few men have.

If the record were to stop right now, it would show that Floyd has
won thirty-six of thirty-eight fights, twenty-five by knockouts. The public image of the man who fires the punches is not, however, a true representation of the man I know. What I want to try to do now is present
Floyd as he is, the way the record book can never show him, but the
way his friends know him.

I remember, for example, the day I went up to see him at Greenwood
Lake, New York. Three weeks before, he had knocked out Archie
Moore to win the heavyweight championship and he was back in train-
ing already at the Long Pond Inn.

On the ground floor of the inn there is a bar and dining room. The
living quarters and gymnasium are over it. When I checked with the
bartender, he said that Patterson was up in his room and I went up
there and we shook hands.

"What time is it?" he said.

"One o'clock," I said.

"I'll be down in the dining room in a half hour," he said.

I waited in the dining room for three and a half hours. As I sat there, the place came alive with teen-agers who had been ice-skating on the lake, but who had come in to play the juke box and dance. Finally, at 4:30, one of Patterson's sparring partners approached me.

"Floyd says he'll meet you in the gym in five minutes," the sparring partner said. "He apologizes."

"That's fine," I said, a little sore. "Where has he been?"

"Up in the room," the sparring partner said. "He came down a couple of times, but when he saw all these kids here he went back. He was embarrassed to come in."

He was already the heavyweight champion of the world.

Two nights later, we were standing and talking by the pool table beyond the bar. A couple of sparring partners were shooting pool and I was working Patterson around slowly, trying to get him to elaborate on the feelings he had when he saw the dining room jumping with those kids.

"You're the heavyweight champion of the world now," I said. "Doesn't that give you the security to walk through a room of teen-agers?"

"No," he said. "I still don't like to be stared at."

I thought of John L. Sullivan.

I kept coming back to this. Patterson is not a man you can push, but he will try to answer your questions as few men will if you just rest him between runs. This time we were standing in front of the Long Pond, waiting for one of his sparring partners who had been dispatched to town to buy morning newspapers.

"But you're going to be stared at a lot," I said.

"I know," he said.

"When did you first realize that this was going to be a problem?" I said.

"The day after I won the title," he said. "Just before the fight my wife gave birth to our daughter, so right after the fight, these friends and I, we got in the car to drive back from Chicago. The next day, we stopped at one of those roadside restaurants and we went in.

"By then the fight was all over the front pages of the newspapers, pictures and all, and I could see the people around the place recognizing me and starting to whisper. I figured we better get out of there quick, so we didn't even finish our meal."

Just before he won the title, Patterson bought a ten-room house in Mount Vernon, New York, for his mother and the eight youngest of her eleven children. The mayor of the town, an ex-fighter, staged a torch-light parade for Floyd after he beat Moore.

"How was the parade?" I asked Patterson.

"I was ashamed," Patterson said.

"Why?" I said.

"Me sitting in an open car and waving to people," Patterson said. "Those are things you only see kings or a President doing."

It was the same with the dinner jacket. A heavyweight champion has to spend some time banquet-hopping, so Cus D'Amato, who manages Patterson, made him buy a tuxedo.

"I don't care to wear it," Patterson said, "and I don't like to go to formals. I don't feel it's my walk of life. That's for people who were born and raised that way. I wasn't."

I thought of James J. Corbett.

After Patterson knocked out Roy Harris, nine months went by before he fought Brian London. During seven of those months he lived with his wife and their daughter in their St. Albans, New York, home. Three or four days a week, though, he would come into New York to loosen up, and one afternoon I met him at the Gramercy Gym, on East 14th Street.

"Are you doing road work?" I asked.

"Only twice a week," he said.

"What time do you run?"

"Well, in camp I don't get up until 6:30," he said, "but here in the city I get up at 5:30 so I get finished before the people start to work and see me."

"Doesn't anybody ever see you?" I said.

"Usually I run on Saturday and Sunday when everybody doesn't get up so early," he said, "but one day I ran during the week. It was a Thursday and after I finished in the park where I run the fella who was supposed to pick me up was late. About an hour passed before he came, and there I was sitting on the park bench with my heavy clothes on and all sweaty and a towel around my neck. All these people were going to work by then, and they were looking at me like I was crazy."

"Didn't anyone recognize you?" I said.

"No," he said. "I was the champion, so I hid my face."

"Shyness is so deeply ingrained in you," I said to him one night at the Long Pond, "that I suppose one of your earliest memories is of being embarrassed in public."

"I guess that's right," he said. "I remember when I was just a little kid. I used to have long hair and my father would comb it. Then he'd send me around the corner for cigarettes, and I remember one day a lady stopping me and running her fingers through my hair. I was so embarrassed that I wanted to cry, and I ran."

He thought about it. It was after dinner and we were still sitting at the table.

"I had to be just a tiny kid for a lady to do that," he said, "but I never forgot it."

Patterson's mother is a serene, sympathetic, soft-spoken woman of forty-eight. While rearing her family of eleven children in the Bedford-Stuyvesant section of Brooklyn, she also worked as a domestic and, for a while, in a bottling factory.

"I would take Floyd to school," she said, sitting in the living room of her home in Mount Vernon, "and as long as I stayed there he would stay, but when I left he would sneak out. I think the large number of children in the classes frightened Floyd."

"Where would he go?" I said.

"He'd hide," she said. "I remember once when he was six years old he found a friend in the school. Then he and the friend disappeared and later they found them hiding together in the basement of the school."

As he grew older, Patterson hid in movie theaters. If you live in Brooklyn and you're interested, he used to hide in the Regent, the Apollo, and the Banko.

"That was when I had the money for admission," he said. "Otherwise I would spend the time in Prospect Park, watching the animals in the zoo. I liked to watch the animals."

Often at night he would sleep in the park. Some nights he slept in subway stations.

"How much was the admission to the movies in those days?" I asked.

"Eighteen cents," he said.

"How much cash have you got in your pocket right now?" I said.

This was some months before he fought Ingemar Johansson the first time. We were sitting on the ring apron in the Gramercy Gym, and Patterson had on a pair of handsomely tailored dark brown slacks and a heavy-knit light tan sweater.

"Oh," he said, "I'd say between eighty and a hundred dollars."

"Do you also carry a checkbook?"

"Yes."

"When you started to be a fighter, did you ever think that you'd have eighty dollars in walk-around money and a checkbook in your pocket?"

"I never even dreamt that a day like that was possible," he said.

"Are you bothered by the sight of blood?" I once asked him.

"How do you mean?" Floyd said.

"Have you ever been scared, as a child or since, when you've been cut?"

I asked this question because a fighter must regard lightly the changes his business makes upon his physical person. He must also be relatively unaffected by the hurt he inflicts upon others.

"No," he said. "I've seen my blood flow from me when I was younger. One time I got a nail stuck in my foot and I kept it in there for three hours, until my mother came home from work. You see, there was this lady, babysitting for us and I was scared to tell her about the nail because she was very mean and she would beat you. So when I got this nail in my foot, I kept it there and stayed in the front room for three hours until my mother came home and then I told her about it."

"What about seeing blood on others?"

"On somebody else?" he said. "Well, this hasn't happened lately, but in the wintertime, when it's cold and my nose feels cold, I'd sometimes see two people fighting in the street. I'd actually see a guy with a big fist hit the other guy square on the nose or face. You know?"

"Yes."

"Well, when I'd see that, I'd feel it myself. It really seemed that I could actually feel it, and I would rather be fighting the one guy and taking the punishment than to see the other guy taking it, because I could just imagine how it feels to get hit when you're cold like that."

The first time Patterson was down in a professional fight was when Jacques Royer-Crecy dropped him to one knee with a right hand in the first round at the St. Nicholas Arena in New York. Floyd came up before the count, but in the dressing room later, fight writers asked him about it.

"He slipped," Cus D'Amato said.

"No," Patterson said. "He knocked me down. I know he hit me because I don't remember going down. Otherwise I'd remember."

Patterson's first loss as a professional was to Joey Maxim, who just managed to move him around enough at the Eastern Parkway Arena in Brooklyn to grab the decision. Eleven of the twelve boxing writers at ringside thought Patterson had won and they told him so in the dressing room.

"Don't you think you beat him?" a fellow said.

"The officials could see it better than I could," Patterson said. "I was too busy fighting."

Patterson won an Olympic gold medal at Helsinki in 1952. Pete Mello coached the United States boxing team that year, and one afternoon I went down to the CYO gym on East 17th Street in New York to see him.

"Tell me about Patterson," I said.

"I'm in this business about forty-one years," Pete said, "and this is the nicest kid I ever handled."

"Give me an example," I said.

"We're over in Helsinki," Pete said, "and we have to line up for chow. I noticed that Patterson used to gather himself three or four steaks, so I watch to find out what he's doing."

"What was he doing?" I said.

"Some of those Finns didn't have too much to eat," Pete said, "so Patterson was making up packages of food for them."

Most fighters will carry a mental image of the next opponent while they run on the road or punch the bag or shadow-box. Before Patterson fought Archie Moore for the title, he boxed the fight many times in his mind.

"I fought Moore when I was awake," he said, "and when I was asleep. One night I dreamt I'd already fought him, and I'd already won. When I woke up, for three or four seconds I thought I was the champ. I lay there with my eyes open, and then the realization came to me that the fight was still a week off. But I'd already had that good feeling of being champ."

"What were your feelings," I said, "when you actually knocked out Archie?"

"I felt good," Patterson said, "and then I felt sorry for Archie Moore. I knew how I'd have felt if he had knocked me out. I put myself in his place, and I looked at him and I could see how badly he felt."

When Patterson was a kid, his idol was Joe Louis. Floyd kept scrapbooks filled with clippings and pictures of Joe. After Patterson won the title, the two finally met at a dinner.

"What was it like?" I asked Patterson.

"Well," Patterson said, "I said to myself: 'Is this really Joe Louis? Am I finally meeting the man who is my idol?' I almost couldn't believe it."

"But you were the heavyweight champion of the world," I said. "You had his old title."

"It seemed to me," Patterson said, "like Joe Louis was still the champion, and I wasn't."

Patterson hid out from five schools before they sent him to Wiltwyck, a school for emotionally disturbed boys at Esopus, New York. There classes were smaller and he received individual attention. There he wore boxing gloves for the first time. One afternoon I went to see Ernst Papanek, the Wiltwyck director, and Walter Johnson, the resident director.

"When Floyd came to us," Johnson said, "he was only about eleven years old, and I can best describe him as very impressionable and a great sufferer. He was suspicious of help and he didn't want to be with others, so our problem was to get him involved in some group activity.

"We tried several things and then I thought of boxing. I put him in a tournament and he won his first three bouts. For the first time he had found success in the group, and we had found the tool whereby he could relate to others."

"But he's unlike any other fighter I've ever known," I said.

"That's right," Papanek said. "I did not expect him to be a boxer. He is so very gentle. I do not mean he is weak, but he is soft. Do you remember what happened in Chicago?"

"Yes," I said.

In January 1953, Patterson fought Chester Mieszala in Chicago. The week before the fight, the two were training in the Midtown Gym, but Patterson refused to watch Mieszala.

"I'd be taking unfair advantage," he told Cus D'Amato. "I learn a lot watching another fighter, and he wouldn't have a chance."

During the fight, Patterson knocked Mieszala's mouthpiece out, and Mieszala stopped and bent over to recover it. He was having trouble picking it up with his glove, so Patterson stooped down to help him. When the mouthpiece was back in place, they touched gloves. Patterson finally finished Mieszala in the fifth round.

"That's what I mean," Papanek said. "I believe Floyd does not want to hurt people."

Patterson once had Tommy Harrison out on his feet in the first round. He dropped his hands and waited for the referee to stop it. In another fight, Floyd opened a cut over Roy Harris' left eye, then began punching to the body.

"Were you sorry for Harris?" I said.

"It wasn't necessary for me to ruin him," Patterson said. "I was way ahead on points anyway."

One afternoon in the Gramercy Gym, Jacob Lofman, a photographer, was taking pictures of Patterson and listening to us talk.

"May I ask you something, Floyd?" Lofman said.

"Sure," Patterson said.

"Does it make any difference to you if it's a white man you're fighting?"

"No," Patterson said. "Absolutely no."

"But do you ever feel that you're representing your race when you're fighting?" I said.

"Only that time with Roy Harris," Patterson said. "I heard some things that were said about the fight. I knew the South was all backing him up, and most of the colored people, you know, they didn't want to see me get beat. When I got up in the ring, though, none of that even entered my mind. He was just another man like everybody else has been, so I didn't notice his color or how much was involved."

"Thank you, Floyd," Lofman said.

After Johansson knocked him out in the third round of their first fight, Patterson went into seclusion for a month. When he came out of it, he set up a training camp in an abandoned roadhouse in Newtown, Connecticut. I guess I visited him there at least a dozen times in the next nine months.

"Do you resent Johansson?" I said to him, the first time I saw him after the fight.

"No," he said. "I was inclined to at first, but then I realized that all he did to me was what I tried to do to him, and there was no reason to resent him."

"At any time when you were down in that fight," I said, "did you recognize anyone at ringside?"

"Yes," he said. "I recognized John Wayne. I think it must have been the third knockdown, because there I was on the floor, looking right at John Wayne and John Wayne was looking right at me."

"Do you know him?"

"I've never met him," Patterson said, "but he's my favorite movie actor. He's always the good guy or the sheriff cleaning up the town, and I think I've seen him in every picture he's made. At first I couldn't figure out how I could be seeing him there at ringside."

"He was plugging a movie during the broadcast of the fight," I said.

"I know that now," Patterson said, "but all I knew then was that I'd seen John Wayne in person, and when I got up I was still thinking of that and I was embarrassed that John Wayne had seen me down."

One day we were sitting in the kitchen of the Newtown club. Dan Florio, who trains Patterson, was boiling a couple of eggs and Patterson was glancing at a newspaper.

"Have you seen Johansson on television?" I said.

"Not with Dinah Shore," Patterson said, "but I saw him in that play."

"*The Killers,*" I said.

"That's right," he said.

"That would have been the first time you saw him since the fight," I said. "Did it bother you?"

"Well, I heard he was going to be on," Patterson said. "At first I didn't know whether I'd watch him or not. Then I decided to watch, and the first time they showed him, he was lying face down on a bed."

"That's right," I said.

"Then I lowered my eyes," Patterson said, "and I said to myself: 'Now this is Johansson. You have to look at him. You have got to accept him.' Then I slowly raised my eyes and I looked at him and I could accept him. I thought he was good in the play."

"Well," I said, "he played the part of a Swedish heavyweight."

"I still think he was good," Patterson said.

The day of the second Patterson-Johansson fight they weighed in at noon at the Commodore Hotel. The big room was crowded with sports-

writers and photographers and members of the fight mob, and I ran
into Johnny Attell. Johnny was a matchmaker for many years around
New York, and while we were talking, Billy Conn walked over.

"Who do you like tonight, Bill?" Johnny said to him.

"Me?" Conn said. "I like the Swede for his punch."

"I don't know," Johnny said, shrugging. "Patterson's got the equipment to take him if he fights him right."

"You hear what somebody had Patterson say?" Conn said.

"What?" Johnny said.

"Floyd said that when he gets a guy out he lays off the eye and hits
him in the belly," Conn said. "You know somebody told him to say
that, because he'd pour salt in a cut if he could."

"No he wouldn't," Johnny said.

"Are you kidding?" Conn said.

"No," Johnny said. "This guy Patterson is really that way."

"Then he's got no business being a fighter," Conn said.

Left hooks and the only anger he has ever carried into a ring won the
second Johansson fight for Patterson. The anger was born of a resentment, not of Johansson but of the many who Floyd said deserted him
and of the many sportswriters who maligned his ability. Twenty minutes after the knockout, the anger was still there. In the crowded, noisy,
humid Polo Grounds dressing room, Howard Cosell, the sportscaster,
held his microphone in front of Patterson.

"How do you feel, surrounded by sportswriters," Cosell said, "most
of whom picked you to lose?"

"I'm looking right in their faces," Patterson said.

I thought of something else he once told me.

"When I was small," he said, "I could never look people in the eye.
When I tried to look them in the eye, it always seemed that they could
read my mind. There was nothing on my mind, but it seemed they
could read it anyway. I tried very hard, and then one day I woke up
and I could look people in the eye. It had kind of sneaked its way in."

"When I left the Polo Grounds," Patterson told me some days later,
"the promoters had a car and chauffeur for me. I was sitting in the back
seat alone, and when we drove through Harlem and I saw all the people
celebrating in the streets, I felt good."

"You should have," I said. "There's been nothing like it since Louis
knocked out Billy Conn."

"Then I thought about Johansson," Patterson said. "I thought how he would have to drive through there, too, and then he would have to go through what I went through after the first fight. I thought that he would be even more ashamed than I was, because he'd knocked me out the first time. Then I felt sorry for him."

"Do you think," I said, "that you can call up the same kind of anger and viciousness the next time you fight Johansson?"

"Why should I?" Patterson said. "In all my other fights, I was never vicious, and I won out in almost all of them."

"But you had to be vicious against this guy," I said. "You had to turn a boxing contest into a kind of street fight to destroy this guy's classic style. When you did that, he came apart. This was your greatest fight, because for the first time you expressed emotion. A fight, a piece of writing, a painting or a passage of music is nothing without emotion."

"I just hope," Patterson said, "that I'll never be as vicious again."

That's what I mean when I say he wasn't cut out to be a fighter, but don't get me wrong. He is a good fighter. It's just that he's a better man.

The Kid's Last Game

Ed Linn | **1 9 6 1**

Wednesday, September 26, was a cold and dreary day in Boston, a curious bit of staging on the part of those gods who always set the scene most carefully for Ted Williams. It was to be the last game Ted would ever play in Boston. Not until the game was over would Williams let it be known that it was the last game he would play anywhere.

Ted came into the locker room at 10:50, very early for him. He was dressed in dark brown slacks, a yellow sport shirt and a light tan pullover sweater, tastily brocaded in the same color. Ted went immediately to his locker, pulled off the sweater, then strolled into the trainer's room.

Despite all the triumphs and the honors, it had been a difficult year for him. As trainer Jack Fadden put it: "It hasn't been a labor of love for Ted this year; it's just been labor." On two separate occasions, he had come very close to giving it all up.

The spring training torture had been made no easier for Ted by manager Billy Jurges. Jurges believed that the only way for a man Ted's age to stay in condition was to reach a peak at the beginning of the season and hold it by playing just as often as possible. "The most we can expect from Williams," Jurges had said, at the time of Ted's signing, "is

186)

one hundred games. The least is pinch-hitting." Ted played in 113 games.

Throughout the training season, however, Ted seemed to be having trouble with his timing. Recalling his .254 average of the previous season, the experts wrote him off for perhaps the fifteenth time in his career. But on his first time at bat in the opening game, Ted hit a five-hundred-foot home run, possibly the longest of his career, off Camilo Pascual, probably the best pitcher in the league. The next day, in the Fenway Park opener, he hit a second homer, this one off Jim Coates. Ted pulled a leg muscle running out that homer, though, and when a man's muscles go while he is doing nothing more than jogging around the bases, the end is clearly in sight.

It took him almost a month to get back in condition, but the mysterious virus infection that hits him annually, a holdover from his service in Korea, laid him low again almost immediately. Since the doctors have never been able to diagnose this chronic illness, the only way they can treat him is to shoot a variety of drugs and antibiotics into him, in the hope that one of them takes hold. Ted, miserable and drugged when he finally got back in uniform, failed in a couple of pinch-hitting attempts and was just about ready to quit. Against the Yankees, Ralph Terry struck him out two straight times. The third time up, the count went to 3 and 2 when Williams unloaded on a waist-high fastball and sent it into the bullpen in right-center, four hundred feet away.

The blast triggered the greatest home-run spurt of Ted's career. Seven days later, he hit his five hundredth home run. He had started only fifteen 1960 games and he had hit eight 1960 homers. When he hit his five hundred and sixth (and eleventh of the year), he had homered once in every 6.67 times at bat.

Cold weather always bothered Ted, even in his early years, and so when he strained his shoulder late in August, he was just about ready to announce his retirement again. He had found it difficult to loosen up even in fairly warm weather, and to complicate matters he had found it necessary—back in the middle of 1959—to cut out the calisthenics routine he had always gone through in the clubhouse. The exercising had left him almost too weary to play ball.

Ted started every game so stiff that he was forced to exaggerate an old passion for swinging at balls only in the strike zone. In his first time at bat, he would look for an inside pitch between the waist and knees, the only pitch he could swing at naturally. In the main, however, Ted was more than willing to take the base on balls his first time up.

He stayed on for two reasons. Mike Higgins, who had replaced Jurges as Sox manager, told him bluntly: "You're paid to play ball, so go out and play." The strength behind those words rested in the fact that both Williams and Higgins knew very well that owner Tom Yawkey would continue to pay Ted whether he played or not.

In addition, the Red Sox had two series remaining with the Yankees and Orioles, who were still locked together in the pennant race. Ted did not think it fair to eliminate himself as a factor in the two-team battle. He announced his retirement just after the Yankees clinched the pennant.

Four days earlier, Ted had been called to a special meeting with Yawkey, Higgins, Dick O'Connell (who was soon to be named business manager) and publicity director Jack Malaney. This was to offer Ted the job of general manager, a position that had been discussed occasionally in the past.

Ted refused to accept the title until he proved he could do the job. He agreed, however, to work in the front office in 1961, assisting Higgins with player personnel, and O'Connell with business matters.

The coverage of Ted's last game was at a minimum. It was thought for a while that *Life* magazine wanted to send a crew down to cover the game, but it developed that they only wanted to arrange for Ted to represent them at the World Series. Dave Garroway's *Today* program tried to set up a telephone interview the morning of the game, but they couldn't get in touch with Ted. The Red Sox, alone among big-league clubs, have offered little help to anyone on the public relations front—and never any help at all where Ted Williams was concerned. Ted didn't live at the Kenmore Hotel with the rest of the unattached players. He lived about a hundred yards down Commonwealth Avenue, at the Somerset. All calls and messages for him were diverted to the manager's office.

The ceremonies that were to mark his departure were rather limited, too. The Boston Chamber of Commerce had arranged to present him with a silver bowl, and the mayor's office and governor's office had quickly muscled into the picture. By Wednesday morning, however, the governor's office—which had apparently anticipated something more spectacular—begged off. The governor's spokesman suggested the presentation of a scroll at Ted's hotel, a suggestion which Ted simply ignored.

The only civilian in the clubhouse when Ted entered was the man from *Sport,* and he was talking to Del Baker, who was about to retire, too, after fifty years in the game. Ted looked over, scowled, seemed about to say something but changed his mind.

Our man was well aware what Ted was about to say. The Red Sox have a long-standing rule—also unique in baseball—that no reporter may enter the dressing room before the game, or for the first fifteen minutes after the game. It was a point of honor with Ted to pick out any civilian who wasn't specifically with a ballplayer and to tell him, as loudly as possible: "You're not supposed to be in here, you know."

Sure enough, when our man started toward Ted's locker in the far corner of the room, Ted pointed a finger at him and shouted: "You're not supposed to be in here, you know."

"The same warm, glad cry of greeting I always get from you," our man said. "It's your last day. Why don't you live a little?"

Ted started toward the trainer's room again, but wheeled around and came back. "You've got a nerve coming here to interview me after the last one you wrote about me!"

Our man wanted to know what was the matter with the last one.

"You called me 'unbearable,' that's what's the matter."

The full quote, it was pointed out, was that he "was sometimes unbearable but never dull," which holds a different connotation entirely.

"You've been after me for twelve years, that flogging magazine," he said, in his typically well-modulated shout. "Twelve years. I missed an appointment for some kind of luncheon. I forgot what happened . . . it doesn't matter anyway . . . but I forgot some appointment twelve years ago and *Sport* magazine hasn't let up on me since."

Our man, lamentably eager to disassociate himself from this little magazine, made it clear that while he had done most of *Sport*'s Williams articles in the past few years, he was not a member of the staff. "And," our man pointed out, "I have been accused of turning you into a combination of Paul Bunyan and Santa Claus."

"Well, when you get back there, tell them what . . . (he searched for the appropriate word, the *mot juste* as they say in the dugouts) . . . what *flog-heads* they are. Tell them that for me."

Our man sought to check the correct spelling of the adjectives with him but got back only a scowl. Ted turned around to fish something out of a cloth bag at the side of his locker. "Why don't you just write your story without me?" he said. "What do you have to talk to me for?" And then, in a suddenly weary voice: "What can I tell you now that I haven't told you before?"

"Why don't you let me tell you what the story is supposed to be?"

our man said. "Then you can say yes or no." It was an unfortunate way to put the question since it invited the answer it brought.

"I can tell you before you tell me," Ted shouted. "No! No, no, no."

Our man had the impression Williams was trying to tell him something. He was right. "Look," Williams said. "If I tell you I don't want to talk to you, why don't you just take my word for it?"

The clubhouse boy had come over with a glossy photo to be signed, and Ted sat down on his stool, turned his back and signed it.

Although we are reluctant to bring *Sport* into the context of the story itself, Ted's abiding hatred toward us tells much about him and his even longer feud with Boston sportswriters. Twelve years ago, just as Ted said, an article appeared on these pages to which he took violent exception. (The fact that he is so well aware that it *was* twelve years ago suggests that he still has the magazine around somewhere, so that he can fan the flames whenever he feels them dying.) What Ted objected to in that article was an interview with his mother in San Diego. Ted objects to any peering into his private life. When he holes himself up in his hotel, when he sets a barrier around the clubhouse, when he disappears into the Florida Keys at the end of the season, he is deliberately removing himself from a world which he takes to be dangerous and hostile. His constant fighting with the newspapermen who cover him most closely is a part of the same pattern. What do newspapermen represent except the people who are supposed to pierce personal barriers? Who investigate, who pry, *who find out?*

Ted's mother has been a Salvation Army worker in San Diego all her life. She is a local character, known—not without affection—as "Salvation May." Ted himself was dedicated to the Salvation Army when he was a baby. His generosity, his unfailing instinct to come to the aid of any underdog, is in direct line with the teachings of the Army, which is quite probably the purest charitable organization in the world. Even as a boy, Ted regularly gave his thirty-cent luncheon allowance to classmates he considered more needy than himself, a considerable sacrifice since the Williams family had to struggle to make ends meet.

When Ted signed with San Diego at the age of seventeen, he was a tall, skinny kid (six feet three, 146 pounds). He gave most of his $150-a-month salary toward keeping up the family house and he tried to build up his weight by gorging himself on the road where the club picked up the check. One day, Ted was coming into the clubhouse when Bill Lane, the owner of the Padres, motioned him over. In his deep, foghorn voice, Lane said: "Well, kid, you're leading the list. You've got the others beat."

Ted, pleased that his ability was being noted so promptly, smiled and asked: "Yeah, what list?"

"The dining room list," Lane said. "Hasn't anyone told you that your meal allowance is supposed to be five dollars a day?"

Nobody had. "Okay, Bill," Ted said, finally. "Take anything over five dollars off my salary."

Bill did, too.

Even before *Sport* went into details about his background, the Boston press had discovered his weak point and hit him hard and—it must be added—most unfairly. During Ted's second season with the Sox, one reporter had the ill grace to comment, in regard to a purely personal dispute: "But what can you expect of a youth so abnormal that he didn't go home in the off-season to see his own mother?"

When Williams' World War II draft status was changed from 1A to 3A after he claimed his mother as a dependent, one Boston paper sent a private investigator to San Diego to check on her standard of living; another paper sent reporters out onto the street to ask casual passers-by to pass judgment on Ted's patriotism.

Reporters were sent galloping out into the street to conduct a public-opinion poll once again when Williams was caught fishing in the Everglades while his wife was giving birth to a premature baby.

A press association later sent a story out of San Diego that Ted had sold the furniture out from under his mother—although a simple phone call could have established that it wasn't true. Ted had bought the house and the furniture for his mother. His brother—who had been in frequent trouble with the law—had sold it. The Boston papers picked up that story and gave it a big play, despite the fact that every sports editor in the city had enough background material on Ted's family to know—even without checking—that it couldn't possibly be true. It was, Ted's friends believed, their way of punishing him for not being "cooperative."

Ted had become so accustomed to looking upon any reference to his family as an unfriendly act that when *Sport* wrote about his mother, he bristled—even though her final quote was: "Don't say anything about Teddy except the highest and the best. He's a wonderful son." And when he searched for some reason why the magazine would do such a thing to him, he pounced upon that broken appointment, which everybody except himself had long forgotten.

After Ted had signed the photograph the day of his last game, he sat on his stool, his right knee jumping nervously, his right hand alternately buttoning and unbuttoning the top button of his sport shirt.

When he stripped down to his shorts, there was no doubt he was forty-two. The man once called The Splendid Splinter—certainly one of the most atrocious nicknames ever committed upon an immortal—was thick around the middle. A soft roll of loose fat, drooping around the waist, brought on a vivid picture of Archie Moore.

Williams is a tall, handsome man. If they ever make that movie of his life that keeps being rumored around, the guy who plays Bret Maverick would be perfect for the part. But ballplayers age quickly. Twenty years under the sun had baked Ted's face and left it lined and leathery. Sitting there, Ted Williams had the appearance of an old Marine sergeant who had been to the battles and back.

Sal Maglie, who had the end locker on the other side of the shower-room door, suddenly caught Ted's attention. "You're a National Leaguer, Sal," Ted said, projecting his voice to the room at large. "I got a hundred dollars that the Yankees win the World Series. The Yankees will win it in four or five games."

"I'm an American Leaguer now," Sal said, quietly.

"A hundred dollars," Ted said. "A friendly bet."

"You want a friendly bet? I'll bet you a friendly dollar."

"Fifty dollars," Ted said.

"All right," Sal said. "Fifty dollars." And then, projecting his own voice, he said: "I like the Pirates, anyway."

Williams went back to his mail, as the others dressed and went out onto the field.

At length, Ted picked up his spikes, wandered into the trainer's room again, and lifting himself onto the table, carefully began to put a shine on them. A photographer gave him a ball to sign.

Ted gazed at it with distaste, then looked up at the photographer with loathing. "Are you crazy?" he snapped.

The photographer backed away, pocketed the ball and began to adjust his camera sights on Ted. "You don't belong in here," Ted shouted. And turning to the clubhouse boy, he barked: "Get him out of here."

The locker room had emptied before Ted began to dress. For Ted did not go out to take batting practice or fielding practice. He made every entrance onto the field a dramatic event. He did not leave the locker room for the dugout until 12:55, only thirty-five minutes before the game was scheduled to start. By then, most of the writers had already gone up to Tom Yawkey's office to hear Jackie Jensen announce that he was returning to baseball.

As Ted came quickly up the stairs and into the dugout, he almost bumped into his close friend and fishing companion, Bud Leavitt, sports editor of the Bangor *Daily News.* "Hi, Bud," Ted said, as if he were surprised Leavitt was there. "You drive up?"

A semicircle of cameramen closed in on Williams, like a bear trap, on the playing field just up above. Ted hurled a few choice oaths at them, and as an oath-hurler Ted never bats below .400. He guided Leavitt against the side of the dugout, just above the steps, so that he could continue the conversation without providing a shooting angle for the photographers. The photographers continued to shoot him in profile, though, until Ted took Leavitt by the elbow and walked him the length of the dugout. "Let's sit down," he said, as he left, "so we won't be bothered by all these blasted cameramen."

If there had been any doubt back in the locker room that Ted had decided to bow out with typical hardness, it had been completely dispelled by those first few minutes in the dugout. On his last day in Fenway Park, Ted Williams seemed resolved to remain true to his own image of himself, to permit no sentimentality or hint of sentimentality to crack that mirror through which he looks at the world and allows the world to look upon him.

And yet, in watching this strange and troubled man—the most remarkable and colorful and full-blooded human being to come upon the athletic scene since Babe Ruth—you had the feeling that he was overplaying his role, that he had struggled through the night against the impulse to make his peace, to express his gratitude, to accept the great affection that the city had been showering upon him for years. In watching him, you had the clear impression that in resisting this desire he was overreacting and becoming more profane, more impossible and —yes—more unbearable than ever.

Inside Ted Williams, there has always been a struggle of two opposing forces, almost two different persons. (We are fighting the use of the word schizophrenia.) The point we are making is best illustrated through Williams' long refusal to tip his hat in acknowledgment of the cheering crowds. It has always been his contention that the people who cheered him when he hit a home run were the same people who booed him when he struck out—which, incidentally, is probably not true at all. More to our point, Ted has always insisted that although he would rather be cheered than booed, he really didn't care what the fans thought of him, one way or the other.

Obviously, though, if he really didn't care he wouldn't have bothered to make such a show of not caring. He simply would have touched his finger to his cap in that automatic, thoughtless gesture of most players and forgot about it. Ted, in short, has always had it both ways. He gets the cheers and he pretends they mean nothing to him. He is like a rich man's nephew who treats his uncle with disrespect to prove he is not interested in his money, while all the time he is secretly dreaming that the uncle will reward such independence by leaving him most of the fortune.

Ted has it even better than that. The fans of Boston have always wooed him ardently. They always cheered him all the louder in the hope that he would reward them, at last, with that essentially meaningless tip of the hat.

This clash within Williams came to the surface as he sat and talked with Leavitt, alone and undisturbed. For, within a matter of minutes, the lack of attention began to oppress him; his voice began to rise, to pull everybody's attention back to him. The cameramen, getting the message, drifted toward him again, not in a tight pack this time but in a loose and straggling line.

With Ted talking so loudly, it was apparent that he and Leavitt were discussing how to get together, after the World Series, for their annual post-season fishing expedition. The assignment to cover the Series for *Life* had apparently upset their schedule.

"After New York," Ted said, "I'll be going right to Pittsburgh." He expressed his hope that the Yankees would wrap it all up in Yankee Stadium, so that he could join Leavitt in Bangor at the beginning of the following week. "But, dammit," he said, "if the Series goes more than five games, I'll have to go back to Pittsburgh again."

Leavitt reminded Ted of an appearance he had apparently agreed to make in Bangor. "All right," Ted said. "But no speeches or anything."

A young, redheaded woman, in her late twenties, leaned over from her box seat alongside the dugout and asked Ted if he would autograph her scorecard.

"I can't sign it, dear," Ted said. "League rules. Where are you going to be after the game?"

"You told me that once before," she said, unhappily.

"Well, where are you going to be?" Ted shouted, in the impatient way one would shout at an irritating child.

"Right here," she said.

"All right."

"But I waited before and you never came."

He ignored her.

Joe Cronin, president of the American League, came down the dugout aisle, followed by his assistant, Joe McKenney. Through Cronin's office, the local nine-o'clock newsfeature program which follows the

Today program in Boston had scheduled a filmed interview with Ted. The camera had already been set up on the home-plate side of the dugout, just in front of the box seats. Cronin talked to Ted briefly and went back to reassure the announcer that Ted would be right there. McKenney remained behind to make sure Ted didn't forget. At last, Ted jumped up and shouted: "Where is it, Joe, dammit?"

When Ted followed McKenney out, it was the first time he had stuck his head onto the field all day. There were still not too many fans in the stands, although far more than would have been there on any other day to watch a seventh-place team on a cold and threatening Wednesday afternoon. At this first sight of Ted Williams, they let out a mighty roar.

As he waited alongside interviewer Jack Chase, Ted bit his lower lip, and looked blankly into space, both characteristic mannerisms. At a signal from the cameraman, Chase asked Ted how he felt about entering "the last lap."

All at once, Ted was smiling. "I want to tell you, Jack, I honestly feel good about it," he said, speaking in that quick charming way of his. "You can't get blood out of a turnip, you know. I've gone as far as I can and I'm sure I wouldn't want to try it any more."

"Have we gone as far as we can with the Jimmy Fund?" he was asked.

Ted was smiling more broadly. "Oh, no. We could never go far enough with the Jimmy Fund."

Chase reminded Ted that he was scheduled to become a batting coach.

"Can you take a .250 hitter and make a .300 hitter out of him?"

"There has always been a saying in baseball that you can't make a hitter," Ted answered. "But I think you can *improve* a hitter. More than you can improve a fielder. More mistakes are made in hitting than in any other part of the game."

At this point, Williams was literally encircled by photographers, amateur and pro. The pros were taking pictures from the front and from the sides. Behind them, in the stands, dozens of fans had their cameras trained on Ted, too, although they could hardly have been getting anything except the number 9 on his back.

Ted was asked if he were going to travel around the Red Sox farm system in 1961 to instruct the young hitters.

"All I know is that I'm going to spring training," he said. "Other than that, I don't know anything."

The interview closed with the usual fulsome praise of Williams, the inevitable apotheosis that leaves him with a hangdog, embarrassed look upon his features. "I appreciate the kind words," he said. "It's all been fun. Everything I've done in New England from playing left field and getting booed, to the Jimmy Fund."

The Jimmy Fund is the money-raising arm of the Children's Cancer Hospital in Boston, which has become the world center for research into cancer and for the treatment of its young victims. Ted has been deeply involved with the hospital since its inception in 1947, serving the last four years as general chairman of the fund committee. He is an active chairman, not an honorary one. Scarcely a day goes by, when Ted is in Boston, that he doesn't make one or two stops for the Jimmy Fund somewhere in New England. He went out on the missions even on days when he was too sick to play ball. (This is the same man, let us emphasize, who refuses to attend functions at which he himself is to be honored.) He has personally raised something close to four million dollars and has helped to build a modern, model hospital not far from Fenway Park.

But he has done far more than that. From the first, Williams took upon himself the agonizing task of trying to bring some cheer into the lives of these dying children and, perhaps even more difficult, of comforting their parents. He has, in those years, permitted himself to become attached to thousands of these children, knowing full well that they were going to die, one by one. He has become so attached to some of them that he has chartered special planes to bring him to their deathbeds.

Whenever one of these children asks to see him, whatever the time, he comes. His only stipulation is that there must be no publicity, no reporters, no cameramen.

We once suggested to Ted that he must get some basic return from all this work he puts into the Jimmy Fund. Ted considered the matter very carefully before he answered: "Look," he said, finally, "it embarrasses me to be praised for anything like this. The embarrassing thing is that I don't feel I've done anything compared to the people at the hospital who are doing the important work. It makes me happy to think I've done a little good; I suppose that's what I get out of it.

"Anyway," he added, thoughtfully, "it's only a freak of fate, isn't it, that one of those kids isn't going to grow up to be an athlete and I wasn't the one who had the cancer."

At the finish of the filmed interview he had to push his way through the cameramen between him and the dugout. "Oh ——," he said.

But when one of them asked him to pose with Cronin, Ted switched personalities again and asked, with complete amiability, "Where is he?"

Cronin was in the dugout. Ted met Joe at the bottom of the steps and threw an arm around him. They grinned at each other while the pictures were being taken, talking softly and unintelligibly. After a minute, Ted reached over to the hook just behind him and grabbed his glove. The cameramen were still yelling for another shot as he started up the dugout steps. Joe, grinning broadly, grabbed him by the shoulder and yanked him back down. While Cronin was wrestling Ted around and whacking him on the back, the cameras clicked. "I got to warm up, dammit," Ted was saying. He made a pawing gesture at the cameramen, as if to say, "I'd like to belt you buzzards." This, from all evidence, was the picture that went around the country that night, because strangely enough, it looked as if he were waving a kind of sad goodbye.

When he finally broke away and raced up to the field, he called back over his shoulder, "See you later, Joe." The cheers arose from the stands once again.

The Orioles were taking infield practice by then, and the Red Sox were warming up along the sideline. Ted began to play catch with Pumpsie Green. As he did—sure enough—the cameramen lined up just inside the foul line for some more shots, none of which will ever be used. "Why don't you cockroaches get off my back?" Ted said, giving them his number-one sneer. "Let me breathe, will you?"

The bell rang before he had a chance to throw two dozen balls. Almost all the players went back to the locker room. Remaining on the bench were only Ted Williams, buttoned up in his jacket, and Vic Wertz. One of the members of the ground crew came over with a picture of Williams. He asked Ted if he would autograph it. "Sure," Ted said. "For you guys, anything."

Vic Wertz was having his picture taken with another crew member. Wertz had his arm around the guy and both of them were laughing. "How about you, Ted?" the cameraman asked. "One with the crewmen?"

Ted posed willingly with the man he had just signed for, with the result that the whole herd of cameramen came charging over again. Ted leaped to his feet. "Twenty-two years of this bull ———," he cried.

The redhead was leaning over the low barrier again, but now three other young women were alongside her. One of them seemed to be crying, apparently at the prospect of Ted's retirement. An old photographer, in a long, weatherbeaten coat, asked Ted for a special pose. "Get lost," Ted said. "I've seen enough of you, you old goat."

Curt Gowdy, the Red Sox broadcaster, had come into the dugout to pass on some information about the pre-game ceremonies. Ted shouted, "The devil with all you miserable cameramen." The women continued to stare, in fascination, held either by the thrill of having this last long look at Ted Williams or by the opportunity to learn a few new words.

A Baltimore writer came into the dugout, and Ted settled down beside him. He wanted to know whether the writer could check on the "King of Swat" crown that had been presented to him in his last visit to Baltimore. Ted wasn't sure whether he had taken it back to Boston with him or whether the organization still had it.

"You know," he told the writer, "Brown's a better pitcher now than he's ever been. Oh, he's a great pitcher. Never get a fat pitch from him. When he does, it comes in with something extra on it. Every time a little different. He knows what he's doing."

Ted is a student of such things. He is supposed to be a natural hitter, blessed with a superhuman pair of eyes. We are not about to dispute this. What we want to say is that when Ted first came to the majors, the book on him was that he would chase bad balls. "All young sluggers do," according to Del Baker, who was managing Detroit when Ted came up. "Ted developed a strike zone of his own, though, by the second year."

When Ted took his physical for the Naval Reserve in World War II, his eyes tested at 20/10 and were so exceptional in every regard that while he was attending air gunnery school he broke all previous Marine records for hitting the target sleeve. But Ted has a point of his own here: "My eyesight," he says, "is now 20/15. Half the major-leaguers have eyes as good as that. It isn't eyesight that makes a hitter; it's practice. *Con-sci-en-tious* practice. I say that Williams has hit more balls than any guy living, except maybe Ty Cobb. I don't say it to brag; I just state it as a fact. From the time I was eleven years old, I've taken every possible opportunity to swing at a ball. I've swung and I've swung and I've swung."

Ted always studied every little movement a pitcher made. He always remained on the bench before the game to watch them warming up. From his first day to his last, he hustled around to get all possible information on a new pitcher.

It has always been his theory that we are all creatures of habit, himself included. Pitchers, he believes, fall into observable patterns. A certain set of movements foretells a certain pitch. In a particular situation, or on a particular count, they go to a particular pitch. There were certain pitchers, Ted discovered, who would inevitably go to their big pitch, the pitch they wanted him to swing at, on the 2-2 count.

And so Ted would frequently ask a teammate, "What was the pitch he struck you out on?" or "What did he throw you on the 2-2 pitch?"

When a young player confessed he didn't know what the pitch had been, Ted would grow incredulous. "You don't know the pitch he struck you out on? I'm not talking about last week or last month. I'm not even talking about yesterday. Today! Just now! I'm talking about the pitch he struck you out on just now!"

Returning to his seat on the bench, he'd slump back in disgust and mutter: "What a rockhead. The guy's taking the bread and butter out of his mouth and he don't even care how."

In a very short time, the player would have an answer ready for Williams. Ted always got the young hitters thinking about their craft. He always tried to instruct them, to build up their confidence. "When you want to know who the best hitter in the league is," he'd tell the rookies, "just look into the mirror."

Among opposing players, Williams was always immensely popular. Yes, even among opposing pitchers. All pitchers love to say: "Nobody digs in against *me*." Only Ted Williams was given the right to dig in without getting flipped. Around the American League, there seemed to be a general understanding that Williams had too much class to be knocked down.

Waiting in the dugout for the ceremonies to get under way, Ted picked up a bat and wandered up and down the aisle taking vicious practice swings.

The photographers immediately swooped in on him. One nice guy was taking cameras from the people in the stands and getting shots of Ted for them.

As Ted put the bat down, one of them said: "One more shot, Teddy, as a favor."

"I'm all done doing any favors for you guys," Williams said. "I don't have to put up with you any more, and you don't have to put up with me."

An old woman, leaning over the box seats, was wailing: "Don't leave us, Ted. Don't leave us."

"Oh hell," Ted said, turning away in disgust.

The redhead asked him plaintively: "Why don't you act nice?"

Ted strolled slowly toward her, grinning broadly. "Come on, dear," he drawled, "with that High Street accent you got there."

Turning back, he stopped in front of the man from *Sport*, pointed over his shoulder at the cameramen and asked: "You getting it all? You getting what you came for?"

"If you can't make it as a batting coach," our man said, "I understand you're going to try it as a cameraman."

"What does *Sport* magazine think I'm going to do?" Ted asked. "That's what I want to know. What does *Sport* magazine think I'm going to be?"

Speaking for himself, our man told him, he had not the slightest doubt that Ted was going to be the new general manager.

"*Sport* magazine," Ted said, making the name sound like an oath. "Always honest. Never prejudiced."

At this point, he was called onto the field. Taking off his jacket, he strode out of the dugout. The cheers that greeted him came from 10,454 throats.

Curt Gowdy, handling the introductions, began: "As we all know, this is the final home game for—in my opinion and most of yours—the greatest hitter who ever lived. Ted Williams."

There was tremendous applause.

"Twenty years ago," Gowdy continued, "a skinny kid from San Diego came to the Red Sox camp. . . ."

Ted first came to the Red Sox training camp at Sarasota in the spring of 1938. General manager Eddie Collins, having heard that Ted was a creature of wild and wayward impulse, had instructed second-baseman Bobby Doerr to pick him up and deliver him, shining and undamaged.

It was unthinkable, of course, that Ted Williams would make a routine entrance. Just before Doerr was set to leave home, the worst flood of the decade hit California and washed out all the roads and telephone lines. When Williams and Doerr finally arrived in Sarasota, ten days late, there was a fine, almost imperceptible drizzle. Williams, still practically waterlogged from the California floods, held out a palm, looked skyward, shivered and said in a voice that flushed the flamingoes from their nests: "So this is Florida, is it? Do they always keep this state under a foot of water?"

Williams suited up for a morning workout out in the field, jawed good-naturedly with the fans and got an unexpected chance to hit when a newsreel company moved in to take some batting-cage shots.

The magic of Ted Williams in a batter's box manifested itself that first day in camp. The tall, thin rookie stepped into the box, set himself in his wide stance, let his bat drop across the far corner of the plate, wiggled his hips and shoulders and jiggled up and down as if he were trying to tamp himself into the box. He moved his bat back and forth a few times, then brought it back into position and twisted his hands in opposite directions as if he were wringing the neck of the bat. He was set for the pitch.

And somehow, as if by some common impulse, all sideline activity stopped that day in 1938. Everybody was watching Ted Williams.

"Controversial, sure," Gowdy said, in bringing his remarks about Ted to a close, "but colorful."

The chairman of the Boston Chamber of Commerce presented Ted a shining, silver Paul Revere bowl "on behalf of the business community of Boston." Ted seemed to force his smile as he accepted it.

A representative of the sports committee of the Chamber of Commerce then presented him with a plaque "on behalf of visits to kids' and veterans' hospitals."

Mayor John Collins, from his wheelchair, announced that "on behalf of all citizens" he was proclaiming this day "Ted Williams Day." The mayor didn't know how right he was.

As Mayor Collins spoke of Ted's virtues ("Nature's best, nature's nobleman"), the muscle of Ted's upper left jaw was jumping, constantly and rhythmically. The mayor's contribution to Ted Williams Day was a $1000 donation to the Jimmy Fund from some special city fund.

Gowdy brought the proceedings to a close by proclaiming: "Pride is what made him great. He's a champion, a thoroughbred, a champion of sports." Curt then asked for "a round of applause, an ovation for Number 9 on his last game in his Boston." Needless to say, he got it.

Ted waited, pawed at the ground with one foot. Smilingly, he thanked the mayor for the money. "Despite the fact of the disagreeable things that have been said of me—and I can't help thinking about it— by the Knights of the Keyboard out there [he jerked his head toward the press box], baseball has been the most wonderful thing in my life. If I were starting over again and someone asked me where is the one place I would like to play, I would want it to be in Boston, with the greatest owner in baseball and the greatest fans in America. Thank you."

He walked across the infield to the dugout, where the players were standing, applauding along with the fans. Ted winked and went on in.

In the press box, some of the writers were upset by his gratuitous rap at them. "I think it was bush," one of them said. "Whatever he thinks, this wasn't the time to say it."

Others made a joke of it. "Now that he's knighted me," one of them was saying, "I wonder if he's going to address me as Sir."

In the last half of the first inning, Williams stepped in against Steve Barber with Willie Tasby on first and one out. When Barber was born

—February 22, 1939—Ted had already taken the American Association apart, as it has never been taken apart since, by batting .366, hitting 43 home runs and knocking in 142 runs.

Against a lefthander, Williams was standing almost flush along the
inside line of the batter's box, his feet wide, his stance slightly closed.
He took a curve inside, then a fastball low. The fans began to boo. The
third pitch was also low. With a 3-0 count, Ted jumped in front of the
plate with the pitch, like a high-school kid looking for a walk. It was
ball four, high.

He got to third the easy way. Jim Pagliaroni was hit by a pitch, and
everybody moved up on a wild pitch. When Frank Malzone walked,
Jack Fisher came in to replace Barber. Lou Clinton greeted Jack with a
rising liner to dead center. Jackie Brandt started in, slipped as he tried
to reverse himself, but recovered in time to scramble back and make
the catch. His throw to the plate was beautiful to behold, a low one-
bouncer that came to Gus Triandos chest high. But Ted, sliding hard,
was in under the ball easily.

Leading off the third inning against the righthanded Fisher, Ted
moved back just a little in the box. Fisher is even younger than Barber,
a week younger. When Fisher was being born—March 4, 1939—Ted
was reporting to Sarasota again, widely proclaimed as the super-player
of the future, the Red Sox' answer to Joe DiMaggio.

Ted hit Fisher's 1-1 pitch straightaway, high and deep. Brandt had
plenty of room to go back and make the catch, but still, as Williams returned to the bench, he got another tremendous hand.

Up in the press box, publicity man Jack Malaney was announcing
that uniform number 9 was being retired "after today's game." This
brought on some snide remarks about Ted wearing his undershirt at
Yankee Stadium for the final three games of the season. Like Mayor
Collins, Malaney was righter than he knew. The uniform was indeed
going to be retired after the game.

Williams came to bat again in the fifth inning, with two out and the
Sox trailing 3 to 2. And this time he unloaded a tremendous drive to
right center. As the ball jumped off the bat, the cry, "He did it!" arose
from the stands. Right-fielder Al Pilarcik ran back as far as he could,
pressed his back against the bullpen fence, well out from the 380-foot
sign, and stood there, motionless, his hands at his sides.

Although it was a heavy day, there was absolutely no wind. The flag
hung limply from the pole, stirring very occasionally and very faintly.

At the last minute, Pilarcik brought up his hands and caught the ball
chest high, close to four hundred feet from the plate. A moan of disap-

pointment settled over the field, followed by a rising hum of excited conversation and then, as Ted came back toward the first-base line to get his glove from Pumpsie Green, a standing ovation.

"Damn," Ted said, when he returned to the bench at the end of the inning. "I hit the living hell out of that one. I really stung it. If that one didn't go out, nothing is going out today!"

In the top of the eighth, with the Sox behind 4 to 2, Mike Fornieles came to the mound for the seventieth time of the season, breaking the league record set by another Red Sox relief star, Ellis Kinder. Kinder set his mark in 1953, the year Williams returned from Korea.

As Fornieles was warming up, three teen-agers jumped out of the grandstand and ran toward Ted. They paused only briefly, however, and continued across the field to the waiting arms of the park police.

Ted was scheduled to bat second in the last of the eighth, undoubtedly his last time at bat. The cheering began as soon as Willie Tasby came out of the dugout and strode to the plate, as if he was anxious to get out of there and make way for the main event. Ted, coming out almost directly behind Tasby, went to the on-deck circle. He was down on one knee and just beginning to swing the heavy, lead-filled practice bat as Tasby hit the first pitch to short for an easy out.

The cheering seemed to come to its peak as Ted stepped into the box and took his stance. Everybody in the park had come to his feet to give Ted a standing ovation.

Umpire Eddie Hurley called time. Fisher stepped off the rubber and Triandos stood erect. Ted remained in the box, waiting, as if he were oblivious to it all. The standing ovation lasted at least two minutes, and even then Fisher threw into the continuing applause. Only as the ball approached the plate did the cheering stop. It came in low, ball one. The spectators remained on their feet, but very suddenly the park had gone very quiet.

If there was pressure on Ted, there was pressure on Fisher, too. The Orioles were practically tied for second place, so he couldn't afford to be charitable. He might have been able to get Ted to go after a bad pitch, and yet he hardly wanted to go down in history as the fresh kid who had walked Ted Williams on his last time at bat in Boston.

The second pitch was neck high, a slider with, it seemed, just a little off it. Ted gave it a tremendous swing, but he was just a little out in front of the ball. The swing itself brought a roar from the fans, though, since it was such a clear announcement that Ted was going for the home run or nothing.

With a 1-1 count, Fisher wanted to throw a fastball, low and away.

He got it up too much and in too much, a fastball waist high on the outside corner. From the moment Ted swung, there was not the slightest doubt about it. The ball cut through the heavy air, a high line drive heading straightaway to center field toward the corner of the special bullpen the Red Sox built for Williams back in 1941.

Jackie Brandt went back almost to the barrier, then turned and watched the ball bounce off the canopy above the bullpen bench, skip up against the wire fence which rises in front of the bleachers and bounce back into the bullpen.

It did not seem possible that ten thousand people could make that much noise.

Ted raced around the bases at a pretty good clip. Triandos had started toward the mound with the new ball, and Fisher had come down to meet him. As Ted neared home plate, Triandos turned to face him, a big smile on his face. Ted grinned back.

Ted didn't exactly offer his hand to Pagliaroni after he crossed the plate, but the young catcher reached out anyway and made a grab for it. He seemed to catch Ted around the wrist. Williams ran back into the dugout and ducked through the runway door to get himself a drink of water.

The fans were on their feet again, deafening the air with their cheers. A good four or five minutes passed before anybody worried about getting the game under way again.

When Ted ducked back into the dugout, he put on his jacket and sat down at the very edge of the bench, alongside Mike Higgins and Del Baker. The players, still on their feet anyway, crowded around him, urging him to go out and acknowledge the cheers.

The fans were now chanting, "We want Ted . . . we want Ted . . . we want Ted." Umpire Johnny Rice, at first base, motioned for Ted to come out. Manager Mike Higgins urged him to go on out. Ted just sat there, his head down, a smile of happiness on his face.

"We wanted him to go out," Vic Wertz said later, "because we felt so good for him. And we could see he was thrilled, too. For me, I have to say it's my top thrill in baseball."

But another player said: "I had the impression—maybe I shouldn't say this because it's just an impression—that he got just as much a kick out of refusing to go out and tip his hat to the crowd as he did out of the homer. What I mean is he wanted to go out with the home run, all right, but he also wanted the home run so he could sit there while they yelled for him and tell them all where to go."

Mike Higgins had already told Carroll Hardy to replace Ted in left field. As Clinton came to bat, with two men out, Higgins said: "Williams, left field." Ted grabbed his glove angrily and went to the top step. When Clinton struck out, Ted was the first man out of the dugout. He sprinted out to left field, ignoring the cheers of the fans, who had not expected to see him again. But Higgins had sent Hardy right out behind him. Ted saw Carroll, and ran back in, one final time. The entire audience was on its feet once again, in wild applause.

Since it is doubtful that Higgins felt Williams was in any great need of more applause that day, it is perfectly obvious that he was giving Ted one last chance to think about the tip of the hat or the wave of the hand as he covered the distance between left field and the dugout.

Ted made the trip as always, his head down, his stride unbroken. He stepped on first base as he crossed the line, ducked down into the dugout, growled once at Higgins and headed through the alleyway and into the locker room.

He stopped only to tell an usher standing just inside the dugout: "I guess I forgot to tip my hat."

To the end, the mirror remained intact.

After the game, photographers were permitted to go right into the clubhouse, but writers were held to the fifteen-minute rule. One writer tried to ride in with the photographers, but Williams leveled that finger at him and said: "You're not supposed to be here."

Somehow or other, the news was let out that Ted would not be going to New York, although there seems to be some doubt as to whether it was Williams or Higgins who made the announcement. The official Boston line is that it had been understood all along that Ted would not be going to New York unless the pennant race was still on. The fact of the matter is that Williams made the decision himself, and he did not make it until after he hit the home run. It would have been foolish to have gone to New York or anywhere else, of course. Anything he did after the Boston finale would have been an anticlimax.

One of the waiting newspapermen, a pessimist by nature, expressed the fear that by the time they were let in, Ted would be dressed and gone.

"Are you kidding?" a member of the anti-Williams clique said. "This is what he lives for. If the game had gone eighteen innings, he'd be in there waiting for us."

He was indeed waiting at his locker, with a towel wrapped around his middle. The writers approached him, for the most part, in groups. Generally speaking, the writers who could be called friends reached him first, and to these men Ted was not only amiable but gracious and modest.

Was he going for the home run?

"I was gunning for the big one," he grinned. "I let everything I had go. I really wanted that one."

Did he know it was out as soon as it left his bat?

"I knew I had really given it a ride."

What were his immediate plans?

"I've got some business to clean up here," he said. "Then I'll be covering the World Series for *Life*. After that, I'm going back to Florida to see how much damage the hurricane did to my house."

The other players seemed even more affected by the drama of the farewell homer than Ted. Pete Runnels, practically dispossessed from his locker alongside Ted's by the shifts of reporters, wandered around the room shaking his head in disbelief. "How about that?" he kept repeating. "How about that? How about that?"

As for Ted, he seemed to be in something of a daze. After the first wave of writers had left, he wandered back and forth between his locker and the trainer's room. Back and forth, back and forth. Once, he came back with a bottle of beer, turned it up to his lips and downed it with obvious pleasure. For Ted, this is almost unheard of. He has always been a milk and ice-cream man, and he devours them both in huge quantities. His usual order after a ball game is two quarts of milk.

Williams remained in the locker room, making himself available, until there were no more than a half-dozen other players remaining. Many of the writers did not go over to him at all. From them, there were no questions, no congratulations, no good wishes for the future. For all Ted's color, for all the drama and copy he had supplied over twenty-two years, they were glad to see him finally retire.

When Ted finally began to get dressed, our man went over and said: "Ted, you must have known when Higgins sent you back out that he was giving you a final chance to think about tipping the hat or making some gesture of farewell. Which meant that Higgins himself would have liked you to have done it. While you were running back, didn't you have any feeling that it might be nice to go out with a show of good feeling?"

"I felt nothing," he said.

"No sentimentality? No gratitude? No sadness?"

"I said *nothing*," Ted said. "Nothing, nothing, nothing!"

As our man was toting up the nothings, Ted snarled, "And when you get back there tell them for me that they're full of. . . ." There followed a burst of vituperation which we cannot even begin to approximate, and then the old, sad plaint about those twelve years of merciless persecution.

Fenway Park has an enclosed parking area so that the players can get to their cars without beating their way through the autograph hunters. When Ted was dressed, though, the clubhouse boy called to the front office in what was apparently a prearranged plan to bring Williams' car around to a bleacher exit.

At 4:40, forty-five minutes after the end of the game and a good hour after Ted had left the dugout, he was ready to leave. "Fitzie," he called out, and the clubhouse boy came around to lead the way. The cameramen came around, too.

The locker-room door opens onto a long corridor, which leads to another door, which, in turn, opens onto the backwalks and understructure of the park. It is this outer door which is always guarded.

Waiting in the alleyway, just outside the clubhouse door, however, was a redheaded, beatnik-looking man, complete with the regimental beard and the beachcomber pants. He handed Ted a ball and mentioned a name that apparently meant something to him. Ted took the ball and signed it.

"How come you're not able to get in?" he said. "If they let the damn newspapermen in, they ought to let you in." Walking away, trailed by the platoon of cameramen, he called out to the empty air: "If they let the newspapermen in, they should have let him in. If they let the newspapermen in, they should let everybody in."

He walked on through the backways of the park, past the ramps and pillars, at a brisk clip, with Fitzie bustling along quickly to stay up ahead. Alongside of Williams, the cameramen were scrambling to get their positions and snap their pictures. Williams kept his eyes straight ahead, never pausing for one moment. "Hold it for just a minute, Ted," one of them said.

"I've been here for twenty-two years," Ted said, walking on. "Plenty of time for you to get your shot."

"This is the last time," the cameraman said. "Cooperate just this one last time."

"I've cooperated with you," Ted said. "I've cooperated too much."

Fitzie had the bleacher entrance open, and as Ted passed quickly through, a powder-blue Cadillac pulled up to the curb. A man in shirt sleeves was behind the wheel. He looked like Dick O'Connell, whose appointment as business manager had been announced the previous night.

Fitzie ran ahead to open the far door of the car for Ted. Three young women had been approaching the exit as Ted darted through, and one of them screamed: "It's him!" One of the others just let out a scream, as if Ted had been somebody of real worth, like Elvis or Fabian. The third woman remained mute. Looking at her, you had to wonder whether she would ever speak again.

Fitzie slammed the door, and the car pulled away. "It was him," the first woman screamed. "Was it *really* him? Was it *him?*"

Her knees seemed to give away. Her girl friends had to support her. "I can't catch my breath," she said. "I can hear my heart pounding." And then, in something like terror: *"I can't breathe."*

Attracted by the screams, or by some invisible, inexplicable grapevine, a horde of boys and men came racing up the street. Ted's car turned the corner just across from the bleacher exit, but it was held up momentarily by a red light and a bus. The front line of pursuers had just come abreast of the car when the driver swung around the bus and pulled away.

There are those, however, who never get the word. Down the street, still surrounding the almost empty parking area, were still perhaps a hundred loyal fans waiting to say their last farewell to Ted Williams.

In Boston that night, the talk was all of Williams. Only 10,454 were at the scene, but the word all over the city was: "I knew he'd end it with a home run. . . ." and "I was going to go to the game, but—"

In future years, we can be sure, the men who saw Ted hit that mighty shot will number into the hundreds of thousands. The wind will grow strong and mean, and the distance will grow longer. Many of the reports of the game, in fact, had the ball going into the center-field bleachers.

The seeds of the legend have already been sown. George Carens, an elderly columnist who is more beloved by Ted than by his colleagues, wrote:

"Ted was calm and gracious as he praised the occupants of the Fenway press penthouse at home plate before the game began. Afterwards he greeted all writers in a comradely way, down through his most persistent critics. In a word, Ted showed he can take it, and whenever the spirit moves him he will fit beautifully into the Fenway PR setup."

Which shows that people hear what they want to hear and see what they want to see.

In New York the next day, Phil Rizzuto informed his television audience that Ted had finally relented and tipped his hat after the home run.

And the *Sporting News* headline on its Boston story was: SPLINTER TIPS CAP TO HUB FANS AFTER FAREWELL HOMER.

A New York Sunday paper went so far as to say that Ted had made "a tender and touching farewell speech" from home plate at the end of the game.

All the reports said that Ted had, in effect, called his shot because it was known that he was shooting for a home run. Who wants to bet that, in future years, there will not be a story or two insisting that he *did* point?

The legend will inevitably grow, and in a way it is a shame. A man should be allowed to die the way he lived. He should be allowed to depart as he came. Ted Williams chose his course early, and his course was to turn his face from the world around him. When he walked out of the park, he kept his eyes to the front and he never looked back.

The epitaph for Ted Williams remains unchanged. He was sometimes unbearable but he was never dull. Baseball will not be the same without him. Boston won't be quite the same either. Old Boston is acrawl with greening statues of old heroes and old patriots, but Ted has left a monument of his own— again on his own terms—in the Children's Cancer Hospital.

He left his own monument in the record books too. For two decades he made the Red Sox exciting in the sheer anticipation of his next time at bat.

He opened his last season with perhaps the longest home run of his career and he closed it with perhaps the most dramatic. It was typical and it was right that the Williams Era in Boston should end not with a whimper. It was entirely proper that it should end with a bang.

So, the old order passeth and an era of austerity has settled upon the Red Sox franchise.

And now Boston knows how England felt when it lost India.

Part Three | 1961–1965

The Untold Facts Behind the Basketball Scandal

Jimmy Breslin | **1 9 6 1**

Three kids had come into the living room of Connie Hawkins' apartment to see him, but the one who had done the work on the project was doing all the talking.

"You want to get down with us on a bank job?" he said to Hawkins.

"What bank?" Connie said.

"National Bank," the kid said.

"You all sick," Connie said.

"No we not. We got a plan all made out and everything. You want to see it? I'll show it to you."

"I don't want to know about anything," Connie said.

The kids had just walked in off the street with an idea to rob a bank. It was always like this where Connie Hawkins comes from. He comes from Bedford-Stuyvesant, which is in Brooklyn and is very bad. Connie is nineteen and is fast and strong and, like everybody in the neighborhood tells him, his big hands would make him the best mugger anybody ever saw. But right from the start, Connie just listened to the propositions, then he laughed at them and walked away. He never had a day's trouble in his life. He had to go to college and be around nice people before he got into trouble.

You've probably never heard of Hawkins. Which is the way it is always going to be now. He is a kid who is six feet six and change, and he is the best basketball player to come along in maybe the last ten years. He had one of the great careers ahead of him. But last May, a kid came into his freshman dormitory at the University of Iowa and said the basketball coach, Sharm Scheuerman, wanted to talk to him and when Connie got over to the field house Scheuerman introduced him to a guy named Richard Bernhart and this one was from the district attorney's office in New York. Bernhart told Connie to get his clothes; he was going back to New York to testify in front of the Grand Jury investigating the basketball scandal.

The 1961 college basketball gambling scandal, which ruined the careers and, chances are, the lives of Hawkins and thirty-four other players, is the most serious problem ever to come up in sports. The whole thing frightens you. To begin with, the dumpers and the people they did business with were uncovered by only two law enforcement agencies, the New York District Attorney's office and the North Carolina State Bureau of Investigation. (Fix arrests made by Florida and Michigan authorities concerned football, which, as we're going to see, probably is a story in itself.) Now investigations are being conducted in other parts of the country.

There was one morning this summer, for example, when Abe Saperstein sat at the desk of his Chicago office and kept shaking his head while he talked about the college scandals.

"Fellows who should know," he was saying quietly, "hear this now, these aren't just talkers, these are fellas who know; well, they tell me things about the Midwest out here that I can't believe. But I got to believe it because my business is hiring basketball players, both for the Globetrotters and for my new league. I don't know what to do about it."

Exactly ten years before this latest scandal was made public, the country was shocked by arrests of players at eight major schools. They had been in on eighty-six dumps or point shavings. It was a helluva thing. It also was nothing more than a warmup for the situation we have on our hands today. This new scandal is worse.

The most basic part is that a basketball scandal involves human beings; young ones; ones who have promise and every chance in the world for a fine life ahead of them; and when you are around to see what it is like when their lives are wrecked it doesn't really matter whether this scandal is bigger than the last or not.

What matters is that once you walked down Fourth Street in Louisville and you saw how Ralph Beard was making sure he didn't meet anybody who would talk to him about basketball as he came along. You saw him and you said, oh, could he play that game. Then you said thank the Lord no more kids are going through what he has since he was in the University of Kentucky mess. You said that, and then one night last summer you wound up in a place called the Savoia Pizzeria on Myrtle Avenue in Brooklyn and it was 1951 all over again and here was a kid telling you he didn't know what he was going to do with the rest of his life because the D.A. had bagged him on the basketball scandal.

It was Connie Hawkins who was sitting at the bar, but it could have been Sherman White or Eddie Roman or Gene Melchiorre or any of the others from ten years ago. It doesn't matter, because it was the same and it was just as bad.

Hawkins had played a record on the juke box and he had his big hand on a piece of pizza pie and he was talking about what had happened to him.

"What are you going to do?" we asked him.

"I don't know," he said. "When this man Bernhart came to school it was right before finals. He said did you hear about the latest break in the basketball scandals and I said I didn't. But I figured that was why he was there. Well, he said I'd only be two days in New York. Wound up I was in his office every day for two weeks.

"When I got through, I call up the coach and he says 'come out to school.' I fly out there, the district attorney had given me the round-trip ticket, and when I get there the coach says nothing can be done, the best thing for me to do is drop out. So I come home and here I am. I play ball at the park every day. All day. That's all I do. I don't know what else to do."

He had on a brown plaid shirt and chino slacks and big (size 14) basketball shoes. He sat on the barstool and talked matter-of-factly about how he got into the whole thing. He didn't realize he was talking about how he had blown what may be the only chance of his lifetime. But he's only nineteen. Someday, when he's older and things get tough, he is going to think about it clearly and it is not going to be good.

"Last summer," he was saying, "I was playing around the parks in tournaments and things. I was up in a place called Kelly Park, near Kings Highway, and I met Jack Molinas. I saw him a lot after that. Manhattan Beach, Rockville Centre, wherever there were games. He was playing in them. He's a good player, you know. Man, the best."

Jack Molinas came out of Columbia University and in 1953 he was as fine a basketball player as the National Basketball Association had.

But in November he was suspended from the league for having made ten bets on his team to win. He sued the league for three million and after turning down a settlement he lost the case in court. He is a successful New York lawyer now. In his off hours he plays basketball at these summer games around New York. In the basketball season, he is player-coach for Hazelton (Pennsylvania) in the Eastern League. The league is a weekend professional circuit and he takes care of his law business during the week.

"One day," Connie was saying, "I came up to his office. He introduced me to this fellow Joe Hacken. Then Jack went into his own office to work and Hacken and I sat in this other office and Hacken talked to me.

" 'Do you know basketball players well enough to introduce me to them?' Hacken asks me. I said yes. He said that's good, he'd like for me to introduce him to some. I said all right. That was that."

Joe Hacken was a client of Molinas'. He is a guy who originally came out of Blum's pool hall on 188th Street in the Bronx. It is a street that always has been hot when it comes to fixing basketball games. Hacken used to be called "Joe Jalop" up there. He hung out on the sidewalk between two candy stores which handled plenty of action. You always could find him with Joe Green and Aaron Wagman, both jailed as this year's fixers. Neil Kelleher, who did a year and a day in the can for his part in trying to fix Manhattan College players in 1951, used to be around, too.

Hacken hustled bets around 188th Street and used to work with fighters in the Uptown Gym. It was out of there that he got in trouble in 1954. He made a move on middleweight Bobby Jones and offered Jones $15,000 to blow a fight. Jones told the D.A. The cops hit from four sides and Hacken did time for it.

Now here was Connie Hawkins talking about meeting him in a lawyer's office.

"I only saw him twice after that," Hawkins was saying. "At the Garden during the Holiday Festival Tournament when I was home from school. The second time I saw him was in my house and that got me in trouble.

"I saw Molinas, though. I remember one night me and Roger Brown [Dayton freshman also in trouble], we both had our girls to the games at the Garden and after it we went with Jack to this restaurant. Then when we wanted to go home it was raining and we thought we could take a cab. Jack says why take a cab. Take the girls home nice. He had a lot of credit cards and he said he'd get us one of those Hertz cars to go home with. He was going to get a Lincoln but they didn't have one so we got a Chrysler Imperial."

He laughed. "We impressed those girls good."

"How did Hacken get you in the trouble?" we asked him.

"During Christmas," he said. "Back at school the coach had given me two hundred dollars to pay my dormitory fees and I had spent the money and now I needed it. So I called Hacken. He come to my house."

Hawkins looked up in the air.

"It was a hundred-dollar bill and two fifties," he said. "That's how he gave it to me. I said I wanted it as a loan. He said sure."

"It was a loan that you could pay back when you started playing," Bob Allen, an old knock-around guy who was drinking with us, said.

Hawkins moved his shoulders. "It was a loan," he said.

"What did the district attorney say when you told him that?"

"Those people wouldn't believe me if I told them my own name," he said. "When they brought me back from Iowa they had Roger Brown, too. They had brought him in from Dayton. They put us in a hotel for two weeks. And every day, for eight hours, we had to go to the district attorney's office.

"The minute we got there, this man Scotti [Alfred Scotti, rackets bureau chief] says 'You lie it's five years for perjury.' Then they turn us over to the detectives. Every day, it was the same thing. They said I was trying to protect Molinas.

"The detective would get me in this office and he'd start in on me. He'd say 'You're lying. Now tell me just what he said to you and did for you.' And I'd say, 'I can't tell you anything that didn't happen. Molinas left the room before I started talking to Hacken.'

"Then they'd go right back at me again. Then all of a sudden the guy would look at his watch and he'd say, 'Gee, it's time for lunch. Do you care for a couple of sandwiches?' The minute I finished eating them, he'd go right back at me again. The man only wanted one thing. And I just couldn't tell it to them. They don't believe me yet."

"Listen," we said to Hawkins. "You're not sitting here trying to tell me this thing all happened out of one meet with a guy. Somebody must have done something else for you. You don't set up a guy this easy."

The kid looked down at his hands. He nodded his head yes.

"Broads?"

The kid shook his head yes.

"They got you New York broads?"

"Uh huh."

"It's a beautiful world," Bob Allen said.

We put Hawkins in the car and drove him home. He lives on Lexington Avenue, which is a murderous strip of blacktop running between decaying three-story houses. Floyd Patterson came from a couple of blocks up Lexington Avenue from Hawkins' house.

The first time we ever saw Connie he had only one set of clothes to wear and he was playing for Boys High School. He was the best basketball player at his stage we ever saw, outside of Wilt Chamberlain. Then the colleges got on him. In the spring of 1960 Indiana, Iowa, Colorado, Michigan State, Ohio State, Illinois, Kansas, Northwestern and Seattle flew him out to spend weekends.

"I was offered two hundred and fifty dollars a month to go to Seattle," he says.

He picked Colorado at first. He went to summer school there last year. But the people at Iowa did not give up easily. There was a short, stocky little guy in a blue suit who owned a feed business and he always had made a fuss when Connie came to Iowa City. Hawkins was at Colorado when Iowa people got hold of him. He wound up at Iowa.

"For money," he was saying. "I went for money. It wasn't as much as five hundred dollars a month. But it was pretty good money. About three hundred? Well, right around there."

For ten years now, people have been telling colleges that as soon as you start throwing airline tickets and money and attention on a kid because he can play basketball, then there are twenty guys on the streets who know how to get to him with money to make the kid do tricks during a game. The colleges didn't do a damn thing about it. Now they cry like suckers when they get jacked-in with a basketball fix. How silly can you get?

You had to think of that when Hawkins got out of the car and said good night. The stoop of his house was mobbed with people. The apartments inside were too hot and lousy to stay in. They would have paid Connie Hawkins $25,000 a year to play professional basketball someday. Now he was walking back to his apartment without a thing in the world going for him. He shouldn't have taken the money, they'll tell you out at Iowa. And when they do that, somebody ought to ask Iowa what the hell Connie Hawkins from Brooklyn was doing out there in the first place. Which is something we are going to look into, too. But right now, on this hot night on Lexington Avenue, all you could think of was what Connie Hawkins had thrown away once he got away from kids who wanted to rob banks and he went to college and became a big basketball player.

It was a lousy night. But it was anything but a surprise that you were spending some time, just as you did in 1951, with some kid who was in trouble because of a basketball scandal. All you had to do was be around town drinking for the last few years to know that. The thing came as anything but a shock.

The first story we ever heard in connection with the scandal this time came in February of 1957 when the remarkable Mr. Toney Betts of the New York *Mirror* came into Madison Square Garden to cover a college doubleheader. Toney is a racetrack man, but the horses were in Florida and somebody on the paper was off that night, so he filled in. For his first edition story, which came out a little before the games started, Mr. Betts did what he thought was a natural. He called a bookmaker in Brownsville and got the prices on the night's games.

After giving him the line, the bookmaker said, "Watch out for this. These are those private schools. We may get a big move later on."

With this information in mind, Toney walked into the Garden lobby, where he was met by Ned Irish, who still is promoting college basketball games for the profit of a commercial arena. And the colleges love it. This thing gets sillier as you go on. Well, anyway, Irish on this night was upset. He had seen the *Mirror* first edition and he did not like the idea that a newspaper was printing gambling prices on his college games. After all, Irish said, we just got through 1951. Why start gambling news again?

Mr. Betts is one of the most learned men we've ever met on newspapers. His knowledge of the English language is extensive. But in this case his answer was clear, concise and unprintable.

The little by-play got around and as guys in bars talked about it they wondered, naturally, about the conduct of the games. If anybody would have gone around 188th Street in the Bronx and had a drink at the Roma Café and made a connection with somebody out on the street they might have had a chance to find something out. They would have found that Joe Jalop Hacken was busy paying off Mike Parenti and Bill Crystal of St. John's University $4450 each for bagging games at Madison Square Garden during that season.

A year later you could see that college basketball had to be heading for a mess. The editors of *Sport* asked for a story on the college basketball situation. In wandering around to put it together you wound up listening to tales of the unbelievable recruiting which went on for such as Wilt Chamberlain and a boy from Minden, Louisiana, named Jackie Moreland. There was good betting going on all over. There was talk about a referee doing business in the Midwest. There was, in fact, only

one thing you could say and the title of the *Sport* piece summed it up—
"Is Basketball Heading for Another Scandal?"

Now we go to February of 1959 and the bar of one of those good
steak houses in New York City. It was one of those places where the
glasses are thick and feel good in your hand and there is good lighting
because the ice cubes in a Scotch on the rocks always gleam when you
raise the glass. A bookmaker sitting at the bar reached into the inside
pocket of his jacket and pulled out a packet of money which was held
together by rubber bands at each end.

"New bills," he was saying. "The guy'll feel great getting these. Look.
Twelve thousand he beats me for."

"What did he beat you on?"

"Basketball. Ain't that something? I wish you could tell me what the
hell I'm doing with basketball. But here I am. Those kids must be doing
something. I don't know what the hell it is. But I figure something must
be up."

A few weeks later, after a big upset, bookmakers all over let out a
scream. The morning after the game, a guy called long distance from
Reno, Nevada, and he was saying, "I got murdered on that game. All
the money come out of Evansville, Indiana. You ought to do something
about it."

So they were betting big again, and there was talk around, the same
kind of talk you heard before the 1951 scandal, and it all added up to
only one thing—when would it happen?

In March of 1960, New York University flew down to Charlotte,
North Carolina, to face West Virginia in the opening game of a two-
night program which would send the winner out to Los Angeles for the
NCAA championship round. It was one of the most tremendous games
of basketball we ever have seen. The game ended with Jerry West of
West Virginia driving toward the basket in a man-to-man, shoulder-
against-chest duel with Tom (Satch) Sanders of NYU. This was in overtime and NYU had a one-point lead. Here came West, on the left side,
and here was Sanders on him and then at the last second, just as West
was going up to try and shoot over Sanders' hands, Ray Paprocky of
NYU cut across from under the basket and he went up, too, and now
West could see nothing and he had to throw the shot up blind and he
missed.

NYU was to play Duke the next night. The afternoon of the game,
we called New York to get the price on the game.

"What's doing?" we said to the bookmaker.

"Nothing. That Sanders is too good for them kids, isn't he?"

"Yes. Is anybody making a move on the games?"

"Just normal stuff. Nothing's going on with these big games."

Now this was a big bookmaker, a guy who had been around for years. He should know everything. But he didn't know the NYU game of the night before had been bought and paid for as a dump, but that the dump hadn't come off. Our guy didn't know anything about it. It gives you an idea of what you're up against trying to break open one of these scandals.

NYU beat Duke easily the next night and after it there was a party and while everybody was around Lou Rossini, NYU's fine coach, and talking about how his team won the games, Bob Quincy, the sports editor of the Charlotte *News*, came over to have a drink and talk.

"We got a mess down here," he said quietly. "There's been something the matter here all season long. I just can't get at it yet. The state bureau of investigation is on it. They won't tell me anything. If you happen to hear anything up North you let me know and if I hear anything down here I'll let you know. Sure as we're here, there is trouble."

The next morning we got on the plane back to New York and for a while during the trip we sat with Raymond Paprocky. He is a six-foot-one, blond-haired kid who comes from the Ridgewood section of Queens and at this time he was on the way to making a fine name for himself as a ballplayer. With a little work on his outside shot—he was only a sophomore at the time—he could have made a living in the NBA.

"How is everything?" we asked him.

"I don't know," he was saying. "When I got married I figured with the subsistence the school gives and my wife's salary, seventy-five dollars a week, we could get by until I finish. But now she's pregnant and I don't know what to do."

By subsistence he meant a quaint practice of New York schools. If you attend school on a basketball scholarship, but live home, which nearly all do, you are paid about $150 a month for room and board. The schools figure this is what it would cost them to house the boy, anyway. The fact St. John's, which does this, too, does not have a dormitory at all doesn't seem to enter the picture. The boy still has his room and board paid for. This thing gets more insane as we go on.

"You know," Paprocky was saying on the plane, "I can't hold any kind of a job during the season. And when the season ends I have to catch up on studies. So it only gives me the summers. I've got to get a good job for the summer and save money or I don't know how I'm going to make it. I'm in a jam. I don't have any money to pay the doctor for the baby."

"Well, whatever the hell you do," we told him, "don't take any money on this basketball thing."

"What do you mean?"

"I mean don't take any money to blow a ball game. They're doing it, you know."

"Me? Never. I don't know anything about that stuff."

"Well you better not. For yourself, for one thing. And for another, you better not dump any games that I go to. I'm supposed to know about this stuff and it would make me look bad. I'll break your legs if you do anything."

He laughed.

A week before, Joe Hacken had sat in a car in front of Paprocky's house and he had handed Paprocky $1000 to make sure NYU lost to West Virginia by more points than the line called for. The next season, Paprocky blew games to Wake Forest and St. John's and he wound up, one morning last April, walking into District Attorney Scotti's office and sitting down and listening to Scotti tell him:

"It is five years for perjury every time you lie. You're going before a grand jury.

"Now what about you taking money to fix basketball games?"

"I don't know anything about it," Paprocky said. "I haven't done anything."

"What about the thousand you took from Joe Hacken for the West Virginia game at Charlotte last year?"

Now Paprocky knew it was all over. He talked. For eight weeks, eight hours a day, Ray Paprocky sat in the district attorney's office and they kept going over his story, trying to get him to remember every last step of his movements in the fix.

With Paprocky, the basketball scandals all started right in the hallways of his school between classes.

"I must have had five guys come up to me and talk, guys who were going to the school. They talked roundabout, but you know how it is, you get the idea of what they mean. It looked like everybody was trying to fix games. Then before the St. John's game last year (March 1960) somebody told me I could make some money selling tickets to it. You know, it was a big game and it looked like a sellout, just like the old days. This fellow told me to go up and see a fellow named Charley Tucker and he gave me his address. Tucker was living in a one-room apartment up in the Bronx. On University Avenue. I bring him the tickets and he's laying down on the studio couch and he pays me fifty dollars for them.

"Then he says, 'Do you want to make any real money playing basketball?' I told him I was interested. There goes my life right there, but I told him I was interested.

"Couple of days later he calls me on the phone and asks what I think and I say yes, I'm interested. Then he tells me this fellow Hacken will be around to see me. So I go meet Hacken in front of the house. First he wanted me to do business on the St. John's game. I said no good. That's too big a game for the school. So he says how about West Virginia and I said sure. He gave me a thousand for it.

"He was, oh, slimy like and I'm sorry I ever met the guy. He told me I'd hear from Davey Budin after that. I knew Davey from around. He played at Brooklyn College and I always saw him around the summer leagues and that.

"Well, we went down to Charlotte that time I was with you, and at first I was trying to lose the game, and we were way behind. I wasn't hurting my teammates or anything. I just wasn't scoring myself or taking care of my man right. Then we started to pull up close and I got excited and I forgot all about the points and I played my heart out. After the game, this Tucker and Joe Green were there, they said to me, 'That's all right. Sanders was just too much for them. You tried for us.'

"Then the next season, I always saw Budin. I'd meet him in a car under the Williamsburg Bridge in Brooklyn and we'd talk about what was to go on and what I was going to get and all that. The next thing I knew the district attorney is after me."

We were sitting in a place in Ridgewood having a beer, but it could have been in Storrs, Connecticut, where Peter Kelly of the University of Connecticut took $750 to blow a Colgate game. Or at State College, Mississippi, where Jerry Graves of Mississippi State took $1500 to blow a game to Ole Miss. Or in Philadelphia, where Ed Bohler of La Salle was to get $1250 for messing up a game against Duquesne, but he didn't play that night and they gave him $750 for solace. Or at Chapel Hill, North Carolina, where Doug Moe of the University of North Carolina took just $75 as introduction money, but once he had it in his pocket he was through. Or at any of the other places—at the University of Detroit, or Tennessee or St. Joseph's of Philadelphia; any of the places where the scandal touched. Because the story always is the same. Kids went for money and they went for it quickly and easily. The number who turned it down is small. The number who took it and haven't been caught has got to be staggering.

And the people who were giving them this money are strange. Aaron Wagman, whose arrest on a football fix attempt broke the case open, is an example. This is a guy from the Bronx who all of a sudden, last fall, wound up at Gainesville, Florida, talking to fullback Jon McBeth of the University of Florida. And he was counting out fifteen $100 bills in front of McBeth as they talked.

"Fumble the ball a couple of times," Wagman was saying. "Just make sure you beat Florida State by less than thirteen points. There'll be plenty more money for you, too. The guy I'm working with bets ten grand here, ten grand there on games."

"I drooled when I saw the money," McBeth said.

Then he said he'd have to think about it and he went to his coach and told him what was going on. Police arrested Wagman and Phillip Silber, a Florida undergraduate who had brought Wagman around to talk with McBeth. They grilled Silber and Wagman. Out of it came information that Davey Budin, on the same weekend, had been in a motel at Ann Arbor, Michigan, and he had been trying to get an Oregon halfback to blow a game to Michigan.

Budin, Wagman and Silber all were from New York. It was a simple thing, the New York district attorney's man tells you, to figure out something was going on. So the check began. Wagman and Budin and Silber were questioned by New York authorities.

"We broke the thing open in the questioning," the D.A.'s man said. "One of them told us everything. Let's leave it at that. Well, anyway, all we had to do was start working. We wound up with a list of players a foot long. We started calling them in. Art Hicks and Hank Gunter of Seton Hall. Then Kelly from Connecticut. Then Paprocky. They gave us information against Hacken, Wagman, Tucker and Green and the rest of them. That took care of the case. So far. The grand jury has been extended until December, you know."

The 1961 fixers did it in the grand, take-chances style of the old fixers. If you can remember Gene Melchiorre of Bradley in 1950 moving around the Convention Hall in Philadelphia in a pre-game warmup and holding out his thumb and sticking it down so the fixers would know he was going under the points against Temple, then you can understand Joe Green grabbing Fred Portnoy of Columbia as the kid came out of the locker room to start the second half against Penn last season.

Portnoy was the last player out of the room as the team headed up the stairs to go out on the floor of the small Columbia gym. Penn was ahead by four. Portnoy's agreement said Penn should have been ahead by thirteen.

"What are you doing?" Green said. "This is business. These guys are going to think I don't have you."

Portnoy went out and took the first shot of the second half against Penn. He just threw it up. It went in. He shook his head. In the stands, Green exploded.

Then Portnoy settled down, didn't shoot any more and blew the game.

Late one afternoon last August we went to the eighth-floor law offices of Jack Molinas in New York City and sat at a desk with him and talked about the whole thing.

Molinas had on a white shirt and college-striped tie. He was smoking a cigar and he kept throwing the ashes from it out the open window behind him. He is an alert, pleasant guy of thirty whose close-cropped dark hair is starting to reach low tide along his forehead. But he is still flat in the middle. He keeps himself in condition. Except for the hair, he looked the same as he did when he was the most promising rookie in the National Basketball Association.

We talked for an hour and twenty minutes. We talked about the Eastern Basketball League and whether there is a chance the kids caught in the present scandal could ever play in that league. Molinas didn't think so. We talked about Abe Saperstein's new American Basketball League. Molinas said he wanted to play in that league and had been in touch with them about it. He said he had a fine law practice and that playing basketball was his hobby. You could see he must be a fine lawyer. If we had a case, it would be great to have him represent us. Talk to him and you can see he is good.

Then we talked about the basketball scandal and the fact his name had been mentioned in the papers during it.

"Innuendoes," he was saying. "They put my initials in gossip columns. Then Harold Weissman had a story in the New York *Mirror*. It said that I defended Roger Brown in a case that came up when he was driving my car. Which I did. One night we were playing in Brooklyn and after it Roger said he and Connie Hawkins wanted to drive down to Nathan's in Coney Island and get their girls something to eat. I said fine, go ahead. On the way back Brown got into a little accident. It was nothing. So I defended him. Then Weissman's story said I introduced Brown to Hacken in a restaurant. That's all it said. Nothing else. Do you know how long I know Hacken? Twenty years. He has been a client of mine. In fact, I am co-counsel on his present case. I'm not doing the paperwork or anything like that. But I know basketball and I know the law. So I have special knowledge. I can sit in court and help the case.

"Look, I know just about every one of these fellows in this situation. I know them from basketball. You meet everybody if you're playing basketball. There are games all over. I like to play. So I go and play in them. Roger Brown, Connie Hawkins, anybody else you want to name, too. I must know just about everybody playing basketball, the same as they know everybody else in the sport.

"But all of a sudden they put my name in stories. Or they say 'an ex-Ivy League player who was in the NBA and is now a lawyer.' Now that is libel by innuendo. There is only one person like that. Me. Well, anyway, the district attorney started to have me followed. Every place I went I started to see these guys and I said, well, they're welcome to come along. But I'm going to have some fun with them. So I'd go into a house and leave by another door and take off. I'd be staying out until four, five in the morning. I had them crazy.

"Everything I did they tried to make something big out of. They brought one kid into the district attorney's office who used to play for Louisville. He comes from Brooklyn. What's his name now? Mantel, that's right. Red Mantel. Well, they say, 'Did Molinas ever buy you anything?' He says yes. They jump off their chairs. 'What?' they say. He tells them, 'After a game we went out and he bought me a soda.'

"I was always around playing. After the games we'd go and get a sandwich someplace. Well, who is going to pay, some nineteen-year-old kid? I'd pay. What would it cost, three, four dollars? Now, I'm through with that. The other night I'm playing in the schoolyard at Grover Cleveland High School and they say that this little fellow who used to play at George Washington, Jon Feldman, that's it, well, he wanted to meet me. I said, 'Please, don't introduce me to anybody any more.' I'm through with that! From now on, I just go home after the game. I won't even buy a soda.

"Take this kid Portnoy. They start a big story about me giving him two trotters at Yonkers Raceway. Do you know what happened? I'm at Yonkers one night and he comes up and says, 'Gee, I'm broke. There are two races to go.' So I say, oh, something like, 'Bet the six horse in the eighth race and the five horse in the ninth race.' That's all. Didn't mean anything. But he took the information and bet and the kid won a couple of hundred dollars for himself. I didn't even think about it.

"A funny thing, a client of mine was in here and when I stepped out of the office he used my phone to get down a twenty-thousand-dollar bet on a game early last season. It wasn't one of the games they said was fixed, either. I didn't even know he made the call until he told me. And he won. It was a Villanova game. Well, the district attorney must have that on tape someplace. The phone has been tapped."

We shook hands and went down and got into a cab and had the driver go to a joint called Moochie's, which is by the docks on the East Side. We got some paper and put it on the bar and began to make a list of all the kids who were involved and where they come from and what schools they go to.

Then we said to hell with it and threw it away and started drinking beer. We'll wait until the final returns on this thing come through. There may be more names to use before this thing ends. And there is also an awful lot of blame to pass around. We hope they place it where it belongs.

Back at the Polo Grounds

Murray Kempton | **1 9 6 2**

The return of the Polo Grounds to the National League was like the raising of a sunken cathedral. It is a place sacred in history and hallowed in the memory. Christy Mathewson used to make his home on the bluff above the Polo Grounds. When he was working, Mrs. Mathewson could look out her window at the scoreboard and, when the seventh inning came, put the roast in the oven secure in the knowledge that her husband would be finished and showered and home from the plough in an hour.

When the Mets brought the National League, or anyway its shadow, back to New York, there was no place for them except this old shrine. The Mets' permanent stadium at Flushing Meadows is a year from completion; and the City of New York had long ago leveled Ebbets Field and sowed a housing project on its site.

So George Weiss, the Mets' new president, took the Polo Grounds from necessity more than sentiment. Weiss, of course, is the deposed general manager of the Yankees; and the Yankees are the authors of that age of elegance and class distinction in baseball which really began with their Stadium Club, a response to the corporate expense account.

Weiss's prospectus for Flushing Meadows would be garish for a trotting track: "The stadium will be triple-tiered with twenty-one escalators

to speed fans to and from their seats. . . . A 1500-seat comfortably dec-
orated main dining room will be available to season box holders. . . .
There are fifty-four public rest room installations conveniently located
on all three levels: twenty-seven for women, twenty-seven for men.
Each women's rest room has its own lounge or powder room."

But all is a total affront to the tradition of the National League in
New York, where Ladies Day was never for ladies and where there was
absolute democracy in the affliction of misery upon rich and poor alike.
Dodger fans had every vulgarity but the vulgarity of wealth; Giant fans
had no vulgarity at all. The mere age and squalor of the Polo Grounds
comforted its customers; you could as easily catch some bronchial disease in its dank recesses as you used to be able to catch malaria at night
in the Roman Colosseum, and both contagions carried the romance of
history.

The New York of the Giants, Dodgers, and Yankees was an annual
re-evocation of the War between the States. The Yankees were the
North, if you could conceive a North grinding along with wealth and
weight and without the excuse of Lincoln. The Giants and Dodgers
were the Confederacy, often undermanned and underequipped and
running then because it could not hit. You went to Yankee Stadium if
you were the kind of man who enjoyed yelling for Grant at Richmond;
you went to the National League parks to see Pickett's charge. George
Weiss, a displaced quartermaster-general of the Union Army, does not
understand that persons committed to endure losing causes do not care
about escalators.

The old Dodger fans were the kind of people who picket. The old
Giant fans would be embarrassed to do anything so conspicuous, but
they were the kind of people who refuse to cross picket lines. Yankee
fans are the kind of people who think they own the company the picket
line is thrown around. It is impossible for anyone who does not live in
New York to know what it truly is to hate the Yankees. As writer
Leonard Koppett has said: "The residents of other cities who hate the
Yankees really only hate New York." He has noticed they even hate the
Knicks, the most underprivileged established team in the National Basketball Association. But, if you live in New York and you're not a Yankee fan, you hate them the way you hate Consolidated Edison or your
friendly bank.

George Weiss, being insensitive to these nuances, could not, even for
one year as tenant, let the Polo Grounds rest as the raddled, gray, pi-
geon-speckled old rookery its mourners had left, for what everyone as-

sumed was the last time, after sacking and looting it after the Giants lost their last game there in 1957.

Weiss has in Mrs. Joan Whitney Payson, the Mets' owner, the most generous of patronesses. He had spent $450,000 of her money decking the Polo Grounds in orange, blue, and green paint and ornamenting its walls with faintly abstract advertisements for cigars, Scotch, pomades, salamis, and breath sweeteners. As a woman, Mrs. Payson may have been enchanted at first glance; but, as a sport, she must have been saddened to see that Weiss had painted out the numbers which used to remind all present of the distance to the foul poles and which were so much the controlling mathematics of its epic history at the Polo Grounds.

It is 257 feet to the stands in right field; and, for its prior active years, the Polo Grounds had proclaimed that terrible statistic unashamedly on its fence. Bobby Thomson's home run against the Dodgers in 1951, the most famous in baseball, traveled barely 300 feet to left. Hitting in the Polo Grounds is like playing a pinball machine. Those numbers were symbols reminding us how in life we are in the midst of death and that the afternoon could end, as so many uncertain struggles had ended before it, with the ridiculous accident of a high fly 260 feet to the wrong field.

Carl Hubbell once pitched forty-six straight scoreless innings as a Giant and this string remains a National League record. Sal Maglie, a Giant almost as sacred in the memory as Hubbell himself, came closer to any other National League pitcher to breaking that record. Maglie was in the Polo Grounds one August afternoon in 1950, two-thirds of an inning away from Hubbell's scoreless total when a young Pirate outfielder named Gus Bell hit a line drive that traveled 257 feet to the foul pole for a home run. The devils who tenant the Polo Grounds had punished Maglie for affronting Hubbell; being long in memory, they have now punished Bell by bringing him back here to finish his career as a Met. For the Polo Grounds, being storied and ancient, is also cursed.

That curse was upon the Mets on opening day in the Polo Grounds. It had rained much of the morning; there was the chill of old night in the air. An usher pulled the collar of his new orange windbreaker up around his chin. "You better watch out," said a colleague. "Mr. Weiss wants our collars down at all times." Casey Stengel was in the dugout with photographers, reporters, and the withdrawn and brooding eminence of Rogers Hornsby, who has been hired to coach hitters who either already know how but no longer can, or, if they learn how, are unlikely to be able to.

Stengel complained that his arm was still sore from throwing plastic baseballs at the lower Broadway crowd which had welcomed the Mets to New York. Behind him, Dan Topping of the Yankees was sitting in a box; you thought of Khrushchev on a state visit to Bulgaria and there was a sudden, useless urge for Casey's Mets to get fifty runs. The Mets came out running earnestly and heavily on a wet track; they were loudly cheered by a cluster of children in right field, an odd demonstration of the persistence of buried tradition, since none of these greeters could have been older than six when the National League fled New York.

George Weiss was suffering in Mrs. Payson's box behind the Met dugout. The devils of the Polo Grounds had devised for him a special torment. The groundskeepers, in their spring-cleaning, had come upon two rusted iron chairs and, presumably to save the long walk to the scrap heap, had thrown them into Mrs. Payson's box, like dead rats in a garden. When he owned the New York Giants, Horace Stoneham would have sat unprotesting ankle deep in coffee cups and hot-dog wrappers because he took it for granted that this was the normal environment of his playground. Weiss waved a pallid hand, a fear-stricken smile upon his pallid face. "Please," he said to one of the special guards, "this is Mrs. Payson's box. Can't you do something about it?"

Down below, Stengel thrust his head through a floral horseshoe, clowning for the photographers. He rarely spoke with his players. Instead he capered and tested the rain and always posed, a reminder that he had been hired as much for his showmanship as for his managing skill; perhaps more. Showmanship and salesmanship are important to the Mets, who have more television sponsors than Jack Paar had. We describe the future they represent when we remember they started the season with one tested and still possible major-league pitcher—Roger Craig—and three tested major-league announcers.

Weiss had bet his future more on memory than on hope. Only Sherman Jones, the pitcher in his first home lineup, bore a name not indented in the memory of the customers. Six of the starters against the Pittsburgh Pirates had played in the Polo Grounds in its last prior season five years earlier. Gil Hodges, a fifteen-year man, would certainly have started if he had been able to walk; and Joe Ginsberg, Stengel's catcher, was no less pickled with brine than his colleagues and would certainly have qualified as a Polo Grounds initiate if he had not spent most of his eleven major-league years in the low-rent district of the American League.

A visitor went down to inspect the Met Lounge, which is reserved for season ticket holders only and where "gentlemen must wear coats, ladies, inclusive of girls twelve years of age and over, will not be permitted to wear slacks of any type or abbreviated clothing." There he was first inspected for dress and credentials by a pretty girl in a pin stripe jacket and with eyes like a house detective. This ordeal entitles the elite to a fifty-cent hot dog.

Stengel's old horses took the field with heart-breaking determination of stride and common impression of haunch. The noise was suddenly immense, almost a profanation at the Polo Grounds, which was always a cloister. It was also unexpected from a crowd of twelve thousand; we were back at Ebbets Field where six thousand customers used to maintain a roar in an ordinary game against the Cubs, which always left any outlander with the suspicion that the management had installed a record-player that was blasting "Crowd noise—Dempsey-Firpo 1923" somewhere in the stands. So this was a Dodger crowd; Weiss had staked his appeal there, with Hodges, Craig, Don Zimmer, and Charlie Neal. Bobby Thomson was absent; but Ralph Branca was there, with an abject grin, to be photographed pointing to the fatal spot in left field and to explain again that it would have been a home run nowhere else.

Still, an inning and two-thirds had to go by before everyone was carried back to that lost time in the mid-fifties when the Giants were sixth. Smoky Burgess got the Pirates' first hit, and then Don Hoak sliced a fly 270 feet to the wrong field, off the wall for a double to score Burgess. Jones had been introduced to that curse of the Polo Grounds, and Hoak, who knew it of old, may be excused for the indignant reflection that he had been cheated of a home run. Then Bill Mazeroski hit a drive well over 370 feet to right center, the afternoon's first evidence of lust but normally an out in the Polo Grounds, the tallest and thinnest park in the big leagues. Richie Ashburn and Gus Bell ploughed and floundered and waved under it, and before Bell could complete the salvage, Mazeroski was on third and Hoak was home. Jones had been introduced to his outfield and was two runs down and innocent.

In the third inning Jim Marshall entered history by walking, the first Met to reach base safely. The first Met hit had to wait until the next inning and belonged to the pitcher. The first Met extra-base hit—a double—came in the fifth and could be credited more to mud than to muscle; Marshall lifted a fly near third; Dick Groat fell chasing it. After two outs it came Jones's turn, and Stengel had to dispense with this young man, already so much more sinned against than sinning. A claque behind first base began crying for Hodges; Stengel sent up Ed Bouchee instead and was rewarded with an honest single to center and a run. It was the old man's first trip to his bench, a thing of tatters; for one brief and wonderful moment, the devils had suspended their curse for Stengel's first command decision.

In the end the Mets lost 4 to 3. The first two of those four runs were tawdry; the third was the comparatively honest consequence of two singles and a wild pitch; and the last the direct result of two wild pitches. That is the balance of their dreary future; and it was underlined by the reflection that, in two of the three Pirate scoring innings, the Met pitcher had stopped the first two batters.

Groat finished the game caked with mud to his hips, from the occasions when he had fallen down, going first to his right and then to his left. But he had made plays he had had to make. The new uniforms of the Met infielders were immaculate as they dragged home to the clubhouse; none of them fallen down, not because they do not have desire but they no longer have possibility. They cannot get close enough any more to the doubtful chance to make use of the desperate dive. People are always saying that one-eighth of an inch is the difference between winning and losing baseball. With the Mets, it is three inches. No one could count the afternoons there would be like this one.

But the first day had been distorted by climate and the illusion of accident. The following Monday, the Mets greeted the new Houston Colt .45s. Hodges was at first; the sun was out; the cries from the stands were faint and infrequent; there were only three thousand customers, the Dodger fans having already struck the colors. We were back on one of those long slow afternoons remembered from sixth place at the Polo Grounds in 1956.

The Mets went on to tie the Colts in the ninth and lose in the eleventh, a pattern picked up from the 1955–57 Giants. Those Giants were the subject of the only baseball short story written in the fifties with a legitimate claim to a place in the canon of that art form. Called "Seven Steps to Heaven," after the beer commercial, its author was E. B. White, and it was about what baseball has become in the electronic age, since its hero never went to the park but watched the disasters of the Giants as shadows on his television screen. But the Mets are not those Giants.

Those old Giants had Dusty Rhodes or Hank Sauer in left, and neither had ever pretended to be a fielder. Rhodes departed cursed and cherished. But who has a right to curse Frank Thomas?

Weiss wanted to assault the sentiment of New Yorkers with what would have been a respectable, if Mays-less, All-Star National League outfield in 1954—Thomas in left, Richie Ashburn in center, and Gus Bell in right. But it does not make you feel sentimental to see Ashburn thrown out on a deep grounder to third when he would have been safe just two years ago. It only makes you feel sad. It makes you sad, too, to see Hodges stand at the plate, trying to chip to the wrong field, a device of shortstops. These are men of great personal class; no one can enjoy seeing that what is hard for them now is what used to be precisely the easiest thing.

More than anything else, this condition must account for the brooding sorrow which chokes the Mets' dressing room after every defeat. The atmosphere has been compared to the dressing room of a team that has lost the World Series. Still a World Series is a transient thing; for those losers, there is always next year. But for the old men on the Mets, there will be no next year; this is where it ends; every afternoon is a reminder that the flesh is grass.

But then Weiss has always had a colder attitude toward old ball-players than the rest of us do. The Met customers in left field occasionally express that difference by bringing along a banner painted "Rod Kanehl Fan Club." Rod Kanehl is a thirty-two-year-old outfielder-infielder who had never appeared in a big-league game before this year. His future is dim, but then so is his past. He carries no memory of departed glory for any spectator to regret; and this demand that he play every day is in some way a protest for the dignity of greater names. These fans would rather look at a faint hope than suffer with a damaged memory.

Hot Rod Hundley

The Man Behind the Clown's Mask

Bill Libby | **1962**

He never had much, not a family, nor a home, nor even a place to call his own. As a child he was raised by strangers who were poor. He slept on a bed behind curtains, under the stairs, and later in a bare room in a small hotel, and after that in a boarding house. He had few friends, because everyone had more than he, and he did not feel he belonged with anyone, anywhere. Even when he married a girl he thought he'd known all his life, he found her a stranger and the marriage went flat in three years.

He did have a certain youthful charm. He still does. He is tall, slender, baby-faced, with crew-cut blond hair, laughing brown eyes and an impish grin. He has a brass front, a silver tongue, a golden smile. He can be a great clown and a lovable eccentric. With these weapons, he found early in life he could make people love him. He wants this love and he has it, but he doesn't trust it for he knows it is shallow. They don't love him, they love what he appears to be. They love the mask Hot Rod Hundley wears.

This was March of 1962. The Los Angeles Lakers led the Western Division of the National Basketball Association by ten games. This night, in L.A.'s Sports Arena, the Lakers led St. Louis by twenty points with six minutes to play. There could not have been a much less significant or exciting moment in the sports year, yet the customers remained seated and buzzed with anticipation.

They didn't have to call for Hot Rod Hundley, for they knew Laker coach Freddie Schaus would bring him off the bench. He did, and in the next six minutes, Hot Rod turned the sporting hall into the Palace Theater. He dribbled between his legs and behind his back and juggled passes into a remarkable eleven assists. He also took an unearthly variety of shots, including a lazy Goose Tatum hook from far out. When it swished through, Hundley strutted in front of the scorer's table, extending two triumphant fingers.

The crowd loved it all and finally went hysterical when, with seconds left, Hot Rod intercepted a pass and cradled the ball as though it were a beloved child. In the dressing room after the 130–107 Laker victory, Rod told a newsman: "My interception was the turning point of the game."

The next day, although Jerry West had scored thirty points and fetched seventeen rebounds, the headlines went to Hot Rod Hundley. "CLOWN HUNDLEY PUTS ON REAL SHOW," one of them read.

After he had finished dressing, Clown Hundley turned a sour face on a teammate. "Big creepin' deal," he said. "Let's go find a beer."

There was a time when the search for that one beer would have magnified into multiples. A beer would have been the least of his findings. He has pursued a versatile career as one of the sporting life's most prolific night owls. He's been not only the court jester, but the carefree boy, who'd rather go fishin', the gay boulevardier, who'd rather go funnin'. Life has been a ball, never to be taken seriously. Only after the wee hours were spent would Rod wander lonely home, wherever that was.

No one has ever hated him for it. Schaus, who has coached him in college and pro ball, says, "Rod never hurt anyone but himself."

This time, however, it really was only one beer, and he got home early, for there was a home, and someone who waited, and almost a family. There was his pretty second wife, Florence, pregnant with his first child. There was the apartment in a building he half owns, and the home he soon would move into, a new $45,000 house in the expensive section of Malibu. He can't afford it. He now has responsibilities he's not sure he can meet. He does not clown when he speaks of these responsibilities. "I don't like basketball," he says, "but I got to keep playing because I need the money. We both work. The kid's coming. We've bought this house. It's out of our class, but we want it, so we're taking a chance. You want to know something? I'm scared."

A few nights after the St. Louis game, he duplicated the vaudeville in another breeze, against Detroit, with some varieties. He has, at various times, shot while kneeling, sitting and reclining. He has drop-kicked for field goals, passed for phantom touchdowns, pitched strikes and batted homers.

After the Detroit game, Willie Jones, the young Piston guard, slouched angrily in the dressing room, exhausted from trying to defend Rod. "Wait'll we get these guys in Detroit," Willie said, "*We'll* put on the show there." They didn't. It was just another ball game. Just like all the revenge rematches that turn out tame and timid.

Many pros talk about "getting even," about "getting Hot Rod," but Rod says, "I'm not looking to make enemies. I've never tried to show anyone up in particular, even when I've been tempted, because someone maybe made me look bad. Sure some guys get mad. More used to in college. Why, for creepin' sakes, one Pitt guy practically wanted to tussle with me! In pro, I'd be silly to show anyone up when we have to play the same guys so often. I guess some guys are bound to take it wrong, that's all."

Some players do get annoyed. "This is a serious business to most of us," says one NBA star. "Who the hell does he think he is?" Rod Hundley can't understand such a philosophy. The traveling, the long days in strange hotels and strange cities, the seemingly endless schedule wear him down. He is intensely nervous, coiled as though caught in a trap. He broods through the basketball part of his life, bored, restless. He makes plane flights almost as a last resort. He ducks practices. He sits on the bench as if he were a teen-ager forced to attend an opera.

A star in college, Hundley has become a fringe player with the pros. He has not accepted all that goes with bench-warming. He refuses to become a cheerleader even though he knows it might prolong his career with the Lakers and coach Schaus. "I'm not gonna sit on the bench and yak it up," he says. "I'm not gonna join hands in the huddle and cry real tears. I didn't in college and I can't now. If one of the boys comes to me on an off-day and says let's shoot baskets, I ask him if he's lost his mind. Play golf, sure, but shoot baskets when you don't have to? Wow! If Freddie says the practice for an off-day is strictly voluntary, for those fellows who feel they need a workout, most of them will take the hint and show up, but there's not a chance in the world I'll be there. It just doesn't mean all that much to me. Well, that hurts me with Schaus and I know it, but it's the way I am."

Rod has turned to a referee during a game and said, "Isn't this drivel ever going to end?" Rod has stared in astonishment at a player's temper tantrum and said, "It's just a game played with a little round ball, after all." Rod has scowled at a teammate's game-delaying argument and said, "C'mon, baby, you're prolonging this nonsense, the world is waiting outside."

While many of his teammates enjoy him, there are some to whom the game is a religion, who are unhappy with such irreverence. One says with disgust: "What a waste! He could have been as big as Cousy."

"Cousy? Who's he?" Rod may say, grinning. But in private, he says: "I'm no Cousy. I'm no Jerry West, no Elgin Baylor. I'm a second-string pro, a sub. Why should I kid myself?" It is as though he has known all along that the fame and fortune, the glory and glamour were to be his but briefly. The days as a star are gone and at twenty-eight Rod is renowned only as the clown.

He seems to relish the role, but if you look close, you will see he does not often smile when he is clowning, only when it is part of the act. Perhaps he never did. Anyway, now, he is usually poker-faced, almost methodical about it. He does it as if he were angry, as if he were mocking someone, something, the whole world, perhaps, which has hurt him.

His wife says, "I don't like for him to clown. I'm embarrassed by it. I look the other way. But I think he really does enjoy it."

"It is expected of me by now," Rod says. "You know, everyone's so stupid serious in this game, I don't have to do much. All I have to do is maybe wave at the crowd and they break up. Well, if that's what they want, what the hell, I've been doing it so long I don't know if I'd know how to stop now. What else have I got to do, anyway? What the hell's the difference anyway?"

It is, in its way, part of that front, the mask he wears. Rod puts up a big front. He poses boldly. When someone asks him if he is a good basketball player, he'll smile and say something like: "Well, I never saw anyone any better." No humble bit for him. "You know, I'm only six-four, which is not big in this league. When I go around with some of those giants, I look out of place," he explains. "Like sometimes when I get on an airplane, the stewardess, who's maybe a doll, looks at those six-ten giants, and she asks me: 'Are you a basketball player, too?' What am I gonna tell her? So I say, 'You better believe it, baby, one of the best.' And she believes me. And she should," Rod grins. " 'Cause I am."

In the off-season, Rod works as a salesman and public relations man. He solicits the business of real-estate firms. Recently his boss, Stan Goethals, said, "Rod is wonderful with the customers. When he walks in, he has a big smile on his puss and he says: 'I am not one of the three wise men, but I come bearing gifts.' He's not with them five minutes before he's got them eating out of his hand. He has a saying when he leaves: 'Well, it's been a little slice of heaven.' They love it and they love him. They don't get tired of him, like they do of some others. Some just seem like wise guys after a while, but not Rod. It's a gift to be able to carry it off, and he has it."

Rod sat on the side, listening to this description of himself. There was a faint smile on his lips. He shrugged his shoulders. "It's business," he said. "It's not hard for me. It comes natural. I been turnin' it on all my life."

Is he, himself, sure what's real now, what he is and who he is? It is doubtful. In private the mask sometimes slips. "I've always had an inferiority complex," he said a while ago. "It's hard to believe of me, maybe, but it's true." He grinned sadly, in shy confession, looking away, down at his hands. "Oh, I put up a big, bold front because that makes it easier. They think that's me, that that's all there is to me, and they leave me alone, and it's easier that way."

He was born Rodney Clark Hundley on October 26, 1934, in Charleston, West Virginia. He had a fancy name but he was a poor boy who came into a shabby world as the Depression was running out. His parents divorced when he was two years old and his mother couldn't earn enough money to support him. She turned him over to outsiders, George and Mamie Sharp, to be raised, and contributed whatever she had.

"I never knew my folks, not as a kid," Rod says. "My dad was a meat-cutter by trade, but he spent a lot of his time around the pool room. Lou was his name, everyone called him Butch. Cora was my mother's name. After they split up, she went to Washington, D.C., where she could get a job. She left me behind. I guess I don't blame her. Maybe she came to see me a couple of times all those years, I don't really remember, but not often. I don't hold it against her. She had her own life. She married again, a fellow named Sam DeCico, and they have a restaurant-bar in Washington. I write now and then and go to see them once in a while. They have my basketball pictures all over the wall, so they're proud of me, I guess.

"My dad was around all those years, but we didn't have anything to do with each other. When I go back now, I see him once in a while. I'll go in the pool hall and he comes in, like always, but he won't speak to me, unless I speak to him first. I mean he sort of hangs around the back, watching me out of the corner of his eye. I guess he feels bad, 'cause he never did anything for me. But when I speak to him, then he's glad, and I'm pretty sure he's proud of me, too.

"These people that raised me, they were old, in their late fifties probably, when I was brought to them as a baby. The husband died not long ago, but she's still there and she must be eighty now. They were good people, really, and they were strict with me, but they didn't have much control over me. And they were poor people. He was a bottle-washer in an ice-cream plant. He never made much money and he never could give me much. But I never had to work, I had my three meals and I had a place to sleep. It was a small house and I used to sleep behind the curtain under the stairs. Oh, damn, it used to get cold.

"My last year in high school, I lived with a freind, Tommy Crutchfield. His mom, Mrs. Ida Crutchfield, owned a small hotel, and she gave me a room there. Lots of kids probably envy the freedom I had all those years, always able to come and go, no real parents to tell me what to do, so I guess it was O.K. But I used to look at those kids with families, real families, and it was like they were in another world from me. I wanted to belong very badly, but I didn't and I knew it. I never fit in. I was always like a round peg in a square hole, always on the outside looking in."

West Virginia is a state of lingering depressions, where men work hard, in the mines or mills, when there is work to be had, and families are often hungry. "Oh, God, yes," Rod recalls. "It's a poor place, soiled and run down. I don't know what would of happened to me if I'd of had to stay. Lots of my friends were hoodlums, really, who got into trouble, because it's the kids who don't have much that get into trouble. I didn't, only because there was basketball for me, right from the start, and I could see it was a way out.

"Baseball was my first love. I threw two no-hitters, but I wasn't really good. I had a tryout with the Giants. They told me to stick to basketball. So I did. I had no choice. I never liked basketball, really, but I found a place for myself there. I belonged there. I was something when I was out there, so I used it. Oh, sure, I was a real genius! I could throw a ball through a hoop. I was so good the YMCA let me in for free!"

Basketball came easy to him. In junior high school he set state scoring records of 441 points for a season and thirty-seven points for a game. He averaged twenty points a game, another record. In high school he broke the state's four-year scoring record in three years, averaging more than thirty points a game. In the post-season high-school exhibition all-star game against Kentucky, he scored forty-five points. He was All-State, of course, and he was selected to an All-America schoolboy team. Forty or fifty colleges pursued him, offering him fat scholarships.

He was cool through it all. It was part of an act he picked up from the public images of his idols. His idols, then, and in college, were not athletes, but Marlon Brando and Jimmy Dean. He did not clown, at least not on court, but he dissipated with an awesome dedication. He did his training at parties. He began to go steady with Nancy Hammond, but he would not hold still.

"All those colleges were after me, all those newspaper people writing me up," he recalls, shaking his head with sad wonder. "Me! I'd never had anything. Suddenly, I was a big hero. The Big Ten wanted me. The Ivy League wanted me. Everyone wanted me. Man, it was really something!" The most convincing bid came from North Carolina State.

"Two summers they took me down to live on the campus," Rod says. "The first time was after my junior year, when I was still in high school, the second time was after my senior year. Ev Case was a great coach and a great fellow. Kids were being flown in from Indiana and New York, everywhere. We played basketball against the varsity fellows during the day and lived it up the rest of the time. They took good care of us. We had a good place to live, good food, everything. They even got us jobs. Some jobs! For a while, I was a lifeguard. All those chicks in bikinis! Crazy!"

He was sold. After the second summer he returned home to gather his belongings before enrolling officially. He picked up a newspaper and the headlines told him the NCAA had cracked down on State for recruiting irregularities. "I called up Wallace Wade of Duke, who was conference commissioner," Hundley says. "He told me I was in the clear because I'd never enrolled, but that I would be wise to forget about State or any other school in the conference."

Time was running out then, so Rod accepted the scholarship offer of his home state university, West Virginia. People all around the state were delighted, but he wasn't. He was the hero of the campus right from the start, but he felt like a jilted lover who'd drifted into the wrong arms on the rebound. Twice he jumped school, once as a freshman when he was going to transfer to Morris Harvey College and once as a sophomore when he was going to bestow his talents, more ambitiously, on the Philadelphia Warriors. Philly, by NBA rules, couldn't sign the undergraduate, but did offer him a job with a farm affiliate. Both times, Rod changed his mind and returned to Morgantown.

The school, which had invested in a knee operation for him between his freshman and sophomore years, restrained itself to paternally slapping his wrist and pleading with him to mend his ways. When he began to cut up, they looked the other way. Schaus, who had just become West Virginia's coach, insists the only real trouble he had with Rod was "getting him to attend classes."

Rod brags he never cracked a book in high school or college. Twice he had to attend summer school to make up classes he'd flunked, so he could stay eligible. He admits he cut classes regularly. "I'm a nervous guy," he says, "always have been tense and nervous ever since I was a kid. It wasn't just that I wasn't real interested, but even when I tried, I couldn't bear being cooped up in a classroom. I'd sit there and get all fidgety and depressed, not able to smoke or anything, wanting to get the hell out."

He let off steam away from campus. He had his own room at a boarding house run by Anna Dinard, who had long mothered Mountie sports stars, but who'd rarely had a pup like Hot Rod. As a campus celebrity, he was immediately pledged to Phi Sigma Kappa, but he never felt like a fraternity boy. He was disinterested in conformity, left the fraternity a couple of times and never lived at the frat house. He was still going with Nancy, a student there by then, too, but she needed an elastic leash.

In his first game as a freshman he scored fifty points. In a later game he scored sixty-two. The team played a soft schedule and the monotony of murdering misfits wore on Rod, until one night he began to clown around. "That was the first time," he recalls. "I did it every game after that. I'd go into the fancy dribble or the fancy pass or hoke it up some way and the crowd loved it, so I kept it up. We were good, better than the varsity. We used to draw big crowds, playing before the varsity games, and lots of the fans would leave when our game ended." He clowned more than he shot, but averaged thirty-four points a game. Athletic director Red Brown said, "We could be playing the Girl Scouts and he'd fill the joint."

As a sophomore Rod used weighted shoes to strengthen his knee from the summer operation. Coach Schaus used him cautiously as the varsity season began, but started him in the third game and Rod scored thirty-one points. Rod started the next game and protected a lead by dribbling out the last ninety seconds. He finished the game with a flourish, hurling the ball into the rafters with such precise timing that it fell into a fan's hands just as the final buzzer sounded. Hot Rod Hundley was off and running.

Hundley averaged just under twenty-five points a game in his three-season college career. Six times he scored forty or more points in a game. Nine times the team scored one hundred or more points in a game. With Schaus coaching and Rod igniting a dynamic fast break, the Mounties soared to national prominence, winning three straight Southern Conference titles.

Rod filled out his act with flourishes, such as hanging from the basket rim and calling for a pass, and faking free throws while the eager rebounders pitched forward in surprised confusion. He was good enough to get away with it and Schaus was a tolerant coach—up to a point. Once or twice it backfired. Once, in the Dixie Classic, Rod rolled the ball behind his back twice and both times Duke players stole the ball and charged in for baskets that tied the game. Schaus took him aside and warned him never again to cut up when his team had less than a twenty-point lead. "Since then," Freddie recalls, "he's never hurt the team or cost a game."

One time, clowning cost Rod a record. West Virginia had the Southern Conference tournament's title game wrapped up and with time running out, Rod, who needed one point to tie Dick Groat's tourney scoring record, drew two free throws. He hooked the first and tossed the second from behind his back. He missed both and blew the record. He didn't really care. He was riding high. He had become not only a campus hero, but a national celebrity. He was not only a great athlete, but a unique personality, and the press loved him.

"Houdini . . . Magician . . . Genius," the writers called him. "Magnificent . . . Tremendous . . . Dazzling . . . Fabulous . . . Refreshing. A fierce Competitor . . . Most Colorful . . . A Great Clutch Player . . . A Great Star." One writer said, "His shooting arm seems eight feet long." Another said, "They said he was sensational, but he's really only slightly terrific." After one game, a national magazine wrote, "It was the kind of playing that can change collegiate basketball into the exciting spectacle it was meant to be." An opposing player said, "You have to see him to believe him." Veteran referee Lou Eisenstein said, "He's the best crowd pleaser I've ever seen in college basketball. He can do things with a basketball the pros couldn't begin to do."

On Rod's first visit to New York, he gave the impression of being the ultimate "shotgun." On one play he was caught far behind his teammates on a fast break. They were already under the basket as Rod was just reaching midcourt. But he was waving frantically for the ball. "C'mon, baby, give ol' Rod the ball," was his rallying call. He shot from every angle and posture and passed so seldom one fellow doubted

Rod knew his teammates by sight. He scored thirty-eight points and had twenty-two rebounds against NYU. He threw the ball away and lost it plenty, but he shrugged it off later and gave the big city writers the sort of copy they expected from him. But he didn't like New York. "I stood on the corner of Times Square for two hours," he said, "and I didn't see one pretty girl."

About this time he led his teammates in an assault on Miami's Gold Coast during a visit to the Orange Bowl basketball tournament. Wearing only shorts, he clambered up a palm tree and waved a basketball as though it were a coconut. A reporter cornered him and Rod put him on to the extent of one of the classic interviews of sports history. "This clown was asking stupid questions, trying to make me admit something," Rod recalls. "He wanted to know if I was getting the moon. So, I told him I was. It's what he wanted to hear.

"He asked me if I was doing all right, so I asked him: 'Is five hundred dollars a month doing all right?' I told him: 'It's better than high school. I never had a Cadillac in high school, only a Ford.' When the guy asked me if I was doing good in my schoolwork, I told him I didn't have time to go to classes, I was too busy trying to decide whether I could help mankind best by going to work for the government after the college gave me a degree in chemical engineering.

"He printed it all, every word," Rod recalls with an impish grin. "It went all over. But the school wasn't too upset with me. They knew me by then and they just took it in stride. The truth is, I did all right, with my room and board, tuition and books, laundry money and expenses money and stuff like that, but nothing great, nothing out of proportion, nothing to get rich on. Hell, I didn't even have a car. And by my last two years, I wasn't even running around. I was married by then. When I was a junior I married Nancy. I'd been goin' with her a long time. That sort of held me back.

"They were good to me in school and I came to like it. I'm grateful to them. Later, after I was graduated, I helped talk Jerry West into going there. Like Schaus and myself, he's a West Virginia boy, too, of course. I didn't sell Jerry a bill of goods, but I pointed out how much it had done for me to go there, and he went along with the idea. He picked up where I'd left off and wound up breaking some of my records and beating me out on the Lakers, but he's a good boy."

Many of the countless school records Rod set still stand, however, including the single-game scoring records of fifty-four points at home and forty-seven points on the road. Rod became the fourth player in all NCAA history to surpass 2000 points, scoring 2180, and after the

1956–57 season, he was the NBA's No. 1 draft pick. Cincinnati chose him and traded him to the Minneapolis Lakers for Clyde Lovellette.

Rod had his troubles with Minneapolis. He had been a forward in college, but at six four was too small to play up front with the pros. He was converted to a guard where it was hoped his ballhandling abilities would pay off. But he was a shooter, not a passer, and they wanted a passer, not a shooter. It was a big, lumbering mediocre club, not suited to Rod's speed and sleight-of-hand. He didn't clown and he didn't play much. He had a succession of coaches—George Mikan, John Kundla, Johnny Castellani, Jim Pollard—who couldn't figure out what to do with him. "If you're a Baylor," Rod says, "it doesn't matter who's coaching. If you're a Hundley, maybe it does. Anyway, we changed coaches like they were going out of style.

"I thought I was the greatest when I came in. After a while, I wasn't sure I was any good at all. You don't improve in college ball, which is uncomplicated and doesn't offer much competition. Then you get in the pros and you find you've got a lot to learn. But it's hard to learn and improve when you're not playing.

"It's a hard life, much different than college. The schedule is three times as long. It's too damn long, too damn many games, too damn much traveling. I wasn't playing, and I lost a lot of confidence and desire. I was mixed-up and depressed. It was a while getting through to me that I wasn't the big star, but just another player. I come off a plane and people will look right through me and ask, 'Which one is Baylor?' It hurts. It was a while before I got used to not being the big shot. Oh, man, you miss that spotlight, once you've had it."

Rod went looking for other spotlights. He was still a pro, after all, still had something of his flashy name and reputation left. He was making the first real salary of his life, and he could still put up the big front. So the fellow who might have been Bob Cousy tried to be Errol Flynn instead.

By then, Flynn had replaced Dean and Brando as Hot Rod's idol. Rod still tells newsmen that Flynn's autobiography is the only book he's ever read. His Minneapolis teammate Bob Leonard autographed it for Rod one playful evening: "To Rod, My Best, Always, Errol."

"The chicks flipped when I showed them that," Rod recalls with a big grin. There are favorite watering places for athletes in every town. In Minneapolis, it was "Buster's." "Bobby and I hoisted a few in there, you might say," Rod says, smiling. "But we hit other places, too, the good spots, at home and on the road. I went with the best and I about killed myself."

Rod's marriage to Nancy broke up in its third year and they were divorced. "Maybe it never was right. Maybe we were too young, maybe we weren't ready for it. It was a lot of little things, I guess. It just didn't work out," he says now, with a shrug.

The terrible toll of NBA travel and his own nocturnal wanderings would have weakened a lesser man, but Rod Hundley, lover and laugher, says, "It was the night life that kept me going. I slept all day and went out all night and squeezed in the ball games in-between. If anyone called me before noon, I thought they were out of their minds. I still do. You know, if you hit the sack an hour or two after a game, then you're gonna wake up at nine in the morning and have all day to kill in some crummy place before the next game. What can you do in the daytime? It doesn't make sense. Who goes to bed as soon as they get home from work? If one of us stays up to, say, four or five in the morning, well then you sleep to the middle of the afternoon, and you feel fine when the game comes up. Hell, they weren't using me much anyway, so why should I have worried?"

Rudy LaRusso, the big Ivy Leaguer who joined the Lakers a few years after Rod and was assigned as his roommate in an attempt to culture the clown, recalls Rod's activities with a touch of wonder. "Rod's car would start up all by itself around midnight," says Rudy.

In his third season Rod began to improve. He got a chance to play regularly. He averaged almost thirteen points a game and was one of the team leaders in assists and rebounds. He played fourteen minutes in the All-Star game, and scored fourteen points. He began regaining his old confidence. And he began dating Florence Pellman, a girl from a little town, Mantador, in North Dakota, who was working in the Western Union office in Minneapolis.

During the off-season, the Laker franchise was shifted to Los Angeles and Rod hurried out as his own advance agent. He scouted out the town's favored sports watering spot, "The House of Serfa's," to replace "Buster's," and staked out some claims. However, while sizing up the local starlets and camp followers between sips, he found he missed Florence. He sent for her and they were married. "He's settled down a lot since we've been married," Florence says.

Rod had another good season in 1960–61 as his team opened in Los Angeles. The West Virginia trio was reunited as Schaus came in as a coach and West as a rookie. Rod's scoring average dipped to eleven points a game, but his assists went up and he snared a lot of rebounds. He scored ten points in the All-Star game. In a game in January he tied an L.A. Sports Arena record with five assists in one quarter, and in a deciding semi-final playoff game against Detroit he made eight assists in a quarter and fifteen in the game, tying two league records set by Bob Cousy. Afterward, Laker owner Bob Short said, "Rod is one of our untradable players, along with Baylor and LaRusso." Rod was so relaxed and happy he began to clown again, for the first time since he joined the pros.

But last season he was more clown than player as the bottom suddenly fell out of his dream world. The Lakers were coming fast now and Hundley and his buddy Leonard were squeezed out. Bob was cast off to Chicago in the expansion draft. Hundley hung on, but Frank Selvy and West beat him out for the starting guard positions.

Soon the Laker offense became simple: give the ball to Elgin Baylor or Jerry West. The two super-stars knew what to do with the ball. They shot—and they scored. Selvy and the rest of the strong Laker supporting cast modestly accepted bit parts and played them well. But, used sparingly, Hundley had his worst scoring season, falling off to five points a game. He had the spotlight only in those games which featured large Laker victories and his clowning.

The Lakers didn't discourage his clowning. Gil Smith, the Lakers' publicity director, says, "Schaus, who is one of the few coaches in this league stronger than his stars, could stop him if he wished, but he knows Rod clowns only at the proper times and has helped make the team a big success here in its new home town."

Schaus says, "Since that first talk back in college, Rod has always exercised good judgment and has never clowned when a game was in jeopardy. Colorful athletes are all too few. I don't think Jim Piersall has hurt baseball, for example, and I don't think Hundley has hurt basketball. This is still a growing league and things which help make it more exciting and popular are all to the good. This is why fewer people actually criticize Rod or me than you might imagine. The game and winning has to come first, of course, but the coach who thinks he doesn't owe it to basketball and the league to help make the game more attractive is wrong. The sort of thing Rod does, Bob Cousy does, too, of course, only in a different way. Hundley does it out in the open."

Behind the clown's mask, Rod had a serious year. Late last season, Flo told him they were going to have a baby. "It overwhelmed me, just overwhelmed me," Rod recalls, shaking his head with wonder. "I'd been married twice, over five years, and I'd never had a kid before. I still can't get over it. You know something? I want that kid. I want it bad. Maybe it's that I want the kid to have a life like other kids have, like I never had. I don't know. But, I know I can't hardly believe it. It's like a dream. I can't wait."

It has made changes in Rod, who had already begun to change. The party-boy had already bought a half-interest in two Los Angeles apartment houses. In the summer of 1961 he went to work for Stan Goethals' Great Western Financial's Liberty Escrow Group office. In 1962 he bought a new three-bedroom home in the plush Sunset Mesa tract of Malibu on the hills overlooking the foaming Pacific. "Lana Turner was looking for a house in the area," Rod says. "Everyone told me it was too much for me, that I had no business going in hock for this sort of place, but isn't it something! Oh, man, with it and the baby, money is going to be some problem! We're all liable to wind up behind a curtain, under the stairs, back in West Virginia somewhere."

To stay reasonably secure financially, Rod is very anxious to stick with the Lakers another season or two. "Moving to Los Angeles was the best thing that ever happened to me," Rod says. "It's a wonderful, beautiful place to live, the best. I love it and I won't ever leave it. If the Lakers trade me, I won't go. I'll quit. I hope they don't trade me. I'm tired of basketball, but I can still play and I think I can still help the club. I want to, and I'll tell you, baby, I need to—it'd help me in business, and there's all that lovely money."

Schaus thinks Rod can continue to help the club. "We don't ask Rod to shoot, so he may not be as sharp at that as he once was," Schaus says, "but he can do everything very well. He can really get a club to moving, which is his job. Rod knows how I feel. In his junior and senior years he was as good a college player for his height as you could find. He's been in the pros five years, which takes some doing, so he's been a good pro. But he could have been a great pro. Truly great. And he hasn't been. He hasn't lived up to his potential.

"It's pretty much up to him now. If he wants to play, he can play. If he goes in half-heartedly, it may be a different story. He had a fair year last year. He was great at times. He was not so good at other times. The real test of a top pro is consistency. Rod didn't give us this. In games he was right, and hustling, he was a big help. In other games, well . . ."

"I give it all I can in a game," Rod says. "That's in a game, if I had practiced more, trained harder, taken the game more seriously, maybe even put on a big act, like it was a religion to me, I might have done better. But, maybe not. You know, sometimes it's a matter of the club you land with. Who's much better than Sam Jones? But he landed behind Cousy and Sharman with the Celtics and it took him years to become a starter. If I'd landed with the Knicks where they wanted a shooter, if I'd been given Richie Guerin's job of scoring, maybe I'd still be a big star. If I hadn't gotten rusty sitting on the bench, maybe I'd have been a big star here.

"But you know something, I realize now I'm not a West or a Baylor or an Oscar Robertson, so why should I kid myself? I can play basketball and I can help this club, but more than that? You know the most helpless I've ever felt on a basketball court? Playing Robertson. Once Oscar intercepted a long pass downcourt and came dribbling back toward me. I was the only man back on defense and he had a teammate on either side to pass to. He came down on me with those ten thousand moves of his and I looked at him and I said, 'Oh, baby, this is the living end!' Did I stop him? Hell, no. He's the greatest! Who stops him? Not Rod, baby!"

But Rod may be better than he knows. Playing part-time, he's scored 3365 points and has averaged just under ten points, four assists and four rebounds a game. And he's a smart player, too. One thing he would like to do, which would salve some of his wounded pride, would be to coach. At first glance, this may seem far-fetched, but Schaus supports the possibility. "Whenever I couldn't coach in recent years," Schaus says, "I gave Rod the job. Of course, after playing under me all these seasons, if he doesn't know my way of thinking, no one would. But, it's more than that. He's an intelligent man, no dummy, and he can be serious. He has a tremendous personality and he's very popular with the other players. He has as good a judgment of a player's ability as anyone I know. He has a natural instinct for the game, a real good basketball sense. He likes to pretend he doesn't care or doesn't know, but he knows the game forward and backward. He could make a great coach on any level."

Rod thinks this may be true, though he reasons his reputation is against him. Still he'd love the chance. "You know the biggest thrill I've ever had in basketball?" he says. "It wasn't playing, but coaching. Last season when Freddie was ejected one time and had some sickness in the family another time, I took over for two games with St. Louis. We were behind in one and I took over and we won.

"The other time we were losing by a lot with time growing short. Freddie got into the place and I knew he was standing right behind me. I don't usually play myself when I'm coaching, but this time I put myself in with West and Selvy, so we had three guards, and used two forwards, LaRusso and Hawkins, so we had fast boys and no big center. We kept stealing the ball and running and scoring. It wound up with me stealing the ball and passing to West who put it in for the winning basket. It was real unorthodox strategy, but we won, and it was me who'd made those moves. I want to tell you that was a real thrill!"

Maybe part of Rod's future does lie in coaching. He's been involved in the game for fifteen long years and, says Schaus, "Rod may pretend basketball doesn't mean anything to him, but down deep I think he's realistic about it. This game has been everything to him and I'm sure he knows it."

Not long ago, Rod and his wife were talking to a fellow about the game and the glory it once brought him. Much of the glory is gone, but Rod has all the old magazine stories and clippings. They help him remember. "I didn't know anything about basketball when I met Rod," his wife said. "I never knew him when he was a great star. Now I can only look at those old stories. I'm sorry about that. But he always knew it wasn't basketball that attracted me to him. By now, of course, I've come to know the game, and I love it, and I think he does, too. I don't like him to clown, but I want him to play, even if only to clown, because even if he won't admit it, I see how bad he feels when he hasn't played at least some. I've come to see that the game's been good to him, too. I think he'll miss it a lot when he leaves it, more than he knows, probably, and certainly more than he'll admit."

Rod thought a second. His eyes narrowed. "Sure it's been good to me," he said. "What the hell would I have wound up with without it? I got no kicks. I even like it now some. And when I have to leave it, I'll miss it some, I guess, sure. But it's a crazy business. Take this 'Hot Rod' stuff. Sure, it's fine when it's a nickname, but do you know some people call me 'Hot Rod' off the court, too? 'Hello, glad to meet you, Hot Rod.' Now, isn't that just a little silly? Don't they know it's not my real name? No, it's a crazy business. I'll keep playing and clowning as long as they'll let me and if they'll let me coach, I'll sure try that. But I don't think I'll be all broken up about it when basketball is finally behind me for good. Maybe it's been too much for me too long. There must be other things and I'll have to look into them."

He paused and grinned. "Now, how about a beer, buddy? One for the road, if we can find a joint that's open."

The Twilight Crisis
of Y. A. Tittle

Steve Gelman | **1962**

Six nights a week from September through December, Y. A. Tittle sleeps soundly. On the seventh night, Sunday, he wrests. He lies in bed, energies exhausted, emotions exploding. He twists, he turns, he tosses; he wrests from within himself the fury he forged playing in the afternoon's football game. Regardless of the game's result, regardless of his own record, he continues playing it, in his mind, through a troubled night.

"It's been that way since I played my first game of professional football," Tittle says, "and I imagine it will be that way until I play my last." It could be no other way because he brings to football a competitive compulsion matched by few men.

Normally, Tittle is a gentle man. He speaks softly, he speaks kindly, he side-steps controversy with a diplomat's flair for dodging. But when victory and defeat are involved, the competitive compulsion brings a drill-sergeant's tone to his voice and violent words to his mouth. It brings him charging into the locker room after a game as if the shower he's headed for were the linemen who've just tried beheading him. It brings tension. It brings torment. It bubbles over in a bouillabaisse of emotional reactions.

"Y.A. wants to win," says veteran football star Hugh McElhenny.

"And he wants to win in everything—even cribbage. Why, you've got to watch him while he's pegging up his points."

McElhenny knows. McElhenny was Tittle's teammate for nine years with the San Francisco 49ers. He saw him suffer and storm through nine seasons of football games. He saw him spend his energies playing quarterback, then, with the defense at work, pace the sidelines for a few plays, sit on the bench for a few plays, squat in front of the bench and haul up hunks of grass for a few more. And he knew Tittle's sorrow, for it was his sorrow, too. In ten years with the 49ers, and in three previous years with the Baltimore Colts, Y. A. Tittle, the man dedicated to victory, never won even one division championship.

Last year, finally, the sorrow ended. Traded to the New York Giants, Tittle starred for them all season and, largely because of his season-long skills, the Giants clinched the National Football League's Eastern Division title on a gray Sunday in December. It was December 17, a day Tittle will never forget, and on that day, he charged through the locker room, feeling the full flush of victory for the first time and hearing behind him the cheers of the Giants celebrating their championship.

While they celebrated, he walked, swiftly, assuredly, past the lockers and around a corner to the clubhouse telephone. His helmet off, sweat streaking his long, lean face and lined, leathery neck, he placed a call to Atherton, California, where his wife, Minnette, who had long shared his sorrow, would finally share his conquest. Presently the call was connected and Minnette was on the line.

"Hello, honey. We won," said Y.A., and so ended the spoken conversation. Only tears followed. First, Minette's. Then her husband's. "We cried for a full four minutes," Tittle says. "It was the most futile call I ever made."

The bouillabaisse of emotional reactions brought tears that time. Other times it's brought tirades. Tittle's best friend among the Giants is Del Shofner, the end, but in football, friends are forgotten. Recently, in practice, Y.A. snapped a long, spiral pass downfield. It was a perfect lead pass, the type that puts six points on the scoreboard during a game, and as Shofner sprinted full steam for the ball, Tittle spurred him forward.

"Drop that ball," he hollered, "and you better keep right on running."

"That Y.A.," says Shofner, "he's all over my back."

Other backs, too, for Tittle is the quarterback, the man in command and, at thirty-six, he assumes his responsibility with a rookie's enthusiasm and a veteran's efficiency. "When he joined the Giants," says Lee

Grosscup, who played with them last season, "he surprised the hell out of us. It was his enthusiasm. That's a reason he caught on so quickly. He was a veteran, a guy who'd been around a dozen years, and the fellows expected him to be tranquil. But he wasn't. And everybody was surprised. He gave us a boost with his enthusiasm. He was a perfectionist, a real battler. We'd make a mistake out there, he'd be like a school kid, slamming his helmet to the ground, sounding off."

Against Dallas last season, Tittle took a snap from center and slapped the football into the belly of rookie running-back Bob Gaiters. All that week Giant coach Allie Sherman had been telling Gaiters: "Don't wait to see a hole open. Blast off! The hole will be there when you get there." But the rookie hesitated for a split-second after taking Tittle's handoff and ended up on the ground, tackled for no gain. Tittle ended up on the ground, too, shouting into Gaiter's ear. "That's the last time you do that," Tittle bellowed. "Bust in there. You take that ball, you hear, and point your head straight thataway."

Gaiters, so shaken he forgot to hesitate again, gained 129 yards in the game.

"Personally," says Tittle, "I feel chewing out players is the responsibility of a coach. We're all out there working at a job and the coaches are out there eagle-eyeing us. But I'm guilty, I know, of getting hot and bothered."

No Giant begrudges him this guilt. Not the rookies, who stand in awe of his reputation, not the veterans, who know his petulance means points in a game. In practice at Connecticut's Fairfield University a week before the current season, Frank Gifford, essentially a running back in his eleven NFL years, was switched to the flanker slot. The day of the switch, after formal practice, Tittle asked Gifford to remain on the field for a special workout. Enlisting Ray Wietecha to center the ball, Y.A. lined up in his quarterback's position and directed Frank to the flank. Again and again, with Tittle commanding, they practiced a basic maneuver of Gifford's new position—a flight eleven steps downfield by Frank and a quick turn to the outside, where the ball, thrown by Tittle, would be waiting for him.

After a while, Gifford told Tittle he'd like to make a slight change in the way he ran the pattern. The quarterback stared at him sternly. "I don't care how you get there," said Y.A., articulating with authority. "But you just better be there."

Later that day Tittle sat in the university faculty lounge, talking with a writer. With his bald head, open-necked white shirt and white cardigan sweater, he looked indeed like a college professor lounging. "I work individually with all the pass receivers," he said. "I have to. You have to practice. You have to do things right." The words came slowly and Tittle squirmed in his seat as he spoke. "Look, I've got to tell you," he said, shifting subjects and squirming. "I don't go for this talking stuff. I hate to see the word 'I' in stories about me." He flipped a plastic bottle of nose spray into the air. "I try to avoid direct quotations." Flip. "I'm shy about publicity." Flip. "Look, a player wants the respect of his teammates and opposing players." Flip. "I don't like to talk in a braggative manner about myself. I don't like to talk critically of others." Flip. "I . . . well . . . I just don't like to talk."

In an interview Y.A. acts as if a wrong word would touch off nuclear warfare. When he's not squirming, he will sit pensively, a hand cupping his cleft chin, his deep-set, blue eyes solemn. "Let me word that right now," he will say. Or, "I have to be careful how I answer that." Or, on a question he considers particularly probing: "Well, how would you react to something like that?" In the Fairfield lounge, discussing the speeches he is called upon to make during the off-season, he said, "I don't really enjoy it. No, not really." He paused. "But I don't mean to say I'm ungrateful for it. I mean, I have to be careful how I answer that. People are liable to say, look at all that football's done for him and now he's ungrateful." He stared at the writer. "But let's say someone said to you, 'Go over to town today and make a speech about writing.' Now, you'd rather be playing golf or spending time with your family, wouldn't you?"

When called upon to make a speech, however, Tittle, through years of practice, is entertaining and reasonably eloquent. There is humor in his phrasing and animation to his anecdotes. He has, from his boyhood years in Marshall, Texas, the sound of the Southwest in his speech (the football command, "Set!" comes out of Y.A.'s mouth as "Say-it!") and a set of sayings that lend a warm folksiness to his manner. When the Giants played Cleveland in their final game last year and a loss coupled with a Philadelphia Eagles' win in Detroit could have thrown the division into a tie, Sherman ordered his players not to look at the scoreboard. "Now, that," Y.A. will say in recollection, "was like not looking at a rattler at your feet." When talking about the Giants' string of championships through the years, sometimes won with strategy criticized by other teams, Tittle will say, "No sir, you can't criticize a trapper who's got the skins on the wall."

But despite his skill at making speeches, he would rather, as he and almost every athlete will say, pursue free-time pleasures. He'd prefer playing golf or tennis or taking part in any of the other outdoor sports which provide off-season release for his competitive compulsion. Mostly he'd prefer relaxing in his $75,000 Atherton home with Minnette, his two sons, Mike, ten, and Pat, nine, and his daughter, Dianne, twelve. With them he is the mild man, shy, warm, sensitive. One Halloween he was observed walking the rounds with Dianne, then four, as she filled a paper sack playing trick and treat. She was wearing a Red Riding Hood costume and he was wearing a red face, caused by blushing each time he said thank you for a treat she failed to acknowledge.

Continually that evening he'd remind her to say thank you and Dianne, in the way of small girls, would forget. His commands, immediately snapped to on the football field, carry neither the crispness nor the authority at home. "I guess," Minnette once told a writer, William Worden, "you'd say he doesn't know much about managing kids."

"Whereupon," wrote Worden, "Mike comes through [the living room] blowing a tin horn. His father says, 'Mike, don't do that,' so Mike blows it again, and louder. Dianne comes through and turns up the TV sound. 'Dianne, don't do that. We're talking.' So Dianne turns it up again, a little louder than before."

When he speaks about his children, Tittle's eyes light up and his voice fills with a parent's pride. His devotion to them flowers forth and it was this devotion that almost caused him to retire from football last season when the 49ers traded him to the Giants. He knew the reason for the trade—San Francisco's new Shotgun Offense required the passer to be a good runner, too, and Tittle, in his words, "can run about as good as my little daughter." But he did not like the idea of spending a season away from his family.

"I didn't want to be away from my wife for three months," he says, "and she couldn't leave the children and come with me. We couldn't take them with us because I knew nothing about housing and schooling arrangements in New York. In fact, I didn't even know where we practiced."

The dilemma was solved swiftly, though, by Tittle's mother-in-law. She was visiting him at the time of the trade and volunteered to return for a large share of the football season, freeing Minnette to join him in New York.

Still, there were other considerations influencing Tittle toward retirement. A college contemporary of Johnny Lujack, Glenn Davis, Harry Gilmer, and Charlie Trippi, all long ago retired from football, he had been absorbing the aches and bruises of pro ball since 1948. He had been injured often, hospitalized occasionally. With 17,900 yards gained through the NFL air, he had already secured his place among pro football's premier passers. Was there a reason, really, for him to go to a new team in a new town, where, in the words of the coach he'd be playing for, he was expected not to be a star, but only insurance behind the number-one quarterback, Charlie Conerly? Was there a reason to once more inflict upon himself the mental and physical punishment and once more fear the asthmatic attacks that came at their worst when they came on the football field and made special pills for him part of the team doctor's standard equipment?

There was a reason. He still wanted the chance to win a championship. And another reason. Pride. Tittle did not feel he was finished at thirty-four and he wanted to show the football world how he felt. And one more reason, perhaps the most important reason.

"I enjoy football," says the man to whom the game has been a way of life for so many years. "Maybe it's foolish for someone as old as I am, but if you retire and decide at forty-three, say, you'd like to come back and play one more season, you can't. So I had to think if I was fortunate enough to have the talent to play at my age, why shouldn't I have continued? I was in shape. Good shape."

So, Y. A. Tittle, his long, astonishingly muscled arms still powerful and his 192 pounds and six feet still trim, decided he'd head for the Giant training base. But first he stopped at the 49er training base. He had something to say to the players and he asked coach Red Hickey for permission to say it. Hickey agreed and presently Tittle stood speaking to his former teammates, his eyes and face announcing his emotion.

"First of all," he said, "I don't want to hear any griping about this trade. When the 'Shotgun' came, old Yat knew time was running out. The heart may be willing but the legs just aren't there.

"I've enjoyed myself with the 49ers. If I'd been in Hickey's place, under the same circumstances, I'd have made the same deal. I just want to thank everybody for all you've done for me."

"Reaction to the speech," a man who was there says, understating, "was emotional."

Tittle went to Atherton and packed. He put some fresh pieces of adhesive tape on the tattered shoulder pads he'd been wearing for thirteen years and, with that good-luck charm in his luggage, left for Salem, Oregon, where the Giants were training for an exhibition game with the Los Angeles Rams. Meanwhile, coming a reverse route, Lou Cordileone, the young guard who had been traded from New York for Y.A., summed up majority reaction to the deal. "Me for Tittle?" said Cordileone. "You mean, just me?"

Tittle knew he'd have to make tough adjustments that would begin on, but range far beyond, the football field. He knew that at thirty-four, almost thirty-five, he'd have to learn a new football system and make a new set of social contacts. "I knew the faces of the Giant players," he said. "Especially the defensive players, the way they swarmed in on me when I played against them. But I only knew the faces. I knew none of the players personally."

After a few days of practicing at Salem, Tittle traveled with the team to Los Angeles for the game against the Rams. At 6:00 p.m. the night they arrived, he stood in the lobby of the Ambassador Hotel, watching the Giants go off in groups to dinner. He waited to be asked along. He waited until all his new teammates had passed him by. Then, alone, he walked slowly out of the lobby and into the street. Deliberating, he approached the doorman and asked if he knew where any of the players had gone. The doorman mentioned a restaurant several blocks away and Tittle, deep in thought, walked toward it, down to Wilshire Boulevard. When Y.A. reached the restaurant, he saw six Giants sitting around a table with seven seats. He walked over and asked if he could occupy the seventh seat. No one objected.

The football adjustment was infinitely tougher than the social adjustment, though, mostly because of one play in the exhibition game against the Rams. On that play, his first as a Giant, Tittle missed the ball on a center snap and as he fell on it, two Ram tackles fell on him, cracking two transverse processes in his back and putting him out of action for five weeks.

"The injury," says Tittle, "was the toughest part of the whole year. It held me back mentally as well as physically. I was having trouble with the numbering system (the play numbers). I had to learn a whole new numbering system and the best way to do that is to keep applying what you learn in game conditions. I couldn't do that. I'd sit in on meetings and study play books and all, but still, it was all mumble-jumble."

"What Y.A. had to do," says Giant center Ray Wietecha, "was learn a new language. Sure, every team runs basically the same plays, but the words they use to set them up are different. The first thing a quarterback has to do in a huddle is set up the play. He can't just call a dive or a sweep or an option and give the number, he's got to set it up. For example, the first thing our quarterback might say is 'Balanced Right.' That gives everybody their position. The right end is in tight. The right halfback is out on the right flanker. The left half and the fullback are in their regular positions and the left end is split out about ten yards.

"Well, in a case like that, Tittle would come back to the huddle and say, 'Over right inside.' We would stop him and ask, 'What the hell does *that* mean?' Then he'd have to explain where he wanted everybody. Halfway through the explanation, someone would catch on and say, 'Oh, you mean *balanced right*.' It didn't make things easy, but Y.A. was great in spite of it."

Quickly, though, Tittle learned to recite the signals by rote. Kyle Rote, the veteran end, "was a big help to him," Wietecha says. "We'd come back to the huddle and Y.A. would tell Kyle, say, 'I want to throw a square out. Call it for me.' So Kyle would call the play that Y.A. wanted, but in our nomenclature. He was Y.A.'s interpreter in the huddle. And that's all he was there."

Wietecha's message was clear. Though Rote did the translating, Tittle remained the top-kick. "The quarterback must be in charge out there," Y.A. says. "I'll enlist the support of others. I want guys to tell me things. We have to see things together. But it can't be like a mad scramble in the huddle."

Despite the language barrier, Tittle was a master of play manipulation through the season. Sherman had designed a wide-open, imaginative offense that could work only when directed by an imaginative quarterback. It worked best beginning with the second game of the season when Tittle assumed the quarterback's command. He hadn't played in a game since suffering the back injury but the inactivity hardly hurt him. Replacing Conerly, he completed the first eight passes he threw and, with ten completions in twelve attempts, was the man most responsible for New York's 17–14 victory over the Pittsburgh Steelers.

Afterward, Sherman wouldn't publicly proclaim Tittle the Giants' number-one quarterback, but Y.A. was quickly taking over. He threw for 315 yards against Washington the next week and New York won, 24 to 21. Against St. Louis he threw for 105 yards, against Dallas, 117. The Giants won both games. Presently they pressed the Philadelphia Eagles for first place in the Eastern Division and on November 19, passed them.

On November 19 the Giants played Pittsburgh again, and the Steelers, well aware of Y.A.'s skills, fought full fury to stop him. Through the game their big linemen drummed a rattling rhythm on Tittle's ancient anatomy. The more they battered him, the more they stirred his competitive storm. He completed nineteen passes for 314 yards and beat them, 42 to 21. But he had been beaten, too, particularly by their defensive bruisers, Lou Michaels, 235 pounds, and Big Daddy Lipscomb, 288 pounds. On one play Michaels chased Tittle out of bounds, leaped a sidelines bench and smashed him. On another, Big Daddy chased him out of bounds, then hit him so hard he opened a gash above Y.A.'s left eye. Tittle remained in action, blood dripping from his wound. So violent were Big Daddy's assaults that after the game, when he came to the New York locker room to congratulate the winners, his buddy, Giant tackle Rosey Brown, stared stonily at him. "Big Daddy," said Brown, shaking his head, "sometimes I gotta wonder about you."

Off to a side of the clubhouse, Tittle stood talking to his two sons, who had never before seen him play football. "How'd you all like the game?" he said.

"Fine," said Mike.

Y.A. reached out and rumpled Mike's hair. Then he rumpled Pat's. "You all really liked it fine?" he said, beaming with pride.

"Just fine," said Pat.

Tittle pointed to the mass of tape he had unwound from his legs and ankles. "Boys," he said, "if it wasn't for this old adhesive, I'd be in bad shape."

Elsewhere in the locker room, the talk was all about Tittle.

"He didn't make a poor play choice or a poor pass all game," said Rote.

"He was the perfect quarterback," said Alex Webster.

"Tittle," said Conerly, a man who would know, "was a master all the time he was out there."

He had been. Not only as a passer, but also as a play-caller. After many early-season problems with the calling of automatics (play changes at the line of scrimmage), Tittle quickly made the checkoffs one of his strongest points. Against Pittsburgh, not only did he improvise on his huddle calls with automatics, but he also improvised on his automatics. Four times in the first half he called an automatic—"Orange, ten," let's say—which sent Shofner scurrying out to catch a short pass on a hitch pattern. The fourth time Tittle shifted to that play at the line of scrimmage, the Steeler linebackers remembering the words, shouted, "The hitch, the hitch!" Moments later, with the Giant offensive team on the sidelines, Tittle huddled with Shofner. "Look, they're keying on our number," Tittle said. "Next time I automatic the hitch to you, don't hitch. Fake it and run a fly."

Lining up for a second-half play, Tittle hunched behind center Wietecha and studied the Steeler defense. He swung his head left and right, shouting out an automatic. "Orange," he shouted, then, looking straight at Steeler middle linebacker Myron Pottios, "Ten."

"The hitch, the hitch!" Pottios yelled. "The hitch!"

Wietecha snapped the ball. Tittle faded back, his feet moving quickly, his eyes following Shofner's flight downfield. Suddenly, following the hitch pattern, Shofner hooked back toward scrimmage. Tittle pump-faked a pass and, as the defensive back cut in front of Shofner, Del swung around and raced downfield. Tittle spiraled the ball into Shofner's hands for a thirty-five-yard gain.

Tittle continued confusing opponents the next week. And they continued clouting him. He completed seventeen passes against the Cleveland Browns, some of them on reflex. "I was feeling goofy out there," he said. "They were hitting me, hitting me too much after I got rid of the ball. They were hitting me so much I was yelling at them."

He was impressing them, too. "Why don't they give *me* a guy like Tittle," Cleveland coach Paul Brown said after taking a 37–21 beating. "Tittle was the man who beat us."

The Cleveland players agreed. "You'd expect one thing," said defensive tackle Floyd Peters, "and he'd hit you with another." Peters paused. "Tittle," he said, summing up his team's reaction, "mixed us up."

While pro football players and coaches were most impressed, perhaps, by Tittle's subtle skills, pro football fans respected him most last season for his basic skill, throwing the ball. Fair enough. Counting his two-year record in the All-American Football Conference, Tittle began the current season with 1859 pass completions, more than any other quarterback in professional-football history. He considers himself a passer, first and foremost, and speaks on the subject with enthusiasm and pride. "I like to throw the ball," he says. "To me, the pro game *is* throwing. I may be wrong, but I feel putting the ball in the air is the way to win."

Tittle puts the ball in the air with a variation of a baseball pitcher's motion. He holds the ball with an unusual grip (he does not spread his fingers across the laces; he keeps his two middle fingers together), leads with his left side and puts his weight back on his right foot. Then he moves forward with his left foot, right arm and shoulder, releases the ball and follows through. To throw short he bends his knees slightly. To throw long he goes into a deep crouch.

Tittle throws longer less these days than he did when he first became a pro passer. He releases the long pass now only after careful calculation, setting it up with running plays and short throws. "The element of surprise is important when you're throwing the 'bomb,'" he says. "You've got to use it carefully. It took me a while to figure out, too, that I'm just as well off throwing a ball to a guy fifteen yards away and letting him run the other fifty yards for a touchdown."

Following this philosophy Tittle threw for 2272 yards last year and they took the Giants to a championship. "Tittle was the difference," said Don Heinrich, then the team's backfield coach. Sherman agreed. So did Paul Brown, who drew an interesting image. "In football," said Brown, "the quarterback is the point of the spear. The Giants had that point in Tittle."

They knew it. At a dinner in Jim Downey's restaurant, celebrating their championship, the Giants listened with interest to the speeches. When the last listed speech ended, a rumble ran through the room. "Y.A. Y.A. We want Y.A." The man they'd passed by in the Ambassador Hotel lobby five months earlier stood. Slowly, spontaneously, sincerely, he spoke to his teammates. He spiced his speech with humor, too, making several references to the extra-curricular job he held, "chaperoning that bachelor boy, Shofner." He captured them with his words the way he had captured them with his quarterbacking.

By then, of course, Tittle did not lack friends among the Giants. Every man respected his wise ways and enthusiasm on the football field and enjoyed his good-natured needling off it. He was particularly close to Shofner. He was also close friends with the defensive players. The attraction there was basic. "Never," says Tittle, "have I seen guys with such great competitive spirit."

A while after the dinner at Downey's, the Giants played Green Bay in the NFL championship playoff game. They lost 37 to 0. The big championship had eluded Tittle and now, with time running out on his career, he is wrapped up in his pursuit of it. "I want to win one," he says, and he doesn't have to elaborate. The tone in his voice tells how much he wants it. Each competitive crisis he goes through is part of a bigger crisis, a chase toward the NFL championship in the twilight of his career.

Last year, in the only game he ever played for an NFL championship, Tittle played poorly. But he made no excuses. "I've had my share of pats on the back," he said. "Now let them criticize me. I have it coming. It was just a miserable performance. I was miserable. The whole team was miserable. The Packers were great. We were beaten by a great football team. It was like a bad dream, a nightmare."

But more pats on the back were coming. Newspaper Enterprise Association gave him the Jim Thorpe Trophy, awarded to the most valuable player in the NFL. He was picked for, and played in, the Pro Bowl Game. Clearly, he was at the peak of his pro-football career, secure in job, secure in his stature.

Still, less than a year later, as the Giants were practicing for the 1962 season, Tittle said, "When I joined this team last year, I felt I had to prove myself. But I feel the same way this year." He paused. "In this game," he said, presenting a platitude of his trade, "you have to prove yourself over again every year."

The man sitting opposite him sneered cynically. "Let me explain," said Y.A. "Let me get this right now. What I mean is in baseball, say, you've got 162 games. If a .300 hitter has a bad slump, even if he's benched, he'll get back in there and hit his .300. But in football, where we have only fourteen games, a quarterback can have one bad game and really start talking to himself. I know I do. He has two or three bad games and even if he's an excellent quarterback, there's a good player behind him who's going to move right in. There's no time to wait. And there are so many elements that go into a quarterback's success—pre-game preparation, analysis—as well as the things he does in a game that he can't afford to think he's proven himself. He has to be constantly striving for perfection."

Tittle, the compulsive competitor, began striving for perfection, he says, in high-school sports in Marshall, Texas. He remembers Marshall as a pine-timber and railroading town of about twenty thousand people, located near the Louisiana border. He was born there October 24, 1926, acquired his father's name, Yelberton Abraham, and, some years later, a measure of football instruction from his older brother, Jack, who played the game at Tulane University. It was only a small measure of instruction, though, Tittle says, and he quickly clarifies. "If I say my brother tutored me in football," he says, "that would be wrong. But if I say he didn't teach me football, that wouldn't be right either. It was just a normal relationship of brothers, the older one showing the younger one a thing or two."

Y.A. lived comfortably on the outskirts of town on the income his father earned as a post-office employee and he made a name for himself in the center of town, at Marshall High School, playing varsity baseball, basketball and football. "But baseball and basketball," he says, "weren't my long suit by any means." Football was. He won a scholarship to Louisiana State University.

"I had some other scholarship offers," Y.A. says, "but it was during World War II and most of the schools had armed-service programs. There were older fellows, in service, stationed at the schools and playing ball there. I picked LSU because it was a civilian school. I'd be playing ball there with boys seventeen and eighteen, boys my age."

As a freshman at LSU in 1944, Tittle was a reserve tailback on the varsity. He didn't play often but did get a chance to go a considerable route in the last game of the season, against Tulane. Completing his first twelve passes and a total fifteen out of seventeen, he was the hero of LSU's 25–6 victory. His passing particularly impressed his coach, Bernie Moore, who named Tittle the No. 1 quarterback when LSU switched to the T-formation in 1945.

Since he'd never played the T-formation before, nor seen much of it, Tittle had a tough adjustment to make. But he learned quickly. He still does. This year, two weeks before the season opened, Sherman introduced a screen-pass variation to the Giant offense. It was basically a double screen, with the fullback swinging to one flank, the halfback swinging to the other, and the quarterback throwing the ball to one of them after employing some faking finesse. The third time Tittle threw on the new pattern, Sherman shook his head in wonder. "Y.," he said. "You gettin' to look like you invented that play."

In the 1962 opening game, against the Cleveland Browns, Tittle completed that pass the first time he threw it. It came at a key moment, while the Giants still had a chance to win, but it was hardly the highlight of the game for true Y. A. Tittle fans. Their biggest moment came when Y.A., enraged at a blown scoring opportunity, hurled his helmet twenty yards, exposing the gleam of his bean and bringing to mind some winsome words from Prescott Sullivan, a San Francisco sports columnist with an eye for the absurd and a flair for putting it across.

"Tittle will be missed by the fans," Sullivan wrote when Y.A. was traded by the 49ers. "No doubt, the seagulls will miss him, too. Tittle's shining pate served them as a navigational guide to Kezar (Stadium) whenever Y.A. removed his hat.

"With the beacon light gone, many now may have trouble locating the field, or in keeping from overshooting it.

"The birds had a valued friend in old Y.A."

Tittle's baldness and sensitivity on the subject began building while he was at LSU. He wore a hat whenever possible. He asked photographers to take his picture only from side angles. He was frequently posing for photographers, but mostly they were local men. Nationally he was overshadowed by such college stars as Glenn Davis, Doc Blanchard, Lujack, Trippi and Gilmer. In the South many people felt Y.A. was being done an injustice (oh, yes, there was Choo Choo Justice, too) because in his personal battles with the more famous All-Americas, Y.A. usually outplayed them. He was the man most responsible for LSU's 32–0 victory over Georgia, led by Trippi, and 32–21 victory over

Alabama, led by Gilmer. But of all the games he played against All-Americas, Tittle's most memorable was the 1947 meeting with Mississippi and Charlie Conerly.

Late in the last quarter, with Mississippi leading 20 to 18, Tittle leaped high on the LSU thirty-yard line and intercepted one of Conerly's passes. Away he went, legs churning, football tucked under his arm, blockers before him. One by one the Mississippi men fell away and finally, one man remained in his route. Squirming out of the man's hands, Tittle was clear, only normal speed needed to move him into the end zone.

He raced on. Past the fifty. The forty. Suddenly, he felt his forward motion slowed. The last Mississippi man had taken a piece of Tittle's equipment with him. His belt. Swiftly, Y.A.'s pants began to slip. He was at the thirty-five, the pants were at his hips. He was at the thirty-three, the pants were at his knees. He was at the thirty-one, the pants were at his ankles. He made a quick choice—propriety over points. Reaching for his pants, he fell thirty yards from the goal line.

"The saddest part of the story," Y.A. says, "is that we never scored from where I fell. We lost the game 20 to 18."

Tittle's troubles at LSU were well overshadowed by his success, of course, and he was drafted in 1947 by the Cleveland Browns of the All-America Football Conference and the Detroit Lions of the National Football League. He signed with the Browns but never had a chance to play with them. In some sleight-of-hand, designed to strengthen the league, Tittle and young, promising players from other teams, were re-assigned to the Baltimore Colts. Though the Colts had an outstanding quarterback, Charley O'Rourke, Tittle reported to their training camp at Sun Valley, Idaho, confident he could win the first-string job.

"I'm always confident," Tittle says. "Even when I feel I have to prove myself, I always feel I *will* prove myself. But I'm confident, not cocky. There's a big difference."

The difference, Tittle says, can be found in a story circulated his first year with the Colts. Reportedly, Tittle sat on the bench during an exhibition game with the Los Angeles Dons and, watching the Dons build up a large lead, said to his coach, Cecil Isbell: "Get me in there, coach, or we'll sure lose this game."

"Actually," says Y.A., "I said that to one of the guys on the bench. And, of course, I was kidding."

When he did get into the game, Tittle moved Baltimore to a touchdown in four plays and, continuing his heroics, was the No. 1 quarterback when the season opened. In the opener, against the New York

Yankees, he broke four All-America Conference records, passing for 346 yards, gaining a total 354 yards and averaging 31.5 yards per pass completion and 16.5 yards per pass thrown. The league's outstanding rookie in 1948, he finished fourth in passing yardage and he experienced for the first time the frustration of losing a division championship. The Colts were second, beaten in a division-title playoff by the Buffalo Bills.

The next year, though Tittle excelled again, the Colts won only one game. Still, when the AAC was absorbed by the NFL at the end of the season, Baltimore was one of four teams (the others were the New York Yankees, Cleveland Browns and San Francisco 49ers) to be taken in. Literally the Colts were taken in, because they received only one player from the four disbanded AAC teams while other clubs split up the harvest. Outclassed, Baltimore won one game and lost eleven in 1950 and was eliminated from the league after the season. The players were assigned to other teams (today's Colt franchise was not built with them but took root years later with the remnants of the '50 Yankees) and Tittle joined the San Francisco 49ers' football family.

To play quarterback at San Francisco, Tittle had to dislodge Frankie Albert, who had been a local hero for more than a decade. The first year, 1951, they shared the position. The second year, Y.A. was the No. 1 man, a rating he held for almost ten years, beating back competition from such talented young men as Earl Morrall and John Brodie. While he was beating back the competition, the San Francisco crowds began to turn toward the younger men and against him. Through his last four or so seasons in San Francisco, Y.A. was booed frequently enough to give him some first-hand thoughts on the cause of crowd hostility and its effects on football players.

"It's foolish for me to say I didn't hear the boos," he says, speaking of the effect first. "I will say this. The boos didn't bother me after a while, but they didn't help me. Sometimes the crowds get on you for doing things that were wise to do. Like throwing the ball out of bounds. All the crowd knows is that the ball was thrown out of bounds. A quarterback knows his receiver was covered."

When he made a mistake, Tittle needed no reprimanding from the grandstand. He was then, as he is now, a relentless competitor, a man continually reprimanding himself. He stormed inwardly and outwardly and, through his ten seasons at San Francisco, he stormed mostly at his team's failure to win a title. The 49ers had Tittle at quarterback and more talent at other positions through those years—Hugh McElhenny, Joe Perry, Bob St. Clair, Leo Nomellini, Billy Wilson, R. C. Owens—

but it never jelled into a champion. The four men who coached the team in Tittle's time—Buck Shaw, Red Strader, Frankie Albert, and Red Hickey—struggled and sweated and devised special strategies. One year, even with wise old Y.A. at quarterback, the strategy was to call signals from the bench. It was, probably, the worst experiment of all.

"We had too many veterans attuned to the old system," says Tittle. "It didn't work. Personally, I feel signal-calling is the job of the quarterback, with help from the coach and the men in the huddle. But that's just my thought. I can't go criticizing Paul Brown. He's won the league championship a helluva lot and if he says, 'Let's compare blue ribbons,' I don't have a one to show him."

The closest the 49ers came was in 1957. It was a year filled with football drama. Three teams, the Detroit Lions with veteran quarterbacks Bobby Layne and Tobin Rote, the San Francisco 49ers with veteran quarterback Y. A. Tittle, and the Baltimore Colts, with a young, surprising quarterback star, Johnny Unitas, fought to the last day of the season for the Western Conference title. Tittle was hurt at mid-year, but to keep opposing players from aiming at it, the whereabouts of his injury was kept secret, and he kept on playing. He was able to take part, therefore, in the most spine-shivering single moment of the season, the final one of the November 3 Lions game.

The Lions were leading 31 to 28, and seven seconds remained in the game when Tittle quickly called his team into the huddle. He snapped out the signals and the 49ers lined up. Y.A. hunched behind the center. End R. C. Owens was split out on the flank. They were the men who mattered most on the play.

Tittle's head, sweat-streaked and dirt-decorated, swiveled left and right as he shouted his signals. Owens pressed his cleats into the dirt, digging in for a swift start. The ball came back and Tittle faded, taking small steps, meaningful steps. Into the protective pocket he went. Down the field Owens went.

Y.A. faded and faked, faded and faked and, finally, crouched, snapped forward and released the football, a long spiral into the end zone, perfectly placed into a pack of Lions.

Out of the pack came Owens, like a basketball rebounder, leaping as he'd done all the times they'd practiced the play. The ball was where he knew it would be, hanging for him. He was where Tittle knew he'd be—using the most phenomenal leap in football to get to the ball. Owens went up, up, up. And came down with the football. The score was San Francisco 34, Detroit 31.

The extra point that followed was simply scoreboard dressing. Y.A.

and R.C. had teamed up on their famous Alley-Oop pass play and it was the biggest day for initials in San Francisco since the U.N. was organized there in 1945.

"I remember that game," says Tittle. "Of course, I do. It was one of the biggest moments of my life. But I remember our last game with the Lions that year even better."

The last game took place December 22. On December 15, the final Sunday of the regularly scheduled season, the Colts had lost to Los Angeles, falling out of first place, and the 49ers and Lions had won, ending up tied for first place. In the special division playoff game on December 22, San Francisco led 27 to 7 early in the second half, but lost the game 31 to 27. "We just fell apart," says Tittle.

The 49ers fell to fourth in 1958, remained there in 1959 and advanced a small step to third in 1960. More significant to Tittle's career in 1960 was the groin injury he suffered in the fourth game. "I kept trying to come back," he says, "but I never did get well." With Tittle injured, Hickey began experimenting with the Shotgun formation, featuring quarterback John Brodie in the tailback-type position. Red decided after the season that the Shotgun was the formation most likely to preserve his future in San Francisco and before the '61 season, traded Tittle to the Giants.

By then Tittle had become deeply rooted to the town. His nicknames—Yat, Ya-Ya, Colonel Slick and Bald Eagle—were part of every sports fan's vocabulary. His family was settled in Atherton, thirty miles outside of San Francisco on the northern peninsula, which Tittle describes as the finest country in California. His non-football occupations, Y. A. Tittle's Sports and Summer Camp and the Tittle-Iverson Insurance Company, were lucrative. A sensible, intelligent man, he feared the businesses might suffer if he left town and this added to his doubts about joining the Giants. But, as he found out, it was an unfounded fear.

"After the season with the Giants," Tittle says, "I found my insurance business doing better than ever. In fact, it's gotten so that with all my business commitments and the speeches I have to make in the off-season, I find it more relaxing in a way during the football season. Then I've got a routine all set. I know I have to go to bed at a certain time, get up a certain time, eat a certain time. I can't let anything interfere with the routine."

Tittle thrives on his routine like a career infantryman thrives on an Army routine. It is an accustomed way of life, a mapped-out route. And, like an infantryman's routine, Tittle's prepares him for combat. In comparison it is inconsequential combat, of course, but it brings, for Tittle anyway, a physical and emotional explosion.

The buildup begins Tuesday with an afternoon workout and meeting. Wednesday, Thursday and Friday, from 9:00 a.m. until 3:00 p.m., there are meetings and practices, more meetings, more practices. The strategy is shaping. Tittle's competitive fury is building. He studies movies, reviews records, plots plays. He works out half an hour Saturday, then leaves practice. He thinks about the game, thinks some more about the game, tries hard not to think so much about the game. He sleeps soundly, reports for a team breakfast Sunday, eats little or nothing. At last, hours later, the game begins. He is at the pitch of his compulsion, playing hard, rooting hard, forgetting himself in his fury. Abruptly the game is over and he's at his locker, unwinding adhesive tape, unwinding his emotions . . . unwinding . . . unwinding through a troubled night.

"I lie in bed," he says, "and the anxiety of the game is still with me. Pass patterns run through my head. Numbers of plays rattle around. I spend so much time winding up for a game I can't just unwind the instant it's over. It takes time. I don't really start unwinding until the next day. Then, finally, I start relaxing."

And then?

"And then," says Y. A. Tittle, the old soldier, "I start winding up all over again."

Davey Moore's Last Days

Bill Libby | **1963**

Los Angeles' Main Street Gym is on skid row. Drifters, drunks, panhandlers and prostitutes litter the soiled streets. Up one flight, the boxers work out. On this day, early in 1963, the boxers were mostly preliminary boys. But there was a champion, too, skipping rope, humming a jazz tune.

The champion, Davey Moore, dropped his skip-rope and bundled a robe around his sweating body. He wiped his brow, picked up a towel and sat down on a bench. I asked him about Sugar Ramos, who wanted to fight him for his featherweight title.

"Me afraid of Sugar Ramos? Haw! 'Tain't so." He laughed. "Davey Moore is the champion. Davey Moore ain't afraid of no one. They put the money up, I'll fight Ramos, I'll fight anyone. Till then, let him wait. I had to wait. Ain't gonna hurt him to wait some."

"Do you think you can beat him?"

"I think I can beat anyone," he said.

"But Ramos . . ."

"He no different than no one else." Moore shrugged. "Maybe he can beat me. Till he does, I ain't gonna believe it. Ain't no one been beatin' me lately."

Moore had lost only one fight in five years, that one in 1960, when Carlos Hernandez knocked him out.

"He didn't knock me *out,* man," Moore said. "I had an impacted wisdom tooth, only I didn't know it at the time. He hit me on the left side of my face in the second round and he broke my jaw. Every time he hit me after that he hurt me like hell. I was never out, but I couldn't help from goin' down a lot."

"How many times?"

"Eight times."

"You kept getting up."

"I kept getting up. Finally I quit."

"What round?"

"After the sixth."

"You fought with a broken jaw for four rounds?"

"Damn near five," Davey said, smiling proudly.

"Any other fighter ever knock you down?"

"Charley Riley. That was back in '54. I was just a punk kid. I had no manager. I wasn't goin' nowhere. I wasn't in shape. He knocked me down. Only time I ever been dazed in my life. But I got up and I beat him."

"You won the fight?"

"That's all I won. Promoter ran south with the money," Davey said. "Only good thing was ol' Riley didn't get paid either." He chuckled.

Davey Moore had been a pro ten years and was twenty-eight years old. He was small, five feet two and 126 pounds, but built big, like a miniature heavyweight. He had a scar on his forehead, an Oriental mustache on his lip, and he wore a scowl when he fought. "Do I really look so mean?" he said when I mentioned it. He was surprised and pleased.

"You in shape?" I said.

"Pretty good," he said. "Davey's always in pretty good shape these days. I mean: I'm in town, now. I'm doin' a little participatin'. I got to squeeze in all the whatjimicallits now, before I go to camp. I don't get in real good shape till I get to camp. I'll be goin' down soon."

"You like it in camp?"

"Like it? Man, I hate it. It is boring and lonely. But I got to do it. I'm champion. I got to protect that. I got a fight, I got to be ready. No one's got any sense, he don't go into a ring when he ain't ready."

Moore got up, took off his robe and began to thump the heavy bag.

The training camp is in Gilman's Hot Springs, in the desert, two hours out of L.A. It is a hot, dusty, bare place. I visited Davey Moore there shortly before his fight with Ramos. He sat at a plain wooden table in his barracks-like living quarters. Jazz music drifted out of his old record player. We talked of Emile Griffith who had killed Kid Paret in a fight for the welterweight title.

"You know Griffith?" he asked.

"I know Griffith," I said.

"What's he like?"

"He's a good boy," I said.

"I hear he's ladylike. Paret said it."

"He's not. That's what made Griffith mad," I said. "Paret said it at the weigh-in. When Griffith got him hurt, he went after him angry."

"Man, you don't go after a man angry, you got no business in there," Moore said. "You not angry, you got to make yourself angry. It's part of fighting. You not gonna do it right, you shouldn't do it at all."

"You ever been really angry in a ring?"

"I fought this Spanish kid in Texas," Moore said. "He had a pin in the laces of his glove. Every time he hit me, he cut me up. I fought him back dirty and I beat him. I'd like to fight him again, I'd kill him."

"You ever felt sorry for someone you were fighting?"

"When I knocked out Cisco Andrade. He was my friend. That was the only time I can remember. I felt bad about having to hurt him. But I didn't think about it while I was in the ring. I had to do it, so I did it."

"You're a pretty good finisher," I said.

"Most fighters today, even the good ones, they get a man on the hook, they lose him. That's a waste. I don't believe in it. I take my time and I pick my spots and I land my best punches. I try to think real calm and clear. I don't show no mercy. There's no room for mercy in boxing."

"Griffith showed Paret no mercy."

"He shouldn't of. He was in a fight with him. He didn't have no gun. He had two fists. Paret had two fists. There was a referee in there. There was doctors at ringside. It just happened. It was an accident." He paused, his dark face solemn. "How do you think Griffith will take it?"

"He'll take it all right. He's a good boy, not a hard boy, though he's hard in the ring. He's intelligent enough to know it wasn't his fault. He'll feel bad. He'll get sick of being asked about it. But he'll accept it."

"I hope I never have a man die on me in the ring," Davey said. "It must be tough."

"It's tougher to die," I said.

He smiled. "Yes."

"Back in New York, I knew Roger Donoghue," I said. "He killed Georgie Flores in a Garden semi."

"Did he keep fighting?"

"Once or twice. He wasn't any good at it after that."

"Was he any good before?"

"I guess not. He was really just starting out. Maybe he had something, I don't know. I know he didn't have anything after."

Willie Ketchum, Moore's manager, had walked over. "Donoghue had fought Flores before, hadn't he?" Ketchum asked.

"Yes, a few weeks before. He beat him bad and knocked him out."

"Flores had no business going right back in against a man beat him bad," Ketchum said. "Paret took a bad beating from Gene Fullmer before he fought Griffith again. What really killed Paret was that beating from Fullmer, a bigger, stronger man, he never should of fought. Fighters like Paret get hurt because no one takes care of them."

"That's right," Moore said.

"There are managers don't care if their boxers never learned how to fight or to protect themselves, and who put them in with anyone and let them take one bad beating after another. You got managers never said no to nobody. No fighter fights everyone. Jack Dempsey didn't. No one did. All along I've made sure Davey learned how to fight and was always in shape and was never overmatched. Let them take care of fighters like they used to and there'd be no one wanting to stop the sport, which is a great sport."

Ketchum had had a couple of champions who drank too much, drove motorcycles too fast, chased women and battled in bars. Ketchum always said Moore was his first straight fighter, who never gave him any concern.

"There are a lot of things you can get crippled up or dead doin'," Moore said. "Football. Hockey. You can get hit by a baseball, you can get yourself killed. You get killed driving race cars. Remember Vukovich? He was a champ. He got killed. No one wants to stop them sports."

"They want to stop auto-racing," I said.

"They shouldn't. Race drivers know what they're doin', jus' like boxers know. There's risks, but we know it. I go to the Indianapolis '500' every chance I get. I can't go there, I go some other race. Those cats take real chances, man. Bad as a fighter. We all take chances."

"Sure you do," Ketchum said. "What about guys wash windows in those big buildings? Or work on construction? There's lots of dangerous jobs some people do for a living."

"Some people like to jump out of airplanes," Moore said. "Fact, some even like to ride in them." He grinned. "You can get killed crossing the street. You can get killed slipping in the bathtub."

"Accidents," Ketchum said. "Accidents. They happen in boxing, too. But you take the right care, they're not gonna happen very often."

"You taking care?" I asked Davey.

"I'm taking care," he said.

"Doesn't this business scare you?"

"No. I don't think about it. I ain't scared of dying. I ain't scared of being hurt. I don't wanna be dead. I'm the most live man you ever saw. And I don't get hurt. I haven't had any real, real tough fights. If I had, maybe I'd be scared. I haven't had, so I can't be scared."

"What about the two fights with Kid Bassey, when you won the title, then kept it. Those were rough fights. Didn't he hurt you?" I asked.

"Them *was* rough fights," Moore admitted. "Sure he hurt me. This is a hurtin' business and he was good at it. But he didn't hurt me bad. I was never in no real bad trouble. I was in command of the situation. I came on and beat him both times. And that was four years ago."

"What about Hernandez?" I asked him.

"That was three years ago. That was an accident, him breakin' my jaw."

"But you took punishment."

"Sure I did. I went on as long as I could, but before the seventh round, I quit. There was no sense going no further."

"Whattaya mean, you quit?" Ketchum said. "You never quit. I stopped it. You kept saying maybe you could catch him with a lucky punch and knock him out. But you were hurt so bad, you couldn't do any good, so I finally stopped it."

"Don't tell me that, Ketchum," Davey said. "If I say I quit, I quit. That's the way it was. Davey don't lie. Can you stop any fight I don't want you to stop? No, Ketchum, you can't, and you know it."

Ketchum frowned and shrugged. "Well, I'm not gonna let you get hurt," he said.

"*I* ain't gonna let me get hurt," Davey said. "And when I got no chance, I'm gonna quit. Fans sittin' comfortable at ringside may think it's wrong for a fighter to quit when he got no chance, but not ol' Davey."

"Do you always know in time to quit?" I asked.

"I start acting funny, I'll get out of boxing," Davey said. "I tell my manager, I tell my wife, I tell my friends: 'You see me acting funny, you tell me. You see me doin' anything different, anything ain't like me, you tell me, I'll quit.' Ain't that what I say, Ketchum?"

"That's right," Ketchum said. "That's what you say and that's the way it'll be."

Later, Moore fried a steak and ate it plain. Then he rinsed off the plate, and washed out his underwear in the sink. It was growing dark. Ketchum was gone now. Davey was deep in thought, thinking about Alejandro Lavorante, who lay in a coma in Los Angeles many months after being knocked out in a prize fight.

"You think Lavorante'll pull out of it?" he asked.

"I don't know. I'm no doctor," I said. "But I doubt it."

"If he does pull out of it, will he be all right?"

"I don't know."

"I worry more about hurtin' someone than getting hurt," he said, sitting down and looking at his hard hands. "But I wouldn't want to be punchy. I'd rather be dead than punchy."

There was silence for a moment. Then I said, "You say you don't think about it, but you do."

"Aw, man, you got to think about it some. You don't think about it real hard, that's all. One thing always worried me was getting a cauliflower ear. I always hated the look of one of them. I always said to myself, if I get one of them, I'll get out. It ain't happened yet. It's rough in there, man. I got to do it, but I don't want to get hurt. I be chit-chattin' sometimes and forget what I was goin' to say and I get scared. But I ask people and they tell me that happens to everyone, so I guess it ain't anything. It ever happened to you?"

"Yes."

"See! You get scared?"

"No, but I'm not a boxer. I'm not taking head punches."

"That's right," Moore said. "I only worry about it because I'm a boxer, maybe. I just try not to think about such things."

"I guess you can't if you're gonna be a boxer."

"That's right. And that's what I is. I ain't anything else."

"You proud to be a boxer?"

"I sure is," Moore said. "What I've done, not everyone could do."

"If you knew there was a chance what happened to Paret might happen to you, would you go on with it?"

"Yes. It could happen. I know that. But I can't worry about it. I wouldn't do nothin' no different. What else I gonna do? Dig ditches? Push a wheelbarrow? That's what I done before. I got no education. I never had no chance. This is the only thing I ever had a chance in. Lots of boxers just like me. Boxing gives us our only chance."

"What if you know it was bound to happen. Would you go on then?"

"I don't know."

"But if you *did* know?"

"No, not then. I guess I'd rather dig ditches or push a wheelbarrow. No one wants to die. I got too much to live for. Only thing is, I *don't* know."

Davey Moore was born in Lexington, Kentucky, in 1933 and raised in Springfield, Ohio. He was one of seven children. The father was a minister, who also worked in a construction gang. The father and mother were both strict with their children, who went to church daily. "That's a heap of goin'," Davey once said, grinning.

One of Davey's brothers grew up to be a minister and one of his sisters married a minister. There was no smoking, drinking or cursing in the Moore house. Davey never smoked or drank, even later, though he kept cigarettes and whisky in his own house for visitors. He might curse to outsiders, but he would never curse in front of his wife or family.

As a boy, perhaps, in rebellion to strict religious upbringing, Davey was hard to handle away from home. He was small so others tried to push him around. He fought back and fought well and soon became what he proudly called "the head leader" of his gang. The gang got into various troubles, breaking windows, stealing small. "I mean we wasn't real criminals, but we was just lucky we wasn't caught more," Davy often explained.

Once, when challenged to a fight with gloves, Davey went to the gym and got hooked on boxing. Some of his friends got hooked on narcotics and crime, and some wound up in jail. Later, when Davey would go home, he would see them all, good and bad. "But they couldn't make me go bad," he said.

As a fighter, Davey lost only five of 125 amateur bouts. At nineteen he made the 1952 Olympic team. He had never gone hungry as a child, but he did later on. He quit school in the ninth grade to get married and, after fighting in the Olympics, began raising his family. He turned pro in 1953, but couldn't get a good manager or regular fights. When he did fight, he wasn't ready. He didn't lose often, but he wasn't getting anywhere. He worked on construction gangs, in yards, parked cars, was a trash man and a janitor. He admitted he was a poor worker, disinterested. He lived off his wife, who worked, or on relief checks.

Moore felt the turning point in his life came when he met Ketchum, who believed in him as a boxer and would work for him. At the time Davey was living with his parents. His wife and their first two children lived with her parents. Ketchum bought his contract for five hundred dollars, staked him, put him in a gym, trained him, and got him regular bouts. Moore began to rise.

He won the title from Bassey in 1959. Going into the Ramos fight, he had won fifty-seven of sixty-five pro fights and had successfully defended his title five times. Unfortunately, American promoters and television matchmakers had become disinterested in low-weight fighters. Davey had to become a boxing gypsy. He fought in Mexico, Spain, France, Italy, England, Finland and Japan, where little fighters are appreciated.

It was a hard life. Foreign fans threw chairs, cushions, rocks, broken glass, bottles, blazing newspapers, firecrackers, even live snakes at him. But he was stoic and he won and his popularity overseas grew. He was unhappy because his own people didn't know him. He hated the long, lonely tours, away from home and family. "But I got to do it, to make that bread," he would say.

He and his wife, Geraldine, had five children. He wanted to be with them, raising them, watching them grow. "You only get the one time," he said. He wanted his children to get good educations, enter good professions. He saved money for them.

Moore averaged $25,000 a year, but he was as close with a buck as a man can be. He admitted it openly and even enjoyed being kidded about it. Last year, he made five dollars one snowy day in Columbus helping a man unload a truck. Later in the year, while staying at a Santa Monica hotel, he made friends with the fellow who worked in the parking lot. When the fellow wanted some time off, Davey offered to fill in for him. The world featherweight champion parked cars for fifty-cent tips, and by the time the hotel manager found out, Davey had made sixty dollars. He showed it around proudly. "Nothing wrong with honest work," he said, grinning.

He owned a five-bedroom home and two cars and invested his money in three small apartment houses, real-estate lots and a physical fitness clinic. He paid his taxes and hired an accountant to help him watch over his affairs. He didn't really need help. No one hit him up for money. If someone had a story for him, Davey had a better one to tell. If a friend needed clothes or a bum needed a drink, Davey might provide them, but never money.

Davey didn't spend much on clothes. He often washed his own laundry. He read his newspapers second hand. One day this year he had dinner with Ketchum and paid the check for both. "He never did that before," Ketchum said later. "It scared me so, I couldn't sleep all night. I just knew something was wrong."

Moore's economies were for himself and his family. "Me and my family live good, but we don't throw nothin' away," he used to say.

Not long before the Ramos fight, Moore sat in a small restaurant in midtown Los Angeles. "You should see my home in Columbus," he said proudly. "It is not a home, it is a palace, a livin' palace. And it is paid for, every cent. My wife wants to buy a new dress, she needs it, fine, but she asks me first, even if she has to call me up. No one, not even her, spends a dime of Davey's money without Davey knowin' about it.

"Sure it'd be easy to have a lot of friends spendin' my money. The girls would spend it faster than anyone. If I was to let 'em, that is. I'll never forget what my father used to say. He said that all that counts in life is to have a roof over your head and plenty of food in the house. Don't worry about no bill collectors. Let them fend for themselves. Don't worry about no fancy clothes. You can go naked if you has to. And that's the way I feel.

"Now it happens I can live good. But I take care of what I got. I got it the hard way, the only way I could. It hurts when someone don't know who I is, and that maybe I got to go all over the world to make a livin'. But I'll tell you somethin': I'll always have a good home and plenty to eat as long as I live. I'll have me something when I leave this game."

"And when will that be?" I asked.

"Another year or two, that's all the longer it'll be."

"You're not ready to retire yet?"

"No, not yet. After Ramos, I'd like to fight Carlos Ortiz for the light-weight title. I got to make me some real bread yet. Another year or two, that's all. It's getting near time I got out so I could enjoy life a little. I got a lot of enjoyin' to do."

The Ramos fight was part of an outdoor tripleheader at Dodger Stadium. Emile Griffith was matched against Luis Rodriguez for the welterweight title, and Roberto Cruz against Battling Torres for the junior welterweight. Torres, a Mexican, and Rodriguez and Ramos, refugee Cubans who now live in Mexico City, drew many Latins to the Stadium. Crowds of Mexicans came across the border for the tripleheader.

Fight night, a Saturday night, it was raining hard. The promoters, Cal and Aileen Eaton and George Parnassus, who had a television commitment for the Griffith-Rodriguez fight, put a canvas roof over the ring and announced the show would go on. A few minutes before the first fight, however, the program was postponed to "Monday or Tuesday."

Monday was clear, but to permit a fresh ticket sale, the fight was put off to Thursday, March 21. All the fighters but Davey went back into training. He did not put on gloves until the night of the rescheduled fight.

A crowd of 26,142 turned out Thursday night. Griffith fought first, and lost to Rodriguez. It was a dull fight. Moore fought Ramos next and this was a great fight, savage and hard. Moore was a great all-round fighter and a very hard puncher. Ramos, the underdog, was good, too—not as versatile or as experienced, but younger and faster, not as hard a puncher, perhaps, but a hard one.

Moore went ahead early, but without his usual conviction. My notes show I was puzzled by the way Moore seemed to flounder on unsteady legs, the way he was pushed off balance so easily. I am still puzzled by this. Later, others, including referee George Latka, said they noticed it.

In the fifth round, Ramos began to come. He pumped hard left jabs, he threw hard right crosses. He knocked out Moore's mouthpiece, and later there was talk that the mouthpiece was split and defective. The crowd set up an eerie chant: Rah-MOS, Rah-MOS, Rah-MOS. Moore began to bleed from the mouth, but he rallied in the seventh round. He hit Ramos with seven straight right-hand smashes. Ramos didn't fall.

Ramos resumed command in the eighth. He hurt Moore badly. In the tenth, he draped Davey over the ropes twice and knocked him down twice. Moore returned each time, but he was in trouble. After the bell, he slumped in his corner, bleeding and gasping for breath. Ketchum looked at him, then threw in the towel. Moore said, "Maybe I can still fight."

"No, no more tonight," said Ketchum. "There'll be other nights."

Davey shrugged. He seemed very tired. They squeezed water on his dark, sore face and he lay back in his pain.

The bout was stopped. I turned to my companion. "Moore can be better than he was tonight," I said. "If they fight again, I'll pick him again."

Moore got up to lean over the ring ropes. "Everything will be all right, don't worry about it," he said to a friend. "It just wasn't my night."

An announcer shoved a microphone in his broken face. "It just wasn't my night," he said.

Later, in the dressing room, he spoke to reporters for almost thirty minutes through puffed lips. "It just wasn't my night. No, I don't know what was wrong. But you fellows *know* I can fight better than I did tonight. No, the delay, the weight-making, the not going back into training, none of that stuff made any difference. It was Ramos' night and not mine. It's that simple. Sure, I want to fight him again. I wasn't as good as I can be. I'll get the title back. This just wasn't my night."

Outside, Cruz had already knocked out Torres in one round. The crowd began to drive home. Sportscaster Hank Weaver drove into a telephone pole and suffered a brain injury identical to that suffered by boxers. He lapsed into a coma, in which, despite three operations, he lay for months.

Back in the dressing room, Moore suddenly put his hands to his head, closed his eyes, moaned, and said, "Oh, my head hurts." Then he lay on his side and slid into unconsciousness. Trainer Teddy Bentham and handler Eddie Foy rushed to him. They pressed ice bags to his temples. Ketchum, frightened, called the hospital. A doctor came to Davey. An ambulance pulled up to third base of the now dark and deserted ballpark and Moore, an oxygen mask over his mouth, was rolled on a stretcher out of the dugout.

The unconscious ex-champ was taken to White Memorial Hospital, where doctors examined him. Dr. Phillip Vogel diagnosed the injury as a small, severe bruise at the base of Moore's brain. It was estimated there was swelling, but not the usual bleeding, so there would not be the usual operation. However, a tracheotomy was performed and a tube inserted in Moore's throat to assist his breathing. His pretty young wife Geraldine looked at her husband and leaned back against a nurse for support. "Oh my God," she whispered.

The vigil at the hospital began. Reporters rushed in. "No, I didn't see the fight," Geraldine told them. "I only saw two of his fights, on television, ever. Davey didn't want me to see him fight and I didn't want to, either. No, I don't blame Ramos. This was God's will to make Davey stop fighting. I pray he'll be all right. It's all I can do."

All night Davey lay in his coma. In the morning, fight fans rubbed sleep from their eyes to stare in disbelief at the headlines. "Moore?" one asked, shocked. "Are you sure? Don't you mean Torres? He was the one knocked out in one round. How could it be Moore? I saw him walk from the ring. I heard him talk."

California Governor Pat Brown called a press conference and resumed an old cry for "complete abolition of this barbaric sport."

Ramos, who had not fallen asleep until 6:00 a.m. and then had slept only four hours, had breakfast, then spoke with reporters. "I met Davey Moore once . . . at the weigh-in," he said. "He didn't act like a vain champion. He greeted me well. A very decent hombre. I liked him. . . . Fighters go into the ring to win. But we're all comrades. We're not out to hurt each other. Maybe people who don't know boxing don't understand this. *Fue cosa del destina.* It was destiny."

They got to the other fighters. Rodriguez said, "The fight should have been stopped in the eighth round, but would the public have liked that? They're very demanding, you know."

Griffith sent Ramos a telegram, then said, "I'm sorry for Ramos. I know how he feels." He clasped his hands. "Moore's in the hands of God and everything will be all right," he said.

Willie Ketchum sat in a sort of shock in the hospital waiting room. "This was just an act of God," he said. "Would you outlaw other sports in which there are injuries? I feel that boxing is as clean a sport as you will find." He slumped in his chair. "Davey Moore was one of the finest boxers and sportsmen. He led a clean life and a healthy life. I only hope God sees fit to send this boy safely home. If he does, Davey'll never enter another ring, I swear to God."

Geraldine Moore touched a hand to his shoulder. "He'll make it, Willie, he'll make it," she said. "He'll make it. I know he will."

Her mother and Davey's sister flew in to be by her side.

Unlike previously injured fighters, Davey Moore seemed in top shape and at the peak of his ability, without having had hard fights, much less taken bad beatings, prior to the critical bout. Dr. Cyril Courville said, "I have never seen an injury like this happen from a boxing glove. It's highly unusual. It might have happened through the back of the head striking the floor or the ropes."

On Sunday, Dr. Courville saw films of the fight. These showed clearly that as Moore fell backward, the base of his head hit the bottom ringrope with the full weight of his body's fall. "That was it, I'm sure of it," Dr. Courville said. "A freak accident."

Sunday, Ramos visited Mrs. Moore. "I've been so anxious. I wanted to see him or you. I am very sorry," he said, and began to weep. Geraldine Moore was composed and compassionate. "I want you to understand I'm not blaming you for anything," she said softly, facing him. "I realize it is hard for you to know you aren't to blame, but I'm closest to Davey and I'm asking you not to take it that way. It was God's act. Just please pray for Davey."

"I'm praying every night," he said, and began to cry again.

"Please don't cry," Davey's wife said. "I know Davey will be all right. I have faith in God that soon Davey'll be well again."

Ramos got up to go, hiding his face. As he left, she said, "Good luck."

At 2:20 a.m., Monday, Davey died.

Mrs. Moore, her red eyes hidden behind dark glasses, consented to a press conference. Still with great dignity and composure, she was patient and kind to her questioners. "I can't say anything about boxing," she said. "Davey loved the sport right to the end. I never wanted him to fight. He knew this. But boxing was the most important thing Davey had on his mind. He promised me this was his last year, that he would retire. He never thought it would end like this. It was an act of God, God's will. Someone had to win. Ramos just happened to be the lucky one."

She touched her hand to her head. "Would I let my sons fight? No. Davey wanted the boys to be anything but fighters. He wanted them to be doctors or lawyers. No, they won't fight, not never."

Davey had made $350,000 in his career. His last check, $26,000, went intact to his wife. Their home and apartment houses were estimated to be worth nearly $100,000. His paid-up life-insurance policy and social security would pay her approximately $300 a month. Other income would come from other properties. "I'd rather have Davey," his widow said.

Ketchum, a month later, said, "I'm going on in boxing. I wasn't going to. At first I sort of gave up. I felt terrible about Davey. I still do. I won't ever feel any different. But then I realized boxing is my life and I have to go on in it. I realized what else can a guy like me do?

"What Davey got out of boxing, and he got a great deal, he could not have gotten any other way. If it hadn't been for boxing, he wouldn't have had much of a life. Did he have much of a life this way? I don't know. But, what he had was good, pretty good, anyway. He was someone."

Other people had reacted the same way. When Davey Moore's gold coffin had been flown back to Columbus, his brother Phillip had met it at the airport. "If Davey could speak today," Phillip had said, "he would say: Don't let my death be the end of boxing."

The Time Babe Ruth
Hit One for Me

Jhan Robbins | **1 9 6 3**

Fifteen years ago Babe Ruth stood at home plate in Yankee Stadium for the last time. The occasion was the twenty-fifth anniversary of the "house that Ruth built." High point of the ceremonies was the retirement of number 3—the uniform number Ruth made famous. The microphones could not pick up the weak whisper of the ailing Babe's acknowledgments, but cheers of tribute rolled down from the stands. Only two months later many of the same fans stood in line for hours to shuffle slowly past his black-draped casket at home plate.

I was among them. I was then married with children of my own but as I looked up at the strips of bleacher seats I remembered the day in 1934 when I sat up there, a stubby teen-ager, confidently waiting for the Babe to fulfill his personal promise to hit one for me.

On that morning I could hardly wait for my mother to finish packing my lunch. "There!" she said, tucking a banana into the paper bag and knotting a string around it. "Mind your manners, behave yourself, and don't let anyone cough germs on you!"

I knew I was too excited to eat and I'm sure she knew it, too. I was off to interview Babe Ruth for my school newspaper and to see the Yankees play the Cleveland Indians. I was fourteen and unquestionably one of the "thousands of dirty-faced kids" that New York City's

Mayor Jimmy Walker said represented the Babe's highest responsibility.

Perhaps he was right. My friends and I had heard Ruth condemned in some quarters as undisciplined, loose-living, and not bright. Yet I don't think there is any athlete on any modern playing field who means as much to today's youngsters as Babe Ruth meant to us.

We worried about him. We knew his playing days were nearly over. His absurdly spindly legs were straining beneath the weight of his roly-poly body. Crippled by a bad knee, he could no longer sprint and he covered little ground in the outfield.

Although it was only mid-June, his younger teammate, Lou Gehrig, had hit eighteen home runs. Yet Ruth was still a beautiful sight at home plate. Gracefully arched fly balls flowed effortlessly from a bat that seemed merely an extension of his body. He was baseball, and to me baseball was life itself.

Caught up in a sweating, pushing crowd, I edged my way to Yankee Stadium's bleacher entrance. I knew nothing about press passes in those days. I bought a bleacher ticket. Then I showed a gate guard a carbon copy of my English teacher's elaborate request to "admit a serious student of journalism" to interview the Babe, along with the three-line response signed by Yankee owner, Colonel Jake Ruppert, saying, "Mr. Ruth will expect you."

The guard thrust a thumb over his shoulder at a gate marked "Press." I followed signs that led to the shadowy humid Yankee locker room. Famous faces popped out of the gloom. Vernon "Lefty" Gomez sat on a bench, cussing lightly over a broken shoelace. Frankie Crosetti, "Red" Ruffing, and Earle Combs were huddled in an apparently serious argument. Tony "Poosh-'em-up" Lazzeri leaned against the wall slowly flexing his knees. I puzzled for a moment over the identity of Art Jorgens, a substitute catcher.

Then a deep voice bawled from a corner, "Hey, Jorgens, maybe today you'll get your chance—Dickey looks pretty sick to me!"

I turned and dropped my lunch bag. It was the Babe. He was wearing a pair of brightly striped undershorts. I was surprised to see how tall he was. His pink moon face, lined and drooping even before the game, peered down at me like an underpowered street lamp. He was drinking soda pop and gulping handfuls of salted peanuts.

I said I had come to interview him and offered my credentials. He waved them aside.

"Fine!" he said. "Have a swig." My mother had cautioned me about germs but this was the great Bambino. I seized the cool, slippery green bottle and drank deeply.

"To what," I asked, choking, "do you owe your success?"

He chuckled. "Good, clean living," he said. I wrote it down.

I knew he was hoping to retire to a manager's job and that most sports critics considered it an absurd dream. Only that morning a columnist had written, "Babe can't even manage himself," and referred to his inability to remember signals. I mentioned the problem and was all but floored by a startling bellow of rage.

"That's the trouble with you newspaper guys," Ruth shouted. "You never forget the past! You never give a guy credit for learning anything! Maybe I lived it up in my time but don't forget I did the papers a favor—I gave you plenty to write about!

"I've settled down now," he went on. "All I want is a chance. You know I never made a wrong play on the field in my whole life. I know how to win and I can make other players do the same!"

It was about a half hour until game time, yet he straddled a bench and began to talk about his childhood. Some of the story I already knew from my conscientious study of newspaper clips.

"My old man was a bartender," he said. "I was chewing tobacco by the time I was seven. I was drinking hard whisky when I was ten. My mother died when I was fifteen. Most of my life was in and out of St. Mary's."

He meant St. Mary's Industrial School in Baltimore. A Catholic institution for orphans and neglected children, it was non-sectarian and had also at one time sheltered singer Al Jolson. There, George Herman Ruth, Jr., had learned shirt-making and tailoring—and to play baseball.

He told me that he had started as a southpaw catcher. One day he tossed a practice ball to the shortstop, who fell down complaining that Ruth had broken his hand. They made Ruth a pitcher.

Following my teacher's advice, I asked him to describe his greatest thrill in baseball. I expected him to talk about the big-league home runs that had won him world fame. Instead he replied, "The twenty-nine and two-thirds scoreless innings I pitched in the World Series for the Red Sox." Next, he said, was the 587-foot hit he had in Tampa, Florida, in the spring of 1919.

"I wasn't even born!" I exclaimed reverently. The Babe reached for another bottle of pop and downed it with a swift gurgle. I remembered the stories about his near-death in Asheville, North Carolina, in 1925 when he collapsed at the railway station after consuming a dozen sodas and fifteen hot dogs on a brutally hot day. He was hospitalized and declared in such bad shape that an English newspaper had published his obituary. Now, I nervously sought to keep him talking. I asked him what he thought about when he was in the batter's box.

"Well, you're all alone out there," he answered slowly. "You're expected to belt it. You don't want to let anybody down. But I don't worry about how I'm going to hit. I don't bother trying to outguess the field. I think about the pork chops I had the night before and if there shoulda been more salt in the barbecue sauce. Or I wonder if Claire will like that watch I just bought her as a surprise present. Or if I look good in a tux. But the second the pitcher rears back everything goes out of mind but that ball. What I see is the heart of it. That's what I lean into."

I knew that the Babe always made dramatic copy. He told me about the wisecrack he had made while negotiating his 1932 contract. Colonel Ruppert had said that Ruth's 1931 salary—$80,000—was more than President Hoover's. Ruth had said: "I had a better year."

We talked about his batting slump. He hadn't had a hit in his last seventeen trips to the plate. He told me it was just tough luck.

The other players rose, stretched and began moving out to the field. I rattled on desperately: "I read that you have a prize bull terrier. My uncle has a bull terrier, too."

He grinned. "My manager, Joe McCarthy, looks like a bull terrier. You can print that."

He stood and headed for the field door. "So long, keed," he said. "You going to see the game?"

"Oh, yes!"

"Well, sit tight," he said, "and I'll show you I still got plenty. I'll hit one just for you!"

I forgot I was a "newspaper guy." "Honest?" I gasped.

"Promise," he said. "I'll stamp your name right on the ball."

I still have the faded, dog-eared yellow copy paper on which I recorded the interview. At the bottom is my thoroughly unprofessional conclusion: "The Babe great as ever," I wrote, "and I am about to go down in history!"

The sun was bright and the temperature, as I climbed into the stands, was in the nineties. It had rained lightly that morning and clouds of steam rose from the turf. I made myself a sun helmet from a section of newspaper and, together with a crowd of fifteen thousand, cheered the Yankees and booed the Indians.

Ruth walked his first turn up. Not his fault, I told myself, and I glared at the cowardly opposing pitcher. The next time up Babe struck out. He swung mightily at the third pitch, lost his balance and fell heavily on his bad knee. I was too far away to see his face but I winced with a real pain.

A bushy-haired man in front of me howled, "Ya bum! Why dontcha quit, ya good-for-nothin' has-been!" As Ruth made his way to right field, the man yelled again, "Why don't they turn ya out to pasture?"

I leaned forward slightly and somehow the wad of gum I was chewing fell in the man's hair. I started to tell him what had happened when he bellowed, "Hey, Ruth, want me to bring a rockin' chair out for ya?"

I didn't mention the gum.

Two innings later an infield pop-up stretched out Ruth's no-hitting streak, but Gehrig hit a clean single scoring Earle Combs, and the Yankees went ahead 6 to 3.

Then it happened. Ruth came up at the end of the eighth inning. A hush settled over the wilted spectators. Those who were on their way out stopped in the aisles. It was clear from any point in the stadium that the Babe was straining at the plate, tense and scowling.

I can still hear the crack of leather as the ball took off on the first pitch, high and black against the glaring blue sky. I leaped to my feet screaming with joy. This one was for me. The ball skimmed to the right, along the first-base line, headed for the fence with speed and height to spare. No successful rocket-firing at Canaveral has generated more pride and fellowship in the human heart than I felt at that moment. The Babe could do anything—he was the greatest!

At the last moment a gust of wind pushed the ball across the foul line. Ruth lined out to first on the next pitch.

Although the game ended with a Yankee victory, I walked out of the park downcast. It was that pitcher, I muttered to myself. He didn't give Babe anything good to hit. I decided to wait for Ruth outside the clubhouse. If I felt bad, I reasoned, imagine how he felt.

Ruth emerged onto the sidewalk freshly shaved and even more pink-cheeked than before the game. He was wearing a silk shirt, a bow tie and a bright plaid jacket and smoking a big cigar. I stopped him as he plunged toward a waiting Cadillac.

"Gee, Babe!" I said. "I'm sure sorry! You're still tops even if you didn't hit that homer you promised me. Thanks for trying."

He glanced at me, puzzled. Then he remembered. "I didn't feel so good today," he said, grinning. "I had a bellyache. Maybe too much beer and sour pickles?" He pounded my shoulder. "But tell you what. I'll hit one for you tomorrow! Absolutely! First chance I get! You can take my word for it! Okay?"

He grabbed my scorecard out of my hands and scribbled his name on it. I couldn't speak. He had let me down with his empty boasts and futile promises—and he could kid about it! The Babe returned the card with a flourish. He stepped into the limousine, bellowed a joke at the driver and was driven away.

The subway ride back to my home on the outskirts of Brooklyn took an hour and twenty-five minutes. I jammed the autographed scorecard in my pocket. What good was his signature if he couldn't face up to the truth? He was through! He had almost made a fool of me but not quite —I could see through him now.

The following day was also hot but dry and very clear. I wasn't at the ballpark. My sister and I were detailed to wash windows. As I wrung the chamois, I thought about the Babe. I felt my sense of outrage disappear and a great tenderness toward the aging Ruth took its place. It was no disgrace to be a has-been. Nothing could dim the luster of a batter who could hit sixty homers in a single season. If he needed to believe he still could do so, it was all right with me. I'd cheer him until he could no longer lift a bat.

There were no Yankee radio broadcasts in those days. I kept slipping down to the corner newsstand to wait for the early sports edition. At last it came, hurled from a truck, and the news vendor cut the cord around the bundle. High in the left hand corner of the front page was the second-inning score: New York 5—Chicago 0. And a big black headline read: BABE BLASTS GRAND SLAMMER.

I saw Babe Ruth play only a few more times. My family moved to the Southwest for four years and by the time we returned his career was over. Now my sons and their friends ask me about him. I hardly know what to say. He was a great ballplayer. He was also self-indulgent, dissolute, and a braggart. Still, he helped me to discover compassion and that it is necessary to separate love from idolatry. He was the first person to treat me like a real "newspaper guy," and to make me feel as though I could be one. Years later, having had more complicated conversations with presidents, prime ministers and politicians, I still look back on it as a pretty good interview.

I'm glad Commissioner Frick ruled that Roger Maris' sixty-one home runs in a 162-game season is a separate record and that Babe

Ruth's sixty homers in 154 games still stands. I wonder, sometimes, about the home-run ball he hit the day after I talked to him. I suppose it is still a treasured souvenir on someone's bookshelf. But I shall always believe it has my name on it.

Boxing's Artful Brothers

Myron Cope | **1 9 6 3**

The telephone rang in the office of Chris Dundee Promotions, Miami Beach. Chris Dundee, a stocky, olive-skinned man wearing black-rimmed spectacles almost as thick as magnifying glasses, picked up the receiver and was told by an operator that Tony Zale was calling collect from Jacksonville. "What's he doing in Jacksonville?" said Dundee, talking to himself. "Okay, put it through."

"Chris! Chris! Whaddaya say, Chris?" cried a hearty voice on the other end of the line.

"This is not Tony Zale," replied Dundee, coldly, in his deep, rasping voice.

"Sure it is. I need three hundred dollars real bad, Chris."

"Can you prove you're Zale?"

"Sure."

"Okay, do you remember the New Year's Eve celebration?"

"Sure."

"Where?"

"Norfolk."

"What hotel?"

"The Monticello."

"Who was with you?"

"My wife."

"Who else?"

"It's hard to remember."

"Well, the chief of police was there."

"Oh, yeah. Yeah, the chief."

"What was his name?"

"Gee, I don't remember. That goes back a long way."

Click. End of conversation. Dundee turned from the phone and said, "The chief's name was Mason Holland. Zale would remember. He was stationed in Norfolk when he came back from overseas, and the chief was his buddy."

If you're a fight promoter, you have to be a detective in the bargain. Who needs the aggravation? Why promote boxing? It's dead, isn't it? The obituaries are entitled *Who Killed Boxing?* or *Why Boxing Is Dead* or *Can Boxing Come Back?* The thwacking sounds of fists upon speed bags, the odor of arena cigar-smoke, the shrill but entertaining lies of promoters and managers have faded to the fringe of American sports. But in Miami Beach, Chris Dundee holds out, a survivor of a lost tribe. In fact, he makes a nice living doing it, which is why he puts up with pseudo Tony Zales calling from Jacksonville.

Thrashing upstream against the trend, Dundee promotes a minimum of twenty-five boxing shows a year, most of them in the Miami Beach Auditorium, some next door at the recently built Convention Hall. In the fifties he was able to stage as many as forty bouts a year, yet if he has had to cut back volume somewhat he remains superbly confident that his promotional instincts are being used to whip a horse that is still very much alive. A visionary, Dundee booked a bout between Kid Gavilan and Tiger Jones in the Siam Room of the plush Carillon Hotel in 1958, prompting Miami sportswriter Tommy Fitzgerald to observe that if Sinatra, Bogart, Flynn, and Tone could fight in nightclubs, why not boxers like Kid Gavilan and Tiger Jones?

Gavilan and Jones sold out (at eight dollars tops), so Dundee came back shortly thereafter with Jay Fullmer and Gale Kerwin in the Fontainebleau.

"The trouble with boxing," declares The Innovator, "those fellows in New York, they live in the past. You become an old man living in the past. People say, 'In our day the Twist would have been disgraceful.' What's disgraceful?"

So intent is Dundee on remaining young that with a straight face he gives his birth date as February 25, 1917, which would make him forty-five. His kid brother Angelo, who just turned forty, laughs.

"Chris was thirty-nine for five years," says Angelo, a slight man of mild disposition, "but when I turned forty he couldn't very well stay thirty-nine, could he? So now he says he's forty-five. *I* don't know how old he is, and that's the truth."

Angelo is the same kind of freak as his brother. He, too, refuses to believe boxing is dead, and as a result, he, too, makes a nice living out of it. He trains fighters—Cassius Clay is his Exhibit A today—and works as a "cut man" in corners. He also manages fighters (among them, Willie Pastrano, Ralph Dupas, and Harold Gomes) and acts as a "representative," which means that for a price he will line up bouts for fighters whose managers lack either the know-how, connections, or energy to do it themselves.

As a manager and representative, Angelo is forbidden by law to act as a promoter, but as an advisor and trouble-shooter he is to Chris what Bobby is to JFK, what Milton was to Ike. Together, the brothers Dundee complement one another so well that the sheer clamor of their activity makes it impossible for boxing to die in Miami Beach.

If Grand Central Station suddenly shrank to the size of a phone booth, it would approximate the commotion that goes on daily in the office of Chris Dundee Promotions. The office, located off the lobby of the Auditorium, is slightly larger than a Volkswagen. Stuffed into it are a counter, a desk, a table, a file cabinet, and a small cupboard that hides a bottle of Scotch for occasions. The walls are obliterated by dozens of photographs in which Chris is posed with everyone from Gene Tunney, the boxer, to Gene Tierney, the babe.

As in a Japanese rice paddy, every inch of ground is put to use. The occupants include Chris, Angelo, press agent Herb Lowe, a Cuban exile named Jess Losado who is Chris's publicist to the Spanish media in Miami, and approximately half a dozen old-timers who seem to have some sort of quasi-official status as aides-de-camp. Added to this population is a steady procession of passers-through: Evil Eye Finkel, Sam (The Mumbler) Sobel, boxing commissioners (Miami Beach alone has five), out-of-town newspapermen who drop by nostalgically to hear once again the sounds of a live boxing office, and guys on the bum for passes. It is so quiet you could hear a bomb drop.

A little, shriveled old guy wearing an American Legion cap walks in and does ten knee-bends and a soft shoe dance before the counter. He then announces, "I'm seventy-six years young!" and departs. Nobody notices.

Two telephones on Chris's desk scream at him constantly, like spoiled children. If it is the day before a fight show, he must phone approximately 180 people, whose names and telephone numbers are on a list of prime customers. It is possible they haven't read the sports pages and don't know there's a fight coming up. "Hello!" says Chris to the party on the other side of town. "You're lookin' good!" And so it goes.

Familiar faces and unfamiliar ones continue to drift in and out of the office. Chris turns to Angelo, who is busy pecking out a letter on a typewriter, and says, "Did you see the guy about the thing?"

"Yes," says Angelo. No more need be said. The brothers Dundee, not caring to share their affairs with every fellow who comes by the office, speak in a code that nobody has managed to break.

Chris is on long-distance, trying to persuade a manager to have his boy fight Allan Harmon, a young Jamaican light-heavyweight owned by Angelo. "Harmon is all shot," Chris shouts. "He can't fight." It's a con job and the manager on the other end of the line knows it, but he finally takes the fight. Chris hangs up and Harmon, who has been standing there, says in his British accent: "I shall not fight for you. You said I am all shot, that I cannot fight."

Chris has to calm down Harmon.

Occasionally violence erupts. A while ago two managers, whose fighters had battled to a disputed decision the night before, slugged it out in the Dundee office, between the desk and the counter. "It was a lousy fight," says Chris. "Managers cannot fight."

Chris Dundee has a shrewd head for business and it is reasonable to assume that he might make just as comfortable a living running a nice, quiet shoe store or a five-and-ten. But to his way of thinking, boxing not only is alive but is only now approaching the mother lode. He has a dream:

It is 1:00 p.m. of a Saturday afternoon in Miami, 1967. The contestants are climbing into the ring to fight for the heavyweight championship of the world. The crowd in the Orange Bowl awaits, tense with anticipation.

It is 6:00 p.m. in London, Belfast and Lisbon, where theaters are packed with fans who have paid to see the telecast of the fight. They will have a late dinner, as is European custom anyhow. It is 7:00 p.m. in the theaters of Amsterdam, Copenhagen and Paris—8:00 p.m. in Athens, 9:00 in Moscow. In Los Angeles it is ten o'clock in the morning, but what the heck, it's Saturday, and it's just like getting up to watch a World Series telecast from Yankee Stadium. In Bangkok it's 1:00 a.m. but the fight fans there are so nutty they'd turn out if it were 4:00 a.m.

All over the world fans have paid to see the theater telecast, transmitted over trans-oceanic cables, and the gross receipts will amount to so many millions that one dares not estimate. And back at Miami, Chris Dundee, promoter of the championship fight, is about to become so wealthy that in Philadelphia, where he grew up selling candy bars on trains, they may have to consider listing him in the social register, right up there with Princess Grace and the Biddles.

All this, of course, is his dream, but there is the barest chance it will come true.

"You realize that two, three, five years from now you'll put a fighter on television and people will see it around the whole world?" demands Chris. "Once that cable gets around . . . well, boy, you gotta dream, that's all. You know where the big crowds are today? Europe! Asia! We don't have the big fights in this country. You realize how much money there will be in closed circuit TV going to all of Europe and part of Asia? One hundred million people watching a fight! I don't see how it can be more than four years away."

Chris may sound as wacky as another Chris (last name, Columbus) once sounded, but there are two reasons for at least listening to him:

First, in the year 1950, when television was coming into its own, presaging the death of fight clubs around the nation, Dundee gave up his occupation as a manager of boxers in order to become a promoter in Miami Beach. It seemed like a frying-pan-to-fire suicide, but to this day he has promoted regularly and profitably, twelve months a year for more than twelve years, while boxing has died off in dozens of cities.

Secondly, Dundee may have the connections to cash in on that multimillion-dollar 1967 fight, for he has been installing the wiring for the past year or so. Here's the setup:

The heavyweight of the future is Cassius Marcellus Clay of Louisville. Clay, a 1960 Olympic champion, is owned by a syndicate of businessmen. They hired Angelo Dundee to train Clay. Angelo trains him in Miami's Fifth Street Gym, which is owned by Chris. From time to time Clay fights in Miami Beach, under Chris's promotion. Everybody is getting along fine—Clay, the businessmen, Angelo, Chris. Therefore, Chris reasons, if Clay ever does win the title and then defends it on world-wide television, is it not reasonable to hope that his managers would deal in Chris Dundee Promotions as promoter, or at least as part promoter?

It's a long-shot hope, but what's to lose hoping?

Meanwhile, the Dundee brothers are, in a sense, out of place in their business. They wear clean shirts, speak to fighters civilly, and do not chew unlit cigars.

Angelo is never heard to employ the managerial pronoun—that is,

"I'm fighting in New York Friday." With Angelo, it is "Clay's fighting in New York Friday." Or whoever the fighter may be. Most managers seem to regard such dialogue as a dangerous admission that fighters are people, but Angelo says, "The fighter does the fighting. I don't."

Chris, as he steers the public through his turnstiles, is somewhat more proprietary. "I like to bet I know 90 percent of my faces," he says. "Names I don't remember." If you vacation in Miami Beach and attend a fight, you become the property of Chris Dundee.

Traditionally, fight promoters have been men whose business and social relationships seldom expand beyond a circle of fight men, bookies, used-car salesmen, and gangsters, but Chris Dundee, regarding himself as a legitimate member of the world of small business, belongs to the Chamber of Commerce, the Elks, the Eagles, and the Exchange Club. He has admitted that mobster Frankie Carbo "ain't a bad guy socially" and he doubtless has never gone out of his way to tread on the corns of boxing's tough guys, but he is vocally in step with recent reformations, saying, "I think it's best for all those people to be away from boxing." On a wall in his office he proudly displays plaques awarded him by veterans' organizations, for whom he has staged boxing shows that did not earn him a dime. In short, if somebody doesn't stop him, he is liable to give boxing a bad name by becoming a pillar of the community.

Actually, being the up-to-date man of the sixties that he is, Chris is conscious of the fact that this is an era of mass public relations. While corporations employ expensive advertising and public relations agencies to make the public detergent-conscious or wine-conscious or hair-oil-conscious, Dundee strives to make Miami boxing-conscious. How is it done?

Well, he recently suggested to this writer that we go to the races at Gulfstream. "Meet me at the office at two."

When I arrived I remarked that we would be too late for the double but I wondered whether Chris knew of any good things running in the later races. "I don't go to bet," he replied. "I go to the track to be seen.

"People see Chris Dundee, what do they think of? Boxing! They think of boxing! I make them boxing-*conscious*." (At Christmastime Chris and Angelo fan out their image via some twelve hundred greeting cards.)

We arrived at the track after the fourth race, and Chris proceeded through the crowd shaking hands like Lyndon Johnson campaigning for office. "Those two guys I just said hello to are mayors," he said. "One's mayor of Jersey City and the other's mayor of somewhere else."

I suggested we bet the number-3 horse, Star Trust, in the fifth. "Why not?" said Chris. Star Trust finished second behind the number-1 horse and as I tore up my ticket I regretted aloud that I had touted Chris on a loser. "That's okay," he said. "I also bet the number-1 horse on the sly. I liked the name. Profit and Loss." You can take a promoter out of his box office, but you can't take the box office out of the promoter.

Between races a man approached our box, an expression of deep concern furrowing his brow. "Chris," he said, in a low voice, "I say this as a friend. As a *friend,* believe me.

"The preliminaries, Chris. The last couple of shows, the preliminaries were bad. I had eight people with me at the last show, and they didn't none of them like the preliminaries. I tell you as a friend, Chris."

"I appreciate it," said Chris, earnestly. The concerned man departed, whereupon Chris said, "You see? You learn from the customers. I hadn't realized the preliminaries had gone sour."

"Hey, Chris," said a man, leaning over his shoulder. "You got mustard on your suit."

"How did I do *that?*" exclaimed Chris. "I gotta go wash that off. It's disgraceful! I can't be seen like this."

The would-be community pillar was back for the sixth race and we watched a horse called Jam-Tootin move ahead on the far turn. Chris glanced at his program and arose screaming. "I shoulda' bet that horse!" he cried. "That's Jim Norris' horse! Spring Hill Farm!" The horse won.

Later, driving back to town, Chris explained that Jim Norris once had loaned him $10,000, interest-free, so that he could buy a partnership in a bowling alley. Dundee unhesitatingly declares that Norris, whose International Boxing Club was broken up by the government, was a benefactor to him, for beginning in 1953 Norris assigned him lucrative TV bouts from time to time. "He was good to me," said Chris, "but I was good for them.

"I had an organization. The TV people didn't have to worry that their announcers wouldn't be supplied with the publicity material, or that there wouldn't be emergency prelims ready, or any details like that. They'd come down here, everything would be set."

A stranger visiting Dundee's office may wonder how anything gets done amid such disorganization, but the truth is that nothing is left undone. And that's the main reason the Dundee brothers survive. "Hard work gets you there," says Chris. "Too many people in boxing don't work. Like at Stillman's in New York—they'd gather around and gab all day."

Chris Dundee Promotions has hewn to a formula that seems to have escaped other promoters in these hard times. What attracts steady customers? Consistently interesting shows. What makes interesting shows? Not necessarily outstanding or famous fighters but, rather, outstanding *matches.* One night Dundee suffered through two terribly dull preliminaries at the Auditorium. Planning his next show, he ignored the winners of the two bouts but matched the losers. They put on an interesting fight. Their styles were suited.

While promoters in other cities have waited for a supply of fighters to fall into their laps, meanwhile bemoaning the scarcity of talent, the Dundees have been busy prospecting the gulches.

Item: Chris loses $1200 per year maintaining the Fifth Street Gym, but more than thirty fighters train there. He spends at least an hour a day there to see which fighters are in shape to put on a good show, if only a four-rounder.

Item: If there is a fight show in San Juan, Kingston, Nassau, or Bimini, Chris Dundee will likely be there, scouting for new fighters. "Why should Americans go in for boxing?" says Chris, a keen student of the economy as it concerns boxing. "Conditions make fighters. The way things are today, most of your fighters will have to come from out of the country. Once they show, they'll draw." It is not surprising, then, to find on Chris' desk a copy of England's *Boxing News* (price ninepence) and a copy of *Guia Pugilistica,* the Latin American counterpart of Nat Fleischer's *Ring Record Book.* No isolationist is Chris Dundee. He has taught himself to read Spanish. Angelo can both read it and speak it.

Item: Angelo, as one of the top corner men in the business, travels all over the country, as well as to Paris, London, and South America. He is, therefore, Chris's chief talent scout. "He's like a baseball pitcher," an office hanger-on says. "He's got a book in his head on hundreds of fighters." Angelo, a one-man CIA, employs agents across the ocean to keep him posted on foreign fighters. A recent letter to him from his lookout in Putney, England, concluded: "You have paid a near season on my stuff. No need to send anything for a long time. Thank you anyway. Times are not good but I do not want to be a burden. I appreciate your friendship, which is far more than money."

Who ever heard of such talk in the fight game?

Angelo also has been accused, by implication, of such misconduct as worrying about the physical well-being of a fighter. As cut man for Carmen Basilio, he was in Basilio's corner the night in 1958 when Sugar Ray Robinson gave Basilio as ugly an eye as had been seen in a ring for many years. In the fifth round Basilio's left eye became a large, firmly closed blob. "Let's stop the fight," said Angelo Dundee.

"Oh, no," said Basilio, who detested Robinson. "Nobody's gonna stop *this* fight." Basilio went the distance, though he lost, and in the days following the fight the talk among men in the trade was that if Angelo had cut the eye that is, reduced the swelling by making an incision with a razor blade Basilio might have won.

Angelo has no regrets, however. "I noticed that the blood was coming from the corner of the eye," he explains. "So I figured there must be torn muscles inside. The doctor told me after the fight that if I had cut that eye I should have been thrown in jail."

To this day Angelo has yet to cut an eye. Delivering a short, sardonic lecture on corner work, he says, "The eye is cut with a sterile razor blade, *if there is such a thing.*"

Chris, too, seems to have suffered from an unprofessional soft heart. Back in the thirties, when he was living in Norfolk, Virginia, and having trouble meeting his room rent, he passed up a golden opportunity to slap a libel suit on the Norfolk *Ledger-Dispatch,* one of whose sportswriters had written of a fighter: "He hit the deck and bounced like one of Chris Dundee's checks."

Although Chris and the sportswriter had not been on speaking terms, Chris called off his lawyer when the sportswriter told him the lawsuit would cost him his job.

The sportswriter, Charley Reilly, remained employed and today is an executive of the same newspaper. He has made no secret of the episode, and perhaps that's one reason why sportswriters have helped Dundee at every opportunity since. As a matter of fact, two of them put him where he is today by suggesting, back in 1950, that he set up shop in the new auditorium Miami Beach was building. They arranged for him to be interviewed by city officials, who subsequently awarded him a lease.

Dundee would be the last to say his success in Miami Beach proves that boxing can be profitably promoted in any large city. For one thing he also promotes weekly wrestling shows to insure himself against financial losses suffered in boxing. "We average two thousand people for the wrestling," he says. "I don't make much money but the crowds are consistent." The wrestlers are furnished by a Florida circuit, which makes the matches, takes 50 percent of the gate, and presumably decides who is to win. "They won't tell me," says Chris, "and I don't care to find out. I'll tell you why: If I know who's going to win, it takes the kicks out of it for me."

While the reliable wrestling revenue has helped stabilize the finances of his boxing promotions, Dundee also has benefited from television more than most promoters. At one time, when the networks showed three fights a week, Chris received as many as twelve TV bouts in one year. Network TV fare, however, dropped from three bouts per week to two, and then to one, which means Dundee may expect possibly three TV bouts a year. But he likes it that way. Says Chris: "One TV show a week is better for boxing than two. But don't tell me boxing would be better off with no TV. I think we'd be dead without television. The only way a fighter gets a name today is on television."

Television revenue has dwindled and Dundee's wrestling "cushion" will last only as long as the wrestling craze does, but boxing is his game and he will go on busily promoting it. On fight night he is a nervous wreck—he even delivers Rockne-type pep talks to the fighters in their dressing rooms—and five or ten years from now he'll still be fussing to see that the guys in the $1.50 seats are comfortable.

Meanwhile, if there is a footnote to be added to his thirteen years of fight promotion in Miami Beach, it is the remarkable fact that he has never had to cancel a show.

Some years ago Chief Crazy Horse was arrested the night before he was to box on a Dundee show, but Dundee persuaded the Dade County district attorney to lend him the fighter for a few hours. After the bout, Crazy Horse was whisked back to his cell. When Dundee recently was reminded that the bout had been only a semi-windup, he shrugged.

"You don't like to break up your show if you can help it," he said. With that, he looked across his desk to brother Angelo and in the code said, "Did you call the guy about the kid?"

"Yes," said Angelo. Both of Chris's telephones rang at once, and he picked up the receivers and proceeded to carry on two conversations simultaneously.

Joe DiMaggio and Little Joe

Johnny Lujack

Doak Walker

Jackie Robinson with Don Newcombe

Alan Ameche

Ted Williams

Oscar Robertson at the University of Cincinnati

Floyd Patterson

Stan Musial

Bobby Hull

Zoilo Versalles

Bill Russell

Alex Karras

Tom Landry

Sandy Koufax

Gale Sayers

Pancho Gonzales

Willie Mays

Lew Alcindor

Muhammad Ali

Stan Musial's Last Game

Arnold Hano | **1 9 6 4**

Sunday, September 29, 1963, dawned grayly dismal in St. Louis, but by the time Stanley Frank Musial had put on a black suit with a black shadow stripe, and had gone to an early Mass and returned home, the day had become bright and invigorating. A brisk, nearly chilling wind rustled the young trees in southwest St. Louis, where Musial lives with his family, and an observer could see that the leaves had started to turn brownly gold.

Sunday, September 29 was the last day Stan Musial would play major-league baseball, and Musial's family and a scattering of neighbors stood outside the nine-room house on Westway Drive, to wish Musial luck as he climbed into his blue air-conditioned Cadillac. Before he got behind the wheel, the ballplayer turned to his four-year-old daughter Jean.

"Where are you going to be today?" he asked.

"On the *field*," the girl said.

"That's right." And Musial laughed his delighted, delightful laugh, and tooled the big car from the driveway into the street, to begin the twenty-minute stretch to Busch Stadium.

It was 10:30. Musial had had breakfast—scrambled eggs and bacon —with his family and with actor and oldtime friend Horace McMahon.

Now Musial and McMahon sat in the front seat of the Caddy. In the rear were this writer, a *Life* writer, and a photographer from *Look,* drawn together for the last day in the career of the most enduring ballplayer of our time.

It was an uneventful trip to the park, or, rather, a trip of small events. So was the day. A few blocks from the house, a car pulled alongside Musial's, and a little girl, sitting next to her father, began to bounce in her seat. As the two cars moved along, Musial rolled down the window, and the other driver, flushed with pleasure, called, "I hope you hit a homer today, Stan," and the girl said, "Me, too. Me, too."

Musial grinned. "I'll settle for a little—" And his voice trailed off.

It was a trip, too, of small talk. Musial didn't know how many innings he'd play. He pointed out an area where an amusement park had recently burned down. He showed us his restaurant. He said he was taking a different route on this last day, but did not say why. Nobody asked. He volunteered, "I used to drive fast. I'm not a fast driver any more." He reflected, and said, "I never was a wild driver."

Then he laughed—Musial's trademark, other than a base hit, is his laugh—and made a remark that was to be a recurring theme all this long last day. "I could upset things—tell 'em I'm making a comeback."

In the city proper, Musial nodded his head at new buildings that had become part of St. Louis University, and Horace McMahon asked bluntly, "Why don't you go to college now?"

"I might," Musial said. Then he reflected again. "No. Not to a regular college. I might take—you know—private—"

"You could go," McMahon said. "After a few days, they'd leave you alone. You could take rhetoric, public speaking, the things you're interested in."

Musial drove in silence, and then he said something which indicated where his mind was. "After all this, I don't know what I'm going to say yet." There would be ceremonies on the field, and after the honoring celebrities had spoken, it would be Musial's turn. What does a man say after twenty-three years? Horace McMahon said, "You know what song they should sing on your last day? 'September Song.' "

And memory, nostalgia lulled the car into silence. You could play with the words of "September Song." It had been a long long way, from May to December. The days had already shortened. Life had crested for all of us, in that car, and had started the downhill run. It would have been a cruel choice, "September Song," but a perfect choice.

The car pulled onto Spring Street, outside Busch Stadium, at 10:53, and as has been his habit for years, Musial parked behind an old hot-dog stand. As Musial walked toward the stadium, a man rushed up and grabbed his hand. "You came to the hospital to see my boy, Tommy, when he was shot. You gave him a ball."

"Did he do real good?" Musial asked.

"He's here today," the man said, and Musial nodded, satisfied, and headed for the players' entrance. A woman pushed her son behind Musial. "Don't be afraid, Mike. You'll never see him play again. Go on up and shake his hand." But Musial was wrestling his way inside, and the woman said forlornly: "Well, it's too late." The words of "September Song" were haunting; you can't play a waiting game.

The Cardinal locker room is long and narrow; one end leads to a so-called players' lounge, cold and dreary. The other end opens on a corridor with a shower room, a toilet, manager Johnny Keane's office, and the trainer's room. Busch Stadium is an old and seedy ballpark. The dirt of the infield looks dirtier than the dirt at most parks. The stadium has a scoreboard which may be unique; it has no room for the batting order of the two teams. The park is so cramped and tiny it has an intimate look. It is a throwback field, more like old Ebbets Field than any other park, and the motif carries into the locker room. Cramped, small, intimate. Musial's locker is flanked by Red Schoendienst's and Ken Boyer's. Musial went quickly to the small open cubicle, but the photographers insisted he make another entrance, this time through a different door, and another theme began to assert itself: the essential falsity of photographs. One word is worth a thousand pictures. Musial would be seen entering one door; actually he had come in another. "You guys are going to wear me out," Musial said. And laughed.

Stacked inside one of Musial's spiked shoes were six telegrams. Musial read them. Then he said to Dave Boyer, seven-year-old son of the Cardinal third-baseman: "Dave, you be my secretary?" and the boy nodded and took the wadded telegram envelopes and disposed of them.

Small talk. Small events. Stan Musial is an undramatic man. He has an uncluttered mind. He is not obsessed with the ego problems that infest Ted Williams; he has none of the depressive fears that grip Willie Mays; he cannot showboat like Willie Davis; he has none of the fitful violence of Al Dark or Gene Mauch. He answers your questions quickly and from the surface of his brain. Somebody later asked him if he had a single enemy, and Musial said quickly: "I hope not." He seldom digs deeply into his own thoughts. He has a standard greeting:

"Hi-ya. Whaddya think? Whaddya say?" It is an automatic greeting, and he is not really much interested in what you think or say, but as a gambit it turns the conversation from himself. It may be that Stan Musial is a shy man.

Yet Stan Musial enjoys the limelight. Not because it pampers him, but because it has become habit, and he is a creature of habit, a man made comfortable by old, worn things. If there was tension playing on Stan Musial this last day, it would have to rise from saying good-bye to old worn things.

The day crawled. Musial lit a cigar, sitting on a red stool. He said, "I want to get the uniform on quick—quickly. That's what I came down for." But he didn't put on the uniform for an hour and ten minutes, and you could read what you wanted to read into his reluctance to do something he would never do again. Sam Jones walked into the locker room and sniffed. "Why don't you smoke a dollar *see*-gar? Those two for a nickel jobs gotta go." Musial is close to a chain smoker, and though he is surely not a neurotic man, he is a nervous man. He smokes his factory cigarillos that cost more than two for a nickel, but not much, about an inch down before he throws them away. He is constantly jogging his foot up and down or rubbing his hair or his mouth. He is a man of small quick movements—unlike most athletes who tend to big lazy slow moves, graceful and catlike—and all these mannerisms came on strongly this last day. He smoked quickly and with a frown, and he said to the photographers: "Now, none of these cigar pictures." He meant it. "I'll be able to tell my friends by the cigar pictures I see. I don't want the kids to see me with a big cigar in my mouth." Then Musial strode into the trainer's room, where he hugged trainer Bob Bauman. Bauman loves Musial about as deeply as one healthy man can love another. Bauman says his job will never be the same, now that Musial is gone. In the rubbing room, Curt Flood waited his turn on the table. A radio was playing, and Marty Bronson, a local nightclub entertainer, was singing the current St. Louis hit: "Stan the Man." Flood sang along with Bronson: "The world is better just by knowing"—*beat, beat*—"Stan the Man." Back in the locker room Musial looked around, as the press had thickened, ballplayers arriving, more visitors, more newsmen. "This is like a World Series," Musial said, and Ken Boyer added sourly: "Only thing missing is the money and the Yankees." A man who identified himself as Dr. C. C. Humphreys, president of Memphis State University, came in with his two sons, Hunter, eleven, and Cecil, eight. Musial grabbed the boys and stared closely. "You guys gonna be ballplayers?" and the kids nodded, and Musial said, "Can you hit 'em?" There would be other boys in front of Musial this day, and to each Musial asked the same question: "Can you hit 'em?" But once he got serious. "Don't ever smoke," he said. The boys surely saw his cigars. "I smoke," he said, "but I don't inhale." One boy said, "I'll just puff, too," but Musial shook his head and said sternly: "Don't smoke."

Little else was serious. Sam Jones was scattering sneezing powder. Ernie Broglio looked at Musial coldly and said, "You just gonna sit there all day? Do something for once." Gary Kolb held Musial's bat and said, "You wouldn't think a guy could make so much money out of a little thing like this."

At 11:40, Musial said, "Fellers, I just changed my mind. I'm not retiring." He got his laugh, but it was forced. So had been Musial's remark. He kept forcing it all day.

There was a TV interview on his stool, and Musial said to Horace McMahon: "I don't want *never* to get in your business. How can you relax in front of a camera? What do you take to calm me down—tranquilizers?" A player said, "Cutty Sark and water," and this time the laugh was natural.

A tanned, graying, smiling, silent man came up to Musial, and Musial shouted in joy: "Here's the guy whose place I took." A writer said, "Who's that?" and Musial stared in disbelief. "You don't know Joe Medwick?" A baseball player's world—like any entertainer's—is insular. He cannot imagine anybody not knowing Joe Medwick, even twenty years after Medwick had quit. Later, a heavy-set sandy-haired man would come in, and Musial would greet him as "George," and this observer had to strain his memory to see that it was Whitey Kurowski. The hubbub in the room now increased; the room became warm and funky with fresh sweat. Horace McMahon was saying loudly: "I loved baseball; he loved the theater. That's how we met. I met him in New York in '48, '49. I was in *Detective Story*." Had a man foreign to the event walked in, it would have been difficult to tell why the crowd was there. Musial does not demand the spotlight—like a Ted Williams—nor does it naturally gravitate toward him, as toward a Dizzy Dean. But the crowd's head pivoted when a writer asked, "Will you play until you get a hit?"

"Yes," Musial said.

"Do you know what number hit it will be?"

"No."

Somebody told him he had 3628 hits. Another hit would be 3629.

Musial grinned wickedly. "I would like 3630. I like those round even figures."

"You mean," the writer said, "you'd like two hits instead of one." And Musial laughed.

Then Musial said, "If I don't get a hit, it's not going to worry me. I'd like to get it for the fans, but— How does it go? The best laid plans go —haywire?"

And the *Life* man said, "There you go again, quoting Shakespeare," and Musial said, delighted, "Is that Shakespeare? Me?"

At two minutes past noon, Musial began to undress. "It's kind of cold," he said to himself. "Put on a heavy one." He pulled on a long-sleeved sweatshirt. He kept his back to the crowd, and dressed, and there was a growing rhythm to what he was doing. He began slowly, talking and dressing, tugging on the sweatshirt, buttoning its collar, and slowly putting on the white underdrawers, and then the long white socks, and then his jock, and then, moving slightly more quickly, the colored oversocks, red, with red, white, and dark-blue stripes. Then his pants, with the red piping. His left shoe, his right. Now he was moving quickly, gracefully. The shirt, with the red big number 6, went on swiftly, and Musial's fingers were swift at the buttons, and as he put on the shirt, photographers said, "Wait a minute, Stan, look this way," and Musial said, "Sure," and then photographers on the other side wailed, "*This* way, Stan," and Musial had to unbutton and button again, but he did it all with a smile.

But still he did not leave the room. More people were shuffled up to him. One was Robert Arteaga, who had taken the first published picture of Musial as a Cardinal, in 1941, and Musial again posed for Arteaga. "Haven't changed in twenty years, have I?" Musial kept challenging Arteaga, and Arteaga shook his head. "No, you haven't." Tears glistened in Arteaga's eyes.

Musial shook his head. "I still don't know what to say. Just before I speak, I'll analyze what to say." But he did not trust himself. He closeted himself in manager Keane's room for a brief spell, and made some notes, and then he returned to the locker room, put on his cap, and suddenly trotted out of the room, across the bridgeway that leads to the Cardinal dugout, and onto the field. It was 12:13. Beneath the bridge, kids squealed and then roared, and on faces you saw the sheen of adoration that you see in church, or you used to see on the faces of teen-age girls when Sinatra sang.

Musial took his batting practice. Lloyd Merrick, a former Card pitcher, threw fourteen times to Musial. Stan hit the first four pitches for grounders, took a pitch, and then in a brief interim stood straight, inhaled deeply, and went back into his familiar crouch, wiggled his hips and set himself. Merrick delivered, and Musial uncoiled. The ball soared high and deep, and fell into the seats in right-center field, beyond the 354-foot mark, and the crowd roared. Musial spiked the next pitch on a line, to right field, took another pitch, and then hit a screaming line drive that struck the underlip of the roof, just fair. He ticked a ball foul, hit a line smash foul, skied to center, hit a ground ball sharply past first, and on the fourteenth and last pitch, belted another ball into the right-field seats.

A bell clanged to change the teams, and as Musial ran off, a boy in a box seat held up a sign that read: STAN FOR PRES. Musial laughed loudly. He walked over and autographed the sign for fifteen-year-old Bob Feigenbaum.

Jim Maloney, who would pitch for Cincinnati this afternoon, came out to get in his few batting practice swings, a big blond young man with a sober face. "I had only so-so luck the couple of times I faced him," Maloney said. "I rely mainly on a fastball, but I can't go with just a fastball to him. I'll have to mix 'em up. Move the ball. Keep the ball low. I will not bear down any harder because it's his last day. I won't bear down any less." Maloney looked grim and worn. It had been a great season for the young man—Maloney was a year old when Musial joined the Cards—his first season in the majors uninterrupted by injury or by minor-league work. Now he was shooting for win number twenty-four, one less than Koufax, one less than Marichal. It was heady company.

Musial had disappeared into the players' lounge, to lie down briefly on an old leatherette sofa. But a few minutes later he returned, and resumed signing pictures of himself for his teammates, resumed his cigar smoking. His face was sweaty, his hair tousled. Musial's hair has no discernible gray in it, but it has receded and thinned over the twenty-three years. His face remains youngish, and his eyes—on this early afternoon—were clear and bright. "Last night I had the best rest I've had in —how long?" The day before, Musial's eyes were tiny and red; he'd had three hours of sleep. He'd taken his daughter Geraldine to the opening social event of the St. Louis season, the Veiled Prophet's Ball, a white-tie affair at which the local debutantes are introduced. It is a mark of the distance Musial has come, from the Donora days when he played ball on a sandlot behind Twelfth Street, the son of an immigrant mill worker. Today he would play ball for the last time, and at night Musial would again dress formally, to attend a banquet at his restaurant. One of the guests would be U.S. Senator Stuart Symington.

But that would be later. The last game still lay ahead. The stint on the field, and the sting of balls crashing off his bat, had further relaxed Musial, and when young, college-educated Ken MacKenzie brought over a picture for Stan to sign, Musial grinned and said, "What the hell can I say about Lefty?" Then he wrote quickly, a mischievous grin on his face. He studied the words, and read aloud: "Dartmouth can be proud of you." He looked at MacKenzie and said innocently: "It *is* Dartmouth, isn't it?" MacKenzie said stiffly: "It's Yale, Stan." Musial laughed, and handed MacKenzie the picture. All it said was: "To a great pitcher and a fine gentleman."

Curt Flood brought over a picture, and Musial signed it and said: "You'll like this, Curt." Flood read: "A fine player—and a fielder who helped me out the last few years." Flood—who is normally a man of wit—nodded humorlessly, and said redundantly: "I was your wheels the last few years." But then Flood had things on *his* mind. He had 198 hits going into the final game. He wanted the magic 200.

Musial finally sat up straight and stretched. "No more autographs," and promptly Del Maxvill walked over with a picture, and Musial bent and signed.

Then—for a brief moment—the crush eased, and Musial sat on his stool, eyes downcast and distant, and the room was less noisy. He brooded, sitting, and no man interrupted his thoughts. But it did not last. Trainer Bob Bauman and team physician Dr. Isaac Middleman came in, and Musial was up and buoyant. "These are the guys who kept me going so long," he said. Then manager Keane walked through the room, saying, "Everyone on the field at 1:30." Outside the locker room a crowd was gathering beneath the bridgeway, and a guard could be heard: "Don't block the aisle. Let the people through." An occasional cowbell clanged. At 1:27 Dick Groat walked across the bridgeway, and kids with cameras yelled, "Hey, Dick!" Then from the Cincinnati locker room below, Jim Maloney walked slowly across and onto the field.

Musial trotted out, his hand resting on the arm of clubhouse manager, Doggy Lynch. And the crowd—perhaps 120 people—cried, "Here he is!" Musial smiled and waved, and ran out of sight, into the dugout, and onto the field, and by this time nearly all of the 27,576 people were on hand, and the roar was tremendous.

Musial walked across the foul-line to the center of the diamond where the celebrities sat on two rows of stools, and the two teams stood at right angles to each other. The first thing Musial did was to put his arm around his wife, Lil.

The affair honoring Musial lasted an hour. A few moments were memorable. Two Cub scouts—one white, one Negro—made a presentation of a neckerchief. The white boy made the speech, the Negro boy looped the neckerchief over Musial's head. For a moment, the faces of the ballplayer and the young Negro were inches apart, and you had to remember that this Cardinal team had been one of the last, one of the toughest to crack for Negroes. Baseball had known no Negroes when Musial broke in, in another September, in 1941. Now Jackie Robinson had come and gone, and baseball was different, and better.

Ken Boyer, on behalf of the players, gave Musial a ring, with a number 6 set in diamonds. Later, Musial would hold the ring first one way and then another. "This way it's 6, and I'm me; upside down it's 9, and I'm Ted Williams." Manager Keane said Musial would play his last game with the Cardinals, but what was also true, the Cardinals would be playing their last game with Musial. And Keane said, "I try to picture the clubhouse after the game," and he paused, and Musial began to cry quietly. Ford Frick, with an aged and broken voice, paid this tribute: "Here stands baseball's perfect warrior. Here stands baseball's perfect knight." Finally, the Dixieland band played "Auld Lang Syne," and Musial walked to the microphone.

He teetered nervously on his toes, he nodded, he turned, he rubbed his mouth and his hair and his eyes. Then he spoke. Almost immediately his mind went blank, and he apologized, and the crowd laughed gently, and Musial fished into his back pocket for his notes, scrawled on index cards.

"As long as I live," he said, "this is a day I'll always remember." He began a litany of thanks. He thanked his managers, he thanked all the players, especially those of the 1963 club. "I am proud of the terrific run they made at the Dodgers, this season." They. Not we. He thanked his wife and four children, "to whom I have been a part-time husband and father." He thanked God.

He thanked the people of St. Louis, and the fans cheered themselves. He thanked the press. He spoke of the opportunity America had given him. Then he turned and wiped his eyes, and kissed his wife on the mouth. He had spoken nine minutes, and though he hadn't said a memorable word, it all had been memorable, because it had been so naked.

And the game began.

In the first inning, big Maloney blew down Flood with fastballs, got

Groat to pop to the second-baseman. Musial stepped in, coiled, the shadow of his head and bat over the plate, and Maloney did what he said he would do. He moved the ball, mixed 'em up. The first pitch was a fastball, on the outside corner at the knees, a perfect pitch, and Musial took it. Then Musial had to hand over his bat to Sid Keener, head of Cooperstown's Hall of Fame, and he had to pose for more photographs, before returning to the batter's box, for the second pitch. Maloney jammed him with a fastball at the hand, and Musial fouled it, and then the big right-hander who looked as fast as any pitcher in baseball this afternoon, broke off a slow curve on the outside, and Al Barlick— who had umpired Musial's first big-league game—threw up his right hand, and Musial walked away.

Musial came to bat in the fourth, and again got a great hand. Not a Cardinal had a hit, and there was a growing sense of irony. Suppose, on this, Stan Musial's last day, Jim Maloney pitched a no-hitter? Who would get the headlines?

Maloney stuck to his prescribed course. He threw fast, but outside, for a ball, came back in with a slow curve on the inside corner, and with the count 1 and 1, threw another fastball. But he got it up a bit, above the waist, out over the plate, and Musial slashed the baseball on the ground past Maloney's left leg. Pete Rose, who had been pulled around to right, a step onto the outfield grass, ran over but the ball evaded his glove, and Stan Musial had number 3629. The baseball was returned to the first-base umpire, who handed it to Musial, who handed it to the Cardinal coach, and the game continued.

In the sixth inning, Musial came up again, in a scoreless game. Curt Flood doubled to open the inning—his 199th hit—and Dick Groat struck out.

The time was 3:44. I had asked Johnny Keane in the clubhouse whether he and Musial had discussed when to remove Musial, and the manager had been offended. It was his club to manage; the decision was his alone.

With the count 2 and 1, Musial got his second hit, banging a curveball on the inside corner past the first-baseman into right field, and the Cardinals had the first run. In the press box, reporters stood and applauded. It was hit 3630—the round even figures Musial likes—and it was RBI 1950, more round even figures, and when Gary Kolb emerged from the Card dugout, you knew Keane had chosen well. Musial trotted off, and at first the crowd booed (as they later booed Kolb when he went into the outfield), but when they realized Musial was going to disappear and be gone, the boos stopped, and the cheers mounted, and Stan Musial had run off a playing field for the last time.

In the locker room, Musial said, "I feel so relaxed. It's been hectic. I feel pretty good." Immediately there was an interview on television. "We're going on live," somebody said, and Musial giggled, "Can't go on dead." Then he said, "Throw me a comb, someone. One without all that dandruff." He got his comb, and the TV man called it "an end of an era," and it was four o'clock.

Musial began to undress and drink beer. Though he had not seemed terribly tense earlier, now you could see him relax. He posed, hanging up his shirt, and when the photographers told him to point to the number 6, Musial shook his finger at the shirt and said, "If I say so myself, you're all right." He liked the line, and repeated it. There was another interview at 4:11, and then the sense of anticlimax began to steal over the clubhouse. Ted Williams had known how to do it; a home run, a blast at the press, and gone. Musial sat and waited for the game to end —the Cards now led 2 to 0—and a reporter asked: "You going to spring training in '64?"

"Yes."

"Do some hitting?"

"Yes." He spoke of instructional hitting, but the reporter waved his hand impatiently.

"No. I mean hitting for your own pleasure."

Musial laughed. "I'll hit for my pleasure. It's *almost* the thing I like to do best." He looked at the *Life* man, and he said, "Did I say that right?" And the *Life* man murmured, "There you go, quoting Shakespeare again."

The interviews —on tape, over mikes, on TV—continued, and before one session, Musial said, "I've got mike fright. I'm like Garagiola. *I'm* afraid of the mike. *He's* afraid he won't get it." The interviewer liked the bit so well he had Musial repeat it over the air. The room became quieter, waiting for the game to end, and Musial said, "C'mon, you guys. This is a happy occasion." A reporter asked Musial whether this was a bigger day than his other big days—the three thousandth hit, his five homer day against the Giants, the hit that broke Wagner's record?

"This is the cumulation of all the days and all the years," Musial said. "There is a fuller meaning to today. This is the wrap-up for the whole thing. Those were just days." Then Musial turned and said, "What's a fellow do when you're out of a job?" And he tried to answer his own question. "I'm going to see the Kentucky Derby. The 500 Mile

Speedway race. Take my family on a picnic on July Fourth." Then he
stopped. "What else do they do in the summer? I don't know." And the
closeted life of a ballplayer was never more pitifully clear. Twenty-three
summers—summer is a euphemism, of course; a baseball summer runs
from March 1 to September 30, seven months—ripped from his life, devoted to baseball. Now he was about to start a new life. But, still, he
couldn't. With two out in the ninth, the Reds tied the score. Musial giggled nervously: "I said this might go extra innings. Nothing like giving
the fans their money's worth." A writer muttered, "It wouldn't happen
to Williams, no. It has to happen to Musial."

Curt Flood—lacking his one hit—came in between innings for a pack
of cigarettes. Musial turned up the radio that sat on top of a locker.
Tim McCarver came to bat in the bottom of the ninth. "C'mon, Tim,"
Musial said. "Hit it on the roof." The game crawled on, and the equipment manager, Butch Yatkeman, dragged out a trunk of beer, covered
with a white towel that read: "Webster Groves Public Schools." The
press was warned there was beer enough only for the players. Somebody asked a St. Louis reporter whether Gussie Busch, Card owner,
was cheap—"after all, he *makes* the stuff"—but the reporter said no,
not cheap, just bush league. "They didn't even think of making a spread
this day. It never occurred to them." The Reds left the bases loaded in
the tenth, and it was now past five o'clock. Musial slipped out of his
baseball pants and at 5:20 showered. He was out again in ten minutes,
and Ernie Broglio had gone in to pitch. Musial sat on his stool, in undershorts, socks and shoes. At 5:45 Musial went into the players'
lounge for a nap, and the last ballgame of his life had also become the
very last game of the year. Out on the West Coast, the Dodgers had already been beaten by the Phils; the Giants had beaten Pittsburgh, but
this game straggled on.

In the fourteenth, rookie Jerry Buchek singled for his first hit of the
season, and Curt Flood singled for his two hundredth, and a few minutes later, Del Maxvill hit a blooper to right, and the Cardinals had
won 3 to 2. It was 6:15. The first game Musial had played as a Cardinal,
he had made two hits, and the Cards had won 3 to 2. This time he made
two hits, and the Cards won 3 to 2, and one writer said, "There's been
no improvement at all."

Musial returned from the lounge, to say good-bye to his teammates,
and to pose again with the ballplayers, and Sam Jones again began to
spray the room with sneezing powder. Musial put on his black suit at
6:25 and had his fourth beer, and then he went back into the lounge,
for a postgame interview with Harry Caray, for a hair-tonic maker.

Caray bubbled over how this must have been the most emotional cere-mony ever tendered a player, and Musial reminded Caray of Lou Gehrig Day, and of the days they gave the dying Babe Ruth.

Musial recounted his big thrills. His first hit, off Jim Tobin, a knuckleballer, and his last, off Maloney, a fireballer, and he said wist-fully: "I wished it had been the other way. I wished I could have seen slowballs today. When I was young, I could hit the fastball. But now—"

And then it all seemed to go out of Musial. He slumped, and his voice gentled, and as he talked he shut his eyes and his right hand rubbed his right brow, slowly, back and forth, and the room was deeply quiet. "I love to play this game of baseball," he said. Present tense. "I love putting on the uniform." Present tense. He said he planned to throw out the first ball in the World Series, and then he'd go down to Fort Riley to see his grandson. "And then I'll retire—" He paused, and seemed to hang a question mark on the word "retire." He let its echo sound in the room, as though he were groping to understand the word, trying to make sense out of it. Then he said the word again, more firmly. "Retire—and take things easy." He opened his eyes.

He left the ballpark, through a back door, a few minutes later, and went into the street. That night, the leaves began to fall.

Victory!

John Devaney | **1 9 6 4**

Sinatra was singing on the stereo, but his voice—"Let's fly, let's fly"—could be heard only in snatches above the clatter of glasses and the shouting of the crowd at the bar. Arthur Modell pushed his way through, his hand high, flapping a twenty-dollar bill. "Two Scotches, two bourbons and a double Scotch," he hollered at the bartender. Modell grabbed the drinks as the bartender handed them over, then passed the glasses to the big men around him.

The big men were Cleveland Browns, and this was the cocktail lounge at Newark Airport last October. Modell, the owner of the Browns, and his players had just come from Yankee Stadium where Cleveland had defeated the Giants 35 to 24. In a few minutes, they would board a chartered plane and fly home to Cleveland.

A slim, intense man, Modell moved through the groups of players, patting one on the chin ("I was real proud of you guys today"). He dropped down on a stool between two broad-backed linemen. Modell clinked his double Scotch against a lineman's glass. "Here's to a great football player," he said, "and to a great guy."

In one corner of the bar, the Browns' quarterback, Frank Ryan, slouched on a stool, a bottle of beer in one hand, a half-filled glass in the other. It was his second bottle, and the beer—as the beer drinkers say—was starting to go down good. Though graying at the temples, Ryan looks—and even talks—a little like a younger Jimmy Stewart. He finished saying something to two Brown players standing next to him, then threw back his head and downed the beer in long swallows. One of the players said, "I saw Huff go by me, so I knew I could go maybe ten or twelve yards out. . . ."

Ryan put down the glass, grinning as he remembered. "That's right," he said, "I'd been throwing to the other side and. . . ."

The people, six-deep around the bar, did not realize that these were the Cleveland Browns. With their trim Ivy League suits, slim ties and button-down shirts, their attaché cases (for toiletries and an overnight change) at their feet, the Browns looked like young executives waiting for the 5:36. If you overheard Ryan, you might have figured these were a bunch of guys, a few years out of college, who had come together on a Sunday afternoon to play a game of touch or maybe softball, and now were sitting over beers and rehashing the game.

But this you could tell—right off, no mistake: Whoever they were, whatever they had played, these were the winners.

They acted like winners. I do not know how the New York Giants acted that evening back at P. J. Clarke's or Allen's in Manhattan. But I doubt they put away their beer with the gusto of Frank Ryan, for whom it was going down good. And I am sure they did not clink glasses in toasts to one another. Gusto and toasts are for bridegrooms and other winners.

Winners, though, do react to victory in different ways. To find out how pro football players react to victory, I went along with the winners of four important 1963 NFL games: Cleveland vs. New York, New York vs. Dallas, Baltimore vs. Green Bay, and Baltimore vs. Chicago.

Most of the 130-odd football players I saw in victory had little to say about themselves, a lot to say about their teammates. What lingers in memory, too, is the quiet, almost cheerless way these men accepted victory. They clattered in their cleats down concrete tunnels toward their clubhouses, sweaty, breathing hard, grass stains and occasional splotches of dried blood on their jerseys. There were no shouts, no whoops. They came off solemn, a job done, like miners coming out of the pits.

"Pro football's so close now," said Doug Atkins of the Bears, after they beat Baltimore, "that there's only a little margin between winning and losing. A lot of luck is involved. It's hard to get too excited when you know that you could've lost as easily as you won."

The margin can be so close, in fact, that you'll find a loser in the winner's clubhouse. Like Cleveland linebacker Mike Lucci, whose knee ligaments were ripped apart early in the game against the Giants. When the game ended, he was already dressed in street clothes and stretched out on a table in the trainer's room. As the Browns flooded in, an attendant momentarily forgot about him. The pain showed in Lucci's wet eyes as he yelled: "Where's that unprintable who was going to get the ice pack? Hey, someone, get me an ice pack. Hey. . . ."

But in the confusion, no one heard. Later, though, linebacker Sam Tidmore, who was also injured, leaned over Lucci and talked to him comfortingly, and Lucci—the worry on his twenty-three-year-old face —whispered, "We have the worst luck, Sam, don't we?"

Overall, the spirit of revenge was in the Browns' clubhouse after they defeated the Giants at Yankee Stadium, a place where they had been humbled so often. Sitting on a stool, defensive end Paul Wiggin grinned, the gaps showing in his front teeth. "This was the same Giant team that ran us off the field many times here," he said. "It's good to beat them. Ever since 1956, there's been this rivalry between us, this feeling that we have to beat the Giants to win."

John Wooten, the big Cleveland guard, screwed up his face angrily as he turned on rookie Jim Kanicki. "Whattaya mean?" he snapped at Kanicki.

"All I meant," said Kanicki, his face flushing, "was that when I saw the Giants get that touchdown right off, I thought we were in for a long afternoon."

(The Giants had scored in the first few minutes of the game when Dick Lynch intercepted a pass and ran forty-seven yards.)

"That was only a mishap," said Wooten, glowering. "You gotta accept mishaps. Any time one touchdown will decide an NFL game, you'd better forget it. It'll never happen. You can't give up. They didn't give up when they were down eleven points in the last quarter, did they? The only excuse you got for saying that is because *you're* a rookie. *I* knew that when we got hold of that ball, we'd move it."

"Oh, absolutely," said Kanicki, red-faced. "I knew we'd move that ball all right."

On the bus to Newark Airport, offensive backs Charley Scales and Ernie Green were reading the mimeographed play-by-play sheets. Across the aisle big offensive tackle John Brown laughed and said, "We lose and no one wants to read that stuff."

Frank Ryan was reading stats which showed that he had hit twelve of sixteen passes. Someone hollered to him that he had made a nice six-teen-yard run.

"I didn't run at all," said Ryan.

"Yes, you did," said a writer.

Ryan blinked and said, "Oh, yes, that's right."

Someone asked Ernie Green how he was feeling; he had been knocked out during the game by John LoVetere's clothesline tackle.

"I heard the bells ringing," said Green. "I didn't know who hit me."

"Maybe it was me," said defensive back Jim Shorter, and everybody around him laughed.

Green turned to stare out the window. In a low voice, he said, "Big bad Giants." Then he laughed, a soft laugh, teeth showing, and said again, a little louder now: "Big bad Giants."

The next week the Giants played Dallas at the Stadium. With the Cowboys leading 21 to 14 in the second period, Y. A. Tittle threw a long pass to Del Shofner, who was free on his own fifteen-yard line. Shofner dropped the pass, and the boos rolled down from the tiered stands. The Giants went off at halftime, trailing 21 to 17, and the boos followed them into the dugout.

They came back in the second half blitzing in on Eddie LeBaron, the Dallas quarterback, shutting out LeBaron for the rest of the afternoon. Tittle hit Phil King for one touchdown, Shofner for another, and the boos changed to cheers.

The Giants ran off the field, the winners, 37 to 21. Tittle, who had thrown four touchdown passes, approached the clubhouse door. He saw his two sons, Pat, ten, and Mike, eleven. "Now you stay outside until they tell you to come in," he said, waving a finger. Tonight he was the Hero of the City, but he could have been any father telling the kids to wait for him outside the supermarket.

In the clubhouse, a reporter mentioned the boos to brick-faced Jim Katcavage, the defensive end. "When you're losing," he said, "everybody notices what you do wrong. It's like what the coach [Allie Sherman] told us last Tuesday after we had lost to the Browns. When you win, Allie told us, we don't see the mistakes. But when you lose, we see every little mistake you *ever* made."

In the back of the clubhouse, Tittle was posing for photographers with his sons. "Big deal," said Y.A., "for a third-place club."

"We're tied for second, Dad," said Pat.

"Oh," said Y.A.

Bob Anderson, the former Army All-America, walked quickly through the dressing room. Anderson had played little all season. "It's always great to win, yes, sir," he said with that military correctness of his, "it's real great to win with the pros."

Then he looked away, perhaps seeing other dressing rooms. "Of course," he said, "when you don't play it's different."

Now the clubhouse was empty except for a few attendants and Sam Huff. "You win on a Sunday," Huff was saying, knotting a tie, "but you can't expect them to roll over for you the next week. You've got to go out there the next week and prove you're a winner *again.* And if you win a championship, you got to go out there the next year and prove you're *still* a champion."

In pro football, Sam Huff was saying, there are winners but no finish lines.

Outside Yankee Stadium Dick Lynch grinned as he signed autographs. He had stopped a late Dallas drive by intercepting a pass and running eighty-two yards for a touchdown. The crowd surrounded him, and he laughed when someone yelled, "Great game, Dick!"

As I watched I thought of another laughing Irishman, a second-baseman for John McGraw named Larry Doyle, who had shouted to the world more than fifty years ago: "Oh, it's great to be young and a Giant."

What Larry Doyle had meant, of course, was that it was great to be young and a winner, as Lynch was this Indian summer afternoon, so filled with the joy of it that he trotted off in the middle of a pack of fans, forgetting—for the moment—a pretty girl who walked behind them on high heels, his wife.

The Packers came into Baltimore with Bart Starr's smashed hand in a cast. The rest of the league was looking hard at this game, wondering how much the loss of Starr would hurt the champions. His sub, Johnny Roach, had thrown exactly twenty-three passes in games over the past three seasons.

There was more bad luck for the Packers: halfback Tom Moore was out with a bad neck, and early in the game their big right end, Ron Kramer, was hurt. With Roach looking rusty as he overthrew receivers, the Colts led after one period 3 to 0.

In the second period, Roach was still overthrowing, but a forty-six-yard field goal tied the score. A few minutes later, Herb Adderley intercepted a pass on the Colts' twenty. With Jim Taylor and Elijah Pitts, Moore's sub, carrying, the Packers scored to go ahead 10 to 3.

Another sub, rookie Marv Fleming, replaced Kramer at end and suddenly Roach was zeroed in. He hit on four straight passes, three to Fleming, and the Packers led at halftime 17 to 3.

They were ahead 20 to 10 after three periods. Then a Jim Martin field goal and a long bomb from Unitas to end John Mackey tied the score 20 to 20 with less than five minutes to play.

Roach did not panic. He moved the Packers carefully, running with Taylor and throwing short sideline passes to Max McGee. On the Colt thirty, he sent Elijah Pitts wide to the left, and the halfback turned the corner and scored.

At the Packer bench, Vince Lombardi leaped into the air and shouted, "Eeee-liii-geee!"

There's only a little margin between being a winner and a loser. Watching and listening as Lombardi shouted "Eeee-liii-geee," I remembered a moment earlier in the game when Roach had hit Pitts with a perfect pass, but Pitts—falling to the ground—had dropped it. Lombardi, hands on his hips, had glared angrily at Pitts for a full minute.

But now Pitts was a winner and so were the Packers, who scored another touchdown to win 34 to 20. Lombardi's eyes shone with satisfaction as he sat behind a small desk in the clubhouse, talking quickly, laughing in the nervous way he has. "This was one of my real proud games," he said. "It was a victory won with our substitutes. They sucked in their bellies and stayed right in there, *eck-eck-eck-eck.*"

Lombardi had the look of a man who had faced all the bad luck anyone could expect—and won. If this was the worst that misfortune could hurl into his face, he would prevail.

In another corner of the clubhouse, Roach talked to reporters. "Sure I was uncertain how I would do all week," he said. "You never know. You always say you'll do the job when you get in there, but when the chips are down, you're not sure.

"I wasn't thinking much about the public humiliation—being the goat—if we had lost. The hardest part of losing is knowing you have failed those who are depending on you. Winning this game with these guys"—he pointed around the Green Bay dressing room—"these guys. . . ."

He paused. "This was awfully important to me, you know? Those guys paid me championship money for two years while I was sitting on the bench. They won the money. You have to feel a little funny, a little guilty. . . ."

He stopped. But a little later he came onto the Packer bus, walking down the aisle, looking for a seat, staring right into his teammates' eyes. Johnny Roach was a guy saying, "We're even now," and he no longer had any reason to feel guilty about taking anybody's money.

Someone began hollering out scores, and the players listened intently. They whistled when they heard that the Giants had walloped the Browns 33 to 6 in their rematch. A player in back said, "I'm kind of proud of those guys." I turned around to see who it was. It was Jim Taylor.

The following week the Bears came to Baltimore. As quarterback Billy Wade explained it later, they had one thought in mind: to keep the ball as long as possible, thus limiting Unitas' opportunities to throw.

Keeping mostly on the ground, Wade marched the Bears to a touchdown in the first period. In the third, Chicago got another touchdown on a short pass from Wade to Casares. The Colts came back to trail 14 to 7, but Wade used up most of the fourth period with sweeps, then picked up a field goal and the Bears won 17 to 7.

Wade stood in front of his locker, looking like Jack Lescoulie except that his blond hair was mussed. "It didn't bother me that I didn't get to throw much," he said. "All I wanted to do was win."

The Organization Man was talking in this moment of organization victory.

Off to the side, defensive back Bennie McRae talked for a while how he had covered Raymond Berry and Jimmy Orr so thoroughly that Unitas' passing scored only one touchdown. But then he saw the veteran J. C. Caroline, head down, taking off his shoes at a nearby stool. Earlier in the season, McRae had beaten Caroline out of the job at left corner back.

"You oughta be talking to J.C. here," said McRae, loudly. Caroline looked up and grinned. "You know what J.C. did?" said McRae. "He's on the kickoff team and he made four out of our five kickoff tackles. Now *that's* something, four out of five!"

Caroline, grinning, played the same self-effacing game. "When you're sitting on the bench all afternoon," he said, "you get plenty of rest to make a few tackles."

On the bus to the airport, the Bears talked in low, buzzing tones: *How did Green Bay do? . . . I heard they won. . . . Then I saw Shinnick cut across . . . Unitas was looking at Berry so I figured . . . Green Bay won in the last period . . . I was keying on Pellington but . . . Who's got the right Green Bay score?*

I remarked to fullback Rick Casares how quietly the Bears were reacting to their victory over the Colts, a victory that kept them in a first-place tie with the Packers.

"They're still too keyed up," Casares said in the articulate, soft-spoken way he has, a way that contrasts oddly with his bumpy nose and fighter's face. "But it will build. On the plane there'll be a lot of joking and clowning around. Then when we get back to Chicago, about half the team will come over to my place—Rick Casares' Pro Bowl—and everyone will enjoy the fruits of victory."

He laughed. "Well, not fruit exactly. Tonight we're having spaghetti and ribs."

He lit a cigarette. "That's the big difference between victory and defeat for us," he said. "After a victory we want to be together. We all make plans to go out and do something. When we lose, everyone goes off in his own direction."

The bus stopped for a light; he looked out the window. "All pro athletes," he said, "their emotions are the same. Winning is the whole thing. To the professional athlete, the fact that you get paid even when you lose, that's no compensation at all.

"Some guys might play pro football for the money alone, but after two years they're gone. This is too punishing a sport to play just for money. Look, you earn a season's salary in summer camp. Nobody would endure a summer camp just for money. The season is a joy after that. At camp there's nothing you look forward to more than a Sunday afternoon in the fall."

But what if you lose on Sunday?

"Then you go from the heights to the depths," he said, looking out at the flashing neon lights. "We lost to San Francisco this season. Coming home that night on the plane, that was the worst experience of my life. You keep saying, 'Geez, if we had only done this or that.' Little things.

"Like you're blocking for a field goal. You throw your block and it's a 90-percent block. Almost perfect but not perfect. Your man slips by and blocks the kick. You lose the game by a point.

"That kills you, knowing that if you had given 100 percent, you would have won. Look, no ballplayer gives 100 percent on every play. He can't. But if you don't on a crucial play, one that loses you a game, oh, geez, it tears you up inside."

He was silent for a while. "This game," he said, slowly, "is 20 percent physical and 80 percent mental—the mind forcing the body to give that extra bit of effort. You ask me about winning. That's what winning is in football—getting that little bit more from your body than the other guy. And if you give 100 percent on a play and the other guy gives 90 percent and you win the game on that play, oh, geez, what a feeling."

At the airport, the players from the Bears' first bus were already streaming up the steps into the chartered plane. Someone standing in the aisle of the second bus yelled: "No beer for the second bus to-night!"

But inside the plane there was enough beer for everybody. Two players were popping open cans, passing them forward, and now the voices grew louder, yelling and laughing: *Get me a beer, roomie. . . . I saw the hole open on that touchdown and. . . . The cornerman copped out so I thought I might have room. . . . Hey, bring some more beer back here. . . .*

It was the time after winning, and whether you are drinking double Scotches or beer, when you are a winner, it all goes down good.

How I Wrecked My Life—
How I Hope to Save It

by *Hank Thompson*
with *Arnold Hano*   **1965**

The number on my white shirt is 174819.

There is nothing about a number like that to remind you of a man who played nearly one thousand big-league baseball games, and who once walked off with a check for $11,147.90, before taxes, after the New York Giants walloped the Cleveland Indians in the 1954 World Series.

But then there's nothing big-league about where I am now, or the shirt on my back.

I'm in prison.

On July 13, 1963, I held up a liquor store at gunpoint in Houston. I took $270 from the cash drawer. The police picked me up the same night. Three months later I began serving a ten-year term. With time off for good behavior, with time off because I am a trusty, my discharge date from the Ferguson Unit of the Texas Department of Corrections is October 9, 1968. With the approval of the Texas parole board, I could get out sooner.

Then I'll start all over again. I'll be forty years old this December 8. They say life begins at forty. It better, for me.

The armed robbery of the Houston liquor store was not my only mistake.

I've been arrested seven times.

One time I killed a man.

I was in reform school when I was eleven.

Warden Jack D. Kyle, who runs the Ferguson Unit, says this about convicts—a convict is a man who has run wild.

He's talking about me. At least he's talking about the "me" who entered the prison in 1963, who was arrested for holding up a bar in 1961, who was arrested for punching a woman in 1959, who was arrested for stealing a car in 1958, who was arrested for homicide in 1948, and who was arrested twice back in 1937, once for taking jewelry from a car and once for truancy. Who began drinking when he was fifteen, and was soon an alcoholic.

I hope to God—and I pray every Sunday in the Chapel of the Prodigal Son, here at the Ferguson Unit—that it isn't the same man any more. When I get out I'm going to have to walk down streets with liquor stores and bars, and I'll have a choice—walk past them, and live, or walk into one, and run wild again. You might say the count on me is two strikes. I've got one swing left.

I don't want to sound like a crybaby. The only person to blame is me. So if I blame drink, *I'm* the guy—Hank Thompson—who did the drinking. If I tell you I came from a broken home—my parents were separated before I started school—so did millions of other kids, and I'm the one in jail. If I tell you my father beat me with a strap and he, too, had a drinking problem, I'm in jail, not my father.

Don't ask me to blame society, or the fact I'm a Negro in a white world, or the fact I have a grade-school education, or the fact I was washed up as a major-leaguer when I was thirty-one years old.

I'm the one who kicked society in the teeth, and maybe you won't believe me—but it's the truth—I'm glad society has started to pay me back.

I was born Henry Curtis Thompson, in Muskogee, Oklahoma, on December 8, 1925. We moved to Dallas, Texas, when I was an infant. My father, Ollie Thompson, was a jack-of-all-trades, mainly a railroad worker, but always a man who liked his whisky. My mother, Iona, was a soft woman who couldn't say no to her kids. She was a cook and a domestic. My folks broke up when I was five or six, and got divorced soon after.

So I had one parent to raise me, and she left for work at 6:00 a.m. and got back at six at night. Which meant my sister Florence was supposed to watch me, but I would sneak off and play ball. All I wanted was to play ball. They made me go to school, but I played hooky.

Even when I didn't play hooky, I'd get my ballplaying in. I remember those spring days in Dallas when it stays light pretty late, and I'd get out of school at three and head for the ball diamond. We'd play ball until the sun went down, and the streetlights would go on, and we'd keep on playing, eight, nine o'clock. Who needed supper? (And who was going to do his homework anyway?)

Those were the happiest days of my life.

I never was a big kid. But I always was good enough to play with older, bigger kids. Baseball was the only thing I've ever done well. A man's got to be able to do something well, to keep his head up. I never was good in school. But I always could hit a ball, field it, throw it.

Still, ballplaying didn't keep me out of trouble. I was always on the streets of Dallas, instead of in school, and when some kid snitched jewelry from a car, the police decided I did it. So I was arrested when I was eleven years old, but they finally believed me when I said I didn't do it. I didn't. Then they turned around and got me on a truancy rap. The next thing I knew I was sent off for six months to Gatesville Reform School, 115 miles from Dallas.

That's a long way from home for a kid.

I was treated decent at Gatesville. Let me put this down. I've never been mistreated in jail, either in reform school or county jail or city jail or the Texas state penitentiary.

One thing I learned at Gatesville. I had to obey the rules. I got up at a certain time, ate at a certain time, made my bunk a certain way. I suppose I could have rebelled. But they held a carrot in front of me. At Gatesville, I played on the first organized baseball team I'd ever seen. For that, I'd have swept every corridor and made every bunk.

When I got out, I had to spend a year with my father. I guess they figured it would be good discipline.

I hated it. He and I didn't get along. I cut the wood and mowed the lawn and did the dishes and didn't play ball, but it wasn't good enough for my father.

So he'd beat me.

The way he beat me was humiliating. He made me drop my pants and underpants, and he'd whip me with his belt across the bare buttocks.

I went back to live with my mother. I didn't go to school. I hung around the ballpark where the Dallas Steers played in the Texas League, and after a while I asked to throw batting practice or shag flies. They let me. Somebody saw me and asked me to play with a Negro team in Dallas, and pretty soon I was a local hotshot. On Saturday nights I'd go to dances in Dallas, and drink wine. I was fifteen.

Near the end of the summer of 1942, B. C. Sorrell, of the Kansas City Monarchs—one of the great Negro teams of the day—suggested I try out for the Monarchs the next spring. World War II was sucking up ballplayers. Still, I figured Sorrell was kidding, and I didn't think any more about it until early in 1943 when William Dismuske, traveling secretary of the Monarchs, wired me twenty-five dollars to get down to New Orleans for spring training.

I asked my mother if I could go (it didn't matter what she said) and she said, "If you want to go, go."

I went.

In New Orleans, the Monarchs stayed at the Hotel Page. There was a bar downstairs. After workouts, the players would sit around the bar and drink beer. I hadn't graduated to hard liquor, but I found you get a good buzz on from five or six beers.

It was a fast life. Satchel Paige was on that Monarch team. So were Buck O'Neil, Willard Brown—later he and I would go up to the major leagues, together—and Connie Johnson. They were grown men, and they acted like men. And I tried to act like them. I was seventeen.

I played right field for the Monarchs that first year, and I batted .280–.285. I figured next year, when I knew the pitchers better, I'd have an even bigger year.

There was no next year in baseball for me. I was drafted into the Army in March of 1944, and I got out on June 20, 1946. Once again I found an institution where you were supposed to obey the rules. It wasn't easy. Once I got word from one of my sisters that her baby had died. I asked permission to go to the funeral. My commanding officer turned me down. I went anyway. I was AWOL for two days. I got bawled out, but that was all. I began to drink whisky in the service. I'd go into town and buy rotgut, seven dollars a pint, twelve dollars a fifth. In Little Rock a bunch of us got drunk and got into a fight, and I ended up in the stockade overnight.

I learned to handle a gun in the Army. I shipped overseas with the 1695th Combat Engineers, as a machine gunner. We were in the Battle of the Bulge, holding a position with our .30-caliber machine guns, keeping the Germans boxed in a village. For three days I had maybe six hours' sleep, total. But the Germans finally surrendered, some three thousand of them.

If there was a moment in my life I did something for society, that was it. But you can't make three good days balance off the rest of a man's life.

I got out of service—a sergeant—in June of '46, and rejoined the

Monarchs. We won the pennant in the West, but in the playoffs the Newark Eagles beat us, four games to three. A couple of guys in the Newark lineup could hit the ball. Monte Irvin and Larry Doby.

Then I had myself a ball. I joined up with Satch Paige and other Negro players, to barnstorm against a handpicked major-league team, headed by Bob Feller. This was the gravy train. My share was $7500 for seventeen days' work. Actually we played more than seventeen games. We'd play a game in New York in the afternoon, and one at night in Baltimore. Each team had a private plane. Segregated luxury!

That winter I played ball in Cuba, with the Havana Reds. I began to notice a pretty girl who always asked for my autograph. I asked her in Spanish to have dinner with me. She answered in English, and pretty soon I had a girl.

Actually, I also had a girl back in the States, in Houston, a quiet girl, more a homebody than most girls I'd gone with.

But this girl in Cuba knocked her right out of my mind. Her name was Maria Quesada. We dated. I met her family. It got serious.

But nothing—ever—was more serious than baseball. Yes, one thing. Drink.

The year 1947 was the breakthrough year for the Negro. On April 10, Jackie Robinson joined the Brooklyn Dodgers. On July 6, Larry Doby was signed by Cleveland. Every Negro, in baseball and out, rejoiced.

Meanwhile, back with Kansas City, I was having a fine season. I was hitting .347. Still, I had no idea I'd be one of the next Negroes tapped. I was twenty-one years old. There were experienced stars in the Negro League. As a matter of fact, when scout Hank DeBerry came to look over the Monarchs, he came not to see me or Willard Brown, our center-fielder, but because the St. Louis Browns were interested in catcher Earl Taborn.

After a ballgame on July 16, we got back onto the bus and drove to Madison, Wisconsin, where we stopped for breakfast. I was eating when traveling secretary William Dismuske said, "Get your stuff ready, Hank."

"What for?" I said.

"You're going to the majors."

"Sure," I said. "Just let me finish my breakfast."

Then manager Frank Duncan came into the restaurant. He was crying. And he was walking over to me.

It was true.

The Browns had bought up my contract and Willard Brown's.

On July 18, 1947, I played my first major-league game.

I went hitless and made an error. The Philadelphia Athletics beat us 16 to 2.

I won't spend much time on the thirty-six days I was with the Browns. I hit .256. I played second base, and I think I played it pretty well.

I can't complain much about St. Louis. Hank DeBerry—God rest his soul—had given me my break. Manager Harold "Muddy" Ruel treated me fair. So did the fans. I can't say the same for all the players. They never said anything directly to me or to Willard. But some reacted in ways that were just as clear. You know how ballplayers sit in the dressing room and autograph baseballs? Well, I'd come into the dressing room, and three guys—always the same three—would get up and one of them would say, "When *you* finish, we'll come back."

Three or four men don't make a whole team. John Beradino, Jeff Heath, Bob Dillinger, Walt Judnich, and Vern Stephens went out of their way to make life pleasant for me and Brown. If they'd see us snubbed, they'd sit down and begin signing with us. Stephens in particular would chat with me and Brown, tell us about the other pitchers in the league, talk to me about how he made the double play, so we'd mesh smoothly.

Actually, the Browns signed us to boost attendance. They were in last place. When the Browns went on the road, the press would talk about the Negro players, and there'd be a big crowd for the first game of the series, and me and Willard, or one of us, would play. But then we'd likely be benched the rest of the series. The gimmick worked. People came the first day, and we played, so they came back the next game as well.

In thirty-six games, I got into twenty-seven games, some of them as pinch-hitter or pinch-runner. I batted just seventy-eight times in twenty-seven games.

I didn't burn up the American League but there were rookies who didn't hit .256 and were good enough to stick. Here's what some of my teammates hit: Jake Early, .237; Walt Judnich, .251; Al Zarilla, .233; Billy Hitchcock, .228; and John Beradino, .228. The team was last in hitting, with an average of .239.

Still, I knew the score. On August 23, Muddy Ruel told us we were being released. General manager Bill DeWitt announced to the press that Willard and I "had failed to reach major-league standards."

He was probably right. I wasn't as good as most major-leaguers. But I was as good as some St. Louis Browns who weren't being released. The only thing they had I didn't have was a white skin.

I went to Bill DeWitt and I said, "I'm doing as good as lots of other guys on this club." And Mr. DeWitt looked uncomfortable and finally he said, "There are things I can't discuss with you, Hank."

That ended the conversation. We both knew what those things were.

So that was that. A short trip to the majors. I got paid for the rest of the season, which sweetened the pot, and I rejoined the Monarchs. At the end of 1947, I went down to Havana, to play winter ball, and made more money, and I got myself engaged to Maria Quesada.

Early in 1948, I left Kansas City to report to San Antonio, Texas, where the Monarchs were holding spring training.

The trip took me to Dallas, and I decided to spend the night with my oldest sister, Margaret, and her husband.

It was the worst night of my life. You can leave everything else exactly as is—all the arrests, the time in jail—but if you cross out this one night and tell me it never happened, my whole life don't seem so bad.

Let me jump back a little. When I left the Browns and rejoined the Monarchs, I started carrying a gun. Some older players I knew were carrying guns and I always liked to do what the older guys did. I bought a .32 automatic for twenty-six dollars. I carried it in my pocket. It made me feel like a man.

In Dallas, my sister Margaret and her husband and I went to a beer garden. We ordered a beer when I saw a guy I knew at another table. Buddy Crow. I played sandlot ball with Buddy Crow years before. I'd known him since 1938 or 1939. I'd seen Buddy Crow when he was feisty drunk. I saw him cut another boy with a knife and the boy stood there holding his intestines in his hands.

Buddy Crow said, "Hello, Mr. Moneyman."

He made it sound sarcastic.

"Have a beer, Buddy," I said.

He said, "Don't mind if I do." He took his beer back to his table.

Suddenly there was a loud noise. Buddy Crow had overturned his table. He started walking toward me. He had a knife in his hand.

"I'm gonna get you," he said.

I pulled out my .32 automatic, and I said, "Stop!"

I guess he figured I wouldn't use the gun. He kept coming.

I yelled, "Stop!" a second and a third time, but he kept on coming, and when he was three or four feet away, all I could think of was that boy with his guts bleeding in his hands. I pulled the trigger.

Three times.

I hit him across the chest and he went down. My sister and my brother-in-law took me back to my hotel. I went to bed, scared and sick. I knew Buddy Crow was hurt bad, but I remember I was thinking, "I had no choice." I know better today. I had two other choices. I could have turned and run, or I could have let him cut my throat.

Either one would have been better.

The phone woke me the next morning. It was my brother-in-law.

"Hank," he said, "Buddy Crow is dead."

I got my clothes on and went down to the police station and turned myself in. I was arrested on a murder charge and released on $5000 bond.

The facts were clear enough. Buddy Crow had come at me with a knife. He had a reputation for using the knife. I fired in self-defense. My lawyer argued it was justifiable homicide, and got me out on bond, and I joined the Monarchs for spring training. I didn't miss a day. Two years later, with the help of the New York Giants, the case was dismissed. It cost me $1200 in laywer fees.

But I got off. Like that. No sweat. I killed a man, and the next day I was playing ball like nothing had happened.

Seventeen years later, I haven't got over it. You can't kill another human being easy. No matter how it turns out. For seventeen years I've paid for that life, and I guess I'll keep paying. I deserve to pay. As I say, I'd rather Buddy Crow cut my throat than I killed him. But it didn't work out like that, and part of the monkey on my back all the years since has been the weight of a guy I'd once played ball with when I was a kid and whom I killed one bloody night in Dallas. I had exactly half a beer in me that night, so I can't blame drink. He was drunk, but I wasn't, and I could have run and let them call me chicken, but I'd have gone to spring training without a man's weight on my back. Buddy Crow is heavy.

But I was young then, and I carried him well. I played for the Monarchs and I had a big year. The end of 1948 saw me down in Cuba again, where I got word the New York Giants had arranged to buy up my contract. They wanted to send me and Monte Irvin to Jersey City, in the International League.

I didn't sign right off. Not that I wasn't thrilled. I just didn't like the way I was getting shuttled around, nobody asking my opinion. The big leagues bought me, the big leagues fired me, the big leagues bought me again.

Alex Pompez, who scouted for the Giants in the Caribbean, called me after two weeks had gone by.

"What's the matter?" he asked.

"Nothing," I said. "I just want some money to sign this thing."

"How much?"

"Five thousand dollars."

Who was I kidding? I wasn't going to get no $5000 bonus. But I wanted to assert myself a little.

So Pompez reported to Horace Stoneham, and he called back, and he said, "How about $2500?" and I leaped for the pen.

At Jersey City in 1949, in fifty-five games, I hit .303. I had twelve home runs, and I stole eleven bases.

It was a big year all around. My girl Maria Quesada—I called her Mary—came up to the States in 1949, and on June 9 we got married in Brooklyn.

And on July 5, the Giants called up Irvin and me. Here's how decent the Giants were. They paid me $7500 that year, even though the minimum was $5000.

I had some good seasons with the Giants, and some very good days. One day we beat the Cards 13 to 8, and I hit three home runs. When Cardinal manager Eddie Stanky walked me the fourth time, the Giants waved towels at him. I knocked in eight runs that day; Willie Mays knocked in the other five.

I got into the record book. (Not just because of my race. As a Negro, I got in several times. I was the first to play for the Browns. I was the first Negro to have played in both leagues. The first day I was with the Giants, I faced Don Newcombe. Never before had a Negro pitcher faced a Negro batter, in all of major-league baseball. In the 1951 World Series, I played right field because Don Mueller hurt his leg in the playoffs against the Dodgers, and this was the first all-Negro major-league outfield—Irvin, Mays, and me.) But the record I'm proudest of has nothing to do with race. In 1950, I participated in forty-three double plays. No National League third-baseman, white or black, has ever been in so many.

By and large it was good. Look at my salaries. I got $7500 the first year; then they upped me to $14,000; in 1951 it was $17,500, and a World Series cut; my salary kept going up until I got $32,000 for 1955. And don't forget the winner's share of the '54 Series—the biggest ever up till then. Even in my last year with the Giants—1956—I got $26,000. I made $170,000 in eight seasons with the Giants.

It wasn't all roses. I was Negro. Which means certain pitchers knocked me down regularly. I don't mean brush-back stuff. I mean knockdown pitches, thrown at my skull.

There were five Negroes in the National League when I came up. Me and Irvin, Jackie Robinson, Roy Campanella and Don Newcombe. Monte, Jackie, Roy and I spent lots of time flat on our backs. One time, I hit a home run and as I rounded the bases, the pitcher said: "I'll get you next time, you black unprintable."

The next time we played against that pitcher, he threw at us and hit one of my Negro teammates with a pitch, putting him in the hospital.

Sometimes players would yell from the dugout—"Nigger, what are you doing up here?"—and the white Giants would do the answering back. Monte and I answered with our bats. You want to know who on the Giants were closest to me and Irvin? Eddie Stanky, from Alabama, and Alvin Dark, from Louisiana. When Dark got fired by the Giants in 1964, I found it hard to believe the things they said he'd said about Negroes and Latins. Not once did Al Dark show me any prejudice.

The worst fans were in Cincinnati. Whenever there was a lull, some loudmouth would yell: "Nigger," or "Black unprintable," and you could hear it all over the place.

If things went well on the field, most of the time, my personal life wasn't going good. Mary and I lived at 940 St. Nicholas Avenue, in Harlem. We started bickering. She left me once.

I guess I was mainly to blame. I was drinking heavy. When the game was over, I'd go straight to a bar and have two or three Scotches to get the game out of my system. Then I'd have a big steak dinner, and go home, and drink a fifth of Scotch, or maybe two fifths. In one night. Or I'd go to the Red Rooster or another bar and I'd pull out hundred-dollar bills and I'd set up drinks. Bigshot.

I started wearing tailored suits, made up in Philadelphia. Some of them cost two hundred dollars. I had twenty to twenty-five suits, ten to fifteen sports jackets, twenty to twenty-five pairs of slacks, twenty-five to thirty pairs of shoes. I bought myself a Lincoln Capri for $5000.

I didn't spend it all on myself. I bought Mary a mink stole, and after the '54 Series, I bought her a mink coat, for $5300. When my wife and I split up, I bought another girl a used Oldsmobile, for $3600.

But I still could have made it if I controlled the drink. I used to say to myself: Hell, I'm no alcoholic. I can take it or leave it alone. Except I only would take it.

Actually, I didn't drink before a game. But my stomach would roll and I couldn't eat either. I'd get to the park weak as a cat. Then I'd drink all night. You can't play major-league ball in that shape. I never was big enough to get away with any weakness. I had to have all my strength. At five feet eight and a half and 168 pounds, I'm giving away inches and pounds to overpowering pitchers, and to guys trying to cream me on the bases. My legs started to go. I kept having little injuries. I began to slow down.

In 1955, Frank Shellenback, the Giant pitching coach, asked me whether I was having family trouble. My problem always has been I'd clam up about my problems. If I had a slump I couldn't talk to anybody about it. Just brood over it.

I told Shellenback everything was fine but he said Leo Durocher knew it wasn't. There was talk—Shellenback said—that I was drinking all the time, and Leo said I wasn't the player I was a year ago.

"You better take care of whatever's bothering you," Shellenback said. "Otherwise, Leo will send you down."

Another time Leo told me after a game that Stoneham had reports I was drinking every night, and if it didn't stop he'd kick me off the team.

Horace Stoneham is a lovely fellow. He was like a father to me. Anything I'd want, he'd do for me. Even little things. I'd maybe get an overtime parking ticket, and Stoneham would pick up the phone and take care of it.

But he was a businessman, and his business was fielding ballplayers who were fit to play ball. When the 1956 season ended, I was sent to Minneapolis, in the American Association.

I played until July of 1957. I was in terrible shape. I tore ligaments in my legs. Even when they healed, I wasn't the same Hank Thompson. One day I hit a ball and I knew it was a double so I whizzed around to second, and there was the ball waiting for me. It stunned me. Then in a game against Charleston a batter hit a pop fly over my head. I ran back, but I never did catch up with that simple flyball.

When the game was over, I said to manager Red Davis: "I got to hang it up, Red."

"No, Hank," Davis said. "I want you to stick around. You'll come out of it."

"I can't," I said. "I don't like making a fool of myself."

The Giants paid me off, and that was the end of my baseball career. Thirty-one years old.

I went back to New York. I'd been trying to get along with my wife. Just the year before I'd bought her family a house in Cuba. It cost me $17,000.

But it was no good. We were divorced in 1959. I couldn't blame her.

I lived on savings from July of 1957 to January of 1958. It was hard, going from the big leagues to hunting a job. I missed the sweet life. In January of 1958 I got a job tending bar at Braddock's, on 145th Street.

I made eighty-five dollars a week. I held the job four or five months. I had other jobs. I was a delivery boy, but I wouldn't show up on the big delivery days. I got bartending jobs, but I'd borrow money from the till and leave a note, without asking permission. Finally the owner of the bar would fire me. And I couldn't blame *him*. Six or seven jobs came and went like that.

On the night of November 10, 1958, I went to the garage where I kept my car, but it was way in the back. I saw a friend's car and drove off with it. I knew I'd have it back before he'd need it. Except I drank, and I didn't get it back until morning.

By which time it had been reported as stolen. I was arrested for auto theft. Later my friend showed up and he said, "If I'd known Hank had it, I'd never have reported it." The charge was dropped, but the arrest is on my record. Stealing a car.

The next year I got into an argument with my girl friend and we had too many drinks, and I lost my head and hit her. She went to the police and I was arrested again. I pleaded guilty, and the judge gave me thirty days or one hundred dollars' fine. I spent seven days in jail, and then I couldn't stand it, so I paid the fine.

You can see what a terrible empty life I was leading. Nor was I hanging around with the best crowd. In the summer of 1960 I got a .25-caliber gun from a fellow in Brooklyn. He needed money. I lent him five dollars. He gave me the gun as collateral. He never paid me back, so I had a gun. I kept it with me all the time.

Then on February 26, 1961, I was riding in a car with a friend, when we got hit by another car. My right arm was out the window and the window came up and broke, cutting an inch-long gash across my wrist. They rushed me to a hospital and took three or four stitches.

The next night I was drinking in a bar in Harlem, feeling sorry for myself. I was sore at my ex-wife, sore at my girl friend, sore at the world. And my arm was sore. Maybe the whisky did it. Something said, "Why don't you stick up a bar and get some drinking money?"

It was crazy. I had a full pint of Scotch in my pocket. But maybe it was like those alcoholics, who have to have whisky in more than one place. You know, a pint in the pocket, one in the kitchen cupboard, one in the glove compartment.

Late that Saturday night I walked into Bill's Place, at 2787 Amsterdam Avenue. I knew the bar. Once when I was broke I hocked my 1954 World Series ring with the owner for $250.

I stood at one end of the bar, and when the bartender came over, I took out the gun with my left hand and said, "This is a stickup."

I got thirty-seven dollars from the cash drawer, and walked out, and a half block later a cop picked me up.

The next morning there was a picture of me climbing into the police van with a big smile on my face. I don't remember smiling, but there was the picture. I think—and I'm no psychologist—I *think* I was saying all that evening: "Will somebody catch me before I hurt someone or before I hurt myself?" They caught me and I was glad.

But it didn't work. Horace Stoneham, Ford Frick and other influential people wrote to the court, saying nice things about me, and I was released on probation.

Don't get me wrong. Stoneham had come through like a champ. But someplace along the line, somebody ought to have said, "See here, he's no good. He's *got* to be punished. He's *got* to spend some time. He's *got* to be put away where he can't run wild, where he can't mock the law."

But nobody did.

Stoneham even got me a job at Casa Grande, Arizona, where the Giants have spring-training camp. I went out there in October of 1961. I cleaned the swimming pool, and when the winter instructional league began, I worked with such young players as Jose Cardenal, Jesus Alou, Jim Ray Hart, Hal Lanier and Cap Peterson. I got three hundred dollars a month, plus room and board.

One other thing happened out there. You remember I mentioned having a girl before I met Maria Quesada? Well, I got a letter from her. She'd read about the trouble I was in. I answered her, and she came out and spent five days in Arizona with me. After all those years, it was the same as it was when we were kids. It was good. Then she went back to Houston where she was a nurse, and I went to California, to visit my father in Bakersfield and my mother in Fresno. My girl joined me in Bakersfield in September of 1962, and we went down to Los Angeles, where I got a job doing interior decorating and painting. I worked with a man named Leonard Spell. Soon I was making $120 a week. She got a job at Bel Air Hospital. We made plans to get married.

Early in 1963, in Los Angeles, she told me I was going to be a father.

Then her mother, back in Houston, got sick. My girl went back home. I went up to Fresno, to see my mother and to wait for my fiancee to return. I intended to stay in Fresno, but I started to fret, and I started to drink, and then I decided to go to Houston and bring her back with me.

She met me at the Houston bus station, and I saw her body was all flat. I said, "What happened?" and she said, "It was a false alarm. I never was pregnant."

I didn't say anything. But I thought it: *She didn't want the baby.* She had an operation. I didn't say it to her. It ended up stuck in my craw. I wanted that baby, I wanted to start a family with that girl. I began to drink heavily. Once the girl's mother said to me: "You're crazy, Hank. You ought to see a psychiatrist."

The old pattern set in. I said to myself, To hell with the world. I had to get some money. (I could have gone back to Los Angeles and started working for Leonard Spell again. I could have wired him for money. I could have borrowed money from friends.)

I had a gun with me. I always had a gun. I was staying in the Midtown Hotel in Houston. On July 13—a Saturday afternoon—I walked into a nearby liquor store. I asked the owner for a fifth of Scotch. He put it in a bag and turned back to me and I had the gun on him. The cash drawer was open. I cleaned it out of $270.

I had borrowed a car. I drove back to the hotel room and placed the gun in the top drawer of the dresser and put the unopened bottle of Scotch on the dresser. I went over to the Matinee Club, which is a drinking place I knew pretty well.

I began drinking. Naturally, I was throwing bills around. Bigshot.

It didn't last long. A few hours later, a detective rushed in and shook me down.

"Where is the gun?" he said.

"I don't have a gun," I said.

We went back to the hotel and there was the stolen bottle of Scotch. He found the gun. They took me to police headquarters and ran me through a lineup, and the store owner identified me. At the preliminary hearing I had no lawyer. I'd written to one, but he hadn't answered. Meanwhile, the assistant D.A. was trying to get me to plead guilty to a twenty-year rap.

"I'm not going to cop out for no twenty years," I said.

He said the judge wanted to give me ninety-nine years. I still said no.

They kept me in county jail for five weeks, because I couldn't raise $7500 bail. Finally the assistant D.A. came back, and he offered me ten years.

So I pleaded guilty and on October 8, 1963, I entered the diagnostic unit of the Texas Department of Corrections in Huntsville, Texas.

Dr. George J. Beto, director of the Texas Department of Corrections, interviewed me at Huntsville, for classification. There are thirteen separate prison units, spread over the state. When you're at Huntsville, they decide what unit you're to go to. Dr. Beto asked if I'd ever worked with

kids. I told him I'd worked in various baseball clinics. He told me he
was sending me to one of the work farms and if I kept my nose clean
he'd see whether I could be assigned to working with young people.

So I worked in the fields at the Eastham Unit, across the Trinity
River, from October 29, 1963, to February 13, 1964. When *Sport* magazine got in touch with Dr. Beto, about this story, Dr. Beto wrote about
me to the magazine: "As a result of hard work and exemplary behavior,
he was promoted to the Ferguson Unit, where he is assigned to the Rec-
reational Department aiding in the directorship of athletics for first
offenders between the ages of seventeen and twenty-one."

My job at Ferguson is gymnasium instructor and baseball coach. Our
baseball team won the state championship this year.

As a trusty, I don't sleep in a barred cell. I'm in a big dorm, like an
army barracks, a hundred beds on the floor. Each trusty has to clean up
the area around his bunk. We each have a small footlocker, a butt can,
a pair of shower shoes and a reading lamp.

The most important part of my stay at Ferguson has been the Alcoholics Anonymous chapter I've joined. We have A.A. group therapy
sessions twice a week. On Thursday evenings, an A.A. man comes up
here from the Huntsville diagnostic center, nineteen miles away, and
sits down with twenty-five to thirty inmates and we talk about our
problems for an hour and a half. Then he shows a movie based on the
A.A. program. On Sunday nights I sit in with a smaller group, maybe
ten or eleven, and we talk for two and a half hours.

I've been in jail for just about two years. We have at the Ferguson
Unit young boys, seventeen to twenty-one years old. Sometimes I hear
one of them say, "Boy, when I get out, I'm going to get myself a Cadillac, and I'll roll in the money and buy $150 suits."

And I say to them: "It's all a dream. It'll never be."

I had that dream. I even lived it for a while. It's an empty dream. It
doesn't mean a thing. I try to tell them why. I hope to God they listen. I
hope to God *I* listen.

When I get out in the free world, I'll join an A.A. group. I'll get psy-
chiatric help if I can afford it, and I'd better be able to afford it, because
I'll need all the help I can get. I'm going to try to get a job painting and
doing interior decorating. I expect to move to Fresno, where my mother
lives. She's a missionary in the Church of God in Christ. I'll live with
her. There are other things I want to do. I want to go up to San Francisco and see the Giants play ball—I'm still a Giant fan—and I want to
thank Horace Stoneham for helping me. Sometimes in prison I'd see a

Giant game on television, and after it was over I'd start a letter to Stoneham, to apologize for letting him down. But I can't write that letter. Maybe when I get out and see him. I can apologize, face to face.

I do *not* want to get back into baseball, in any capacity—coach, scout, trainer, anything. I want to stay out of the public eye. I don't want people saying, Oh, that's Hank Thompson, ex-convict. Some people will say it no matter where I go, and I've got to expect it, but I don't want to be in the public eye where it will happen a lot. It's not that I'm ashamed (I am, of course), but that I hope by the time I get out, it'll be a different Hank Thompson. It won't be the same Hank Thompson who hit .364 in the 1954 World Series, and it won't be the Hank Thompson of 1963, who held up a liquor store at gunpoint. It'll be another Hank Thompson. It better be.

Which winds me up, I guess. I wrecked my life and now I hope to save it. A writer from *Sport* asked me if I had any advice for other young kids going into baseball that might keep them from repeating what I did. This is what I said:

Get advice about money, how to save it, how to invest it.

Live a clean life.

Stay away from those goodtime people who pretend to be your friends.

Stay away from liquor.

Stay healthy.

Baseball is the cleanest sport we have, so treat it decent.

My Friend the Bruiser

Bill Libby | **1 9 6 4**

The Olympic Auditorium in downtown Los Angeles is a monument to days sadly gone by. It sags and creaks. Its ten thousand upholstered seats leak out their insides from a thousand knife slashes. Its stairs are slippery from blood and spit and spilled beer and millions of shuffling feet. Its air is stale with smoke and sweat, and heavy with the echoes of cheers and boos and profanities.

Clearly, it is a typical old fight arena. It is most especially typical in that for some years now it has been crowded only on wrestling nights.

This was a wrestling night and a great many simple, honest working men, their wives and girl friends, and their children had turned out to see several extraordinary personalities, including Edouard Carpentier, the handsome Frenchman, and Richard Afflis, better known as Dick the Bruiser, the ugly American.

Carpentier entered first, dancing down the aisle to the cheers of his public. The men eyed him in awe, the women blew him kisses and the children jumped up and down and clapped their hands. Carpentier smiled, shook hands politely and paused at ringside to sign autographs.

From the opposite side came the Bruiser, booed by right-thinking people everywhere in the arena. Men curled their lips in curses. A few laughed. Women sneered and shook their pocketbooks at him.

(*337*

Dick the Bruiser is the world heavyweight wrestling champion of Detroit, conqueror of Honest Alex Karras and "the meanest man in wrestling." He is six feet one and 265 pounds, his thickly muscled body is so
wide he seems short, his chest so large that his arms cannot hang naturally at his sides but are curled like an ape's, as though he is ready to
grab you. Instinctively, you step back. Beneath his crew-cut blond hair,
he contorts his round pug's face into ugliness. It has been said he is one
of those persons least likely to sing in a choir. His voice is a low, hoarse
rasp which growls out of his guts.

Now, he spoke. As some adorable children reached out for him, he
rasped, "Get outta my way, you little blanks." He pushed them aside,
no doubt more severely than he intended, for they sprawled on the
floor.

As he reached the ring, he rushed to the crowd surrounding Carpentier and scattered the people, grabbing pens and programs and throwing them aside. He began to "beat up" some women. As he pushed one
lady backward, she seemed soft to the touch and he paused at his la-
bors to examine her. She was brunette and curved.

The heroic Carpentier had to be restrained by others. The Bruiser
sneered, "Come on, you frog, I'm willing." Somehow, they held Carpentier back. The police led the Bruiser back to his side of the ring. The
arena darkened. The National Anthem was played, which the Bruiser
declined to sing. The announcer introduced the contestants as though
they were Maurice Chevalier and Benedict Arnold. The bell rang and
the Bruiser and Carpentier advanced on one another under the bright,
hot overhead lights.

The Bruiser kicked Carpentier in the groin. When Carpentier doubled over, the Bruiser hit him with a kidney punch, then a rabbit punch,
then kicked him in the face. When Carpentier fell on his back, the
Bruiser fell on him. He smashed his fist on Carpentier's nose, probably
breaking it, then seemed to twist it off. He smashed his fist on Carpentier's mouth, probably knocking out all his teeth. He gouged his fingers
in Carpentier's eyes, probably blinding him, then seemed to pull the
eyeballs out of their sockets and throw them into the crowd.

Carpentier's howls of agony filled the hall. They chilled the blood. It
was awful. The crowd was on its feet, screaming at the Bruiser, aroused
by his somewhat unsportsmanlike tactics, screaming at the referee,
aroused by his failure to halt these somewhat unsportsmanlike tactics.
The referee pulled the Bruiser away. Carpentier, a pitiful sight, staggered to his feet, badly hurt and helpless.

The Bruiser grabbed him, pushed him across the ring and began to bat his head against the ring pole, probably splitting one or the other. Then he began to pick Carpentier high up in the air and throw him down. Then he began to jump up and down on his back. Carpentier, every bone in his body no doubt smashed, no longer howled, but lay still as though dead.

But Carpentier was not dead. Incredibly summoning some amazing reserve of courage and determination, he drew his broken body gallantly erect, staggered around shaking off the pain, wiped off the blood, and began to advance on his foul foe. The crowd cheered. Now justice would be done. It was . . . for a while. Using clean, clever moves, the brave, handsome Frenchman trounced his bigger foe for a while. Repeatedly he pressed the Bruiser's shoulders to the mat about to pin him, but at the last instant before the referee could complete his final count of three each time, the Bruiser would work free.

Eventually, the Bruiser regained the upper, or lower, hand. He began to work over Carpentier again. After a while, Carpentier began to trounce the Bruiser again. This went on for about twenty minutes.

Now, Carpentier was in command, administering such a clean, clever, and honest beating that the Bruiser rolled outside the ring ropes, bent on one knee as if in prayer and pleaded for mercy. The crowd howled in delight. "He din' give you no mercy," one fan pointed out to Carpentier. However, Carpentier is a gentleman. He stepped back and waited for the Bruiser to re-enter the ring. It was a mistake.

The Bruiser hit him at once with both arms, both legs and one head. When Carpentier fell on his back, doubtlessly unconscious, the Bruiser climbed to the top of the ropes, balanced a second, then leaped down to land with all his weight on Carpentier's neck, probably breaking it. The Bruiser then lay on him and held his shoulders down while the referee tolled three.

Police had to restrain the fans as the Bruiser, snarling defiance and shaking a fist at them, left the main floor. One fan turned aside miserably. "You have to hand it to the big blank, he's tough," he said.

Carpentier was lifted tenderly onto a stretcher and carried gently back up the aisle while brave men wept and their women prayed. A few poked at him to see if he was still alive. The crowd then began to wait impatiently for the first medical bulletin on his condition—until the next two wrestlers entered the ring and began to smash one another.

In due time, Carpentier, showered-fresh and neatly dressed, holding a small suitcase in his hand, emerged into the dark corridor at the back of the arena, slipped out a door and into the night. A little later, the Bruiser emerged from the same dressing rooms. He wore only his trousers and held an unlit cigar between his teeth. Drops of shower-water clung to his large, bare chest.

"How'd you like the show?" he rasped, smiling.

"It was a fine show," I said with undisguised admiration. "I thought it was a particularly nice touch where you began to beat up on them women right off."

"I hate autograph-seekers," he rasped proudly.

"I also thought it took wonderful timing to jump from that top rope onto Carpentier's neck without hurting him," I said.

"Not hurt him, hell," the Bruiser rasped indignantly. "I went right through his neck. For the rest of his life, he'll talk like me," he said.

He winked wickedly.

Twenty years ago, when we were in our teens, there was no question but that many of us at Shortridge High School in Indianapolis, Indiana, were destined for greatness. It was only a question of how many. Sadly, in the long years since, few made it.

The greatness we wanted was the greatness of true fame. One lad made the front pages and jail, but this is hardly admirable. The jazz fans among us who used to sit in Benny Barth's living room, listening to him copy-cat Gene Krupa records, feel Benny came close. He is now a well-recorded San Francisco jazz drummer. A guy named Vonnegut has done all right as an author. But, of all of us, the only one who really made it big was Bill Afflis, for Bill grew up to become that true immortal of the squared circle, that much-publicized and ever-popular athletic great, Dick the Bruiser.

Afflis' story has been told before, mostly in wrestling magazines, and usually with the clear ring of truth associated only with political speeches. He is perfectly willing to tell his story, only every time he tells it, he tells it differently. Others with whom he has been associated, such as the five colleges for whom he played football, are less willing to discuss his story. However, we, who knew him when, have an edge.

Bill Afflis was born in Lafayette, Indiana, in the late 1920s and moved to Indianapolis as a child. His father, who prospered in the optical business, died just before Bill entered Shortridge. Mrs. Afflis and Bill moved into a fashionable residential hotel on the banks of Fall Creek. Mrs. Afflis, who later became prominent as Margaret Afflis Thompson, former State Probation Officer and current Indiana Democratic Committeewoman, later was re-married to a retired official of Allison's aircraft plant, but she was in those days a lonely widow, striving to raise her only child properly.

Afflis used to read those Charles Atlas ads, as did all of us. You have only to look at him to see he took them seriously. He lifted weights at the Indianapolis Athletic Club until they ran out of weights big enough (he has pressed three hundred pounds), then switched to Hoffmeister's Body-Building Studio, a place up a dark flight of stairs. Small boys went in and large men came out. Afflis was largest.

Once, cops were called in when someone was seen walking on his hands around the narrow ledge of the YMCA roof, eight stories up. It turned out to be Afflis, merely taking his daily workout. A bully kicked sand in his face at the world's largest outdoor pool, Broad Ripple Swim, and Bill carried him to the top of the world's highest slide and threw him off. When ruffians from Tech threatened us, we called him up from the crap game downstairs at the Parkmoor Drive-In or the Country Club basement and our rivals fled.

When we'd cut school and go to the movies or the penny arcade or the Fox Burlesque Theater or sneak into a darkened and deserted church gym to play basketball, truant officers might find us, but they'd take one look at Afflis and back off to hunt smaller delinquents. With him, we could crash the "500." He didn't have to help us over the Speedway walls, he could throw us over.

He was kicked out of his hotel once for hurdling chairs in the sedate lobby while little old ladies huddled in terror in the chairs. When he was pressed for a place to stay, he'd come up to one of us and say, "I'm staying with you tonight, buddy." We never turned him down. After all, his muscles never quit. It was sheer folly to antagonize him.

All things considered, we had a normal, happy childhood. We chased girls. Bill caught them. His true attraction was physical. I recall a girl asking me, wistfully: "Just how in the hell do you tell him no?"

The trick for which Afflis was most famous had something to do with the way he dressed. Even in mid-winter, he covered his ample chest with no more than a T-shirt two sizes too small. When the girls would gather round, Bill would take a deep breath and split the shirt down the middle.

After a while, his poor mother, growing desperate over the cost of keeping him in T-shirts and out of jams, agreed to permit him to return to Lafayette to finish high school. She sent him money by mail weekly while he enrolled at Jefferson High, found a room by himself and began to unwind from the tension of his restricted life in Indianapolis.

Bill had played football at Shortridge, but he was just big, not good, at first. Year by year as he learned to use his size and strength, he got better. In 1947 he made All-State guard at Jeff. The athletic director there, Marion Crawley, recalls, "He was one of the strongest, most aggressive and best defensive players we ever had."

But, Crawley adds, "Bill was more interested in weight-lifting and judo. His body was one of the best developed for an eighteen-year-old I've seen. We here do remember that he was a little unhappy with high-school wrestling because it was rough on him. He dislocated a shoulder."

Nevertheless, Afflis seemed to enjoy the roughness he could find in the town pubs. In time, his mother cut off his allowance. "I guess I got into too many fights," Bill recalls proudly. Purdue promptly began to pick up the tabs. Bill had been scrimmaging the Purdue varsity while still in high school and the coaches there welcomed him with an All-America gleam in their eyes and an athletic scholarship in their hands.

However, as time passed, the Purdue staff grew increasingly restive with his extra-curricular activities, particularly a disastrous association with a town girl, and took to riding him rather hard. "One day I picked up my helmet and hit the line coach over the head with it, breaking my scholarship," the sensitive lad recalls.

After that, Bill became a football bum: "I went to Notre Dame, but the midnight curfew beat me in two weeks." He was shocked to find they read books and attended classes there. He could have told you The Fighting Irish were on their way out as a football power then. "So I went on the Southern tour," he adds. "I visited the fine campuses at Alabama and Miami until they decided my intercollegiate standards didn't measure up. But it was time well spent. Them Southern broads was polite, to say the least."

Changing his name to conceal his past—he changed from Bill Afflis to Dick Afflis—he hopped a fast freight for the Far West, where Nevada U.'s grid coaches awaited him. He found happiness there, in the fine warm college town of Reno. "I played football six months a year and worked as a bouncer at Harold's Club six months a year," Bill recalls. "Harold couldn't lick my grandmother," he points out.

Bill is remembered fondly there by his fellow bouncers, who are called "security officers" now. He, himself, grew so fond of the place he has since booked himself out of Reno and has used the name "Harold's Club" on the back of his robes. It is his real alma mater. He began to wrestle there and he began to get married there and he had his first divorce there.

"All the loot I made wrestling I gave back to the broads and the divorce lawyers," he says. "I never gambled, but dames are more expensive than crap tables. My last divorce there busted me and I was years getting even. Still, I like it there and I liked bouncing. I lasted until I hurt too many stiffs. After a while, Harold had so many lawsuits hanging over his head, he suggested I cut out."

Dick recalls that as a bouncer his average number of ejections was two or three a night. "The suckers would get boozed up or angry at some broad, or blow a bundle on a game, which they figured was rigged, which it never was, and I had to help them to the door," he says. He insists he never lost a decision. "I never met anyone that tough," he growls menacingly.

However, he later wandered to work in a similar capacity at Miller's, a hillbilly joint outside of Indianapolis. A friend picked him up hitch-hiking on the road late one night, looking much the worse for wear, and extracted a sheepish confession from him. "He was," the friend says, "a bouncer who had just gotten bounced." Afflis denies any such memory. "Maybe," he suggests hopefully, "it was a fair fight."

Afflis retired from the profession to answer a summons from the Green Bay Packers, and he played for them four years, 1951 to 1954. He was a good, but not great player, who manned many positions on both the offensive and defensive lines, and was regarded as the team's best blocker, one of its best tacklers, and a bruising customer.

In fact, it was said of him so often that "he's a bruiser," that the nickname stuck. He is so fond of it that he now registers at hotels and takes out marriage licenses simply as "The Bruiser." His wife calls him "Bruiser," too, but his mother does not.

It was also at Green Bay that a stray elbow caught him in the Adam's-apple, rendering him speechless for six months and leaving him with his present voice. "Most guys don't think it's for real, but it is," he rasps, as though someone were strangling him. "A lot of them bums, wrestlers, that is, try to copy me. They think I got a perfect voice for a wrestler."

Afflis enjoyed his years with the Packers. "Green Bay may be small in size, but it's big in fun," he said recently. "Every other house is either a church or a tavern. You can go either way. I don't think I have to tell you which way I went."

He paused, readjusting his overlapping bottom on a bar stool and using up a book of matches trying to light his cigar without success. "We had a lousy team, but a great bunch of guys," he resumed. "We lived good. When we went on the road it was more of the same. I don't think we won a game in Los Angeles when I was with the team. A couple of nights in L.A. and we couldn't have beaten Shortridge, much less the Rams."

Afflis' Packer days were before tough Vinnie Lombardi became the coach. Perhaps Afflis anticipated the arrival of Lombardi or perhaps he got tired of the modest checks given players on teams which win only fifteen games in four years. In any event he discarded his 1955 contract in favor of one to pursue wrestling full time.

"I like football," he says. "I liked knocking heads. In pro, a lot of guys were as big as me, so it took some technique, too. But wrestling was a better buck." Many football players, from Jumping Joe Savoldi to Leo Nomellini to Ernie Ladd, have gone this way. Asked recently if he was a villain from the start, Afflis grinned, "Hell, yes. I'm Dirty Dick. It comes natural." Various wrestlers have pet holds such as "The Dropkick" and "The Sleeper." Dick admits to two: "A punch below the belt and a kick in the chops." Clearly, he has found his calling.

The world of wrestling is a carnival world peopled by actor-athletes with wild names. Every town has its own world champ. Antonino Rocca, Vern Gagne, Lou Thesz, Buddy Rogers, Freddie Blassie, Ray Stevens, Don Leo Jonathon and Pat O'Connor are all world champs. So is the Bruiser.

Mostly, though, wrestling is big business. The wrestlers earn up to six-figure salaries. They play along with the acts and trappings of their con game. They growl, they grimace. Straight-faced, they spout the fan-appealing theatrical lines. One of the Bruiser's rivals says of Dickie: "He's no wrestler, just a big, ugly, dirty bully." The Bruiser's official line goes something like this: "I don't take nothing from nobody, not from promoters, not from wrestlers and not from the dumb slobs in the cheap seats. You don't have to be very smart to be any of those things. They all hate me, but so what? Friends? Who needs them? My friends are my keen mind, my fantastic strength and my guts. When someone gets in my way, I want to tear them to pieces. I'll tell you what makes me the greatest: I don't depend on anybody else. I go it alone and I'm tough."

Whatever it takes in the way of athletic or dramatic ability or a colorful personality to make it big in this dodge, the Bruiser has had it from the start. Perhaps the secret to his success is that he has a genuine mean streak in him, and his best friends would be lying if they pretended otherwise. The fan who pushes him in an arena, the fellow who picks a fight with him in a bar, the policeman who seeks to quell one of his disturbances, is apt to find out that the Bruiser does not know when the act is over. He walks a frighteningly thin line between pretend and for-real.

One of the lovely girls with whom we went to Shortridge once prevailed upon the Bruiser in the name of friendship and old school ties to wrestle at an outdoor charity affair that otherwise consisted of raffles and tea. They set up a ring and the society folk prepared to be amused. They were nearly killed. The Bruiser got out of the ring and emptied a dozen chairs, turning them into kindling. Later, the shaken girl said, "He wasn't getting a dime. He was doing it for fun, to help sweet charity."

Of course, carrying on in the audience is a standard part of wrestling routines, but the Bruiser goes at it with a zest that makes it impractical. He triggered a Madison Square Garden riot in the 1950s that involved three hundred fans and thirty policemen. Many people were injured and one cop got a broken back. Lawsuits pending against him have weighed against his return to New York for years. Anyway, he's suspended. "Suspended, like who needs him?" a commission official says. "I mean it's for real. Even we've got limits. This guy doesn't know when to stop. Somebody's liable to get hurt."

Privately, the Bruiser grins and says, "I guess I go a little wild sometimes. There's no fun like getting in there and really belting. I've been in more jails than Dillinger. I've been suspended longer than the Brooklyn Bridge. I'm suspended in so many places, I have to check the list to see if I can go in my own backyard."

When Alex Karras, the Detroit lineman, was suspended from pro football after the 1962 season, a wrestling match was arranged, Alex *vs.* the Bruiser for Detroit's Olympia Stadium. Grounded one night in town shortly before the match, the Bruiser took a cab to the Lindell Bar, the bar jointly owned by Karras and a tiny fellow named Jimmy Butsicaris. Conceivably, he had it in mind to drum up some publicity. Karras went along.

"You're a bum," Afflis told Karras.

"You were a third-rate football player," Karras told Afflis.

"Pro football's a phony sport," Afflis told Karras.

"You should talk," Karras told Afflis.

Then the fun started. A fellow who was present recalls, "It was like one of those cowboy saloon fights in the movies. But I got the hell out of there when I realized they were really breaking up things, like people."

As the Bruiser remembers it: "I was just having a few beers and making small talk when this little squirt, Butsa-something, tells me to shove off. I refused. They got a pool room in the back and some guys went and got some pool cues and began belting me over the head with them. I got upset."

As Karras remembers it: "He started pushing Jimmy around, so I jumped on him. I was sitting on his chest when the cops came in. One of them belted me and broke my glasses. That made me mad, so I let the Bruiser up. That's when he wrecked the place. They needed eight cops to take him out in chains. He's an animal."

"I woulda killed Karras if it hadn't been for them cops," the Bruiser insists. "One at a time, I can handle any cop. They kept coming at me in waves, two at a time. They knew they were in a fight, anyway, before they got leg irons on me and dragged me off to the cooler. The hell of it was I had to pay more dough in fines and damages than I got for the bout. I lost money on the deal."

Incredibly, when the match was held, the Bruiser won. "Of course I won," he snarls. "He's no wrestler. He's never wrestled again, has he?"

When the damage was toted up, the bar was a shambles, the TV set and jukebox were wrecked, one policeman had a broken arm and another a torn groin muscle, Karras had teeth marks on his arm and scratches across his chest, and Afflis had a five-stitch gash along one eye.

The Bruiser is one of perhaps ten or fifteen wrestlers making $100,000 a year. Only a few, such as Rocca, make more.

The Bruiser has reached the point where he could throw out his manager and agent. His office is his home. The promoters call him. And he is booked up months in advance. If you haven't heard much about him, it's because every wrestler sticks to one area. The Bruiser, who has wrestled throughout the U.S. and Canada, and has turned down offers to wrestle in Asia and Europe, usually stays in the Midwest. He wrestles four or five times a week, two hundred times a year, and makes up to $1500 for a big match.

It is not a soft touch. He is on the go night after night, spending half his time in cars and planes and hotels, often wrestling in crummy arenas in tank-towns before incredible fans who believe so strongly in his villainy that the women actually do sometimes stick hatpins in him and the men slash at him with razor blades. "In an arena, in a crowd, the slobs get brave," Afflis says. "Outside, alone, they usually take one look at me and think better of it.

Whatever else it may be, wrestling is a rough, hard racket. The acrobatics alone are dangerous. A heavy fall can hurt. The ropes can burn. Sometimes the blood dripping down a wrestler's face is actually blood.

Afflis has had more than three hundred stitches in his face and head. A network of small scars trims his lovely puss and trim scalp. He has had most of his teeth knocked out, his nose broken several times and other bones broken in his body other times. "It's about as dangerous as

football," he says. "Even doin' it right, you're gonna get hurt sometimes. But gettin' hurt don't hurt you."

Despite all of this, in his tranquil moments, he really doesn't look
bad.

"Not bad?" He grinned. "I'm better lookin' than I ever was. I get better lookin' every year. Just like Marilyn Monroe. She looked like hell
till she was about twenty-five."

The Handsome Bruiser goes first-class. He gets a new Cadillac every
year, drives to many of his matches, flies to the others, logs about
100,000 miles in travel a year. He stays at the best hotels and motels,
eats good and drinks good. He works out almost every day, usually in a
gym "You gotta keep in shape to get outta shape," he grins. He does
not drink water all day so he can drink beer at night.

Going out at night and in the morning and in the afternoon is the
quaint way he licks the problem of killing time in strange towns. A
writer trailed the Bruiser and the Crusher on a fourteen-hour spree recently. With time out for a bout in between at the local arena, they visited four bars, a strip joint, a twist joint and a restaurant, drank twenty
bottles of beer and ate two twenty-two-ounce steaks apiece, bullied mo-
torists, elevator operators, and waitresses, defied cops, pushed around
two punks and a saloon-keeper, danced with barmaids, sang with
barflies, played pool with each other, and in general had a nice time.

"We got an image to live up to," the Bruiser grins.

In Indianapolis, he owns his own bar, "The Bruiser's Harem Athletic
Club," on North Meridian Strip, which has plagued city officials with
its traffic in vice. "I run a clean joint," Afflis insists. "Nothing fancy. No
eating or nothing like that. Just drinking and having fun. And a little
floor show."

Recently, after kidding "500" racecar owner J. C. Agajanian about
his patronage at another place down the street, Afflis turned to me and
said, "He don't know it, but I own a piece of the other joint, too. Either
way, I get his dough."

Afflis owns eight oil wells in Tell City, Indiana, three of which are
small producers. He owns considerable real estate and has put up a
number of $25,000 homes. "Strictly class," he grins. He also has an in-
terest in a TV firm which is going to syndicate wrestling films nationally.

He has been married four times and has four children, two of whom
live with him now. His present wife was a stripper in Calumet City, Indiana, near Chicago. Cal City is the Tijuana of the Midwest, a place
gaudy with neon and blood. "She's gone straight," the Bruiser says of

his attractive bride. "She's strictly a housewife now. The club and some of my other things are in her name, but she hates to even leave the house. She's a good girl. We've been married so long now, I think it's going to stick."

They live in a plush home on the north side of Indianapolis. A swimming pool and a twenty-two-foot cabin-cruiser (on blocks) are in the backyard. Some summer afternoons, the Bruiser puts on a yachting cap and goes up and sits on the deck. Obviously, he is safe from sea-sickness. He drinks beer and throws the empty cans in the pool.

Recently, while he was on a wrestling tour of California, I invited him to my apartment-house pool. "You probably got no broads to look at there," he said.

"No," I admitted. "Only my wife."

"She's no broad, she's a wife," he said. "You come to the hotel pool. We'll lie in the sun and look at the broads there."

He went through a book of matches trying to light his cigar, then talked of wrestling. "It's a hard life, but a good one," he said. "It's a pretty clean racket these days. Most of the wrestlers are college graduates. They're really not freaks. Most of 'em, that is." He laughed. "We're all in it to make a buck. And there is a lot of loot in it. I could wrestle every night of the week if I wanted.

"The fans give me a laugh. The more they hate you, the more they want to see you. They form fan clubs for me, I cut 'em cold. They put up signs in the arena, I rip 'em down. They come to me for autographs, I steal their pens. Even when I was a kid, I never put no arm on no clown for an autograph. When I was with the Packers, we used to sign Johnny Lujack or any name. When I do sign now, I sign Bobo Brazil or President Truman. The slobs don't even look. They go away happy. They send me money for pictures, I keep it.

A large laugh rumbled in his chest. He shifted in his beach chair, shaking Southern California. The Bruiser used eleven matches and finally got his cigar going. He puffed on it once and it went dead. "It's a buck stogie," he said contentedly.

I asked him if his mother went to see him wrestle. "Sure, she comes with her husband," he said. "They get a kick out of it. Some of the old gang comes once in a while, too. Or they come to the club to touch me up for free drinks. One of the boys is into me for a long tab, and I don't like it no more."

He paused, studying the palm trees. "I don't care what anyone says about wrestling," he said finally. "I think nobody likes it but people."

I asked him how long he expected to stay at it. "Maybe ten more years," he said. "Then I'll quit. I'll go to Florida. I'm big there. And I like it there. I'll sail my boat and skin dive and fish. Naw, I don't catch fish. I jump in the water and chase 'em." He laughed.

After a while, he asked me if I knew any good places to hit that night. I named a few. Then he named a few. I was impressed that he had found his way around so well. "Practice," he grinned. He suggested a beer and we left the pool and walked through the lobby. Everyone turned to stare at him.

He beat Art Neilsen that night at the Olympic before going on the town. He had the next night off, but went to Bakersfield to wrestle as a favor to a promoter friend. Before his match with Carpentier the next day, he was talked into attending the weekly broadcasters' luncheon at the swank Scandia. Olympic publicist Don Fraser felt the publicity would help the show. Perhaps it was because the radio and TV people expected little from a wrestler, but the Bruiser spoke with such natural wit about his school, football, wrestling, and saloon careers he was the hit of the affair.

At the luncheon he anticipated the inevitable question about wrestling's honesty. "Ask me any questions you want," the Bruiser told the broadcasters. "Just remember that I am not bothered by sore shoulders and I do not go out sitting down."

No one asked.

As we were driving down Hollywood Boulevard that afternoon, Afflis asked me to stop by a cut-rate store. He came out with a bag full of cheap sunglasses. When I asked him why, he explained in such a way that I knew my friend, the Bruiser, was still Bill Afflis, who used to split his too-small T-shirts down the middle for the girls back in Indianapolis.

"I need a lot of sunglasses and there's no sense my having good ones," he said, grinning. "I take 'em off, I put 'em in my shirt pocket, I just move a little, flex a little, and they break up all to hell."

What Makes a Champion?

John Devaney | **1965**

This is a steamy morning in the spring at Pompano Beach, Florida. I am inside the Washington Senators' clubhouse. I can hear the public-address announcer read the lineup for the visiting Milwaukee Braves: ". . . batting fourth, number forty-four, Hank Aaron. . . ."

Inside the clubhouse a Senator pitcher whistles, low, admiringly. "Aah," growls someone next to him. "Aaron puts on his uniform the same as anybody else."

"Yeah," says infielder Chuck Cottier, "but *he* puts it on over a different body."

The body of a champion, twice the batting champion of the National League. That's what makes Hank Aaron's body different.

Champion. It is more than a title. It was once a dream for all of us, to be the best in sports or something else. The dream comes true for very few. Somewhere along the way we learn we're not the best, and maybe we wonder why. What did the champion have—more talent, more luck, more energy?

My dictionary tells me that "a champion [is] a winner of first place in any competition . . . excelling over all others." But that I knew before I opened the dictionary.

I go out and talk to champions and those who compete against champions. I ask: What makes a champion?

I am told many things, but this I keep hearing: Skill alone does not make the champion.

Warren Spahn tells me: "I've seen maybe fifty guys in my career who had more stuff than me. But somehow they only reached a certain level and never got any higher."

Carol Heiss, the former Olympic figure-skating champion, tells me: "A champion needs 10 percent skill and 90 percent the other things."

Ed Furgol, who beats the best in golf despite a withered left arm, tells me: "There are dozens of pros on the tour who would be as good as Palmer if they had his outlook. But you can't put something into a man that isn't there."

Chuck McKinley, the 1963 Wimbledon champion, tells me: "You don't get there on natural ability alone. A lot of people are born with natural ability, but few of them become champions."

What, then, are the qualities that make a champion? I look back in my mind at champions I have known and watched.

I remember Ben Hogan, late in his career, standing ankle deep in water, a hundred or so yards away from a green in a tournament I have since forgotten. The ball is submerged in three inches of water; most pros would pick it up and take the penalty.

Not Hogan. He stands over the ball, iron in hand, looking at the ball, then at the green. He swings, and from out of the spray of water, there comes the ball—arching toward the pin in a flawless curve. It hits short, hops once, twice, and rolls dead maybe two feet from the pin.

A champion's shot. And remembering that shot, I submit: a champion must have *skill*.

I remember a cold, gray dawn on Broadway five or six years ago. A cutting January wind blows scraps of dirty, discarded programs under the marquee of Madison Square Garden. Teen-age Carol Heiss, pert and blond, collar up against the wind, runs toward the entrance of the Iceland Skating Rink.

It is a little after seven in the morning. She has been up since five, rattling into Manhattan for an hour on a cold, grimy subway car. At 7:15 she is spinning over the ice, tracing the same figure over and over again, and she will go on tracing it for nearly four hours. Then she will go off to school and come back to Iceland that evening and skate another two hours. At about ten she will be back on the dark subway, riding home, nodding over schoolbooks.

I think of a thousand dawns for Carol Heiss. I think of hundreds of thousands of hours, painstakingly spinning circles within circles. And remembering, I submit that a champion must have *determination*.

I remember the Los Angeles Arena on an April night in 1963, the roaring of some fifteen thousand suddenly going silent as Bob Cousy writhes on the floor, holding a twisted ankle. This is the sixth game of the NBA playoff finals. One more victory and the Celtics will be champions a fifth successive time. And Cousy, who'd announced his retirement, will leave as he'd promised himself he would leave, a champion.

But now, with Boston leading 92 to 83, he is leaving with a limp. "Ten minutes too soon," he says, looking up at the clock. "Ten minutes too soon."

He is helped off the court. As he sits in the dressing room, his ankle being taped, he can hear the big partisan crowd screaming as the Lakers shrink the Celtic lead to one point, 100 to 99.

Red Auerbach jumps off the bench, hands forming a T. The Celtics bunch around him, and then—so suddenly the crowd lets out a surprised shout—out comes Cousy. He is still limping, but he has come back to play.

He plays the Celtics into a 112–109 lead. And with less than twenty-four seconds remaining, he dribbles out the clock, favoring the bad ankle but somehow keeping the ball away from the flailing arms of people like Elgin Baylor and Jerry West. When the buzzer ripsaws through the tumult of noise, Cousy throws the ball high in the air, thanking God—as he said later—he'd been allowed to leave a champion.

And remembering how Cousy limped back, after promising he would leave a champion, I say a champion must have *pride*.

I remember a moment before a meaningless ball game between the Pirates and Cardinals maybe ten years ago. Big Wally Westlake, the Pirate outfielder, jumps out of the batting cage after jerking several pitches into the seats. He sees Stan Musial near the Cardinal dugout.

"Hey, Stash," he yells, "man, do I feel great today. Like I was a lead-pipe cinch to go four for four. Ever get that feeling?"

"Yeah," says Musial. "Every day."

Westlake stares.

And remembering that stare, I say: a champion must have *confidence*.

"It's a cockiness really," says Bill White, the Cardinal first-baseman. "To be a champion you got to believe so much in yourself you're cocky. You're always trying to play it down, trying not to let your cockiness show, but sometimes it'll show.

"Like the other day, a columnist said to me: 'You're a hard guy to find something to write about.' And I said to him, 'Yeah, I guess I am. It must be hard to find something to write about a guy who only hits above .300 every year and drives in more than a hundred runs.' "

White begins to laugh. "That was my cockiness showing through," he says. "Sometimes you can't help it."

Four qualities: Skill. Determination. Pride. Confidence. Put them together in an athlete and is he or she a champion?

I'm not altogether sure.

I'm not sure, at any rate, that those four words—skill, determination, pride, confidence—mean the same thing to champions as they mean to the rest of us.

There are nuances to those words, shadings of meaning so subtle that their true meanings can only be felt emotionally rather than grasped intellectually. "I can talk all day of desire and determination," says Johnny Keane, "but some ballplayers sincerely will have no idea what I'm talking about."

Nevertheless, let us, the non-champions, try to understand those four words a little better by listening to champions and non-champions talk about them.

1. *Skill*

The non-champion is overawed by the skill of champions. "If you have the horses, you're half the way home," Duke Carmel tells me, sweating, his breath coming in gasps as he struggles this spring to make the Yankees as a utilityman. "Some guys come out here and break their backs trying to learn to do something. And maybe they never learn. The ones like Mantle, they just put on their uniforms and they can do it."

But the champion shrugs at his skills. "He's got to work hard to improve himself, just like anyone else," says Joe DiMaggio, who probably had more all-round skills than any ballplayer of his time. "People used to say I was great at coming in on groundballs. Well, I wasn't weak at it, you understand, but I didn't think I was up to the standard I could reach. So each spring I'd work on fielding groundballs. I'd have coaches hit low liners and groundballs to me by the hour, working on picking up the ball and throwing it in one motion. It was hard work, sure, but I don't know of any other way to reach the top."

The champion tries to mesh his skills to his personality. "You got to know yourself," says Cary Middlecoff. "You must learn which tournaments to play in, which ones to skip. You must learn when to lay off for a few weeks, when to start in playing again. You must learn what time of the day is best for you to practice. You must learn what you should be doing during a competition—sitting around with friends at night, or going off by yourself. And finally, you must have the self-discipline to make yourself do the things you've learned that you must do."

"Understanding yourself, that's the key," says Warren Spahn. "Say you're the kind of infielder who gets all tense, thumbs down, in a close game. You got to learn how to relax out there. Another guy, he's *too* relaxed. He's got to study himself to find ways to make himself bear down."

From the bench of champions, Phil Linz has watched Yankee skill in action. "The big thing," he says, "is that the champion—in a crucial situation—makes the play just the way he would make it in an ordinary situation.

"Like it's a World Series game. Two out, the bases loaded, the last of the ninth, score tied, the place in an uproar. Someone hits a groundball at Tony [Kubek]. He'll come in on that ball the same way he'd come in on a ball during infield practice. He makes the play the same way he always makes it.

"You'll see another guy, maybe as good a fielder as Tony. But in a tight situation, you see him come in on that ball a little different, trying to make sure of the play.

"The champion, like Mantle, he goes up with the bases loaded and he swings in the same groove he always swings in. The other guy, he's pressing, gritting his teeth, saying, 'I *got* to hit that ball.' And that's wrong. You do something different from the way you always do it, the way you learned, and you're not going to do it as well."

A champion, then, must have skills, but skills polished by practice, understood, and then mastered so that they quiver not a hair's breadth when destiny points a finger and says, "Now, *you*, be the big man!"

2. *Determination*

Which one of us hasn't known someone who wasted tremendous gifts because he wouldn't, as the athletes say, "pay the price"?

I have seen Stan Musial pay the price—taking batting practice for two hours under a broiling sun at Connie Mack Stadium because he was in a slump, then change his uniform and play a twi-night doubleheader. I've seen Dolph Schayes shoot foul shots for close to two hours, throwing up the ball, retrieving it, throwing it up again, chasing after it

—doing that hundreds of times and then coming back the next day and doing it again. And all because he missed three of ten foul shots in a game.

What makes them do it—the rich, the secure, the famous? What impels this fierce determination to excel? "It sounds trite," Vince Lombardi tells me, "but I think one must have a reason for being a champion. With most people the reason is a hunger—a hunger for financial gain or a hunger for glory."

Glory. A strange word coming from this hard-bitten man, his steel spectacles glinting in the sun. "Oh, yes," he says, laughing that quick laugh of his. "Glory. It can be very important. I have seen many young men, financially secure, who didn't have to take the punishment they must take in pro football. I have seen them come back to play because they wanted—maybe even needed—the glory that goes with being a champion."

I would agree that hunger for money or glory does breed determination. But it is not as easy to explain another facet of determination—the thing athletes call hustle or desire.

They confuse the two terms, in my opinion. Hustle is a physical thing: running out groundballs to the pitcher. Desire is a mental thing, an urge to win so powerful that in a moment of crisis it suddenly triggers a tremendous explosion of energy.

In the eighth inning of a close game, Mantle sprints from first to third on a single to left. The ordinary ballplayer stops at second. On third and three of a touchdown drive, Jimmy Brown pumps his legs one more time, sheds a tackler and makes the down. The ordinary fullback is stopped a foot short. Oscar Robertson shoots, misses, grabs the rebound, shoots, misses, and grabs the ball again. The ordinary ballplayer gets only one shot.

Sudden, amazing bursts of effort—second-effort, third-effort, fourth-effort. For an instant, the champion is superquick, superfast, superstrong.

It can happen to any of us: a son is trapped under the wheels of a truck; his father picks up the front of the truck, releasing the boy.

But for us, it happens rarely, maybe only once in a lifetime. It happens day-in and day-out with the Mantles, the Browns, the Robertsons.

I don't know whether this desire comes from a hunger for money or glory, or from some inner need to prove something to themselves and the world. But I do know it is there in only a few. "You can make a man hustle by fining him," says Johnny Keane. "But you can't teach him desire. It's there or it isn't.

"You see it plainly in some, like the Eddie Stankys. But it's there in the quiet ones as well as the holler guys. It's like a button that they press inside themselves, and suddenly they're bigger than they really are."

3. *Pride*

"Oh, it's a real thing, all right," says Brooks Robinson, who has looked across a diamond sundry times and seen it on the faces of the Yankees. "That club, they have it. Hank Bauer talks to us about the pride of the Yankees, but he doesn't have to; you can feel it when you play them."

In an individual this pride is there from youth, believes the Reds' Jim O'Toole. "Some guys start off hoping they'll just make the big leagues," he says. "But the champions, they start off figuring they're going to be the best there ever was."

"A champion is someone who can't settle for second best," says Warren Spahn. "He's not the guy who's hanging on. He figures he's the best on the club, the best in the league—yeah, maybe the best ever."

Pride nags the champion when he loses, hounding him to come back a winner. "The champion knows what winning means," says pro basketball's winningest coach, Red Auerbach. "A champion, when he loses, realizes to the fullest extent what he has missed. The other guy, he doesn't know."

It is pride, says Bud Wilkinson, remembering the goal-line stands of his national champion Oklahoma teams, that brings out the best skills of a champion when he is under pressure. "The pride of a champion," he says, "impels him to respond with a superior performance related to the strength of the challenge."

But pride eventually drives some of them into early retirement. Joe DiMaggio, still a powerful hitter but hobbled in the field by a bad heel, quit rather than be a part-time player. Bob Cousy, still among the league's top scorers, retired when he couldn't get himself "up" for top performances game after game. Rocky Marciano stepped out of the ring when his paper-thin nose could be made to spout fountains of blood by feather punches.

In others, the pride fades before the skills. "It isn't age," says Ed Furgol, who's forty-eight and still feels the pride swelling inside him. "It's a kind of complacency that sets in. A guy starts thinking more about living than competing. He thinks, 'Why all this work, why all this sweat? I don't have to prove anything any more.' And then you know the pride is gone."

Around the NFL there are some who will tell you that last year's Baltimore Colts lacked the pride to be champions. After clinching the Western title, they played Detroit and were badly beaten. "The Colts couldn't have cared less," said one Detroit lineman later, shaking his head. "I mean they were joking with us and carrying on. Just playing out the string. They had it made and didn't want anybody to get hurt. They just didn't care."

The Colts went on to play the Browns in the NFL championship game. And lost.

4. Confidence

"There is a certain kind of personality," says Phil Linz, "the kind who believe in themselves more than other people do. When they lose, they're surprised."

But I doubt this. For example, no matter what kind of personality you have, if I beat your brains out in ping-pong twenty times out of twenty pretty soon you're not going to be surprised when you lose.

Confidence, I think, comes after skill plus determination plus pride have built victory after victory. To a point, Linz agrees. "This Yankee spirit," he says, "part of it comes from knowing we've won so much. A guy comes to this club, knowing all the championships this team has won, he gets that confidence that the rest of the team has."

"It's like with Arnold Palmer," says golf pro Dave Marr. "He's done Frank Merriwell so many times he's making Frank Merriwell look like a bad finisher. When you finish like that so many times, you get the confidence that you're always going to be coming from behind to win. You're shocked when you don't."

What makes a champion? A champion must have basic skills which he polishes with hard work, then masters by gearing them to his own personality. He must have a determination to excel, a determination born out of hunger for fame or money, plus a desire—no, a *need*—to win that sets off spectacular explosions of energy. Also, a pride in himself, in his team, or in *his* achievements that keeps alive this determination and desire after reaching the top. And a confidence that comes with triumph after triumph.

My answer, I know, is not complete. For example, I will not try to weigh how much of each quality there must be in a champion. I would doubt that skills weigh only 10 percent as Carol Heiss maintains, but I suspect that the percentage varies widely from champion to champion, some having more skill than others.

I do maintain that some meaningful measure of *all* the qualities must be present. Let determination disappear, and skill rusts from disuse. Let pride disappear, and skill fades before its time. Let confidence disappear, and skill trembles in crises. And if skill disappears, then you can have all the determination, pride and confidence in the world and you still will know only galling disappointment and defeat.

I would agree with Carol Heiss that luck is important. "Good luck that you are not injured," she says. "And also having the good fortune to win at the right times, when determination is beginning to slip and you're beginning to wonder if all the work is worth it."

And I would especially agree with this from Dave Marr. "When I think what makes a champion," he told me, "I remember Arnold after the 1961 Masters. You remember: He'd come to the eighteenth needing only a par four to win. He shot a double-bogey six, and Player beat him by a single stroke.

"*A six!* It wasn't that he'd been beaten. He'd blown it. Oh, you could see that it was killing him, watching them put that green jacket on Gary. He had to be wishing he was a thousand miles from there. But he just sat there, that tight smile on his face, and I remember thinking: It's easy to be a winner, but champions really show what they're made of when they lose, and there—right there now—there's a champion."

John F. Kennedy

His Legacy to Sports

Arnold Hano | **1 9 6 4**

Our athletes cheat us. We root for a man who is adept at shooting baskets, but we must swallow the knowledge he uses his elbows on rebounds. We marvel at the pitcher with the sweeping sidearm delivery, but we wince as he throws the ball at a man's throat. So it goes. We are the fans, the dreamers; we swap our identities in the dark arenas where we can suddenly be great and triumphant, but as we do we keep up a running argument. So what, he's a dirty player. So what, he uses the laces in the clinches. He's a high-sticker, kidney puncher, faceguard-grabber? So what. He steals a hundredth of a second at the starting blocks? So what.

The ideals we set up must be downgraded. The dream is defiled. The man's great, but. We settle for second best.

A series of second bests has sullied sports in this nation. It has sullied the nation. These are the heroes we emulate. The heavyweight champion is an ex-con. We go to the arenas to watch a man strain himself in a test of strength, courage, and skill—but the real reason he wins is because he puts spit on a baseball. We tolerate the cheats. This is the ugly legacy of sports. The best you can say (and perhaps the worst) is: That's life.

Until November 22, 1963, it was possible to accept this halfway heroism, this sullied idealism, this spit-stained legacy. Not any more.

(*359*

On November 22, 1963, a man died.

Something of all of us died that day. "The wound is mortal and is mine," a poet said, in another context, nearly twenty years earlier. The poet? Aldous Huxley, who—incredibly—would die that same November 22, 1963. The wound was mortal and is ours.

But something in us was exalted by the death of John F. Kennedy. Something rose up out of that Texas street. Blood cleanses. Fire purifies. He had said—in his Inaugural—that he had been given a torch, he and his whole generation, a torch that had been lighted when this nation was born and which still burned. When he fell in that Texas street, we took the burning torch. The image is athletic.

He ran a leg of a relay race and passed the baton to us. Now we must run and carry, for ourselves. He showed us how. We have a new legacy.

He was, in the narrowest and broadest senses of the word, an athlete. Francis Bacon defined athletics as "the art of activity." The narrow sense. "I wasn't a terribly good athlete," John Kennedy said, "but I participated."

He played ball all his life, he swam, he sailed, he played golf, he walked, he ran. The day before he was nominated by the Democratic National Convention in Los Angeles, John Kennedy shot a round of golf at Cypress Point, California, and came within inches of a hole-in-one on the 150-yard fifteenth hole. After the nomination, he went back to the place of his childhood activity, the beaches of Cape Cod. "I played here as a boy," he explained, "and I relax here as a man."

You had just to look at him to sense his athletic nature. "The figure tapers like a boxer's," William Manchester wrote, in a book on Kennedy. Manchester kept noting the hand that made a sudden, spastic fist, the drumming fingers, the animal vitality. Activity drove Kennedy. "I can't hold back the stops," he said. "I have to go flat out, all out." The image, the words of an athlete.

Flip through photographs of Kennedy. The shot of Kennedy on his feet at a baseball game, his head thrown back, laughing, as a foul ball ticks past. Tossing out the first ball. Striding into a room of reporters, for a press conference. Shouldering his way out of the surf at Santa Monica, enjoying the press of bodies about him. We laughed at the way he said "vigah." But we admired the way he practiced it. He spoke the prose of an athlete, supple, sinewy words, with an athlete's sense of balance. He stripped the fat from words. The words became darts, truly thrown.

And he surrounded himself with athletes. Byron (Whizzer) White, All-America football player from the University of Colorado, and National Invitation Tournament basketball star. Kenneth O'Donnell, captain of Harvard's football team. Stewart Udall, also an NIT basketball player, from Arizona U., a man who plays tennis, hunts, fishes, and climbs mountains. The director of the Internal Revenue department, Mortimer Caplin, used to box. John M. Bailey, Democratic National Committee chairman—selected by Kennedy—played football and basketball at Catholic U., and captained the baseball team. Orville Freeman was a college quarterback. When Kennedy wanted a federal mediator to visit racially torn Birmingham, he sent Earl (Red) Blaik, former Army and Dartmouth football coach.

Nor did he have to go out of his family. The fifty-mile hike, test of a man's fitness, is associated today with his brother Bobby. The Kennedy men made touch football a national vogue. Kennedy's older brother, Joseph, Jr., taught the boys to sail and swim, to play football and baseball. After his death, John took over.

Above them all—in that vigorous family—stood Joseph P. Kennedy. Love him or hate him (and the old man has been loved and hated), he instilled in his children a sense of competition. He whetted their urge to win. Achilles' father commanded his son "ever to be the best and to surpass others." Of John F. Kennedy's father, author William Manchester wrote: "If young Joe and Jack lost a sailboat race, his rage was a caution; the only way to avoid it was to win." But it was not competition only for competition's sake, or victory's sake.

The importance of early athletic competition—Joe Kennedy suggested—is that it prepares for the more meaningful, more exacting competition of life. The boy who fought his brother Joseph with his fists in the Hyannis Port house—with nobody interfering—is the same man who later stood eyeball to eyeball with another powerful man over the issue of life and death for all men. It is possible that in the entire history of mankind, there has never been so important, so meaningful a demonstration of strength and courage as John F. Kennedy displayed over the issue of Russian missiles in Cuba. The lesson of an athletic competition had been magnificently taught.

And so, as a boy, John F. Kennedy sailed a yawl on Nantucket Sound. He competed in ocean sailing races. He swam backstroke for Harvard. He courted Jacqueline Bouvier aboard a twenty-four-foot sailboat. He caught a giant sailfish while honeymooning, at Acapulco. It seemed only natural that it was to John F. Kennedy that Floyd Patterson first confided he would fight Sonny Liston for the title.

These are the things he did, the affinity to sports that marked the man. He urged the creation of national parks, where hunters and fishermen, hikers and climbers—sportsmen—would have an opportunity to be active. In his 1033 days of Presidency, three national parks were established, including Cape Cod National Seashore Park where he played as a youth.

Sports knew how much he had given, and honored him. He received a gold medal from the National Football Foundation for outstanding service to football. John F. Kennedy, friend of athletes. If this had been his sole legacy, it would have been enough, the fruit of Woodrow Wilson's prediction that future Americans would one day pick their President from "wise and prudent athletes." It would have been a healthy link back to Eisenhower, an athlete in his youth; back to Roosevelt, who swam though crippled, and whose forearm muscles were admired by Jack Dempsey; back to Theodore Roosevelt, espouser of the vigorous life, hunter, boxer, conservationist; back to Lincoln who outwrestled a bully; back to John Adams, who swam in the Potomac. It would have carried us back to the British, who thought wars were won on playing fields, back to the Greek concept of a sound mind in a sound body.

And indeed, John Kennedy spoke out as such a President, link to a past where vigor was not to be scoffed at, but emulated. The words are not original, but then, this is still Kennedy, artist of activity. Two quotes suffice:

"Our struggles against aggressors throughout our history have been won on the playgrounds and corner lots and fields of America."

"We do not want our children to become a generation of spectators. Rather, we want each of them to become participants in the vigorous life."

Yet there was more than this pursuit of vigor. John F. Kennedy looked into athletics, and saw a moral core. A life of slothful ease was not simply a repudiation of man's vigorous instincts. It was immoral. Before he became President, he said, "We have, as a nation, gone soft—physically, mentally, spiritually soft. With a tough test facing us for a generation or more, we seem to be losing our will to sacrifice and to endure. We are in danger of betraying our traditions. We have altered our national scale of values. The slow corrosion of luxury—the slow erosion of courage—is beginning to show."

And suddenly the concept of *athlete* becomes more than activity, greater than an aptitude for throwing a football. A nation that became physically flabby became morally flabby. In such a nation, courage must erode and die.

It is a difficult lesson to plant.

John F. Kennedy demonstrated its validity. He set an example. This is his true legacy to sports, to America.

We think of sports as a test of manhood. A man pits his skills and strengths against a foe, or against the demanding standards of time or distance. But there must be more. A man must reach for more than strength, when his strength is spent. What he reaches for, then, is *courage*.

John F. Kennedy was a man imbued with courage, obsessed with courage, "most admirable of human virtues." He borrowed from Ernest Hemingway a definition of courage: "Grace under pressure." You must have grace, that oldest characteristic of Christianity, that gift of God. In the tests of courage, in the crucible of pressure, it is a moral decision you must make.

John F. Kennedy lived the lesson. He put himself out on the extreme edge of life, out on the brink, and—alone—he met the tests of pressure with moral strength. We need not fully detail the harrowing days and nights of early August 1943 when his PT boat was sliced in two and John F. Kennedy was thrown into the sea. But mention must be made.

"I thought—this is what it must feel like to die," he said. And then he went about the business of living, of making sure others about him lived. His back, injured while playing football at Harvard, was painfully injured again, but he swam and towed a man with his teeth and endured, his courage a visible thing in the black sea.

He and his mates could have huddled on the first island they reached, and have been found either by friend or by foe. But that would have been like quitting. A man doesn't quit so long as he can move, breathe, live. And so the swimming and the towing went on, agonizing hours, an endurance tested beyond belief, and the rescue was made as John F. Kennedy wanted it. They reached a friendly island. They hadn't quit. Quitting was immoral.

He assumed and resumed the lonely vigil we so often think of as only the athlete's: the pitcher on the hill, the runner racing a ticking clock, the prizefighter entering a ring, the skier descending the awful slope before rising to the majestic sky. What sustains you on the hill, in the ring, near the tape, in the sky—or in a sea infested by sharks and enemy guns—is courage. This is John F. Kennedy's legacy, and lesson, to sports.

And he knew—while he endured on the lonely edge of life—exactly what he had bargained for. *New York Times* Washington bureau chief

James Reston, on the day after the assassination, recalled a speech in which Kennedy suddenly drew out of his pocket a scrap of paper, and read aloud Blanch of Spain's words, in Shakespeare's *King John*:

> The sun's o'ercast with blood. Fair day, Adieu!
> Which is the side that I must go withal?
> I am with both; each army hath a hand,
> And in their rage, I having hold of both,
> They whirl asunder and dismember me.

These are the forebodings of death, and it is part of his legacy to sports. The athlete must take risks. When there is no daylight for the fullback to run to, he must make his own. The bullfighter, the jockey, the boxer all dare death. So did Kennedy. "His whole life has been a hunt for challenges," William Manchester wrote. It has been, and more. It has been a taunting of death. Look again at those men Kennedy surrounded himself with. Orville Freeman—the Minnesota quarterback—had his face shot away by a Japanese bullet. He had to learn to speak again. Kenneth O'Donnell was a fighter pilot. Pierre Salinger—that fat, affable, cigar-smoking man with a talent for music—was a teen-age minesweeper captain. Byron White was a PT boat officer.

Death was a companion to John F. Kennedy. He knew its face full well. He nearly died, out on the sea, and later he was given the last rites of his church when infection set in after a spine operation. His brother Joe, Jr., had been killed in the war. His sister Kathleen died in a plane crash. Her husband had died fighting with the Coldstream Guards. Sister-in-law Ethel's parents were killed in a plane crash. A daughter of John and Jacqueline Kennedy was stillborn. A son had lived less than two days. Death, and all Death's friends. A sister is mentally retarded. His father has suffered a paralyzing stroke.

Some of this obsession, this grim companionship with death and with its ally, pain, grew out of his family upbringing. Some of it grew out of the harsh soil of the place where he played as a child. Cape Cod is a barren windswept spit of land that sticks a bony foot into the gray Atlantic. You may think of it as sunny and wafted by ocean breezes, a place to swim and loll, but that is a summer thought. It was at Hyannis Port that John F. Kennedy spent his Thanksgivings and his Christmases. Think of the Cape then. Grim and wet, with a cold that reaches to the bone. Such a land demands its inhabitants be tough, whether they be Harvard-educated millionaires' sons, or Portuguese fishermen. This is where he played.

And yet despite its rigor, there is a cleanness about the Cape, and its salt and bleached sand and water. Somehow, this, too, was John Kennedy. He was a totally clean man. He enjoyed the look of health, in himself and in others. When Commander Alan B. Shepard came to Washington after his flight into space, Kennedy said of the astronauts: "They are the tanned and healthy ones; the others are Washington employees." But Kennedy was one of the tanned and healthy ones. This health went through him. Somebody once said Kennedy never told a dirty joke. Dirt was foreign to Kennedy. And it is all linked—this athletic stripping away of fat, from word and from flesh; this eliminating of the flabby mind, the flabby wit, the flabby spirit; this distaste for the salacious; this instinct that courage erodes or builds with a corresponding building or lessening of softness. A man was either soft or he was athletic, and the distinction touched him from skin to soul.

We are led, finally, to the realization that Kennedy's roots go back farther than the land he played on, farther than his family's roots here and in Ireland, farther than the roots of athletically inclined American Presidents. We go back to that other clean, heroic, athletic, sea-living, sea-loving people, the Greeks. We are today amused by a modern man who tries to be heroic. It is almost anachronistic. Who needs to be a hero?

That is the question, and Kennedy answered it. Just as that other athletic people answered it. The Greeks insisted man needed to be a hero to fulfill his manhood. The gods they created could throw thunderbolts, shake the earth, support the firmament. In short, their gods were super-athletes. And Greek men set out to emulate them. To the Greeks, if the gods were athletic, then athletes must try to be godlike. Kennedy, the Christian, capitalized the "G." Kennedy said: "A man does what he must—in spite of personal consequences, in spite of obstacles and dangers and pressures—and that is the basis of all human morality."

The world of sports—Kennedy knew, the Greeks knew—provides that first early test where a man meets obstacles and dangers and pressures. It is here a man begins to excel.

This is the legacy. Second bests won't do. Mediocrity won't do. Placing spit on a baseball won't do. You devote yourself to the pursuit of excellence, outwardly, inwardly. You begin on the playground—or on the sea—and you continue to pursue it all the days of your life. John F. Kennedy pursued excellence right on down a Texas road. The very last thing John Kennedy did was throw back his head and laugh, and expose his throat.

This athlete has not cheated us. He martyred himself to excellence, and was slaughtered by mediocrity, but he made us see the difference. No longer shall we be satisfied with the defilers of our dream. This is his legacy to sports.

Part Four | 1966–1971

The Unknown Side of Bill Russell

Fred Katz | **1966**

Bill Russell was very intent because he had this theory and he wanted to make sure it was understood. "Two a.m. is no good," he said, shaking his head. "No, two a.m. is too early. And six a.m., that's too late. But four a.m. . . ." Russell's eyes shone with approval. "Four a.m. is just right. I've even set the alarm to wake me. Four a.m. Then I pick up the phone and call my friend Harold Furash and I say, 'Hi, Harold. I had to go to the bathroom and I thought about you. Did I wake you up?' " Russell's whooping laugh crashed into the corners of every room in the house.

Russell was enjoying himself in his home in Reading, Massachusetts. It is a house built for privacy and ornamented with luxury. It belongs to a man making $100,000 a year as the Boston Celtics' center, captain and most valuable player. Outside, there's a swimming pool, and a stable to be filled as soon as Bill's three kids get their way. Inside, the six nine and three-quarters Russell is dwarfed by the towering beamed ceiling in the living room. And music—always there is music. This is Bill Russell's hideaway. It is crammed with creature comforts, yet it would mean nothing to Russell if it didn't offer more. It does. It provides a place where he can laugh at the practical jokes of the past and the humor of the moment.

"My boy Buddha came up to me one day," said Bill, "and he went 'Whew!' I said, 'What's the matter?' and he said, 'Boy, I'm tired.' I said, 'You kiddin' me?' And he said, 'Gee, Dad, it's *hard* to play all day.' " Russell's lips parted in laughter and the eyelids on his pliable face were drawn nearly shut. The sound that came out was once described this way by writer Ed Linn: "If thunder were played on an English horn instead of a kettledrum, you would have some idea of the pitch and tone of Russell's laughter."

Laughter is very important for Bill Russell. Without it he might be a difficult, hateful man; with it he is merely complex. A small segment of the public might be surprised to learn that Russell has ever *smiled,* much less laughed. A larger segment might doubt that he does either very often. Give Russell a lot of credit for this image; he's worked very hard to build it.

Russell once said, "I owe the public nothing and I'll pay them nothing. . . . I refuse to smile and be nice to the kiddies. . . ." He spoke those words as a militant Negro impatient with the white man's hypocrisy. He reinforced them with a scowl and a refusal to sign autographs. The words, the scowl, the refusals still stand as ready reminders to the public that the further it stays away from Russell, the better he likes it. DANGER. KEEP BACK. BEWARE OF THE MAD NEGRO.

The reasons for Russell's militancy are many, but he rarely recites them. "I don't care if people don't understand me," he says. "I don't make it easier for them to understand me. I avoid that as much as possible. People who are realistic are non-conformists because they do what they want to do without caring what others think. I'm that way."

Russell's public pose seems an extreme way of being recognized as an independent thinker. But life for Bill Russell has always been a series of extremes, with rarely a middle ground. He once was poor. Now he's well on his way to becoming a millionaire and, probably, a multimillionaire. As a high-school sophomore he barely made the junior varsity. Today many people consider him the most valuable basketball player in the world. When men around him were growing mustaches, Russell grew a beard. When his stereo or car radio is on, it is always a few hundred decibels too loud.

The extremes roll on. As a youngster he went to church four times every Sunday. Today, he never goes. "Religion left me a long time ago," he says, and though he doesn't foster his beliefs on his family, he is extremely cynical of the Christian ethic.

"When I lived in the South," he says, "I realized that teachers and preachers were selling Negroes down the river. When I travel all over the world I see that where religion is strongest, the people are poorest. There is a church in South America that took three hundred years to build and is gold from the ceiling to the altar. Outside, on the steps, the people are starving."

And so today Russell claims he has as little need for organized religion as he does for the public, that he snubs both for the same reason: hypocrisy. It's easy enough to ignore religion, but the public is a different matter and Russell must work extra hard to keep the battle running. He is, however, well-armed with ammunition. He can cut down a stranger with one deft thrust. Last year a man said to Bill: "Mr. Russell, I have a son who thinks you're just the greatest." Replied Bill: "Well, I have two sons who aren't a bit impressed."

Yet, curiously, Russell himself will seek out people—as long as his anonymity is guaranteed. He enjoys seeing how they'll react. Driving toward the Mystic River Bridge near Boston one day, Bill glanced out the rear-view mirror. "I think I'll pay the toll for that man behind me," Bill said to his wife, Rose. Russell handed the attendant two quarters and slowly drove off. Bill's beneficiary reached the toll booth and tried to pay, but the attendant shook his head and pointed toward Russell's car. Bill and Rose, meanwhile, were laughing hysterically at the sight of the two men arguing. The other driver finally gave up and started pursuing the crazy man up ahead. Bill stepped on the gas and disappeared from the man forever.

Another time Bill stopped for a red light on a narrow crosstown street in Manhattan. Off to his left was a young couple changing a tire on a Volkswagen. It was cold and snowing and the couple didn't look very happy. Russell pressed the window button on his Lincoln convertible and, looking over the side, said: "You mean to say Volkswagens get flat tires?" The girl looked up blankly. Said Bill, straightfaced: "I always thought Volkswagens were perfect." Russell pressed the window button and drove off.

Bill says he meant to lighten their burden, but it might be hard to convince many people of his good intentions. If you've ever seen Russell ignore a pleading six-year-old's cry for an autograph, you'd have to believe that he'd just as soon poison the kid's porridge. That is, you would until you saw Bill some night at the Boston Garden when he is the last to leave the locker room and a flock of kids is still waiting. More than likely he'll sign for all of them—punctuating his signature with a warning not to tell.

The inconsistency of the man can be overwhelming and people close to Russell can be subjected to it just as much as strangers. This past December Bill was on the phone going over plans to be out of town the next day. When he hung up, his wife said, "Do you know what tomorrow is?"

"Yeah," said Bill, "it's December ninth and I'll be married nine years. Don't rub it in." Bill laughed but Rose was hurt and returned to the sink to wash dishes. The next day, while Bill was keeping an engagement he couldn't break, Rose sewed.

Contrast that with Rose's birthday last summer. Bill had to go to Africa to check on his Liberian rubber plantation. Before he left he arranged for the Ford dealer in town to drive Rose's present—a red station wagon—to the house on her birthday. "Sometimes," says Rose, "people just don't understand that Bill is more than a hard shell."

Harold White, a lawyer, found out about that shell first-hand. He finally pierced it with a lawyer's best weapon—sharp words. He told Russell he couldn't deal with him in his best interests until he stopped fearing him. Bill let down the barrier and today he and White are good friends.

But even after one is admitted into this exclusive inner circle, the battle is not over. Last summer was a nightmare of confrontations and run-ins between Bill and his friends. "In their friendship people had worshipped him as Bill Russell," says Rose, "and they thought of him as the best father, the best businessman, the best this and that. Everybody had a different pedestal for him and when he didn't measure up to this, he was no good. For an insecure man like Bill, it can be squashing. He was trying to establish his humaneness. Now most of these people are trying to relax and let him be himself."

At thirty-two, Russell still seems unsure of who he is. Given the chance, he'd like to emulate his grandfather and, to a lesser extent, his father. "I don't think I've really ever been able to talk to my grandfather," Bill said recently. "He's so much of a man that I've been almost afraid."

Russell laughed when he was reminded that people have said the same thing about him. "That's because I'm big. My grandfather's only five six, five seven. I never remember him having a job, never remember him working for anyone. He always supported himself and never took charity. As for my father, he always maintained his manhood in times when it was particularly difficult. There were times when he'd go looking for a job every morning for months. When you're a poor kid it's very important never to have been on relief—my father was always able to be head of the household."

You cannot envy the position Bill Russell is in. He must uphold the legacy of two generations of fierce independence. He no longer lives in Monroe, Louisiana, and he no longer is poor, so it should be easier for him than it was for his forebears. Yet it is not easier. He is a man who feels deeply about things—so deeply that he has had to cultivate the protective coverings to withstand the blows. And how do you resolve going your own way when it bothers you to know that it will adversely affect a friend?

"Once Bill really brooded about hurting a certain person," Rose recalls. "He touched me so much. He said, 'I'll be glad when I die and then I'll be alone and I won't hurt anyone again.' " Bill's conversation is constantly shrouded with references to dying.

Rose Russell traces her husband's sensitivity to a childhood and youth filled with loneliness and rejection. "He played alone a lot because his mother died when he was young," says Rose. "And his first real deep loves all backfired. When he was just plain Bill Russell he wasn't good enough, not until he became known nationally. So what is mistaken today for a dislike of people is really a fear of people and a fear that they may not like what's there. With or without a crowd, Bill is still very lonely."

Russell is fortunate to have a lovely, intelligent wife with uncommon insight. He also has two devices that help numb the inner pain of reality. One is his career with the Celtics, now in its tenth year. Bill calls pro athletics "a fantasy world, an artificial life," so it offers, to him, an escape. The other pain-killer is his sense of humor which flashes in a dazzling spectrum. There is the whimsy, the one-liner, the practical joke, the joke-on-himself, the put-on, the sarcasm, the shocker, the squelch and the insult. Sometimes Russell's humor can be unfunny, even cruel. The cruelty is very special. It is reserved for the people Bill likes.

Before a recent game a photographer came into the Celtic locker room. "Hi, Jerry," said Russell, "how's your health?" Jerry said it was okay. "Maybe you'll die soon," said Bill. "I hope." Jerry walked to another part of the room. "Nice fellow," Bill said quietly.

Russell's humor. You do have to be prepared for it. A guy got him on the phone at practice one day and, after talking for a while, told Bill to ignore the message he had left for him at home. "Okay," said Bill, "I was going to, uh, do that anyway." Russell waited until he heard the caller laugh and then he too broke up.

Bill loves to put people on. The first time his newsboy saw Bill's license plate which reads "Celtics 6," the boy's eyes grew big. "You play with the Celtics?" he asked Bill excitedly. "You play? Who are you?"

Bill deadpanned, "Sure, I play with the Celtics. I'm Bob Cousy."

The boy blinked and stared at the dour Russell. Then he blinked again. "Nah," he decided finally, "you're not Bob Cousy."

For a short while early this season Bill's humor was restrained considerably. The trying period began on December 3, in Boston. Philadelphia 76er co-owner Isaac "Ike" Richman died of a heart attack during a game which the 76ers eventually won. The death deeply affected Russell. Richman was well-known for his generosity—particularly to Wilt Chamberlain and the 76ers' other Negro players. Chamberlain and Russell are good friends and during their occasional meals together at Bill's home, Wilt undoubtedly spoke kindly of his boss. This meant a lot to Bill, who has learned to be suspicious of a white man's dealings with a Negro. When Richman died, Russell felt the loss of a man he probably would have liked to have known better.

The next night Russell's miseries mounted. He strained a hamstring muscle in St. Louis, the only NBA town he dislikes. His hatred stems from the racial goings-over he got there as a rookie in 1956–57 when he was the only Negro on either the Celtics or the Hawks. Bill admits St. Louis isn't nearly as bad any more, but his feelings haven't softened. "I can appreciate a change, a legitimate change," he says, "but I'm not going to forgive or even *try* to forget."

Boston went on to win the Hawk game without Bill, but it lost the next night in Cincinnati. To the delight of the crowd, Russell sat on the bench in street clothes. Royal fans obviously have no love for Russell as a player because he, more than any other, stands between the Royals and a championship.

After an off-day the Celtics flew to New York for a 6:30 game with the Hawks. Bill tried to sleep between 3:00 and 4:45 but received about fifteen phone calls. He looked groggy as he let a visitor into his room but said he was actually getting more rest these days than ever before. At the end of the '63–'64 season Bill had made headlines by saying his weariness over the course of the season and his fear of flying, among other things, might force him to retire. "If he's looking for sympathy from me," said coach Red Auerbach, "he'll get zero."

So last season—his ninth season—Bill went through what he calls "an adjustment period," and started getting more sleep. "I can even sleep on planes for the first time," he said with slight amazement. "Takeoffs are the worst—they still bother me. But I sleep on flights. Maybe I sleep too much."

Bill picked up the phone and made one last call before leaving for the game. "I feel two hundred years old," he said, laughing into the receiver. "All they got to do is lay me down and close the box."

After he hung up Bill said it always makes him nervous when people ask him how he is. "When I was a rookie I was naïve," he said. "There was, shall we say, the bookie element in Boston, and I thought everyone who asked me about my health was a gambler. Men would call up and say they were taking their sons to the games so they wanted to make sure I was okay. They were just checking." Bill chuckled softly.

Russell got into the hotel elevator, along with an elderly couple of about seventy. The man asked Bill a question several times, and Bill tried to answer, but it was difficult to decipher the strange accent. Finally Russell figured out that the man wanted to know where Bill played basketball. "Everywhere," said Russell, staring straight ahead. The man's face brightened and, as the elevator reached ground level, the man playfully punched Russell in the ribs. "Sure are tall," he giggled. The door opened and three women in their thirties nudged each other as Russell stepped out. "He must be a basketball player," said one. "No," said Russell, without breaking stride, "I'm a jockey."

When Bill reached the Celtic locker room at Madison Square Garden, his entire personality seemed to change. He doesn't normally speak loudly, but now his was the loudest voice in the room. He instigated most of the wisecracks, moving swiftly from one player to the next. He was fulfilling his role as elder statesman and captain.

Surprisingly, there was a time when Russell appeared to shun responsibility. Cousy expressed this concern during his last season (1962–63). "He doesn't seem to want to take over as leader," said Cousy. "But if they're going to win, he must." Auerbach forced the role on Russell by appointing him co-captain the next year. As strange as it must seem to the fans who view Russell as an insensitive brute, Bill's big problem was that he didn't want to hurt anyone's feelings by making corrections.

At first Russell reacted to his new position as he often does in a strange situation—in the extreme. He had been co-captain less than two months when he told a luncheon audience there was nothing wrong with John Havlicek that some coaching couldn't cure. And as for Tom Heinsohn. . . . "Well," said Russell, "Auerbach should play him some night until he falls down and then pour water over him and make him play some more."

If Auerbach stayed in character, he probably commended Bill on his enthusiasm and then suggested that a little discretion wouldn't hurt either. Today Bill combines both and there isn't a man on the team who doesn't feel the Celtics have the best captain in the league. Russell's pride—both in himself and the club—were virtual guarantees that he would succeed in his relatively new role. Bill now knows, too, that a captain can lead without making public critiques. Russell did, however, make an exception this past December. He told the press that a certain player hadn't been hustling and was out of shape and had better start playing up to par. The player's name, he hastened to add, was Bill Russell.

"We like to think it's a special kind of guy who becomes a Celtic," says Russell. "He can't be selfish and play for this team. A while back we had a veteran who tried to spread dissension by saying 'Hurrah for me, the hell with everyone else.' He wanted to return for another season but he wasn't invited back. There's no room for prima donnas around here."

Russell's pride often forces him to be tough on himself and on others—particularly rookies. In camp he'll test the newcomers with an extra shove, a needless elbow, a protruding hip. To Russell all rookies on trial have the same name: "Boy." If they try to get friendly, he walks away. "When you get to like someone and he leaves," says Russell, "you lose something." Bill seemed to be speaking from sad experience.

As Russell says, there are no prima donnas on the Celtics, and even as he tested his valuable leg in Madison Square Garden the scene seemed underplayed. Most of the players appeared intent on something else as Bill kicked and stretched and pivoted. Still in tie and shirttails, Russell walked over to Auerbach and shrugged his shoulders. "Now we've got to run on it," said Bill.

Russell could have played that night if he had been needed. But his backup man, Mel Counts, did a fine job on the Hawks' Zelmo Beaty, and, as it developed, Bill proved more valuable on the bench. He had to take over as coach when Auerbach got thrown out early in the second half.

The Celtics won 112 to 96, so, of course, their post-game locker room was a pleasant place to be. Russell's big laugh hacked through the dull roar of the exhaust fan as fellows congratulated him on his "fine coaching job." "Hey, Red," said Bill, "I'm sure glad you got a lot of money—the way you kick those hundred-dollar bills around." Russell simulated a placekick and broke up.

Bill's occasional stint as Red's replacement is good for laughs, but it wouldn't be if it were a steady thing. "Red can have that coaching," says Bill. "I get frustrated and can't do anything about it. When I'm through playing, that's the end of basketball. Way I think now, anyhow."

Despite his past threats to retire, Bill seems to want to cling to his playing career just as long as possible. If he refrains from straining his hamstring muscles, and if his arthritic knees don't hobble him, and if a chronically ailing Achilles' tendon doesn't act up—well then, Bill figures he has two more seasons after this one. By then he just might have led Boston to its tenth straight world championship and Bill always did like round numbers. And he especially liked the round figure of $100,000 times three which appeared on the three-year contract he signed last summer.

Immediately after the Hawk game Russell returned to Boston and rested at home the next day for the Los Angeles game that night. Bill's home in Reading is about a twenty-five-minute drive from the Boston Garden and he likes the town very much. He likes it, he says, because he has good neighbors. And he has good neighbors, he says, because they don't bother him. There are four or five other Negro families in town and Bill hasn't met them all.

The Russells' previous house was on Main Street. They lived there several years, but the house was broken into twice and a supermarket opened across the street and the growing community began to crowd in on Bill. So he took part of the wealth he had begun to accumulate and moved to a home where you can stare out the kitchen window and see open field and trees that seem to dwindle into jagged matchsticks on the horizon.

Bill also has a nice front lawn which a group of teen-agers admired so much that they used it for an impromptu beer party one night when Bill was out of town. "If they have enough nerve for that," says Russell, "they might have enough nerve to come in sometime." So Bill has bought Rose a .22 pistol and taught her how to use it. There was, in fact, a night when Bill feared he might have taught her too well.

Rose was home with the children when, in the middle of the night, she thought she heard strange noises. She got the pistol and turned on all the lights, including the floodlights that illuminate the lawn. Apparently no one was there, but Rose was so keyed up she couldn't go back to sleep, so she started pacing in the kitchen—the pistol still in her hand. It was 4:00 a.m. now and Bill was just getting back from a road trip. As he drove up to the house, he wondered why all the lights were on. Then he walked into the kitchen, only to be greeted by his gun-toting wife. Suddenly Bill visualized himself in the morning headlines:

CELTICS STAR SHOT BY ANGRY WIFE. "What'd I do?" he screamed at
Rose. "What'd I do?"

Bill laughingly recalled the incident as he sat in the kitchen a few
hours before the Los Angeles game. He appeared more at ease here
than in any of the other several settings around which he revolves during the season: hotel, locker room, basketball court, airplane. And it
was indeed a scene of domestic contentment. Rose was cleaning up
while wearing a crimson apron with the imprinted warning: "Don't kiss
me, I'm busy!" Buddha, eight, in his Cub Scout uniform, was doing his
homework, and Jacob, six, and Karen, four, were drawing trucks.

Yet despite the pleasant setting and Bill's own frequent outbursts of
good humor, Bill still seemed incapable of controlling his moodiness.
He sat with a visitor at the table, but frequently, without warning, he
broke off the conversation by turning his attention to the newspaper in
front of him. At times Rose and the visitor found themselves talking
about Bill in the third person as though he weren't there. What's more,
Bill seemed to enjoy the imaginary eavesdropping—cocking an ear and
looking up with a quizzical smile when something intrigued him.

He appeared to be disinterested as Rose talked about his preoccupation with death. "He uses death as an excuse for a lot of things," said
Rose. "Say, for example, he feels he's not as close to the children as he
should be. So he'll rationalize by saying, 'I'm Bill Russell the basketball
player and businessman and I'm busy and I might die any minute.'

"It's also shown by a selfish desire to achieve and be an economic
force. 'I'll get all this and retire young and then I won't have to worry
about dying.' " Rose's voice rang heavy with irony. "Then I'll be a rich
widow and the kids will be in good shape." She walked away from the
table.

Bill kept his finger on his place in the paper and looked up. "Sure I
think about death," he said. "It doesn't scare me. Sometimes I think:
'*I'm going to die.*' " He said it without drama, as casually as if he were
talking about going to the market for a loaf of bread. "I just hope I can
do most of the things I want to do."

The phone rang and Bill answered it. The woman on the other end
said, "Mrs. Russell?" "Not unless her voice has changed," said Bill before handing the phone to Rose. Rose's friends dread that Bill will get
to the phone before Rose does. If one of them says, "Can I speak to
Mrs. Russell?" Bill is likely to reply with mock disgust, "If you insist!"

Of course, Bill often has a few surprises on the phone for his own
friends, too. Former teammate Ben Swain called one day. "Hello, Bill?"
he said.

"Very solly," came the high-pitched reply. "This is Cathay Café. Ah so. You want Chinese food? Egg loll, shlimp chow mein, egg foo young, chicken flied lice. Velly nice." Swain kept saying he didn't want any Chinese food, but the "proprietor" of the Cathay Café wouldn't take no for an answer. For five minutes Bill recited the restaurant menu. Swain finally hung up and a minute later Bill's phone rang again. "Hello, Bill?" said Swain. "Yeah," said Russell in his normal voice. "Boy," said Swain, "you're not going to believe this but I got a wrong number and this Chinaman wouldn't let me off the phone." "No kidding?" said Bill.

Russell has always been one for the practical joke. The only problem is, he peaked too soon and all his adult life he has been waiting for the golden moment to top the thing he pulled off as a kid. It seems Bill's parents were friendly with a very superstitious neighbor couple. The woman was enormously fat and the man had a pegleg and they would come over to Bill's house and talk about ghosts by the hour. One night when the couple was visiting, Bill and his brother took some white sheets, went down the road and hid. After a while the couple started on their way home. At just the right moment the two little ghosts filtered into the moonlight. *"Oooooowww,"* they moaned, *"oooooowww, oooooowww."* The couple's eyes popped and they suddenly realized they had a very important decision to make: Which was closer, the Russell house or their own? They chose the Russells' and made it in record time. "That was a race," says Bill. "A pegleg and a fat broad. It was a dead heat, believe me."

Bill was in a rollicking mood now as he recalled his past conquests and the mood continued at the dinner table. After Buddha said grace, Bill called the boy over and whispered into his ear. Buddha then walked over to the visitor. "Do you know what Wilt Chamberlain is?" said Buddha.

"No," said the visitor, "what is Wilt Chamberlain?"

"Wilt Chamberlain is a fink." The children all giggled and Bill tried unsuccessfully to keep from laughing too.

By six o'clock the babysitter had arrived, Bill and Rose had dressed and the children lined up for their father's farewell ritual. Each one approached in turn, arms extended. Without bending over, Russell lifted each one straight up, planted a kiss and lowered the child straight down. He is both firm and tender and they love his sense of humor. Saturday morning is a good time because if Bill is home he gets up to watch the Bugs Bunny cartoons on TV with them. And he seems almost determined that if they are to admire him at all, it be solely as a father, not as a well-known basketball player. The children rarely go to the games and only once or twice has Bill shot baskets with Buddha.

Bill has provided extraordinarily well for his family, but as Rose had indicated, Bill's financial aims extend well beyond being merely a good provider. Rose had mentioned the term "economic force," and as Bill drove toward the Boston Garden, he explained exactly what that meant.

"Having money is one thing," he said, "but it's the kind of money you have that counts. Do you follow me? Now. Say I buy stocks and bonds and end up with six hundred million dollars. What kind of influence do I have? Perhaps very little. But if I have ten percent of General Foods, say, I have a certain amount of power.

"That's what I want. You have to become a participating part of industry—maybe steel, aluminum, chemicals, automobiles—to have influence. Do you see? Like when a certain steel company raises prices and others have to follow suit—that kind of influence."

So far Russell has diversified his business interests. He has his rubber plantation in Liberia which provides jobs for a couple of hundred Africans. He owns a popular restaurant in Boston, works for a Ford dealer, has designed and is in the process of manufacturing his own basketball sneakers, and has various real estate investments. It is obvious that once Russell quits the Celtics he intends never again to work for anyone else. You don't become an economic force by punching someone else's timeclock.

Bill was one of the first Boston players to arrive at the Garden and once more he was center-stage. "I sure learned something from you cats last night," said Bill, pausing for the proper effect. "I learned it's more fun to be a shooter than not." Bill laughed.

Sam Jones walked in wearing a conservative gray suit. "Nice suit, Sam," said Bill.

Ron Bonham, standing next to Bill, said quietly, "Better than that fluorescent one he had last night."

Russell cringed in mock horror. "Sam, you hear that? Bonham's cuttin' your clothes again."

"I didn't say a thing," said Bonham.

"Yes he did, Sam. He's lyin'. Look at that, his palms are up." Russell roared as Bonham tried to turn his hands over.

Mel Counts walked past Russell and that was all the cue Bill needed.

Turning to a reporter, Bill said, "Listen to this and you can quote me: Mel Counts owns Zelmo Beaty. Yes, sir. Mel Counts owns Beaty. No doubt about it." Counts, who had gotten fourteen rebounds against St. Louis the night before, was as embarrassed as he usually is when Russell kids him.

Russell stretched his right leg out on the bench and placed a heating pad under the hamstring area. A fellow walked in who couldn't have been taller than four six. "There," said Bill, loud enough for all to hear, "is our next pivot man."

"Hey, Russ," said K. C. Jones, "you playing tonight?"

"It's a spectator sport, isn't it?" said Bill. "Well, I just might spectate. I haven't had much of a chance to study the multi-skilled endeavors of such outstanding performers as Thomas "Satch" Sanders, Don Nelson, and John Have-a-shot—er, I mean Havlicek."

Auerbach walked in and Larry Siegfried began talking about the speaking engagement Red had set up for him in a Catholic church. "My church doesn't even allow me to go in there," said Larry.

"Don't worry," said Red, "I'll get a special dispensation for you."

"That's right, Larry," said Bill. "That's the man you want when you're layin' out there in purgatory. He's got a hot line to God."

Like the night before, Russell could have started the game, but he and Red agreed to wait until a crucial moment. The time came with two minutes left in the third period, the Celtics trailing 85 to 81. The crowd's roar as Russell took off his jacket reminded you of kids at a Saturday matinee when the cavalry finally arrives. Russell played seven minutes and in addition to rebounding fiercely, knocked away a pass that forced the Lakers to lose the ball on a twenty-four-second violation. When Bill went back to the bench, Boston led 96 to 92.

Suddenly the game reversed itself. Three straight times the Celtics missed their first shot and couldn't get the rebound. With 3:05 remaining and the score tied at 102, Russell went back in. The one-man cavalry again. He immediately broke open the game. Bringing the ball down he spotted Sam Jones, who broke for the basket, caught Russell's pass and scored. Russell got the next defensive rebound, started a fast break and Havlicek hit from twenty feet. In a minute and twenty seconds, Boston made three straight baskets. The Lakers scrambled and scored twice, but the possible tie-making shot by Rudy LaRusso was blocked by Russell. The Celtics got the ball and, finally, the game—108 to 106.

In ten minutes Russell had grabbed ten rebounds. He had provided a textbook demonstration of how to be the most valuable player on the court without scoring a point. Only Russell could write such a book, and somewhere in it he would have to tell you how to play on a murderously throbbing leg.

Like a diamond, Russell is a multi-faceted wonder who sparkles in different ways at different times. But there's no mistaking Russell's "plane of cleavage"—that critical point which unveils the secrets of an uncut stone. The secret to understanding Russell is to accept him as a man who must, for better or worse, pursue an independent course. Put no bindings on the man because he will throw them off. He wants power—hungers for it—but only certain kinds. He says he could never be a politician: "too confining." Russell as a politician? Shaking strangers' hands? Kissing babies?

If Bill fails to get wherever he wants to go, he wants it to be *his* failure and no one else's. If he makes it, it will be *his* triumph. "You hear a lot of guys say that 'I couldn't have done it without my wife,'" says Russell sarcastically. "Well, how can your wife give you the drive you don't have? Now I don't treat anyone the way I treat Rose. She's a very special person. She's the one person I picked to spend the rest of my life with and to me that's a big deal. But success, contrary to popular belief, is the result of hard work and that work probably started before you ever met your wife."

Russell's drive is unlikely to sputter as long as he remains as unimpressed with his past as he is now. One day while he was sorting records he was asked what his proudest accomplishment was. Twenty seconds passed. "I don't know," he said. "I haven't given it much thought." For the next minute he gave it some thought. "I don't know," he said again. "I guess it's because I really haven't done anything—not really. So far I've just lived my life as it's come. I haven't been the master of my own destiny."

Somehow Russell didn't seem quite sure whether he was searching for the obtainable. Was that destiny as real as the record in his hand? Or was it merely a mirage shimmering with mocking grandeur? Whichever the case, it was clear Bill Russell could never be a contented man until he found out.

Zoilo Versalles

How a Problem Child Becomes an MVP

Jerry Izenberg | **1966**

Underneath the mud and grime, the station wagon is a gunmetal gray, blending with the dull January sky like a set of matching bookends. The road from Minneapolis to Dresser, Wisconsin, winds icily ahead. In Cuba, whatever else may have happened, the mangoes still bloom and the warm water still rushes to meet the sand out of Miramar Beach. But here, on a December night in Minnesota, the snow drifts endlessly beside the highway and the wind cuts like a double-edged axe and the St. Croix River has already begun to hibernate beneath the ice floes.

Up front, Tony Oliva hunches forward like a diver with the bends, draws his muffler tightly against his neck and tries to crawl into the car's heater. In the rear, Rich Rollins looks out the window at the snow and speaks of skiing and ice skating because this is his home and his kind of weather. Next to him, Zoilo Versalles sinks deeper into his rich, blue overcoat, hands thrust heavily inside his pockets. It is not his kind of weather.

December and January and February are the cruelest months for Zoilo Versalles. Later that night he would say, "There is nothing worse to a man than to lose his home. I am cold. The people are nice but the snow is on the ground and I am cold. Cuba is my country and they don't let me go home."

(*383*

He is twenty-five years old and he is the most valuable player in the American League. A whole world is caught in a social revolution but it is not his battle and he doesn't want to fight anyone. He began his fighting a long time ago with an empty belly and a cast-off fielder's glove and he won his war by himself, which is the way it had to be because most of the time it was himself he was fighting. But now when he has reached a type of maturity, when the tantrums and the sulking are gone and he is the acknowledged best at what he does, the banquets and the awards and the speeches have a dull, hollow ring. He is cold, and Havana and Washington have erected a wall between the two halves of his life. The wise bamboo bends with the wind but it still needs its roots.

On this particular night, Versalles and Rollins and Oliva are on their way to Dresser (population 600) to make a good-will appearance for the Minnesota Twins. The Twins belong to the people of Minnesota and Wisconsin and the Dakotas and even part of Canada. They work this caper hard and well. And in the off-season, Zoilo Versalles, who once fed on temperament and moodiness, works it for them.

Versalles left school in the second grade to run on the streets of Havana and at eighteen he came to a strange country with a strange language and absolutely no ability to communicate. Now it is eight years later and he makes speeches in small town halls and in big hotels and the people hear and understand and appreciate.

"If the situations were reversed," Rich Rollins asks a visitor, "could you do it?"

It is no small way to measure a man.

The town hall in Dresser used to be the elementary school before the village outgrew it. Workmen are setting up plain wooden tables and the mayor is there and everybody seems to know everyone else. Zoilo Versalles smiles and he shakes hands and he stands a bit back from everyone else and then he and Oliva check into a motel for a nap. Two hours later, Rollins and the visitor return. The motel room is a wall of steam. Moisture bathes the windows and runs down them in little tributaries.

"It's very pleasant in here," the visitor says, groping through the heat waves.

"Yes," Zoilo says.

"The thermostat reads eighty-four."

"That's nice," Zoilo says.

"Man," Tony Oliva shudders, "it's gonna be cold out there."

This is a typical off-season night for Zoilo Versalles, who is also a member of the Twins' promotional staff. He sits at the make-shift head table with the mayor and throughout the meal he signs autographs on cracked fielder's gloves and bats and bits of paper. He picks at his food and he smiles and later he makes a speech. It is a short speech and it draws warm laughter and applause and when he sits down, he turns to a man and says: "You understand my speech? You think they understand it?"

"Sure," the man says.

"Good," Zoilo nods but he is unconvinced. A lot has happened to Zoilo Versalles in the past eight years; the problem child has been replaced by the man, but doubts still crowd his mind.

The night in Dresser, Wisconsin, is over. The autographs have been signed and the pictures distributed and outside the temperature continues to drop. On Highway 95, a million miles from home, Zoilo Versalles begins to talk about the way it was and the way it is.

"The sun," he says. "In Havana the sun could burn you pretty good. No snow . . . no cold . . . only sun . . . everywhere. Sure I remember the way it was. I remember my home . . . just one room and in this room I dream to myself that someday maybe I can get to be somebody. It was like this."

Calle Norte 3919 was a horseshoe-shaped tenement in Havana's Marianao District. There were thirteen one-room apartments with common walls and each family lived and bred and died within the confines of its single room. A single naked light bulb hung from the ceiling on a half-naked wire in each apartment. A single water spigot and a single out-house served all thirteen families.

"My stepfather," Zoilo says, staring off into the Minnesota night, "he make three dollars a day . . . pick and shovel . . . not so bad for where we live. My mother, she cook and clean in the beeg houses in Miramar Beach. My brother is Lasaro. The four of us live in the one room. Sometimes my mother doesn't come home until nine-thirty, ten o'clock at night. My father is always tired. My mother is always tired. Sometimes late at night she ask me about the baseball that afternoon and I tell her and then she take my arm and put it next to her cheek and she say, 'Zoilo, some day this arm gonna make lots of thousands of dollars.' She die before I get to beeg leagues.

"How it was?" he says more to himself than his companion. "Well, I could be much beeger, you know, but nobody beeg on my block. How you get beeg with coffee for breakfast and coffee and bread for lunch and beans and rice for supper?"

The beans and rice kept him out of school. Every morning he would walk by himself to the Mesa Domingoes School and afterward he would play baseball in the streets in his bare feet ("Well, you had to save the shoes for Sunday, you know") and when the feet began to bleed on the broken bottles and cobblestones it was not a very big thing because that only made you exactly like everyone else in the game.

But in the second grade Zoilo dropped out of school. "My mother was working," he explains now in the station wagon. "My father was working. Lasaro was working. Everybody work. So somebody has to put the beans and rice on the fire. My second-grade teacher—she was the last teacher I ever had—she was short and fat with white hair and very mean. I stay home after that to make the supper.

"But you have to understand something here. The life was not so bad as it sounds. Sometimes, Juan and Miguel and Teodoro—they were keeds on my block—sometimes we go across the road where the beeg house is and we climb the fence, steal mangoes to eat. And sometimes I chop wood for the laundryman's fire for thirty-five cents and we go out and have crackers and jelly.

"But I tell you something. This is the best education. To start from nothing . . . to have nothing. The neighborhood was not so tough. A lot of bluffing, you know, but baseball is more important than fights. But you start here, you don't forget. Like I say, this is the best education. When you have been poor, you remember."

There were a lot of things which could have happened to Zoilo Versalles in this environment. He could have quit on life and grown mean and hard. A second-grade education, after all, does not qualify you for very much in this world. This is not a small point to bear in mind when assessing the sulking and the confusion which marked the early part of his major-league baseball career. What it did do to him, however, was to make him acutely aware that baseball was an escape route and he attacked it with the kind of desperation which gave ammunition to his early critics. There were many critics and, in truth, reasons for criticism.

The life of Zoilo Versalles, like Caesar's Gaul, has been divided into three parts. There was the childhood that never was, then the belated adolescence, which was marked by swagger and moodiness masking fears. Finally there is Zoilo Versalles today, who speaks with more authority and, perhaps, more honesty and has only begun to scratch the surface of what will some day be the sum total of his professional achievements.

Phase two, the adolescence, began to take shape when his stepfather's brother, a journeyman ballplayer named Carlos Paula, gave him a discarded baseball glove. It was black and scarred and the leather was cracked but it was the first such glove to appear anywhere along Calle Norte and it made a very large boy of Zoilo. He began dreaming of playing for Alemendares, a local professional baseball team. "The blue uniform of Alemendares," Zoilo says, "I could think of nothing else. I wanted to be part of that so much."

His brother, Lasaro, got him a tryout as a second-baseman with a team in a very fast semi-pro league. Zoilo made the team and, at fifteen, he was the baby. "The peetcher," he recalls, "was thirty-five. They were men. I was good hands, plenty courage and no heet. But the manager sent me to Cambria."

Joe Cambria was a scout for the Washington Senators. His base was Cuba and he shipped a steady stream of hungry kids North.

"My mother and me," Zoilo says as the station wagon heads from Dresser to Minneapolis, "we go to the big Pan-American Building in Havana to Cambria's office. I sign there."

"You get a bonus?" a man says.

"Bonus? Sure we all get bonus. You know the bonus we get? Carfare, that's the bonus.

"Hey, Tony," he says, leaning forward to Oliva, "you get a bonus? You ever hear of any Latin player who gets a bonus?"

Oliva laughs and answers in staccato Spanish.

"He says no," Versalles laughs. "I'll tell you, everybody knows us. Everybody knows we have the poverty. We have the hunger. All we want is to play ball. So, hokay, no bonus. Latin boys never get no bonus. I don't like this thing but I don't tell you for complaint. I tell you so that you will know the way it is."

Cambria sent Versalles north in the summer of 1957. "I fly to Key West," Versalles says. . . . "I don't know no English. I get to bus station and right away I get in trouble because there is segregation. Well, this I don't understand because this is supposed to be land of democracy but I'm just a visitor and some nice white lady help me out. So then I have to eat but I don't have no English so I point to picture of hamburger on wall and I get something to eat.

"Now we go on the bus and every town we pass I run up to the driver and I say, 'Hey, is this Charlotte?' That bus driver get to know me pretty good before we get there. Then we work. Then they say, 'Zoilo, go home and grow.' I go home. I don't grow but next year they sign me anyway."

Zoilo hit .292 at Elmira in 1958. The next spring a private meeting took place in the Senators' camp at Orlando, Florida. Present were manager Cookie Lavagetto, owner Cal Griffith, farm director Sherry

Robertson, traveling secretary Howie Fox, Cambria and the coaching staff.

The Senators were a bad ballclub and their shortstops were even worse. "They are plain lousy," Lavagetto said. "I need a major-league shortstop. I don't care if he only hits .100."

"I got the kid," Cambria said. Cambria always seemed to be saying that and people rarely took him seriously.

"Listen," Sherry Robertson said. "Why don't you try selling the other clubs on your kids. That way maybe we can make a trade."

"I mean it, Cookie," Cambria said. "I got a kid with one year's pro experience. He has a major-league arm. He runs like a major-leaguer. He fields like a major-leaguer. Maybe someday he'll learn how to hit like one. Right now he can't hit a lick. Maybe you can teach him to bunt .100."

"I don't know," Lavagetto said.

"He'll only take up time and space," Robertson said.

"Uncle would try it," Cambria said, appealing to Calvin Griffith. Uncle was Cambria's pet name for Calvin's father, the late Clark Griffith.

"All right," Calvin said. "It won't hurt to look."

Enter Zoilo Versalles, skinny and scared. He arrived at Orlando and announced that Luis Aparicio was the greatest shortstop in baseball but Zoilo Versalles would be even better. He came in talking and the talk, of course, was a cover for his fright. After one practice, he sat in a car with Camilo Pascual and a reporter and the reporter said with a large needle: "You look good, kid. But let me tell you about Aparicio. One day in Comiskey Park he makes a catch against the left-field fence, right, Camilo?"

"That's right," Pascual said, picking up the gag.

"He do that?" Zoilo said. "He do that? I dunno. Take me two more years before I can do that."

And so it went. But while Zoilo talked incessantly to the irritation of some of the veteran players, he performed amazingly in the field. The Senators were a bad ballclub and Orlando, Florida, cared even less about them than Washington, D.C. But suddenly the natives were turning out just to see the skinny kid with the big arm work infield practice.

"He was the biggest hot dog you ever saw," says a former teammate of Zoilo's. "But he had an amazing feel for what people wanted to see. You could sense it there in infield practice and you can sense it now if you ever go out and hear him make a speech. He read the paying customers perfectly. Unfortunately, he couldn't do the same with some of his teammates back then."

The brass agreed on Zoilo and they also agreed that they were going to make every effort not to rush him. They shipped him off to Fox Cities in Wisconsin and recalled him late in the year. In 1960, they sent him to Charleston, where he hit .278, and when he joined the Senators late in the season, they were playing the White Sox and for the first time Zoilo Versalles and Luis Aparicio were on the same field.

In the bottom of the eighth inning, Harry Simpson slammed a lead-off pinch-hit double for the Sox. The next hitter was Aparicio, who rifled a shot past pitcher Camilo Pascual and toward center field. And suddenly here came Versalles, skin and bones defying gravity and common sense. He flagged the ball down in shallow center, pivoted and unhesitatingly threw toward third. Simpson, who had rounded the bag, was out.

While Versalles only played fifteen games that year for Washington, it was apparent that the trips to the minors were over. The following season the club moved to Minneapolis. Zoilo left for spring training and discovered that he couldn't go home again. The bars between Cuba and the United States were real and solid. Suddenly, everything began to fall apart.

It was a strange year. The best thing about it for Versalles was the chance to play in New York. It enabled him to go to the Metropolitan Opera House. Ballplayers—or at least many of them—find this a little hard to understand, especially in light of Zoilo's limited education. But he is a man of deceptive duplicity. He used to bring his recorder to the clubhouse and play Verdi's *Il Trovatore* and Mozart's *Don Giovanni*. This went over so large with the literati that he had to take it home again.

Things went from bad to worse as 1961 progressed. Zoilo began to hurt. There was a story around the league that he would develop back trouble if he struck out early in a ballgame. His development lagged. His wife, Josefa, and his children were still in Cuba. He ran up astronomical phone bills. He spent money he did not have. "I was beeg-leaguer with only twenty dollars in my pocket," he says. He was in the majors and he was broke. Then he developed stomach trouble.

If there is a single low point in the major-league career of Zoilo Versalles, it has to be a July afternoon in 1961. The White Sox were in town for a day game. Zoilo had become moody and even more introspective than usual. He said his back hurt. Other people said it didn't. He said his stomach hurt. Other people said it didn't. The lack of money—he was already overdrawn on his salary—rankled him. He announced to nobody in particular in the Twins' clubhouse that he was going to quit.

For three days he brooded at the Maryland Hotel in Minneapolis. He went from his room to the coffee shop and back to his room. He had become the biggest story in town by playing the reluctant dragon. On the third day, a local family called and offered to take him in. Homesick, confused and a little bit angry at himself or the world or both, Zoilo accepted.

He did, indeed, have a stomach ailment, which was treated and cured. The back remained a point of debate, but he joined the club three weeks later. Soon afterward, Josefa and the children arrived from Cuba. He had turned the corner.

The crowds reacted immediately. Armed with his instinctive showman's flair, he won them back. Life around the clubhouse, however, did not fall into shape quite so easily. Sam Mele was the manager now. He gave Zoilo every chance but there were times when even Sam began to doubt his eagerness to play. In 1961, Zoilo Versalles hit .280 but 1961 was a lousy year.

The change in Zoilo began to shape itself slowly in 1962. For one thing, the three-week AWOL stint had drawn national publicity. In the spring of '62, writers from other cities began to seek him out in Orlando. Zoilo was on center stage now. He spoke freely. He did not have a good season but the following year he did. He displaced Aparicio as the All-Star shortstop. This was important to him. Teammates recognized this and congratulated him at each opportunity. Still he had doubts.

In the spring of 1964 he sat in the visitors' dugout at the Yankee camp in Fort Lauderdale and suddenly broke a moody silence. "Listen, you think I got it made. No. How can that be?"

"Come on Zoilo," a guy said. "You're the All-Star shortstop. Nobody is going to take your job. You're going to be here a long time."

"Listen, you don't understand. You still got to make the play. I come here like crazy kid and run. Now I learn you got to know how and why you run, hokay. But you got to keep learning. This game is not so easy. I joke and laugh with you, hokay. But this my business. I got to be good. I got to stay good. When time comes I no good, you know what they say? They say, 'Goodbye Zoilo.' I don't have it made. Only stupid man says that."

Inch by inch, Zoilo Versalles had begun to mature. The final breakthrough began on a cold, snowy night at a bar called Duff's in Minneapolis. Versalles walked into the bar between the 1964 and 1965 season and saw Twins coach Billy Martin sitting in a booth.

"Hey, Zoilo," Martin called, "come here. I gotta tell you something."

"What you want, Beely?" Zoilo asked.

"I just wanna tell you that with a little effort you are going to be the most valuable player in the American League this year."

"Oh, Beely," Zoilo said, "you very fonny fellow."

A week later, in the Twins' offices a few blocks from Zoilo's home, they met again.

"Get a good rest," Martin said. "When we go south you are going to start becoming the MVP."

"Sure, Beely," Zoilo said. "Sure."

In Orlando, Martin kept after him. In Zoilo's own words: "You know he talk so much MVP beesiness I start to get very interested in this thing."

Versalles grew closer and closer to Martin. In a spring-training game, manager Mele and Zoilo had a well-publicized run-in, in which Zoilo said he'd play for Martin, not for Mele. Mele, of course, fined Zoilo heavily and Zoilo came around. He got along well with Mele from then on and he also remained close to Martin.

Early in the season, Zoilo began to assault the ball like a wounded snail. "Hey, Beely, you please tell me," he said, "how I gonna hit .227 and be MVP. I jus' like to know that, huh?"

But Martin carried the verbal war to Zoilo every day—on buses, on airplanes and in hotel lobbies. As the Twins came hammering down the stretch toward the pennant, it suddenly occurred to Zoilo Versalles that Billy Martin had a hell of a shot at making all-league prophet.

"You could see the change," Mele says. "Suddenly we had a leadoff hitter. We had tried him there before. But now he was cutting down on his strikeouts and he was running the way we thought he should be running.

"We had a rookie [Frank Quilici] playing next to him at second and Zoilo picked the kid up. He started to become the leader of this team. Martin would talk to me about Zoilo every day and we were pretty much in agreement. He seemed to mature. For the first time, we were able to turn him loose."

The effect of this last was apparent on the customers as well as the enemy. There had been a moment in the second game of one of the strangest World Series ever played, when the Twins were about to put the Dodgers away for the second time. Suddenly, there was Zoilo jumping up and down off first base and the crowd was chanting, "go . . . go

. . . go," and this wasn't supposed to happen at all because people said Zoilo played in the cheesecake league and the Twins were not going to run on the Dodgers.

"I only wish we could have run him more in that series," Mele says. "I think he is going to do things that will keep people talking for a long time."

"Zoilo Versalles," says Rich Rollins, "is so good he has no idea how good he is. He makes more errors because he gets to balls that other shortstops wouldn't have a prayer at. He is amazing. And he's different now. That car ride we took to Dresser. Listen, two years ago he would have sat there like a stone. Two years ago he seemed to be living inside himself."

In a way, part of Zoilo's new-found maturity stems from his off-season speaking job with the Twins. He has an innate curiosity about people, dating back to Calle Norte and the freedom of the streets. Last year he and Rollins and Jerry Snyder, who works in the Twins' public relations department, stood alone in the snow, looking up at Mt. Rushmore. They visited Deadwood, South Dakota, the stamping grounds of Wild Bill Hickok.

"There," Versalles says, "they take us to this beeg bar and they show us this table and the man say, 'Right here, Zoilo, they shot Wild Beel dead.' So then we go to another bar and another man say, 'You see that table? Right there they shoot Wild Beel dead.' Well, you know, we see so many places where they shoot Wild Beel I don't know if he was a man or a cat."

The morning after the excursion to Dresser, Zoilo Versalles sat in his living room at 9101 Oliver Street in Bloomington. It is a clean, small home. The living room is furnished with the neat transience of people who raise their family well but know in their hearts that home is somewhere else.

In the kitchen, ~~Josefa Versalles~~ an attractive dark-haired woman, was trying to keep her four small daughters' minds on breakfast. The oldest, Amparito, four, was eating toast in front of the television set.

Framed in the distance through the big picture window behind Versalles were the light towers of Metropolitan Stadium. A 1966 blue Cadillac stood in the adjacent garage. Josefa answered the doorbell and took an armful of clothes from the driver of a cleaner's truck.

"I was waiting for you," she said.

So was Zoilo, who had to make a personal appearance that afternoon at a local supermarket and had no intention of wearing last night's suit.

"Clothes," Zoilo said, opening a subject on which he has drawn much criticism from ballplayers who say he is not saving enough money, "I have fifteen suits. I have fifteen pairs of shoes. Who tells me not to buy them? The guys who wear one suit all season.

"Look, this house is hokay. My family eats. My children grow strong, hokay. These guys, they don't tell me nothing when they speak. They don't tell me what it means to be poor. I know. I told you how we live when I was a keed. Hokay, don't nobody have to tell me what it means to be poor. God gave me a talent. He give one to everybody. So you supposed to enjoy it. I have no education. What I learn, I learn on the street but I learn when you have no shoes, then shoes are something you want. Those guys, in the hole when they put you there because you are dead, you can't take no money with you."

"Zoilo," a visitor said, "you are the first Latin to win an MVP award and. . . ."

"Yes," Versalles said, "and this is big thing for me. Latins have much emotion. Sometimes, I guess, this makes the trouble. People try to treat us the same but we are not the same . . . not the same language . . . not the same ideas . . . look, I don't say this because I am MVP."

"Why not?"

"Hokay, maybe is good thing because if MVP says it then maybe people will listen. Most of us, we don't have the education other boys got. Our parents don't have it either. Most of us, we have only poverty in the beginning. Maybe this is why we never get no bonuses. But that's not important. We want to play and they give us the chance. Hokay.

"But look, they bring us here, right? We are the latecomers. Hokay. We don't want to say this is the way you should do things but I think is good idea if the commissioner's office gets somebody who understand us to help settle problems keep them little ones instead of big ones. Now look, I don't tell commissioner his business. They tell me he is pretty good man but we do need somebody to try to find out what we theenk. So we got problems, too, but we don't talk English so good so maybe it's hard for people to understand.

"When the season ends, we can't go home, I mean the Cubans can't. Hokay, so we like to play in Latin countries. They won't let us. They say major-league Latin takes away some Triple A boy's chance to play winter ball. But then the Triple A boy, he take away some Class A Latin boy's chance. But he could play with us.

"And if we go and play in Mexico and Puerto Rico and Venezuela I think is not such a bad thing for this country. It is much goodwill.

"I love these people up here but I don't wanna stay here all year and catch cold . . . the snow . . . the cold . . . I don't want to tell anyone how to run his business but like you say, I'm the MVP so if I speak maybe somebody will say, 'Hey, that's not bad idea.' "

There is a great deal of thought behind much of what Zoilo Versalles says. The Cubans, for example, have a special problem. "You remember the day we cleench the pennant," Zoilo said. "Everybody drinking champagne . . . much hollering . . . everybody happy. I stand in front of my locker with Tony [Oliva] and Camilo [Pascual] and Sandy [Valdespino] and we don't say nothing. Tony cries. I think, this is beegest moment I ever have and I can't go home to tell nobody. It's not our fault Castro is there."

Zoilo went back inside to help out with the baby and Amparito slipped into the living room and stood there looking up at the stranger.

"You want to see something?" she asked in a very brave voice.

"Yes, I do," the man said.

She took his hand and led him down to the basement, which had been finished off into a kind of den.

"That's my Christmas tree," she said. "I helped mommy fix it up."

It was a large tree and there were presents underneath it and a colored spotlight was tilted upward at the base. A photographer was coming this morning to take a family picture.

In the corner of the basement there was a large oil painting of Versalles in his Minnesota Twins uniform. Next to it, the trophies were lined up neatly on a long shelf. There was one from the women's auxiliary of the Minneapolis Chamber of Commerce and on the day Zoilo had received it, he had stood up in the main ballroom of the Radisson Hotel and he had said, "This is a great honor and a very heavy trophy. It means much to me to be the MVP. For one thing, it means a bigger paycheck." And the joint had broken up over that, prompting Calvin Griffith to take the microphone and urge Zoilo to come in and talk contract before somebody else decided to give him another trophy.

Next to it there was the Golden Glove Award for fielding excellence and a large vacant area in the center where the American League Most Valuable Player Trophy will ultimately stand. Finally, off by itself in the corner, there was a small gold cup: *"a Zoilo Versalles"* the top line read. *"Exilados en Minnesota"* was engraved beneath that. This was a gift from other Cubans who cannot go home and its meaning is self-evident.

The photographer had begun to set up his equipment in front of the Christmas tree and Josefa and the rest of the family were being told where to sit. Upstairs, Zoilo paused for a moment at the head of the stairs to listen to the hi-fi set, which had been playing all morning. The song was "Linda Cubana" with Barbarito Diez. The complete record was a medley of Cuban tunes, the ballads were soft and undulating . . . the others were up-tempo with a touch of fire in the beat.

Versalles listened for a moment, then carefully raised the needle and shut the lid. He came downstairs and took his place in the middle of the family group.

"Lift up the baby, Zoilo," the photographer instructed. "All right everybody, now let's have a nice big Christmas smile."

Outside, the weather was turning cold again.

The Price of Fame
for Bobby Hull

Bill Furlong | **1 9 6 6**

The phone rang at 6:30 in the morning. Bobby Hull picked it
up and began to work. "A 'beeper' interview for the radio show I do,"
he said. Hull still led the National Hockey League scorers even though
he'd missed four games because of an injury to his left knee. Until that
injury, he'd been off to the most fantastic scoring start in hockey history: in the first six games, Hull had scored as many goals personally as
the entire Toronto Maple Leafs team had scored in eight games. Suddenly he found himself a prisoner of his own fame. Though his knee injury prevented him from playing for the Chicago Black Hawks, he
found his work going on . . . and on . . . and on. He bought a heifer
for a highly publicized appearance in the International Live Stock
Show in Chicago ("finished ninth in a field of ten"). He made personal
appearances at sales promotion parties thrown by an automobile dealer
("I figure I can pay for our new car this way"). He showed up in a tuxedo for the opening of a store that rents formal wear ("they seemed to
like the appearance"). He taped radio and television reports ("only on
the day after a game"). And he made an appointment to consult with
his accountant for year-end tax planning (carrying his financial records
around in an old grocery sack).

This is the toll of fame: it is always there—always demanding. It filters into the quiet corners of the mind. It consumes time, energy, the precious gift of privacy. It breaks some men. It exalts others. In Bobby Hull, it brings out his drive, his ambition, his vision of the future. It brings out also that special quality: he has mastered fame—he hasn't let it master him.

At the heart of his fame is a simple fact: at the age of twenty-seven, Bobby Hull is the greatest hockey player in the world.

This describes but does not define him. He has the hardest shot in hockey—"the hardest *ever* in hockey," says his teammate, goalkeeper Glenn Hall. His slap shot has been timed at 118 m.p.h., or 19 m.p.h. faster than the fastest pitch ever recorded in baseball. It has inspired terror in goalies, awe in the fans. "He can miss with one of his blasts and the goalie, thanking the fates for this momentary escape, starts looking for the nearest exit," says Jack Griffin of the Chicago *Sun-Times*. "And from the crowd comes this rumble over what they've seen. When Bobby warms up with those two little rabbit hops of his and starts down the rink, the entire arena begins to tremble in anticipation." It was that quality which endowed Babe Ruth with his unique place in baseball. "This is not just in the madhouse that is the Chicago Stadium," Griffin went on. "It's also in staid Toronto, in blasé Montreal, and in New York and Boston and Detroit. He's the draw—the guy who fills the house."

In short, he has that matchless gift called color. Bobby has had it ever since he came up to the major leagues at the age of eighteen. To be sure, the years since cost him something of himself. His nose has been battered often. His face is laced with scars, some of them imperceptible, some of them angry and red—such as the one over the rise of his left eye. His once-plush blond hair is thinning a little. "Bobby just ain't pretty no mo'," says one friend. Yet it is the *image* of Bobby Hull—square, handsome, as fully charged as a young tornado—that endures. He is *color* personified—the hero as he should be: strong, dauntless, upright, unyielding under pressure, unflinching under attack. He is the wish-dream in all of us, the personification of what-might-have-been.

His skill and his color have given him a special stature in sports: he is alone at the peak of his game. No other man in the world so dominates his sport as Hull dominates hockey. Baseball? There's Willie Mays *and* Sandy Koufax. Football? There's Jimmy Brown *and* Johnny Unitas. Basketball? Wilt Chamberlain *and* Bill Russell *and* Oscar Robertson. Hockey? Bobby Hull. He stands alone.

Hull dominates all thought about the game; he changes its traditions and shapes its rules. Once in Canada he made some comments about a Black Hawk coach—a violation of athletic niceties that set teeth on edge. In print, at least, the players must maintain a sufficient servility pleasing to the owners. Hull was, in his view, merely telling the truth; he never expected his comments to creep back to Chicago. Instead of fining Hull—or trading him—the front-office men of the Black Hawks merely gritted, "When a player produces, he's got a right to his opinions." Within a year the coach was replaced. Even the league changes its rules for Hull. One of the most hallowed of rules over the years has been the one that bars players who haven't signed their contract from playing in the league all-star game. Last autumn, Hull hadn't signed his Black Hawk contract on the day of the all-star game. The league repealed the rule. "We would have looked foolish to stage our all-star game without Bobby Hull," said Clarence Campbell, the NHL president. Hull *then* signed his contract.

His fame offers Bobby Hull power, opportunity—and burdens. He has not recognized the power. He has recognized the opportunities, for he is one of the New Breed in Sports—the athlete who not only accepts fame but uses it. He sees it not as the reward of greatness but as a tool of the future. He has his goals though he has a tendency to understate them. "I'd like to play long enough so that when I'm finished, I won't have to go out and dig ditches or punch timeclocks." He wants to lead the good life, to indulge its security, its comfort, its meaning. It is what fame might yet return him.

He is ready to accept its burdens. It happens that he is temperamentally inclined to work hard to match those burdens. Indeed, he *has* to be up and working. "I really can't sit still long," he says. "On Sunday at home on the farm, I just can't sit around. I've got to get up and go look at the herd." Nor can he really enjoy vacations. Last summer, he and the family went to Hawaii for a vacation that was supposed to last two weeks. But he couldn't take it—just lying around on the beach in the sun. "After five days, we came home," he says.

Some burdens are not physical. They wear at the emotions and the mind and they penetrate deeply into the texture of family life. Bobby hates to part—as he must—with his three small sons when the Hawks go on road trips. "The children don't understand," he said last spring. "They can't understand why I don't stay home with them all the time. Why just the other day Bobby, Jr., told my wife, Joanne, to take my suitcase away from me." And when his daddy had to join the team at a special Stanley Cup retreat, three-year-old Blake Hull began to cry.

Said Bobby: "When I got into the car, he turned to Joanne and asked, 'Why is daddy leaving? Have I been a bad boy?' "

Still other burdens demand a devotion to commitments that might embarrass him. Last autumn, for instance, he'd hoped to show one of his yearling bulls at the International Livestock show in Chicago but the bull fell ill. Without his own steer, he'd have preferred not to enter the show at all. "But they'd put out so much publicity that I felt we had to come up with something," he says. So he bought a heifer from another farm in Canada and had it shipped to Chicago. "I led it into judging myself," he says grimly. The animal didn't have quite enough meat on her—"they've got to be so fat they can hardly walk," he says. "You've got to start getting her 'fit' from the time she's a calf." He didn't like finishing ninth—and he couldn't explain to the public that the heifer hadn't been bred on his farm. He simply accepted the fact that he *had* to appear and he made the most of it.

It hasn't always been easy. "Bobby is a very complex man," says one friend who's studied him for eight years. "He was one of the most poised eighteen-year-olds I've ever encountered and he's maintained this poise all through his career. "I think there's a lot of the Canadian farm boy in Bobby, but he knows that this game is played in the big cities and that's where his income is. So he's learned to play the sophisticated role—the kind of person they *expect* him to be in New York and Chicago. But I'm not sure he really likes it. I think he'd be perfectly happy staying on that farm back in Ontario."

Hull himself concedes the contradiction in his nature. One day not long ago he sat in the Black Hawk suite of offices in the Chicago Stadium and considered one particular question like a man weighing the insoluble prison of being: "Who would you like to be if you could choose to be anybody else in history?" Outside, the afternoon dusk was beginning to eat like a river into the winter light. Hull was the picture of the young executive—à la Paul Newman of the movies. He has an ineluctable sense of dress and he can look perfectly groomed in a cable-knit sweater or—as he was dressed this day—in clothes suited for a meeting of the board of directors. He found the question an intriguing one; it reflects the imagination and desires of the inner man. Mickey Mantle once told me he'd rather be Frank Sinatra. Bill Veeck said he would like to have been Robin Hood, who stole from the rich to give to the poor.

Now it was Hull's turn. His answer: "Tom Jones!" He looked a little abashed at the candor of his choice. Tom Jones was the swashbuckling character in Henry Fielding's novel of England's more picaresque life in the eighteenth century; he achieved a somewhat wider celebrity in a movie adapted from the novel, which illustrated—among other things —how to be a slob while eating. A lecherous slob. "I'm not sure I should have said that," said Hull, looking prim and proper, "but I've often thought I'd like to live in the days when people were not so prim and proper."

If his world is sometimes prim and proper, it is also immensely varied and stimulating. For his fame has been a passport to a knowledge of many lives—as athlete, farmer, businessman, celebrity. At the centrix of them all is the life of the hockey player.

The shelter in that world is the locker room. It is located in the grimy bowels of the Chicago Stadium, hard by storage rooms with old lumber, by the workshops and concessions storage rooms, by a kennel penning a snarling black German shepherd behind a door that says: "Bad dog—Man Eater!—Keep out!" The locker room itself is immaculate, well-lighted, the most modern in the business. It has the usual equipment: a training room, an equipment room, an office for the coach. But it also has a sauna bath ("temperature runs 140, maybe 160") just off a modern shower room. And it has a "slumber" room where the players can relax and sleep after taking a sauna and shower. Bobby Hull's cubicle—a hard wooden bench with hooks on the back wall for his clothes, hooks on the top frame for his skates—is in the far corner of the locker room, away from the door. His neighbors on his right are his linemates —rangy, outgoing Phil Esposito, the center; chunky, agile Chico Maki, the right wing. Billy Reay likes to keep his lines together as much as possible. On Hull's left, as the cubicles turn the corner, are two defensemen—open-faced Doug Jarrett, burr-headed expressive Matt Ravlich, who grew up in Sault Ste. Marie with Esposito and Maki, who played junior hockey with Hull in Ontario. (Dennis Hull, Bobby's brother— who's almost six years younger than Bobby—has a cubicle across the way, near the players he normally joins on the ice. When Bobby was hurt, it was Dennis and Ken Hodge who replaced him on the left wing.) There is always an undertone of joshing and happy needling going on around the Hull cubicle: his friends pay him the high tribute of wiseguy affection. ("Samson lost his strength when he lost his hair," warns Ravlich.) Hull takes the needling with embarrassed smiles: his friends are more accomplished at it than he is. He is never imperious about hockey: he speaks with his skill, not his mouth.

One morning Hull sat in his cubicle and looked down at the floor. He was bothered about his hockey sticks. He'd picked one off the rack and taken it to the work table outside the locker room. The work table has a vise, a saw, and a plane and it gives the players a chance to tailor the sticks to their own desires. He cut two inches off the end of the stick, then planed down the heel. "I don't know what's wrong with these sticks—I don't even think they're mine," he said. He dismissed the fact that the handle had his name burned in black on it. "They can still make a mistake," he said. The sticks have a deep curve in the blade. "Stan really started it," he says of Mikita. Hull adopted the curved blade in the season he scored fifty goals—1961–62. ("They used to take the old sticks and put them under their doors at night so they'd get a little bend in them," Dennis Hull has recalled.) Today the sticks have the deep curve manufactured into the blade—"it would take me quite a while to get used to the straight blade again," says Hull. What's the advantage of the curved blade? "You can pull the puck into you"—with a sweep of the stick—"and shoot it at the same time," says Hull. The puck spins off the end of the blade, a little as if flung from a sling. "If you tried the same thing with a straight blade, you'd just pull the puck into the corner."

He finished wrapping tape around the stick and stood up. He was wearing only sweat clothes and a rakish scarlet sports-car cap. He was only going to "break a sweat" in the workout; there'd be no supervised scrimmage. But now he remembered that he'd forgotten to put the leather brace on his left knee. "Well," he said tentatively, "nobody's going to hit me in the knee today, I hope." He stomped on his skates across the vinyl and out the door.

While he was gone, the other members of the Black Hawk organization talked about him matter of factly, not with wonder but like a surgeon describing his finest operation. "He's so powerful," said Glenn Hall, "that defensemen only want a piece of him—they don't want to take him head-on." On this day, Bobby weighed 191 pounds. He stands only five feet ten inches tall but his muscles are so well-developed that he looks like he should be hunted, not played. His biceps are bigger than Cassius Clay's. He has to get custom-tailored jackets because his chest is size 44 and his waist is size 32. He is a physiological phenomenon: the "perfect muscular mesomorph," reported the Sports College of Canada and Fitness Institute. It found that Bobby is the fastest man in hockey when carrying a puck—he was recorded at 29.4 m.p.h. His speed and strength not only intimidate defensemen but force him to make his decisions and his dekes (fakes or feints) quickly. "His deke is *real* quick," says Hall. "He's coming in on the goal so fast he's *got* to make a real quick move. He uses it more than he used to, particularly when he's coming in tighter on the goal."

In the office of Billy Reay, the coach, several men gathered to discuss hockey and Hull. "When Bobby first came up," said one man, "he was playing center on a line with Nester [Eric Nesterenko] and Ron Murphy. All three guys were the same kind of player—they'd be all over the ice, nobody knowing where anybody else was. Rudy Pilous"—then the Black Hawk coach—"was strictly a by-the-book man." That is to say: he liked his players to hold their position and organize for plays, not to play free-wheeling hockey. "He'd look out and see these three guys free-wheeling it all over the ice and all it meant to him was confusion." Eventually, Rudy shifted Bobby to left wing and the discussion in Reay's office turned to what kind of players should play on the same line with Hull. Why, for instance, should Stan Mikita not play with Hull?

Mikita, too, is an extraordinary player. He's led the league in total points for the last two years. The enormous variety and consistency of his skills lead some Canadian newsmen—particularly those in Toronto, who helpfully like to foster dissension elsewhere—to declare that there is jealousy between Mikita and Hull. Nonsense, says Mikita. "I've known Bobby since he was playing with the junior team in the town I grew up in. He was a star then and a good guy with it. He's the star here and the same good guy." Says Hull: "We were actually in business together. He's a great hockey player and I admire his skill."

Actually, there are good strategic reasons for playing Mikita on one line and Hull on another.

"They're both the same kind of player—they're both the kind of guys you want carrying the puck," said one of the men in Reay's office. Hull carries it on a power burst down the left wing: what he lacks in subtlety he makes up in the whirlwind force of his charge. Mikita carries it down to harass the defense with his finesse; he's like a muscular mosquito who can't quite be swatted. They are at their best with their individual skills and the Hawks feel it makes more sense to exploit those individual skills instead of sublimating both by trying to match them on the same line.

The discussion turned—as it must, in discussing greatness in hockey —to the skills of Hull's contemporaries: Gordie Howe, who is in his twentieth year with the Detroit Red Wings and Maurice "The Rocket" Richard, who retired several years ago after a distinguished career with the Montreal Canadiens. Richard was the first player to score fifty goals

in a season and he did it in the days when there were fifty games in a
NHL season. Hull did it later in a seventy-game season (and so did
Bernie Geoffrion of Montreal). Richard finished an eight-year career
with 544 goals in regular-season play. Howe has scored more than 600
goals so far—and he's still playing. Early in his ninth season, Bobby
Hull had 280 goals; he was the only player in NHL history to collect
250 goals in less than ten seasons.

"Bobby is a combination of both Richard and Howe," said Reay.
"He has the explosive potential and the strength and durability of
Howe. He can skate better and faster than either one and he shoots
harder."

Actually, the comparison with Howe has to be more subtle because
Howe's skills embrace everything from defense to the sly forms of punishing an opponent. Hull lacks Howe's finesse and experience. "Howe
makes the game look easier," says Tommy Ivan. He coached Howe
when Gordie was sixteen; he coached Hull when Bobby was seventeen.
"Bobby has a shorter stride than Howe; he *looks* explosive when he's
going down the ice," says Ivan. "Howe is a much more deceptive
skater. He has a longer stride so he doesn't look like he's skating as
hard as he is." Hull, of course, has a much faster shot. And Hull shoots
a much 'heavier' puck," says Ivan. One goalie stopped a Hull shot with
his glove and found it numbed his entire arm. Another said: "You
catch it with your hand, it still breaks off and goes into the net."

Among the greatest assets that Hull possesses are his relative youth
and his ability. "Bobby has become an outstanding two-way player,"
said George "Red" Sullivan, until recently the coach of the New York
Rangers.

Claude Provost of Montreal, who often is assigned to guard Hull,
says, "You can't give him any room to get started." That is the most
common strategy for stopping Hull—other than fouling him outright.
The idea is to check and harass him before he can get his speed up, for
after that he's virtually unstoppable. "He'll beat you unless you stay
right on top of him and it's harder than ever to do that." Leo Boivin of
Boston, who also shadows Hull, adds that "you have to try to get him
over to the boards." In that way, the defenseman can use the boards as
an ally in crowding Hull. "It isn't easy," conceded Boivin. "He's like a
bull."

Perhaps the most remarkable aspect of Hull's skills is that he does it
against the odds—indeed, it seems, against the very wishes of the en-
trenched force of the NHL. In the 1961–62 season, for instance, Hull
was officially credited with scoring fifty goals, thus tying Maurice Rich-

ard's record. Actually, he scored fifty-one goals but the other goal was credited to a teammate, Ab McDonald. The disputed goal took place in a game between the Black Hawks and Red Wings on February 21, 1962. Hull shot the puck toward the net. It deflected off the stick of Detroit defenseman Warren Godfrey and went into the net. But in the same melee, McDonald took a swing at the puck. Later he told the official scorer, Ozzie Bluemel, that he couldn't be sure whether he'd ticked the puck or the leg or skate of another player. Bluemel had instinctively credited McDonald with the goal but he was willing to change the decision if he'd been wrong. Unfortunately, he couldn't locate Godfrey before the Red Wings left the Chicago Stadium. When he next saw Godfrey, the Detroit defenseman told him that the puck had been shot by Hull and was deflected off his stick. He also told Red Wing Coach Sid Abel, who took the matter up with Clarence Campbell, president of the league. They thought, in justice, that Hull should get credit for the goal. So did Bluemel. "On the basis of the information I've received since then," he said before the season ran out, "I think Campbell should reverse his decision." Campbell didn't—and Hull remains credited only with a tie, not with breaking the record.

Even more startling is the easy acceptance of the league—and its referees—of illegal play used against Hull. Reay mentioned one player whose technique for guarding Hull is "Let's face it: hooking and holding." Last season, Tommy Ivan began complaining out loud about the way the officials ignored the abuse given Hull. "It's not that Bobby isn't playing well enough to score fifty-one or sixty-one goals," he said. "He's just not being allowed to play his game. . . . The referees don't call a quarter of the penalties they should against the players trying to check him. He's hooked and held and tripped more than any man in the league and, because he's as great as he is, the refs ignore what these guys do to him. Holding is holding and hooking is hooking, no matter whether the man being hooked or held is Bill Smith, Tom Jones, or Bobby Hull. And that's the only way penalties should be called. Refs have no business taking the person being victimized into account."

Hull had started the '64–'65 season by scoring thirty-five goals in thirty-seven games, then lost his momentum in a tangle of holding and hooking. "The average player will be knocked down by the stuff they pull on Bobby," said Ivan. "But the guy is tremendously strong and he has great pride. They can't drag him down often, no matter what they do to him. He won't take a dive to impress officials."

He does absorb punishment. Some six years ago, he lost six teeth to a stick wielded by Doug Harvey. In 1963, his nose was splattered all over his face; it took ten stitches to close the cut and the orbital bones near his nose around his eyes were smashed. He missed one game, then came back to join the Black Hawks in the Stanley Cup playoffs. Last season, shortly after Ivan's remarks, he suffered a disabling injury to one knee because of a check, then—when he returned—tore the ligaments in the other because of another check. He didn't regain his health until the end of the season; he missed nine games and couldn't play at full effectiveness in the games he did play. When the Stanley Cup series opened, the Hawks heard that one team was drawing a bead on his injured left knee in an effort to stop him. "I just don't understand something like this," said Billy Reay. "A good solid check—yes. But to deliberately cripple a player . . ." Hull's reaction was dramatic: he scored ten goals and seven assists in fourteen games to carry the Hawks into the final game of the series.

Hull has both the temperament and the muscle to retaliate memorably when goaded to exasperation. All he needs is the proper incentive. Last season Chicago buzzed with reports that he'd taken umbrage at vulgar and indiscreet remarks made at a social gathering by a huge defensive lineman on a professional football team. The lineman prided himself on his roughness and his toughness. He was six inches taller and sixty pounds heavier than Hull. Hull—according to the reports—merely knocked him cold with one punch.

When he decides to act, Hull acts violently. Last year he got only thirty-two minutes in penalties and won the Lady Byng trophy for sportsmanship. This year, he had twenty-seven minutes in his first twelve games and is not likely to win the Lady Byng trophy. One reason: he became embroiled in a fight in Montreal with three seconds left to play in one game and escalated to such heights of violence that he drew fifteen minutes in penalties and fifty dollars in fines.

Upstairs, in the chilly empty arena—where the red chairs and yellow aisles of the second balcony gleamed in the artificial light—Bobby Hull finished his workout. He clumped back into the locker room on his skates, still worried about his stick. "I'll take the one I used last night as a spare in Boston," he told the equipment manager. On the green chalk board, the departing time for the plane was marked: 8:00 a.m. the next day. Stan Mikita looked at it unhappily, then chalked beneath it: "An earlier plane leaves at 5:00 a.m. for those who desire." Hull began peeling off his sweat clothes and tape. "Maybe I'll take a little heat," he said. Normally he doesn't like to go into the sauna bath. "It takes something out of you," he says. He also doesn't have much time to relax: when he leaves the stadium, he goes on to work elsewhere. The Black

Hawks don't object to his outside interests. "They know that when I step on the ice," he says, moving his head to indicate the rink upstairs, "I'm ready to go."

What they do get uneasy about is his gift of candor. He has a genius for saying exactly what he thinks—something that escapes most renowned athletes. "I'm sure if I didn't say I wanted to win the Hart award, you'd think there was something wrong with me," he says. On more controversial subjects he is just as outspoken. In 1962–63, for instance, his goal production dropped from the record-tying fifty per season to thirty-one. It had been known that the Hawks had been working very hard all year—in practice as well as in the games. To the conscientious player, hockey is as demanding a sport physically as pro football —except the players play two or three games a week and frequently scrimmage in practice between games. "I was sick of hockey when the season started," Bobby said at the time. "They worked us to death in training camps. We played seventeen exhibitions and had two tough practices a day."

Even in his best year, he was not a fast starter. In his record-tying year he'd gotten his fifth goal in his seventeenth game, his twentieth goal in his forty-third game. He got thirty goals in his last twenty-five games, one of the most torrid performances in hockey history. But by the middle of the following season he still felt the fatigue in his bones. Now, under Billy Reay, the Hawks have a more relaxed practice schedule. Recently the Hawks had three games in four days—and had only one workout, one "sweat-breaking session" and two skull sessions in the days that followed.

From time to time, Hull discovers that his fame gives much wider circulation to his remarks than he ever anticipated. Last July in Hawaii, he told a reporter that he thought he might seek $100,000 from the Black Hawks for a new contract. He'd just completed a five-year contract—which was said to pay him $20,000 a year, or $100,000 for five years—and he was aware of how his value had grown in those five years. But he had no set amount in mind at the time. "I should have told him $200,000 so he'd of known I was kidding," he said later. Actually, his economics was sound: the Black Hawks—and all of hockey— have been drawing incredible crowds in the last few years. And Hull has been the big magnet.

In the end, Bobby didn't get anywhere close to $100,000. Nor did he expect to. But his fight made it possible for all hockey players to look toward greater income, particularly when the NHL expands. Indeed, he will tell any other player in the NHL exactly what he's earning so that the player can better negotiate for his own salary. He doesn't intend to lead a union movement; he merely believes that information is at the heart of establishing a player's market value. That doesn't mean every player will act on the knowledge; some of them—as he acknowledges—"are afraid they might get sent back to the minors" if they bargain too sharply.

Hull's own negotiations last autumn were complicated by a problem rarely encountered by other players: the Black Hawks barred his sons from the locker room. Bobby himself learned to skate when he was four years old. He started teaching his sons to skate when they were two. They learned on the Black Hawk ice. The two older boys—ages six and four last autumn—frequently accompanied their father to practice. Blond and fair-skinned—like their father—they'd play in the locker room or in the grandstand while their father was working out with the team. And like young boys, they had an energy that confounded their elders. "They called them 'The White Tornadoes,' " says one friend of Hull's. To prepare for the 1965–66 season, the Black Hawks decided to train in Chicago at the Chicago Stadium. And at the start of training, they barred the children of the players from the locker room.

Hull tried to reach Jim Norris, co-owner of the Hawks, who was staying out of touch of Hull in Florida. But Norris managed to get through to the newspapers. Hull, he said, is "taking a spoiled boy's attitude toward the training rules." He made an indisputable point: "It's hazardous having little children running all over the place unsupervised during practice." He insisted that "we certainly couldn't make an exception in Hull's case."

Said Hull: "I don't think I'm being big-headed about this. I don't like not working and playing when the other guys have to, but this is a matter of principle with me . . . The Black Hawks can't be too interested in where players are coming from if they want to discourage two little boys from skating and getting to know the game."

Eventually, the matter was resolved through compromise. The boys could work out on the rink in the stadium when the Black Hawks weren't using it—i.e., when their daddy was in a meeting with the rest of the team. But they weren't to roam through the stadium alone. When everything had calmed down, Hull conceded that the issue had grown beyond all proper proportions. But that is a price he must pay for his fame.

There is, however, one change that his own fame will never alter: his joy in the land. Here is the focus of his world away from hockey: the land. Bobby owns two farms and two homes. During the season, he lives in the three-bedroom ranch house he built in Addison, Illinois, some seventeen and a half miles west of Chicago's Loop. He was raised in a small town: Point Anne, Ontario—"about four hundred people and five hundred dogs," he says. He still likes to see the stars at night and smell the fresh sharp air of winter. So he doesn't live in the city. His other home is a nine-room Cape Cod on a bluff on an island in the Bay of Quinte in Ontario, about four miles by water and twenty-eight miles by land from Point Anne. It is from this home that—during the off-season—he directs his farming operations. Though he didn't live on a farm as a boy, he visited relatives' farms often. He still thinks that living on a farm is an exultant experience. "Anybody who's been raised in the city can never forget a farm," he told a city boy recently. The first farm he bought, in partnership with a man named Ralph Edwards, is a 250-acre spread in Demorestville, Ontario, about four miles from his home on the island. He raises cattle—Polled Herefords—on the spread.

The town that Bobby was raised in is a "company town." Point Anne is built around a cement factory, a factory where Bobby's father worked "since he was about fifteen years old." The houses are "company houses," built by the cement factory to house its workers. Most of them are stucco and frame. The Hull family—which blossomed to eleven children—is now in its fourth "company house" as the company keeps knocking down older structures. "The folks just moved into it," says Bobby.

When he was four years old, his sisters taught him to skate. The town of Point Anne is on the shore of the Bay of Quinte and there was plenty of opportunity to skate, both on the Bay and on a rink in town. "I used to get up at five o'clock in the morning and build a fire and go out to skate before going to school," recalls Bobby. He never had to do muscle-building exercises to acquire his muscles—and he doesn't have to do such exercises to keep them. "When I was eight years old," he has recalled, "I started going into the wood near Point Anne with my grandfather. I chopped down trees with an ax and that helped develop my arm and back muscles. I also walked to and from school four miles a day and during the winter I shoveled snow from morning till night."

When he was ten Bobby began playing in organized hockey, with Belleville, Ontario, which was about six miles from Point Anne. He recalls himself as being "short and squatty—not particularly muscular." He played bantam hockey for three years and then Bob Wilson, a scout for the Black Hawks, spotted him. He was put on the "negotiation list" of the Black Hawks, which meant he was reserved for them until they released him or until he quit hockey. He played junior hockey with several Hawk farm teams, winding up with St. Catharines, where in one year—1956–57—he scored thirty-three goals and twenty-eight assists in fifty-two games. The town was two hundred miles from his home and almost every weekend his mother and father would drive over to see him. "I don't know what I would have done if they hadn't," he once said. "But that's part of growing up in Canada if you want to make the NHL."

At that time, the Black Hawks trained at St. Catharines. Bobby trained with the farm clubs at night; the major-league team practiced during the day. So Hull's schedule was simple: he'd go to high school during the day, practice with the high-school football team in the afternoon, and then practice with the hockey club at night. One afternoon, he scored two touchdowns in a scrimmage, then turned up for dinner about six o'clock. He learned that Bob Wilson had been trying to reach him: the Hawks wanted him to play that night against the New York Rangers. He bolted down his dinner, rushed over to the rink—and scored two goals against the Rangers. "That night," he says, "the Hawks signed me to a major-league contract." He was seventeen years old.

Bobby scored thirteen goals in his first year and eighteen in his second. Then in his third season he began to stamp his mark on the record book: he led the league in goals (thirty-nine) and total points (eighty-one). He was to do it twice more in the next four years—and suddenly the work had turned to fame.

At the same time, his brother Dennis was moving up through the Black Hawk ranks. He joined the Hawks last season, rejoined them this season. "If anybody has a shot as hard as Bobby, it's Dennis," says Reay. But he lacks Bobby's know-how—the experience acquired in more than eight years of big-league hockey. One day not too long ago, Bobby was pacing through an underground corridor in the stadium and talking of Dennis. But what he was saying reflected the way he looked at hockey and its discipline:

"All he needs is some more ice time—a little more experience about the moves. The only way you can learn the moves is by playing. I don't care if you can go sixty miles an hour, if you don't make the moves you won't beat the goalkeeper. By playing—if you play enough, eventually they start coming fluently. That's what I like to think about my playing —when I'm ready, I'm fluent out there. My moves are *fluent*. And the only way you get them is by work. You know what you should do. You see what you should do. And then suddenly you can do it—automatically . . . without thinking."

His footsteps splintered in the gloom. Now he was climbing the steps to the world outside of hockey. It would demand work and more work. There was a lot to be done before sundown. And tomorrow would be another day. It would begin at 6:30 in the morning.

Alex Karras

"Right or Wrong, I Say What I Think"

Myron Cope | **1 9 6 6**

In the dimness of the Lindell A. C. Cocktail Lounge, downtown Detroit, Alex Karras came across like a meaty barn owl peering through the night. He has a dark, pudgy face and black-rimmed glasses whose thick lenses caught the meager light and seemed to hold it like two shiny puddles. "Funny thing," Karras was saying at a corner table. "Some of these ballplayers who do cigarette commercials don't even smoke. They got to be taught how to hold a cigarette. Now *I* smoke but I don't get the commercials." That he does not is no surprise. Although he is an All-Pro defensive tackle for the Detroit Lions, Karras has been more or less the ranking pariah of the National Football League ever since 1963, when Commissioner Pete Rozelle kicked him out of football for a year because he had placed bets on NFL games. "I haven't had one television commercial, not one," he said.

"That's because you're an undesirable character," a man at the table replied. "Maybe you could do a commercial for the Costa Nostra."

"Yeh, that's the ticket. How's this? 'Dey ain't so bad. Dey ain't so bad as everyone tinks. An old, established firm dat's proud of its reliability. So if dere's anyone you want to get rid of, we'll fix a little bomb and it's up, up, up and away she goes.' "

Whatever the merits of NFL justice, Pete Rozelle's theatrical instincts were sure when he cast Karras in the role of pug-ugly. Because of his appearance it is a fair guess that if Alex ever enters the movies his first line will be, "Please, boss, lemme break just one of his arms." He has Greek-olive skin, a heavy shock of straight black hair, and those evil-looking glasses without which he can scarcely distinguish one man from another.

"Hey, Al, that's a nice sweater," a man called to him from another table. Karras was wearing corduroy slacks and a green velour sweater that had an emphatic turtle-neck collar. "Thanks," he answered. "I got my submarine out the back." Karras describes his nearsighted vision as "zero-zero, blind" and characterizes his line play as a system of Braille employed upon bodies. (Says his wife: "He tried contact lenses for two exhibition games in 1959 and was so thrilled to see what was going on he played his two worst games.") Playing defensive left tackle for the Lions, Karras continually amazes teammate Wayne Walker, who was now standing at the Lindell bar relating anecdotes about Alex's faulty vision.

"Couple of years ago we were playing the Bears," Walker was saying, "and as you may know, Al's brother Teddy was playing offensive guard for the Bears. He played left guard but a guy got hurt so they switched him over to the right side to replace the guy for a few plays." There Teddy found himself perilously close to brother Alex across the line.

"Al knocked him down, then kicked him in the stomach," Walker went on. "I hollered, 'Al! What are you *doing?*' And he said, 'Who *was* that miserable crud?'"

Karras is a big, bulky man but not a giant. At six feet two and 240 pounds he actually is a watch-charm tackle, more suited in size to play offensive guard. But he is astonishingly nimble, a squat tank of a man who unexpectedly tippy-toes through the blur of opposition that rises before his squinty eyes. He is probably the finest pass-rusher in football. Shortly after Rozelle reinstated him in 1964 he suffered a double groin injury that tore at both sides of his crotch and limited his maneuverability, but last year, at age thirty, he was All-Pro for the fourth time in his career.

A short man named Tom Moreno—a potato broker in a blue suit—sat down at Karras' table and said, "Tell the story about the Green Bay rookie, Al." Karras shrugged off the suggestion, so the potato broker told the story himself.

"This rookie, he's playing against Al in '64, and Al's got the groin injury so he can't handle the rookie." At the time, neither the rookie nor any of Detroit's opponents knew of Karras' ailment, for it was kept a secret lest opponents run all their plays at him. "The rookie done him up good," Tom Moreno went on, "and later he pipes up and says, 'Karras can come straight ahead, but that's it. He's got no moves.' "

"Yes, he said I'm just a bull-rusher, that's all," said Alex. "But don't knock him for talking like that. That's how a football player ought to talk when he beats you."

"Last year Al's healthy," Moreno went on. "What he did to the rookie was statutory, believe me. It wasn't even halftime, Lombardi takes the kid out of the lineup. He's going off the field and Al says to him, 'What do you think of *those* moves, you creep?' "

The corner of Karras' upper lip curled into a wry smile. Off the field, the put-downs he delivers are not quite so coarse. The night before, he had appeared on a Detroit television show answering questions phoned in by fans, one of whom declared in a falsetto voice, "Thay, I think the quarterbacks th'd get more protection from the linemen."

Karras replied, "Really, now, they get more money than we do, sweetheart."

Actually, the essence of Alex Karras is that he says precisely whatever comes to his mind and has utterly no regrets in the aftermath. He is full of opinions, which he quickly points out may be dead wrong but are honestly stated. "I sleep good," he says. His scene with Rozelle three years ago was a bad one that caused him to emerge in the public prints as a sort of overgrown reformatory type who would not take his medicine gracefully from the soft-spoken father-commissioner. While agreeing that he was wrong to bet on NFL games (though none of his bets were against his own team), he vociferously argued that Rozelle was abusive to fine him $25,000, the amount of salary he would lose from a one-season suspension. Alex had placed five fifty-dollar bets and lost three of them. "Fine me $2000 and I'll agree it's fair," he told Rozelle. Perhaps correctly, Rozelle was making an example of Karras, but the logic of such extreme punishment is never easy for the victim to appreciate.

"I have some friends and that's all I care about," says Alex, refusing to prostrate himself before the American public.

Undoubtedly Rozelle put across his point to NFL players when he suspended both Alex and Green Bay halfback Paul Hornung, but the epilogue that followed the commissioner's crackdown tells something sad about a sport that has bound itself ankle and wrist to the gimcrackery of marketing and public relations techniques. Hornung, no slouch at public relations, quickly consulted with advisors to formulate a public reaction to his suspension. He hung his head and publicly begged forgiveness, with the result that during his year in exile he busily earned as much money from endorsements and public appearances as he would have gotten from the Packers.

By contrast, Karras would not allow the NFL's boat to stop rocking; so even after he was reinstated and had played his way right back to the top, he got no TV commercials, which probably was just as well for the ad agencies. He might have taken one drag on their cigarette and said, "Tastes like rope."

Happily, the NFL's war with the American Football League has made Karras, of all people, so financially secure at thirty-one as to be the envy of every professional athlete who has gone before him. When the AFL's Miami franchise asked him to jump the NFL last May, the Lions frantically fought back by tendering an unprecedented seven-year contract, which will pay him a quarter of a million regardless if age relegates him to a management job before the contract runs out. The commissioner's office must have swallowed hard when it okayed the contract, for even in the days before the AFL gave Karras his wedge he was burning the ears of officialdom. Hating sham, he said: "I get absolutely tired of these guys who appear with their chins dropping on that NFL *Countdown to Kickoff* television show. 'Joe, how come you had such a good game against the Rams?' And Joe says, 'Oh, I was lucky.' I get sick of this. All of these guys in pro football are egotistical. You've gotta be good to survive, so if they've survived they know they're good. Just once I'd like to hear a guy say, 'I had a good game because I was a lot better than the guy I played against and I knocked the hell out of him.'

"Listen," Karras went on, "I've been whipped a million times by a million guys in this league, but on the other hand, you've gotta be pretty good to last nine years. If I tell you I'm good it's the truth. But now a guy catches twenty-five passes and goes in for five touchdowns and then comes on the television and says, 'I just happened to be there.' Oh, it makes me sick."

But not so sick that he cannot view such goings-on with a compensating sense of amusement. Hard-guy Vince Lombardi's Green Bay coaching staff collapses Karras. "Lombardi gives it one of these," he said, folding his arms stiffly across his chest, "and his coaches give it one of these." Karras thrust his hands to his hips and said, "Lombardi gives it this, and his coaches give it this." Then Karras ran his thumb up his nose, adjusting the bridge of his glasses, and said, "Lombardi does this, and his coaches do this, even if they don't wear glasses."

Nothing if not blunt when he discusses his own work, Karras then launched into a detached presentation of football's realities. "You have to be a sadist on the field, no question about it. I'm not talking backs, I'm talking linemen. If I said to you I don't enjoy ripping Bart Starr's head off, I'd be lying to you. Knocking down an offensive lineman and breaking his head open," Alex added with a touch of exaggeration that made the point, "is something I enjoy."

He comes from a football family. His eldest brother, Louie, now a businessman, played offensive tackle two years with the Washington Redskins before he suffered a detached retina. Teddy, seventeen months older than Alex, has played offensive tackle and guard, first for the Steelers, then for the Bears, and last year for the Lions. Kid brother Paul had a brief football career at the University of Iowa before a knee injury sidelined him. "Louie was real tough," says Alex. "Teddy is vicious. I've seen Teddy knock them down and stay at them. This is what separates a guy from playing three years in the league or nine years."

Alex's own viciousness, or whatever it is that describes the ecstasy of wrenching a quarterback off his feet, wells up from a hot temper that in recent years he has learned to control off the field. He is good-naturedly patient with strangers who park themselves at his restaurant table and abruptly ply him with questions as if they were CBS News. He walks away from potentially violent situations, but when his patience occasionally runs out, as it did two winters ago in the town of Belleville, Michigan, people hark back to his record in J. Edgar Rozelle's files and say, "He's always been an animal."

Alex had gone to Belleville as a member of a basketball team composed of Lion football stars. Playing a team of local youngsters, he judged that one of them was going out of his way to rough him up, in order to prove his courage. "I begged him off twice," says Alex. "I said, 'Please don't do that again.' I'd taken my little boy, Alex, Jr., to the game, and you know I wouldn't want to put on a bad scene in front of him, but finally I had to hit the guy on the button. I made page one: KARRAS SLAUGHTERS HIGH-SCHOOL BOY. He weighed about 240, stood about six four, six five." Karras adds sarcastically, "They love me in Belleville."

One evening not long ago, Alex and his tall, attractive wife, Joan, visited an Italian restaurant named Larco's, not far from their Detroit home. After barging into the kitchen to bid a hearty hello to the chef, Alex sat down at a table but decided he would not have dinner. He had gorged himself on sausage all afternoon and felt slightly out of sorts. To the waiter he said, "I'll have lukewarm water and soap suds and a syringe if you got it." He settled for a bottle of Chianti while his wife sighed, "The day I met this man was Bad Day at Black Rock."

In his individualism, which runs the gantlet from angry defiance to whimsical humor, Alex resembles his late father, a stark figure who, judging by the account that Alex now related over his Chianti, was more or less a counterpart of Dr. Sam Abelman, the gruff good Samaritan of Gerald Green's *The Last Angry Man.* Dr. George Louis Karras, a heavy-set man with curly black hair, had emigrated from Athens to Chicago at the age of three, and had studied at the University of Chicago and interned in Canada. There he met and married a Canadian nurse and with her settled in the steel city of Gary, Indiana.

"He was a family doctor and a surgeon," Alex said. "He was a happy-go-lucky guy but oh, yes, hot-tempered. He'd yell and scream at his patients but they knew him and knew he didn't mean it. Every mooch in town used to get five and ten from him. He delivered babies for only twenty-five bucks, and when he died everyone owed him money." Alex was thirteen at the time, and his mother had to go back to nursing to support four sons and a daughter.

Alex himself peddled newspapers and programs, and from the age of sixteen spent his summers working in the steel mills, first as a member of a labor gang and then banking furnaces in the open hearths. Gary was a tough town, the grimy backyard of Chicago, a place populated by middle-European immigrants and first-generation Americans. Making his own way in that environment, Alex was no stranger to the seamy side of life. "In Gary everyone bet," he says. "You took betting for granted and nobody thought it was wrong. You would think Rozelle would have given my background at least a little consideration, but he comes down on me like I've been writing numbers or selling dope."

The Rozelle affair was by no means Alex's first run-in with authority. For the fact is that until he turned professional, he hated football and everything about it—hated it, as he says, with a passion. Chiefly, he hated the contact, because it made no sense to him to put himself on a plot of ground where eleven men would come banging at him from all directions. Later, as a pro, he came to love the contact for the simple reason that it paid him money, but in the beginning he played the game only because he had little choice.

"Emerson High had this big football tradition, you know," Alex explains, "and my brother Louie made all-state there. So automatically, when he made it big, the other Karrases got grabbed. Teddy was next in line and he got grabbed and made it big. So now I'm a freshman and it's automatic—'You're a Karras, here's the shoes, kid.' I was only four-teen but I was six two already and weighed 185, filling out like hell, and I even stopped smoking on the chance that cigarettes were making me grow. They had a freshman team there but I was a Karras so I got put on the varsity."

Right away, Alex made second-string tackle, which delighted him be-cause the circumstances could have been worse—he might have made *first* team. Second string appeared to be a fairly good situation, for as a football player he would have a certain status with the girls and yet if he were lucky he would not have to see much action. In the opening game of the season, however, the first-team tackle went down writhing in pain on the very first play of the game.

"Man, don't let it be who I think it is," Alex muttered from the bench. Alas, the injured tackle had suffered a broken leg, so at fourteen Alex was a full-time player.

"The thing is, we only had thirty-seven guys on the ballclub and they had no one else to play," he says. "I was a hot body." Alex searched his heart but found no supply of courage. "I was scared to death I'd get hurt. I mean, those other guys had hair under their arms, and I figured they must be forty-three years old, you know. We won nine straight, but I didn't make a tackle all year. Teddy was a junior then and he played right alongside me at guard and did both our jobs. He was furi-ous with me. I wanted to ask out but I was scared he'd punch me."

Frantic to preserve his body in one piece, Alex inventively took measures to avoid a broken leg. He forced himself to run with short strides so that when hit his knees would be in close juxtaposition. (Thus the dainty style that has made him so elusive to opponents was the product of a terrified mind.) With a hand saw, Alex shortened his cleats so that his feet would not be locked into the ground when an opponent blasted him. Today he is one of the few veteran linemen in pro football untroubled by bum knees, and it may be noted that many physicians and trainers, catching up with the method conceived by the high-school freshman, now prescribe Ripple Sole shoes for players who have knee histories.

Emerson High's head coach, A. J. Rolfe, was a hard-bitten single-wing man who in practice sessions ordered two-on-one drills that lasted fully thirty minutes and convinced Alex that football is a game for men who are not altogether sane. Yet as his high-school career proceeded, it became somewhat less aggravating to him because the coach shifted him to end and then fullback. Says Alex, "We had real big linemen there, so that was beautiful because the coach kept moving me farther from the line of fire."

Alex was not entirely anti-athletics. He loved basketball and baseball. In basketball, the rim may have looked different to him than it did to others, but it stood in one place so he was able to average twenty-one points while refusing to wear glasses. At an early date he regarded himself as a major-league catching prospect but changed his mind because, he says, putting the rap on football again, "my eyes went bad from all that contact."

Meanwhile, back at the football purgatory, Alex somehow made all-state in each of his last three years. The motivation behind his brilliant performances was largely one of self-preservation, but then, too, he discovered that whenever Emerson High won a game he received a type of reward that one can put in the bank. Each time, a local attorney (who in fact worked less at the law than at underworld enterprises) came to Alex and without explanation handed him one hundred dollars. The attorney asked no favors, and Alex asked no questions. It may very well be that the man was setting him up to buy a fixed game, but Alex will never know. For in his senior year the attorney no longer was able to come around with his cash.

"Some fellows put three holes in his head. They trussed him up and stuffed him into the trunk of a car and left the car out by the gate at the Joliet penitentiary," Alex explains.

A C-average student, Alex cared little for classwork but he figured he might as well go to college on the chance that eventually he might be able to earn a living in professional football. So he accepted an invitation from coach Forest Evashevski to come to the University of Iowa and sign up for physical education.

Four years later, after he had played his last game for Iowa, the university's publicity department was to turn out a release that glowingly summarized his collegiate career as a "rags to riches story" in which the hero had repented his lack of desire, settled down to hard training, and battled to glory in the best tradition of Big Ten football. That was not precisely the case, says Alex, who goes on to provide his own summary.

"I hated the university, I hated the coaches, I hated football," he says. "By actual count I got kicked off the team seventeen times, put on probation twice, and was suspended three times. That's not too bad a record."

"What was the bone of contention?" Alex is asked.

"Football. I hated college football with a passion. I wouldn't walk across the street to see a college game—all those poor guys out there killing themselves for nothing. Anyone who thinks it's glamorous ought to go out and get the hell beat out of him like I do every Sunday, and then he'll see how glamorous it is. Now I'm not saying I was right about Iowa, about Evashevski, or about anything else, but I just didn't like school and I didn't like rah-rah coaches. And on the other hand, I'm not saying I was wrong either."

A tackle once again, Alex showed great promise playing with the freshman team. He weighed 223 pounds then, and when he reported for spring practice with the varsity he weighed 230 and carried the poundage well. Evashevski exulted over the future that lay ahead of his new tackle and labeled him a key man. Unfortunately, Alex ate nicely over the summer and reported for fall practice weighing 263 pounds. The extra thirty-three pounds touched off a war between him and Evashevski.

Each day, practice sessions opened with calisthenics, so Alex carefully timed his arrival to be ten minutes late. "From September 1st to 14th, Evashevski kicked me off the team three times," he says. "Now I was still out of shape, so then he began to run me every day till I'd drop. I did that for three days before I figured out the answer. I'd run for two minutes and then drop. He put me on the fat man's table, which consisted of one guy, me, but the other players would steal food for me and I'd eat it in my room. Evashevski couldn't understand why I wasn't losing weight."

The second game of the season, against Wisconsin, was for all practical purposes the swan song of Alex's sophomore season. Early in the game a Wisconsin guard peeled out of the line leading an end run and threw a clip on Alex, injuring his ankle. For nine weeks, he says, the ankle kept locking on him, but because it had not swelled and X rays had shown no tear, the Iowa coaching staff eyed him with doubt. "They figured I was dogging it," he says. "We had a disastrous year—3-5-1—so Evashevski blamed the whole season on me."

In his second year of varsity football, Alex and Evashevski found a way to coexist. This pact resulted from an incident that had occurred in the final game of Alex's sophomore season. In a close battle with Notre Dame at South Bend, Alex was resting comfortably and fresh on the bench, feeling sorry for a first-string Iowa tackle who looked as though he would drop from exhaustion. With time running out the score was 14 to 14, and Paul Hornung, then the Notre Dame Golden Boy, was preparing to kick a field goal.

The exhausted Iowa tackle found a hole in the Notre Dame line, says

Alex, but was so tired that he could not get to Hornung in time to block the kick. The ball sailed through the uprights to give Notre Dame the victory. In the dressing room, says Alex, Evashevski approached him and told him, "Gee, I don't know why I didn't play you on that kick." Alex did not know either and having no taste for puzzles, he marched out of the dressing room and thumbed his way home to Gary. "I was going to go down to Tennessee," he says, "but I heard they were even rougher there." When Evashevski phoned to ask that he return to Iowa, Alex relented after negotiating a point. He explains that he and Evashevski agreed that they would not speak to one another unless absolutely necessary.

Therefore, prospects for a tolerable junior season were looking up, inspiring Alex to report in good playing condition. He decided that if he was going to be a pro he had better first become a regular at Iowa. Quickly clearing a path to the first team, he became imbued (perhaps infected is the word he'd prefer) with the Hawkeye spirit. "I was really getting college gung-ho," he recalls, "though of course I caught myself in the end."

The season was to open with a game against Indiana at Bloomington, a short distance from Gary, and Alex happily anticipated turning in a good performance before relatives and family friends. Shortly before kickoff time Evashevski announced the starting lineup. It did not include Alex, who plunged into a sulk. Although Evashevski put him into the game a few minutes after the kickoff, and notwithstanding the fact that he played superbly in a 27–0 victory, Alex was not mollified. In the dressing room the coach said to him, "Well, you've finally made it."

"What do you mean?" replied Alex. "I quit. You're not going to embarrass me in front of all my relatives."

Evashevski argued that Alex would be making a grave mistake to leave Iowa, whereupon Alex finally agreed to stay. Says Alex: "I told him, 'Okay, but don't do it again.' "

Now Alex settled down to a regular job at tackle and proceeded to attract the serious attention of pro scouts, but this is not to say his relationship with the university contained any ardor on either side. As a matter of fact, his conduct off the field kept the administration fairly busy suspending him.

By way of explaining his first major altercation, Alex says of Iowa: "That state is a quiet state. They don't want to hear too much noise. They're nice people but quiet, you understand?" It seems that Iowa had just won the Big Ten basketball championship, whereupon Alex and three buddies decided to celebrate the occasion by organizing a panty raid. They rounded up a mob of fifteen hundred male students at the dormitories. "Now what we'll do," Alex told them, "is rush the front door of the girls' dorm and grab some panties and leave." Unfortunately, security had not been airtight and word of the impending raid already had leaked out.

Alex led the charge on the girls' dorm and was the first man to crash the front door. There he was met head-on by the flash of a camera as a newspaper photographer recorded him in all his panty-raiding glory. The university set him down for three weeks.

Alex is candid about his second suspension. "I got caught cheating in a math final," he says. He was suspended for two weeks this time.

For a while Alex lived at a dormitory, but the proctor in charge of the dorm was fast running out of patience with him. The proctor's attitude stemmed from the fact that Alex and a 280-pound lineman named Mish (which in Serbian means Little Mouse) Nahod were fond of knocking on one another's doors and hurling buckets of water in each other's faces. Late one night they collaborated to work out a somewhat more imaginative prank.

Alex climbed on Mish's shoulders and covered both of them with a raincoat they had borrowed from a basketball player who stood almost seven feet tall. In the dead of night they knocked on the proctor's door. Waking to see a monster before him in the shadows, the proctor raced panic-stricken down the corridor and bumped into a wall light fixture, starting a small blaze. "That was my third suspension," says Alex. "No, come to think of it, we didn't get suspended. We just got kicked out of the dorm and had to find refuge elsewhere."

For the benefit of anyone who is wondering why Iowa continued to put up with scholar Karras, it should be explained that he was fast becoming the best college lineman in the country. He made All-America in his junior year, and in his senior year he not only won the Outland Trophy, which goes to the nation's best lineman, but finished second in the Heisman Trophy balloting for the nation's number-one college football player. (Paul Hornung finished first—in retrospect, a one-two finish that proves college football adept at producing matching sets of weekend gamblers.) Trophy upon trophy and certificate upon certificate piled up on Alex and today may be viewed in the showcase by the front door of the Lindell A. C. Cocktail Lounge, an exhibit location that Alex obviously chose as a sardonic commentary on college football.

In any case, his senior year at Iowa was not without a pleasant aspect, for it was then that he met Joan Jurgensen, a sorority girl from a well-to-do family in Clinton, Iowa. Seldom has a more incongruous match been made. A mutual friend brought the two together on a blind date, which Joan had accepted out of curiosity—after all, Alex was famous by now. "I thought this was going to be a joke," says Joan. "I thought that at the last minute I'd go down the stairs and it wouldn't be Alex Karras at all."

But it was Karras, and he ushered her through the rain into an old Hudson convertible he had borrowed. "You'd better move over to the middle," Alex advised her. "The roof leaks over there." Joan checked the roof, found it in perfect order, and remained put.

"My poor wife," sighs Alex today. "Here she comes, a girl from nice stock, from nice wealthy folks, a sorority girl. And I come out of right field, without a glove." Joan's father, Reynold P. Jurgensen, is an executive (in charge of research and other technical matters) of the Clinton Corn Processing Company, a division of Standard Brands, Inc. As Joan politely puts it, she had never met anyone from an environment similar to Alex's and was taken aback. "I had a real good time," she told a sorority sister after her blind date with Alex, "but I don't believe I could ever fall in love with him." Less than six months later she married the man.

By now, of course, there was no doubt that Alex would make his way in professional football. The files of the Detroit Lions still contain a scouting report turned in by Sonny Grandelius, who gave Alex the best possible marks on speed, blocking, lateral movement on defense, and pass-rushing. "No doubt about his making it," the scout concluded. The Lions made Alex their No. 1 draft choice for the 1958 season.

Nick Kerbawy, then the Lions' general manager, did not exactly approach Alex with hat in hand, for there was no American Football League in existence to bid up the price. Recalls Alex: "I was in San Francisco for the East-West game, and Nick was out there at the time so he figured, 'Well, I may as well go talk to this jerk.' He came to my hotel room and said, 'Have you any idea how much money you want?' I said, 'Yeah, I want $9000.' Nick walked out and slammed the door behind him, and I said to myself, 'Well, that's it. I'm not going to play professional football.' Four minutes later Nick opens the door and says, 'I thought it over and I'll give you $8500.' I said, 'That's fine.' "

Actually, Alex's fortunes quickly took a turn for the better when a Des Moines wrestling promoter signed him to grapple in the off-season as Crippler Karras, with a $25,000 one-year guarantee. His spirits up, Alex left Iowa with a flourish. At a banquet for senior athletes he listened while his teammates delivered their humble farewells to the university and then took his turn at the dais. Glaring at an assistant coach, Alex told the audience, "I want to thank this man for calling me a fat greaseball for four years. Get a look at *him*, will you?"

The next order of business for Alex was a trip to the land of his fore-fathers, Greece—an expense-paid junket that came about through Alex's quick thinking when he received a phone call from an official of a Greek-American society, the Order of Ahepa. The man informed Alex of the society's intention to organize a track-and-field squad of Greek-Americans to compete in the forthcoming Balkan Games at Athens. Was Alex, by any chance, conversant with the discus and shot?

Certainly, answered Alex, who then quoted a few impressive statistics from a track-and-field career that he was able to invent in an instant. The fact was that although he had dabbled in the shot-put event in high school, his hand had never held a discus. Now, having finagled a free cruise to Europe (and with it a six-weeks' vacation on the Continent), Alex adroitly solved the matter of the Balkan Games.

"I threw the shot fifty-two and a half feet," he says, oblivious to the fact that no shot-putter ever *throws* a shot, "which wasn't too bad, but I never did throw the discus. In the discus, I kept falling out of the ring so they'd think I'd gotten rusty."

Back from his European jaunt, Alex reported to the training camp of the College All-Stars in Evanston, Illinois, where he lost little time de-ciding that he should have dallied a while longer in Europe. All-Star coach Otto Graham, now head coach of the Washington Redskins, conducted calisthenics with a whistle in his mouth. At the command of the whistle the players would fall down, and at the next command bounce to their feet. Up, down, up, down. After several minutes at this exercise, Alex advised Graham: "Kid, I don't need you."

"Hey, where do you think you're going, Karras?" demanded Graham. "We're going to scrimmage now."

"*They* might be scrimmaging," answered Alex, "but I'm not. For a hundred and fifty bucks I don't need it. I can get two-fifty a week in the steel mills."

Joan Karras listens to her husband's account of his sojourn in the All-Star camp and thoughtfully observes, "Now I know why you came to Detroit with the reputation of a troublemaker."

"Yes," says Alex. "Otto Graham told George Wilson"—then the Lions' head coach—"I wouldn't make the grade. He told Wilson, 'You'll cut this kid his third day into camp.' "

Here, Graham overlooked the bedrock of Alex's philosophy on football—namely, that one cannot enjoy the game playing without pay (or for only 150 bucks) but that the game can become fun when the knocks and bruises translate themselves into National Football League dollars. All to the better, the Detroit Lions—from coach Wilson down through the playing ranks—proved to be Alex Karras' kind of people.

On the field they were hard; off the field, hearty. Quarterback Bobby Layne, the veterans' ringleader, took an immediate fancy to Alex, perceiving that his peculiarly nimble, tippy-toe method of slipping past blockers was a talent that would keep him in the pro game for many years. Layne nicknamed him Tippy and, by way of demonstrating his interest in the rookie, appointed him his personal chauffeur. On the Lions, rookies disregard the wishes of veterans only at their peril, so Alex dutifully acceded to Layne's wishes, though the hours were long.

Layne was a jazz buff. "The band," says Alex, "would say, 'Please, Mr. Layne, we've gotta go home. We're dead tired.' But Bobby would throw them a hundred-dollar bill, which never failed to freshen the musicians for another set." Unlike Layne, who never required more than a few hours' sleep, Alex plodded through practice sessions bleary-eyed and not entirely sure that he would survive the squad cuts, but as it happened, George Wilson knew of his chauffeuring duties and was greatly amused.

To say that Alex was an immediate success in the NFL would be a gross exaggeration. "I stunk in my rookie year," he says. "I was just horrible. Wilson played me, but again, just as in my freshman year of high school, it was a matter of my being a warm body. One of the guys had got hurt and I was forced into the lineup. We played San Francisco on the coast and Joe Perry and Hugh McElhenny slaughtered me. Perry had 174 yards rushing, all of it over me. I'll tell you how bad it was. The newspapermen put it in the papers, and how many times can a newspaperman truthfully say Joe Perry ran 174 yards over one guy? Well, Joe Perry did.

"I don't remember which lineman I was playing against," Alex goes on, "but he just killed me. The 49ers wished they could put me in their traveling bag and play against me every week. My second year in the league was lousy, too, but nothing could have been as bad as that first year."

Actually, toward the end of Alex's second season, he began to emerge as a first-rate tackle, for experience was teaching him that he was neither big enough nor strong enough to bowl men over. He was learning to finesse them, to slip around them. His teacher was defensive coach Buster Ramsey, a fierce, impatient man who has stirred the ire of many players but who, in Alex's opinion, was a coach of rare skill. "He kept prodding me," says Alex. "He used to scare hell out of the ball-players but he never scared me. Anyhow, if a guy is making mistakes he shouldn't get mad when he's told about them."

In the early years Alex worked hard in practice, for he did not carry sufficient importance to test his coaches' patience. But once established, he prescribed his own practice pace, which consisted roughly of three parts inertia and one part boredom. He says: "I practice hard for two weeks, which puts me in good shape. From then on, they won't get any practice out of me. Some ballplayers you have to pamper, some you have to kick in the tail, and some you have to leave alone. With me, the best thing is to leave me alone. I won't do it on Thursdays because I don't get paid to do it on Thursdays."

Karras always has been ready on Sundays, keyed up so intensely that he vomits just before kickoff time. Moreover, notwithstanding his dis-taste for practice, he comes better prepared than most players, for he is a fanatical film-watcher.

Because he plays without contact lenses and sees the action as a blur, he spends long hours boning up on his opponent. Each week he studies (with glasses on, of course) a minimum of six game films, digging out his opponent's weaknesses so methodically that in the game he will spot them immediately, however blurred. "I find out how a guy makes a move and why," Alex says. "By the time I get my glasses off, I know what I have to do to beat him." Still, one can safely guess that Norm Van Brocklin, the Minnesota Vikings coach, had Alex's eyesight in mind one Sunday in Minneapolis when the Vikings unexpectedly took the field in white jerseys similar to the Lions'.

Five minutes into the first quarter, Karras demanded the Vikings change into their purples. (He suspected that in the opening minutes he had tackled teammate Darris McCord three times.) When told by Van Brocklin that the Vikings had not gotten their purples back from the cleaner, Alex replied: "Man, you better get knocking on that cleaner's door right now."

The game was held up while a truck was dispatched to the Vikings' office for the purples.

Today Alex Karras emerges as a man of somewhat contradictory fac-ets—a man of wonderfully whimsical humor and yet one who is capa-ble of almost brutal candor. When the Lions are on the road, a cluster of them can usually be found whiling away the last hours of Sunday morning in Alex's room. Stretched out on the bed, Alex projects himself into a world of fantasy in which he has led a succession of lives, usually as an aide or relative of historic figures. "Hitler was not an ordinary Joe," he expounds. "You knew that when you were around him as much as I was. He had this obsession to hold his breath for more than three minutes."

Could he do it? "Nowhere near. He got red in the face very quickly, and there'd be this little popping sound when the air came rushing out. He never lasted more than eight or nine seconds—shortest-breathed man I ever saw."

Abruptly, without warning, Alex emerges from his fantasies, transported into a being who is literally sick with pre-game tension. Once he has vomited in the dressing room, he plunges into the game with such ferocity that he cannot bear to be let down by a teammate. At various times he has told teammates—quarterback Milt Plum was one—that they ought to be embarrassed for having shown up.

"After I cool off I say I'm sorry," Alex points out. "I think the players know me and know I say things I shouldn't say, but I apologize later."

It is a matter of sheer frustration to Karras, meanwhile, that in his career with the Lions they have never won a division championship, though they were strong enough to finish second in three straight years —1960, '61, and '62. "In '62 we lost three games by a total of eight points," he says. "Green Bay"—the champions that year—"beat us 9 to 7 on three field goals." The Lions consistently were formidable on defense and George Wilson was an excellent coach, says Alex, who contends that the club fell into trouble because of an inability to replace aging players with talented young ones. The repeated second-place finishes deprived Detroit of top draft choices, he says, and the American Football League picked off some of the Lions' better ones—men such as John Hadl and Earl Faison. Before the '65 season the front office pressured Wilson into resigning, having decided more or less that too much nonsense had been tolerated by the Wilson regime. Under Harry Gilmer, Wilson's replacement, the Lions finished 6-7-1, next to last, as the players adopted an attitude close to insurrection. Karras, a Wilson disciple, is his usual frank self on the subject.

"See, we have a ballclub that's older than most—the nucleus is older men. Gilmer can't get as close to a club as Wilson could. He's just no Wilson. But we haven't really given Harry a chance because we've been indoctrinated to Wilson. Harry is just not the same type, but he should realize you just can't change a team overnight. I don't think we did anything detrimental to Harry, but there has been a lot of griping and the majority of it is based on the fact that he hasn't been very close to his club. As a player I know I respond more to a fellow I have a little warmth for than one I really don't know."

The techniques of coaching are a subject that engrosses Alex, partly because he would like to become a coach when his playing career ends, and his theory of coaching is one that interestingly separates a football squad into layers. "If I'm a coach," he begins, "out of my forty ball-players in this league I might have twenty-five good ones. Of the fifteen remaining, the also-rans, ten of them will go along with the nucleus. The other five are misfits, so you don't worry about those five.

"Now the ten also-rans who are going along with the nucleus, they'll go down on the kickoff for you and take care of that sort of thing," Alex goes on. "So what you have to do is take care of the twenty-five, the nucleus. Of these, six will be the core of the nucleus—the ones the other nineteen look up to. If you can keep those six happy, the other nineteen are happy. This is what my theory is and I think it was Wilson's. We won games for him we had no business being in. So when you get down to it, getting a little more out of the ballplayers is what coaching is about in this league."

Alex has no illusions that he will ever receive an opportunity to put his coaching theories into practice. "I'd love to be a coach," he says, "but I don't think I'll ever be a head coach, because I'm no politician."

As a pro football star, Alex attaches no particular importance to himself and by the same token has no use for anyone who believes he ought to come on with a line of wholesome platitudes in order to set an example for American youth. Integrity, so far as Alex is concerned, is being oneself, devoid of poses.

That form of integrity is, perhaps, a luxury—one that only the independent can afford—but even before Alex Karras got a seven-year contract with the Lions he was guarding his independence jealously, seeing to it that he remained free of obligations. "I've saved my money real well," he said last winter. "I'm not hurting. I have a tightwad wife. I'm free of ties, so if the club wants to trade me, let them trade me." He was selling autos for the Northland Chrysler Company of Detroit. With his wife and three children—Alex, Jr., Peter, and recent arrival Carolyn Joy—he lived in an attractive six-room Colonial-style house, but one that cost him only $18,000. He had steered clear of expensive houses that mean costly mortgage payments, for he never wanted to be at the mercy of the front office.

If Alex Karras continues to be remembered as the bad boy who
back-talked Pete Rozelle, so be it. "Right or wrong, I say what I think,"
he insists. "That's the way I am. I'm not going to try to change. I'm not
going to go to the Salvation Army and ring a bell."

Koufax, Clemente, Mays

The Key Men Down the Stretch

John Devaney | **1966**

The Pirates stomped across the boards of the dugout, swinging bats, staring out at the floodlit greenness of Dodger Stadium, while some 45,000 throats yelled "Charge!" Roberto Clemente, sitting near the end of the dugout, turned to a young ballplayer beside him and saw something that made him smile.

"Your hand shake a little," Clemente said. The young ballplayer flushed, then grinned self-consciously.

"Never mind," said Clemente. "Some of us shake on the outside, some of us on the inside, but when it comes down to games like this, we all shake a little."

Bob Clemente lied. He was being nice to a scared teammate, but Bob Clemente does not shake even a little. "I never get nervous," he told me later. "I love this, in September, when you are in first or second place, and each game means something, and there are a lot of people watching me. Who wants to play in a game that means nothing?"

This game, between the Pirates and Dodgers on the steamy night of September 15, 1966, meant a great deal. The Dodgers were in first place, the Pirates one and a half games behind in second, the Giants three games behind in third. Only three games separating three teams with fewer than twenty games left to play. I was in Los Angeles to find

(*429*

out what it was like down the stretch for the key man on each team—
Roberto Clemente, Sandy Koufax, Willie Mays.

The three, I will tell you now, came down the stretch without shaking, almost casually, yet each was inwardly driven to collect first of all,
a pennant, and then something else that was uniquely personal to each
of them. A pennant means $11,000 or so a man, a year's salary for a lot
of ballplayers. But $11,000 is not so staggering a figure when you earn
from $70,000 to $125,000 a year, as these three do. They went down the
stretch wanting to win that $11,000, of course, but each hoped to take
something else out of this 1966 pennant race.

On September 15, a few hours before the start of a three-game Pirate-
Dodger series, I discovered what Bob Clemente yearned to extract from
the race. We met in the lobby of the Hotel Biltmore, "at 4:30 sharp," as
he had promised. He looked as sharp: gray sharkskin suit molded to his
muscular body, an angular face that vaguely resembles Harry Bela-
fonte's. "I am tired," he said, "and I am not very hungry, but let's go
and I will try to eat something."

Over a dish of calves' liver, which he toyed with, he told me in his
Puerto Rican accent: "I cannot sleep at night. I don't know what it is. I
go to bed at eleven o'clock, but I can't get to sleep until two or three."

"Is it the tension of the race?"

"No, no," he said, waving a fork. "I always have this trouble sleeping. I go to the park tonight, I will be too tired to take hitting. If I try to
hit, I be too tired to play when the game starts."

Clemente has a reputation for being interested in physiology, his
own, and now he was covering the subject from head to toe. He talked
of aching feet, sore arms, working his prognosis up to his right shoulder.
"This shoulder was real sore," he said. "About a month ago I caught a
fly ball. I throw hard to home and I tell you, it hurt plenty."

"Would you have thrown as hard if the Pirates were in sixth place?"

"You bet not," he said candidly. "Why risk your career on a game
that mean nothing? But when you're up here in first or second, you got
to give your best."

If the Pirates won, I said, the writers might vote him the league's
Most Valuable Player Award. Clemente was silent. The MVP award is
a fever sore on his memory. In 1960, when the Pirates last won the pennant, Dick Groat was named MVP. Clemente finished tenth in the vot-
ing, a ranking he considered an insult. To this day he does not wear
his 1960 Series ring.

"It will be either you, Mays or Koufax," I said. He looked at me like a man who'd done a lot of thinking about the subject. "Well, I tell you," he said, "even if we don't win, you think they give it to Mays? What's he hitting around .295?"

At the moment Clemente was hitting .327 with twenty-three home runs and 110 runs-batted-in. For Bob Clemente, a stretch run is for a pennant, first of all, and for a chance to heal a fever sore.

By 10:30 that night, Clemente's average had dropped to .324 after he'd gone 0-for-three against Don Drysdale. But the game was not yet over. With two out, in the ninth, the Dodgers ahead 5 to 1, Clemente came up for his fourth at-bat. He hooked into a slow curve and drove it six rows into the left-field stands. The next batter, Willie Stargell, jerked a home run over the right-field fence and in came Phil Regan. The Dodger crowd, some 47,000, came up shrieking as Donn Clendenon hit Regan's first pitch to the wall in center, but Willie Davis overtook the drive. The game was over, the Dodgers 5–3 winners. And now Pittsburgh was two and a half games out.

Los Angeles, September 16—Sandy Koufax came into the clubhouse at 5:15, dressed California casual: white turtleneck shirt, black slacks, a royal-blue cardigan. Tonight he was the starter. I asked if he'd prepared himself in any special way for this game.

He stared at me, seemingly astounded. "Why?" he said, his deep voice rising. "Why? Look, you do things no differently whether you're in first place or in fifth place. You have a responsibility to your team. You are paid to win so many games, and you're supposed to go out and do your job, win those games, no matter whether you're in first place or in sixth place."

"But isn't there pennant pressure?"

"I don't think so," he said, his dark face crinkling in the smile of someone who has just heard a silly remark. "To me the pressure is game to game, inning to inning, batter to batter, pitch to pitch, and it's that way in May, June, September—any month."

He lit a cigarette. "In September there is more fan interest," he said, "more press coverage. But to the ballplayer, he doesn't feel any more pressure on the field in September than he does in May. Hell, you win a game in May, it's as important as a game you win in September."

"Isn't there a special thrill to winning a big game in a September stretch run?"

"No," he said firmly. "Suppose you start the season and you're, say, one-and-two. You win a game and now you're an even .500. That game could be a real big one for you, because it puts you even and now you can get started on winning a string of games and building a base for a real good year. That game in April could mean more to you than any game all year."

He pulled off the turtleneck shirt. "I will say this," he said. "You lose in May and you've lost one for yourself. You lose in September, when there isn't so much time to make up that game, and you may be losing for twenty-four other guys. Naturally you feel bad, but that's not pressure."

I nodded, said thanks, and started to leave, but he spun on his stool toward me and said, "People have a lot of wrong ideas about a pennant race. There are three teams in this race. They're bunched together because they won during the first five months of the season. If they'd lost in April or May, people would say, 'Well, they just had a bad year.' But if they lose in September—and *someone* has to lose, someone has to get beaten—then they'll say, 'The Pirates choked,' or 'The Giants choked,' or 'The Dodgers choked.'" He smiled and threw up his hands.

"There's only one difference between a game in May and a game in September," he said after a moment. "You lose in September, there's less time to get it back."

"But isn't that a big difference?" I said.

"Well, maybe," he said. "That may be true." He said it as if it might very well not be true as far as he was concerned. A little later another Dodger told me: "I've got butterflies in my stomach. For the first time this season. Everybody here"—he waved a hand around the clubhouse —"they tense up just before a game. But I don't know about Sandy. He's different. The game starts and he shuts himself in a closet inside himself, he concentrates so hard. But what he's really feeling I can't tell you. We don't communicate much with Sandy."

Watching Sandy try for his twenty-fourth win that night, I thought about what he had told me. Koufax is paid something like $125,000 a year to win something like twenty-five games a season, and he goes out virtually every four days intent on winning one of those twenty-five. That, as he said, is what he is paid to do, and it doesn't much matter whether the day is in April or September. He pitches as coolly down the stretch as he does in April and it is important for a team in a tight race to play behind a pitcher who has no butterflies. Nevertheless, as Sandy Koufax pitches down the stretch, I suspect that twenty-five victories are almost—not quite but almost—as important to him as a pennant. They are unassailable proof that this proud man is worth each of his $125,000.

On this night he had little trouble winning his twenty-fourth. Only in the seventh, ahead 5 to 0, did he appear ruffled. There were runners on first and third, one out, Andre Rodgers batting. With the count three and one, Koufax threw ball four filling the bases.

Koufax's temper, once much in evidence but well contained in recent years in that inner closet, flew out. He stomped around on the mound, yanked his cap, kicked up dust. Then he settled down, yielded only one run and went on to win 5 to 1.

In the clubhouse afterward I asked Jeff Torborg, his young catcher, what had upset Koufax. "I confused him," said Torborg, the sweat running down his dirty, fuzzy face. "He wanted to pitch inside to Rodgers on that last pitch, but I forgot and set outside. He came out of his motion, after looking at the runners, saw me setting outside, and it ruined his concentration. That's why he walked the man."

A rumpled, wet Koufax slumped on a stool in front of his stall, sipping a soft drink. Someone asked about the walk to Rodgers. "There was a mix-up," Sandy said.

"Did the catcher mix you up?"

"It was my fault," said Koufax crisply. "I walked the man."

A little later I asked Torborg: "Did Sandy's arm hurt him tonight?"

"A couple of times it did," he said. "You can see his face tighten up."

"How often do you see that?"

"Maybe, if he throws a hundred pitches, five or six times in a game," he said. "But gee, I shouldn't be telling you this. Sandy doesn't like to talk about it."

Reserve outfielder Al Ferrara ran down an aisle, nude except for a sombrero. "Sweet Mets!" he yelled. The Mets had beaten the Giants 5 to 4. The Dodgers now led the Pirates by three and a half, the Giants by four.

Outside the stadium, Clemente waited to board the Pirate bus. Some people clamored for autographs, and he signed, laughing with friends. He does not go down snarling.

Los Angeles, September 17—Clemente stretched on the rubbing table. Today there was pain in his foot. "I tell you something about pennant pressure," he said, putting aside the newspaper he'd been reading. "Yesterday I go up there with a man on base and I am thinking, 'Home run.' That's bad. You try to hit the home run, you make out. Bad. Ruins your swing. Bad."

The talk came around to Koufax. "I don't care what anyone say," said Clemente, who really doesn't. "They say he got a sore arm. He don't have a sore arm when he pitches. He may have a sore arm *after* he pitches, but no one can throw like that with a sore arm. I once had a sore arm, and my arm hung like this." He hung it limply toward the floor. "Koufax won fifty games the past two seasons. If he won all those games with a sore arm, this league is a joke."

Clemente, the man who worries steadily about his own health, shook his head in disbelief that another man could pitch in pain and accept it so well. That afternoon Clemente got one walk in four tries, and the Pirates went into the seventh losing 3 to 2 and staring into their grave. But Clendenon kept them alive with a three-run homer and they got four more runs in the eighth and they won 9 to 5.

At six that evening the Pirates flew to San Francisco, trailing the Dodgers by two and a half with San Francisco now three behind.

San Francisco, September 18—It seemed like a Sunday morning, which it was, in the Giants' rambling clubhouse, the laughter of Willie Mays pealing through the room like church bells. "Is that right?" he was shrieking, his face bunched up with laughter. "Is that right?"

"That big Los Angeles crowd yesterday," I was telling him, "they were standing, watching that lighted scoreboard flashing the play-by-play of your game here. They were cheering each Giant out, and when the lights flashed, 'Hart up,' they were ready to yell at the final out, and then—oops!—on blinked the words, 'Hart homers,' and you could hear that crowd go dead."

Mays screamed laughter. "I guess," I said, "you were pretty excited on the bench."

"No," he said. "There is nothing in baseball that can get me excited any more."

"Not even a big homer in the stretch?"

"No," he said. "I *got* to stay calm. We have so many kids on this ball-club, it's my job to stay calm."

There were black circles under his eyes. He is thirty-five now, Willie Mays, but those black smudges made him look older. They are the coal-black kind you see on sick men in hospitals. "Are you very tired?" I asked.

He shrugged. "The season, it seems longer and longer."

"Is this the toughest pennant race for you?"

"Shoosh, no," he said. "The first one is the toughest. After that you're used to them."

"Your first one was 1951."

"Yeah," he said. "I didn't know what it was all about then." He laughed. "I was so frightened, I didn't get a hit the whole last two weeks."

"You can't let that happen to these young ones."

"Sure can't," he said. Willie Mays, captain of the Giants, got up slowly from the chair, wincing slightly when he put weight on his right foot. He'd hurt it stealing a base a few days earlier.

He walked around the clubhouse, gossiping and giggling, challenging young catcher Bob Barton to a golf game.

In the game that afternoon he went nothing-for-three and in the seventh, the Pirates ahead 3 to 0, he was replaced by Frank Johnson. Woody Fryman was throwing a one-hitter for the Pirates until the ninth when Tito Fuentes led off with a homer. Now the score was 3 to 1, and the Giant crowd that had been quiet most of the afternoon began a rising, hungry roar.

The next batter, McCovey, leveled on a fastball and it jumped off his bat on a high arc toward the right-field fence.

Clemente ran back, grabbed the wire fence with his bare hand, ready to climb it. Then he relaxed, took one step forward as the ball, caught by the wind, dropped like a dead bird. Clemente, as casually as someone swatting a mosquito, snatched it with one hand. The crowd's roar faded to a whine.

Moments later they were up again, screaming, watching Frank Johnson's liner rocket down the right-field line. Clemente ran into the corner, jumped against the fence, his glove straining near the top. The ball hit his glove, showed white in the pocket as Clemente slammed into the wire. But as he tumbled to the ground, he grabbed the ball with his bare hand and held on to it. A moment later Fryman got the third out and the win.

The Pirates whooped into their clubhouse. "You magician you," yelled Al McBean at Clemente, shaking his hand. "Congratulations, Mr. MVP," shouted Jose Pagan. Clemente smiled.

"You caught that ball of McCovey's kind of casual-like," I said. "You drop it and you'd be the goat of this pennant race."

"That's the way I always catch a ball," he said. "You do something different from the way you always do it—you try to make sure of it—you may mess it up."

"Was that catch of Johnson's liner the biggest of the season for you?"

"Why a big catch?" he said. "Because it's now? How about the catches I make in May? They win games too; nobody around to see them, but those games in May as important as the games in September."

Mr. Clemente, meet Mr. Koufax.

In the Giant clubhouse Mays pointed to his right foot. "I can't swing off it," he said. "If you can't swing, what's the good of playing? That's half the game right there—swinging."

He stared at the foot. "There's no use worrying about it," he said. "Just one of those things. Ain't going to do any good worrying about things."

San Francisco, September 19—Mays' foot was still sore. "I won't start," he was saying in the clubhouse. "But I expect I'll be in there before it's over."

Coach Cookie Lavagetto watched Mays talk with young Ron Herbel about a post-season basketball team they may organize. "I'll tell you what's it like for Willie," said Lavagetto. "The ordinary guy gets two hits, he feels he's done his job. Willie gets two hits, he knows he's expected to get two hits tomorrow and the day after tomorrow. That's a big load to carry and it wears him down and he gets sick or we have to rest him."

That afternoon the Pirates, behind Bob Veale, went into the ninth ahead 1 to 0. The first Giant batter, Jim Ray Hart, singled up the middle. Jack Hiatt hit a one-hop scorcher to Bob Bailey at third, who threw to Bill Mazeroski at second. Baseball's best second-baseman pivoted, saw he had plenty of time for the double play at first. He aimed, threw softly—and the ball sailed high over the first-baseman's head. Hiatt was on second.

I remembered what Celmente had said earlier: *"You do something different from the way you always do it, you may mess it up."*

Jesus Alou popped up. Two out now, and the expectant roar of the crowd, some 40,000, told Veale who was coming to bat.

Willie Mays came out, swinging bats, and then the pinch-hitter stepped into the batter's box.

The count went to two and two on Mays, the crowd howling on every pitch. Then Veale threw a slider tight and Willie lashed at it. The ball shot under Bailey's glove into left field, tying the score.

The crowd stood, applauding, as Mays came back to the dugout, replaced by a pinch-runner. There was a painful grimace on his face and he limped.

The game was still 1 to 1 in the eleventh. Clemente, who'd gone o-for-10 since his home run off Drysdale in Los Angeles, led off. On a 2-and-2 count, reliefer Frank Linzy threw an inside breaking pitch and Clemente swung, picking the ball off his belt buckle and undercutting it 340 feet over the right-field wall for his twenty-fifth homer and the Pirates led 2 to 1.

Air seemed to hiss out of the Giants and the Pirates scored four more runs and won 6 to 1.

I was the first reporter in the Pirates clubhouse and found Clemente wandering through the trainer's room. "What are you looking for?" I asked.

"A sleeping pill," he said. "I got to get some sleep tonight."

Reporters clustered around, asking about the home run. "Well, I got this sore foot," Clemente was soon saying. Having already heard extensive reports on his health, I ducked away.

In the Giant clubhouse Mays sat alone, the black under his eyes looking almost ghoulish. "How will this loss affect the club?" I asked him.

He looked up, solemn and unfriendly. "I'm sure you know," he said. "But you go ask him." He waved a hand toward manager Herman Franks' office. "You get no quotes from me."

He stood up and walked toward the shower. On the way he met Len Gabrielson. Willie said something, began to laugh, and Gabrielson laughed too. Mays was still laughing in the shower room.

The next afternoon I flew back to New York, the pennant race coming down to the final week with the Giants seemingly out of it, the Dodgers one and a half games ahead of the Pirates—the same lead they'd had when I'd picked them up. The race would not be decided until the season's final weekend when Koufax won his twenty-seventh game to clinch the pennant.

I had watched three tired men playing with as much fierce devotion as they could muster through a stretch run for a pennant. In that run, I am sure, more than one hand trembled (the Giants made four throwing errors in one game). But the hands of Koufax, Clemente and Mays did not tremble. Each had been in one of these things before, each came with confidence and skill, each knew how to accept skill's responsibilities. "You win or lose and there's nothing you can do about it," said

Clemente. "*Someone* is going to get beaten, *someone* has to lose," said Koufax. "Ain't going to do any good worrying," said Mays.

At the end of the stretch the three key men—Roberto Clemente, Sandy Koufax, Willie Mays—had proven their worth. And then one man went into the World Series and the other two went home.

Lee Evans' Grim Education

David Wolf | **1969**

When Lee Evans returned home from the Olympics last October, a hero's welcome would not have been out of place. Here was a proud, twenty-one-year-old black man who had risen from bleak poverty to become a world record-holder at 440 yards and 400 meters, and a winner of two Olympic gold medals. This should have earned him recognition from the white community of San Jose, California, where Lee lives and goes to school. And, of course, he should have been even more of a hero to the black community. He had helped lead one of the first black student protests, stood in the vanguard of the Olympic boycott movement, and had undergone excruciating pressure before demonstrating on the victory stand at Mexico City.

"But when I got home," says Evans, "I caught hell from both sides. The white people were mad *and* the black people were mad. Can you imagine how I felt? I was never so alone."

To some, Evans was too militant. To others, he was too moderate. Many whites condemned him for wearing a Black Panther–style beret on the victory stand. Yet many blacks, including some of his closest friends, felt Lee had copped out by not being as defiant as Tommie Smith and John Carlos, who had clothed upraised fists in black gloves.

(*439*

An influential black commentator began calling Evans "a Judas." While Smith and Carlos went to banquets and rallies, Evans was conspicuously uninvited.

"When people see me coming they drop their eyes and walk the other way," nineteen-year-old Linda Evans said at that time. "People who used to make me feel proud to be Lee's wife don't want to say anything to me now."

"They turn against you so quick," Lee says. "I had arguments with guys who used to be the most fantastic [Uncle] 'Toms.' Now they were asking me why I didn't do more? Guys I thought were my friends, like Harry Edwards' brother James, were against me. He said, 'When Evans flies home, the white people gonna give him a big parade. But we're gonna give one for Smith and Carlos.' It was just a lie. Nobody was giving me a parade."

Lee's problems increased when the city of San Jose offered him a job which he thought entailed working with ghetto children. When the newspapers carried the story, the announcement said Lee Evans would be working as a trouble-shooter for the police force, a symbol of oppression to so many blacks. Lee quickly called a press conference and turned down the job. "I feel I will be used against my black brothers if I were a member of the police department because of its racist nature," he said. "Black people do not need the police. What they need is to organize themselves."

But it was too late. The damage had been done. And it was compounded when John Carlos, the tough, opinionated street-kid from Harlem, who now runs track for San Jose State, began telling college audiences that Lee was a member of the police force. Carlos referred to Lee as "Mr. Cop," Linda as "Mrs. Cop" and their two-year-old son Keith as "Junior Cop."

"Once Carlos and me were tight," says Lee. "In Mexico City what I did was fine with him. But when he got home and found out what the white press was saying, he changed. Finally I called him up and told him to cut it out. We argued and when he hung up I was so mad I went lookin' for my gun. I mean it. I was going to shoot him. But then I remembered what a friend once told me: 'Whoever shoots Carlos will be even stupider than he is!' So I forgot about the gun and just headed for his house."

Outside Carlos' home they argued for some time. Just when tempers were beginning to cool, their wives joined the shouting match. The women had to be dragged apart.

Several months later, Evans sat in a New York restaurant eating a pre-race steak. Soon he would run in the Millrose Games' 600 against Larry James of Villanova, who finished second to him at Mexico City. "The adrenalin is starting to flow," he said. "But I can't say that I'm really up. Maybe James wants this race bad because he's never beaten me, but after Mexico there isn't much that's gonna get me real tense."

He spoke carefully, as he often does around white people, trying to pluralize the proper words, keep the correct tense, and avoid the dialect of the cotton fields from which he comes. John Lilly, a white middle-distance runner, entered the restaurant and waved a friendly black power fist at Lee. Evans grinned and returned the gesture. Normally, he is as amiable as a big teddy bear and, of all the militant blacks, is the most popular among the white athletes who sympathize with the blacks' cause. He also is the team captain at San Jose State. "The white guys at school respect me and I respect them," he says. "They're cool dudes. A couple of nights a week we meet at someone's house and listen to stereo. We can talk about racial things. But that doesn't make me a 'Tom.'"

That night Evans received the usual mixture of boos and cheers when he was introduced at Madison Square Garden. The big applause was for Larry James, but it didn't last long. Although Lee was far below the physical peak he reached in Mexico City, he simply would not allow himself to become a loser on the indoor circuit. He'd been beaten only once all winter, on a night when he was sick.

James, smooth, long-legged and graceful, took the early lead. Lee, his stocky, broad-shouldered frame hardly the classic build for a quarter-miler, suddenly accelerated and swooped past James with a lap and three quarters to go. At the top of the stretch James made his move and the crowd rose, shouting. But this is when Lee Evans is at his best, for Lee is probably the most ferocious competitor in track and field. Broad features contorted in a pained grimace, mouth open and teeth bared in sharklike fury, shoulders rolling, head snapping from side to side, Evans pumped his knees high and strained ahead once more. His style is clumsy, like a steam engine gone out of control, but it works for him. He leaned into the tape just ahead of James.

Afterward, as he sat happily with friends in another restaurant, Lee was asked about his reception in San Jose. He waved a hand in disgust. "In Mexico City I decided for the first time that I wasn't going to do what somebody else wanted. I want to help black people, but I want what's best for Lee Evans too. I don't have any regrets about what I did."

It sounded good. But Lee didn't really feel this way. Actually, the pain of his icy reception was heightened by his own disappointment in himself. He resented the ease with which many of his militant friends ostracized him his first month at home, yet he did not excuse himself.

This was apparent a week after the Millrose Games. Evans was back in New York for another meet, and as he sat in a friend's darkened living room, he stared at his lap and inhaled deeply. "If I had it to do over again I would do something more on the victory stand," he said slowly. "What I did wasn't enough. I know now. I know now. I should have done more."

This was not the speech of a man doing penance. Lee had come too far and accomplished too much for that. Rather it was an agonized admission that he had not fulfilled his own expectations.

Why did Lee Evans become a leader of the boycott ("The Olympic Project of Human Rights") and consider forfeiting a gold medal at Mexico City? Why does he believe that black people are oppressed and must establish their own identity and pride? And why, therefore, does he feel that his demonstration at the Olympics was not sufficient? The reasons are not uncommon. Except for his athletic skills, Lee might be typical of thousands of young blacks on campuses all over the country.

In college there was a contact with black culture and history and the philosophies of black power, a realization that his people were rioting and dying in the ghettos—and an awareness that all this related to him. For much in Lee Evans' youth had been an assault on his dignity and a reminder that he was poor, unequal and powerless.

Almost as soon as he could walk, Lee was on his knees baking in the summer sun as he picked grapes and cotton among the migrant laborers in the San Joaquin Valley—where *Grapes of Wrath* is a reality. The pay for cotton was three cents a pound. He picked 250 pounds a day, then prayed he wouldn't be cheated when he brought his cotton to the scales.

"I can still see it," he says, his voice almost a whisper. "One day the boss put his foot under my sack—that makes it lighter on the scales— and I saw him. But I was too scared to say anything. There was this look on his face, like 'I'm the white man and you're the little black boy and ain't nothin' you can do about it.' Our whole family was out pickin' and if I'd made any trouble they'd have sent us all away. So I stayed quiet. But I was ashamed. I think about that day a lot, even now."

In Fresno, home was a leaky cement structure, so cold in winter he could see his breath each morning. Lee and his four brothers slept in one room. "Three of us were in the same bed," he says, "and there was this problem with wetting. Maybe it was our diet; we couldn't afford any meat but pork. It was bad. I didn't stop wetting that bed till I was thirteen years old.

"But school was the most embarrassing thing. I had holes in my pants and cardboard in the bottom of my shoes. The white kids could afford a hot lunch. I had one peanut butter sandwich. The 'bloods' and the Mexicans, we'd sit in the corner with our paper bags lookin' hungry as hell. I was too ashamed to take out my sandwich. I'd just stick the bag up to my mouth.

"I learned to read quick and I got good grades at first, but the teachers never let you forget you was black," he recalls. "You walk in the classroom and right away it's the 'bloods' and Mexicans in back. The teacher doesn't pay any attention to you. She's always smiling at the little girl with the long blond hair sitting up front. Right then they stereotype you—and you start stereotyping yourself. You're black, so you must be dumb. 'Evans,' she'll say. 'You and Santos don't have to do this assignment. I don't think you can handle it.' Right in front of *everyone!* Not *too* embarrassing! Soon the white kids assume they're better. Then, in high school you don't know what's happening. The counselor puts *them* in college prep courses and puts *you* in metal shop and choir. Even after I got athletic scholarship offers they kept telling me I couldn't handle academics. And all along, the white kids are coming back from vacation with their new cars, tellin' you about what they did at the beach. I'm tellin' them about killin' snakes in our tent at some migrant camp in Oregon."

Evans also thinks a lot about what happened to his brother Doug, once a high-school All-America football player. "He was big and rough and could really kick tail," Lee says. "The coaches would let me ride in the bus to the games. Doug was five years older than me and I idolized him. That's how I got interested in sports."

But when Doug left high school his life came apart. He flunked out of junior college in one semester. Then there were some bad checks. Then a year in jail. Now he loads sheet rock onto trucks in San Jose. "I owe a lot to him," says Lee, "because every time he messed up, I told myself I wasn't going to let that happen to me. But I keep thinking it might have been different if he wasn't poor and black. In JC he'd be playin' well, but the coach would take him out for a white dude. Maybe that's why he didn't try out when the Oakland Raiders invited him. He was a black man in the system gettin' messed on. He couldn't relate to what they taught in college. All he knew was playin' football and pickin' grapes. I've felt the same way. I never had a steak till I was in college.

The first time I was in a restaurant was at the State Meet in L.A. my junior year in high school. I looked at the menu and the only thing I understood was chicken. So I ordered it. I was nervous when the waitress came around. Man, I didn't even know what to say."

Track gave Lee his chance. "By tenth grade I was winnin' all the time, so I started trainin' hard. It was the biggest thing that ever happened to me. I was somebody. I was *doin'* something. I wasn't just a fast cotton picker." At San Jose City, a junior college, Evans became the nation's top quarter-miler. In the spring of 1966, in New York, he ran down favored Theron Lewis in the final sixty yards to win the AAU national championship.

There were many offers from four-year colleges, but Lee chose San Jose State, to run for Bud Winter—dean of the sprint coaches—and on the relay team with Tommie Smith, holder of eleven world records, Evans improved quickly. Winter smoothed his form a bit and taught him the "high knees" style that is the San Jose trademark. Inspired by the inevitable competition with Tommie, Lee established a training routine that would probably give any of the world's other top quarter-milers a double coronary. In the fall he ran fifteen miles a day with the cross-country team. During the track season he worked out with the sprinters *and* the middle-distance men, running three-mile warmups, instead of the usual one, and practicing 660s and 550s, instead of 440s. That spring he won the AAU 440 again and established himself as an international star.

But Evans' real growth took place away from the track. In a year he changed from a naïve, subservient youngster who thought newspapers were for plugging the holes in broken windows, to a fairly well-informed, quietly outspoken black man and a good student. "When I first met Lee," says Harry Edwards, the twenty-six-year-old sociology professor who organized the boycott, "his hair was slicked back and he was wearing a 'Nigger shirt'—one of those loud cheap things they keep around stores because they know some Nigger will be fool enough to buy them. You never saw a more brainwashed cat. He was grateful to the white folks for bein' nice enough to let him run."

Tommie Smith is more succinct: "When Lee came here, man, that cat was just a big dummy."

A major influence on Lee was Art Simburg, then sports editor of the student newspaper. Easygoing, unaffected and moderately radical, Art was one of Tommie's closest friends. "At first," Simburg recalls, "it seemed Lee's thinking was hopelessly shallow. But as we got to know him we realized how intelligent he is and that he had a real hunger for learning."

It was Simburg, a white man, who gave Lee *The Autobiography of Malcolm X*. The book deeply affected Evans' future thinking. Like many young blacks of this generation, Lee saw much of himself in Malcolm's story and, when he looked around, saw many of the injustices of which Malcolm wrote.

"We were both growing, opening our eyes for the first time," says Smith. "At first we didn't realize we were being stereotyped as dumb black athletes when the athletic department recommended we take easy courses we didn't need, like Badminton and Football Appreciation. And when we'd sit down next to a white girl in the cafeteria and people'd start peepin' over the tops of their newspapers, we actually thought, 'Man, we're just great athletes, that's why they're staring at us.' "

"The more we learned and read, the more we could see how somebody is always steppin' on a blood," says Lee. "We began respecting people like Malcolm who stood up to that crap."

After competing on several national teams during the summer of 1967, they weren't surprised to learn that the United States Olympic Committee (USOC) was leading a campaign to return apartheid South Africa to the Games—although the South Africans had eliminated hardly any of the racist policies for which they had been barred. Like many black athletes, they became increasingly aware that coaches were always white and that AAU and Olympic officials were middle-aged, conservative, and out of touch with the competitors, especially the blacks.

"In Germany we were driving to a meet to represent our country," says Lee, "but we had to stand on the bus so the AAU people could sit. In Rome, Ollan Cassell of the AAU took Carlos' seat on a plane to New York and Carlos had to wait in the airport six hours. In Austria, I walked past a bunch of crackers from the U.S. and one says, 'We can't ever get away from them God damn Niggers.' Next day, I win my race and the same dudes want my autograph."

That fall Lee and Tommie joined Harry Edwards' boycott program. But first they were instrumental in one of the earliest campus black power demonstrations. Edwards, who organized the United Black Students for Action, tied up the San Jose campus for a week in September and forced cancellation of a football game. They demanded that the school move against segregated housing, outlaw all-white fraternities, establish a program for minority group students and eliminate such athletic department practices as grouping blacks in a corner of the locker room, entertaining prospective athletes in segregated fraternities, and encouraging blacks to take unnecessary 'gut' courses to keep them eligible for sports. The administration finally announced that the demands were valid and rectified most of the grievances.

"Harry used Tom and me a lot to get things started," Lee says with pride. "Our names were known to the other students. We really got something done."

Evans was involved in political action for the first time. It gave him a sense of fulfillment. But he was not a real activist—and he is not one today. It is easy to forget that he and the other militant black athletes are still in their early twenties and that sports, not demonstrations, is really "their thing." In a strange city, Lee checks out the movie theaters, not the local black power organization.

But Lee's beliefs are strong and he overcame his shyness to become one of the "Olympic Project's" most active spokesmen. Neither he, Tommie, nor Carlos, who came to San Jose that fall, really expected to boycott. Their hope was to focus attention on the absence of blacks from national sports administrations (particularly the USOC), expose the segregated practices of the New York Athletic Club, generate pressure for barring South Africa and, in the process, display solidarity with less fortunate blacks. But they were prepared to boycott if they had to.

They didn't have to. When several nations threatened to join the American blacks' boycott, the International Olympic Committee (IOC) reversed itself and ousted the South Africans. In Los Angeles, after the first Olympic trials, the black athletes voted not to boycott—but decided overwhelmingly to make some significant gesture at Mexico City.

At the Lake Tahoe training camp, however, they couldn't get organized. Edwards was in the East working on his Ph.D. They were distrustful of whites, like the Harvard crew, who offered support. Lee was too easygoing, Tommie too reserved, and Carlos too erratic to take over the leadership.

"Everybody was sayin', 'We gotta call a meetin',' " Lee says, "but we all had our minds on the competition and adjusting to the altitude. When we finally met we couldn't agree on something we could all do. Black socks were suggested—and we thought we'd agreed on that—but then some guys said they couldn't run in socks. People talked about black shoes, a black scarf, a black bow on the uniform. Nothing. We finally just decided that everybody would do his own thing."

In Mexico City, Lee was deeply affected by his contact with many black Africans. He came away with numerous friends and the assurance that such stars as Keino and Temu of Kenya supported the black protest.

But the atmosphere was clearly hostile. Avery Brundage, the eighty-one-year-old IOC president who supported South Africa, had already issued a warning that demonstrations would be dealt with harshly. Later, a photographer, whose pictures of black protestors had appeared in a national magazine, was hounded by a top Olympic press official. "I'm giving you trouble," the PR man shouted, "because you took pictures of those damn jungle bunnies!"

The protests began mildly, with many black athletes—including Carlos, Smith and Evans—competing in black knee-socks, ironically issued by the USOC as part of the dress uniform. Then, after finishing one-three in the 100 meters, Jim Hines and Charlie Greene, usually both moderates, let it be known they would not accept their medals from Avery Brundage. And Brundage was absent from the ceremony.

That day Lee and Tommie pondered the same problem. "I won't shake his hand," said Lee. "But what do we do if he shows up?"

"Let's get some black gloves," Smith suggested. "We can put them on if he tries to shake our hand. That ought to shake him up."

The next morning Linda Evans and Denise Smith went shopping for black gloves. But after Tommie had overcome a pulled muscle to set a world record and win the 200-meter final, he decided to carry his protest further. When he and Carlos, who finished third, appeared on the victory stand, Smith was wearing a black scarf and Carlos a black shirt. Their shoes were off to display their black socks. When "The Star-Spangled Banner" was played, they lowered their heads and each thrust a gloved fist into the air. "It was a protest to show that what we had won was for all black people," Smith was to explain. "Our goal was black dignity."

As the demonstration took place, Evans stood in the stands with black gloves on both hands, repeating the gestures. "People were yellin' and cursin' at me," he says. "But what we were doin' made me proud."

In the next few days, those black athletes who didn't already know found out what it was in the society and the sports establishment that Smith and Carlos were demonstrating against. The USOC suspended Tommie and John and ordered them from Olympic Village. "We recognize," USOC President Douglas Roby said later, "that these incidents may be the results of granting athletes what might be considered excessive freedom in the cause of human rights. . . ."

From every direction came pressure on athletes—black and white—

to remain silent. Several were contacted by pro football teams and re-minded that demonstrators were not likely to be drafted. American ath-letes on leave from the Army heard quickly from their commanding officers. Athletic departments, ROTC units and employers pounded home the message. A rumor circulated that the IAAF, which controls amateur athletics, was ready to bar anyone who violated regulations. The all-white Harvard crew almost came to blows with members of the U.S. rifle team, who were hanging a "Win with Wallace" banner from their window in Olympic Village.

Some disagreed with the tone of the black glove protest, but almost all the blacks—and a significant number of whites—shared its senti-ment and were furious at the suspensions. Yet they were frightened and leaderless and few acted. As one black runner put it: "The reason I'm okay is because I acted like a 'Tom' in the first place. . . . And I got the word I better 'Tom' it on the stand tomorrow."

Evans and the other U.S. 400-meter finalists, Ron Freeman and Larry James, had planned to warm up in black berets they'd brought from the States and then wear black socks on the victory stand. Now everything had changed. James, Freeman and Vince Mathews, their partner in the 1600-meter relay two days hence, were moderates—and easily frightened. Smith and Carlos had each other for support. Lee Evans, a twenty-one-year-old political novice, was alone. The pressure was focused on him.

Lee learned of the suspensions on his way to breakfast. By the time he arrived he'd made a decision. "You realize we can't run today," he told Freeman and James. But his teammates were uncertain.

"We decided to have a meeting later," Lee says. "Then I started back toward the dormitory. I couldn't believe what had happened. On the way an Olympic Committee cat comes up and smiles and says, 'Hi,' like nothing had happened. I grabbed him.

"Listen, Mother," Evans rasped, "don't even talk to me after what you done to my partners!" The man broke Lee's grasp and ran. Lee walked into the dormitory lobby, where a female reporter was waiting to interview him. Shaking with rage and on the verge of tears, he still agreed to answer her questions. But just then another Olympic Com-mittee member came in and ordered the woman to leave. "The dude grabbed her arm," says Lee, "and soon as I saw that 'Olympic Commit-tee' on his jacket I went for him. I shoved him backwards against the wall and I don't know what I'd have done to him if coach Winter hadn't come over just then and pulled me off."

In the elevator, going up to his room, Evans met Olga Connelly of the U.S. women's team. "She told me that she wouldn't compete if I didn't," Lee recalls. "That really meant something to me. She said she and her husband, Harold, knew a lot of whites who were mad enough to leave."

Evans was lying on his bed, tears running down his cheeks when John Carlos walked in. "I told him," says Lee, "that I wasn't running unless he told me to."

"Listen, man," Carlos said, "I want you to run. Get all the gold you can. *Then do your thing.*"

Moments later, Lee saw his tall, fiery wife Linda standing in the doorway. Always more militant than Lee, she had been especially proud of his involvement with the boycott. "Linda was worried 'cause she'd heard I'd been fightin'," Lee recalls. "I told her I was all right and that Carlos said I should run. I could see she was real mad. She kept sayin', 'You got to do somethin'. You got to do somethin'.' "

When Evans got to the stadium he found James and Freeman vacillating. Finally he snapped: "I'm wearing the damn hat. That's all. Are you?" James and Freeman nodded.

Five minutes before the 400-meter final, Roby confronted the three athletes, now at an emotional peak for competition, and began to lecture them. "Now boys," he began, "I don't want to upset you, but. . . ."

As Evans, James and Freeman bounced nervously in front of him, Roby made a half-hearted disclaimer that the suspensions of Smith and Carlos weren't really the fault of the USOC—and then proceeded to warn them that "any further demonstrations [will] be dealt with to the full extent of the USOC's powers."

Evans, emotionally spent, would have surprised no one by losing. Yet he ran the greatest race of his career, leading a one-two-three sweep for the black Americans. His time was a world and Olympic record of 43.8 seconds.

An hour later, when they appeared for the medal presentations, Evans, Freeman and James wore their berets and black socks—and had their fists tucked into their shirts. The crowd murmured, expecting a reappearance of the black gloves. But when the fists emerged, they were bare.

In contrast to the solemnity of Carlos and Smith, the three quarter-milers were smiling. On the stand they waved their fists in the black power sign, but it was not a defiant gesture. And when the anthem played they removed their berets.

"I feel I won this gold medal for all black people," Lee said, echoing

Tommie, at a press conference later. "Tommie and I learned a lot in the boycott movement. If I had it to do all over again I'd support it."

But when asked the significance of the berets, Lee just smiled at James and Freeman and said: "It was raining. We didn't want to get our heads wet."

Lee anchored the U.S. 1600-meter relay team to another gold medal two days later. Again the blacks wore their berets and socks. And Lee gruffly refused to shake Roby's hand during the ceremony. The team members did not appear at the post-race press conference.

There were a few other small signs of black displeasure. Bob Beamon appeared in black socks and Ralph Boston barefoot after finishing one-three in the long jump. The women's 400-meter relay team dedicated its gold medal to Carlos and Smith. But that was all.

Thus, compared to the other black athletes, Evans expressed himself dramatically. In fact, had his demonstration come before Smith's and Carlos', it might have been Evans, James and Freeman who were suspended. Their act was significant—and it took guts. But, in light of Lee's own beliefs, was it enough? He feels now—and he probably knew then—that it wasn't.

Evans had been a leader in the black athletes' movement since it began. The USOC and the IOC had tested its strength by the suspensions. Unfair as the role may have been, it was up to Lee to prove that the black athletes would not be intimidated. He was only partially successful.

Now, four months later, he sat in his friend's living room trying to explain why he had not done more. "After the 400 meters I really thought I was doing something. I didn't know how it would be taken by the white press. But then I got some phone calls. I wasn't ignorant about it after the relay. But I didn't know what to do. I just didn't know. It was the most difficult time of my whole life," he said, choking on the words. "What to do?

"The first time on the victory stand I was debating: should I leave the beret on during the national anthem? That would have shown I stood with Tom and Carlos, 'cause what they did was during the anthem too. But I took the beret off 'cause I wanted to run in the relay. I didn't want to get suspended yet. If I didn't have another race coming up, I was so mad then I would have left it on. That's all I would have had to do.

"But man, I was so afraid of being shot. Do you know what kind of targets we were on that stand? You wouldn't believe the feeling in the air. I really thought the chances of being shot were seventy, eighty percent if I did what Tom and Carlos did. Every second I was up there I was scared. When the boycott started we got all that hate mail and guys threatened our lives. I had a dream Tommie and I got shot at a meet in San Francisco. I couldn't get it out of my mind.

"You know something?" he said, shaking his head. "I even had a black glove in my pants during the ceremony. It was there in case Brundage showed up. But I couldn't have done what Tommie did. Why didn't I?"

Evans paused. He was breathing quickly. His eyes were beginning to water. "One, I'd built it up in my mind that I was going to do what Lee Evans wanted. See, I'd gotten all these letters, tellin' me to do this and that. But it wasn't my bag to do what someone told me. Then, like I said, I was scared of being kicked off the team before the relay and I was scared, so scared of being shot. And, okay, I was worried about what would happen to my future."

Now the words were tumbling out, as though they had been waiting a long time. "If I had it to do over again, I'd probably leave the beret on. But, no matter what, I'd be more militant than I was.

"I think about it a lot at night. Maybe I shouldn't have showed up for the ceremony at all. Or maybe I should have gotten something that would make a big black cloud and set it loose when they started the anthem. And I'd be gone when the cloud cleared away."

For a moment, Lee laughed at himself and the foolishness of his idea. Then he fell silent. "Linda didn't say she wanted me to do anything specific," he said at last. "But I know anything I did that was more militant than Tom would have made her happy."

His eyes were wet again. "God, it depresses me to talk about this. I've never said it before. But I tell you, what I did in Mexico City, it affects my whole life. All those people turned against me so quick."

But not everyone. Tommie Smith stood by Lee. "I wasn't disappointed in him. Surprised, but not disappointed. The cat did more than the rest," says Tommie. "And he had scared rookies like Freeman and James to pull up too. Lee may not be as stout in 'thinking black' as Carlos, but he's really in earnest about what he's trying to do. I told Carlos to get off the man's back."

Recently, Lee's status in the black community has improved somewhat. One reason is that it's very hard to be around Lee Evans and still dislike him. He is just too bouncy, bumbling (last summer he managed to miss the meeting where the boycott was voted down, and then prematurely announced it to the press), enthusiastic (he loves track so much, and wants a winner so badly at San Jose, he has personally helped recruit most of the team's best runners), and good-humored.

"I've got a money-making project," he suggested after the Olympics. "I'm gonna sell bumper stickers that say 'Brundage Wears Black Socks.'"

Although there are loud rumblings that no pro football team will draft either Evans or Carlos (Smith was taken as a red-shirt choice two years ago), Lee still can joke about his future: "I'll play next fall at San Jose State, become an All-America cornerback and flanker, and sign for $400,000. When I retire I'd like to coach track in Kenya for a couple of years. Then I could come back, get a college job and recruit all the Kenyans for my school. Can you imagine what kind of team I'd have?"

The ice between Evans and Carlos has even melted a little. Their families have exchanged visits; Carlos invited Lee to stay in Harlem while both were in New York for a meet (Lee declined), and they will be co-captains at San Jose. Carlos may also be impressed that even the ridicule of some of his own people has not stopped Lee from being involved in black causes.

In February, when the San Jose NAACP chapter invited Smith, Evans and Carlos to receive awards at a banquet, it was Lee who told the others that Roy Wilkins, the NAACP executive-secretary, had just spoken out against black studies programs and black campus facilities —something they all support. "Smith and Carlos didn't even know about it," Lee laughs. "I guess they don't read the papers much. Me, the 'Tom,' I had to tell them. Well, we told the local chapter they'd have to renounce the Wilkins statement before we showed up. And they did."

A week later, Lee conned Jesse Abramson, meet director of the Olympic Invitational Meet at Madison Square Garden, into admitting that the USOC, which was sponsoring the event, had ordered him not to invite Smith or Carlos. "Who's coming?" Lee asked innocently.

"Oh, everybody who's good," Abramson replied.

"Can Ronnie Ray Smith come?" asked Lee. Smith is another San Jose State Olympian.

"Why yes," Abramson said. "We want everybody from the Olympics and some of the best ones who didn't go. We're making a big show for the people who couldn't get down to Mexico."

"Are Smith and Carlos invited?"

There was a long silence. "No, but it wasn't my decision," Abramson said hurriedly. "It was a high-level decision by the Olympic Committee.

They say Carlos and Smith are still suspended. Somebody has to set a policy on this."

Lee set a policy by not attending. He also talked to Wyomia Tyus, the women's 100-meter gold medalist, who was going to present an award to the winner of a fifty-yard dash held in her honor. On the day of the meet she told the committee she would attend just as soon as "brothers Smith and Carlos are invited."

There are some black militants to whom Evans will always be a "Tom"—for he is not a separatist, not a revolutionary and not an advocate of violence. Many whites will also dislike him increasingly, because he intends to keep pushing, in his own way, for what he believes in. But still Evans is emerging from the shadow that has haunted him since Mexico City.

He isn't likely to be leading many demonstrations in the future, but there will be other "Mexico Citys" in Lee's life and he can be expected to put his experience to good use.

"I think we accomplished a lot with the boycott movement," Lee says with pride. "We closed down the New York Athletic Club meet for good; we kept South Africa and Rhodesia out of the Olympics; we got people to realize that the Olympic Committee is racist and undemocratic; we got schools to start hiring black coaches, and we got a lot of black athletes—like me, involved—starting to think about black people. And I'm still learning. We're just gettin' started."

"Are You All Right, Smoke?"

Al Hirshberg | **1967**

The day after Smoky Burgess arrived at the Chicago White Sox spring-training camp in Sarasota, Florida, infielder Al Weis greeted him in the locker room, saying, "How do you feel, Smoke?"

"Felt pretty good when I got up this morning, Ace," Burgess said. "But I got over it."

"How's the ulcer?" asked manager Eddie Stanky.

"Bad, Ace," Burgess said. "Real bad."

Then Burgess went out and hit five straight line drives. It was the first time he had held a bat since the end of the 1966 season.

"He's ready," Stanky said. "He'd be ready Christmas day with six inches of snow on the ground."

Smoky Burgess is always ready. He's a grandfather, fat, forty, gray at the temples, asthmatic, ulcered and hypochondriacal, but he's still the best pinch-hitter big-league baseball has ever known. Last year he got twenty-one hits in sixty-seven at bats for a .313 average. He also collected eleven walks, managed to get hit twice and drove in fifteen runs. His 136 pinch-hits in the major leagues is an all-time record.

Once he was a pretty good catcher, but he got over that, too.

"I caught five innings last year, Ace," he told me. "My ambition this year is to catch none. I didn't even bring a glove."

454)

Burgess doesn't need a glove. All he needs is a bat and a pitcher to throw to him. He can hit anything that doesn't hit him, and almost every pitcher who ever faced him has jagged-edged memories of Smoky's bat. Burgess came into the majors back in 1949, and he is always running into pitchers who look the other way when he approaches them.

Like Marv Grissom, once a top reliever for the New York Giants. A former California Angels coach, Grissom began a new job as pitching coach for the White Sox this year. When Burgess first saw him in Sarasota, he said, "Hi, Ace. Remember me?"

"Go away," said Grissom, as he shook hands. Then Grissom went away and Burgess said, "I'm with the Reds in a tie game against the Giants in Cincinnati one night, and we get the bases full with two out on Grissom. Manager Birdie Tebbetts sends Steve Bilko up to pinch-hit and Grissom gets two strikes on him. Then Tebbetts yanks Bilko and sends me up, with one strike left. What do you think happens, Ace? Grissom tries to brush me back. He hits me on the shoulder and the winning run comes in."

Burgess threw back his head and laughed, then wandered into the trainer's room.

"You sick again?" said Tommy John, who was lying on one of the two training tables. "You want me to get up?"

"You stay right where you are, Ace," Burgess said. "I'll take this one."

With some effort he climbed on the table. Charley Saad, the new White Sox trainer, said, "You all right, Smoke? You want a rub or something?"

"I'm all right, Ace," Burgess said. "Just tired."

He lay on his back, and his stomach piled up above him, turning the training table into a small hill. Young, flat-bellied, hard-muscled athletes came in, stepped on scales, frowned, and walked out. Burgess watched them, a little smile playing about his lips.

"How much do you weigh, Smoky?" I said.

He turned over on one side, then lifted his head high enough to get his elbow under it. "Darned if I know," he said. "I haven't weighed myself lately."

"What's your playing weight?"

"Whatever it happens to be," he said. "I don't keep track."

Whatever it happens to be has to be well over two hundred pounds even though he's listed at 198. Because he stands only five eight, it's even hard to estimate his weight. Suddenly Burgess yawned, sat up, stretched, climbed off the table and went back into the locker room. He was just in time to hear a rookie pitcher named Tony Alessi say, "I don't make it to the big leagues this year, I'll hang 'em up."

"How old are you, Ace?" Burgess said, lowering himself onto a trunk.

"Twenty-two," Alessi said.

"How long you been down?"

"A year. Since I got out of college."

"Less than a year then," Burgess said. "You know how long I was down? Eight years, counting a couple after I had a shot with the Cubs. I got out of the service, my arm was so bad I couldn't throw the ball back to the pitcher, so I learned to throw left-handed and monkeyed around in the outfield. That's how bad I wanted to play ball."

"I want to play," Alessi said. "But I don't want to waste my life in the minors."

"One, two years more, what's the difference?" Burgess said. "And when you get to be my age, there's other things you can do. I've got an automobile agency up in North Carolina."

Hoyt Wilhelm came in and Burgess said, "Look at Hoyt, Ace. He's even older than I am." He turned to Wilhelm. "How long were you down, Ace?"

"Nine years," Wilhelm said.

"You got anything else going for you now?"

"Coupla things," said Wilhelm.

Burgess turned back to Alessi. "See?" he said.

"Sure," said Alessi, "that's great for Burgess and Wilhelm. But who ever heard of me?"

Later, I asked Burgess, "Did you really learn to throw left-handed when your arm went dead?"

" 'Course not," Smoky said. "I can't throw with my left. But I don't want that kid quitting. He's a pretty good prospect."

"How often have you caught Wilhelm?" I asked Burgess. "You guys are the oldest battery in the majors." Burgess was forty last February. Wilhelm will be forty-four in July.

"We ain't no battery, Ace. I've never caught Wilhelm and never will. Even in the bullpen I used to stand aside with my glove stuck out. I didn't want the guy hitting me in the face."

Burgess climbed off the trunk and led the way back to the trainer's quarters, for he is a restless soul, torn between compulsions—to find a place to sit, lean or lie on and to see what's going on somewhere else.

As Burgess made himself comfortable on one table, young pitcher Fred Kovner strolled toward the other with a pained look on his face.

"What's the matter?" asked Charley Saad.

"I gotta blister on my hand," Kovner said.

Burgess and Saad chorused, "Aw—" in such perfect harmony that even Kovner laughed. "He's great with blisters, Ace," Burgess said. "Your little hand'll be all better before you know it."

As Saad was treating the blister, Rich Austin came in. Austin, trainer of the White Sox farm club at Evansville and Saad's spring-training assistant, also had the job of preparing the locker room lunches for the ballplayers. Burgess, who was intently watching Saad's blister work, never lifted his eyes as he said, "Hey, Ace, your soup is lousy."

"What's the matter with it?" Austin said.

"All it's got in it is tomatoes," Burgess said.

"Soup is soup," Austin said. "You want me to make something special for you?"

Burgess looked up at Austin. "Y'know, Ace, that's a fine idea."

As Smoky settled back, Moose Skowron, puffing heavily from a tough workout, came in and walked to the scales at the foot of Burgess' table.

"What a life, Smoky," Skowron said, wiping the perspiration from his brow.

"Rough," said Burgess, without changing his position. "Real rough."

Duane Josephson appeared. The big rookie catcher, who hit .324 at Indianapolis last year, looked as tired as Skowron.

"How ya feeling, Ace?"

"Fine," Josephson panted.

"You keep this up, you'll be in shape all right," said Burgess.

"How about you?" Josephson said.

Burgess yawned. "I'm always in shape."

Jim O'Toole, the starting pitcher in an exhibition game that afternoon, climbed on the other table for a rubdown. As Saad began working on him, O'Toole accidentally slid too close to the edge.

"Move over," Saad said.

"And be sure it's in the right direction, Ace," said Burgess. "Otherwise you'll fall off. A guy can get very badly hurt falling off a training table."

"You ought to know," O'Toole said.

By now, Burgess had been in the same position on the training table for half an hour. When he finally stood up, I asked him if he had ever fallen off one.

"No, but I came close a couple of times," he said. "You have to watch yourself on training tables. They're pretty narrow."

He held his hands together as though holding a bat, then twisted them as though turning the handle.

"What are you doing?" I said.

"Working out," he said.

"Is that all the working out you do?"

"No, sir," Burgess said. "I run. I help the boys play pickup."

Pickup is a game in which one man rolls a ball while the other runs, bends, picks it up and tosses it back. The ball-roller gives himself as much or as little exercise as he feels like taking, while working the picker-upper to exhaustion.

"Do you roll or do you pick up?" I said.

Burgess looked at me as if I were out of my mind. "Roll, of course," he said.

"How about calisthenics?"

"They're bad for my ulcer," he said.

Burgess has lived with his ulcer for so long that he speaks of it with the affection of a master for a pet poodle and coddles it in the same spirit. Without his ulcer, Burgess wouldn't be Burgess. Partly because of it, he told White Sox general manager Ed Short that he wouldn't be back this season.

Concern for his wife and his business interests in Forest City, North Carolina, were the real reasons for his retirement decision last fall, although he threw the ulcer in out of pride in it. His wife was facing surgery and his automobile agency was making increasing demands on his time. When the surgery was successful and Burgess's partner assured him he could be spared for the baseball season, Burgess brought his ulcer back to the White Sox.

The Sox bought his ulcer from the Pirates in September of 1964. When he reported to the team in Detroit, where the White Sox were finishing a series, manager Al Lopez said, "I got you for your bat, not your glove. All I want you to do is hit." Which wasn't exactly a shock to Smoky.

That night, Lopez sent him up in the ninth inning with two out, a man on and the White Sox a run behind. Burgess hit Dave Wickersham's first pitch into the upper deck of the rightfield stands. It was foul by three feet. However, two pitches later, he hit a screaming line drive into the lower deck for a home run that won the ballgame.

"You got the idea," Lopez said, as Smoky trotted into the dugout.

Burgess also got the idea on the last day of the 1956 season when he went to bat as a pinch-hitter late in the game, with the Reds needing one home run to tie the single-season major-league record for team homers, 221, then held by the Giants.

"Home run or nothing," said manager Birdie Tebbetts.

Burgess hit the first pitch out of the park.

In the years between 1959 and 1962 he was the Pirates' regular catcher and rarely pinch-hit. During that period his batting average was never under .294 and once soared to .328. Bob Skinner, a teammate for years, marveled at him. "He looks like a butcher in a supermarket," Skinner once said.

Burgess appears to be a lot of things he isn't. Despite his beer-barrel belly, he never drinks. Despite his nickname, he never smokes. And despite his ailments, real and imagined, he's never unable to swing a bat.

Although Pirate manager Danny Murtaugh often platooned him behind the plate with Hal Smith, a right-handed batter, Burgess, who bats from the left, doesn't care which arm a pitcher throws with. Once he steps into the batter's box, nothing much matters to him.

"That Smoky Burgess," said Dick Groat, when the two were in Pittsburgh together, "will hit left- or right-handed pitchers. He'll hit on hot days or cold. He'll hit late in a game or early. He'll hit with men on or with the bases empty. He just doesn't care."

Burgess isn't especially choosy about the pitches he goes after either. The ball doesn't have to be in the strike zone as long as it's within reasonable reach. He prefers it on the tight side, since he is a pull hitter. However, when there are two strikes on him, he'll punch an outside pitch to left if need be.

"A hit is a hit, Ace," he told me. "What do I care where it goes as long as it's in fair territory and out of everybody's reach? At my time of life, I can't be fussy."

"Is that the secret of your success?" I said.

"Not really," he said. "The secret of any good pinch-hitter's success is to swing at the first pitch if it's over the plate. How many times do you see a guy watch the first one come right down the middle? That puts him behind the pitcher, who then can monkey around. You don't want the pitcher monkeying around—you want to do that. You've got to make him come in with your pitch, not his. And most of the time, your pitch is his first one. You may not see another like it."

"Doesn't every pitcher in the league know you'll go for the first one?"

"I suppose so," Burgess said.

"Then aren't you likely to see little to hit on that first pitch?"

"No," Burgess said. "The pitcher isn't any more anxious for me to get ahead of him than I am for him to get ahead of me. He'll try to get the first pitch over. If he doesn't, I'll let it go by for a ball and still have three swings left. He can't afford to let me do that."

Burgess liked manager Eddie Stanky's idea of permitting the same pinch-hitter to come up at two different times during a game, but disagreed with his boss on letting the replaced man stay in the game. While Stanky felt he should be allowed to, Burgess felt he shouldn't.

"Once a guy is out of the game, he should stay out," Burgess said. "Otherwise, I think the idea is great."

For various reasons, Burgess didn't have much chance to see how it worked for him in actual practice. Although the American League approved it as an experiment for spring training, the National League didn't, which prevented Stanky from doing it more than half the games the White Sox played in Florida. And, since Burgess rarely left Sarasota, somebody else was the "designated" pinch-hitter, the man who could bat twice, when the club was on the road.

The first time Burgess tried it, he went o-for-two.

"Hit the ball good to right first time up, but it was caught by a guy perfectly positioned," he said. "Second time I struck out on a three-and-two pitch, but I wouldn't have in the regular season."

"Why not?" I said.

"It was a sinker outside," he said. "I would have punched it to left, or got a piece of it or something. But I don't like to change my natural swing in spring training."

"Hey, Smoke," somebody yelled. "You coming? The game's starting."

The White Sox took such a big early lead over the Houston Astros that Burgess obviously would do no pinch-hitting that day. In the seventh inning, he strolled out to right field with Gerry McNertney, who began running with a couple of other ballplayers. While they sprinted back and forth between the foul line and right-center, Burgess leaned against the fence and talked to the ball boy.

After a while, Smoky started trotting with Jim Hicks and Buddy Bradford, who quickly pulled away from him. Burgess responded to the challenge by slowing down to a near walk. He stopped in right-center, then turned as if to trot back. But, fortunately, he spotted Ron Hansen working out in a screened-in batting cage and he ambled over and talked to him.

Then he walked back to the foul line, where he noticed that Walter (No-Neck) Williams had left his glove. Burgess casually kicked it against the fence, turned and jogged back toward right-center, passing

Williams on the way. At the foul line, Williams stopped, looked for his glove, then put it back on the foul line. When Burgess returned from his round trip, he kicked the glove against the fence again. Williams put it back when he arrived there, Burgess kicked it aside when he got there. This went on until Burgess got tired of all that trotting, which was very soon.

Burgess then got involved in a game of pickup with Bill Voss, a young outfielder. Smoky is one of the game's great ball-rollers. For a few minutes, he worked bending over, but after a while he went into the catcher's squat. While Voss dashed madly back and forth, bending, stretching, picking up the ball and tossing it back to Smoky, Burgess moved only the hand that rolled the ball. When Voss, his face streaming, finally quit, Burgess hadn't even worked up a sweat.

Later, Eddie Mathews and Jim Landis of the Astros, both in street clothes, wandered over to say hello. Burgess, who hadn't stopped to talk for some twenty minutes, greeted them like long-lost brothers.

"I see you're in shape, Smoke," Mathews said.

Burgess grinned, patted his stomach, and said, "I don't hit with this."

"How old are you, Smoke?"

"Forty, Ace."

"You'll be hitting when you're ninety," Mathews said.

"If I make it to then," said Burgess.

When the game ended, Burgess trotted to the locker room to shower and change into street clothes. I met him later in the lobby of the nearby Sarasota Terrace Hotel, which the White Sox own and where their unattached ballplayers stay during spring training. Burgess is not only a great pinch-hitter, a great ball-roller and a great talker, he is one of the last of baseball's great lobby-sitters. When he's not eating, sleeping or at the ballpark, he can almost always be found in hotel lobbies.

In the Terrace lobby, a local artist had painted his picture, which was up on the wall, along with other examples of the artist's work. Each drawing had a price tag. Burgess' was ten dollars. On the same panel was a picture of President Johnson, priced at twenty dollars.

"How come your picture is worth only ten bucks and the President's twenty?" I said.

"Beats me, Ace," Burgess said. " 'Specially when you realize the President couldn't hit a fastball down the middle to save his life."

He shrugged, stood up, patted his stomach and said, "Chow time. I hope the ulcer can take it."

Tom Landry

God, Family, and Football

Gary Cartwright | **1 9 6 9**

It is Saturday afternoon, early November. A chilled old-time wind chases the fire and baked bronze of dying leaves, and Tom Landry sits in his office on the eleventh floor of a suburban tower in North Dallas, looking down with the sort of detachment that Baron Frankenstein must have experienced as he watched the villagers fight fear with sticks and hayforks.

The Monster is loose again!

The extent of his capering again will be apparent in the agate type of the Sunday sports pages. Ohio U. defeats Cincinnati 60 to 48. Virginia holds off Tulane 63 to 47. Yale tears up Princeton 42 to 17. *Yale!* The blunderbuss of the dime novel, the twenty-three-pound turtleneck sweater in grandpa's attic, scoring with basketball propensity. Even Landry's old school, the University of Texas, is lacing TCU (47 to 21) with unparalleled freedom of expression.

Records fall like leaves, then blow away under the gusts of new records. Someone named Mike Richardson (forget that name) wipes Kyle Rote and Doak Walker from the SMU record book. Michigan's Ron Johnson is a jet-age ghost, cremating the memory of Grange and Harmon in his fantail. In a radio interview former Los Angeles Rams' center Art Hunter refers to O. J. Simpson as "the best of Jimmy Brown and

Gale Sayers rolled into one." And Texas' Chris Gilbert, the little tail-back who has broken all the Southwest Conference rushing records and threatens more ot the same to every career rushing record in the history of college football, will have difficulty making it as a first team All-America.

What was once a game of patience, prudence and pogroms enacted more or less in the geographical center of a seven-diamond defense now looks as though it were invented by the French. Even the college teams who are not, strictly speaking, relying on the "pro-type" offense, are gaining three or four hundred yards a game. "Ten yards and a cloud of dust"; that's how Texas Tech coach J. T. King describes the University of Texas attack.

The Monster is everywhere, legends tumbling on his vibrations.

"I still feel that the defense will stand up to the test," Tom Landry is saying on this particular Saturday afternoon. Landry is seemingly oblivious to the riots that are at this moment taking place on the campuses across the land: Landry is talking of the National Football League, specifically of the game in the Cotton Bowl Sunday between his Cowboys and the New York Giants, a game that will go a long way in settling the winner of the Capitol Division. There are those in football, Giants' president Wellington Mara among them, who feel that Tom Landry has perfected, maybe even invented, football's modern defense. Landry credits the invention to Steve Owens, the genius of the Giants from 1931–53, though it was Landry who defined the relationship of the line-backer to the width of the playing field, thus establishing what Mara calls "the inside-out theory of defensive football"—protecting the middle while trusting the flanks to hot pursuit.

Landry was one of the first to recognize tendencies and traits in his opposition, and one of the first to devise "keys" which would unlock the secrets of the mysterious huddle. Many coaches eventually reached that conclusion, but *Landry did it as a player.* And when it was perfected—and when the Giants were the most feared defense in football —Landry started experimenting with offensive weapons which could conceivably destroy his life's work. It was a restless imitation of art and life: from the missile came the antimissile came the anti-anti-missile. . . .

But listen to Landry on this Saturday afternoon:

". . . The defense will stand up. But sometimes you wonder (he says this with some irony in his normal monotone; his oyster eyes twinkle; his Ice Age smile, collected through centuries of slow but constant seepage, is alert to history's carnage). . . .

"You see what's happening to college football. The two-platoon rule opened it up to the multiple offense, and the multiple offense created an impossible situation in terms of how a college team can defense it. The key to *defense* is execution; in order to execute well enough to contain a multiple offense a team must play together four or five years . . . at least that long . . . which is impossible for the colleges. As long as colleges play a multiple offense . . . a T-formation offense, with quarterbacks in the pass pocket . . . as long as that happens, the colleges will never be able to defense it: they will never have enough experience to cope with the many problems. The colleges must either return to one-platoon football or resign themselves to big scores."

Somewhere in the corners of your mind you hear Baron Frankenstein speak, identifying his work, preaching caution, almost amused at the misunderstanding. Lay aside your hayforks, melt down your silver bullets: your icons are powerless, your dogs less than useless. The Monster is not the creation but the creator. It is the *Landry Monster,* that gangling apparition of spreads and slots and double-or-triple wings and men-in-motion and abrupt shifts, coordinated to wreck anticipation, delight the fans and make supermen from human tissue.

They used to laugh at it. Such great-but-stylized coaches as Buddy Parker used to warn Landry that the multiple offense would never work, that it would strangle on its own complications; and for a time in the early 1960s it seemed as though they were right. But Landry *had it in his mind* when he resigned as defensive coach of the Giants to take the head job with the newly formed Dallas Cowboys in 1960.

His conviction never wavered. "It was, and still is, the only way to attack the basic 4–3 defense," Landry says. On the other hand: "If you have the time and patience to coordinate your defense . . . the experience to handle all the complicated sets . . . defense will prevail."

In his ninth season with the Cowboys, Tom Landry is the dean of NFL head coaches. He had five straight losing seasons before his team broke even in 1965. Since then the Cowboys have dominated the Eastern Conference, barely losing to Green Bay in two NFL Championship games. Landry's is the first expansion team in modern sports history to achieve championship status, and his ideas on multiple offense have filtered down to the most primitive level of football. If the Dallas Cowboys appear awesome on your television screen, they are nowhere near as awesome as Landry intends.

Like brilliant men in every field, Tom Landry is self-made. Or, as Landry chooses to put it, he is the product of destiny, and divine counterplay.

"It is hard to put your finger on why you make the decisions that you make," says Landry. "I'm a great believer in my own convictions, but I pray a great deal that I'll make the right decision. I have no doubt that there is something other than man himself that leads man."

That something, of course, is the Christian God. There was a time eight or nine years ago, in the scruffy, early years of the Cowboys, when some of the older players referred to their coach as *Pope Landry I.* Less pious in recent years, Landry expresses his deepest beliefs in the stereotype of selected banquet speeches, and in answers to direct questions. "If Landry has ever saved any souls," says one current player, "he did it without anyone knowing."

In the early years many players found Landry confusing and non-communicative. "He would never pat you on the behind and tell you 'good job,'" complained one former defensive back. "If you intercepted a pass, Landry looked at you like *that's what you're supposed to do!*" But that is Landry's style taciturn without being shy, confident without being boastful; he exudes rather than expounds his philosophy. Except for the practice field or meeting room, Landry permits himself almost no personal contact. There is one minor exception: he sometimes lifts weights with the players in the off-season. Landry is as trim and maybe as strong as any man on his team. With Tom Landry, the priority is God, family and football.

"I grew up in a Christian home," says Landry, "but I wasn't truly converted to Christ until 1958. I lived a moral life but I wasn't a true Christian. Most people go through life always looking . . . always seeking. I found out that a Christian commitment is the only real purpose in life."

Landry says that he did not have "a religious experience" in 1958 so much as he "matured in to it."

"You could never get Tom to talk about his background," recalls Father Benedict Dudley, the Giants' chaplain.

Says Cowboy president Tex Schramm, "Tom isn't the easiest man in the world to communicate with. You have to hit him with a two-by-four to get his attention; but once you get it, you get his whole attention. Tom has a rare perspective. For instance, he is known as a progressive coach, but in a lot of ways he's very conservative. He holds strong with tradition, yet he is an innovator. If you remember, he used to alternate quarterbacks (before Don Meredith reached maturity). He recognized this wasn't the ultimate answer, yet there we were in 1962 leading the league in offense. And with *nothing!*"

Sportswriters who have known Landry for a few years find him strikingly honest, easy to interview. I remember a party in 1963 after team owner Clint Murchison, Jr., destroyed Landry's original five-year contract and signed him to a new eleven-year contract, an unprecedented vote of confidence.

Everyone was whooping it up but Landry who was sitting alone in one corner, serene as a Ming vase. "Why aren't you living it up?" someone asked him. "This is your party."

"No," said Landry. "This isn't my party. This is the team's party."

Later that night his wife, Alicia, told me: "No one will ever have to fire Tommy. He would quit if he didn't win. The new contract is a vote of confidence in the *football* team, not in *Tommy!*"

Tom Landry takes his aspirations seriously—and one at a time. Aside from beating the Green Bay Packers in a championship game, Landry's idea of personal fulfillment is to have a positive influence on as many young men as possible. This is his passion and it traces back to his own boyhood which was, in a contemporary sense, unique.

Landry was born in 1924, a half block from the First Methodist Church of Mission, Texas. Mission is a small town with a large Mexican-American population in the lush citrus valley between the Gulf of Mexico and the Rio Grande. Tom's father ran a garage; he served as Fire Chief and superintendent of Sunday school at the church down the street. Tom played every sport in season, made mostly A's in his school subjects, and had an exemplary Sunday school attendance record.

"Mission was a great place for a boy to grow up," he recalls. "I learned something playing in the sandlots . . . something that today's youngsters aren't able to experience. Here is where you learn to cry and to fight . . . to overcome all situations according to your own abilities and initiative . . . without some (adult) supervisor always looking over your shoulder."

With characteristic clarity Landry remembers that his final high school team (1) played the Notre Dame box formation; (2) went undefeated in twelve games; (3) allowed only one touchdown—on a pass interference penalty. Landry was a good college player at the University of Texas, a standout passer until he broke the thumb on his passing hand, at which time he was forced to surrender his starting position to another passer of some ability, Bobby Layne. Converted to fullback in the week between the thumb injury and the game against North Carolina (the Choo-Choo Justice team), Landry ran for more than one hundred yards that Saturday afternoon. Though he had less speed than your average pulling guard, Landry played six seasons at cornerback

with the Giants (1950–55), the last four as a player-coach. By the late
1950s he was such a valued assistant coach with the Giants that head
coach Jim Lee Howell referred to him publicly as "the best coach in
football."

The Giants in those glory days were pretty much the product of two
assistant coaches—Landry on defense, Vince Lombardi on offense.
"Jim Lee Howell gave them a lot of leeway," admits Wellington Mara.
"He kept the power of veto, but he recognized their abilities. I recall
back about 1956, everyone was defending the end sweep by dropping
off the ends (who became linebackers) and forcing the play inside. Landry wanted to defense it inside-out, stop them up the middle with the
idea that the pursuit would take care of the outside. Quite simply, Tom
was talking about today's 4–3 defense—where the four (defensive) men
(up front) are charged with the responsibility of keeping the five
(offensive) linemen from getting a clean shot at the middle linebacker.
Jim Lee accepted Tom's idea; the rest is history."

In 1959 Lombardi heard the call, moving to Green Bay. *His* success
is football cliché. Not long after, Landry tentatively accepted a position
as head coach of the new Houston Oilers of the AFL, but destiny was
squeezing curious patterns. In the middle of the 1959 season, while the
Giants were posting a 10–2 record and winning another Eastern Conference championship, Mara called Landry, advising him that the new
NFL franchise in Dallas had expressed interest in him. If Mara knew at
the time that Jim Lee Howell would announce his retirement at the end
of that season ("Those ten victories," said Howell, "don't make up for
the two defeats"), Mara did not mention it to Landry; but the opportunity to remain in the NFL (not to mention the opportunity of challenging Lombardi) prevailed. So Landry took the Dallas job.

Much of the fascination in Landry's rise is that he came up through
the ranks: from player, to player-coach, to coach. Only Don Shula of
the Colts has approached Landry's success both as a player and a
coach, making the transition while still retaining respect and command.

The message is one of pace and temperament. "The day Landry became a non-playing coach," recalls Giants' publicity man Don Smith,
"it was as though he had been *coach* for twenty years. You pull a shade,
you go to sleep, the next morning you wake up with a lifetime of wisdom under your pillow. There is no sense of time passing. Even today
when I run into Tom I get the feeling—there has been *no passage of
time.*"

"Landry is a born student of the game," says Em Tunnell, the great defensive back who played with (and later for) Landry. Tunnell had been with the Giants two seasons when Landry came as part of the peace package negotiated when the old All-America Conference folded before the 1950 season. The Giants and the New York Bulldogs each picked five players from the newly defunct New York Yankees. On the recommendation of Gus Mauch, the Yankees' trainer, the Giants selected three of the four members of the Yankees' secondary—Otto Schnellbacher, Harmon Rowe and Landry. By 1951, the Giants had the best defensive backfield in football.

"Landry was sort of weird," Tunnell recalls, "but we were a unit back there (in the secondary), getting closer and closer. I remember when we shut out the great Browns' team in 1950, didn't even let 'em get close enough to try a field goal. After the game me and Schnellbacher and Rowe would go out for beer, but Tom would disappear. He was always off with his family. You never knew what was going through his mind. He never said nothing. He just always knew what was going on. We didn't have words like 'keying' in those days, but Tom made up his own keys and taught 'em to the rest of us."

Landry remembers it well: "By training I was an industrial engineer." (He was on his way to a career in engineering when the Yankees signed him as a punter and defensive back in 1949; he also played running back with the Yankees.) "I had to know what was going on. It was my nature. I couldn't be satisfied trusting my instincts the way Em did. I didn't have the speed or quickness. I had to train myself, and everyone around me, to key various opponents and recognize tendencies."

Where Vince Lombardi was a gurgling volcano, blistering everyone in his path, Landry was placid as a mountain lake. These contrasting personalities had no small effect on the Giants.

"Lombardi was a much warmer person," says Mara. "He went from warm to red hot. You could hear him laughing or shouting for five blocks. You couldn't hear Tom from the next chair. Lombardi was more of a teacher. It was as though Landry lectured to the upper 40 percent of the class and Lombardi lectured to the lower 10 percent."

Again, that was Landry's style. Intellectual but non-aggressive. At the same time Landry's physical presence went unquestioned; it was a lineal strength that ran through the team, a central nervous system. He had been one of them through all kinds of hell.

When the Giants lost both of their quarterbacks in a game with Pittsburgh in 1953, Landry came over from defense and ran the team for most of the last half. Though Landry had never worked at quarterback, he was obviously the only man on the team who might be expected to play the position cold.

"I was lucky," Landry recalls. "Pittsburgh was the only field in the league where you could draw plays in the dirt."

The Giants lost 24 to 14. The following week against Washington, New York again lost 24 to 21. Landry played fifty-nine minutes of this game, directing both the offense and defense.

That mystical and saintly presence which sustained the Giants (in ways that it took them years to realize) has never abandoned Tom Landry.

"He tells you what's going to happen," says Cowboy halfback Dan Reeves, "and on Sunday it happens."

Says Don Meredith: "Landry used to be ultra-frustrating. I thought I knew a *little* about football. But Landry would be up at the blackboard saying, 'Okay, we'll do this . . . then they'll do that . . . then we'll . . .' You'd interrupt him and say, 'Coach, what if they *don't* do that?' . . . Landry would just look at you and say, *'They will.'* "

But this is a Saturday afternoon, early November 1968. Landry is absorbed by new peril, not old glory. Until two weeks ago his team was undefeated, rolling Packer-like to another conference championship, true to the vow he made in training camp: *this time,* Landry vowed, the Cowboys would be more than a match for the Packers in the championship game. But it is beginning to look as though Landry is wrong. For one thing, the Packers show scant inclination to win their own division; coach Lombardi is now *Mr.* Lombardi, elder statesman to pro football. Then two weeks ago in the Cotton Bowl the erstwhile headless horsemen of Green Bay rode through Dallas as though it were Sleepy Hollow. It was no contest.

"They were the Packers of old," Landry is lamenting. "They tested us in areas (of defense) that we thought we had under control. You never know how good you are . . . or how far you've come . . . until Green Bay tests you. It's always been a measure of my defensive team how well we've been able to do against Green Bay, and up until now we have never matched them with experience and execution. When we do, we will have arrived."

Anticipating that the Packers are somehow still the team his Cowboys must beat, Landry made one key change—he moved Mel Renfro, his talented free safety, to leftside cornerback. Meanwhile, the Cowboys must win their own division. If they beat their only challenger, the

Giants, on Sunday, they will have a three-game lead with five games to play. Since New York in its last two games lost to lowly Atlanta and was shut out by Baltimore, victory seems simple, if not assured.

But now it is Sunday, a dark, cold, windy afternoon. Meredith's first pass is crippled by a thirty-mph headwind and falls into New York hands. Dallas gets it back on a fumble recovery, but Meredith can't get it going and after an exchange of punts Fran Tarkenton takes New York in for a 7–0 lead. Bruce Maher intercepts a second Meredith pass and runs it eighty-nine yards to the Dallas six. Tarkenton throws and New York has a 14–0 lead.

On the sideline Landry watches his pass rushers play Chinese chess with Tarkenton: "Tarkenton's uniform won't be sent to the cleaners this week," moans a Dallas sportswriter. Landry's face is tight as a coffin when he tells Meredith: "They're outhitting us. They're outplaying us every way. We've got to get tough."

Now Meredith is brilliant. He first hits Bobby Hayes, then Lance Rentzel, with touchdown passes. The Cowboys struggle to a 14–14 tie by halftime. The second half opens with Tarkenton throwing a sixty-yard touchdown pass to Homer Jones.

"Get tough!" one of Landry's assistants yells from the sideline. The Cowboys are on the march. Meredith scrambles for six yards and a first down, then he comes limping to the sidelines: Meredith is back in the game after three plays, but his knee cartilage is torn and won't be sound for the remainder of the 1968 season. It's more pain for Meredith, Landry knows. Fullback Don Perkins bolts for seven yards. The Vikings have just defeated the Packers, announces the public address system. Dallas halfback Les Shy drops a touchdown pass at the goal line. The Cowboys continue to march. On a great second effort, halfback Craig Baynham, who has replaced Shy, pounds over from the New York one; the game is again tied 21 to 21.

In the final quarter Dallas goes against the wind, New York with it. Tarkenton throws thirty-five yards to Homer Jones, then Pete Gogolak kicks a field goal, pushing New York in front 24 to 21.

"All the way, Lance-*baby!*" an assistant coach shouts from the sideline, but Lance Rentzel signals for a fair catch and fumbles in a gust of wind. Gogolak kicks another field goal. New York has a six-point lead. Landry has never seemed more composed. He glances at the clock. A little more than two minutes remain.

First and ten, Dallas has the ball on its forty-five. Things look normal, which is to say they look good. The *toughness* to pull a game out, the sacrifice of a self-extracted wisdom tooth, that has been Landry's lesson to his team. Now Meredith rolls right, now Lance Rentzel is open near the Giants' twenty, now the pass hangs on the wind, and now Spider Lockhart is making the sweet interception.

Landry is four feet out on the playing field, shouting, "Dammit, why did you . . ." but he never says who, he never says what. It is dark now in Dallas. The lights are on; dew collects on the pale green grass. It seems much later than it is and Meredith jogs back to the sideline, his face broad with wonder, twisted with regret. The whole thing must seem too stupid for words: while the Cowboys were losing two of their last three games, Meredith went from *third* to *first* on the league passing chart. Too stupid for words . . . too painful. Landry wears that same expression you have seen so often on the lead film preceding all NFL telecasts, that classic eyes-closed-to-earth muffled sob, that God-imploring anxiety caught on film as Landry realized that an illegal-motion penalty had sealed Dallas' defeat in the 1966 championship game in this same stadium, in this same paralyzing dark cold, in this same and endless quest for something attainable in an unattainable sort of a stupid way.

"You don't think it didn't hurt to walk off that field?" Landry asked writers at his press conference the following Wednesday. "There's no criticism *you* could make that could hurt like that."

In Landry's mind it was simple. He had taught them offense, he had taught them defense. He had taught them how to come from behind; he had provided the leadership that gives a man confidence in the system, if not in himself. In some cases . . . in Meredith's case, for example . . . Landry had in fact saved a soul. For what? For what came *next*.

What comes next, Landry is quick to explain, is toughness. He will have to remind them of toughness. Chances are good that they have already reminded themselves, but he will call it to their attention with some very hard work.

"You don't build character without somebody slapping you around," Landry tells his press conference. "We got to the point where we thought we could take it easy and win. Why even my wife was talking of an undefeated season. That's a sure sign of death. . . . I'll tell you this, we'll be a different team *next* week."

Willie Mays, Yesterday and Today

Roger Kahn | **1 9 6 9**

He is sitting on the three-legged stool they give to ball-players and milkmaids, and he looks enormous and supple and strong. He has a massive flat chest and bulging arms and shoulders and the kind of muscled stomach I remember from comic-book drawings of Tarzan. Still, he is thirty-eight years old.

"What do you do to stay in shape, Will?" I say.

"Nothin' special," Willie Mays says. "I walk a lot and I play golf now, 'stead of pool. And I don't eat too much and I never did drink, except three times, when we won pennants." A smile briefly lights the handsome brown face.

"Well, you look like you can go on forever."

"I won't lie to you," Mays says. "It gets to be work. Sometimes when I get tired and all that pressure, it gets to be work. I knew when I was sixteen years old, I never did want to work for a living." Again the smile.

"You want to manage?"

"Yeah. I think I'd like to."

"What about handling pitchers? Could you do that?"

"You're a manager," Willie says, "man, you get to *hire* help."

It is eleven o'clock the morning after a night game and Willie will

472)

play this afternoon. The team is not going well and last night in the ninth inning, with the count three-and-two, he guessed curve. Then Ron Taylor of the Mets threw a fastball by him. Willie is not playing for fun today, but from a sense of obligation. He has come out early so we can talk in an empty locker room, and the conversation sweeps across a broad range. We go back a way together and when Willie trusts you, he is warm and open and droll and humorously sly. Together, we consider divorce and alimony and child-raising and financial security and how time, the subtle thief of youth, steals from you, me and even Willie Mays.

A spring, fifteen years ago, comes back in a rush and I see again the wide pellucid sky, the baked hills wanting grass, and the desert winds blowing whirls of sand. I hadn't wanted to come to Phoenix. I hadn't wanted to cover the Giants. For two previous years I'd been assigned to the Dodgers. This nurtured a condition, described in a general way by the late nonpareil of sports editors, Stanley Woodward. "Baseball writers," Woodward observed, "always develop a great attachment for the Brooklyn ballclub if long exposed to it. We found it advisable to shift Brooklyn writers frequently. If we hadn't, we would have found that we had on our hands a member of the Brooklyn ballclub rather than a newspaper reporter. You watch a Brooklyn writer for symptoms, and, before they become virulent, you must shift him to the Yankees or to tennis or golf." Woodward was gone from the *Herald Tribune* by 1954. I was shifted, under protest, to the Giants.

The ride from New York to Phoenix was interminable. We had to change trains in Chicago, wasting time, and somewhere near Liberal, Kansas, we stopped dead for ten or twelve hours in a snowstorm.

Perhaps fifty hours after we had left New York, the train pulled into Phoenix and we stepped out into a cool and cloudless morning. Louis Effrat of the *Times* alighted with me, and looked about the station. A few Indians were sleeping. In the distance lay brown hills. "Three thousand miles," Effrat shouted. "I leave my wife, my daughter, my home and travel three thousand miles." He inhaled before bellowing, "For what?" He was making a joke, but that was the way I felt.

My outlook did not improve immediately. The Giant manager, Honest Leo Durocher, offered me tidbits on his swelling romance with a post-virginal actress, but was more devious when asked about the club. The ballplayers were decent enough, but I didn't know them, or they me, and I was starting from scratch, building up confidences and new sources. And aside from that, the team bored me. I was used to the explosive Dodger atmosphere, with Jackie Robinson holding forth and Charlie Dressen orating and Roy Campanella philosophizing. The Giants seemed somber as vestrymen.

While I struggled and wrote a story a day, plus an extra for Sunday, Willie Howard Mays, Jr., was struggling with an Army team at Fort Eustis, Virginia, hitting, as he later put it, ".470, or something like that." They were all waiting for him. The Giants had won in 1951 with Mays. Without him in 1952 and '53, they lost. Each day in the press room, one of the regular Giant writers or one of the officials would tell anecdotes in which Willie was always superman. In exasperation, I sat down and wrote a story for the Sunday paper that began:

"Willie Mays is 10 feet 9 inches tall. His arms reach from 156th Street to 154th. . . . He has caught everything, hit everything, done everything a centerfielder can possibly do."

"Look," I told Charles Feeney, the Giant vice-president, amid the amber torrents of the Phoenix press bar. "There are a couple of other centerfielders, too. Ever hear of Mickey Mantle or Duke Snider?"

Mr. Feeney erupted in song. "In six more days," he choired, to the tune of "Old Black Joe," "we're gonna have Willie Mays." He may have sung it "going to." He is a Dartmouth man.

Each day Feeney warbled, amending the lyrics cleverly enough, say changing the word "six" to the word "five." The song, like the sandy wind, became a bane.

M Day, as I came to call it, dawned like most other days, with a big bright sky. Durocher had scheduled an intra-squad game and was elaborately underplaying things. The post-virginal movie star was gone, making him somewhat irascible.

"Nothing unusual," Leo announced in the lobby of the Hotel Adams early M Day. "Just a little intra-squad game, boys, that's all." Then he walked off, barely able to keep his footing for his swagger.

The Phoenix ballpark was typical medium minor league. Old stands extended part way down each foul line. A wood fence ringed the outfield. The players, Monte Irvin, Whitey Lockman, Alvin Dark, were in uniform and, as always in spring, it seemed odd to see great major-leaguers in a minor-league setting.

Willie was coming by plane, we all knew that, and in Phoenix you can see great distances. Whenever an airplane appeared, one of the writers or Giant officials leapt up with a cry, "Willie's plane." Two Piper Cubs, four Beechcrafts and one World War I Spad were positively identified as the transcontinental Constellation bearing Mays.

"Feeney," I said, "this is ridiculous."

This time he chose the key of C-sharp minor:

> "In no more days,
> We're going to have Willie Mays!"

The athletes were still playing catch, the intra-squad game had not started, when a trim figure in slacks and a dark open-collared shirt appeared in the dugout. He was blinking at the sunlight, mostly because he had not been to sleep, and seemed to be trying to hide, to be as unobtrusive as possible. "There's Willie," someone cried in ecstasy, and the sportswriters swarmed.

Mays stood next to Irvin, probably the closest friend he has had among ballplayers in a curiously lonely life. Irvin was very poised, very strong, very sensible.

"Hey, Willie," someone shouted, "what you got in that bag?" He had dropped off his large suitcase, but clung to a smaller one.

"Not much," Willie said. "A couple of things."

"What?"

"Just my glove and my jock."

Durocher hugged him repeatedly for joy and for the news photographers. Monte, who felt like hugging him, shook his hand.

"He's shaking hands with the pennant," Barney Kremenko, one of the baseball writers, proclaimed.

"Hi, roomy," Irvin said.

"Hey, Monte."

Irvin smiled. "Roomy," he said, "how's your game?"

Willie shook his head. "What you mean my game, Monte? You talking about pool?"

"No, Willie," Irvin said. "I'm talking about your game, about baseball."

"Oh yeah," Willie said, as if surprised there should be a question. "My baseball. I'm ready any time."

A few minutes later, when the intra-squad game began, Mays remained on the bench. Durocher, with his sure sense of drama and his always brilliant sense of handling Willie, was letting the elements cook. The game proceeded without much excitement. The most interesting thing at the Phoenix ballpark was watching Number 24, striding back and forth, looking at Durocher, asking with his eyes, and being ignored.

Halfway through the game, he was sent in to hit. Willie sprang from the dugout. He ran to the batter's box. He took a tremendous swing at the first pitch. His form was flawed. There was a little lunge in the swing. But I don't believe I have ever seen anyone swing harder. Three swings, and mighty Willie had struck out.

"The thing about Snider," I told Kremenko in the press box, "is that his butt doesn't fly out of there when he swings."

"Now, listen," Kremenko began, as though I had assailed the family honor. And I suppose I had.

The first unusual thing that Willie did was snatch a sinking liner off the grass. The ball came out to center field low and hard and Willie charged it better than anyone else could have and dove and made a graceful somersault and caught the ball. "Nothing," Kremenko shouted. "For Willie that's absolutely nothing."

The next time he came to bat, I resolved to look for specific flaws in his form. I was doing that when he hit a fastball 420 feet and out of the park. An inning later, and with a man on first, someone hit a tremendous drive over Willie's head. He turned and fled and caught the ball and threw it 300 feet and doubled the runner. Pandemonium. The camp was alive. The team was alive. And Willie had gone through the delays of a discharge, then sat up all night in a plane. I conceded to Kremenko that given a little rest, he might show me something.

Then I sat down and wrote an account that began, "This is not going to be a plausible story, but then no one ever accused Willie Mays of being a plausible ballplayer. This story is only the implausible truth." It ran quite long and I had no idea whether the *Tribune* copydesk would eviscerate it, until a day later when a wire came from Red Smith in Florida. Red was the columnist in the *Tribune*, a thoughtful man, and his telegram, a personal gesture, was the first indication I'd had in a month that my stuff was getting printed and was syntactical.

That night Feeney, selecting the rather cheerful key of D Major, honored me with the final version of his aria:

> "Gone are the days,
> When we didn't have Willie Mays."

After Willie's debut and Red's wire, I was genuinely surprised to hear how much Feeney's voice had improved.

Willie conquered me. I had not come to praise him and sycophancy annoys me, but he brought to the game the outstanding collection of skills in our time and the deepest enthusiasm to play I've seen. He was the ultimate combination of the professional full of talent and the amateur, a word that traces to the Latin *amator,* lover, and suggests one who brings a passion to what he does.

They used to play pepper games, Leo and Willie, sometimes with Monte Irvin as the straight man. Willie has what his father, Kitty-Kat Mays, described as oversized hands, and Durocher was one of the finest defensive shortstops. They'd stand quite close and Leo would hit hard smashes at Willie's toes, or knees, wherever. Mays' reflexes were such that he could field a hard line drive at ten or fifteen feet. And he liked to do it. He threw, and Leo slugged and Willie lunged, and threw and Leo slugged again. Once in a while Willie bobbled a ball. Then he owed Durocher a Coke. Durocher made great shows of cheating Willie. One morning he hit a hard smash on one hop, well to Willie's right, and Willie knocked the ball down with a prodigious lunge.

"Coke," Leo roared. "That's six you owe."

"Ain' no Coke for that," Willie said. His voice piped high and plaintive. "That's a base hit."

"Six Cokes you owe," Leo insisted.

"Monte," Willie pleaded at Irvin. "What you say, Roomy?"

"Six Cokes," Irvin said, solemnly. Willie's mobile face slumped into a pout. "I'm getting the short end," the expression said, "but I'll get you guys anyway."

Sometimes Irvin hit, and then there was added by-play. Not only did Durocher and Mays stab smashes, they worked to rattle each other. Durocher seized a line drive, wound up to throw to Irvin, and with a blur of elbows and hands tossed the ball to Mays at his left. Leo has the skills and inclinations of a juggler. Willie caught the toss, faked toward Irvin and there was the ball floating down toward Leo. Durocher reached and Mays slapped a glove into his belly.

"Ooof," Leo grunted. Willie spun off, staggering through his own laughter. It wasn't long before people started coming to the ballpark long before the game, just to watch the pepper. The clowning would have done honor to Chaplin.

Willie ran and threw and hit and made his astounding catches and slowly that spring I began to get to know him. I was the youngest of the baseball writers and that helped. We had little conversations after the workouts and the exhibition games, and he always became very solemn and gave me serious answers. "Who suggested," I asked one day, "that you catch fly balls that way?" The technique is famous now: glove up, near the belt buckle.

"Nobody," Willie said. "I just start it one day. I get my throw away quicker."

"Nobody taught you?"

Willie's eyes, which sometimes dance, grew grave. "Nobody can teach you nothing," he said. "You got to learn for yourself."

On another afternoon we were talking and Ruben Gomez, a pitcher from Puerto Rico, came up and said, "Willie. That man in New York. I forget the name. I sign a paper for him."

Willie mentioned a New York agent.

"That's him," Gomez said.

"You sign a paper," Willie said, "and you worried because you haven't got your money."

Gomez nodded.

"Well, don't worry," Willie said. "Long as you sure you signed. It may come soon, or it may come late, but long as you sign something, you'll get money." He looked at me. "Ain' that right?" I thought of leases, installment contracts, and overdue bank loans, but I said, "Yes." Maybe it would always be that way for Willie, spring and youth and plenty of cash and laughter. But it wasn't, not even that spring.

Along with the Cleveland Indians, a team wealthy with pitchers, the Giants flew to Las Vegas for an exhibition game late in March. The Giant management did not want the ballplayers spending a night in Las Vegas. The Stoneham regime is paternalistic and the idea of a troop of young ballplayers abroad among the gamblers and the bosoms of Vegas was disturbing. The team would play its game with the Indians. The players would be guests for dinner at one of the big hotels. They would watch a show and seek as much trouble as they could find up until 11 p.m. Then a bus would take them to the airport for a flight to Los Angeles, where two other exhibitions were scheduled. We wouldn't get much rest.

It was a gray, raw afternoon in Vegas, and Bob Feller pitched for the Indians. Sal Maglie opposed him. My scorebook is lost, but I believe the Giants won by one run. Afterward we wrote our stories and took a bus to the hotel that invited us all. We ate well, and I caught up with Willie in the hotel theater, where Robert Merrill, the baritone, was to sing. As I joined Willie's table, Merrill began "Vesti la Giubba," the famous aria from *Pagliacci* in which Canio, the clown, sings of having to make people laugh, although his own heart is breaking.

Merrill gave it full voice and all his passions. When he was done, Willie turned to me amid the cheering, "You know," he said, "that's a nice song."

An hour later, he was in a gambling room. He was standing quietly amid a group of people close to a dice table. Monte Irvin and Whitey Lockman were fighting a ten-cent one-armed bandit. Sal Maglie, looking like Il Padrone of Cosa Nostra, was losing a steady fifty cents a game at blackjack. I walked over to Willie. "How you doing?"

"Oh," Willie said, "I'm just learnin' the game." We both grinned.

I moved on. A stocky gruff man grabbed me by the arm. "Hey," he said, "wait a minute."

I shook my arm free.

"That guy a friend of yours?" said the man. He pointed to Mays.

"I know him."

"Well, get him the hell away from the dice tables."

"What?"

"You heard me. We don't want him mixing with the white guests."

"Do you know who he is?"

"Yeah, I know who he is, and get that nigger away from the white guests."

If there was a good answer, except for the obvious short answer, I didn't come up with it. Very quickly I was appalled, unnerved, and angry. What unnerved me was the small significant bulge on the man's left hip.

"Do you know that boy just got out of the Army," I said.

"That don't mean nothing. I was in the Army myself."

"You bastards invited him down to your hotel."

"Who you calling a bastard?"

We were shouting and Gary Schumacher, the Giants' publicity director, suddenly loomed large and put a hand on my shoulder. "What's the trouble?" Gary said.

"This guy," the tough began.

"I asked *him*," Gary said, nodding at me.

I had a sensible moment. "No trouble, Guv," I said to Gary. I took my wallet out of a hip pocket and withdrew the press card. "This joker has just given me one helluva story for the Sunday New York *Herald Tribune*."

The hood retreated. I walked over to Irvin and told him what was happening. Lockman listened briefly and then, taking the conversation to be personal, stepped back. "Maybe Willie and I'll get on the bus," Irvin said. It was his way, to avoid confrontations, but he was also worried lest Willie be shocked or hurt.

Now a hotel vice-president appeared, with a girl hard-faced but trimly built. He asked if "my assistant and I can buy you a drink, Mr. Kahn."

We went to the bar and the man explained that he had nothing against a Negro like Irvin or Mays playing one-armed bandits. It was just that the dice table was a somewhat different thing. As far as he, the vice-president, was concerned, Negroes were as good as anybody, but he had to concern himself with customers. That was business.

"We're really in the South here," said the brunette.

"I thought the South was Alabama, Georgia, Texas."

"That's it," the brunette said. "We get a lot of customers from Texas." She glanced at the bartender, and I had another drink. "We're really a very liberal place," the girl said, "even though we are in the South. We not only book Lena Horne to sing here, but when she does, we let her live on the grounds. We're the only hotel that liberal." She leaned toward me, a hard handsome woman, working.

"Why did you invite him if you were going to crap on him?" I said, and got up and joined Monte and Will in the bus.

Later Irvin asked me not to write the story. He said he didn't know if it was a good idea to make Willie, at twenty-one, the center of a racial storm. That was Monte's way and the Giants' way and Willie's way, and you had to respect it, even if dissenting. I never did write the story until now.

In the visitor's locker at Shea Stadium fifteen years later, the headline on a folded newspaper cries out: "CITY COLLEGE TORN BY BLACK AND WHITE STRIFE." The times are different and I have heard a prominent Negro criticize Mays as self-centered. It was the job of every black to work for a free society, he said. To the militant—a Stokely Carmichael or a Rap Brown—Willie is the embodiment of the well-fed de-clawed Tom.

"They want me to go out on some campus?" Willie says. "Why should I lie? I don't know nothin' about campuses. I never went to college. I wanted to play ball."

"Well, what about the whole black movement."

"I help," Willie says. "I help in my way." His face becomes very serious. "I think I show some people some things. I do it my way." He is a good fellow, serious and responsible, never in trouble, never drunk, never in jail.

"Do you speak out?"

"Like what?"

"On schools, or full employment or whatever?" He eyes me evenly. "I don't think I should. I don't know the full value of these things. I'm not the guy to get on the soap box." He pauses, then announces with great assurance and pride, "I'm a *ballplayer*."

In the autumn of '54, after Willie led the Giants to the pennant and a sweep over the Indians in the World Series, our paths crossed again. I was putting together a book featuring articles by All-Star ballplayers on the qualities that made one an All-Star. I sent questionnaires to many like Ted Kluszewski and Bob Lemon. I telephoned Stan Musial. I went to see Willie in the flesh. He had made his classic World Series catch, running, running, running, until he was 460 feet out and grabbing Vic Wertz's liner over his head. He had taken Manhattan, the Bronx and Staten Island, too, and was in demand. At the Giants someone gave me the name of his agent.

After hearing what I could pay, the agent said Willie would let me have three to four minutes on a slow Tuesday afternoon, but while we talked he might have to sign four endorsements, accept six speaking engagements, get his shoes shined and telephone for a date. His business was being handled brusquely, although not, we were to learn, very well.

A few seconds before the appointed minute I appeared in the agent's office. Willie was in an anteroom only signing endorsements. When I appeared he waved and smiled, relieved to see a familiar face. "Hey," he said, "Roger Kahn, is that you? I didn't know that was you. What you want to talk to me about?"

I explained.

"You writin' a book?" Willie said. "That's real good, you writin' a book."

Disturbed by gratuitous friendliness the agent vanished and Willie held forth on playing centerfield. "The first thing," he said, "is you got to love the game. Otherwise you'll never learn to play good. Then, you know, don't drink, and get your sleep. Eight hours. You sleep more, you get to be lazy.

"Now in Trenton, where I played when I first signed, I was nowhere near as good as I am now, but I have my way to learn things. People tell me, 'Willie do like this, like that,' but that ain't the way."

He sat in a swivel chair, which he had tilted back. His considerable feet were on a desk. "Well, how do you learn?" I said.

"Some things maybe when you're real little, you got to be told. But mostly you got to be doing it yourself. Like once I was a pitcher and now I'm in the outfield. Watch me after I get off a good throw. I look sort of like a pitcher who has thrown.

"You got to be thinking, 'What am I doing wrong?' And then you look at the other two outfielders and think, 'What are they doing wrong?' And you're thinking and thinking and trying not to make the same mistake three times, or four at the most, and you're also thinking what you'll do if the ball comes to you. Understand?"

"Pretty much."

"You don't want to be surprised," Willie said with finality.

But on what Branch Rickey called the best catch in baseball history, Mays was indeed surprised. The Giants were playing in Pittsburgh, where centerfield runs 457 feet deep, a good stage for Willie. Rocky Nelson, a left-handed hitter, smashed a tremendous line drive and Willie, calculating at a glance, turned and sprinted for the wall. Nelson had hit the ball so hard that there was a hook to it. While Willie ran, the ball drifted slightly to the right.

At precisely the right instant, Willie looked. He had gotten back deep enough, a mini-miracle, but now the ball was to his right and sinking fast. He might have been able to reach across his body and glove the ball. Or he might not. We will never know. He simply stuck out his bare right hand and seized the liner at the level of his knees. Then he slowed and turned, his face a great, wide grin.

"Silent treatment," Durocher ordered in the dugout. "Nobody say nothing to him."

Willie touched his cap to acknowledge the crowd and ran down the three steps into the Forbes Field dugout. Everyone avoided Willie's eyes. Durocher was checking the lineup card. Bobby Thomson was pulling anthracite from his spikes. Hank Thompson was taking a very long drink. The silence was suffocating.

"Hey, Leo," Willie piped. "You don't have to say, 'Nice play, Willie.' I *know* that was a nice play."

A minute later a note from Rickey arrived. "That," Rickey wrote, "was the finest catch I have ever seen and the finest catch I ever hope to see."

I finished the story by Willie with a comment that he offered in the agent's office. "You got to learn for yourself," he said, "and you got to do it in your own way and you got to become much improved. If you love the game enough you can do it." It reads right after all the years, and true, but even as I was finishing I understood that no book was likely to help a young man play centerfield like Willie Mays.

In Shea, we start talking about the old times. "New York was a good town for centerfielders," I say, "when you were here with Mantle and Snider."

"Yeah," he says, "Mick and I broke in together, but he had a real bad body. Legs."

"How do you feel being the only one left?"

"Proud. Proud that I'm still playing."

"Lonely?"

"There's more new faces, but . . ." He turns his palms up and shrugs. "That doesn't bother me none.

"I worry, though," he says. "I get worried now that I can't do the job. 'Course I always was a worrier. I get the ball out, but I can't get it out as often as I used to."

"About old friends," I say.

"You know," Willie says. "I don't have many friends. People I know, people to say, 'Hi, Willie,' there's a million of them. My friends, I could count them on a few fingers."

I went calling in 1956, four days after Willie had taken a wife. Because he is handsome and country slick, and also because he is famous and well-paid, he does not lack for feminine attention. Joe Black, the Dodger relief pitcher, told me Willie was getting married. We played winter basketball together and after one workout, Joe said he hoped Willie knew what he was getting into.

"I'm sure of that," I said.

"I mean I hope he doesn't get hurt."

"What's the girl like?" I said.

"The *girl*," Joe said, "is older than Willie and has been married twice before."

A number of people counseled Willie against getting married, but he doesn't like to be told how to run his life, and each bit of counsel was a shove toward the altar. Then, in February, he gathered Marghuerite Wendelle, stuffed her into his Lincoln, and set off for Elkton, Maryland, where one can marry in haste. On the way, he picked up a fifteen-dollar fine, for driving seventy in a sixty-mile zone.

He set up housekeeping in a tidy brick home not far from LaGuardia Airport. East Elmhurst was one of the early colonies open to the black middle class and I remember the white taxi driver looking at the clean streets and detached houses in surprise. "Colored people live here?" he said.

Mrs. Mays received me with a cool hand, tipped with pointed fingernails. She was a beautiful woman, who stared hard and knowing when she said hello. It was midday, but Willie hadn't come downstairs. "Just go on up," Marghuerite Mays said. "I have to go out to the beauty parlor."

I found Willie sitting in an enormous bed, gazing at morning television, a series starring Jackie Cooper and a talking dog. Willie was wearing tailored ivory pajamas. "Sit down," he said, indicating a chair. "What you doing now? How come you don't come around? You okay?"

I had left the newspaper business and gone to work as a sportswriter for a newsmagazine. The salary was better and the researchers were pretty, but the magazine approached sports in an earnest, sodden way. One of the supervising editors had been a small-town sportswriter once and then become a sportswriter on the newsmagazine. The change of fortune downed poorly. He alternately tried to relate great events to his own experiences, perhaps covering a playoff game between Bridgeport and Pittsfield, or he demanded scientific analyses of the events and men. A great story on Mays, he told me, would explain in complete technical detail how Willie played centerfield.

In the bridal bedroom, I told Willie I was fine. I was wondering how to swing the conversation into a technical analysis. I asked what had made him decide to marry.

"Well," Willie said, "I figured that's it's time for me to be settling down. I'm twenty-four years old."

"You figure being married will affect your play?"

"I dunno," Willie said. "How am I supposed to know? I hit fifty-one home runs last year. Man, if you come to me last spring and tell me I was gonna do that, I woulda told you you were crazy." Willie shook his head and sat straight up. "Man," he said. "Tha's a lot of home runs."

On top of the TV set rested three trophies. The largest was a yard-high wooden base for bright gilt figurines of ballplayers running, batting and throwing. It bore a shiny plaque which read: "To Willie Mays, the most valuable player in baseball."

"What are you hoping to do this year?"

"I dunno," Willie said. He frowned. "Why you askin' question like that?" he said.

I stopped and after a while we were talking about marriage. "You hear some people say they worried 'bout me and Marghuerite," Willie said. "Same people last summer was saying I was gonna marry this girl and that girl. But they was wrong then, like they're wrong now." He thumped his heart, under the ivory pajamas. "I'm the only guy knows what's in here."

They didn't know what to make of my story at the newsmagazine. They cut out chunks of it, and devoted equal space to the picture of a

2-to-5 favorite winning a horse race. Willie's lovesong was not news-magazine style.

The marriage went. I like to think they both tried. They adopted a son and named him Michael, but some years later they were divorced. "Foundered on the rocks off the Cape of Paradise," is how the actor Mickey Rooney likes to put it, but there is nothing funny about the failure of a marriage or having to move out from under the roof where lives your only son.

In Shea before the game against the Mets, Willie is talking about the boy. "He's with me, you know," Willie says.

"How come?"

"He was with Marghuerite, but when he started gettin' older I guess he missed me and we kind of worked something out.

"Michael is ten years old," Willie says, "and there's a lady who keeps house and she looks after him when I'm away. A real nice boy. I send him to a private school, where they teach him, but they're not too hard with him."

I think of the iron worker's son with a boy in private school.

"I've made a deal with him," Willie says. "He needs a college degree in times like these, and the deal is I send him to good schools, put it all there for him, and after that it's up to him to take it."

"You think he will?"

"He's a real good boy."

Two men have come into the Mets' clubhouse to see Willie. Paul Sutton is a patent attorney and David Stern is a vice-president of Sports Satellite Corporation. Willie hopes that these men and a Salt Lake businessman named Ernie Psarras will build his fortune up to seven figures. For now Willie is concerned about filling the house he is building on an acre, in Atherton, down peninsula from San Francisco.

He stands to greet Sutton and Stern and says, "Hey, what about the furniture?"

"We're seeing about it," David Stern says.

"Man," Willie says. "I got to stay on you guys."

"Willie doesn't like to pay retail," Stern explains.

"I don't like to *pay*," Willie says, and he laughs.

Larry Jansen, a coach who pitched for the old Giants, approaches and asks Willie about a doctor or a dentist. Willie gives him a telephone number. Willie owns the keys to the kingdom in New York.

When the Giants moved to San Francisco after the 1957 season, I lost touch with Willie. I read he was having problems. He moved into a white neighborhood and a Californian threw a soda bottle through his living-room window in protest. It was a good thing for the Californian that Willie didn't grab the bottle and throw it back. With that arm, he would have cut the man in half. Later, at least as we got word in New York, some San Francisco fans felt disappointed in Willie. They didn't appreciate him as we had; a number said they preferred Orlando Cepeda.

I was paying less attention to sports, and writing more about other things, but I knew Willie was not disgracing himself. He kept appearing in All-Star Games and driving homers into the high wind over Candlestick Park. But I wondered if the years and the franchise shift and the divorce had dampened the native ebullience.

It was 1964. Forces that would explode into Black Revolution were gathering and an editor asked me to spend a few months in Harlem, "a part of New York that white New Yorkers don't know."

"*I* don't know it," I said.

"You've been there," the editor said.

"Sure. Whenever I took a taxi to the Polo Grounds, I'd ride right through."

This time I got out of the taxi. I went from place to place on foot, trying to grasp the bar of music, the despair, the life and death, the sour poverty, the unquenchable hope of a black ghetto. It was different from living in a press box.

To shake off the gray ghetto despair, a man can stand a drink, and one evening I walked into Small's Paradise, with my new blond wife on my arm. Across the bar a major-leaguer was drinking hard, although he had a girl with him. She was quite young, a soft off-tan, and wore an enormous round black hat. The athlete and I raised glasses to each other's ladies. Suddenly Willie walked in.

It was a cold day in January, but his stride was bouncy. Willie wore a beautifully tailored topcoat of herringbone charcoal. He has unusual peripheral vision and he covered the bar with a glance. Then he bounced over with a smile.

"Buy you a Coke?" I said.

Willie shook his head. "How are you? You okay? Everything all right? What you doing around here? Who's that girl over there with . . ." And he mentioned the other major-leaguer's name.

"I don't know."

"You sure you okay, now?" Willie said.

"Fine." I introduced him to my wife.

Willie put an elbow on the bar and placed a hand against his brow and fixed his gaze at the girl. "Who is that chick, man?" he said.

None of us knows what happened next. Willie was around the bar quickly, greeting the other ballplayer, talking very fast to the girl. Then he bounced out of the bar, calling, "See ya, man." Five minutes later the other major-leaguer was drunker and the pretty girl in the big round hat was gone. "That," said the blonde on my arm, "has to be the smoothest move I've seen."

You don't judge a man's vigor only by the way he pursues fly balls.

Back at Shea, Willie is asking if he'd given me enough to write an article and I tell him I think so.

I find his father sitting in the dugout. Kitty-Kat Mays has his son's big grin and says sure, he'd like to talk about the boy. Kitty-Kat is smaller than Willie. He has a round belly. He was a semi-pro around Fairfield, near Birmingham, Alabama.

"I was down there, Mr. Mays, when Bull Connor was the police commissioner."

"Things are a lot different now," Kitty-Kat says.

"You still live there?"

"No. I'm up here. I've got a good job."

The man knows baseball and I ask when it first struck him that his son was going to be a superlative ballplayer. Kitty-Kat screws up his face, and I can see that he is going backward in time. He says, "Well, you know we lived right across from a ballfield, and when Willie was eight he had to play with older kids."

"I mean even before that."

"Soon as he started walking," Kitty-Kat says, "he's about a year old, I bought him a big round ball. He'd hold that big round ball and then he'd bounce it and he'd chase it, and if he ever couldn't get that ball, he'd cry."

"I knew he'd be a good one, with those oversized hands." Mr. Mays extends his own palms. "I was pretty good, but my hands are regular size. Willie gets those big hands from his mother."

Willie emerges, taps his father's shoulder, and goes out for batting practice. He does not take a regular turn in rotation. He hits for three or four minutes, then sits down. That way is a little gentler on the legs.

He doesn't dominate the series. The Mets do. In one game Ron Swoboda hits a 430-foot home run to left-center field. Willie sprints back, the way he can, but this is not the Polo Grounds. He has to pull up short. He is standing at the fence when the ball sails out. In his time, and in his park, he would have flagged it.

Later, he crashes one single to left so hard that a runner at second couldn't score, and then he says he wished he'd hit it harder. He hits a long double to left that just misses carrying into the bullpen for a home run. He leads off the ninth inning of a close game with a liner to left that hangs just long enough to be caught. The Giants lose three straight and, in the way of losing teams, they look flat.

When we say goodbye in the clubhouse, Willie seems more annoyed than depressed. The last game ends with the intense frustration of a Giant pitcher fidgeting, scrambling and walking in the winning run. "What can you do?" Willie says. "You got to play harder tomorrow."

For an aging ballplayer, he seems at peace with himself. He went through money wildly in the early days, borrowing from the team, spending August money by April. "You're really okay financially?"

"Oh, yes," Willie says. "Very good." His face was serious. "I ought to be, I've been working a long time."

Back in the Arizona spring we wore string Western ties and we worried about flying DC-3s and we ate in a restaurant where a man dressed like a medieval knight rode a charger and pointed with his spear to show you where to park. Who would have thought then that the Giants would leave New York, and that my old newspaper would fold, and that in another spring, my hair showing gray, I would sit in a strange ballpark and ask Willie Mays about legs, fatherhood, investments and fatigue?

Driving home, while Willie flew to Montreal, the spring kept coming back. I saw in flashes a hit he made in Tucson, a throw he loosed in Beaumont, how Leo made him laugh, and I could hear how the laughter sounded. The racists were appalled that year. A Cleveland coach snapped at me for praising Mays and one writer insisted on betting me twenty dollars Willie wouldn't hit .280. We made it, Willie and I, by sixty-five percentage points.

All this crossed my mind without sadness. Once Willie was a boy of overwhelming enthusiasm. He has become a man of vigorous pride. I don't say that Willie today is as exciting as Willie in '54, but what he does now is immeasurably harder. Playing centerfield at thirty-eight was beyond the powers of Willie's boyhood idol, DiMaggio, or his contemporary rival, Mantle. Willie stands up to time defiantly and with dignity, and one is fortunate to write baseball in his generation.

I guess I'll look him up again next trip.

"Mr. Howe, Before I Die, Please Tell Me How You Can Skate So Gracefully"

Tom Fox | **1969**

It was a Sunday in October, the final day of the 1966 baseball season, and the Los Angeles Dodgers, needing one more win to clinch the National League pennant, were in Philadelphia for a close-out doubleheader with the Phillies.

The Dodgers blew the first game 4 to 3, and the fans booed. Phillie fans would boo a funeral cortege, which is what the first game brought to mind.

The Dodger defeat, plus the cackling from the fans, was just too much for Herbert Khaury to bear. Herbert Khaury is a Dodger fan from New York City, a very resolute Dodger fan. Herbert Khaury cracked.

He jumped atop a seat in the boxes along the first-base line and, a limp wrist to the temple, he shrieked.

"Oh-h-h-h-h-h."

He brought both hands to his face, brushed back his rumpled, shoulder-length mane of dark hair, and he shrieked again.

"Oh-h-h-h-h-h."

"What the hell's eating you, buddy?" a Phillies fan asked.

"Oh-h-h-h-h-h," said Herbert Khaury in a Nora Bayes soprano, "if you only knew the feeling of depression deep, deep down in here." He pointed to his heart.

"Oh-h-h, I promise myself not to get excited, but the game is such an intimate thing with me. I take it more inwardly, deep, deep in here." He pointed to his heart again.

"Oh-h-h-h," he said, "I feel spiritually numb. What anguish! Oh-h-h-h, I must be alone for a few minutes."

Herbert Khaury picked up a paper shopping bag. The shopping bag contained Herbert Khaury's personal effects—a Dodger cap, a transistor radio, two scorecards, four pencils, two spongy sandwiches, a jar of sunflower seeds, a fresh shirt, six neckties, a change of underwear, a toothbrush and a ukulele.

Herbert Khaury is a tall, fortyish-looking man with a large, hawkish nose. He is built like a milk bottle: narrow, stooped shoulders, bulging hips and thick, heavy legs, like oversized fire hydrants. He was wearing a rumpled sportscoat, a plaid checkered shirt and a bright blue-and-yellowish paisley tie with a knot the size of an orange. The dark, flowing hair was witch-long. He looked like a leftover from a Halloween seance.

Herbert Khaury, shopping bag in hand, tried to make his way through the jammed aisle to the grandstand, but a crowd had gathered behind the box. The booing had stopped and everybody in the park seemed to be craning to get a look at Herbert Khaury. Every time Herbert Khaury tried to move, a cheer went up.

"Hey, buddy," a Phillies fan asked, "what's in the bag?"

"Oh-h-h-h," Herbert Khaury uttered, "oh-h-h-h, why, my ukulele. I am a singer, you see . . . oh-h-h-h, yes, I'm from Greenwich Village."

Now the crowd behind the box had turned into a mob and they told Herbert Khaury that if he wanted out of the box seats, he would have to get out the ukulele and sing a few songs, which Herbert Khaury did, of course. He strummed a few bars on the ukulele and, in a sky-high soprano, he sang "Tiptoe Through the Tulips." He sang it in that utterly-flutterly, you're-putting-me-on style that, a year later, would skyrocket him to fame as Tiny Tim, the new flower of American manhood.

Nobody in Connie Mack Stadium that sunny October afternoon in 1966 had ever heard of Herbert Khaury or Tiny Tim. At the time, Tiny Tim was working as a $41-a-week supporting act at Steve Paul's The Scene in Greenwich Village. He had taken a train ride down from New York to see the Dodgers, his favorite baseball team, win the pennant. Recently, he recalled that peculiar scene.

"Oh-h-h, well, you see, they threw me out of the ballpark," said Tiny Tim. "I sang 'Tiptoe Through the Tulips' and 'I'm So Happy' and I was in the middle of 'He's a Real Good Guy,' when this gentleman-policeman came up and said, 'Is that you doing the singing?' I said, 'Oh-h-h, why, yes.' And he said, 'Well, come with me.'

"People began throwing things and the booing started all over again, but the gentleman-policeman took me to the gate and said, 'This way, Mister Songbird—O-U-T.'

"Now, I did feel bad," said Tiny Tim, recalling the anguish of it all, "but in a way, I was glad. You see, I had to consider the law of averages and I realized, immediately, that had I remained for the second game, the odds would have favored the Dodgers' losing. Again. And, perish the thought, losing the pennant in the process.

"The thing was, you see, I had seen the Dodgers play six times that season and they had won only one of the six games. So I said to myself, 'Well, now, let's see what happens if I'm not there.' So-o-o-o, you see, putting me out of the park was the perfect move. The percentages were all there. And my Dodgers won. Mr. Sandy Koufax pitched a wonderful game and Mr. Lou Johnson hit that luscious home run in the third inning and the Dodgers won the pennant. Oh-h-h-h my, oh-h-h-h, it was so, so festive."

Tiny Tim, even today, calls everybody Mister. He also shakes hands lefthanded. And blows kisses to strangers. And comes on like a test pilot at a broom factory. It works, too. He may have peaked early this year but he still earns $25,000 a week. He is big in nightclubs and on the *Laugh-In* show and makes all that money. And he would, he says, give it all up in a minute if only they would make him hockey commissioner.

"Oh-h-h, my yes, I would love to be the hockey commissioner," says Tiny Tim. "But I don't know if I have the qualifications. You see, I can't skate. Not even on one foot."

His voice quivers and his dainty hands flutter when he talks of his love for hockey. Herbert Khaury grew up in a first-floor apartment at 601 West 163rd Street in New York City and fell in love with radio, the old Brooklyn Dodgers and the Toronto Maple Leafs, in that order. And today he may be the biggest baseball-hockey fan in the world. Certainly, he is the most original fan of them all.

"I listened to every Dodger game, starting in 1943, from the opening pitch to the final out. I didn't care if the Dodgers were ahead by two, or trailing 10 to 1, in the last inning, I would never leave the house until the game was over. Never. Aw-w-w-w, radio was so intimate, so exciting and glamorous, you see. Why, Mr. Red Barber was at the thing and what glorious drama, what suspense. Oh, my, I was spellbound."

Tiny Tim talks about the Dodger heroes of his boyhood with deep reverence. "I loved the spray hitters, you see," he explains. "Mr. Pete Reiser and Mr. Luis Olmo and Mr. Arky Vaughan and Mr. Billy Cox and Mr. French Bordagaray and, aw-w-w-w, Mr. Joseph Michael Medwick. They were clutch hitters, singles and doubles hitters, although Mr. Medwick could sock the old long ball, you know. These were the men who won the close games, the men who stole and slid and walked and socked the old apple in the clutch. Every pennant winner has them, you know. There was Mr. Joe DiMaggio, but there was Mr. Phil Rizzuto, too. It was my spray hitters who stood up to the pressure, day after day, by bunting and running and stealing and squeezing. Oh-h-h-h-h, the suicide squeeze. It's one of my favorite things."

The "Oh-h-h-h-h" was a slip back into the Tiny Tim façade. Herbert Khaury smiled and steadied down again. The voice was controlled and the hands were stilled, with only an occasional pounding of a clenched fist on the arm of a chair to make a point.

"You see," says Herbert Khaury the sports zealot, that other creature momentarily forgotten, "with me, baseball and hockey are much more than a hobby. Oh, much, much more. Really, I'd say it's more like a romance. It's something that affects me every day. When I'm on the stage, for instance. If it's the hockey season, why I feel like I'm in the nets. I'm Mr. Johnny Bower, of the Maple Leafs, turning away the hard slap shots. If the crowd boos or jeers, I simply ignore the crowd.

"In the baseball season, I feel like I'm batting in the clutch. I'm Mr. Maury Wills, or Mr. Danny Cater. The winning run is on second with two out. Ah ha, that's a pressure situation. When I'm on the stage performing, I'm really not on the stage at all, you see. I'm on the field, on the ice.

"Now, let us say that the audience begins to boo, or someone makes a remark. I'm ready for that kind of pressure, because, you see, I've already built myself up mentally to handle the situation. I simply say to myself, 'Now, you're Danny Cater and you're going to sock that old ball through the hole between short and third' . . . or I'll say, 'Steady now, Mr. Bower. Here they come down the ice. Keep your eye on the puck.'

"Oh-h-h-h, let me tell you, baseball and hockey fit in fantastically with the stage. When I'm performing in the spotlight, I really feel like a twenty-year-old rookie, I really do. . . . I'd love to play baseball, even now, but I have this one great fear, you see: I'm afraid of the ball. I fear those awful hooks the pitchers throw."

The last time Herbert Khaury played a game of baseball was when he was nine and at a summer camp in the Catskills. "I struck out," he says, "I struck out three times. The camp director said, 'Why don't you try hitting left-handed.' So the next day I batted left-handed. I copied the batting stance of the great Mr. Ted Williams. Oh, what a spectacular hitter Mr. Williams was. I copied his stance and I socked the old ball into right field. A clean hit, you see. But I was so slow, they threw me out at first. It was a crisis, but I had to accept the truth: I was not baseball material. So I decided to become a skater. Oh-h-h-h-h, that was a disaster, too. I couldn't even stand up on skates, not even on roller skates. And that's how I became a fan, a true-blue, 'Let's Win This One For Uncle Wilbert Robinson' Dodger fan and, of course, a lover of the Leafs. Oh, how I do, do love my Leafs."

The romance with the Maple Leafs reached full bloom in the early 1950s, when Tiny Tim was serving his apprenticeship in show business. He bought balcony seats to Maple Leaf-Ranger games at the old Madison Square Garden. "I couldn't afford the good seats in those days," says Tiny Tim. "I was forced to buy in the balcony, but when I changed my singing style and let my hair grow and grow and grow, which was in 1954, you see, I had to forsake the economy of balcony prices. You see, they began throwing beer on me. Oh, those nasty, nasty Ranger fans. I felt bad about it, of course. Who wouldn't feel bad if beer is thrown on them? But it took those beer throwers to make me realize that the balcony was the wrong move for me. I belonged down on the ice with my Leafs. From then on, I sat in the four-dollar seats."

In those days at the old Garden, Herbert Khaury was called "Alice" by the Ranger fans. He came early, stayed on to the very end and generally made a nuisance of himself by taunting the New York stands with a series of zany antics. "One night," he says, "the Leafs were superb. The Leafs scored ten goals. Imagine! Oh, the Ranger fans died that night. Died. Died. Died. After the sixth goal, I jumped up—I jumped up in the middle of hundreds of Ranger fans—and I shouted, 'Splendid, splendid—let's have more, more, more!' Oh, now, that got them. It got them and they screamed.

" 'Sit down you witch,' they yelled. 'Sit down you rotten witch.' Ah-ha-ha, it was a little bit of heaven, you see."

Tiny Tim's fascination for the Maple Leafs launched him on a short-lived career as a horse player in the early 1950s. His parents who worked in the garment district couldn't afford to buy young Herbert the two-hundred-dollar Zenith shortwave radio he desired so much. With that radio he could catch games from Toronto on the Canadian Broadcasting Company. "Now I really, really needed that Zenith," says Tiny Tim. "Where we lived in New York, radio reception was disastrous.

You couldn't hear a thing. If I wanted to hear the game, I'd have to sit in a friend's Volkswagen and freeze to death. So, you see, I just had to have that Zenith. I had to have it, so I took one of my many, many one-day jobs. I went to work—for ten dollars a day—at Grumbacher Paints. With malice aforethought, you might say.

"You see, at the time I was following the trotters at Yonkers and I had this very strong feeling about a horse named Diamond Feet. Diamond Feet was running at Yonkers that very night and he was fifty-to-one in the morning line. Oh-h-h-h, my one day at Grumbacher Paints was a calamity. I couldn't work because all day long Diamond Feet kept growing on me. Naturally, at the day's end I was fired for a very, very poor performance, but I was paid the ten dollars nevertheless. I took a Greyhound bus to Yonkers. My feeling for Diamond Feet grew stronger and stronger. He was thirty-five-to-one on the board, the longest shot in the race. And he came in. He paid seventy-four dollars for two, but, foolishly, I had bet him as part of the Daily Double.

"When they posted the Daily Double combinations, Diamond Feet and the horse I had in the second race—I can't remember the beast's name—would have paid over a thousand dollars. Oh-h-h, what ecstasy, what divine anticipation. My horse in the second race led from the gate into the stretch. In the middle of the stretch, he was ahead by two lengths. I'll tell you, I was down to the ground with expectation. I looked again and he was still leading by a length and coming on strong. Oh-h-h-h, I was seeing three Zenith radios.

"But there, right there, the beast quit. Quit dead, do you hear! Two other horses went S-W-O-O-S-H and passed him at the finish. I was down to a bus ticket."

Tiny Tim is really hung up on his "feelings." He claims they live within him and afford him a sixth sense about baseball players and managers. "I had a very strong feeling about Mr. Gene Mauch, a feeling that he would be named commissioner of baseball. But, of course, someone else got the job, didn't they? What was the new commissioner's name?

"Oh, you can't remember it either. Now, that's amusing, isn't it? Oh, dear, the negative spirits must be in the air today."

Tiny Tim says he is convinced the negative spirits abounded when Mauch and the Phillies blew the pennant in 1964. "There is no doubt about it," he said. "You see, there is no way to defeat the negative spirits. Now, one way to rout them would be by prayer, but no one prays any more. No one prays in the clubhouse.

"But I did have this feeling that Mr. Mauch would be named baseball commissioner. I saw him as a fearless commissioner. As a manager, he was a stern disciplinarian. Judging from his record, Mr. Mauch doesn't take anything from anybody. He's having an affair with baseball. Baseball is Mr. Mauch's mistress. I can tell. . . . Oh-h-h-h, yes, I can. Oh, gracious, what a scrumptious commissioner he would have been.

"Now, I do have a feeling about this new commissioner, the one whose name no one can remember. My feeling—and this is a very, very positive feeling, you see—is that this new commissioner may surprise us all. There."

We were talking in the reception room of Tiny Tim's dressing quarters in the Latin Casino in Cherry Hill, New Jersey. It was between shows and his "feelings" were particularly strong.

"Mr. Hammerman," he shrieked, "Oh, Mr. Hammerman, if you please."

Mark Hammerman, Tiny Tim's manager, stuck his head in the door.

"Mr. Hammerman," said Tiny Tim, "my shopping bag, please."

Hammerman returned with a multicolored shopping bag and placed it at the feet of his client and then began lecturing him. "My God, Tiny," Hammerman said, "you've been talking for two hours and you've still got another show to do. You're going to lose your voice."

"Oh, now, Mr. Hammerman, please," said Tiny Tim. "I've been talking baseball and hockey and that is music to my ears."

Tiny Tim dug into the shopping bag, pulled out the *Baseball Digest* and began looking for pencil marks he said he had made the night before.

"I've had feelings about some great players," he said. "I had strong feelings about Mr. Vada Pinson and Mr. Bill Virdon and, yes, Mr. Lou Brock, when the Cubs traded him to the St. Louis Cardinals."

He thumbed through the *Baseball Digest,* suggesting that notes be taken on his latest crop of "feelings." For a starter, he cited Bill Russell of the Dodgers. "I'm not sure what position he plays, but Mr. Russell will become a splendid spray hitter. I feel it . . . and the Yankees have a secret find in Mr. White—is it Bill White or Ron White? Whichever Mr. White the Yankees have, that Mr. White is going to be sensational. My feeling about Mr. White is very positive."

The "most positive feeling" Tiny Tim ever had, he says, was the year the Dodgers won their first World Series—the 1955 conquest of the Yankees in seven games. He was between jobs at the time, but on the morning of the sixth Series game, he was interviewed for a promising position. It was suggested that he start work that afternoon, but Tiny Tim refused. "What?" he said. "Why, the Dodgers are playing in the Series this afternoon. I can't work at a time like this."

The prospective employer agreed that might be asking too much, so it was decided that Mr. Khaury would begin his duties the next morning. "But I never took the job," says Tiny Tim. "I went home and sat in front of my radio and died. The Dodgers lost. I called the gentleman who offered me the job and I said, 'Look, I'm very, very sorry, but I can't come in tomorrow. The Dodgers lost today. I just can't take it.'

"My mother and father were livid. They said, 'How can you give up a job like that? How can you turn down a good position, just for a baseball game. What's baseball going to give you?'

"I told them. I said, 'Honey, the Dodgers are going to give me spiritual satisfaction.' And the next afternoon they did. They beat the Yankees. Mr. Sandy Amoroso made that fantastic catch in left field. Let me tell you, there was more than just a player involved in that catch. That was a miracle. There was something heavenly going on in left field in Yankee Stadium that afternoon. And what a day for a miracle."

Herbert Khaury's parents couldn't understand the miracle. There are several things Herbert Khaury's parents don't understand about their son. They are in their late seventies now and retired from the garment district and they still can't understand why Herbert carries on about baseball as if it were the Democratic Party or something. And they still pray that someday Herbert will find a nice girl and settle down.

"They simply refuse to understand my romance with baseball," says the son. "Baseball and hockey are fantastic for romance. The girls you see. . . . Not too long ago, I met this beautiful angel in a nightclub. She was breathtakingly gorgeous. I asked her for her telephone number and she obliged, but, at that very moment, I realized I didn't have a pen or a pencil. Now, that was an error. But to top the error, I pulled another boner: the mental lapse. I told her to wait, I would get a pencil and be right back. But when I returned, the angel was gone. Gone forever. Oh, what a rock that was.

"But it taught me a lesson. A few weeks later I met another angel, a Miss Margaret Foot. She was fantastic, a dream, a lunch, a delicacy. She not only gave me her telephone number, she asked for mine. And two days later, in midafternoon, she telephoned me. She said, 'This is Miss Margaret Foot. Will you come over to my apartment right away and walk my rabbit George?'

"I said, 'Miss Foot, I am leaving immediately.' And I slammed down the phone. I didn't give her a chance to change her mind. You see, had I conversed with Miss Margaret Foot, I might have made a bad pitch. I might have thrown a hanging curve.

"So I dashed from the apartment. My mother said, 'Herbert, where are you going in such a hurry?' And I said, 'Mother, when I get a telephone call from a beautiful girl like Miss Margaret Foot, I must leave at once—remember, Mother, never let a pitch hang.'

"Oh-h-h-h, sometimes I forget who I am, you see."

Some people just don't understand Tiny Tim. Walter Alston is one. For years, Tiny Tim dreamed of meeting Walter Alston, a man he regards with saintlike devotion. One day last summer he met Alston in an elevator in a Chicago hotel. The elevator stopped at a floor and in walked Walter Alston and Tiny Tim lost his breath.

"Oh-h-h, Mr. Alston," he said. "Oh, hi . . . hello, there . . . Oh-h-h-h, Mr. Alston I have always dreamed of meeting you, sir."

Alston, who has the quiet demeanor of a preacher, was speechless.

"Everybody in the elevator held their breath," says Tiny Tim, "but when the car stopped at the next floor, who got in but Mr. Wes Parker, the great Dodger first-baseman. Mr. Parker and I had met before at a concert, and so Mr. Parker smiled and said, 'Hi, Tiny.' Then Mr. Parker spotted Mr. Alston standing in the back of the car and Mr. Parker stood at attention the rest of the trip down."

Tiny Tim had a different sort of an experience with another one of his idols, Gordie Howe. Tiny Tim was on the Johnny Carson show one night last winter. "If you were dying," Carson asked Tim, "and wanted someone to talk to before you died, who would it be?"

"Why, Mr. Gordie Howe," said Tiny Tim.

"Who's Gordie Howe?" asked Carson.

"Oh-h-h," said Tiny Tim, "Mr. Howe is a very fine hockey player with the Detroit Red Wings."

"A hockey player?" said Carson. "Why would you want a hockey player at your death bed?"

"Oh-h-h-h-h," said Tiny Tim, "I would ask him, 'Mr. Howe, before I die, please tell me how you can skate so gracefully down the ice, with three or four hockey players in front of you, and still manage the puck so magnificently. Tell me, Mr. Howe, how are you able to stick control the puck so beautifully in that kind of situation?' "

Gordie Howe, who caught the telecast in Detroit, was flattered. Howe mailed Tiny Tim an autographed copy of his new book, *Number Nine*, and they got together later in Detroit.

"I told Mr. Howe it was an utter joy to meet him," says Tiny Tim.

"Mr. Howe asked if he could call me Alice and, of course, I consented. Mr. Howe invited me to work out with the Red Wings while I was in Detroit, but, horrors, I had to decline. I was compelled to inform Mr. Howe that I do not know how to skate. Oh-h-h-h-h, would that I could stand up on the ice."

Perhaps, someday, our Tiny Tim *will* be named hockey commissioner, and then will learn how to stand up on the ice. Perhaps, then, they will let him play goalie, let him fulfill his fondest dream, of turning away those hard slap shots. Herbert Khaury smiled beatifically at the thought. "Oh-h-h-h, that would be scrumptious, just scrumptious."

Gale Sayers

The Hard Road Back

Al Silverman | **1 9 7 0**

Gale Sayers lay on his bed in a motel room in Washington, D.C., a day before the Chicago Bears' first exhibition game of the 1969 season. He was wearing white jockey undershorts and glistened like a bronze god. A friend, Henny Young, had come in the room and noted immediately that Sayers' skin was a deeper brown than usual. "You got a tan!" Young exclaimed. "Where'd you get that tan? You been sittin' in the sun?" Sayers laughed, a flashing, self-assured laugh, showing his white teeth and sharing his secret with no one.

The bronze body was hard and lean and the five-inch scar that ran along the inside of his right leg, thigh-bone to knee-bone, knee-bone to leg-bone, that jagged badge of fellowship among professional football players, was not noticeable. But it was there and it filled the room with its presence; unspoken questions, urgent questions, were in the air.

The knee had been cut into last November 10 and cartilage removed and ligaments sewn up and now the finest runner in professional football the last four years—until November 10, 1968—was about to play in his first game since the injury.

Finally, a question was asked, not to Sayers but, warming up, to Sayers' roommate, Brian Piccolo, who lay on his own bed, the whiteness of his skin a startling contrast to Gale's bronze look.

"There's one big difference in Gale now," Piccolo said. "He runs all right until the knee starts to wobble." He laughed and Gale laughed and the visitors in the room laughed and, suddenly, the air was lighter.

Piccolo played fullback at Wake Forest. He was born in Massachusetts but raised, he said, in Fort Lauderdale, Florida.

"By way of He-Hung-High, Mississippi," said Sayers.

Pick grinned. "Don't get me started, Massa Sayers," he said. But he was started. The two had become roommates two years ago in Birmingham, Alabama, before an exhibition game, when the Bears decided hastily to room men according to position.

"Of all the places to spring it on us," said Piccolo. "I came up to the room and saw Gale and said, 'What are you doing here?' But it's been okay. We talk about everything, whatever goes on."

"Mostly race relationships," said Sayers.

"We're okay," said Piccolo, ignoring Sayers, "as long as he doesn't use the bathroom."

Someone asked Sayers, "Who would you want as a roommate if you had a choice?" He replied, "If you're asking me, what white Italian fullback from Wake Forest, I'd say Pick."

Some people find it difficult to understand the black humor, the needling that goes on between Sayers and Piccolo. The two keep it up even on the field. When Ross Montgomery, a rookie running back from Texas Christian, first heard it, he was astonished. Sayers and Piccolo use it therapeutically, as a way of easing into each man's world, a world that has been vastly separate for so long. The needling helps take the strangeness from each man's world, and it lessens tensions.

Sayers said, "Pick, show him the letter you just got." The letter had come from Chicago, from a man who had actually signed his name. It began: "I read where you stay together with Sayers. I am a white man! Most of the people I know don't want anything to do with them. I just don't understand you. Most Italians I have met say that they stink—and they really do."

Piccolo interrupted. "Well, of course that's true. You can't get away from that."

Sayers roared, shaking his head. "I don't like your racist attitude," he said.

The rest of the letter described how the Bears smelled, how they had no quarterback, no receivers, no offensive line. And, it ended: "Sayers will fold up like an accordion when he gets hit."

That was one question Sayers hoped to settle right away in the game with the Redskins. But he was disappointed to learn, earlier in the week, that he would not start, that he would be used only to run back kickoffs and punts.

Jim Dooley, a tall man with curly hair, who wears horn-rimmed glasses and looks more like a scoutmaster than the head coach of the Bears, explained why Sayers would not be starting. "He's fine," Dooley said. "I know he wanted to start this game. I told him, 'Gale, look, we got an inexperienced line. Two of our regulars are out. They make a mistake—boom.' When he scrimmaged last week someone made a mistake and Butkus hit him. He understood afterwards."

Perhaps he understood, but he was not happy. "They're babying me," he said, "I know they are."

All along, Sayers had refused to baby himself. He would not use crutches when his leg was in a cast. Right after the cast was removed, he began to lift weights on the leg. He started jogging in early February. He was examined on February 27 and Dr. Theodore Fox, who had performed the operation, told Sayers, "If there were a game this Sunday, you'd be able to play."

Dr. Fox believes in Sayers. He once defined the special quality that made Sayers the finest runner in football. "Factor X," he called it. "This stands for drive and motivation," he said. "Factor X elevates a player one plateau. It makes a star out of an average player and a superstar out of a star." Dr. Fox said that his operation on Sayers' knee would contribute 60 percent to Sayers' recovery and "Gale's strong desire to return—Factor X—will add the other 40 percent."

There could be no doubt about that desire. "I worked hard to get up there," Sayers had said mid-point in his recuperation period, "and I'm going to work twice as hard to stay up there." At that time, an article in a Chicago newspaper suggested that running backs with knee injuries rarely come back to top form and that Sayers might have to spend the rest of his career as a flanker or at some other position. The article infuriated Gale. "I saved it," he said, "because when I do come back as a runner, I'm gonna show it to him." And then, as if to underscore his determination, he drew out the words—"I . . . Will . . . Be . . . Back."

When rookie camp opened in Rensselaer, Indiana, in mid-July, Sayers was there. His first day in camp, he insisted on taking part in the scrimmage. On one play he started running to his right. Willie Holman, the Bears' huge and mean defensive left end, came across and blindsided Sayers, crashing him to the ground. Others piled on. Sayers got up by himself. He continued to play. Finally, the scrimmage was over. He had carried the ball a half-dozen times, gaining six yards through the middle once, five another time. But no one said a word to him. Sayers felt he was being ignored by the coach, the trainer, the Bears' doctor. But that was the game plan. Trainer Ed Rozy says, "The instructions on him were don't even mention it. Make him forget it."

In desperation Sayers went up to Ed McCaskey, who is the Bears' treasurer, a son-in-law of George Halas and a confidant of Sayers.

"How'd I look?" Sayers asked.

"You're all right," McCaskey said, and turned away.

When the veterans came in to camp, Gale was used sparingly. The younger backs, Mike Hull, Ralph Kurek and Montgomery, did most of the hitting. Dooley was going easy with Sayers, but also with veterans Piccolo and Ronnie Bull, who had a record of preseason injuries. But the lack of contact drills worried Gale because of his timing. "With Piccolo or Bull in there," he said, "the timing is different. The guards can be a little slower. But with me in there they've got to go full speed. I'm much quicker, so they have to set up their blocks fast. When I'm in there, I'm running up their backs."

But he did scrimmage a bit. In the Saturday scrimmage before the Redskins' game, he went up the middle. Someone grabbed him by the legs and Dick Butkus rammed him in the chest. Ed Stone, who covers the Bears for *Chicago Today*, was there and says that Sayers seemed to show his old moves. "I talked to Johnny Morris, who's on TV now," Stone says, "and he said that on a sweep it looked like Gale might have the slightest hitch. But," Stone said, "I can't see anything. It looks like it's all there."

On the morning of August 2, at breakfast, Sayers and Piccolo talked about Vince Lombardi and Washington and playing the first exhibition game of the season. Both men were dressed casually, in T-shirts and shorts. A waitress came over to Sayers. "Can I ask you your name?" she said to him. Pick mumbled loud enough for all to hear, "They all look alike."

Piccolo said he thought he would like to play a little bit for Lombardi before his career was over.

"I can arrange that," Sayers said.

"Would you? I'm tired of playing in your shadow. I want to be a legend in my own time."

The game was less than twelve hours away and they talked about what it meant to them. "You can't treat it as any game," said Sayers. "Do that and you have a short season. Every game is important, and you always like to start off with a win after all that training."

"But it's not like life or death," said Piccolo. "Lombardi and Washington is not the same as Lombardi and Green Bay. Certainly, you want to beat Vince, but it's not the same as beating him with a team that's in your division."

"I know Lombardi's going to be up," Sayers said. "The Redskins are going to be up." His thoughts suddenly became disconnected. "I hate to lose," he said. Then, as if the real meaning of the game had just come to him, he said, "I just want to show people I'm ready."

That was it—to show people that he was ready. It was a secret he had carried around for eight months, and even he did not know the answer. He had jogged, played handball, basketball and touch football. He had run full speed, he had made his patented Sayers cuts, he had been hit in camp and, through it all, the knee had held up. Now there was one more test, contact in battle against another team. He was twenty-six years old with four glorious and rewarding years behind him and now he must know about the future.

While Sayers attended a mid-morning team meeting, I talked with the Bears' trainer, Ed Rozy. He is a grizzled Walter Brennan type who has been with the Bears for twenty-two years. "I'd say Gale's 99 percent now," Rozy said. "The big thing to overcome is the mental attitude, the subconscious feeling—is it or isn't it? See, he's got to believe it, it's got to be proven to him. Better than that, he's got to prove it to himself. That's why he had to go right out that first day in camp and scrimmage and try to get it over with."

Rozy talked with admiration about Sayers' dedication. At Rensselaer, Sayers would come down to the basement at 8 a.m. each day. He would take a whirlpool bath for ten minutes to loosen up the knee, then go into the weight room and lift sixty pounds on the knee, lift those sixty pounds fifty times. Morning and night he would be down there lifting. "That's the mark of a champion," Rozy said. "The guy never quit on himself."

Rozy talked abstractedly about the injury. "It was a beautiful shot," he said of the film clip and still photo of the injury. "It shows Gale planting his foot with pressure applied to the outside of the leg. A beautiful shot," Rozy repeated, as if he were admiring a Picasso painting.

Sayers himself saw little beauty in the shot. One night last March he brought home the Bears' 1968 highlight film to show some friends, including his teammates George Seals and Frank Cornish. When the film came to the injury—the first time Sayers had seen it—Seals hollered, in jest, "Get up! Get up!" And a chill, almost like an electric shock, went through Sayers' body. After the guests had gone, he told his wife, Linda, "I'm never gonna look at that film again as long as I live." A couple of days later when he had to show the film to a group, he left the room just before the injury sequence. Eventually, he got over it, said to himself, the hell with it, and stayed and watched.

It was, no doubt, the most traumatic moment of his life. The Bears were at home and, in the second quarter, held a comfortable 24–6 lead over the 49ers in the ninth game of the season. Sayers had gained 32 yards in ten carries. That gave him 856 yards rushing for the season so far, well ahead of all the NFL runners; he seemed on his way to the best year of his career, perhaps a record-breaking year.

In the huddle, quarterback Virgil Carter called for a toss to Sayers. Gale broke left, hoping to go outside the defense behind the blocking of tackle Randy Jackson. The 49ers' right linebacker, Harold Hays, began to string along the line, keeping his hands on Jackson in order to control him and prevent Sayers from breaking to the outside. Right cornerback Kermit Alexander, who also had the responsibility of turning the play inside, was trying to strip his blocker. Hays was controlling Jackson and defensive tackle Kevin Hardy was barreling down the line toward Sayers. So Gale knew he couldn't go wide and he tried to slip inside the blocker, as he often does.

At the instant he planted his foot, Alexander hit him with a low, rolling block. The cleats of Sayers' right shoe were anchored in the turf, preventing give and the knee took the full shock of the blow.

Sayers knew immediately that the knee was gone. He thinks he turned to Alexander, who was standing over him, and said, "It's gone." He remembers motioning to the bench to come and get him and putting his arms around a couple of the Bear players. Then he passed out.

He came to as he reached the sidelines. Dr. Fox was there. "It's gone, Doc," Sayers said.

Dr. Fox checked the knee. "It's okay," he said, and started to walk away.

"Come back here!" Sayers screamed. "Tell it to me straight."

Dr. Fox looked at Sayers for a moment, then said, "Yes, you have torn ligaments in your knee."

At that moment, Sayers felt an overwhelming sense of loss, also of self-pity. He asked himself, why me, why did it have to be me? And he began to cry.

He was operated on late that afternoon. The quicker the surgeon can get in there, the better job he can do. "You wait twenty-four hours after one of those things," Dr. Fox said, "and the injury is like a bag of mush. It really would be like trying to stitch together two bags of cornmeal mush."

In medical slang, Sayers' injury is called "The Terrible Triad of O'Donoghue." This describes the tears of the three ligaments in the knee and is named after Dr. Don H. O'Donoghue of the University of Oklahoma, the dean of football physicians. It is a common operation now. The estimate is that there are fifty thousand football victims each year, fifty thousand who require knee surgery.

The operation took three hours and when Sayers came out of it he remembers the doctor saying, everything's okay, and Sayers not believing him. "You wouldn't lie to me? You wouldn't lie to me?" he kept repeating. Linda Sayers was there and she says that Gale actually got up and started screaming to Dr. Fox: *"You wouldn't lie to me?"*

He is much more emotional than has been generally understood. He is much deeper, too. In his first couple of years with the Bears he was very shy, a little frightened, unsure of himself off the field and wary, very wary, of strangers. He began to change about two years ago. Symbolically, he stopped cutting his hair short for football. He wears a natural now and someone wrote him a letter blaming his knee injury on his "long" hair. He became a stockbroker for Paine, Webber, Jackson and Curtis in the Chicago office. He worked on his public speaking. He began to respond to people, and to the world around him. Recently, Ed McCaskey has helped make a reader of Sayers. McCaskey gave Sayers *The Autobiography of Malcolm X* and Sayers devoured it in three days. In quick succession he read a novel, *Siege,* Eldridge Cleaver's *Soul on Ice* and the classic Ralph Ellison novel *Invisible Man.* All are on Negro themes and all seemed meaningful to Sayers. "Something," he says, "keeps you going into books and you don't want to put them down." He seemed to relate most to Malcolm X. "He was a drug addict for so many years and got out of it," Sayers said. "I believe he could do anything he wanted."

He admires people like that, people who can overcome. He is that way himself. In his rookie year, he would vomit before every game. Finally, he decided he had to stop, that he was using up too much nervous energy. "I would go out of the dressing room," he said, "tired, beat." So he started talking to other players, thinking of other things and he disciplined himself to stop vomiting.

Now the discipline, the fight, concerns the knee. He rested in his Washington motel room an hour before the team dinner, which would be followed by the ankle taping and then the bus ride to Robert F. Kennedy Stadium and a football game. The television set was on. The Baltimore Orioles were playing the Oakland Athletics and Sayers watched idly. And as he watched, the question was slipped to him:

"Do you think about the knee?"

"I think about it," he said, "I never stop thinking about it. When I'm in my room listening to records, I think about it. Every day a thought about it goes through my mind. I know it's fine, but I think about it."

He has considered seriously about going to a hypnotist. "I remember Don Newcombe went to one about his fear of flying. If I knew of a hypnotist in Chicago, I would probably go to one." But then he said he was not sure that he was the type to be hypnotized.

His mind was a jumble of emotion. He thought of an old teammate, Andy Livingston, who had hurt a knee against the Packers a couple of years ago, and was never the same again. But he also thought of the old Bear halfback, Willie Galimore, who had survived two knee operations and come back fine (only to die in an automobile crash); and of Tommy Mason, who has had six knee operations and still plays. Gale blamed the failures on human weaknesses. "They didn't work at it," he said. "I worked at it." He groped for words. Finally, words came. "I consider this my game. A damn injury like that is not going to keep me out of it."

Looking at Sayers in the Bear dressing room deep beneath RFK Stadium, the strong statement he had made a few hours earlier seemed remote and irrelevant. He sat slumped in front of his locker. It was five minutes to seven and he would have to go out on the field for pregame drill in fifteen minutes. He was wearing his cleats, his white game pants with the orange piping down the side, and a white T-shirt. He sat on a folding chair in front of his locker. He was bent over. His head was bowed, his eyes were closed. He was leaning on his elbows, holding his head in his hands, his two thumbs resting between his eyes. He sat there quiet as stone, as if in a trance. He was unapproachable.

George Seals, the 265-pound offensive guard, the man Sayers had ridden behind for so many of his long-gainers, was dressing in a corner. A close friend of Sayers, he was asked whether he felt any extra pressure to protect Sayers because of the knee. Seals shook his head. "To me," he said, "that would be conceding something. Football is a very emotional game. When you step out onto that field, you cannot concede a thing. Gale certainly wouldn't want it that way."

Seals, who had his own knee operation last March and was still far from being 100 percent, was with Sayers when the cast was removed from Sayers' leg. He was astonished to see that there was very little atrophy in the leg. "He's not human," Seals said. "After he got that cast off, he'd go out in the afternoon, morning, every night, doing things constantly. Many athletes come back from knee injuries lacking quite a bit. I feel if Sayers comes back, he'll be the one that comes back all the way."

And still Sayers sat there, bent over, trancelike, almost in the fetal position. Bennie McRae, the Bears' veteran defensive back came over, leaned down and whispered to Sayers: "Are you ready, man?" Sayers nodded. "You all right? You're gonna be all right," McRae said soothingly. "You're ready, I know you're ready." He put an arm on Sayers' shoulder. "Hang loose." Sayers nodded again. McRae drifted away and Sayers remained cast in stone.

I was thinking various things. I was thinking about the knee . . . how it happened, could it happen again, how would it hold up . . . hoping I could make it through the game. That's the mental torture of football and I think this is going to afflict me as long as I play this game.

Finally, it was 7:10 and the players started out. Backfield coach Ed Cody came close to Sayers and said, "About a minute, Gale."

Sayers shook himself, rose, slipped on his white jersey with the big navy-blue numerals, 40, picked up his helmet and clattered out of the room.

As you come through the runway leading up to the field, a distorted sound hits you, an eerie sound, like a piece of heavy machinery sucking out air. It is only when you get through the runway and hit the dugout that you finally recognize the sound—it is the roar of the crowd.

It was a stifling night. The temperature was in the eighties, there was no breeze stirring and the humidity menaced the soul. The weather forecast was for scattered thundershowers, but the clouds in that Washington twilight looked benevolent.

Sayers was throwing left-handed with Ronnie Bull, he and Bull trotting up and down the field exchanging passes. Then the Washington Redskin players poured out of their dugout and milled around the entrance. Sam Huff was leading them. He stood there, waiting for them all to come out before leading the charge across the field. "Everyone up?" he asked. Vince Lombardi, wearing a shortsleeved shirt, black tie, black pants and the look of a bus driver, grew impatient with Huff. "Okay," Lombardi barked, "let's go, let's take 'em." There was joy and exhilaration in his voice as he ran out on the field with his men. Clearly, he was glad to be back in the game.

Sayers, taking part in a passing drill, caught a short pass and ran by

Lombardi. The Redskin coach stopped him. They shook hands. "I'm very glad to see that you've overcome your injury," Lombardi said. Sayers mumbled his thanks.

Sayers remembered meeting Lombardi in Commissioner Pete Rozelle's office in New York last spring, the spring of his recuperation, the spring of his anxieties. Lombardi said to Sayers, "How do you feel, son? I hope to see you out there this fall." And Sayers said, "You'll see me August 2." And so he had.

Now it was 7:30 and two Bear players started the kicking drill. The punts came out of the sky like fireworks, except that the boom was heard first, then the ball was seen soaring in the air. Sayers caught the first punt and ran it back fifteen yards, crouched, darting, making the moves that had thrilled people for the last four years. He caught another punt, then a third, and a fourth. Then he was in another pass drill. He went down and out, toward the Redskin side of the field, taking a long pass over his shoulder. Two skinny Redskin kids, Number 5 and Number 3, the field goal kickers, were together when he went by. They looked at Sayers, then turned to say something to each other, gossiping like a couple of old maids at a soda fountain.

Finally, the drill was over and the Bears returned to the dressing room to put on their shoulder pads and wait for the start.

It had been raining for five minutes when the teams lined up for the kickoff, a hard, slanting rain with thunder and lightning and a rising wind. The field, especially the skin part, the Washington Senators' infield, was already filling up with puddles.

The Bears were the receiving team. Gale Sayers was deep, at his five-yard line, with Ross Montgomery stationed just in front of him. Just as the kicker moved forward, Sayers hollered to Montgomery to deploy right. Sayers, who captains the kick and punt return team, always tells the other deep back where to go. The idea is for Sayers to cover three-quarters of the field, to make sure that he gets the football.

He got the football. He took it easily on his six-yard line and started straight up the middle. One man broke through the wedge and came on to challenge Sayers. "I feel I can always beat any man one-on-one," Sayers has said, "and two on one I can beat 75 percent of the time." Sayers gave the one man his inside move, a head and shoulder fake, and the man was out of it and Sayers was flashing to the right, toward the sidelines.

"The thing that makes Gale different," Brian Piccolo had said earlier, "is the way he's able to put a move on somebody and not lose a step.

He gives a guy a little fake and he's full speed. I give a guy a move like that and it takes me fifteen yards to get in stride."

Sayers was in full stride now, streaking down the sidelines. Two Washington defensive backs angled in on him around the Redskin forty. One lunged at him and Sayers just pushed him away with his left arm. The other threw himself at Sayers, jostling him momentarily. But Sayers kept his feet, regained control and sped triumphantly into the end zone. There was a purity, a shining purity to that run, that contrasted in a strange and rather beautiful way with the indecent weather and the spongy field. The first time he had carried the ball in combat since his knee injury, which was the worst kind of a knee injury you can have, he had broken one. It was as if all the questions had been answered, all the doubts resolved about the condition of Gale Sayers. It was an illusion, of course; it was much too early to form a judgment on Sayers' recovery. But the illusion was heightened by the clap of thunder that accompanied Sayers' last step into the end zone.

One illusion was, however, quickly dispelled. It was not a touchdown after all. The referee ruled that Sayers had stepped out of bounds on the Redskin twenty-five. Sayers said later that he could not see the sideline markers because they had been obscured by the rain. But it was still a sixty-nine-yard run and surely it held some meaning for Gale Sayers, for the Chicago Bears—and maybe for those fifty thousand players who fall victim to a knee injury every at."

And that was all there was to the game, really. Later, the Bear coaches had to throw out the films of the game because nothing could be seen. After the Sayers' run the rain intensified and the entire first half was played in a blinding cloudburst that ruined the field and left the players dispirited. The Redskins won 13 to 7. Sayers came out on the field twelve times, but carried the ball only once more. Dick Butkus took a short kickoff and lateraled to Sayers who piled seventeen yards up the middle before he was pulled down in the glop.

The next morning Sayers was eating breakfast at 7:15. He had hardly slept that night. He says it usually takes him a day and a half to unwind after a game. He ordered ham and eggs but ate sparingly.

He listened while a friend read accounts of the game from the Washington morning newspapers. Sayers, it seemed, had almost gotten equal play with the Redskins. One story began this way: "It took the sellout crowd of 45,988 at RFK Stadium last night only a matter of seconds to see for themselves that Gale Sayers is as good as ever. . . ."

He grinned when he heard that. He thought it was true and now he felt more assured because he had passed the first test. After months of hard work, months filled with doubt and pain and the mental torture that only a knee victim can understand, he had passed his first test. He knew it was only a beginning, but it was a good beginning.

At Rare and Lovely Times, He Is Still Pancho Gonzales

James Toback | **1970**

It is summer, 1969, and Richard Gonzales, called Pancho, born in 1928, is walking off the court at Forest Hills. He and doubles partner Ron Holmberg have just won an early-round match in the U.S. Open Championships. From the distance of the other side of the court, Gonzales' body had looked hard and lean, the muscles long like a swimmer's, the skin tight and olive brown. But as he crossed the net, coming closer, he seemed thinner in the arms and legs, his shorts loose, skirtlike on his thighs, his calves withering down to ankles as thin and delicate as wrists.

Now he is near and his large, dark brown eyes shift in their sockets, darting from side to side, down, up, side, down. He looks pale and tired. His face is lined and the black hair is gray along the hairline and at the temples, and he has a one-inch scar on his left cheek that splits in two directions down to the corner of the mouth. It is a face that will not tolerate pity. I walk alongside of him for twenty yards, heading toward the clubhouse.

"Lend me your ear."

"What do you want?" he says, eyes still down.

"I want to talk to you. I'm going to write about you."

He looks to his left. I am on his right. His voice is quiet and even, a baritone with potential in tenor range.

"What are you getting paid?"

I tell him.

"I want half of it," he says.

"Okay. I'll give you half from my pocket."

His head whips around and he stares at me.

"I don't want it from you. I want it from them."

"If you want it, it will have to come from me."

"I need to concentrate on tennis. I can't be talking while I'm playing."

"Okay." I start away.

"Listen," he says, "I'm playing singles tomorrow, but come by the clubhouse the next day."

At the foot of the stairs a boy asks for his autograph. Gonzales ignores him at first, then stops, turns back, reaches for the boy's program and signs. Then he rushes up past the bar, edging his way through players and members and officials and disappears.

If Pancho Gonzales had been an ordinary tennis star, he would now be playing senior tennis. Senior tennis is what a gentleman plays when his chest begins to sag, his stomach to swell, his chin to double, and his hairline to recede. In his twenties and early thirties, the future senior tennis player wins his share of tournaments, fights for his country in the Davis Cup, achieves national ranking, and, perhaps, tours and prospers as a professional for a few years. But now he plays only on weekends; now he is a stockbroker, a banker, an investor; now he plays only in one tournament, the senior tournament, at Forest Hills, with boys his own age. He is a gentleman. Ten years ago "he" was Frank Perry, Don Budge, Sidney Wood, Bitsy Grant, or Frank Shields. Today "he" is Gardner Mulloy, Billy Talbert, Bobby Riggs, Vic Seixas, or Jack Kramer. Fifteen years from now "he" will be Clark Graebner, Bob Lutz, or Stan Smith.

Pancho Gonzales is not such a "he." His chest and chin are tight, his waist is thin, and his hair has not retreated an inch from the line it held in 1948 when he won the United States Nationals and contributed to an American Davis Cup victory. And, above all, he is not a gentleman; not, at any rate, the sort of gentleman that the River Club, the Racquet Club, the Merion Cricket Club, and the West Side Tennis Club are wooing to their dining rooms. For twenty-one years he has yelled at linesmen, abused ballboys, challenged spectators, insulted reporters, flayed officials and publicly feuded with a long line of players and promoters who have all faded into varying shades of national oblivion even as he, Pancho Gonzales, has grown into world legend.

Gonzales is not content with the memory of two amateur titles, and the satisfaction and money of a decade (1953–1962) of merciless domination of professional tennis. He wants more. He wants once again, absurdly, to be the best. And although he is perpetually threatening to retire, he continues, under the aegis of George MacCall's National Tennis League, to play in tournaments all year and around the world. His last "retirement" came in September, right after the U.S. Open, but within two months he was playing again, in the British Indoor Open. And even when he was defeated, 6-1, 6-2, by Tom Okker, Gonzales said he would go right on playing. Until the next time he retired, of course.

His victories in the first half of 1969 earned him $24,000. In June, at Wimbledon, although he did not win, or even reach the semi-finals, he played the longest match in British tennis history. It went five sets, lasted five and a half hours of playing time and was split over two days. The match serves as a metaphor for the man.

Gonzales' opponent was Charlie Pasarell, ranked first in America in 1967. They battled evenly through forty games of the first set, before Pasarell broke serve to win 22 to 20. Gonzales, grateful for the evening darkness, started off the court to begin his rest before resumption the next day. He was stopped, however, and informed by referee Mike Gibson that another set was to be played before he could leave. ("You can't let yourself feel sorry for the older man," Gibson would say later that night. "It would have been unfair to Pasarell. Conditions were the same for both.") Incredulous, then enraged, Gonzales bitched, whined and cursed his way through a pathetic second set in which he was lucky to win one game. The center court Wimbledon spectators, the most restrained tennis fans in the world, hissed and jeered as he walked away.

The next day, presumably in no shape for more than a brief exhibition, he played his best tennis of the year and ran off three consecutive sets, 16-14, 6-3, 11-9, for the match. Salvaging seven match points, he closed the fifth set with a crescendo of eleven straight points. The center court Wimbledon spectators, the most restrained tennis fans in the world, gave him a standing ovation.

The summer passes to late August and we again pick up Gonzales at Forest Hills. This U.S. Open Championship (men's, not seniors'), is a tournament second only to Wimbledon in world tennis esteem. Gonzales is seeded thirteenth in a field of 128, a field which includes Rod

Laver, who needs only this tournament for an unprecedented second grand slam, Arthur Ashe, America's best player and the defending Open champion; and the ranking players from twenty-three other countries. But Pancho Gonzales has not come for sentimental reasons or as a gentleman. Nor has he come for money alone. Jimmy (the Greek) Snyder quotes him at 35 to 1 but Pancho Gonzales has come to win.

On opening day, August 27, Gonzales plays Bob Potthast, a "qualifier," who has had to win an elimination match to gain formal entrance into the tournament. Gonzales' victory is in straight sets, 6-3, 6-3, 6-4. The doubles match with Holmberg comes the next day, and on the third afternoon Gonzales is to play Ray Ruffels. Ruffels looks like a fox terrier. His body is stocky and smooth, his thick red hair brushed straight back, the bones of his face sharp. But there is a nastiness in his small eyes and a belligerence in his swagger. He is the best amateur player in Australia and twenty years younger than Gonzales, but he is unseeded in the Open, and Gonzales is supposed to dispose of him without inordinate difficulty.

The first set goes according to plan, Gonzales breaking serve early, holding his own, then breaking again for an easy 6-2 opener. But in the second game of the second set, serving, behind love–1, Gonzales' lobs, on which he has come to rely each year, begin to fall short, and Ruffels clouts two violent overhead winners for a 30–40 edge. Ruffels nets a forehand drive for deuce but then crouches down to drive a backhand by Pancho at the net and then breaks serve on a hard return to the forehand which Pancho, failing to bend, coming up too soon, hits weakly into the middle of the net.

Behind 3-5, Gonzales must break Ruffels' serve to salvage the set. The stadium benches have filled, and by now there are ten thousand spectators expressing loud support of the old man.

"Get him, Pancho," a boy yells as Gonzales walks head down, to the baseline to receive.

"He looks exhausted," a woman says.

"There's more noise!" Gonzales cries suddenly, whirling around, glaring in the direction of the woman. Silence.

At his best, ten years ago, Gonzales would have been next to invincible in a situation such as the one he now faces. Behind, the pressure intense, he would have called on his hardest, cleanest, surest strokes and broken even the finest of serves. Ruffels' is not the finest of serves. His first ball is hard but lacks the wicked angle, and his second serve doesn't move, doesn't surprise. Pancho decides to play as he did ten years ago, to step out and swing, to cut the lobbing on which he has been relying up to this point in the match and which has been failing him in this set. He drives a solid forehand return back at Ruffels who shoves a volley to the baseline. Pancho strokes another forehand which whistles by Ruffels and hits an inch inside the baseline. Ruffels thinks the ball was out. He looks at the linesman in disbelief, then disgust. Then he looks up to the crowd, imploringly, asking for what Gonzales never has asked for and never would accept, sympathy.

"Go on, play; it was in by a mile," a man yells.

Ruffels frowns, walks heavily back to the baseline, and serves. In this point, as in the next three, he follows his serve into the net and plants himself in the middle of the court, blowing back Gonzales' ground strokes until he can put one of them away or force Pancho into an error. Each time he succeeds. Gonzales is hitting with all his force, but he cannot drill the ball through Ruffels or angle it by him. The set is over and, even when Gonzales comes back to take the third set 6-3, it is obvious to everyone that Pancho's chances of winning the tournament are meager indeed.

When he loses the fourth set, thoughts shift simply to winning this match. Even that is now in doubt.

Serving at 1-1 in the fifth, Gonzales hits an anemic lob on the first point and Ruffels cracks it so hard the ball bounces into the second row. A young boy catches and hides it, his Gonzales souvenir. One of the ballboys, hands on hips, looks up, waiting.

"Come on, ballboy, let him keep it," yells Gonzales, and the crowd again goes wild.

Pancho recovers and holds serve, edging ahead at 2-1, but a haze has descended on Forest Hills and the sun is setting behind the stadium. Gonzales hates the late hours, fears that his eyes are getting weaker as he grows old. Ruffels holds serve easily to draw even and Gonzales knows that at this late time in the match and in the afternoon, to be broken on his serve would be fatal. Ruffels knows it too and makes his supreme effort to conquer in the fifth game. Of the forty-five games in the match, this is the most tense, most brilliantly played and most critical of all.

Pancho, his service groans taking on emphysematous dimensions of agony, blurs a flat, titanic blast down the middle. When Ruffels starts his swing, the ball is already making contact with the backstop. Fifteen –love. Pancho shoots for another ace, but this time Ruffels, springing on his toes, chops a sharply angled forehand crosscourt for a winner.

Gonzales licks his dry lips, slaps the sweat off his left brow, tosses the ball in the air, leans back and, moaning, hits an awesome shot to Ruffels' backhand, charging doggedly in behind it. Ruffels, confident of the success of his last angle, goes cross-court again, softly, precisely. Pancho lunges but the ball is by him and he is behind. Heaving with exhaustion and rage, sucking in his cheeks, biting them inside, he wipes his left arm across his face. Too worn for power, his next serve is sliced short to Ruffels' forehand and he waits back at the baseline. Ruffels drives a hard low shot down the line and starts in toward the net. Pancho takes two long strides, reaches, and catches the ball cleanly, whipping it back deep. Ruffels shifts direction awkwardly, right foot stuck, left sliding back, and chips back a drop shot which Gonzales, rushing in, picks off his shoe and shoves back to the baseline. Ruffels, retreating, outruns the ball and arches a backhand lob, low, long, heavy with spin. Gonzales, suspended, stretches arm and racquet in desperation for a piece of the ball. But he is too low and too late. Jerking around, looking back, he hopes. The ball drops, perfectly, an inch inside the baseline. Double break point.

Half the spectators stare at their feet. The only noise is the ticking of typewriters in the reporters' section of the marquee.

Gonzales, looking up into the pallid sun, takes one deep breath, lifts the collar of his shirt, viscous from sweat, and strides evenly to the service line. Toss, grunt, swing, ace. Thirty–40. Two steps to the left. He waits for Ruffels. Toss, grunt, swing, ace. Deuce. Ruffels has not had a chance to bring back his racquet in two points. The crowd is delirious. Ruffels' face is red. If there were no net between them, Ruffels would drop his racquet and charge.

Sapped, and seeking to jar Ruffels with a new rhythm, Pancho hits a soft twist serve down the middle. Ruffels, however, is not fooled, goes with the bounce, and then pummels the ball low across the net. Approaching, Pancho blocks the shot in front of his right ankle and whips back his racquet immediately, causing the ball to bounce back toward him once it has crossed the net and hit safely on Ruffels' side.

"A dink shot!" yells a short bald man in the middle of the inarticulate roar of the crowd.

Pancho goes back to a flat, hard serve, bidding for an ace. Ruffels comes around fast and strikes a forehand behind Gonzales coming in, but the old man reaches across his body and back, touching the ball gently, wheedling it up onto the tape at the top of the net and over. It drops dead, ten feet in front of Ruffels and the game is over.

Ruffels has made his tap-out bet and lost. He has put his courage on red and watched the ball roll black. He struggles desperately in the sixth and eighth games and wins, but in the tenth, down 5-4, Gonzales forces him into two errors at net with solid forehand returns. At 30-all, he double faults and then hits long on a forehand drive. Defeated, he flings his racquet across the ground. Pancho, exhausted, grim, shakes Ruffels' hand, then the umpire's, picks up his four aluminum racquets, and, towel around his neck, walks slowly off the court.

The crowd is still applauding long after he is gone, but it is a hollow sound, an echo in an unlighted tunnel, because there is no one, not a single person of the ten thousand who have seen this match, who doesn't know that before this tournament is over Pancho Gonzales will lose.

The next day the Gonzales-Holmberg team is upset by Mark Cox and Peter Curtis of England, a modestly talented but abundantly practiced unit. I go to wait for Gonzales in the main room of the clubhouse. A short, dark man of about seventy sits down next to me. His arms are still sturdy and muscled and his eyes, bright blue, study me.

"Your arms are in great shape."

He smiled, his face wrinkling.

"My arms? Look at my legs!" He draws up the right leg of his loose brown pants and displays a mammoth, granite calf muscle which he flexes proudly. "It's from soccer. I was the best player in Mexico for many years." He has a heavy Spanish accent.

"I'll bet."

"You waiting for Pancho?"

"How did you know?"

"You look like you're waiting for Pancho."

"Well," I say, "your intuition is impeccable. Did you see the match?"

He nods sadly.

"He's getting old. You know why I say that? Because he don't get mad the way he used to. He don't hit balls at people. He don't throw his racquet, and he don't scream. I've been watching him for twenty years, all over the world. He used to be the terror. No more."

He shakes his head. Then suddenly, he smiles.

"You know Billie Jean?"

"Sure, she's the best."

"Well, I'm Manuel Casals. My daughter's Rosie Casals!"

"And Pablo's your uncle?"

He laughs. "Yes. Pablo's my uncle. They say he's ninety. But you know how old he is? He's a hundred and five. Now Rosie, I teach her everything she knows about tennis. She's playing doubles with Billie Jean."

"She has good claims on her own."

Manuel shrugs modestly.

"You not the only one waiting for Pancho. Everyone come to see Pancho. Always been like that. They used to come to see him because they hate him. Now he's old man so they come because they love him. When he was the best they want him to lose. Now they want him to win."

"He still might," I say.

Manuel chuckles. "I hope so. I love to see it. But I don't think so." He looks me over carefully again. "You handsome young man. You want to meet my daughter?"

Gonzales, wearing a yellow sport shirt and black pants, moving easily, looking rested, sees us, comes over and sits down.

"You don't lose your temper so much any more," says Manuel.

"I never did here," Pancho says flatly. "Not at Forest Hills."

Manuel says he is going to look for Rosemary.

"You meet her later," he says. I shake his hand, which is very strong.

"Why?" I ask Gonzales.

"Why what?"

"Why don't you lose your temper at Forest Hills?"

"Because," he says, his voice and face serious, "there's really no excuse here. Everything is so relaxed. It's not like the tours we used to go on, barnstorming, fifty cities in six months, playing every night, eating badly, missing sleep. Then you tend to be on edge, you don't have the control. You're fighting your nerves. Here it's different."

"But doesn't the rage help?" I insist.

"Only if you turn it against yourself." His eyes are set at mine for the first time. Then they start darting again, the only part of him that moves. "It's good to let anger come to the surface, but you can't direct it at someone else. Big men use rage to perfect themselves. Small men use it to tear down others . . . bigots."

He lights a cigarette and looks at the floor.

"I'm getting lazy," he mutters. "I'm not chasing the ball anymore."

"Are you serious?" I say. "Players half your age don't go after shots the way you do."

"Well, the really young ones, they'll learn."

"No," I say, "most of them won't learn, they just won't get to be too good."

He laughed. "I guess you're right. You know, that's why Laver is so good. He plays every game as though he were behind 5–love. And his concentration is so intense. It seems to come naturally to him. His mind is all there all the time. I used to be like that, but not any more. I have to fight with myself to keep my mind obsessed with the match."

A man about forty with a crew cut and a brown suit, field glasses around his neck, has been standing five feet from us, and edging closer.

"What do you want?" Gonzales snaps at him suddenly.

"I'm just listening," he says with an awkward smile.

"Well, my friend and I are having a personal conversation, so maybe you'd better move on."

"I'm just listening," the man repeats in flat Midwestern tones. "I guess that's the price you have to pay if you're famous." He smiles again.

"I don't have to pay any price to you," Gonzales says, and glares at him. The man walks away quickly.

"There's only one thing I owe people," Gonzales says in agitation, "and that's preparation. If I practice, stay in shape, go for regular check-ups, sharpen my game, then I can give them my best and that's what they're paying to see. But, you know, I'm not what I used to be. Preparation used to bring me to a point where I could play at 100 percent of my capacity about 85 percent of the match. And I could always call on my best when I had to."

"Like Willie Mays hitting an extra-inning home run," I say, "or Sugar Ray, behind on points, putting someone out with a left hook, or Jim Brown breaking three tackles for a touchdown on fourth and goal."

Gonzales smiles. "That's the idea. But I can't do that any more. I get a feeling a few times during every match that I'm going to catch fire. And I do. But it only lasts for a few points of a few games, and then it's gone and I have to wait for it to return. A set today seems like what a match used to be."

"You play by instinct?"

"Not exactly. I usually have a plan, and if it goes well, I should be following it instinctively before too long. But if it isn't, I have to shift gears and find a new idea."

"Like in the Ruffels match yesterday. You saw your lobbing, dink game wasn't working and you started to step out and hit."

Gonzales shakes his head sadly, his lips tight. "That was too close. I almost lost that match."

"You knew you would win it, though, didn't you?"

He stares into my eyes again. "No, I was sure I was going to lose!

Even after the third set when I was ahead 2-1, I didn't think I could win, I don't know why; it happens often now. I always used to know I was going to win, but now I take nothing for granted, and sometimes, like yesterday, I have no confidence at all."

"Well, you know you'll beat Ulrich tomorrow," I say, smiling. Ulrich, the best player in Denmark for twenty years, is forty, the only player at Forest Hills Pancho's age.

"I don't," he says quietly. Then, almost irritably: "I don't know anything anymore. I have to take one match at a time. I can't take anyone for granted. I want to win very badly, but, you know, as I get older I get more and more interested in the state where a player performs beyond his ability. The moment when he coordinates all of his talent and power. The true beauty of sports is to go beyond the idea of winning or losing. That's why I love tennis so much. It gives you the sense of total loneliness and self-reliance, a stage on which you can create your own beauty. I could have played baseball or football, but they're team sports. Someone else can always interfere with your moment. In tennis it's up to you alone."

He frowns and the lines of his face are deep. His eyes rattle from left to right to left, suspiciously searching other people in the room. Abruptly, he leans back and relaxes.

"I guess I'm very lucky. I have achieved all my goals in tennis, all the titles, the Davis Cup; a lot of success and a lot of money along the way. I used to feel less of a man when I lost, but by now I have had enough satisfaction that I can lose and accept it. I've satisfied myself that I'm a winner, so now I can accept defeat. I hate it but I can live with it. I am growing old without becoming . . ."

"A megalomaniac."

He smiles: "Yes."

Jack Kramer walks by on the terrace. Kramer is neat and clean and from Southern California. His face, even after a half century, is unlined and soft and thin, his hair still flaxen thick. But his nose is fleshy and it is not a strong face, not a face one would remember if one had not seen it on the cover of a hundred magazines over the past thirty years and on television with considerable regularity. It is the face of the social secretary or sports director of an Episcopalian country club. Kramer ruled professional tennis while Gonzales was making his mark as the finest amateur, and when Gonzales turned pro himself in 1950, a confrontation between the white Titan and the brown Prometheus was arranged in the form of a nationwide, year-long series. Kramer demolished Gonzales in city after city and established undisputed claim as the world's best player. Although Gonzales took full control two years later, and maintained it far longer than Kramer had, the devastation of his 1950 defeat scarred his pride and set the tone for future personal, as well as athletic, competition with Kramer. The two fought insistently, publicly, often through the press, over the next twelve years, first as player against player, then as promoter (Kramer) against champion.

"What do you think of Kramer now?" I ask.

"We have a mutual respect," Pancho says, his face tightening. "Naturally, when he was number one, I was out to get him, just as I (and everyone else) am out to get Laver now, just as they were all out to get me when I was the best. But I think we have learned from each other and I believe we have benefited from our wars."

"Did it ever bother you that he was accepted not just as a player, but as a club man, welcome anywhere under any conditions as an American hero while you were the villain, invited only for tournaments, not socially right, too brown?"

"I suppose it did, sure. But I didn't let it get to me too much. If I walked into a club and they asked me to leave, I left. I'd just as soon play on public courts. That's where I learned to play in the first place. In fact, I don't know why the hell they don't build more public courts. It would keep the kids off the streets. If you love the game it doesn't matter where you play. And if you start thinking about vendettas when you're on the court—vendettas against Kramer, fans, clubs, officials, bigots, or anyone else—you're doomed. There's enough pressure from the match itself."

"But weren't you aware," I go on, not giving up, "of metaphorical dimensions of your matches with Kramer, how violently crowds took sides; every spectator with rebellion in his breast feeling victory when you won and defeat when you lost?"

"I know," says Gonzales, voice soft, face severe, "but that wasn't always a good thing. People tend to let others represent what they themselves would like to become and, as a result, they relax on themselves and tend to shirk their own responsibilities and development. You have to do it on your own, for yourself, alone."

Gonzales is right about Ulrich. Had he taken him for granted he would have walked away a loser. As it is, he needs five intense, exhausting sets to edge to success. Ulrich has a full blond beard and long blond hair, banded into pigtails, and he smiles beatifically after every long rally, no matter who wins the point. He refers to Gonzales as "the Master," but he makes "the Master" run and sweat and wheeze for every game he wants to win.

In the dressing room after the match, Gonzales is in pain, his legs aching with cramps. His brother Ralph wraps hot towels around his legs and massages them. Several reporters stand by, waiting for Pancho to speak, but afraid to ask a question. Finally, Pancho turns to them and says, "You know, if I were smart, I'd announce my retirement as soon as this tournament is over." He is silent for three counts as the reporters shuffle awkwardly. Then he smiles and says, "But I'm not smart."

He has the next day off and then, because it rains, the two after that. On the fourth day he meets Tony Roche, ranked second only to Laver, a rugged, left-handed Australian shepherd whom Gonzales stunned with a straight-set victory the year before at Forest Hills. But Roche has won each of their six matches since then and has been playing at the peak of his game all week. The court is soggy and footing is treacherous, but referee Mike Gibson, imported from Wimbeldon, has told Gonzales that he cannot wear spikes. Disgusted, sluggish, impotent before Roche's power, Gonzales loses the first set 6-3.

In the second, he knows that defeat will mean virtual loss of the match and elimination from the tournament. He chases every ball frantically, works into a consistent groove of control and force, and stays even through eighteen games. In the nineteenth, he is behind 15-30 on his serve and tries for a winner on a backhand volley, but he slips while making contact with the ball and nets it. On his way back to the baseline he slips again and nearly falls down. "God damn!" he bellows furiously. "You can't wear spikes, you can't wear *nothin'!*" Roche and ten thousand spectators sense the end. But Richard Gonzales is about to enter into one of those periods, one of those three- or four-game segments, one of those sustained moments of beauty, where no one alive, not even Rod Laver, can beat him. He runs off four consecutive points for the game and then, three games later, breaks Roche's serve to win the second set 12-10.

The inspiration runs into the third set as Pancho holds serve and then breaks Roche again in the second game. The delirious crowd, Tony Roche, and perhaps even Gonzales himself are beginning to think he may once more pull off the miraculous and win. But, suddenly, as suddenly as it had come, his power goes. Roche breaks him back in the third game, then again in the eleventh and walks off the court for intermission with a 2-1 lead in sets.

When Gonzales comes out for the fourth set, he is pale and stiff. There is no spring left in his legs, no tension in his arms, no lash in his strokes, no cunning in his game. Roche, with the certainty of a prizefighter who has his opponent pinned in a corner unconscious on his feet, slugs away freely, drubbing the ball, whipping Gonzales six games in a row. But even at the bottom, even in the agony of utter helplessness when this man who has always sought solitude is most totally alone, he has his moment of ecstasy and pride. He is behind 0-4 and 15–40 and he walks to the service line, beating the sweat from his brow with his left index finger, driving back his hair with his hand, rolling up his right sleeve. He glowers at Roche, then tosses the ball, parabolically, over his left shoulder and, weight thrust up from his right leg and buttocks into his shoulder and right arm, cocks and shoots for all, groaning—no, shrieking this time—and the ball blisters, invisibly, past his rival. An ace. An ace to remind the delirious crowd, Tony Roche, and, yes, Richard Gonzales too, who he once was and who, at rare and lovely times, he still is now.

Lew Alcindor's Life as a Pro

Roger Kahn | **1970**

The motel was called Quality Court, which means this was no Plaza Suite, and the black man lying under the brown blanket seemed endless and you had to wonder what was going to happen when he stood up. Would there be room for all of him under that low plasterboard ceiling?

"I have a hyperactive mind," the black man said. He threw his head from one side to another, as though in pain. "I have to clear my mind to play basketball, see? I can't have it all cluttered, man. That's why I look relaxed, but I'm not relaxed." He paused. His moments are full of silences. Then, "I'm all worked up, man, deep down inside."

The tall and troubled black was Ferdinand Lewis Alcindor, Jr. It had been difficult to get an appointment to see him. His employers at the Milwaukee Bucks appeared cowed, as well they might. The personage of Lew Alcindor may be more consequential than the Milwaukee basketball franchise. Certain press reports described Alcindor as mercenary, rude, possibly antiwhite. Finally, he had an unnerving recent record of aggressiveness toward opponents: one broken jaw, one knockout and one foiled attack in a few months. You go into this kind of interview carefully, preparing all the questions, gauging your subject, wondering about your own jaw.

That was how it had been but now it wasn't that way at all. Now I was sitting in this dreary room in St. Louis with a bright, sensitive, esthetic young man, wondering if he was going to bump his head and wondering, too, about the rest of us and the society that had made him both millionaire and nigger.

"I want to talk to you about race," I said.

Alcindor gazed at the wall. It was four o'clock in the afternoon of a game; the drapes were drawn and the only light came from a reading lamp on the night table. He was lying on his side, the great legs bent under the brown blanket, and the upper part of his body supported by an elbow. His body was curled so that he could lie with his head on the pillow and stare at the wall.

"How do you see your role in the black movement?"

He blinked. No other sign or motion.

"When Jackie Robinson broke in, it was enough, it was significant, for him to get base hits. That was enough."

Only his mouth moving, Alcindor said, "Because white people thought he wasn't good enough to do it."

"But it isn't enough anymore. Black intellectuals don't want black athletes for leaders. They feel there've been enough black symbols in sports and jazz."

Alcindor made a spasmodic nod. "I know that," he said. He lunged from the bed and began to stride. He bent slightly at the waist. There was room between his head and the ceiling, but he had better not jump.

"I'm figuring it out," Alcindor said, pacing, towering. "It's fragmented, man. Some go to church. Some go to school. Some do nothing. Some want revolt."

The black community at large. That was what he had decided to talk about. "Where do you stand?" I said.

"Try to get change as quickly and painlessly as possible." Alcindor returned to the bed. "Try to stand for something positive. Be something positive."

"What about violence?"

The body shifted under the blanket. Alcindor resumed considering the wall.

"What about violence on the basketball court?"

"You want to know what happened in Seattle. Tresvant hit me couple times. Bob Rule got a finger in my eye. Man, I went for Rule. And I spit. And a kid, some big-mouthed teen-ager, I gave him a shove. And I want to stand for something positive and I managed to have everyone

in the whole arena dislike me. I was a protagonist." Alcindor shook his
head. I thought he might spring up again. "These things you want me to
talk about," he said. "They're hard to put into words." He smiled and
scowled, as though in a private dialogue. I wondered if violence was
something he disliked.

"Lew. When you went for Bob Rule, did you mean to hurt him, or
just give him a shove?"

Alcindor turned and looked directly at me and said, quite evenly,
"When I went for Rule there was murder in my heart."

It is not going to add up. Of that, you can be assured. In a society
that does not add up, the Lew Alcindor phenomenon, frozen in full
flow, which is what we are trying to do, is not going to provide one of
those comfortable *Reader's Digest* summations, with smooth beginning,
anesthetic middle, tidy end. The Alcindor phenomenon is a mix of
rough edges, and incompleteness and immaturity and wisdom and
misinterpretations and rages and regrets. It makes Ray Patterson, president of the Bucks, discuss dimensions of maturity; and John Erickson,
the general manager, speak of uneven development; and Larry Costello, the coach, long for days which may never have been, when professional basketball players concerned themselves only with professional
basketball. These things are important, but important, too, is what Guy
Rodgers had to say. "Lew is a very nice guy, with a fine sense of humor,
a terrific person."

We were sitting over steak in a Milwaukee restaurant late at night.
Rodgers, at thirty-four, had played a brilliant game against Los Angeles, and his young wife, Lita, had just learned that their seven-month
old baby, who has an eye disorder, was not going to need an operation.
It was a cheerful time.

"Lew is your teammate," I said. "Suppose you didn't think much of
him? What would you tell me then?"

Rodgers was wearing steel-framed spectacles and an ascot. "You
didn't know me in Philadelphia," he told me.

"I was wondering," Lita said, "why we're having dinner with him, if
the story he's doing is about Lew."

Rodgers winced slightly.

"I wanted to have this dinner," Rodgers said, "because there are a
couple of things people ought to get straight.

"Ask anyone who really knew me in Philadelphia, and they'll tell you
I'm a pretty honest guy. If I didn't like Lew, maybe I wouldn't knock

him to you, but you can bet we wouldn't be having dinner right now. What I'm trying to say is that this is a special kind of kid, and I played with Wilt in the beginning and I've been in this league for a long time. Believe me, this kid is a rare human being."

That is something to remember as we work our way across the jagged edges. Alcindor at twenty-two has won the warmth and admiration and friendship of a fine old professional.

I had heard of Alcindor a long time ago, a gifted black from Inwood, which is a hilly section of Manhattan, far north of Harlem, with trees and grass and integration, to which vanguards of the black middle class escaped during the 1950s. He was Roman Catholic, or his parents were, and he burst upon us, a gloriously gifted young giant, at Power Memorial Academy, a Catholic prep, accompanied always by a white man, his coach, Jack Donohue. The coach hid Alcindor from the press and seemed to be his closest advisor, and right or wrong the word was that Jack Donohue was going to hang on to Alcindor's Achilles' tendons and follow him to a college job. The recruiting of Alcindor—he could have gone anywhere—produced at least one charge that Donohue was writing himself into the letter of intent. But then, to general surprise, Alcindor fled to UCLA, far from his old schoolyard, far from Donohue and far from his parents, who had moved to Queens.

The Alcindor era was the finest in UCLA basketball annals. The Bruins pivoting around him were chronic national champions. After that the only question was where he would play professionally and for how much. He was fortunate to graduate at a point when two leagues were battling. The Milwaukee Bucks, for the NBA, and the New York Nets, for the American Basketball Association, made offers. Alcindor settled on Milwaukee, a lovely city in many ways and in many ways a backwater, for a supposed $1,400,000. That is roughly $200,000 per foot and also, when you consider it, possibly more than the owners of a new and rather modest NBA franchise carry in a checking account. Then Alcindor began playing, with enough potential to draw this from Bob Cousy: "Alcindor is the only man I've seen with the possibility of combining Bill Russell's mental concentration with Wilt Chamberlain's physical dominance."

Later Alcindor crashed into print, selling three installments' worth of memoirs to *Sports Illustrated* for a reported $20,000, or about a dollar a word, which is more than John Keats or Langston Hughes ever earned. The memoir paired Alcindor with a talented, busy author named Jack Olsen, and offered us this quite early:

I'm going to tell you my life story . . . and if you think that it takes a lot of conceit for a 22-year-old basketball player to tell his life story, then that's your hang-up. The way things are in America today—and have been for 200 years—the story of any black man has meaning, even if he's a shoeshine "boy" or porter or your friendly neighborhood Uncle Tom.

That was the general tone. The story described how being called "nigger" had wounded Alcindor; friendly neighborhood coach Donohue had told him once, "You're acting just like a nigger." It presented background and outlook and anecdote, but always with a kind of insolence, which, I was to learn, was not entirely fair. It is a weakness of the genre, the collaborative form, never to be wholly true to either party. Two egos are working and sometimes clashing. When one man is white and the other black the conflict becomes more complex, and when both are working to provide a black life for a magazine that caters to affluent whites, the impure art form must be discolored. What we have is not pure Alcindor and not pure Olsen. Instead we have a hybrid: Olsendor.

On the telephone, John Erickson would not comment on the stories. "As general manager," he said, "it's my job to be concerned about Lew on the court. I make it a point not to interfere with other matters. He had every right to do those stories and he has every right to see or not to see whom he pleases."

I was making a pro-forma call before flying to Milwaukee. It is always a sound idea to check in with management; professional athletes are busy people, not always punctual or even reliable, and it can be helpful to have management arrange introductions.

"When can you get us together?" I asked Erickson.

"I can't get you together."

"But you're the Bucks."

"That's right, but as I say, aside from what goes on during the games, Alcindor is on his own."

I telephoned a newspaperman who had been covering Alcindor. "He can be very difficult," the newspaperman reported. "Says very little. Gets into fights. Not always cooperative."

After two more calls to the Bucks, one to the commissioner of the NBA and two to a California stockbroker who was supposed to be Alcindor's confidant, I mounted the jet to Milwaukee. There was not going to be any trouble seeing him, I was assured. And sure enough, when I went to the Milwaukee Arena there he was, in a sweatsuit of forest green and white, practicing lay-up shots—swish, swish, slam. The Bucks were going to play the Cincinnati Royals, who offer Oscar Robertson and an interesting supporting cast, with Connie Dierking, a somewhat fleshy six foot ten, playing center.

Alcindor seemed listless during the warm-up. His face was expressionless. Often he stood by himself. There was no enthusiasm to his moves, no adventure. He does not go out of his way to stuff shots and several times I had to remind myself of Cousy's quote and of another observer's remark: Alcindor possessed so much ability that he is a basketball third force all by himself.

Alcindor won the tap, but the Royals stole the ball. Robertson dribbled, jumped and scored. Then the Bucks drove. Alcindor, moving slowly, trailed everyone else. A shot missed. The Royals stormed. There were two fast passes. Suddenly Johnny Green laid up an easy shot. Where was Alcindor?

Two minutes into the game, Lew put in a pretty hook, spinning toward the center from a post on the left. Quickly Tom Van Arsdale hit a jump and Robertson drove, faked, fed to Dierking, who sank a lay-up. Alcindor looked confused. At the end of the quarter, Cincinnati led 33 to 20. Rodgers stirred the Bucks in the opening minutes of the next period but Dierking hit from the circle, then with a hook, then with a running lay-up. Alcindor still trailed plays, got himself boxed out, seemed out of things. Halfway through the second quarter, he was out of things. Larry Costello sat him down in favor of Dick Cunningham.

Alcindor returned for the second half and the Royals, more or less ignoring his presence, ran five straight baskets. Connie Dierking was dominating underneath. He scored at the rate of a basket a minute, until, four minutes into the half, Costello yanked Alcindor again. The Royals walked in that night, 129 to 104.

It is difficult to describe this late November performance except in terms of negatives. Alcindor did not often get position for rebounds and when he did, he would not fight for the ball. The statistician credited him with five rebounds for the first half, when the issue was in doubt, while Rodgers, more than a foot shorter, grabbed six. Overall, Alcindor took thirteen shots, several from underneath, and sank five. He scored just thirteen points. He was not a third force or any force at all. He was a cipher.

The Bucks' dressing room is closed for a time after each game, but on the other side, coach Cousy was smiling and relaxed and smoking a large cigar. "It isn't fair to comment on Alcindor's play tonight," Cousy said, making a comment. "He's a rookie and he's having troubles. It's hardest for rookies at center. But everything I said about his potential still goes."

The Bucks dress in cramped quarters; when I got there Larry Costello was obviously upset. "What is there to say about something like this?" he told Bob Wolf of the Milwaukee *Journal* and Lou Chapman of the *Sentinel*. "They didn't come to play."

"*Anything* good tonight, Coach?" Chapman said.

Costello made a little laugh. "In a game like that?"

"Rodgers," Chapman prompted.

"That's right," Costello said. "Guy did a good job."

I wandered toward Alcindor, who was dressing quickly, silently. He was neither friendly nor hostile. He was civil. "How's 4:30 tomorrow?" he said.

"Fine."

I returned to Costello, who was becoming more upset. The performance was disturbing him slowly but surely, like a bad clam. "I don't understand some of these guys," he said. "Here they play a terrible game like this, and now they're taking off, going their separate ways. It wasn't that way when I was playing." Costello gulped a soft drink from the bottle. He has a flat, pleasant, tough Irish face. "If we played one like this, we'd want to sit around for a long time and talk, talk among ourselves." At that moment, not twenty feet away, Alcindor slipped out of the dressing room alone.

"So many outside interests," Costello said. "So many things on the side."

"What about all that money?" a reporter said.

"Look, the more money a guy can get, the more power to him. And everybody on the team feels the same way. I'm just saying when it goes bad, sit around and talk. Stick around. Hang together like a team."

"You speaking of anyone in particular?" a reporter said.

Costello blinked. "Nah," he said. "Nobody in particular. I'm talking about the whole team."

The situation was charged in a community with an unhappy recent sports history. Milwaukee tried to support professional basketball in the early 1950s—Ben Kerner's Hawks. The community failed and the Hawks moved on to St. Louis, where they prospered until hockey swept down the Mississippi. Now the Hawks play out of Atlanta. In 1953, the Braves became the first of baseball's floating franchises by shifting from Boston to Milwaukee. There they were treated regally, plied with free beer, ogled by blondes and responded by becoming a National League power. A slight slump and whoosh, quicker than you can say capital gains, the Braves are in Atlanta. "If General Sherman were still alive, they wouldn't dare try that stuff," one of the Milwaukee blondes, now graying, pointed out recently.

Enter the Bucks, organized by a syndicate that includes Wes Pavalon, a man of means and a goatee, who rides chauffeured limousines thanks to his invention, Career Academy. The new spirit has moved someone to song:

> "Milwaukee Bucks! That's the name of our team,
> And they will win, with an effort supreme.
> Milwaukee Bucks! How they handle the ball,
> And they break great, whether they're short or tall."

They did not break great a year ago. The Bucks won twenty-seven games, finished last in the East and the NBA guide spelled their name "Milwuakee." At about this time, when the rustlings of spring 1969 stirred, the downbeat Milwaukee trail and the upbeat road of Lew Alcindor intersected.

The NBA operated with a draft and since Milwaukee and Phoenix, last in each division, were expansion teams, commissioner Walter Kennedy drew cards to see who would have the first pick, then the call. The card came up Phoenix. The call was heads. The coin came up tails. Milwaukee had won.

"Whooop!" cried Wes Pavalon, embracing John Erickson and burning one of Erickson's ears with his cigarette. That was the beginning of Milwaukee's Alcindor ambiguities.

In Encino, a San Fernando Valley city where Alcindor holed up with a friend, Lew was aware that a fortune awaited. But he was conscious too that blacks were once peddled from the slavers' block. He didn't want that; it had been humiliating. There is a song Paul Robeson used to sing: "No more auction block for me." "There won't be any bidding for me," Alcindor decided. "Each team [Milwaukee and the New York Nets of the American Basketball Association] can make one offer. Then I'll pick the one I like."

Everyone, from Pavalon to Alcindor, promised that the Milwaukee offer would be kept secret. The figure of $1,400,000 comes from an excellent source, but that source can provide no detailed breakdown. "Probably it will be spread at about $300,000 a year." Suffice it, then, that Alcindor appears to have been paid three and a half times what Joe Namath appeared to have been paid to become a professional athlete.

Lew talked to Milwaukee on a Monday and to the New York Nets on a Tuesday. He decided quickly for the Bucks. "All things being equal, it would have been easier to play in New York, but things were not equal."

When his decision became known, an ABA spokesman made the doomsday bid. To play for the Nets, Alcindor could have a $500,000 cash bonus, five years each at $200,000 salary, an annuity of $62,500 a year for twenty years starting at forty-one, 10 percent of a proposed ABA television contract and 5 percent of the Nets franchise. Alcindor declined. "I told each of them," he said, "to make one offer. I'm sticking to that. I'm going to Milwaukee."

Pat Boone, the singer, is one of the ABA's backers. "Our negotiator blew it," Boone announced in California. Lawyers for the ABA brought an action against the NBA charging that the teams in the older league "conspired to jointly purchase a superstar through the use of defendant's combined powers." What that means, aside from the point that lawyers split infinitives, is that the ABA did not believe Messrs. Pavalon et al. carried a spare $1,400,000. Instead, the ABA was asserting that there had been a kind of subscription throughout the NBA to finance the Milwaukee bid, and thus keep Alcindor out of the new league. This litigation may be one reason why neither Erickson, nor Alcindor, nor Pavalon will disclose the terms of the signing.

At any rate, on Wednesday, April 3, Alcindor affixed his Ferdinand Lewis to a Bucks contract. "It's a dream come true," Pavalon said. John Erickson said he was thrilled not only because of Alcindor's skill, but "because of the quality of the person. He carried on his contract talks with the greatest trust and integrity I've been a part of." Larry Costello said he expected to play Lew at both a high and low post. "Lew has the talent to shoot from outside," he said, "but since he's seven four, I'd rather have him under the basket."

Officially, Alcindor was, and is, seven feet one and three-eighths. Had Costello let something slip? One more mystery. Erickson moved to the microphone and said smoothly, "Lew appears to have grown today because he has entered the business world."

Alcindor then answered a few dozen questions courteously and for the most part well. Yes, the ABA actually had made that $3,250,000 offer, but only after it appeared in the newspapers. Yes, he thought the ABA had demeaned itself. Yes, he did look forward to dunking again because it would be good playing basketball the way it was meant to be played. Yes, he had a boyhood idol, Jackie Robinson. Yes, he'd had some bad experiences with the press, but 85 percent of the experiences were good. No, he couldn't describe his impressions of Milwaukee. He hadn't really seen it yet. The Milwaukee press was delighted and after touching base with his parents in New York, he flew back to California, a dignified, literate and now wealthy man who had only "a few inconsequential courses" to complete for his degree and who had earned a little time for quiet breathing.

Trouble shattered the quiet in June. Playing what is described as a pick-up game at a Los Angeles high school, presumably for fun, Alcindor suddenly lost control of himself. According to one witness, Alcindor's team was taking the ball out of bounds when "Lew turned and threw a punch and walked off the court and left the gym." There is enormous leverage in those lank arms: Alcindor's punch struck the jaw of one Dennis Grey, six feet eight and 215 pounds. The jaw was fractured and surgeons at Hollywood Presbyterian Hospital had to wire it together.

Grey was under contract to the Los Angeles Stars of the ABA. A teammate, Warren Davis, said, "There was the usual shoving that occurs when guys are tired, but Dennis couldn't understand why Lew hit him." Grey consulted a lawyer and presently sued Alcindor for $750,000. "Frankly," said Grey's lawyer, Paul Caruso, "the injury may have ruined Dennis' basketball career."

The suit was still pending when Alcindor joined the Bucks and, despite a sprained ankle, he worked out impressively. The Bucks were not simply a changed team. They were a new team, capable on any night of defeating anyone. They would not be last and although they would not win, they were certain of reaching the NBA playoffs. Lew could drive and dribble as no big man before him. He had a remarkable eye. He had speed and quickness, which are different things, and grace and intelligence, and he was tough.

On October 31, the Bucks defeated the Philadelphia 76ers for the first time since the dawn of man, and that night, Alcindor's temper burst again. It was rough under the boards. Darrall Imhoff, who is shorter than Alcindor but just as heavy, had been shoving and elbowing underneath. Suddenly, in the second quarter, Alcindor swung his right elbow full force into the back of Imhoff's neck. Imhoff fell forward onto all fours, the way fighters sometimes do, and stayed there on knees and elbows too dazed to move. Alcindor walked to midcourt. He placed both hands on his hips and watched impassively. Imhoff could not play again until the second half.

The Philadelphia crowd began to hoot. When Alcindor fouled out

late in the game, he responded smartly to the boos. He gave a "V" sign
—victory and peace. The boos continued. Alcindor clenched a fist and
held it high. Black Power.

"I have no comment," he said in the dressing room.

A Philadelphia sportswriter said, "Could it be that you wanted to hit
Imhoff, but not around the head?"

"I have no comment," Alcindor repeated.

But Luke Jackson, six feet nine and 240, had a comment for Philadelphia. "That was dirty," he said. "Deliberate and malicious. If I'd had
an opening later, I would have nailed him."

Trouble with the Milwaukee press flowered the next month. In Milwaukee nearly everyone reads the *Journal*, a fine, fat afternoon and
Sunday paper. Each weekend the *Journal* carries a slick, nicely written
magazine section called *Insight*. Because Alcindor was important autumn news, George Lockwood, who edits *Insight*, assigned a writer
named Evans Kirkby to prepare a feature. The story was cast as a visit,
a rather easygoing account of a reporter's adventures and impressions
as he pays call on a celebrity. Conversation gives a "visit" thrust; the
subject, ideally, is voluble.

Whatever Alcindor's natural inclinations, he had already made his
$20,000 arrangement with *Sports Illustrated*. For the money he had to
promise not only his life story, but also exclusivity. In effect, until the *S.
I.* series appeared, he could grant interviews only provided they were
dull.

Trying to be true to his word to the national magazine, Alcindor an-
tagonized the man from the local paper. "My first attempt to meet Alcindor," Kirkby began, "had been a social and professional failure."
He found the rookie "aloof in speech and habit." Alcindor was brusque
and late. "When the photographer said he thought he had what he
wanted," Kirkby wrote, "Alcindor turned, a West Pointer doing an
about-face, and strode off to change his clothes. He did not say good-
bye." Kirkby called his article "A *Short* Visit with Lew Alcindor." It's a
fact that bad press feeds itself. If one experience is sour, why try to
make the next sweet? Damn 'em all.

In Detroit, Alcindor walked into a press conference arranged for him
by the Pistons and, according to Detroit *Free Press* columnist, Joe
Falls, "Never have I seen such a discourteous display." By Falls' account, Alcindor refused to answer questions or made one-word answers
or simply grunted. "Farewell, Alcindorella," Falls began an ensuing
column. Alcindor, he added, "is one of the smallest men I have ever
met."

Finally, at about the time I was asking Erickson about arranging an appointment, came the Seattle blowup. The Bucks held a three-point lead, before thirteen thousand at the Seattle Center Coliseum, with fifteen seconds to play. Alcindor held the ball near a foul line, looking to pass. Then Bob Rule tied him up. The referee called a jump. In abrupt fury, Alcindor lunged at Rule. All four teammates grabbed him. The Bucks called time.

As the team huddled, Larry Costello said, "Let them shoot. We've got three points. Just don't foul. We don't want to give them a three-point play."

When action resumed, Alcindor lost the jump. Three seconds later he fouled Lucius Allen, an old UCLA teammate, as Allen took a short shot. Costello gazed in agony. The ball dipped into the basket and spun out. No three-point play. Still Allen would have three chances to make two free throws.

That was Alcindor's sixth foul and as he walked off, fans jeered. He responded by spitting on the court. Allen made only one of three, the Bucks won by two points and as they started toward the dressing room, a teen-ager ran toward Alcindor shouting, "You big bum." One sweep of the giant arm, and the teen-ager was knocked to the floor.

In the dressing room, a reporter said, "Were they too rough out there?" "Yeah," Alcindor said. He picked up his suitcase and stormed out.

Greg Smith, a young Milwaukee forward, stood nearby. "Look," he said to the reporter, "this is not a good time for him."

Costello was less charitable. "This is a game where there is a lot of contact. Guys are bumping you all the time. If Lew ever gets mad like that at the beginning of a game, he might ruin his whole game."

So there we were, a few days and that terrible Cincinnati night later, in the motel room in St. Louis, Alcindor and I trying to understand what was happening.

"It gets me," he said from under the brown blanket, "the way people say now you've got the money, you've got contentment. The money makes for a stability, but there are pressures, man. Out there you're a vector for all the hostility in the stands. It all comes and they're shouting that I'm not hustling and that I stink and I'm a bum. Maybe there are some bad calls; the refs miss some or call something they shouldn't. And all that's happening, you know, and you're trying to be positive and you know if you let all this upset you, you can lose your mind. Sometimes I think about what Wilt said in the beginning. Turn on. Tune in. Get out."

He talked about his background after that. He has traced his family back to the Caribbean, through a great aunt, and he had heard of a forebear who stood almost six ten. "I don't know how well he moved. They say he had flat feet. The name Alcindor is originally Moorish," he said.

"I know 'al' means 'the.' What about the rest?"

"The firebird," he said. "You know, the bird that rises from its own ashes. That's what Alcindor means."

His father, a trombone player, attended Juilliard, one of the finest classical music schools on earth, but because classical musical organizations retain frightful prejudices, he had to go to work in the New York subway. Imagine years spent studying Brahms and Bach and Beethoven, great longings expressed in exquisite sound, and then, because of the color of your skin, having to listen everyday to the subway's atonal, grinding roar.

"I don't turn on to Beethoven myself," Alcindor said. "I don't know why. A Miles [Davis] record was fine, but not the classical stuff. My Dad, he's the expert in that area."

Growing, Alcindor went from six three to six eleven in two and a half years, from the seventh to the ninth grades. He was a good all-round athlete, swimming, running track, playing baseball, and he says he did not mind the tremendous rate of growth, although for a while his knees hurt constantly. He always wanted to win in whatever he did; he took pride in winning.

"What about your temper?" I said. "Has that always been a problem?"

He sat up in the bed. "It was when I was very small, until about the sixth grade. Then I got it under control and I thought I had it under control until this year."

Bob Rule is black; Alcindor has gone after blacks and whites with fine impartiality. Still I wondered about the fan in Seattle.

"There was nothing racial there," Alcindor said. "I just didn't like what he said. I shouldn't have spit and I should have ignored the kid."

"Do you get much racial needling? Does that trigger things?"

He shook his head. "I don't hear any of that; just once in a while in the mail I get a letter that calls me a no-good nigger."

We talked about Jackie Robinson, and how Jack had heard nigger almost daily in the beginning, and how Eddie Stanky once held up a pair of shoes in the St. Louis dugout and screamed at Robinson, "Hey, porter. Shine these."

Alcindor seemed surprised. "Stanky did that? What did Robinson do?"

"He took it; he had to take it, but maybe he stole an extra base."

We considered the press. Alcindor insisted that he would never give up his right to privacy. It was very difficult in Milwaukee. "I like to walk and I could walk in California, but in Milwaukee as soon as I step outside I get mobbed." He had been interviewed while at UCLA, but that was nothing like what was going on now, when the press wanted him all the time, it seemed.

"You better get used to it," I said.

He turned and gazed.

"You're going to play for a while, maybe fifteen years. Well, you better be ready for fifteen years of interviewing. That's part of what all the money is for."

"I don't have to give up my privacy," Alcindor said. "I'm not peddling that."

I remembered Roger Maris and the year of his sixty-one home runs; sixty-five journalists attached themselves to the Yankees and put questions to him day after day. The same faces asking the same questions.

Alcindor grimaced.

"He got good questions," I said, "and stupid questions and rude questions. Somebody from *Time* magazine asked if he played around on the road. He handled all the questions pretty well."

"What bothers me," Alcindor said, "are stupid questions. Somebody asks a stupid question, man, I think, Why are you taking up my time?"

Sometimes a seemingly stupid question is a reporter's way of starting a subject talking. (Other times, to be sure, it is simply a stupid question.) But what seemed to me to be the point for Alcindor was that he accept the questions with grace. Like jump shots, they are a part of his professional life.

He mentioned feeling good about his past. He had left the Catholic Church to become an orthodox Muslim because that was his true heritage. The book that influenced him most was *The Autobiography of Malcolm X*. He spoke a number of languages, including Yoruba, a West Nigerian dialect. At length in the motel, he seemed to enjoy talking; seemed happy to be able to describe himself and his heritage; seemed relieved to be able to say that yes, the press vs. personal privacy was a problem; seemed unburdened to review the story events of Seattle and to concede that he, proud Lew Alcindor, had been wrong. His movements became less spasmodic. He talked in longer sentences. He listened hard. When Flynn Robinson, his roommate for this trip, walked in and began to dab at his hair, Alcindor said amiably, "That won't help. They'll still see your bald spot."

I rose to go and Alcindor stood and from his great height extended a hand. "Good luck, tonight," I told him.

"I'll need it," Alcindor said. Then quite warmly, "If you think we ought to talk some more, I'm available. Just get me the word."

We were a short walk from the restaurant Stan Musial runs. The Bucks were going to play Atlanta that night in the St. Louis Arena. Ben Kerner had arranged the game, which would benefit a local charity and honor a number of old stars from the St. Louis Hawks. I went to the arena on foot, the better to think, and passing Musial's, the contrast was almost too pat. Stan had answered questions with grace and charmed the press (and kept his private life private) with the same ease he displayed when he clubbed a hanging curve. Now here was Alcindor to whom everything, except perhaps the $1,400,000, was coming so hard.

Traffic was filling the St. Louis street. There was going to be a crowd at the arena. I had been here often for hockey, but tonight was basketball and as cars turned by me toward the parking lot, more Negroes were coming than I had ever seen come here to watch the Blues.

It was foolish then to contrast Alcindor with Musial. Alcindor, to you and me, may be one of the great athletes of the era; to himself he is one of the significant *black* athletes. He carries all that heritage within him, a sense of black aristocracy and black dignity and how the Moors were warriors and how his uprooted family was supposedly free in a society which condemned a Juilliard man to work in subways.

Then it was game time.

The Hawks have a fine young center in Jim Davis, but not Davis, nor I suspect Bill Russell, could have done much with Alcindor that night. He blocked a shot by Bill Bridges, then hit a little jumper. Len Chappell and Jon McGlocklin scored and the Hawks were driving hard, but for the first seven minutes Alcindor was as close to perfection as a mortal basketball player can be. In quick succession, he dropped in a beautiful hook, swept the other backboard, came back, dribbled out of a high post, drove like a forward and sank a jump, swept the other board again, raced back and dropped home a fifteen footer. He scored twelve points in six and a half minutes. More than that he showed an incredible combination of speed and cool and quickness. The quarter ended with the Bucks ahead 34 to 22. The difference, of course, was Alcindor.

The Hawks charged back in the second period, but in the end Milwaukee won 130 to 115. "We were collapsing on Alcindor all night," complained Richie Guerin, the Hawks' coach, "but we were collapsing stupid."

Alcindor's opening spurt had confused or panicked the Hawks. That changed the game. He finished with thirty-three points, six assists and thirteen rebounds, but the numbers don't tell it. He dominated. "How do you feel?" I said in the dressing room.

"Redemption time," he said, and grinned.

The next night, back in Milwaukee, he played another splendid game, but my eye was caught by Rodgers, who in a few spurts moved the ball beautifully and drilled passes through openings that had not seemed to exist. That was the evening Rodgers and I were to go out. I stopped at Alcindor's locker and told him how much I'd liked Rodgers' passing.

"I liked it, too," Alcindor said. He looked relaxed. "Hey," he said. "Rodgers could get the ball to Jimmy Hoffa, and he's in jail."

It was my turn to grin and thank him. He was doing one of the kinder things an athlete can do for a writer; he was throwing me a line.

What surely can we take from these few days in the life of Lew Alcindor? Something about the man and something about the times in which we live.

The pressure is enormous. He generates a good deal himself with inner drives, but much of it hangs ominously, there, always there, never dissipating. He is potentially *the* black athlete of this era, as Jackie Robinson was the black athlete of another. His role is not more difficult than Robinson's—after all, the Klan is not threatening to shoot Alcindor for what he did to the Atlanta team. But it is more complex. The black movement has become more complex.

He is no racist; most of his closest advisers are white. Nor is he militant, in the sense that Stokely is. But he is more militant than, say, Willie Mays, because he is of a later generation, and this goes hard with some.

He accepts advice from others on income spreading and such; one suspects that the lawyers who read the *Sports Illustrated* contract for him advised him badly. Starting in a new city $1,400,000 ahead, what should have come first was new relationships, not additional cash. By allowing one magazine to dictate his relationships to all magazines and newspaper and television stations, the lawyers did him no favor. He could have demanded less restrictive terms from *Sports Illustrated,* or simply put off composing his autobiography until he reached the advanced age of twenty-three. By then, working relationships in Milwaukee and around the league would have been established. He feels enough pressure this first year on the basketball court, without a sideshow of fencing with the press.

But he is a great athlete and a strong man and to me a winning person. At twenty-two, this proud, intense black has magnificent moments and dreadful ones which, if memory serves, is what being twenty-two is like. It is going to be a pleasure to watch his poise and understanding grow; almost as much of a pleasure as it will be to watch him play basketball as no one ever has for the next ten or fifteen years.

Terry Bradshaw

The Making of a Number-One Draft Choice

Roy McHugh | **1970**

On this last Tuesday morning of January, in a small room illuminated by harsh winter sunlight, Art Rooney, Jr., sat at the foot of a T-shaped walnut table and waited for a telephone to ring. Neat lists of football players' names were chalked on blackboards hanging from the walls. A football player when he attended St. Vincent College, bushy-haired at thirty-four and wearing oversized black-rimmed glasses, Art Rooney, Jr., is personnel director of the Pittsburgh Steelers, the professional team owned by his father, and in bulk he compared with the coaches in the room. As ten o'clock approached, the room was silent. Exactly at ten, the phone rang. Art Rooney, Jr., the receiver cupped to his ear, listened for a moment and said, "Bradshaw."

The Pittsburgh Steelers, first team to choose in the 1970 pro football draft, had announced their selection. At a desk in a ballroom of the Belmont Plaza Hotel in New York, facing television lights and platoons of reporters, a Steeler representative sped the word to Commissioner Pete Rozelle, who stood by. And soon, with dramatic pauses, Rozelle was talking into a microphone, saying:

"Pittsburgh. . . .

"First choice in the first round. . . .

"Terry Bradshaw, quarterback from Louisiana Tech. . . ."

When the news reached the offices of the Philadelphia Eagles, draft headquarters for BLESTO-V, a talent scouting service available to the Chicago, Detroit, Philadelphia, Pittsburgh and Minnesota teams, eleven men jumped to their feet and cheered. BLESTO-V is a name that resulted from compressing the initials of something once called the Bears-Lions-Eagles-Steelers Talent Organization, the V at the end standing for Vikings, who joined the group tardily. At a meeting in Pittsburgh six weeks before the draft, having assessed and minutely graded a thousand college football players, the BLESTO-V scouts, gathered now in Philadelphia, had pronounced Terry Bradshaw the best of them all.

BLESTO-V's appraisal of Bradshaw was a trade secret. In those considerable areas of the nation where Louisiana Tech is not a household name, it would have dumfounded the average football fan. Louisiana Tech—officially, Louisiana Polytechnic Institute—is in Ruston, Louisiana. Its games with Northeast Louisiana and Southeast Louisiana, Northwest Louisiana and Southwest Louisiana, McNeese State and East Carolina merit one line of type in the Sunday morning editions of big-city newspapers. Accordingly, the world for the most part was unaware of Terry Bradshaw until *The New York Times*, early last November, identified him as news fit to print. A feature story on Bradshaw appeared in the *Times*, but the BLESTO V scouts and their professional rivals had no need to read it for educational purposes. "Lord God," said Jess Thompson, the BLESTO scout who covers Louisiana, Texas, Mississippi, and Arkansas, "*all* of us knew about him."

Scouts are reverent, brave, and possibly also trustworthy when they describe Terry Bradshaw. He reminds them, simultaneously, of Joe Namath, of Roman Gabriel, of Sonny Jurgensen, even of Li'l Abner. Will Walls, a BLESTO scout who caught Sammy Baugh's passes at Texas Christian University, says that Bradshaw has a "better arm" than Baugh did. Scouts use such adjectives as "better" and "best," "strongest" and "quickest" glibly in discussing Bradshaw. The very sight of him spurs them to hyperbole. It was Jess Thompson, at his first glimpse of Bradshaw in the flesh, who saw him as Li'l Abner come to life. Bradshaw has extravagantly blond hair, resembling, in that respect, Daisy Mae rather than Li'l Abner, but a squarejawed, snub-nosed, ingenuous face with deep-set blue eyes. He is big and raw-boned. His mere dimensions, however—six feet two and a half and 215 pounds—do not convey an adequate idea of his appearance, for the massive upper arms, developed by weightlifting and summertime ditchdigging, contribute indeed to an impressive top-heavy look suggestive of Li'l Abner. His actions, in the heat of a football game, are brisk and decisive. Even when he is scrambling or improvising, he always seems sure of his next move. And he throws with a snapping overhand delivery, cutting the ball through the air at high speed for great distances. Y. A. Tittle, no scout but an authority on quarterbacks, having been one, has seen Bradshaw play, and he says the Steelers should charge admission to watch him warm up.

In Art Rooney, Jr.'s office, there's a gray metal filing cabinet. It contained, in the fall of 1966, on a small sheet of paper called an underclassman form, two expository sentences about Terry Bradshaw: "Best arm on a freshman quarterback I've ever seen" and "World's high school javelin champion." (The latter may have taken in a little too much territory. Bradshaw merely held the U.S. high-school javelin record—244 feet 11 inches.) The author of that report was a BLESTO scout named Jim Palmer, Jess Thompson's predecessor in the Louisiana-Texas-Mississippi-Arkansas area. No one had read it except the filing clerk, a gray-haired, middle-aged woman. Terry Bradshaw was a freshman in 1966, and for a scout to report on a freshman is almost unimaginable. Art Rooney, Jr., never looks at underclassman forms. "We have a thousand seniors to think about," the personnel director explains.

If Louisiana Tech was an unlikely place for Jim Palmer to discover the best arm he had ever seen attached to a freshman, the reason Bradshaw was there had nothing to do with anyone's lack of perception. During Bradshaw's last year at Woodlawn High School in Shreveport, Louisiana, he attracted the favorable attention of Baylor University's head coach, Johnny Bridgers, later to become the backfield coach of the Steelers. Bridgers inspected films of Bradshaw, and, certain that he could play in the Southwest Conference, made phone calls and visits to Shreveport and invited him to the Baylor campus.

Baylor is rigidly Baptist and so was Terry Bradshaw's upbringing, with its curfews and rules about Sunday school attendance, its prohibitions against smoking and drinking. Terry's father, Bill Bradshaw, was a self-made man who had been on his own since the age of thirteen, after running away from his home in the Tennessee hills when his parents split up. Construction worker, bus driver, short-order cook, he had staked himself to a patchwork education of numerous correspondence courses and fifty-seven credit hours in "colleges all over Louisiana," his path leading eventually to a plant manager's job with the American Machine and Foundry Co. But Baylor was not for Bill Bradshaw's son.

On a trip through the dormitories, Bill Bradshaw said later, Terry had noticed whisky bottles. Another story, never formally authenticated, was that Baylor had lost interest in Terry because of his score on the college boards test. In New Orleans it has been printed that Terry had failed the test for admission to Louisiana State, which was also recruiting him, but turned down a chance to take it again, having decided on Tech.

With the slightly strained patience of one who is forced to repeat the same explanation over and over, Terry spells out the advantages of Louisiana Tech—its location, "seventy miles from Shreveport," the "real good brand of football," the pro-style offense favored by the coaching staff, the new stadium, "seating 25,000." The lack of publicity never bothered Terry. "I figured if I was good enough to play pro ball, I'd get my chance," he says. "The scouts come around to the small colleges, too."

He was still just a freshman, trying to make the varsity team in spring practice, when Jim Palmer went back for another look. Projecting six months into the future, Palmer wrote: "Has quickest delivery and strongest arm I've ever seen on a sophomore." Filing clerks in the various offices of BLESTO-V clients may have discerned a faintly monotonous quality in Palmer's literary style, but there were also these negative notations: "doesn't scramble well" and "needs game experience."

The game experience came the following season, when Bradshaw divided the quarterback job with a senior the scouts referred to simply as "Robinson." Jess Thompson, replacing Jim Palmer, carefully recorded Bradshaw's passing statistics and labeled him "a fine future prospect." The passing statistics were nothing remarkable, but Thompson, looking back on it, drawls, "Ah don't know, you kind of feel 'em or smell 'em. He was a pro all the way."

In the spring of 1968—Bradshaw would be a junior that fall—the sniffing of the scouts became audible to him. He observed them at practice—big, quiet men with the screaming unobtrusiveness of hotel detectives. The head coach, Maxie Lambright, would say to him, "So-and-so's here for a look at you. Don't worry about it, just get out there and throw the ball like you can." Bradshaw understood that Maxie Lambright was scrutinizing his poise.

"He's a very humble young man," Maxie Lambright once said of Bradshaw. "If he's got any bad habits, I don't know about 'em. He doesn't smoke or drink, but even if he did I think he'd play for us." Enthusiastically, Bradshaw had joined the Fellowship of Christian Athletes. Youth director at the Baptist church in Ruston, he enjoyed giving inspirational talks to audiences of children, telling them that by hard work they could achieve their goals but to bear in mind that the glory belonged to God. Early in life he had thought of the ministry, but decided that "God would rather have me play football," God's eye for a quick delivery and a strong arm being equal, apparently, to Jim Palmer's.

For the preservation of that arm, Bradshaw had given up the javelin. As a junior, he passed for twenty-two touchdowns and almost three thousand yards, Louisiana Tech winning eight of ten games. Before that season was well along Jess Thompson had sent a message to Will Walls, a BLESTO superscout whose job is to check on the area scouts. "We've got a dinger over here," Jess Thompson said. "I think I've seen the best arm I ever saw."

Will Walls was the first scout to say positively that Bradshaw would be a first-round draft choice. There was a striking repetitiousness in the observations the scouts collected from college coaches who had seen Bradshaw play. They were all of the same opinion: that Bradshaw's arm was extraordinary, that his vision was keen, his wrists flexible, his ability to "set up" unexcelled. Art Rooney, Jr., began to read the reports when the 1969 draft was out of the way and Bradshaw's underclassman forms went into the thick, looseleaf, black-covered notebook in which Rooney keeps track of seniors. And Chuck Noll, the new head coach of the Steelers, requested films from Louisiana Tech. His verdict on Bradshaw was: "Boy, he has a real rifle arm!"

Jess Thompson noted that Bradshaw was getting "actual pro-type instruction" from Maxie Lambright, who had been a quarterback at Mississippi Southern when Thompson was line coach there, and from backfield coach Mickey Slaughter, who had played the position at Louisiana Tech and with the Denver Broncos. Last fall Thompson sat in the stands on the Saturday afternoon that Louisiana Tech lost to his and Lambright's old school, now the University of Southern Mississippi; it was Tech's only defeat until the post-season Grantland Rice Bowl. Then and there, Thompson said, he realized Terry Bradshaw was "the number-one boy in the country." "Southern Mississippi," he remembers, wincing, "just physically whipped Louisiana Tech's line and Terry got racked something awful. But he just never quit, he never slowed down, he stood in there throwing the ball like he owned the park, throwing on target all the time, and he passed for 248 yards." Bradshaw, Thompson put down on paper, "could be a superstar."

Art Rooney, Jr., willing to believe, headed for Ruston. He stopped first at Grambling College, three miles outside of Ruston, which in recent years has been an assembly line for draft choices. Eddie Robinson, the black head coach there, said, "Oh, you've got to see this guy Bradshaw, he's the greatest thing going." Rooney drove into Ruston with pleasant expectations.

Ruston is a placid college town, undefiled by the smokestacks of industry. Up north, the weather was getting cold, but in Ruston green leaves clung to the trees and for comfort Rooney drove with the air-conditioner turned on in his car.

Two months before, when the Steelers were in Baton Rouge for an exhibition game, Rooney had taken care of the Tech coaches' ticket needs, and now they received him affably. They set up a movie projector and in muggy darkness Rooney watched films.

Later, at practice, he saw Bradshaw throw. He was deeply interested. After a while Rooney turned to a nearby student manager, who was gathering up footballs and stuffing them into a sack.

"What kind of a guy is Bradshaw?" Rooney asked.

The student manager, tall and dark, paused in his task and straightened up.

"Wonderful guy," he said with a radiant smile.

Rooney kept asking questions about Bradshaw. The student manager's answers grew progressively more lyrical.

"You sound like a relative," Rooney said.

"I'm his brother."

Gary Bradshaw, one year older than Terry, had been a football player until he fell from a tree, breaking his back. Rooney was probing him for "headshrinker stuff." Did Terry respect his father? (Very much, which meant he'd be coachable.) Did he drink? (Whatever Maxie Lambright may have thought, he'd take a beer; and Rooney approved of that, being vaguely mistrustful of ascetics.) Did he like girls? ("He sure does," Gary laughed; once again, Rooney approved.)

Terry Bradshaw was looking better and better. Rooney began to think of him as a player who would be a top draft pick, equating him, for the first time, with Mike Phipps of Purdue, the quarterback most frequently mentioned in newspaper stories about Heisman Trophy candidates. The Steelers, who had won their opening game, were now losing week after week, but there was "no way," Rooney felt, that they could finish with the worst record in professional football and thus be eligible for first choice in the draft. He hoped that by the time their turn came around they would still have a shot at Ronnie Shanklin, an elusive pass receiver from North Texas State.

Art's brother Dan, older and smaller, the Steelers' vice-president and ranking shirtsleeve executive—Art Rooney, Sr., who is sixty-eight, takes no part in the day-to-day front-office management—was not as starry-eyed. On a frosty Sunday in November, watching the Steelers lose disgracefully to the Chicago Bears, his accustomed good humor slipping away, Dan Rooney knew they'd be 1-13 for the season.

The season would end on December 21. On December 10, the BLESTO-V scouts met in Pittsburgh to arrive at their final evaluations of a thousand college players. From that day on, says Art Rooney, Jr., it was certain that Terry Bradshaw would be the first player chosen in the draft. In the BLESTO-V ratings—the lower the rating, the better—Bradshaw scored a 1.3, higher than Norm Bulaich, running back from TCU, or Mike McCoy, defensive tackle from Notre Dame, or Phil Olsen, defensive tackle from Utah State, or Cedric Hardman, defensive end from North Texas, but the ratings are based on a player's probable effectiveness in his rookie year, and because quarterbacks develop at such a leisurely pace, Bradshaw's 1.3 was superior to Bulaich's or McCoy's 1.0. After the BLESTO meeting, a scout walked up to Rooney and said, "This guy's like buying Xerox. There might not be another one like him for twenty years."

Dan Rooney's premonition was accurate. The Steelers wound up with a 1–13 record, losing their final game on a touchdown in the last fifty seconds, but the Chicago Bears also were 1-13. In January, at New Orleans, two days before the Super Bowl game, a coin flip would determine whether the Bears or the Steelers drafted first.

The season had been over just a matter of hours when Chuck Noll and his backfield coach, Johnny Bridgers, were flying to Miami, where college all-star teams from the North and South would be playing on Christmas day. Noll, thirty-eight, compactly built, is a thoughtful and even a cultivated man with a soft, deliberate way of speaking. In the previous three months, though he had tuned in a college game on a television set every Saturday, he had spent little time considering draft choices. In any event, he was not keen on drafting a quarterback, for the Steelers' second-round choice in 1969 had been Terry Hanratty, the Notre Dame cover boy from Butler, Pennsylvania, near Pittsburgh.

Troubled, as most rookies are, by a preoccupation with the opposing team's rush, Hanratty failed to distinguish himself greatly last year. Noll, the truth is, had not expected him to, sharing in the popular conviction that quarterbacks ripen slowly.

But Noll was extremely impressed by Bradshaw in Miami. "He's an athlete," Noll said to himself when Bradshaw walked onto the practice field. Then he saw Bradshaw throw. "I was startled," Noll said. "I knew from the films that he had a strong arm, but a film doesn't measure intensity."

In the lobby of the South team's hotel, Johnny Bridgers chatted with Bradshaw, subtly recruiting him for the second time. Noll met Bradshaw on the practice field. The meeting was brief, just a handshake and hello after South coach Bill Peterson had introduced them, and Bradshaw seemed distant, absorbed, impatient to resume throwing a football.

That day he had pulled a hamstring muscle. Although practice was over, he intended to stay on the field and throw to several willing receivers. The South's other quarterback, Bill Cappleman, happened to be from Florida State, where Peterson was head coach, and Bradshaw could sense that he was not going to start.

The draft, he would say later, occupied just a nook in the back of his mind. " 'Course, I'd be lying if I said I'd forgotten it completely, but no, sir, I never started thinking I'd be a first choice," he went on. "I heard rumors, but I didn't believe it would ever happen. There was Phipps, there was McCoy."

On Christmas day, Phipps started at quarterback for the winning North team. Cappleman, sure enough, started for the South. Bradshaw relieved him in the second and fourth quarters, handicapped, everyone took it for granted, by the hamstring. "Bull!" exploded Bradshaw with an absence of charity that was somewhat surprising in a Christian Athlete. "I didn't play more because the coach wanted Cappleman in."

Noll, back in Pittsburgh, saw the game on television and awaited a copy of the films. Running the team and passing, Bradshaw gave a good account of himself, "but we still didn't have that convinced feeling," Noll was to say. A roll-out quarterback from the Air Force Academy, not regarded by Noll as professional material, had played most of the game for the North, upstaging Phipps.

At this point, according to Noll, Dennis Shaw, San Diego State's quarterback, was worthy of serious contemplation. Shaw had been the most valuable player in the East-West game. In the Steeler offices, Noll and his assistants and Art Rooney, Jr., worked from 9 in the morning until 10:30 at night, looking at films, reading BLESTO reports, "tying information together." They were taken with Mike Reid, Penn State's aggressive defensive tackle. But when defensive line coach Walt Hackett returned from the next all-star game, the All-America Bowl in Tampa, he was trumpeting, "Bradshaw's the guy!"

He wasn't really the guy until Chuck Noll flew to Mobile five days before the Senior Bowl game and stayed for three practice sessions.

Bradshaw did not remember having met him in Miami. He accepted an introduction to Noll and shook hands abstractedly. "I went down there to beat out Cappleman," he would say. "I just went there with the feeling that I would win the position, start, and have a good game." In a forty-yard sprint—Bradshaw's time was 4.7 seconds, very fast for a quarter-back—he pulled the same hamstring. South coach Don Shula offered to send him home, but Bradshaw refused to hear of it. Watching him set up and pass with an injury, watching him respond to the "topflight competition," Chuck Noll shed the last of his doubts about the quarter-back.

So did Art Rooney, Jr. In February, holding up a sheaf of papers, Rooney said, "This might be the thing that swung it." At the request of Jack Butler, BLESTO-V's managing director, Bradshaw had agreed to take a personality test and an IQ test in Mobile. "He came out okay," said Rooney. "Or he wouldn't have been our first draft choice."

There remained the question of whose choice he would be, the Steelers' or the Bears'. On the day before the Senior Bowl game, Noll was in New Orleans for the coin flip. Amid Super Bowl hoopla, while the Bears' man called out "heads," Pete Rozelle flipped a 1921 silver dollar. It bounced on a cloth-covered table and came up tails. "We have no idea who we'll take," said a smiling Dan Rooney, but Chuck Noll talked of Bradshaw with suspicious enthusiasm.

Bradshaw started in the Senior Bowl and was still firing passes with authority at the end of the game, a 27–27 tie. He had ignored, since the third quarter, two broken ribs. The quarterback for the North was Dennis Shaw. Noll, Dan Rooney estimates, made at least ten exhaustive studies of the film.

From early until late, Noll and his staff continued their evaluations. The Steelers have a history of unfortunate first-round picks, reversed by Chuck Noll with his selection last year of defensive tackle Joe Greene, a Big Daddy Lipscomb reincarnate, but what they now had to decide was whether to trade their first choice for established veteran players who could move them up quickly in the standings.

Even before the coin flip, the offers had started coming in, and they were to hear from every other pro team except three. "All I'm going to tell you is this," said Art Rooney, Sr., to his sons and coaches. "If we trade the guy, if we give away a guy who turns out to be great, just make sure we get front-line ballplayers." He assumed, as the Steelers' competitors did, that Bradshaw would be the first choice, and because Bradshaw was a quarterback, Rooney felt apprehensive. "We're experts on quarterbacks," Rooney once said. "We've had Sid Luckman, Johnny Unitas, Len Dawson, Jack Kemp, Earl Morrall and Bill Nelsen and we got rid of them all, every one."

In Dan Rooney's office late on the night of January 26, the night before the draft, Chuck Noll at last said, "Well, let's take this kid." Tacitly, Noll and Dan Rooney had come to an agreement in the sixteen days since the Senior Bowl game that "this kid" was Terry Bradshaw. Now they were deciding that there would not be a trade.

Only one deal had tempted them, an offer from the St. Louis Cardinals, who were drafting eighth. The Cardinals wanted to trade their first choice for the Steelers' first choice and throw in four regulars. If Mike Reid had been available when the Cardinals' turn arrived, the next day, the Steelers would have thought long and hard, but the Cincinnati Bengals, drafting just ahead of the Cardinals, eliminated the Penn State All-America as a pawn.

On the Wednesday before the draft, Art Rooney, Jr., had telephoned Bradshaw in Ruston and found him to be well disposed toward the Steelers. Terry and his father never had given credence to rumors that Pittsburgh was cheap, for in 1952, when the Steelers played an exhibition game in Shreveport, their bus driver—Bill Bradshaw—received a twenty-dollar tip. "The most I ever got from any other team was five dollars," he said.

Terry Bradshaw, destined for bigger money than twenty dollars, heard from Dan Rooney at 9:45 a.m. on January 27. With his mother and father and the neighbors, with sportswriters and sportscasters there, with television cameras set up, he was sitting in the kitchen at home. "Well," he said when he put down the phone, "I'm number one."

The news that Bradshaw was number one traveled swiftly. In February he made a trip to New York to be photographed for a picture layout in *Harper's Bazaar* that would "show how women's fashions are influenced by sports." Said a *Harper's Bazaar* editor named Gloria Moncouer: "I was looking for a fresh new face. Joe Namath is too old, too overphotographed." Beholding Terry in his Steeler uniform, she exclaimed, "Oh, wow, terrific . . . really terrific." From New York, Terry flew to Dallas, where he modeled slacks for one hundred dollars a day. ("I'd wear a dress for one hundred dollars a day," Terry said.) Later in the month he visited Pittsburgh, exciting mini-skirted chicks and young men in Edwardian clothes on a tour of the Market Square nightclub district with Andy Russell, Steeler linebacker. Terry had a couple of drinks—whisky, perhaps. Toward the end of the evening, he casually asked Russell how the veterans would accept him. "Oh, you'll get your share of needling," Russell answered. Looking hard at Russell, Terry said, "Listen, I'm a leader. If anyone gives me trouble in the huddle—I don't care *who* they are—I'm going to sting them." He put Russell in mind of Bobby Layne.

How Jacksonville Earned Its Credit Card

Paul Hemphill | **1970**

It was still early in the season when a Jacksonville television station got carried away and put together a wonderfully hokey sixty-second love poem to its Dolphins: film clips of seven foot two Artis (Batman) Gilmore loping downcourt like a giraffe and little Rex (Robin) Morgan spinning toward the basket like a water spout, all of it synchronized in slow motion to the strains of "The Impossible Dream." That had been the Muzak, the music to work miracles by, as the Jacksonville University basketball team kept on winning, kept on moving up in the national rankings, kept on soaring upward on a collision orbit with the great powers like UCLA and Notre Dame and Kentucky.

After all, fifteen years ago Jacksonville had been a junior college. Six years ago the team had an annual recruiting budget of $250 and played to crowds of less than a thousand. Two years ago they had been losing to Wilmington College and were the fourth-best team in perhaps the nation's weakest basketball state. *One week* ago they had borrowed cash from their play-by-play announcer so they could pay for dinner after beating Kentucky in the NCAA Mideast Quarterfinals. But here they were in the throne room now, coach Joe Williams and recruiter-assistant coach Tom Wasdin of the Jacksonville Dolphins, sitting in a traditional restaurant down the street from the White House on the eve of

(553

the 1970 NCAA finals, ordering brandy milk punch for a gaggle of writers representing big-city dailies and national magazines, giddy and loose and expansive and struck by the wonder of it all themselves.

"Y'all," said Wasdin, "go ahead and order anything you want."

"Sure you can afford it?" a writer said.

"Shoot, we got a credit card now."

Somebody said, "Say it ain't so, Tom."

"Look here, American Ex—"

"No, I mean that story about you dressing up like a member of the booster club so you could recruit Artis. You expect us to believe that stuff?"

"Tell you the truth," Wasdin said, "I'm starting to believe some of those stories myself. The more we win, the better they get. I'll tell you one that *did* happen, though." He is a finely chiseled man with a hint of Kirk Douglas in his bronze face; he is thirty-four, two years younger than Joe Williams. He spread his elbows on the white linen tablecloth and grinned like an old boy about to tell a shady story on the town beauty queen.

"About three years ago we'd kicked off a couple of boys and some others had gotten hurt, and we were down to nine players. Coach Williams wanted to scrimmage one day so he says, 'Why don't you suit up and be the tenth man, Coach?' Well, I did, and after a while one of the kids tried to cut the baseline on me and I sort of laid a body check on him, you know, and it—you ready?—well, it broke his back. Then we had eight." When the nervous laughter had died down, Williams told about the time the elevator in an old hotel in Cookeville, Tennessee, broke down between floors with the entire squad on it ("That's when we were driving all day in cars for a two-hundred-dollar guarantee"). Then Wasdin said JU's amazing season had brought "one real concrete offer" to him and Williams: "The president of the school called us in the other day and said no matter what happens in the tournament he thought we'd done a real good job." And then somebody offered Wasdin a cigar after dinner and he said, "No, thanks, Artis won't let any of us smoke," and then the evening degenerated into burlesque.

Not everybody was laughing, of course. There was nothing particularly humorous to the NCAA Establishment about the arrival of Jacksonville University in College Park, Maryland, for *their* finale. There is an Establishment in college basketball, just as there is in anything else. The NCAA Establishment includes people like Kentucky's Adolph

Rupp, who thinks zone defenses and tall players are Communist threats; UCLA's John Wooden, who has all the sartorial and verbal flair of a funeral director; the anonymous coach who said that a national title for Jacksonville would "set basketball coaching back twenty years," and even the sportswriter who wrote from the University of Maryland campus that free-wheeling, undisciplined, free-form play was "for playgrounds and Jacksonville University."

The Establishment did not like it that the Jacksonville Dolphins were in the 1970 NCAA championships. "What is this, Rent-a-Goon?" said a writer, pointing at JU's two giant black junior college transfers, seven-two Artis Gilmore and seven-zero Pembrook Burrows III. "Just look at them, would you?" said the wife of an NCAA official, nodding toward the entrance to Cole Field House as Joe Williams and his team came to work, smacking gum and horsing around and wearing bell-bottoms and zippered racing jackets, and what she was really saying was *How tacky, the very idea.* Williams, they had read, had no curfew for his players, scribbled his game plans on the backs of cocktail napkins and wore this God-awful "lucky" outfit to every game: white six-button blazer, blue bell-bottoms, psychedelic tie and watermelon-red shirt. And their followers: route salesmen and hardware-store owners and small-town doctors, many of them still trying to straighten out the difference between charging and hooking, self-conscious and still suspicious about any game that's played *in*doors. And the players: good old boys from places like Chipley and Jacksonville, who gorged themselves at the "training" table, drank beer in public, pulled pranks like hiding each other's shorts, and had painted green-and-gold stripes on their shoes when they found out they were going to be on color television at College Park. "Basketball is supposed to be fun," Williams had been quoted, and that was especially disturbing to the Establishment when they realized that Jacksonville University had lost only one of its twenty-seven games and was ranked fourth in the nation.

A lot of this incredulity, this shock, was seen on the Thursday night of the semifinals, just after UCLA had blown past New Mexico State, and Jacksonville had slopped its way over Bob Lanier-less St. Bonaventure to set up the UCLA-Jacksonville championship game. John Wooden would be going after his sixth NCAA title in seven years Saturday afternoon against JU, and when he entered a dressing room off the floor for the post-game press conference the writers crowded in to ask him what he thought about Jacksonville and Williams and the Mod Squad and Artis Gilmore. Wooden doesn't normally delight in talking to the press, but it seemed as though they were all in this thing together this time; Wooden and the big-time basketball writers, making the best of it. Inflections and raised eyebrows and dramatic pauses did the job nicely:

Q—Did Jacksonville impress you with anything besides its height, John? (Laughs)

A—(After thoughtful pause) Depth. Height and depth.

Q—Have you played anybody as good as Jacksonville this year?

A—Yes. (Quick, clipped, definite answer, bringing a burst of laughter) I won't name them, but there are *plenty* of good ballclubs around.

Q—Do you think Jacksonville will out-rebound you?

A—(Acid smile, the Jack Benny delivery) *Well,* they *should.*

The Establishment *knew.* Sitting across from each other at dining tables in the bowels of the University of Maryland fieldhouse, they were passing silent messages. *Jacksonville will get theirs.* They had seen these instant teams blow in from the boondocks before, the boondocks being anywhere basketball is not king. *UCLA isn't exactly Mercer or Biscayne or Richmond.* Class and discipline and tradition would, they were certain, overcome.

It must have been fall of 1962 when I first met Joe Williams. Most newspapermen, at one point or another, succumb to the illusion of public relations—thinking it is the rainbow leading to money and class and peace of mind—and I had just quit writing sports to become the sports publicist at Florida State University. It was football season all of a sudden and I was buried in brochures and eight-by-ten glossies and travel arrangements when Bud Kennedy, the FSU basketball coach, walked in one day and introduced Joe Williams as the new freshman basketball coach. Even then Williams was not the kind to make dazzling impressions. He was quiet and pleasant, tall and hunched-over, a man in his late twenties, who grinned out of the side of his mouth and looked *up* at you, in spite of being six four, through bushy black eyebrows. He was, it seems, sort of a part-time coach while doing graduate study or something. Florida State was just beginning to flex its muscles in football then, and so Bud Kennedy (who died recently) and assistant coach Hugh Durham (now the head basketball coach at FSU) and, by all means, Joe Williams sort of hovered about like extra men at a picnic softball game.

Joe *did* have a beautiful young bride named Dale, whom he had met while he was coaching high-school basketball in Jacksonville. But she was the only outwardly outstanding thing about Joe Williams, and they lived in what sounded like a fishing-camp cabin in the swamps outside Tallahassee, and I suppose I had his picture taken for the basketball brochure and I suppose the freshman team played out its season. I just don't know. I went back to newspapering very shortly and Joe took an assistant coaching job at Furman University, both of us roughly the same age, both of us just looking for a home, and we went separate ways without looking back.

Jacksonville's basketball program was, in those days during the early sixties, almost non-existent. I had seen them play, against teams like Tampa and Valdosta State and Mercer, and it was a twilight zone of dark and airy gyms, small crowds, travel-by-car and intramural offenses. There was a line in the papers about Joe Williams leaving Furman in 1964 to become head basketball coach at Jacksonville University, not the most exciting announcement but at least news about an acquaintance. Jacksonville, you could find out if you bought a Jacksonville paper, got progressively worse—from 15–11 to 8–17 in Joe's first three seasons—and people like me who had known him however vaguely were wondering whatever in the world possessed him to take a job like that.

The Jacksonville Dolphins began getting a little ink outside of Jacksonville in 1968–69 when they finsihed 17–7, but everybody knew they were still playing the same humpties who had once populated a league called the Florida Intercollegiate Athletic Conference. The feeling was the same when the 1969–70 season began and Jacksonville won its first thirteen games: sure, they were averaging 105 points a game, but they were beating up on Mercer and Biscayne and Richmond and Miami, and Florida State had ended the streak with an 89–83 victory in Tallahassee ("The prince has turned into a frog," crowed the Florida *Times-Union* the next morning).

They kept coming, though, Jacksonville did, and now they were in the Top Ten and avenging their loss to FSU and whipping NIT-bound Georgia Tech in Atlanta, and suddenly they had advanced through the first two rounds of the NCAA tournament. And then came that Saturday when everybody in the country was watching the Mideast Quarterfinals on television from Columbus, Ohio, and there was Joe Williams wandering up and down the sideline with a hand in his pocket and the camera zooming in on him and his team, the Jacksonville University Dolphins, advancing to the World Series of college basketball by laying it on Adolph Rupp's Kentucky Wildcats 106 to 100. "Remember?" my wife said to me. "He had a real pretty wife." *My God*, I thought.

There was plenty enough work to do at home, but I found myself on the phone to Jacksonville and Joe Williams Tuesday morning. Lucky I had left my name with his secretary, Joe said, because he had just about stopped returning calls. Some starlet wanted to come out and have her picture made with the team, and the mayor wanted to *work out* with them that afternoon, and he didn't know whether his throat would make it through the next press conference in an hour. Dale was fine, they had two young sons, and the team was flying off to College Park early the next morning.

"It's been a long time since FSU," I said.

"It sure has."

"I didn't believe it, Saturday."

"Nobody did," he said, "but us."

A certain giddiness prevailed at the Interstate Inn, a short mile from the scene of the finals, where Jacksonville's fans and press and players and official family had set up headquarters on Wednesday afternoon. The lobby, restaurant and bar of the motel spilled over with Dolphin fans wearing white straw boaters and oval green-and-white stickers that said J-U CAN DO. The very idea that this school of 2700 students that squats across the river from a cigar factory and a paper mill in North Florida might very well be playing UCLA for the national championship within seventy-two hours was really too much to bear. "The deal is *on*," JU fans would yell, for no apparent reason, sticking thumbs up. "JU can do," would be the reply. "The Big A has come to play," somebody else would yell. And in the midst of all this were Joe Williams and Tom Wasdin, who were back in their rooms tying up the Interstate Inn's three outside lines with calls to some fifty prospects all over the country ("I just wanted to tell you to be sure and watch us on TV this weekend").

The story of Joe Williams is as unlikely as the story of his team. His father was a Methodist preacher, sort of a circuit-rider in Oklahoma, and Joe remembers that on more than one occasion Mr. Williams was paid off in maple syrup for preaching. When Joe finished high school he went to Oklahoma City University and became a so-so basketball player for Abe Lemons, who has been, along with Hank Iba, the biggest influence on Williams' coaching philosophy ("In a way, I was always *against* Adolph Rupp and his coaching, like most kids in Oklahoma were, because he was the enemy"). Two of Williams' brothers also became ministers, but Joe had decided he wanted to coach basketball and he somehow wound up coaching a junior high team and then Ribault Senior High in Jacksonville.

In 1962 he coached the Florida State freshmen, in 1963 he was an assistant at Furman University. In 1964 he was offered, and accepted, the head coaching job at Jacksonville. The administration told him they wanted "a nice program that wouldn't lose too much money."

Jacksonville could afford no more. It was founded as a junior college in 1934 and had been changed to four-year Jacksonville University in 1956.

Joe Williams' recruiting budget for his first year totaled $250 ("I wouldn't go visit a boy until about eight o'clock at night, when I was sure he'd already eaten supper"), and he ran the wheels off his '60 Chevrolet scouring his territory for high-school prospects.

Joe Williams needed ten hands to keep up—he was the head coach and the recruiter and the publicist and the wet-nurse, and in addition to all of that he was teaching five classes at JU and commuting to the University of Florida in the summer for his own studies. "Sometimes it was like trying to climb a greased wall," he has said. He was even arranging for the printing of automobile floormats with Dolphin schedules on them, and organizing a booster club (which now has 125 members, paying one hundred dollars a year each). The 15–11 finish in 1964–65 represented the best record a Jacksonville team had ever had, but then it dipped to 12–11 in '65–66 and 8–17 the next season. About all Williams had to cling to was something told him by Abe Lemons that first year when Oklahoma City and Jacksonville happened to run into each other on the road in Memphis.

"We had been on the road nearly a week," Joe recalls, "riding cars, playing people like Carson-Newman and Tennessee Tech for small guarantees, not even making the bills, and we'd split the trip. Abe started telling us about the fine restaurant they'd been eating in while they were in town playing Memphis State, and he said, 'If you're going to lose or break even, you might as well do it in style.' I think that's when I made up my mind on the 'Four-Year Plan.' "

The Four-Year Plan is something that evolved soon after Williams hired Tom Wasdin as his assistant coach and recruiter in 1966, the year of the 8–17 disaster. They had known each other since junior-high coaching days in Jacksonville (Wasdin was the Duval County coach of the year twice, but lost two of three games he played against Williams' team). Wasdin, like Williams, had also come out of nowhere: he had been a star quarterback on the six-man football team at Waldo, Florida (population 800), and had his Florida basketball career cut short by a sandlot football injury. He and Williams complemented each other, Wasdin being the more glamorous recruiter-type and Williams being the brooding executive, and at the very beginning of their relationship they went to the school administration and said they wanted a chance to build a major basketball program in four years and if they didn't succeed they would leave quietly. The Jacksonville administration didn't necessarily give Williams and Wasdin a *carte blanche*, but they did give their blessings.

The next season the Dolphins broke even at 13 to 13. But things were happening. Super-recruiter Tom Wasdin had rolled up his sleeves and gone to work.

Practice time at Cole Field House on the University of Maryland campus in College Park, the eve of the semifinal round of the 1970 NCAA championship tournament. A chance for the teams to get used to the strange floor and the huge coliseum. At seven o'clock, on Wednesday night, it is time for the Jacksonville University Dolphins, and a crowd of some eight hundred Maryland students and sportswriters surges around the glistening floor to watch. They do not believe Jacksonville. They do not believe that a "pickup" team like this can be the first NCAA team ever to average one hundred points per game during the regular season, or lead the nation in rebounds. They want to see this Artis Gilmore, the seven-foot-two transfer who is the nation's leading rebounder and eighteenth scorer; and that seven-foot playmate of Gilmore's, Pembrook Burrows III; and the little six-foot-five playmaker, Rex Morgan.

The first thing they see is a little bushy-haired black player, Chip Dublin, walk to the side of the court and put a home tape recorder on the floor and turn on the electricity. Dublin has brought a reel of tape filled with soul music. The Dolphins begin shooting basketballs, but then "Sweet Georgia Brown" drifts out of Chip Dublin's tape recorder and Pembrook Burrows III yells, "Show time!!!" and now they are all blurring around Rex Morgan while Morgan goes through his Harlem Globetrotter drill. Then they line up and eight straight men dunk the ball, Gilmore ending the show with a twisting, backward, two-handed dunk that sends the crowd up the wall.

Once the 1969–70 season had ended, Tom Wasdin was being called one of the very strongest recruiters of basketball talent in the United

States. He denies it—"except for Pembrook, we sort of fell into all of these boys"—but when you see the sort of talent he was able to recruit in competition with schools that have so much more to offer than Jacksonville, you have to give him a large amount of credit. Jacksonville has a limit of fifteen basketball scholarships to give out (the Southeastern Conference has twenty-five, for a comparison), there is no freshman team, and it is extremely difficult to lure a hot prospect to a school that plays some of its games in exotic places like Tallahassee and Greenville, North Carolina. It happened this way:

ARTIS GILMORE—Grew up in Chipley, Florida, a depressing little town in the scraggly piney woods of the Florida Panhandle some 250 miles west of Jacksonville. The son of a yard man, he was a good high-school basketball player at the black school in Chipley and—in his senior year, when he became too old to play in Florida—at the black school in Dothan, Alabama. First discovered by George Raveling of Maryland, maybe the premier scout of black talent in the nation, but couldn't get into Maryland and was put under a rock, more or less, at tiny Gardner-Webb Junior College in Boiling Springs, North Carolina. Was averaging twenty-three points per game at G-W but was unhappy there. Wasdin, who had tried to get him out of high school, received a letter from another unhappy G-W player who wanted to transfer to JU and bring "a friend of mine who is seven two." Wasdin went after Gilmore, who wanted to be close to his aging parents and liked Williams, and he got him.

REX MORGAN—From Charleston, Illinois, he was also courted by Wasdin when he was graduating from high school, but decided to go to the University of Evansville in Indiana. Unhappy there (according to one story, he didn't like it because the freshman team was given sandwiches in brown paper bags on road trips), he moved to Lake Land Junior College in Illinois. Still unhappy, he called Jacksonville and came running. "Morgan may be the original tramp athlete," says one cynical writer who has covered the Dolphins, but he gave the team go-power and set the style for it.

CHIP DUBLIN—An all-city prep player in New York City, he signed with Loyola of Chicago but didn't like it and left after four months. Wasdin was in New York trying to recruit another player when the player's coach suggested he forget that one and find Dublin. Wasdin found Dublin working as a clerk at Chase Manhattan Bank on Wall Street and easily convinced him that playing basketball would be a lot more fun.

PEMBROOK BURROWS—Came out of West Palm Beach and was so awkward he didn't make high-school varsity until his senior year, and then scored a grand total of nine points in the two games he played. Started putting it together at Brevard Junior College (in Cocoa, Florida, where Wasdin once coached) and hit 69.4 percent from the field his second year there. This is the one Wasdin had to work on, against stiff competition.

"What's writing all about?" says John Crittenden of the Miami *News*. "It's sticking around and asking one more question and not getting your feelings hurt, and that's Wasdin as a recruiter." Says another writer, on the usual suspicions that arise whenever a small team comes out of nowhere: "Hell, Jacksonville was so broke it couldn't *afford* to cheat." Says Williams: "I just called practice one day and they all showed up." However they got to Jacksonville—these two seven-footers and these transfers—the fever began to rise before the season ever got started. All five of the starters were back from a 17–7 team, and now JU—with Gilmore and Burrows—had the tallest team in the world, probably.

There was a closed-doors practice game against Davidson in Jacksonville before the season started, and the results of it had Gene Pullen writing about a national champion in the Jacksonville *Journal*: "Jacksonville led by 12 points at the half and ate 'em alive. We started going with that game, and everybody was laughing at us." The thing is, the players believed in themselves and in Joe Williams, their hunched-over young coach who listened to jazz and read existentialist authors and visited museums on the road. "What's discipline?" asked Williams. "It's getting them to do what you want them to do."

There were the openers, all of which JU won—East Tennessee State, Morehead State, Mercer, Biscayne. Jax led Georgetown 41 to 26 and Gilmore had twenty-one rebounds with 1:23 left in the first half when a fierce fight broke out. Morgan was belted above the eye and bled like a stuck pig. The Dolphins won it on a forfeit.

They were 13–0 when they went to Tallahassee to play Florida State, and FSU won by 89 to 83 (Gilmore scoring "only" twenty-one points), but it was to be the only regular-season loss.

For the first time, Jacksonville was showing up in the national rankings by the wire services. The legend was growing about "the mod squad" (at Richmond, five thousand showed up for Jacksonville a week after another Spiders' game had drawn less than one thousand). JU was making money now, packing the Jacksonville Coliseum with between six thousand and ten thousand fans a game (they made $10,000 off the

FSU-Jax return match, which drew a state record crowd of 10,500). The year before Williams had gotten to Jacksonville, gate receipts for basketball had totaled $3000 for the year, but if the Dolphins could make it to the NCAA finals they could gross nearly $100,000 for the season.

They made it. They were 23–1 when they went into the NCAA's first round at Dayton against Western Kentucky ("Jacksonville Who?" read a motel marquee back in Bowling Green). Then they knocked off Big Ten champion Iowa and SEC champ Kentucky in a space of three days at Columbus in the Mideast Quarterfinals, and all that stood between them and a national title were St. Bonaventure (which had lost star Bob Lanier to injury) and, most likely, powerful UCLA.

Artis Gilmore was sitting all alone in a booth in the Interstate Inn dining room, working on his fourth Coke and staring through the rain-spattered plate-glass window, when the writers caught up with him on Friday afternoon. It had been a long, restless day for him, and although most of the other Dolphins were already leaving for the movies he looked as though he were going to stay there until he got sleepy. The Jacksonville performance against St. Bonaventure the night before had been listless, even if JU *had* won the game 91 to 83. Artis Gilmore had scored twenty-nine points and taken twenty-one rebounds, but he had been heckled by the St. Bonaventure fans and when thirty sportswriters crowded around him in the dressing room after the game most of their questions implied that they thought he had played badly. And in the morning paper, he was referred to as a giraffe. So it was not a good day for the nation's leading rebounder.

He is a brooding man, a dusky giant with sad eyes and a trim goatee. Few white people beside Joe Williams had ever been able to talk with him. He is courteous to almost everybody, but he simply doesn't unwind and talk about the weather or girls to anybody who comes along. He is a black man from the Florida Panhandle, and maybe that is why. It is poor country, for black and white, and in the past two Presidential elections the area has gone overwhelmingly for Goldwater and for George Wallace. So maybe Artis Gilmore hasn't had much practice with white men.

There were three or four writers who moved in on the booth with Gilmore, all of them traveling with Jacksonville, and Gilmore was reluctant to say much at first. He had had about fifteen offers when he finished at Carver High in Dothan, he said, Florida State not "showing much interest," and when George Raveling had recommended Gardner-Webb Junior College to him he had gone. He didn't like to think about Gardner-Webb, he said.

"Somebody said the coach was always slapping you."

"No slapping," Gilmore said. "Pinching and kicking."

"Did you try to leave?" somebody asked.

"A lot of times I laid in bed and thought about it. But then I thought about losing hours in school and everything. One time I went to the bus station and bought a ticket, but it was late and the coach came and got me and took me back."

"Why did you decide on Jacksonville?" he was asked.

"Because," Artis Gilmore said, "coach Williams was the first white man I ever trusted."

What happened in the finals was, the best team won. UCLA fell behind quickly to Jacksonville, but when Johnny Wooden made some adjustments to shut off Artis Gilmore, the Bruins closed the first half with nine straight points and went on to win 80 to 69.

There was no great joy that night at the Interstate Inn, but neither was there a wake. Of the key players, only Rex Morgan would not be around next season.

"We're in pretty good company," Tom Wasdin was saying. It was almost midnight and he was in the crowded motel bar with the tension off for the first time in months.

"How'd you feel tonight, before?" he was asked.

"I felt like we were a team of destiny."

Throats were cleared and a round of drinks was ordered. Wasdin insisted on buying. "We had a pretty good payday today," he said.

"That's what I understand."

"But don't forget," said Dr. Judson Harris, the crewcut JU athletic director, "we haven't eaten breakfast yet."

The Sunday after the finals the city of Jacksonville honored its Dolphins with a huge banquet. On Monday morning Joe Williams went fishing and Tom Wasdin taught four classes. On Tuesday the Boston Celtics drafted Rex Morgan and forward Rod McIntyre, the latter a star two years earlier, but now buried in the shadow of Artis Gilmore. As though they had just discovered the game of basketball, Florida papers that week after the tournament were pouring out thousands of words about Jacksonville. Then it was announced that Joe Williams was leaving to become head coach at Furman University and would be replaced by Tom Wasdin. The money was one thing, Williams said (he was being boosted from $12,000 to $18,000 a year), but the real reason for the switch was that Furman is a basketball school. "There were too many extra duties at Jacksonville," Williams said, and nobody had to have it explained.

The Lessons of Syracuse

Tom Dowling | **1971**

A balmy autumn day with a warm southern breeze has been promised for the Saturday afternoon kickoff. Syracuse University — a traditional power in the East with twenty straight non losing sea sons as its heritage—will be opening its 1970 home football season against Kansas. It's a hallowed scenario for a weekend of good clean college fun; an occasion redolent of the pageantry of marching bands, busty pompon girls and school pennants fluttering proudly in the stands. Just another exciting college football weekend.

Well, not exactly.

"We may just play ourselves a little cowboys and niggers out there at the stadium tomorrow," muses an older man in a white crew cut. This is at the press party the Syracuse athletic department is hosting the night before the game. "I'll tell you, those Indians found out what happened when they messed around with the white folks and tomorrow those jigs may find out a little something." The man smiles at his companions, one of them a high-ranking member of the Syracuse athletic hierarchy.

"Go ahead, son," the man continues, "take your notes. I don't care. It's this way: you got niggers and you got blacks. The coloreds we got on the Syracuse team are niggers. They don't want to play football. Syracuse was one of the first universities in this country to have jigaboos

(565

on the team and look what it got us: trouble. You go back to Jim Brown, you go back to the first one of *them*, raped a white girl. . . ." The man rambles on, oblivious to all restraints, emboldened with fire-water, positively warmed by the prospects of the "nigger-cowboy" showdown on the morrow.

Who can say when the trouble really began at Syracuse, when it be-came black against white, *them* versus us? For twenty-one years coach Ben Schwartzwalder's Syracuse offense has been slugging into the enemy line, advancing the ball in four- and five-yard bursts, those big black running backs like Jimmy Brown, Ernie Davis, Jim Nance and Floyd Little helping power the Orange to one national championship, four Lambert Trophies and seven postseason bowl games. At sixty-two, Ben Schwartzwalder is the third most successful active major-college football coach in the country (right behind Bear Bryant of Alabama and Johnny Vaught of Mississippi.) Now, after a 42–15 obliteration by Houston, Syracuse is coming home to face its student body and a ra-cially tense city without any big black runners to lug that football, with-out any black linemen to block or tackle.

Eight of the ten blacks on the team—Al Newton, John Godbolt, D. J. Harrell, Rich Bulls, Duane Walker, Bucky McGill, Greg Allen, and John Lobon—have charged Schwartzwalder, his coaching staff, the Athletic Department and the university administration with racism. The accusations range from the use of racist epithets by the coaching staff such as "nigger" and "boy" to the claim that black athletes have been denied the benefits of under-the-table payola given the white ball-players. In between are such assorted accusations as medical malprac-tice by the team doctor, anti-black stacking of the depth charts, double standards in meting out disciplinary actions and in selecting players for away-game trips, and the lack of academic tutoring help for blacks. Two black athletes—Robin Griffin, a defensive back, and Ron Page, a running back red-shirted with a knee injury—agree with none of these charges. All ten are in accord that Ben Schwartzwalder failed to make good on his 1968 promise to hire an assistant black coach for the 1969 season, and, failing that, "an interim" black coach for the 1969 spring practice. As a result, nine of the ten boycotted spring practice and eight of them are now suspended from the 1970 squad. To top things off, the school has at last hired a black coach, Carlmon Jones.

The situation is muddled and embittered. The town and the univer-sity are jittery. There are rumors that four thousand members of the city's black community have bought five-dollar game tickets to storm the field. There is talk of a student lie-in on the football field at halftime. Syracuse Mayor Lee Alexander has threatened to cancel the game, perhaps the whole season, in the interest of public tranquillity. Black and white radical student groups are calling for the suspension of the football season and the firing of Schwartzwalder. Chancellor John Corbally's office is being flooded with anti-black hate mail. Five days before the Kansas game Corbally's office announces that the white players have unanimously invited the blacks to rejoin the team. Five of the eight are immediately declared ineligible, and the other three don't report back.

As promised the weather dawns beautifully on Saturday. Jim Decker, Syracuse's Athletic Director, stands at his office window and peers down at the oval of Archbold Stadium below. He is a gray, morose-looking man with a thin, cadaverous face. Doubtless, I have not caught him on one of his better days. His conversation is punctuated with sudden inexplicable sighs and abrupt, baffled shakes of the head. "Ben always said he was willing to hunt for a black coach, but he didn't promise anything. *They* say he promised to get one, but he didn't say that. He said he'd hunt for one. I was at the meeting and I heard him. Well, we had two vacancies on the staff and the blacks gave us two candidates. One was an assistant coach *in high school,* the guy just wasn't qualified. The other one's salary was way out of line. If we'd hired him we would have had to raise all our other assistant coaches maybe four or five thousand dollars. That's the way it is when you hire a black coach. I talked to one school said it cost them forty-six thousand for their black assistant coach. But the black coach is just a pretext. They're out to get us. If it wasn't the black coach, it'd be something else. It's happening all over. Michigan State used to recruit ten blacks a year, now maybe three. We've all got the same problem. It's just us who's in the spotlight this week."

There is a new six-foot-high chain-link fence circling the football field. Decker notes that the normal security force of forty policemen will be doubled today to eighty, although this figure would later seem greatly on the conservative side. He points to the tunnel at the far end of the field and, with the worried air of a coach forced to dwell on the virtues of his depth chart, explains the rapidity with which police rein forcements can be rushed onto the field, should the need arise.

"It's hard to talk with these blacks," Decker says, "because they say I'm black and you're white and you can't understand me. They keep referring to *their* heritage, as they call it. You wake up one morning and they've made a new claim against you.

"The lesson is you can't give in. The minute you give in on one point, you get weaker for the next time. The black militants are trying to get rid of football, they are attacking the structure of our society. The pattern is football, college, country. It's just like Ben says."

Outside, the campus is deceptively tranquil. An eleven-o'clock rally to urge a boycott of the game is being held on the quad. The turnout is scant. The forty-odd demonstrators, unable to pick up any waverers from the crowd of onlookers, begin to taunt the police with chants of "oink, oink" and whispered slurs. A white girl marches out of the picket line, points a finger in my face and hisses, "You dirty racist bastard." There is nothing left for the demonstrators now but to snatch a rhetorical victory from the ashes of defeat, to assuage the hurt and humiliation of a dead-end demonstration with the ugly language of insult.

After pushing his pants-suited blond wife through the picket line and gaining the ticket gate, a respectable middle aged man in a snazzy sports coat and cuffless trousers turns to face the demonstrators. "You f—— racist scab," someone yells at him. The man's amiable face suddenly curls into a tight smile of defiance and he flashes the middle finger high in the air. He grins at his peers for approval, a grown man inordinately proud of himself for making a rude gesture, coming down to the level of these bitter teen-agers.

This exchange of civilities just about sums up things. The demonstrators would account for the fiasco of their efforts by shrugging off white society as hopelessly "racist." The spectators at the ballpark would have the cushy moral luxury of judging the rights and wrongs of the racial crisis in Syracuse football by the behavior of a few abusive teen-agers. There would be righteous satisfaction in both camps. The neutral ground for bystanders to occupy would shrink, the chances of conciliation would diminish and the game of *them* versus *us* would go on. Pick your side. Cowboys versus niggers. Brothers versus racists.

The game, a success from the law and order standpoint, is a travesty on the field, Syracuse bowing to a somewhat less sloppy Kansas team 31 to 14. The following week the white ballplayers announce that the so-called "unanimous invitation" to have the banished blacks return has been wrung out of them under the duress of having the Kansas game and possibly the whole season canceled.

At the end of the week Syracuse flies to Illinois and is wiped out 27 to 0, running its record to 0–3. The fourth game of the season is at home, against Maryland, one of the certifiably awful teams in the college ranks. More rallies and demonstrations are scheduled to denounce racism and urge a boycott of the game. They fizzle even more spectacularly than the pre-Kansas game efforts and Syracuse goes on to beat

Maryland 23 to 7. Schwartzwalder gets the game ball, and the Orange win their next four games in a row, ending the season at 6–4.

The Syracuse dressing room is jubilant after the Maryland game. It is as if a verdict has been handed down after an immensely long trial: an unqualified vindication. "Today our defense finally jelled," says defensive end Rich Kokosky, "the team is solid. We don't want them back. Not now. We don't need them. We've worked this thing out ourselves. The blacks never even consulted us. When they walked out last spring it was for their own good, to get their black coach. Now they're trying to make their walkout sound like it's for us too, for better medical treatment, all of that bull. And that doesn't work so they say everybody calls them 'niggers.' Well, sometimes we'd say, 'hey, boy, come here.' But we were just joking around. You got to have some fun out there."

Tri-captain Paul Paolisso says, "You just get weary of this racism stuff, the vote on whether or not to take them back before the Kansas game was what broke it. We were split down the middle. Ben said, 'Christ, take them back. Do anything to play the game!' That's what I mean about Ben. The blacks told him right to his face that he was a racist who should get fired, that he's too old for the game. So he's got to be bitter, got to have hostilities toward them, but he says take them back or they won't let us play the ballgame. So we voted to take them back and the university administration puts it out we wanted them back. We wanted them back because otherwise they weren't going to let us play the ballgame. Finally we decided we'd have to explain why we really wanted them back. Not for themselves. They were wrong and we didn't want *them*. Maybe we were wrong there. Maybe we shouldn't have been such big mouths. If we had any dignity at all maybe we lost it by shooting off our mouths. But the university fixed it so we were going to lose face or the blacks were. They were putting it to us, and we shot off our mouths. I tell you, we just want to go back to being kids. We don't want to go on fooling around with these adult games. They throw all these legal terms and decisions at us. What the hell do we know? We're just kids. All we want to do is play ball."

Bill Coghill, a white defensive tackle, says, "We're not the most intelligent people in the world but if we could have sat down with the blacks and hashed things out we wouldn't have had this mess. The kids —black and white—were used by other whites and blacks. The administration wants to use us as a way out when they can't solve the problem. The black players' leaders, Dr. Johnson and George Moody, are using the players to make charges and demands that aren't true and that they can't win. It's too late for understanding between the players now. We don't want them back. I said that publicly and got sixty telegrams from Sparta, Mississippi; Nashville, Tennessee; the Loyal Caucasian Society telling me to hang in there. God, it shows the country has flipped its wig. Now that we've won one maybe we can get back to playing football. That's all we're here for. To play ball. The black guys, too. That's the sad thing."

I talked to the eight suspended black players twice: the day before the Maryland game and the day after. The Syracuse victory had turned things around for them. The validity of their case also turned on the Syracuse won-lost record. For the more games Syracuse won, the more the issue of racism would recede from the public mind. It was a childish way to judge a serious issue, but football was, at bottom, regarded as a boy's game of no great significance, which was one of the reasons the Syracuse student body was almost totally indifferent to the black players' grievances. The day before the Maryland game, with Syracuse 0–3, the blacks were confident, bellicose, almost chipper. The Sunday after the game, with Syracuse 1–3, they were worried, a trifle shaken that they were possibly no longer needed to produce a winning football outing. The future nagged at them. They kept asking if I thought pro teams would draft them, would give them a chance. They were by instinct and background football players and they were struck to the quick with the dawning realization that there would be no more football for them this fall, possibly ever. They were honest and direct, quick to clarify any vagueness, discard any hyperbole one of their number might fall into. They were, like the white players, a pretty decent collection of kids. And that was the tragedy—that these two groups with so much in common should have been driven so far apart.

Yet they looked at things entirely differently. The white players wanted to get to being kids again, where the answers were simple and contradictions could be overlooked. The black players had matured quicker, had been forced into the tricky world of adulthood before their time and they were quick to exploit contradictions.

Black fullback Al Newton says, "When I came here as a freshman I was the lowest-ranked fullback they had, but I worked my way up by playing. That was right. Last spring practice starts and I couldn't understand why I was a starter for two years and the leading ground gainer and here's this Marty Januszkiewicz cat in front of me. I asked Floyd Little why should I be second-team and he says to make you work harder. And I said, well, put Marty behind me and make *him* work harder. It's these contradictions they're throwing at you all the time. Like last spring there were student strikes all over the country dealing with the Cambodian issue and the university comes out with a policy that any student that did anything peacefully would get no reprimand. They stopped classes, put up barricades and nothing happens to these cats. We do things according to the process, a peaceful boycott, and we get suspended. Sure, we're still in school. But football, man, is what we came here for. We're interested in football for a career.

"Like the black coach, Carlmon Jones, they finally got from Florida A&M after we struck to get him here. We laid out three demands: One, that he be a varsity coach so he could deal with us and monitor the situation. Two, that he get a three-year contract. Three, that he get paid ten to twelve thousand a year. So they get him here and he is the assistant to the assistant freshman coach and there are no blacks on the freshman team. He is on a one-year appointment so they can fire his ass any time. And he is making just ten thou a year. They are giving that cat a screwing and he is still out there and Ben can point to him and say there isn't any racism here because Carlmon Jones is still on the team."

Jones is a big, overweight '70 graduate of Florida A&M, who makes no effort to conceal the mystifying complexity of his position, not the least of which is that he is hardly any older than the black players. "I'm the key," he says. "Everybody wants to get me on their side. The black players want me to make a statement about Ben being a discriminator. Only how can I do that? I only just got here. By the same token I'm supposed to keep the ears open. Ben told me if I hear any 'nigger' words to let him know. Only there aren't many blacks around here. Unless the blacks come back how can I judge what it's like for black athletes around here? It's kind of hard. Sometimes I feel it's too much. I'm leading a hell of a life. The black people don't like me and the white people don't like me. There are too many hard feelings. It might not never get solved and I guess it goes back a long time, these charges and all."

Yes, there has been trouble brewing at Syracuse for a long time. The Pittsburgh Steelers' Negro tackle John Brown, who played on the 11–0 national championship team in 1959, recalls, "I look back and I could see this coming. I really could. I mean the ghetto is changing. You don't go down there any more and recruit ballplayers by telling them, 'Hey, Supernigger, you get to come to my school and play us some ball. Just do your thing and you'll be all right, Supernigger.' That was the acceptable attitude ten years ago. I was floundering in the ghetto when the chance came to go to Syracuse. I was grateful for it. Academically and financially it was a groove—socially, morally and spiritually you could shove it. But you accepted that too in those days, if you were black.

You knew you couldn't be a mediocre ballplayer and be black. With black guys you were expected to play and excel, emphasis on the latter. But that was true of every white school that brought in black ball-players back in the 1950s and early 1960s."

According to the black players, Syracuse football had always been racist, based on a double color-standard. The standard had once been unapologetically blunt. That was why Avatus Stone—the team's first black running back in the early 1950s—and Jimmy Brown had both been warned against dating white girls.

In any case the white ballplayers feel Syracuse football should be judged by its present, not its past. "I don't give a damn what someone said or did to Jimmy Brown ten years ago," one white player says. "The question is right now. And right now the only racism around here is coming from the black players who want special treatment and privi-leges no one else gets." As far as the whites are concerned there is only one standard to be discerned; it is harsh, undemocratic, and uniformly unconcerned with human rights. "Ben's idea is you got to fit into the wheel," says white defensive tackle Joe Ehrmann. "You got to be his kind of spoke. You couldn't believe the crap I take for my long hair." "Yeah," chimes in Bill Coghill, "he made me shave my mustache. Ben doesn't like hair. Ben likes to play the sawed-off, tough paratrooper-hit-ting-Normandy role." "Ben is only interested in winning ten games a year," says white senior quarterback Paul Paolisso. "He just wants ball-players. He doesn't care what race you are. To win ten, that's all he cares about. How can that be racism?"

How indeed? Well, racism meant different things to different people. When the black players at Syracuse used "racism" they meant the whole range of discriminatory deeds and thoughts, they referred to the historical context of racism, the ways in which it impinged on their childhood, the ways they assumed it would affect their adulthood. When most of the white players were confronted with talk of racism they assumed it meant an outright act of tangible bias, an instance of vivid locker-room cruelty committed during the 1970 season.

Changing times create new contexts, give words a different meaning, add or detract urgency from the old standards. That lesson has not been learned very well at Syracuse University, certainly not on the foot-ball team.

Ben Schwartzwalder is a dour, strong-willed man, his hair cropped to a burr of white, his mouth sunken inward, as if forced to do without false teeth for a protracted period of time. He is fundamentally a man who looks to the past—those years when his conservative, running brand of football, powered by those big black running backs, had ground out the championship yardage.

"Listen," Schwartzwalder says, squinting in the pale autumn sunlight outside Manly Fieldhouse. "They just want to nail old Ben to the cross." He has just been asked if he has ever called a black player a "nigger" or a "boy." That is one of the frequently aired charges against him, although, when pressed, the black players admit that he has never personally used either word against them. He has frequently, they point out, called them "boys," which is hardly the same thing but in the racially charged atmosphere of Syracuse football has also become a slur. Schwartzwalder says, "Now 'boys' is something you slip on. Now that we don't have these kids [the blacks] on the team anymore it's normal for me to say 'boys' on the field. I don't want to say 'kids.' It's a little formal to say 'men,' right? So I'm saying 'boys' again. And not that I'm being a wiseguy. I've always used 'boys.' It's a category that fits them all. But I've never used the other word."

"Nigger?"

"That's the one. Why would I? I don't regard myself as a racially prejudiced person. I couldn't be a very good citizen and be prejudiced against any group, right? Sure I've used 'Polack' in a joking sense. 'Wop' never! 'Polacks,' yes, because I know a lot about them. And the Germans I'll really abuse. I'll say, 'You're nothing but a stupid, stubborn Kraut. I can say that, right? Being German. Now Rocco, our line coach, can call them 'Wops.' We all can take liberties with our Polish kids, because they know they're almost our favorite kids. They're not sensitive. I've always said I've never had a Polack who wouldn't hit. And they've always had a tenacity about them. They like to be called 'Polacks' because they know it connotes something a little special."

Schwartzwalder was not the most sensitive or foresighted of men. Yet there was in him a rock-like sense of his own rectitude, not to mention innocence—a crusty, obdurate, old-fashioned way of thinking and acting that had been used to make him seem a bigot in the context of 1970.

"They got a gun on old Ben," he says, the tough ex-paratrooper's small, clear eyes pugnacious behind the glasses. "And old Ben doesn't like to operate with a gun on him. They think they got me down in the gutter, but old Ben doesn't like to get kicked when he's down. I don't mind persuasion, but I don't like force."

Well, there is some truth in that. Schwartzwalder has been pushed and insulted, often unjustly, more than a man of his temperament could be expected to endure. But if he is on the ropes, or in the gutter as the case may be, he got there, in large measure, on his own, because he refused to listen to persuasion until it was too late.

According to Schwartzwalder, "I've been put in a position by this thing where they say I have to be a sociologist, a psychologist, too. Well, I say, sure, a football coach has other responsibilities, but a football coach from my point of view shouldn't have to be a sociologist or a politician as good as those folks may be. I shouldn't even be an administrator. I should just be a football coach."

In the fall of 1968 he was forced to have a go at being those other things. There had been a street fight that summer in Syracuse between a white ballplayer and a black citizen, who lost the brawl decisively. It was, on the face of it, an extraneous issue, but the black filed a complaint with the New York State Human Rights Commission, which in turn got Syracuse to order Schwartzwalder to hold a team meeting to discuss alleged charges of racism on the football team. Schwartzwalder took a dim view of the assignment, and in his forthright way doubtless showed his disdain for such obscure sociological side issues.

Black fullback Al Newton recalls, "Ben started the meeting by asking me if there was anything wrong on the team, any racial problems. Well, hell, I wasn't even in town when the fight took place. I was supposed to be his token Negro, I guess. The good guy. So I said 'yes.' It's Ben's tendency to find himself a Negro who will play ball, this is a tendency of society, and I didn't want to play that role for him."

The meeting went downhill rapidly. Black defensive back D. J. Harrell stood up and said sure there was racism on the squad. Hadn't he had a fight with a white player who squirted him with water the year before? And hadn't all the white players cheered the culprit on?

Paul Paolisso remembers. "There wasn't any racism on the team as far as I could see. Oh, a couple of guys who were bitter about blacks. But you always have that. D.J. brought up the white guy who'd sprayed water on him and, even though he won the fight, D.J. was pee-oed because the white guys were pulling for the white guy. We said, yeah. Hell, why fight him just because he sprayed you? He sprayed other guys too, and they didn't want to fight him."

It was a minor matter that could be looked at in varying contexts. Yet the little things multiplied, festered, loomed larger in the gathering clouds of American racial suspicion. Perhaps the crisis was already beyond the redemption of sociologists or the atonement of politicians. In any event, Schwartzwalder had had his fling with sociology and politics. It had not had a very satisfactory outcome, and his temptation was to fall back on the metier he knew best: the authoritarian football coach.

Syracuse had a so-so 6–4 season in '68. In the winter of 1969 several black football players neglected to stand for the national anthem at a school basketball game. Schwartzwalder was incensed. According to Paolisso, "Ben is, well, the guy is a superpatriot. He told the black players: You got to stand for the flag. That's it. Because I won't have it any other way. And they didn't stand at the next game either and Ben was threatening to have them off the team." Before Schwartzwalder could take matters into his own hands the school administration quietly passed the word that students demonstrating at a basketball game was not a football disciplinary problem.

Several weeks after the basketball incident representatives of the black players met with Schwartzwalder, Athletic Director Jim Decker and Vice Chancellor James Carleton to discuss the problem of racism in Syracuse sports. Schwartzwalder was reported as saying that the blacks' only problem was a bad attitude. Nonetheless, the three black representatives emerged from the meeting to announce they had exacted a promise from Schwartzwalder to try and find a black coach. It seemed reasonable to assume that the search would be a fruitful one in a nation of more than twenty million blacks, many of whom knew a fair amount about coaching football. In time two prospects were selected, one of whom had coached Duane Walker in high school, and the other of whom had coached Al Newton. Neither was hired. When the football players reported to practice in the fall of '69 both vacancies on the coaching staff were filled, and by whites.

The black players felt betrayed. In light of Schwartzwalder's recollection of the agreement to hire a black coach it is hard to blame him. "I got hauled off to this meeting with three fellows who're supposed to represent the black players," he explains. "They were a half an hour late and when they get there they start telling me this and that. 'All right,' they said, 'will you look for a black coach?' I said, 'Sure, I'll look all over for one.' Naturally, they nailed me on that one. I got to thinking and I went to Carleton's office the next morning. 'Just so you won't get any wrong ideas,' I said, 'I told those people I'd look for one and I looked all the way home and all the way back to school this morning and I didn't find any. 'No,' Carleton said, 'you committed youself!' Well, I ask you: did I or didn't I commit myself? I said I would look for one, but I wasn't being serious. I had no intentions of being serious and they knew I wasn't serious and I said it strictly out of sarcasm because they were late for the meeting and kept me waiting."

Well, what can you say? That a pledge of the utmost gravity was reduced to the level of sarcastic pique over a half-hour delay in a meeting?

Nonetheless, the black players remained on the team for the '69 season with the understanding that Schwartzwalder would produce an "interim" black coach for the 1970 spring practice. The "interim" coach turned out to be the Denver Broncos' fine running back, Floyd Little, making his annual weekly pilgrimage to Syracuse to review his financial affairs with his business advisor.

Little, as bizarre a diplomatist as Schwartzwalder was a negotiator, promptly unburdened himself of a lecture on the importance of a "good attitude" in making it in pro ball. He told the student newspaper, *The Daily Orange*, that Negro running backs John Godbolt and Al Newton had "very bad" attitudes, while singling out three white players—Ray White, Joe Ehrmann and Bill Coghill—as "great pro prospects." The implication was the whites had "good attitudes." This was not quite what the black ballplayers had in mind from their officially anointed friend at court, not quite the function of a black coach, as they saw it. Besides, the whole "attitude" issue was a recurrent Schwartzwalder *bête noire,* and the black players found it distressingly odd that Little should use the same phrase, especially in light of the fact that he had hardly had a chance to speak to either Godbolt or Newton. Furthermore, they wondered how Little could judge who was a pro prospect and who wasn't since he had not seen any of them practice in pads. Their interpretation was that Little was the artless mouthpiece of Schwartzwalder, a willing houseman imported back to the campus to put his black brethren in their places.

"That was the second time we were betrayed by the university," Al Newton says. Nine of the ten black ballplayers went out on strike, boycotting the remainder of spring practice, although they worked out on their own.

At this point Chancellor John Corbally belatedly entered the dispute. He took Schwartzwalder aside and informed him that the "next vacancy on the football staff will be filled by a black coach. There *is* a vacancy now." Schwartzwalder assured the Chancellor he already had a full contingent of eight assistants. Corbally assured the coach that a full contingent of assistants now amounted to nine. The impasse seemed on the verge of resolution. A black coach would be sought. Schwartzwalder, drawing on his apparently bottomless capacity for the hapless *faux pas*, addressed an SOS to the Baltimore Colts' black tight end John Mackey, the president of the Syracuse Football Alumni Association. The letter began, "We are in the process of securing a black coach. We are more concerned about a candidate's character than we are his coaching talent and ability although we obviously would prefer both."

Mackey, no slouch at dead-pan sarcasm, fired back a "Dear Ben" letter that said, "I can understand that talent as a coach and ability are very important to you. I can see where the character of any man employed by you is important, but I do not understand when you say you are more interested in character than talent and ability, although you would prefer both. I feel that there are many black coaches in the United States that are of great talent and ability, and that I am most interested in helping you secure that type of individual."

Mackey did not hear further from his old coach. Chancellor Corbally winces when reminded of the Schwartzwalder-Mackey correspondence, the memory that his football coach's original missive was not couched in the most useful or subtle language. "No," he allows, "Coach Schwartzwalder is not the subtlest of men. Take his original agreement to look for a black coach. That was seen as a commitment by some very reputable people. At the very least it was an *implied* commitment for immediate and rapid action to get a black coach. It doesn't take a great prophet to know that in 1970 a school that didn't have a black coach needed one. I came here from Ohio State, and Woody Hayes has had a black coach for quite some time."

Corbally promised that the black coach would be on hand by the 1970 season and urged that the blacks return to spring practice. The black players countered that the university had betrayed them twice already and they refused to return on the basis of still another pledge. George Moody, the black player spokesman, said, "We can recognize Corbally as a man, but we must recognize his institutional role as well. It is that role we cannot trust."

This would prove to be their undoing. Up until this point the moral superiority of the black position was obvious, the weight and power of the white university establishment had lined up behind them to accede to their demand for a black coach. Having been rebuffed, Corbally withdrew from the dispute with the warning the black players would have to accept the consequences of refusing to report back to the team.

The consequences were tangled and explosive. Only two of the boycotting players, Rob Griffin and Greg Allen, were invited to rejoin the team by Schwartzwalder. On August 1 Carlmon Jones was hired. A day

earlier some of the black players filed charges of discriminatory practices against the university and the coaching staff with the local human
rights commission. The charges—originally four and ultimately expanded to eight—were meant to be a blanket indictment of Syracuse
football as a racist, repressive and double-dealing institution. The alle-
gations cut across racial lines. In sum, their thrust was that the Syracuse
Athletic Department did not treat players in a very civilized manner,
and had shown an especially "bad" attitude toward blacks. Examined
individually, the charges, even if true, were largely unprovable and
sometimes insignificant. How could you prove, for example, that the
team doctor's incompetence was greater when treating black athletes
than white ones? Why would you even want to prove that the black
players were not given the same illegal opportunity to accept secret
handouts from rich alumni that the whites got? The charges were too
indefinite, too sweeping to stick. A black coach—that was concrete. But
an elaborate laundry list of unsifted rumor and fact—that was merely
confusing.

Nonetheless the line was drawn. For Schwartzwalder to allow the
blacks back constituted a tacit admission of bigotry. For the blacks to
come back without a detailed apology from Schwartzwalder was a tacit
confession that they were prepared to submit to unusually severe discrimination in order to play football. There was too much face involved, neither side could give, and the verbal context of "right and
wrong" hardened like two geological strata of rock pressed together.

Naturally enough, the preamble and five recommendations for reconciliation worked out at the end of August by the university, the athletic department, the black players and the local human rights commission tried to find some middle ground of compromise and was rejected
by the black players, though it certainly reflected more harshly on the
university and Schwartzwalder than on the black athletes.

The hopelessness, the poignant bitterness of the division between
white and black was best summed up by those two competing fullbacks, Marty Januszkiewicz and Al Newton. Januszkiewicz says, "You
have to feel sorry for these black kids because they're not doing the
thing they love: playing football. I think they should have signed the
code for reconciliation. It would have showed they had a little humility,
were willing to bow their heads to come back."

Al Newton says, "How could we go back to a team that says they
were a hundred percent in favor of not having us, but one hundred percent in favor of having us back to play their game? What kind of pride
as humans would that leave us with?"

Pride meant the same thing, but it too came in two different contexts. Neither side was willing to leave the other any of it to cling to.

"This whole university is completely racist," says Dr. John Johnson, the black Vice Provost for Minority Affairs, "and until the whites recognize that there won't be a change here."

It seems a tall order. I ask for some examples of racism at the university.

"We've got an English professor who told his class *Tom Sawyer* was the greatest American novel ever written," he snorts.

"*Tom Sawyer*?" It seems a heretical choice for the honor.

"The one with Nigger Jim in it," he shakes his head, while I am left with recollections of *Huck Finn*, and finally pulls from his desk an old 1967 football program, from which he reads former Syracuse Chancellor William Tolley's thoughts about Syracuse football in days gone by. "Of course, I must not forget Jimmy Brown," Dr. Tolley writes. "Big Jim was a boy who was very difficult to reach. Despite our best efforts and a required course in responsible citizenship we had little influence on his character. In Jim's case perhaps success came too early."

What could you say? Gratuitous racism put out by the university press. But then Tolley is not running Syracuse any more. Corbally is. Nor am I inclined to fault the English professor's judgment on the literary standing of *Huckleberry Finn*. It all seems ancient history, irrelevant in any event.

But then I am forced to remind myself that it has been the mistakes of whites to dismiss the past, to not give a damn what happened to Jimmy Brown ten years ago, that has led to much of the estrangement of the present. And, indeed, much of the racial confusion at Syracuse— and elsewhere no doubt— is compressed in the context of time. To the blacks the present is synonymous with the indignities of the past. To the whites the present is, as always, the deferred apology for the past, the promise that the future will get a little bit better. In a sense, the black players' lengthy list of grievances against Syracuse athletics is a distillation of the collective injustices with which they have always lived, with which they expect to live in the future.

But that does not make the list correct in the context of Syracuse football in 1970. It does not make the grievances provable. And it does not mean that the white players and the athletic department must make reparations for the wrongs of the past.

How far back into the past could you go? I myself thought Jim Brown had suffered from racism a decade earlier, but I thought *Huckleberry Finn* was anything but a racist novel and should be taught at a university. By the same token I thought Schwartzwalder had blundered unforgivably in waffling out his agreement to get a black coach, but I thought he had been unjustly hurt and abused by charges of racism that he had not committed. Corbally had erred, as he himself admitted, in not intervening earlier to force the hiring of a black coach. I was convinced that Moody and Johnson had used the black players to advance their own notions of black *realpolitik* at Syracuse. They saw an issue that appeared to have enough gut emotional power to rally the university to their side, but they misjudged the degree to which they could push it, they overreached themselves and the black ballplayers were left holding the bag. Perhaps the flaw of the black position was that it sought revenge for the past, not equity for the present. Yet it also had to be said that Schwartzwalder had used the white players to his advantage, had employed them as shields against his own past mistakes. His flaw was perhaps to concede in the present what he should have bestowed in the past.

The dogma of football was winning at any cost, no matter who got hurt, and at Syracuse the lesson had been mastered with a vengeance. It was just a game, but it had been played in a way that taught a great many young men how to hate one another. They were—both the black and white ballplayers alike—more charitable and tolerant people than outside circumstances had forced them to become. The responsibility for what had gone wrong in the different contexts of the past and the present was not theirs. Schwartzwalder, Decker, Moody, Johnson and even Corbally had accepted authority. They took credit when things went right and ought to bear the blame when things went disastrously wrong. The point of coaching college football, of advising minority students, of running a university was not to leave the lives of your charges scarred by hate. Any "required course in responsible citizenship" taught that. Jimmy Brown had to take the course. Apparently there were others who should have, and didn't.

Rob Griffin sits hunched forward on the locker-room bench in Manly Fieldhouse, tying the strings on his shoulder pads, the only black left on the team. The muscles in his face are wound up tight like a clock-spring. "It used to be integration, and now all you hear is separation. I'm going to try to recruit blacks to come up here to play football. I think maybe they've learned something from all of this. To give blacks a better shake. I boycotted last spring for the black coach. We had a definite commitment and I had an obligation to. But I've never heard 'nigger' used here. All of the accusations disturbed me. A lot of them were not true. Now we've got the black coach. I know Jones. He will stand up. He will stand if he has to. I'm glad I stayed with the team. I did what was right as far as I could tell it. But, I'll remember this as long as I live. It has torn me up. People have got to learn to give. You don't win anything by calling people bigots, racists, troublemakers, black militants."

That was a reasonable lesson in citizenship. But they didn't teach it on the Syracuse football team.

Pro Football's Dropouts

Roger Rapoport | **1 9 7 0**

Most correspondence reaching St. Louis Cardinal owner Stormy Bidwell comes on officious letterhead bond and talks of television deals, contracts, season tickets, draft picks, trades and league business. But one morning last March a strange item showed up in the mail, a greeting card bearing a picture of a young North Vietnamese "liberation fighter" toting a rifle. Bidwell opened the card to find a poem by Ho Chi Minh which read in part:

> The universe throws off
> its muddy clothes
>
> all the birds sing at once
> Men and animals rise up reborn.

Alongside the poem was a note from Rick Sortun, a twenty-seven-year-old Cardinal offensive guard. The six-season veteran explained he was quitting football to work for creation of a socialist society. Sortun suggested: "Someday you are going to have to decide what is most important to you, the profit you make and the property you own or the establishment of a democratic egalitarian society. In such a society football as a professional sports activity will no longer take place and I hope that when the barricades are drawn you will be on the right side."

Rick Sortun used to be a crew-cut, conservative $30,000-a-year line-man who spent the off-season examining statements for a Seattle bank. Today he is one of the new pro football dropouts. Sortun and other stars have quit the game to pursue radical politics, anti-war protest, communal living, vegetarian diets and yoga. No longer wedded to the football system, they are now out working for social and political revolution.

Sortun's political consciousness blossomed two years ago when he enrolled in a Masters' program at his alma mater, the University of Washington in Seattle. He joined Students for a Democratic Society, was baptized into campus protest and has never been the same since.

Linebacker Chip Oliver dropped off the Oakland Raiders in a different manner. During the hectic 1969 season, the twenty-six-year-old athlete began to unwind with the "One World Family" commune, owners of the Mustard Seed natural food restaurant near San Francisco. When the season ended Oliver decided to find inner peace by moving into the commune's Victorian mansion in suburban Larkspur. Oliver's decision was a mystery to teammates who callously pestered him for blind dates with "hippie chicks."

In May, Oliver disclosed he was severing all ties with the football world so he would be free to live in the commune and work in the Mustard Seed restaurant. Old friends couldn't understand. After all, the son of a San Diego painting contractor might still be flipping pizzas or installing telephones if a USC football scholarship hadn't paved his way to a $25,000-a-year Oakland career. But Oliver countered that he didn't need the money, pointing out that a fifth "went down the drain in Vietnam—now Cambodia" anyway. More important, he could no longer support a game that fosters brutality in an excessively violent world.

Shortly after Oliver quit, Sortun's former teammate, Dave Meggyesy, turned up in Berkeley working on a book for Ramparts Press called *Out of Their League: Why I Quit Pro Football*. Meggyesy's book will tell his Horatio Alger story. Once upon a time he was a poor Ohio farm boy who lived in a house without running water. Fine work on the Solon High School gridiron turned him into an all county fullback, member of the Cleveland *News* dream team and Syracuse football scholarship recipient. Meggyesy played his way straight onto the St. Louis Cardinals where he joined the Falstaff speakers' bureau and extolled the virtues of football to Elks clubs and Boy Scout troops.

But the linebacker began to change when he enrolled in sociology graduate school at Washington University in St. Louis. New friends introduced him to the protest movement. The next thing the Cardinals knew the FBI was on the phone inquiring about Meggyesy's anti-war work. He refused to stand at attention for the pre-game national anthem and castigated pro football in an interview with "New Left Notes," the official organ of SDS. Now, at twenty-eight, a slimmer, hirsute Meggyesy is out to persuade other athletes to "quit working for the edification and glory of the football capitalists."

This brand of heresy is being voiced in more and more locker rooms across the country. Traditionally athletes have been stereotyped as members of the political establishment. But in an increasingly politicized country many of them are beginning to question the morality, integrity and relevance of professional sports. Vietnam, Kent State, Woodstock, pollution, militarism and the draft have broadened the social consciousness of many players. Many are wondering out loud about the future compatibility of pro sports and the individual.

Of course the players drop out with different goals in mind. Some want to start revolutionizing the world while others feel the first priority is revolutionizing themselves. Rick Sortun is deep into political organizing, Dave Meggyesy is anxious to organize athletes, while Chip Oliver wants to rediscover himself. These contrasts seemed clear when I visited all three dropouts recently.

While Meggyesy slaves away every day on his football memoir, Rick Sortun is trying to forget about the game: "This fall will be the first time since sixth grade that I haven't played football and my only regret is that I didn't have the strength of character to get out sooner. I hated playing football. I stuck it out for six seasons because it was the only way I knew to make $30,000 a year and still have six months of freedom."

In his farewell note to Stormy Bidwell, Sortun explained that he had "more socially important work to do than playing football." The Cardinals promptly issued a press release claiming that Sortun had quit "to go into social work."

But Sortun says his former employer didn't get the message: "I don't have any intention of going into social work—socialist work, yes; social work, no."

Unlike some pro players who choose to quit with press conferences, national magazine articles or books, Sortun has shunned the press since he left the Cardinals. He is not interested in a football post mortem. When I visited him in Seattle this summer he was busy casting off his old lifestyle. I arrived just after he traded in the Pontiac he bought his rookie year for a more utilitarian carry-all van. He was about to sell his comfortable suburban home for more modest lodgings. His hair was fashionably long, and staying away from training tables had brought him down to 204, about thirty-five pounds under playing weight. This necessitated a new wardrobe that leaned toward blue jeans and denim.

Sortun was finishing work on a Masters' degree in public affairs at the University of Washington. An active member of the International Socialists (which he joined after a series of schisms in SDS) he was working on anti-war protest and studies in a small basement office filled with books by Marcuse, Fanon, Lenin, Malcolm X, Marx, and Bernard Fall. These were some of the writers who deepened his misgivings about the Vietnam war, lured him away from the Cardinals and into social protest.

Sortun felt pragmatic when he got into the football business: "As a youth I traded very heavily on sports and hoped it would be to my advantage the rest of my life." He began playing in sixth grade, was successful at all stages and easily won a spot on the line at Kent Meridian High School, south of Seattle. Sortun's mediocre grades and limited finances made no difference to the University of Washington, which awarded his agility with a football scholarship.

"My scholarship paid for room and board in exchange for work hours," he recalls. "I didn't have to work very hard, but the time spent on football, work and all the other related activities was tremendous. I figured out that I was making about twenty-five cents an hour for my work. But Washington had just won two Rose Bowls, I was pretty gung-ho and didn't think about being exploited."

Sortun's performance on the field prompted the Huskie coaching staff to label him: "The best blocking lineman on the Washington team. Rick doesn't make mistakes and has a tremendous grasp of football knowledge. Opposing coaches rate him as one of the West Coast's most outstanding linemen."

Midway through his junior year Rick noticed a change in the game. "Until that point the coaches appealed to us on the basis of pride. For example, there was a Huskie tradition to live up to after the Rose Bowl victories. But when we started losing heavily the coaches began punishing us with heavy practices. Every Saturday we played more out of fear than enthusiasm. We knew defeat meant grueling punishment the next week.

"Football became more and more of a job. Considering the money gained and hours worked it was highly exploitive. But I had a real and psychic investment in the game. I treated college ball as apprenticeship to a lucrative pro career."

Sortun was drafted by the Cardinals in the fall of 1963 and was playing in St. Louis before he even completed his B.A. at Washington. In 1965 he finished up his schoolwork and took a business degree.

Rick developed a stoical attitude toward life. He played hard during the season, then coasted into a bank job during the off-season. But by the end of 1967 Sortun felt sandwiched between violence and hypocrisy. "I kept thinking about the way all the guys kneeled down before the game to say the Lord's Prayer. When they were done everyone leaped up, put on their helmets and charged out of the locker room screaming, 'Let's kill the bastards.' "

Sortun began to feel like a soldier in the pro football army. "The head coach can be considered the general, and his assistants the butt-kicking drill instructors, along with a whole coterie of trainer-medics, physicians, waterboys and office helpers. In addition the President can come to the war zone and see how his boys are doing.

"To win you must penetrate the enemy's territory and score. The quickest way to score is to 'throw the long bomb.' An end run is a sweep and there are men at your flanks [flankers].

"The linemen are the heavy equipment which open holes like tanks so the other men can gain ground and hold it until a new line is established for the next surge. Defensively the team tries to hold the line while the linebackers blitz at unsuspecting times."

Much of Sortun's thinking was reinforced through bull sessions with teammate Dave Meggyesy. Early in 1968 Sortun began looking for a way out of football. His first move was enrolling in a Masters' program in public affairs at the University of Washington. Sortun was astonished by the changes on campus since his graduation three years earlier.

"I heard people talk at open forums, read articles in the campus papers about SDS and what was going on in the world. I went to an antiwar fund-raising dinner one night and met some SDS people who invited me to a meeting . I went somewhat timidly but was really impressed with the honesty, openness and straightforwardness of the chapter at Washington."

Rick joined SDS in March 1968 and immediately began working on the "April Days of Protest" against the Vietnam war. His activities caught the eye of campus administrators who gave him a disciplinary "warning" after one protest.

Through demonstrations, reading and studying Sortun began to articulate a socialist philosophy. "When I was an undergraduate I thought socialism was great in theory but wouldn't work in practice.

The Soviet Union was socialist and I didn't want the U.S. to be like that. But I began to realize that the Soviet Union does not have socialism at all because socialism means more than state ownership of the means of production, it means workers' control."

Sortun's new philosophy made his life completely incompatible with the capitalistic world of pro football: "The game exploits the public and it exploits the players. Football has been merchandised very cleverly over the past six or seven years but I don't think people want it any more than the other products advertisers seduce them into buying.

"No matter how much money they make the players are being exploited. A pro signs a standard contract legally binding him to a year's service with an option on his next year's playing rights. You can be sold, traded or released at will. You are carried on the books as a depreciable capital asset and exist like a piece of chattel.

"It is easy for the owners to blackball any player and to set price ranges. The owners, through the draft and merged leagues, have a monopoly on your right to play professional football in the U.S."

Sortun believes a militant players' union could combat the ownership. He wants football players to get a direct share of the profits. But Rick has found little enthusiasm among players for this or any other union cause. During training camp last year he tried to convince players not to eat California scab grapes off the training table, but no one took him seriously.

By the end of the 1969 season Sortun had given up. After the final game in Green Bay he and Meggyesy made a pact to quit football over a bottle of champagne (French champagne, presumably). "People didn't believe me when I told them I wasn't coming back," Sortun says. "They just didn't know me, they just didn't know how much I'd changed."

One reason the Cardinals misjudged Sortun was that much of his political work was done back home in Seattle during the off-season. But there was no mystery about Dave Meggyesy. The linebacker was into all sorts of radical causes during the season. During the late 1960s he was a major figure in the St. Louis anti-war movement. He circulated petitions, organized demonstrations and spoke to college audiences. When a student demonstrator's eye was mashed by a lawman, Dave organized a committee to protest St. Louis police brutality.

The Cardinals knew all about Meggyesy's extracurricular work. For example during the fall of 1967 an FBI agent called Stormy Bidwell to point out that Dave was signing checks for a peace group headed to the

Washington march on the Pentagon. Bidwell asked the linebacker about it. Meggyesy explained he was only acting as treasurer for the group, that he was not actually financing the trip.

Just before the 1968 Democratic convention Meggyesy drafted a petition backing Senator Eugene McCarthy and asking for immediate withdrawal of American troops from Vietnam. Seventeen players signed it and copies were wired to all the Missouri delegates.

During the 1969 training camp Meggyesy and Sortun gave an interview to an SDS newspaper in Chicago. Dave suggested that pro football was racist, pointing out that whites play the brain positions and blacks play the brawn positions: "There are a lot of black defensive ends and no black quarterbacks. You have a lot of black defensive tackles, many black cornerbacks, but few black free safeties."

The interview was picked up by the underground press. Stormy Bidwell saw it and asked Dave not to do that kind of thing again: "I reminded him that he represented the entire Cardinal team and comments like that hurt everyone. Off-season he was a free man but when he wore the Cardinal uniform he represented all of us."

Meggyesy refused to knuckle under and soon caught hell from St. Louis superpatriots. After the Cardinals lost the Minnesota game a local columnist suggested that the Vikings won through better discipline as evidenced by the way they stood at attention for the national anthem. The following week Cardinal coach Charlie Winner ordered his players to stand straight and tall for "The Star-Spangled Banner." Meggyesy refused, lowering his head, shuffling his feet and otherwise raising the ire of patriotic fans. The linebacker was castigated on local radio talk shows and soon fans were displaying signs that said "Big Red Thinks Pink."

In October 1969 Meggyesy persuaded thirty-seven players to sign an anti-war petition. A few weeks later Charlie Winner demoted him to the "bomb squads" because he wasn't spending enough time on football.

Meggyesy's bitterness soon gave way to relief. Dave was sick of football after seven seasons and that final putdown convinced him to quit. When I met Meggyesy at his new house in Berkeley he voiced no regret about leaving the game. "I like being in the protest movement," he said. "It's more fun to be a radical than a straight old up-tight football player."

Like Rick Sortun, he has purchased a carry-all van. Unlike Sortun he is anxious to promote a radical philosophy of football. Dave thinks his story can help convince other athletes to quit the competitive rat race.

He believes the best medium for his message is the new book being co-authored with New Left sportswriter Jack Scott.

"This isn't going to be any Jerry Kramer-type *Farewell to Football.* I'm not going to apologize for the game or praise the sort of fascist organization promoted by Vince Lombardi. I'm going to tell the truth about how football wrecks lives, exploits the public and perpetuates violence in this country."

Meggyesy's disillusionment began with a football scholarship to Syracuse. He learned about Mickey Mouse courses for athletes, the complete pay scale for collegiate amateurs and the way football was exploited to make money for the school. At one point Dave was so fed up he almost dropped out, but eventually he took a more worldly attitude. He figured staying on might win him a piece of the lucrative pro football action. Sure enough Dave was drafted by the Cardinals in 1962.

Dave describes himself as "a very emotional player. I wasn't cool like Rick. I psyched up heavily for the games and loved playing one-on-one situations against guys like John Mackey. But I couldn't stand being treated like an animal year after year. There were all these little sawed-off, five-foot-six coaches who had never played pro ball standing around and yelling that you didn't have any guts, that you weren't hitting hard enough.

"The coaches kept subtly implying that you didn't have the will to hit, that you couldn't get it up to hit, that you weren't being violent enough. They always treated you like some kind of a machine, coming by and grunting, 'How's the knee, how's the shoulder, how's the hip?' You were supposed to depersonalize your body, it wasn't your leg, it was 'the leg.' After fourteen years of football I didn't know my body as anything other than a weapon."

During the off-season Meggyesy used to pick up an extra fifty dollars speaking to civic clubs for the Falstaff speakers' bureau. "I would show them a twenty-minute film of game highlights and hold myself up as a model American. But actually I was representing the worst values of society in terms of violence, monopoly and greed. Of course these days the players are a little more hip. You have guys like Namath projecting an illusion of freedom with the whole *Playboy* mentality. They're saying, 'I'm not oppressed, baby. I got my car, my broad, my bottle, my bell bottoms and long hair. I'm free, I'm really free.' But it's all just an escapist trip played by people who never want to confront reality, find out who they are and what they are really doing with their lives.

"People asked me: 'What are you complaining about? You get $33,000 for six months' work.' But look at the owners, they have all their profit made before the season even begins. Virtually the entire stadium is sold out in advance and the TV rights are disposed of in April. In football you have a few workers putting out for the edification and glory of the capitalists. Even some of the sportswriters are paid by the ballclub to follow the team. You know they aren't going to be very critical.

"It's no accident that Nixon and Agnew have turned out to be gung-ho football addicts, watching games during peace demonstrations, putting the seal of approval on Texas as the No. 1 team. They're really into the whole notion of sacrificing for abstract goals. They're the kind of people who get their kicks watching coaches push grown men around. When the revolution comes football is going to be obsolete."

After talking to Dave for an afternoon I mentioned I was on my way over to Larkspur to visit Oakland Raider dropout Chip Oliver and his commune. Meggyesy suggested we go together and soon we were riding to the wooded suburb on the north side of San Francisco Bay.

Oliver's commune, the "One World Family," lives in a well-kept mansion at the foot of Mt. Tamalpais. When we arrived the blond linebacker had just finished jogging and was changing in his tiny basement room. Makeshift Japanese doors encased a sleeping area in one corner. Oliver propped his elbows on a plank desk held up by a couple of boxes. The boxes promptly gave way, the desk nearly collapsed and Chip decided to sit up straight.

"You know when I realized I was through with football?" said Oliver. "It was during the Cincinnati game. I didn't want to hurt anybody. I couldn't get hostile. That's what happens to vegetarians. When you stop eating meat, you lose your ability to hate."

As the three of us talked, it became clear that Oliver was less political than either Sortun or Meggyesy. While Rick and Dave talked about exploitation, Chip spoke of natural foods, yoga, psychocybernetics and philosophy.

Oliver spoke from wide personal experience. As a child he traveled from Army base to Army base as his sergeant father taught soldiers how to drive tanks. When his dad retired to become a painting contractor in San Diego, Chip enrolled at Hoover High School. He played good football but did not go directly to college after graduation.

From 1962 to 1964 he held a variety of jobs in California and Nevada with Coca-Cola, the phone company and a pizzeria. Marriage to a Las Vegas showgirl ended in divorce eight months later. He resumed his football career at San Diego City College, won a scholarship onto the national championship USC team and was drafted by the Raiders in 1968.

"I found out pretty quickly that pro football ideals are in the gutter. These men are supposed to be the best, but I found they were pretty hung up on money, booze, and sex. I'd try to get them interested in organic foods and they thought I was crazy. They called me 'loose wire.' "

Oliver was surprised to find how heavily his teammates depended on pep pills to get up for a game. "There was a regular pharmacy run from the locker room. They had all sorts of stimulants like dexedrine and benzedrine. I tried the pills a few times but they just messed me up. One time though, a friend gave me half a capsule of mescaline just before practice. I walked on the field and kicked a forty-five-yard field goal. John Madden couldn't believe it."

But by the middle of the 1969 season Oliver could hardly bear coming to practice. He was living in Mill Valley not far from the Mustard Seed restaurant. He made friends with the owners from the commune and went on a vegetarian diet for the last half of the season.

Chip began to dread the locker room. "I'd walk in there and smell the meat coming out of the other players' bodies. I didn't have anything in common with those guys. I mean all you have to do is spend a half hour with the Raiders and you know everything about them."

One day Chip did skip practice and team officials called in a panic. They promised Oliver a bonus for coming back. "I returned and it was just like it had been. They treated me like a kid, sending someone around to my room at 9:30 p.m. to make sure I was in bed, alone."

While Chip continued explaining his decision to leave the Raiders and move into the commune, his friend and yogi, Allen Sri, walked into the room. Soon Sri was hyperventilating, drawing in a quick series of deep breaths. Chip began to emulate him. Dave and I asked what it was all about.

Sri explained that yoga requires a special set of breathing procedures' called pranayama: "Hyperventilating increases the air intake to the organs, gives them a charge and increases their voltage." Sri took off his shirt, loosened his zipper and hyperventilated faster. Then he sucked his stomach in so far we could almost see the outline of his spine. Chip quickly slipped out of his Raider T-shirt and sucked his stomach in too.

"This stomach exercise is called the nauli," explained Sri. A few moments later Dave had taken off his shirt and Sri was teaching him yoga fundamentals. Soon all three of them were doing the nauli, but Sri was clearly the master. Not only could the blond yogi suck his stomach back the farthest, he could roll either side around at will.

Sri told me that Chip was a good student: "It's much easier to work with an athlete, someone whose body is in fairly good shape. This is a lot healthier for him than football. You know, contact sports are dangerous. It's not biologically correct for people to smash their bodies against one another."

In a higher state of consciousness the group walked up two flights of stairs, passing some of the fifteen adults and ten children who made up the commune. On the second floor Sri led us into a turret where his flow art was on display. Everyone praised the paintings and then resumed the nauli. Sri spent about ten minutes with Dave and by the time we left the One World Family Meggyesy had the knack. Sri suggested he come back soon for another lesson. Dave said he would.

The following morning I returned to Larkspur, and Chip showed me dozens of letters from people across the country congratulating him on his decision to forsake football for the commune. Then he let me look at some of the writing he'd been working on. In one essay Chip had said: "There is no reason to measure time when you have eternity, there is no reason to measure love when it is infinite."

Then he walked out into the hall and joined some of the children painting a mural. Later it was time to go upstairs and bake banana bread for the restaurant. I chopped up bananas while Chip got together the baking powder, salt, honey, oil, lecithin, milk powder, water, and chopped nuts. Oliver explained why he had given the One World Family $5000 to open a second commune and Mustard Seed restaurant in Berkeley.

"My aim is to have Mustard Seed natural food restaurants open up everywhere," he said. "I think natural foods make people less aggressive. It certainly helped me escape from the competitive sport ethic, the idea that conflict is inevitable, that you have to be bloodthirsty and hate the enemy.

"What's the point of playing football if you're just going to be uptight and nervous? The game just perpetuates the illusion that we are not brothers, that we don't belong to one another. What's the point of living if you are just trying to beat out the other guy?

"When I played football I was turning people on to violence, competition and greed. Now I bake bread, wait on tables at the restaurant and turn people on to health, love and peace. Our family is demonstrating that you can subsist by turning people on to a better way of life."

Chip, Dave, and Rick fully expect other pros to follow their example. All three of them illustrate the variety of factors chipping away at the pro football ethic.

Sortun's socialism made his life incompatible with pro sports. Meggyesy toyed with the movement, found it more fun and relevant than football and joined up for keeps. Oliver couldn't handle the pressure, decided football wasn't a "game" anymore and opted for a more peaceful way of life.

Sortun and Meggyesy each have a wife and two children to support, a fact that means both will have to find new work. Meggyesy talks of finishing his book and then farming in New Mexico. Sortun is undecided while Oliver has determined he can live without personal possessions.

Football officials at the highest level are watching the new dropouts carefully. They do not want to be taken by surprise anymore. St. Louis Cardinal owner Stormy Bidwell says, "I had no idea how far Dave and Rick had gone in their political thinking. Their decision to quit was a real shock. They were good ballplayers."

Bidwell still keeps Sortun's letter of resignation, that North Vietnamese greeting card, in his desk drawer; "People don't believe me when I tell them how determined these guys are. So I take Rick's card out and show it to them. Then they believe me."

Jim Ryun

What's He Trying to Prove?

Arnold Hano | **1971**

> *"Miami. It makes me sick to think about it. I didn't know it was coming. Jim was tired. Sometimes he wouldn't get up in the mornings to work out. That's unlike Jim. He'd lost his enthusiasm. Training had become a drag. He had quit at Drake–the Drake Relays—but he was hurting then. Physically. It began to play on us—injuries, little nagging injuries. It was no fun. When people wouldn't believe he was hurting, it got worse. Then he ran at Miami. I saw it and I couldn't believe it. When he started to slow down, I said to myself, 'You're not really going to step off the track. Keep going. Keep going.' Then he stepped off the track. I went up to him. We walked through the parking lot. Neither of us said anything. We thought the world had ended."*
>
> —ANNE RYUN

We inflict cruelty on our athletes. Our demands are insatiable. The pitcher with the sore arm must pitch even when his shoulder socket is a pulp of ground calcium. Why else do we pay him $100,000? The football halfback whose knees now contain no cartilage must cut and run, bone rasping against bone. What else are heroes for? The heavyweight champion must keep marching in to a pair of fists like razor blades. That's what keeps him honest. And then we ask our ath-

594)

letes, "What are you guys trying to prove?" That's what keeps us honest.

We're good at these cruelties. We've been especially clever in the case of Jim Ryun.

Jim Ryun made the mistake of running too fast too soon too often. We came to expect it of him. At seventeen he broke the four-minute mile. At nineteen, he broke the half-mile and the mile world records. At twenty, he broke the 1500-meter mark. At twenty-two, we broke his heart. So what that he had a bad back, mononucleosis, pulled muscles; so what that he had to run in air a mile and a half high in Mexico City, with four weeks of training, against a man who'd lived at such altitude for twenty-five years. Haven't we told you? You run until you collapse. And if you lose, you're dogging it. It hurts? Run through it, pal. It's always darkest before the dawn.

On June 29, 1969, in Miami at the AAU Nationals, Jim Ryun found it was just as dark at high noon. In the middle of a race, he wondered what he was trying to prove, what he was doing out there. He quit doing it. He performed an act so sensible it ought to be enshrined in some new kind of Hall of Fame, with a legend under it reading: "I stopped running because it wasn't fun." George Sauer, meet Jim Ryun.

Jim Ryun quit in the middle of a race, disappeared from sight, retired from track. Now he's come back, running again. And the pressures are beginning to build. What's he trying to prove?

If you have followed my peregrinations through these pages over the years, you will know that this is the delayed second part of a look at Jim Ryun. Five years ago I sat down with Jim Ryun in Lawrence, Kansas, in that interim between the world records and the Olympics, that period in which he absolutely ruled the world of track. Since then much has happened. He lost at Mexico City. He lost twice to Marty Liquori, the second time in Miami, when he walked off the track. He quit running. His weight ballooned from 160 pounds to 195. He had married. Soon he would be a father.

But there is an itch in runners. Jim Ryun had run since he was fifteen years old. Stretch out all the miles he's run and he'd circle the globe eight times. Quietly, last May, he began to jog. The jogging quickened. The distances lengthened. Now he is running again, training again, back in a regimen we all once wondered at and then took for granted. He runs some seventy to a hundred miles a week up in Oregon when he isn't running in competition. He runs in brilliant sunshine; the day I saw him in April he ran in heavy rain, a wind so cutting it chilled your bones. I huddled beneath the stands at the University of Oregon outdoor track, and I watched in the wet gloom. Jim Ryun would lower his head and take a convulsive gulp of air, and he would snap his right hand where he held the precious stopwatch, and he would sprint for 330 yards. Then he'd walk 110 yards. Then he'd sprint another 330. Walk 110. Sprint 330. Until he had done this ten times, on an outdoor track in the fading afternoon of a rainy day in Eugene.

Nearby, the University of Washington track squad had just arrived for a dual meet with Oregon the next day. A Huskie runner whined to a coach, "I'll run indoors." No, the coach said. Outdoors. Five laps. "I'll do *ten* laps indoors." No, the coach said. Outdoors. The whining continued, as Jim Ryun kept running by, the slanting rain turning his body into a pale wet sheen, like a birch tree in the spring rain. The first series of ten sprints, ten walks had ended. Now he'd begun a second series. When he finished that, he would run a third series. He had warmed up with seven laps around the quarter-mile track. Finally, when he finished at 5:30 that dark afternoon, he would stand in front of the gymnasium in the pelting rain and wait patiently for his wife to pick him up in their VW squareback. The next morning he'd be up to run before breakfast, along lonely Oregon roads, up pine-studded hills, running.

I flew to Eugene, Oregon, to see about this Jim Ryun, to see this "new" Jim Ryun, to find out why he had come back and if he was a different Jim Ryun from the one I had come to know five years ago.

Over the phone, Jim Ryun had said, "Golly, I don't know. My employer—Bohemia Lumber Company—is awful nice about letting me have time off, but, gosh, I'll have to see. I keep my weekends free for my wife and my daughter. I just don't know."

He called back. Yes, he found time. "And don't bring a raincoat," he sang over the phone. "When it rains here, it's the kind of rain you enjoy being out in."

I flew up, with my raincoat, and I shivered in the rain, as Jim Ryun enjoyed himself. Yet I too enjoyed it. It is a dream of mine. To run like that. Endure like that. I began to think of Munich in 1972. That is how we treat our heroes. That is the cruelty we impose. We insist they live our dreams.

Jim Ryun, unfortunately, makes it easy for us to be cruel. He makes our insatiable demands seem commonplace, our dreams a reality. Brian Glanville's novel *The Olympian* tells about a British youth who is trained to endure pain as a runner by a Mephistophelean coach. The youth breaks the world mile record. He runs in the Olympics but he does not win. He marries; he seems to retire from track for a brief while. He comes back and runs in another Olympics, against a young black runner from Africa. He runs his greatest race, but again he does not win. That is all. Fiction. An author's dream. Yet Jim Ryun has lived it. He laid off track for nearly nineteen months. Then he ran in San Francisco, his first outing, and he won against an inept field in 4:04.4, off by himself. Still, we (I) fretted. Four minutes, 4.4 seconds. Jim Ryun ran again in San Diego, his second time out, and this time he equaled the world indoor record for the mile, 3:56.4. Later he would run in the Kansas Relays, the Glenn Cunningham Mile, and he would win in a smashing 3:55.8, fastest mile in the world in nearly three years. Next he would take on Marty Liquori, the man who beat him the day he quit in Miami.

Jim Ryun is back, living our dreams.

He met me at the airport. "There are a couple of physical differences between now and 1966," he said. We had last talked in '66 after his mile record at Berkeley, and before injuries and illnesses dogged him right up to Mexico City. "I'm not quite as far along in training as I'd like to be because I was out of action all last year. My times are not as fast as I had hoped for in my workouts. I've had a pinched nerve in my calf. I'm a little stiff. I don't have the quickness of 1966. But I'm a lot stronger. I've matured." He put them together, the quickness he lacks because he has not trained enough, and the new strength, and he said, with a quiet confidence, "I feel the physical maturity outbalances the loss of training."

There are two parts of Jim Ryun. One is a modest, self-effacing, almost shy young man, who will never say he is going to win a race or break a record or do anything outstanding. It is the lingering boy in him. The other is an inner man. If there is a real difference between the Jim Ryun of 1966–67 and the Jim Ryun of today, twenty-four years old, it may be that the inner man is coming out more often. Even when he is noncommittal, he seems to commit himself.

You ask him where he intends to run this summer, and he says, "If I were to commit myself to specific competition, the pressure would again become insurmountable." Never—in the old days—had Jim Ryun admitted that pressure truly bothered him. And he does hint at future meets. I told him this article would appear late in June, and he said wistfully, "They'll be running the Nationals up here at Eugene late in June. I'd like to compete." He does more than hint. He ran in Kansas, and immediately announced he'd run against Liquori next, and

Kip Keino, if Keino could make it. He seeks out pressures these days.

You ask him what his personal goals are, and he says, "I don't care to divulge them to anyone except my wife and close friends. The moment I make them known, everyone gets excited. I'm not about to say I'm going to run the first 3:50 mile." Then he adds quietly, "The same desire is still there."

That's divulging a heck of a lot for a man who keeps his goals to himself. You press him further (our demands are insatiable) and you ask whether he expects ever to run back to that 1966 form. His face changes and he cocks his head slightly. A subtle hardness transforms him from boy to man.

"Wouldn't I defeat myself if I thought I was not able to do as well as I once did?"

Is this what Jim Ryun is trying to prove? That he can be as good as he was? Or is it a matter of revenge?

You ask, "Does redemption come into your desire to run again? Are you trying to redeem yourself—for quitting at Miami, for not winning at Mexico City?"

He winces. "It gripes me when people wonder whether I want to 're-deem' myself. I have nothing to redeem myself for."

Yet when you ask what he was thinking when he got ready for his first meet in nineteen months, the mile at San Francisco, he says, "I was more nervous than I'd ever been. I thought about the last time I'd raced, when I walked off the track in Miami. It was on my mind, and it was pretty darn mysterious."

So you think you have pinned him down. Yes, he was trying to redeem himself. Not so, he says, he always thinks of the last race he has run. "The next time I ran, in San Diego, I thought about the race I'd just run in San Francisco. The Miami incident was now closed."

He says. You cannot disbelieve him. He is honest, a young Kansan imbued with the Protestant ethic—honesty, honor, self-sacrifice, modesty, hard work, the whole Puritan philosophy that makes men endure pain not for some elusive goal, but simply to prove themselves fit. Physically fit. Morally fit. You cannot disbelieve him, because he is honest. But you have to wonder. Who ever knows exactly why he does what he does? There is the modest boy who would like to be liked. There is the inner man who desires to triumph. Put the two together and you have a man who runs to win, so he'll be loved. Perhaps this is why Jim Ryun runs. And why I write; and you teach; and she sells; and he engineers; and they play. We must leave a recording behind for people to admire. Didn't Bonnie write poems of her bank-robbing exploits with Clyde and send them off to the newspapers? We can't stay retired; the itch is there, for something—fame, love, applause, acceptance. Is that what we are trying to prove?

What is his goal in track right now? Does he want to run in the 1972 Olympics?

"If at the end of this year I don't want to run, I won't. It's a temptation to run in the next Olympics. But people are not able to comprehend the pressure. The Olympics are like no other meet I ever ran in. I've run in two Olympics."

He has. And lost both times. Once, just a kid, in 1964, shouldered out to the middle of the track in a qualifying race, forced to run twenty yards farther than anybody else, badly beaten. Then in 1968 at Mexico City, running what he calls "a perfectly planned race," yet beaten by fifty yards by Kip Keino's incredible performance. We talk about those races.

"Are you galled by people who keep bringing up the two or three races you lost, rather than the three hundred or so you've won?"

"No," he says. (Nice kid.) "You lose and you win. Losing is an aspect of it."

He talks about the 1968 Olympics with great ease. If it bothers him, you can't see it. He talks about that "perfectly planned race" and its disastrous consequences.

"I never felt such pain as after that. I hurt all over. Chest, head, legs. I was out of it. I remember only pieces of the next fifteen minutes. The idiots—and you can quote me—who said altitude would have no effect on distance were dead wrong. It mattered. I had hoped Keino would run a stupid race, that he would not set a fast pace. Then I'd have a chance to catch him. But he didn't run a stupid race. I wasn't in bad shape after three-quarters—maybe fifty yards behind, in fifth place. I'd won from that distance before. But Keino didn't come back. And I had so much oxygen debt I couldn't do anything. I take nothing away from Keino. He might have won at sea level. But you have to run at altitude twenty-five years to get used to it. It wasn't important we had only four weeks to train. Six months, a year wouldn't have mattered. You still wouldn't have got used to it. When it was over, I went up the entrance ramp, just a slight incline. I felt I was climbing the Empire State Building, on my hands and knees. I barely remember the awards ceremony. I'm not ashamed of that race. I'm proud of it."

He walked over after the awards ceremony to Anne Snider, whom he'd been dating for two years and would marry three months later, and he hung the silver medal about her neck. "I didn't expect him to win at Mexico City," Anne recalls. "I was relieved it was all over. I was pleased he had done as well as he had." But Anne was in tears.

That was Mexico City. He feels there is nothing to redeem. Yet he is tempted to run in the 1972 Olympics, even though the pressure is not comprehensible to us lay folk. It is a meet unlike any other. What is Jim Ryun trying to prove?

And Miami, when he quit in the AAU championships after running six hundred yards? He has said many things about that day. "I don't know. I didn't even know I was doing it. All of a sudden I just found myself off the track. It was a nightmare. . . . I'd been running five years, and I wasn't enjoying myself. I was unhappy and uncertain as to what I wanted to do, and was unable to establish priorities for my wife and myself. . . . I was just about at the end of the rope. I quit because I have to be my own person, my own man. I didn't know what I was doing there in the race. So I just quit. . . . If I had to give an answer, it would have to be pressure. I can't even begin to express what it's like. It wasn't a visible thing. Most of it was inside me. . . . The pace picked up. At that point there was no competitive response, no great desire to run. . . . Yes, I quit in Miami. But I don't think I'm a quitter. . . . All my life I strove for perfection and never achieved it. Not the perfection of winning or setting impossible times, but the perfection of being perfect within yourself."

Today he says he has put Miami away. But he also says, "Miami could be recreated, if I let the pressure get to me. In a sense, it was a good experience. You can learn from your bad experiences."

And what had he learned from that bad experience?

Jim Ryun laughs. It is another difference. He is amused by more things these days. His eyes glint with enjoyment, his mouth curls into ready smiles. What had Miami taught him?

"I learned, one, you shouldn't ever quit. And I learned, two, you'll never be able to explain it to anybody."

Perfection is ceasing to be a real goal, inside or out. Yes, he says, "I am a perfectionist in some ways. I want to do my best. But I dislike the term. It denotes a self-centered person. Put it this way: I want to excel in track and in photography and as a father. I want to excel in all the things I try."

This is Jim Ryun today. He runs seventy to a hundred miles a week. Back in Kansas, Bob Timmons, coach at the U of Kansas and formerly at the high school where Ryun ran, still directs Ryun's training. By mail and by phone, each week the two men correspond, Ryun telling the coach what he's done the prior week and how he felt, and the coach preparing next week's regimen. But this is not all of Jim Ryun's life. When you ask him his goals, you had better specify whether you mean track or life. He distinguishes between the two. "One thing I want," he says, "is to be a good father, a good husband. Happiness is seeing my little girl smile. Happiness is making my wife happy."

He is able to entwine the two goals, running and life. He had said in 1966 that he ran for different reasons at different times. In the beginning, it was a way of life. Then it was to win his letter. Later, the Olympics. Then, travel. Now he says, a bit stiffly, perhaps because it is so personal, "One big motivating force to compete is the desire to share it with my wife. I want her to meet some of the people I have met, experience the excitement I have experienced."

Just as Jim Ryun is shy, Anne Ryun is open, outgoing. She laughs easily, a small fair-haired dimpled girl with a trim figure, an utter delight, the perfect foil for the quiet Jim Ryun. They met on a blind date. Anne Snider was a cheerleader at rival Kansas State; she'd heard about Jim Ryun, what a shy boy he was. She shrugs off things like that. She knows she can open people up. Besides, they had actually met before. Jim Ryun ran his great race at Berkeley, shattering Jazy's mile mark by two seconds, and in the crush that closed in on him somebody stole his track shoes. Ryun was upset. A cute coed pressed up close, asking for his autograph. Curtly, he turned her down. That was Anne Snider. He was anxious to get back to the dorm. "Everybody was trying to rip stuff off my body," he explains. "It's silly. All that adulation. Ripping off my clothes." It humiliates Ryun.

So this first meeting was negative. Bad vibes. Then came the blind date, and Anne Snider found Jim Ryun wasn't particularly shy after all. Anne thinks it isn't shyness so much as the problem of being in the public eye. "Jim had to be cautious. He was more exposed than most people. He always knew what he said and what he did would be recorded."

They dated. They married. Today Anne Ryun says, "He's much more open."

But before the openness came the disaster in Miami, when Jim Ryun stopped running. He'd lost the zest to run. He quit. A world had ended.

"I didn't really retire," Jim Ryun says today. "I stopped my career for a needed rest. Six months later I no longer felt stale. I wanted to return to training, but I couldn't, because of my studies. I needed nineteen hours to graduate."

The Ryuns discussed the question of Jim's resuming training. At dinner and in the evenings, they talked about it. Could they make the time? They knew he'd be coming home terribly tired at night. Anne Ryun was pregnant. She'd be having her baby along about July of 1970. A new baby demands time from both parents. They decided.

On May 18, 1970, Jim Ryun began to jog the streets of Lawrence, Kansas. The first day he jogged three miles; then it was four. Soon it was more. Anne had her baby, Heather. When Anne was up to it, she jogged along. The first time she jogged, she ran two miles, and found it fun.

The tempo picked up. In December the Ryuns moved to the West Coast. They searched for a place to live and a place to work, combing the California coast, beginning in San Diego and hitting Los Angeles, Santa Barbara, and San Francisco before moving into Oregon. In Eugene Jim Ryun, who majored in photojournalism at college, found a small apartment on the outskirts of the city and a job with Bohemia Lumber Company, a conglomerate that makes everything from fence posts to prefabricated modular homes. He says he hates the term "public relations," but that is what he does. He gets on the phone and makes dates for visitors to tour the plant. When he recently went down to run in Australia and New Zealand, he stopped off at Kauai in the Hawaiian Islands, where Bohemia has a plant, and did a photo-story. He is new on the job, and he apologizes when he takes you through the office. "I still don't know all the names of the employees." On the phone to a caller he says, "Oh, golly, I'm afraid I can't answer that. That's too difficult for me to answer. I'm pretty new here." Some things haven't changed.

Other things haven't changed. Yes, he'll take an occasional beer or a glass of wine, but water and Coke remain his favorite drinks. By far. An exciting night out for the Ryuns is a trip to the local pizza parlor. Or maybe a snack at Farrell's Ice Cream Parlour, where a waitress bangs a big drum and stops at a diner's booth while other waitresses throng about to sing 'Happy Birthday to You.' It happened the day Jim Ryun and I had lunch at Farrell's, and Jim Ryun cringed with embarrassment for the poor guy whose birthday it was. Well, that's tough on Jim Ryun. His wife had planned a similar birthday surprise for him at Farrell's at the end of the month.

Some things don't change. His training. The day before I joined him in Eugene, he'd run in the streets for an hour and a half, in one of the worst rains Eugene had ever had on an April day. Naturally he enjoyed it.

His workouts are split into two general types. A sprint workout and a hard distance run. When he runs for distance, he relaxes. "I have a good time. I let my mind go blank." When he sprints, he concentrates. He has to achieve certain times, which he dispatches to Bob Timmons back in Kansas. Timmons digests the material and sends out next week's sked. At first, it was hard. His muscles ached. It's still harder—training is—than it was in 1966. But he adds quickly, "It's not as hard now as it was three months ago." Jim Ryun is coming around.

He also comes around to the theory of pain. Because it is difficult to conceive of anybody submitting himself to the routine of a distance runner, we writers have evolved our own theories of pain, which we hang about the necks of runners like lead medals. Running, we have said, is a dark tunnel with a light at the distant end; men punish themselves in order that they may reach the ever-receding light. Pain, we say, is a barrier which the runner must punch through in order that he gain a mastery of his body. We have said more, and I am not sure any of it is wrong. Jim Ryun thinks most of it is. "I am disgusted with the 'Pain Is the Name of the Game' part of track. So is lifting weights part of the game. So is mental attitude. So is concentration. Pain is secondary. It is not painful. Oh, it is, but it's not. I don't think of pain in literary terms the way writers do. It is *an* aspect of training, but a subtle aspect. I don't think much about it. It's overdone."

Training isn't painful. It is. It isn't. And anyway, it doesn't matter. That is what he seems to be saying.

Anne Ryun says similar things. "Track is a hobby," she says. "But it is a life, too." She lives the life. Jim takes two and a half to three hours out of that life, every day, just to run. "It means no movies or going out at night," she says. "He comes home tired. It's late. We don't eat until eight or eight-thirty. He is tired when he most wants to be full of life." But she does not complain. She has opted for that life. And she submits to her husband when it comes to goals.

"He makes his own. I hope he continues to do what he thinks is right." She has already known the pleasure that comes from his running a fine race. At San Diego, Ryun ran a 3:56.4 his second time out after his comeback. "The morning after," says Anne, "we lay in bed, and I thought back to Miami. *Mmm*, I thought. Quite a change. Oh, it was such a good feeling."

Pain is part of it. But so is pleasure. You run and you win, or you run and you run well, and it makes you feel good. We keep forgetting that part. It makes Jim Ryun feel good. He ran in Kansas, in the Glenn Cunningham Mile, and he won in 3:55.8, and he said, "I think today I indicated I am ready to run."

So what is he trying to prove? He has run since he was fifteen. Now

he is twenty-four. Nine years, with a year off to find the pleasure principle. Maybe he's trying to prove—to himself, to others—that running is
part pain, part pleasure. Like life. He's run back to the first reason he
ever ran when he was a kid. It was a way of life. After nine years it becomes more than a *way* of life. It becomes a life of its own. Part pain,
part pleasure. A universe slips between these extremes. We spend too
much time labeling things. Let it be. He runs. Sit back and enjoy it.
Running has always had a mystique of its own. What does it prove? It
doesn't have to prove. It is. He runs. Once he quit. That was no big
deal. We all quit. I quit a dozen times a day over my typewriter, trying
to avoid it. Housewives dawdle over the TV set to quit facing the iron-
ing board. We all quit. He quit. No big deal. Now he's back. That is a
big deal. He doesn't have to prove anything. He doesn't even have to
win, if we'll permit him. But of course we won't. Our demands are insatiable. Let us take Jim Ryun apart some more. We're good at these
cruelties. See Jim run. Run after him. Rip off his clothes. Those he
wears on his body and those he wears to shield his soul. Strip him
down. Our demands are insatiable. That is the pressure Jim Ryun is
again heading for. I think he knows it. I think he can handle it. I think
he's strong enough now—physically mature, mentally mature—to handle it. God knows, he'd better be.

Muhammad Ali, Then and Now

Dick Schaap | **1971**

In some ways, it seems so long ago: John F. Kennedy was a handsome young senator, starting to campaign for the Presidency of the United States.

In some ways, it seems like yesterday: Richard M. Nixon was starting to campaign for the Presidency of the United States.

It was August 1960 when I first met Cassius Marcellus Clay, when he was eighteen years old and brash and wide-eyed and naïve and shrewd, and now more than a decade has elapsed, and John F. Kennedy is dead, and Richard M. Nixon is President, and those two facts, as well as anything, sum up how much everything has changed, how much everything remains the same.

It is ridiculous, of course, to link Presidents and prizefighters, yet somehow, in this case, it seems strangely logical. When I think back to the late summer of 1960, my most persistent memories are of the two men who wanted to be President and of the boy who wanted to be heavyweight champion of the world.

And he was a boy—a bubbling boy without a serious thought in his head, without a problem that he didn't feel his fists or his wit would eventually solve.

He is so different now. He is so much the same.

We met a few days before he flew from New York to Rome to compete in the 1960 Olympic Games. I was sports editor of *Newsweek* then,
and I was hanging around a Manhattan hotel where the American
Olympic team had assembled, picking up anecdotes and background
material I could use for my long-distance coverage of the Games. I
spent a little time with Bob Boozer, who was on the basketball team,
and with Bo Roberson, a broad jumper who later played football for
the Oakland Raiders, and with Ira Davis, a hop-step-and-jump special-
ist who'd played on the same high-school basketball team with Wilt
Chamberlain and Johnny Sample. And then I heard about Cassius
Clay.

He was a light-heavyweight fresh out of high school in Louisville,
Kentucky, and he had lost only one amateur bout in two years, a decision to a southpaw named Amos Johnson. He was supposed to be one
of the two best pro prospects on the boxing team, he and Wilbert
McClure, a light-middleweight, a college student from Toledo, Ohio. I
offered to show the two of them, and a couple of other American boxers, around New York, to take them up to Harlem and introduce them
to Sugar Ray Robinson. Cassius leaped at the invitation, the chance to
meet his idol, the man whose skills and flamboyance he dreamed of
matching. Sugar Ray meant big money and fancy cars and flashy
women, and if anyone had told Cassius Clay then he would someday
deliberately choose a course of action that scorned those values, the
boy would have laughed and laughed and laughed.

I wasn't just being hospitable, offering to show the boxers around. I
figured I could maybe get lucky and pick up a story. I did. And more.

On the ride uptown, Cassius monopolized the conversation. I forget
his exact words, but I remember the message: I'm great, I'm beautiful,
I'm going to Rome and I'm gonna whip all those cats and then I'm
coming back and turning pro and becoming the champion of the world.
I'd never heard an athlete like him; he had no doubts, no fears, no second thoughts, not an ounce of false humility. "Don't mind him,'he rain-
McClure, amiably. "That's just the way he is."

He was, even then, an original, so outrageously bold he was funny.
We all laughed at him, and he didn't mind the laughter, but rode with
it, using it to feed his ego, to nourish his self-image.

But there was one moment when he wasn't laughing, he wasn't bubbling. When we reached Sugar Ray's bar on Seventh Avenue near
124th Street, Robinson hadn't shown up yet, and Cassius wandered
outside to inspect the sidewalks. At the corner of 125th Street, a black

man, perched on a soap box, was preaching to a small crowd. He was advocating something that sounds remarkably mild today—his message, as I recall, was simply buy black, black goods from black merchants—but Cassius seemed stunned. He couldn't believe that a black man would stand up in public and argue against white America. He shook his head in wonderment. "How can he talk like that?" Cassius said. "Ain't he gonna get in trouble?"

A few minutes later, as a purple Lincoln Continental pulled up in front of the bar, Cassius literally jumped out of his seat. "Here he comes," he shouted. "Here comes the great man Robinson."

I introduced the two of them, and Sugar Ray, in his bored, superior way, autographed a picture of himself, presented it to Cassius, wished the kid luck in the Olympics, smiled and drifted away, handsome and lithe and sparkling.

Cassius clutched the precious picture. "That Sugar Ray, he's something," he said. "Someday *I'm* gonna own two Cadillacs—and a Ford for just getting around in."

I didn't get to Rome for the Olympics, but the reports from the *Newsweek* bureau filtered back to me: Cassius Clay was the unofficial mayor of the Olympic Village, the most friendly and familiar figure among thousands of athletes. He strolled from one national area to the next, spreading greetings and snapping pictures with his box camera. He took hundreds of photographs—of Russians, Chinese, Italians, Ethiopians, of everyone who came within camera range. Reporters from Europe and Asia and Africa tried to provoke him into discussions of racial problems in the United States, but this was eight years before John Carlos and Tommie Smith. Cassius just smiled and danced and flicked a few jabs at the air and said, as if he were George Foreman waving a tiny flag, "Oh, we got problems, man, but we're working 'em out. It's still the bestest country in the world."

He was an innocent, an unsophisticated good-will ambassador, filled with kind words for everyone. Shortly before he won the Olympic light-heavyweight title, he met a visitor to Rome, Floyd Patterson, the only man to win, lose and regain the heavyweight championship of the world, and Cassius commemorated Patterson's visit with one of his earliest poems:

> You can talk about Sweden,
> You can talk about Rome,
> But Rockville Centre's

Floyd Patterson's home.
A lot of people said
That Floyd couldn't fight,
But they should've seen him
On that comeback night. . . .

There was no way Cassius could have conceived that, five years later, in his most savage performance, he would taunt and torture and brutalize Floyd Patterson.

The day Cassius returned from Rome, I met him at New York's Idlewild Airport—it's now called JFK; can you imagine what the odds were against both the fighter and the airport changing their names within five years?—and we set off on a victory tour of the town, a tour that ranged from midtown to Greenwich Village to Harlem.

Cassius was an imposing sight, and not only for his developing light-heavyweight's build, 180 pounds spread like silk over a six-foot-two frame. He was wearing his blue American Olympic blazer, with USA embroidered upon it, and dangling around his neck was his gold Olympic medal, with PUGILATO engraved in it. For forty-eight hours, ever since some Olympic dignitary had draped the medal on him, Cassius had kept it on, awake and asleep. "First time in my life I ever slept on my back," he said. "Had to, or that medal would have cut my chest."

We started off in Times Square, and almost immediately a passerby did a double-take and said, "Say, aren't you Cassius Clay?"

Cassius's eyes opened wide. "Yeah, man," he said. "That's me. How'd you know who I is?"

"I saw you on TV," the man said. "Saw you beat that Pole in the final. Everybody knows who you are."

"Really?" said Cassius, fingering his gold medal. "You really know who I is? That's wonderful."

Dozens of strangers spotted him on Broadway and recognized him, and Cassius filled with delight, spontaneous and natural, thriving on the recognition. "I guess everybody do know who I is," he conceded.

At a penny arcade, Cassius had a bogus newspaper headline printed: CASSIUS SIGNS FOR PATTERSON FIGHT. "Back home," he said, "they'll think it's real. They won't know the difference."

He took three copies of the paper, jammed them into his pocket, and we moved on, to Jack Dempsey's restaurant. "The champ around?" he asked a waiter.

"No, Mr. Dempsey's out of town," the waiter said.

Cassius turned and stared at a glass case, filled with cheesecakes. "What are them?" he asked the waiter.

"Cheesecakes."

"Do you have to eat the whole thing," Cassius said, "or can you just get a little piece?"

Cassius got a little piece of cheesecake, a glass of milk and a roast beef sandwich. When the check arrived and I reached for it, he asked to see it. He looked and handed it back; the three items came to something like two and a half dollars. "Man," he said. "That's too much money. We coulda gone next door"—there was a Nedick's hot dog stand down the block—"and had a lot more to eat for a whole lot less money."

From Dempsey's, we went to Birdland, a jazz spot that died in the 1960s, and as we stood at the bar—with Cassius holding a Coke "and put a drop of whisky in it"—someone recognized him. "You're Cassius Clay, aren't you?" the man said.

"You know who I is, too?" said Cassius.

Later, in a cab heading toward Greenwich Village, Cassius confessed, at great length, that he certainly must be famous. "Why," he said, leaning forward and tapping the cab driver on the shoulder, "I bet even you know that I'm Cassius Clay, the great fighter."

"Sure, Mac," said the cabbie, and Cassius accepted that as positive identification.

In Greenwich Village, in front of a coffeehouse, he turned to a young man who had a goatee and long hair and asked, "Man, where do all them beatniks hang out?"

In Harlem, after a stroll along Seventh Avenue, Cassius paused in a tavern, and some girl there knew who he was, too. She came over to him and twirled his gold medal in her fingers and said that she wouldn't mind if Cassius took her home. *We* took her home, the three of us in a cab. We stopped in front of her home, a dark building on a dark Harlem street, and Cassius went to walk her to her door. "Take your time," I said. "I'm in no hurry. I'll wait with the cab."

He was back in thirty seconds.

"That was quick," I said.

"Man," he said, "I'm in training. I can't fool around with no girls."

Finally, deep into the morning, we wound up at Cassius's hotel room, a suite in the Waldorf Towers, courtesy of a Louisville businessman who hoped someday to manage the fighter. We were roughly halfway between the suites of Douglas MacArthur and Herbert Hoover, and Cassius knew who one of them was.

For an hour, Cassius showed me pictures he had taken in Rome, and then he gave me a bedroom and said goodnight. "Cassius," I said, "you're gonna have to explain to my wife tomorrow why I didn't get home tonight."

"You mean," said Cassius, "your *wife* knows who I is, too?"

A few months later, after he turned professional, I traveled to Louisville to spend a few days with Cassius and write a story about him. In those days, we couldn't go together to the downtown restaurants in Louisville, so we ate each night at the same place, a small restaurant in the black section of town. Every night, Cassius ordered the same main course, a two-pound sirloin, which intrigued me because nothing larger than a one-pound sirloin was listed on the menu.

"How'd you know they served two-pound steaks?" I asked him the third or fourth night.

"Man," he said, "when I found out you were coming down here, I went in and told them to order some."

In the few months since Jack Dempsey's, Cassius had discovered the magic of expense accounts.

But he was still as ebullient, as unaffected, as cocky and as winning as he had been as an amateur. He was as quick with a needle as he was with his fists. One afternoon, we were driving down one of the main streets of Louisville, and I stopped for a traffic light. There was a pretty white girl standing on the corner. I looked at her, turned to Cassius and said, "Hey, that's pretty nice."

Cassius whipped around. "You crazy, man?" he said. "You can get electrocuted for that! A Jew looking at a white girl in Kentucky!"

In 1961, his first year as a professional, while he was building a string of victories against unknowns, Cassius came to New York for a visit with his mother, his father and his younger brother, Rudolph. Rudy was the Clay the Louisville schoolteachers favored; he was quiet, polite, obedient. Later, as Rahaman Ali, he became the more militant, the more openly bitter, of the brothers.

I took the Clays to dinner at Leone's, an Italian restaurant that caters partly to sports people and mostly to tourists. To titillate the tourists, Leone's puts out on the dinner table a huge bowl filled with fruit. Cassius took one look at the bowl of fruit, asked his mother for the large pocketbook she was carrying and began throwing the fruit into the pocketbook. "Don't want to waste any of this," he said.

The first course was prosciutto and melon, and Cassius recoiled. "Ham!" he said. "We don't eat ham. We don't eat any pork things." I knew he wasn't kosher, and I assumed he was stating a personal preference. Of course, Muslims don't eat pork, and perhaps his Muslim training had already begun. I still suspect, however, that he simply didn't like pork.

After dinner, we went out in a used Cadillac Cassius had purchased with part of the bonus he received for turning pro (sponsored by nine Louisville and one New York businessmen, all white), and Cassius asked me to drive around town. On Second Avenue, in the area that later became known as the East Village, I pulled into a gas station. It was a snowy night, and after the attendant, a husky black man, had filled the gas tank, he started to clean off the front window. "Tell him it's good enough, and we'll go," I said to Cassius.

"Hey, man," Cassius said. "It's good enough, and we'll go."

The big black man glowered at Cassius. "Who's doing this?" he said. "You or me?"

Cassius slouched down. "You the boss, man," he said. "You the boss."

The attendant took his time wiping off the front windshield and the back. "Hey, Cash," I said, "I thought you told me you were the greatest fighter in the world. How come you're afraid of that guy?"

"You kidding?" said Clay. "He looks like Sonny Liston, man."

During the middle 1960s, when Cassius soared to the top of the heavyweight division, I drifted away from sports for a while, covering instead politics and murders and riots and lesser diversions. I didn't get to see any of his title fights, except in theaters, and, of course, I didn't see him. But our paths crossed early in 1964; by then, as city editor of the New York *Herald Tribune,* I was very much interested in the emerging Black Muslim movement. At first, I didn't know that Cassius was, too.

Through a contact within the Muslim organization, I learned that Cassius, while training in Miami for his first title fight with Sonny Liston, had flown to New York with Malcolm X and had addressed a Muslim rally in Harlem. As far as anyone knew, that was his first commitment to the Muslims, although he had earlier attended a Muslim meeting with Bill White and Curt Flood, the baseball players (all three attended out of curiosity), and he had been seen in the company of Malcolm X (but so had Martin Luther King).

When the *Herald-Tribune* decided to break the story of Clay's official connection with the Muslims, I tried to reach him by telephone half a dozen times for him to confirm or deny or withhold comment on the story. I left messages, explaining why I was calling, and I never heard from him. The story broke, and I heard from mutual acquaintances that Cassius was angry.

The first time I saw him after that—by then, he had adopted the name Muhammad Ali—he was cool, but the next time, in St. Louis, where he was addressing a Muslim group, he was as friendly as he had ever been. He quoted Allah, he paid tribute to the Honorable Elijah Muhammad yet he still answered to the nickname "Cash." He even insulted me a few times, a sure sign that he was no longer angry.

He had been stripped of his heavyweight title, and he was fighting through the courts his conviction for refusing induction into the armed forces. I could see him changing, but it was never the words he mouthed that signified the change. His logic was often upside-down, his reasoning faulty, and yet, despite that, he had acquired a new dignity. The words didn't make any difference; the actions did. He had taken a dangerously costly step because of something he believed in. I might not share his belief or fathom the way he arrived at that belief, but still I had to respect the way he followed through on his beliefs, the way he refused to cry about what he was losing.

Yet it was during this period, when I sympathized with his stand, when I found that some segments of the sportswriting world were exhibiting more venom, more stupidity and more inaccuracies than I had thought even they were capable of, that Muhammad took the only step of his career I deeply resent. He turned his back on Malcolm X.

I don't know the reasoning. I don't know why he chose Elijah Muhammad over Malcolm X in the dispute between the leader of the Muslims and his most prominent disciple. I can't, therefore, say flatly that he made the wrong choice, even though I believe he made the wrong choice; Malcolm was a gifted man, an articulate and compassionate man. But I can say that Muhammad showed, for the one time in his life, a totally brutal personal—away from the ring—side. It is brutal to turn on a friend without one word of explanation, without one word of regret, with only blind obedience to the whims of a leader. I have tried, since then, to bring up the subject of Malcolm X with Muhammad Ali several times, and, always, he has tuned out. His expressive face has turned blank. His enthusiasm has turned to dullness. Maybe he is embarrassed. He should be.

During Muhammad's forty-three months away from the ring, I bumped into him occasionally and found him still to be the only professional fighter who was personally both likable and exciting. (Floyd Patterson and Jose Torres, for example, are likable, but not often personally exciting; Ingemar Johansson was exciting.) At one point, David Merrick, the theatrical producer, professed an interest in sponsoring a legal battle to get Muhammad back his New York State boxing license; Merrick wanted to promote an Ali fight in New York for a worthy cause, which was not, in this case, David Merrick.

I arranged a meeting between the two, and Muhammad swept into Merrick's office and stopped, stunned by the decor, the entire room done in red and black. "Man," said Muhammad, "you got to be part black to have a place like this. You sure you ain't black?"

It was the only time I ever saw David Merrick attempt to be charming.

The legal fight never materialized, not through Merrick, and Muhammad continued his road tour, speaking on college campuses, appearing in a short-lived Broadway play, serving as a drama critic, reviewing *The Great White Hope* for *Life*. One night, I accompanied him to a taping of the Merv Griffin Show—he was a regular on the talk-show circuit—and during the show, outlining his Muslim philosophy, he spoke of his belief in whites sticking with whites and blacks with blacks.

Afterward, as we emerged from the studio, he was engulfed by admirers, calling him "Champ" and pleading for his autograph. He stopped and signed and signed and signed, still soaking as happily in recognition as he had almost a decade earlier, and finally—because he was late for an appointment—I grabbed one arm and my wife grabbed the other and we tried to shepherd him away. He took about five steps and then looked at my wife and said, "Didn't you hear what I said about whites with whites and blacks with blacks?"

She dropped his arm and Muhammad laughed and danced away, like a man relishing a role.

In the fall of 1969, when the New York Mets finished their championship baseball season in Chicago, Muhammad and I and Tom Seaver had dinner one night at a quiet restaurant called the Red Carpet, a place that demanded a tie of every patron except the dethroned heavyweight champion.

The conversation was loud and animated, dominated by Muhammad as always, and about halfway through the meal, pausing for breath, he turned to Seaver and said, "Hey, you a nice fella. You a sportswriter?"

When we left the restaurant, we climbed into Muhammad's car, an Eldorado coupe, pink with white upholstery, with two telephones. Two telephones in a coupe! "C'mon, man," he said to Seaver. "Use the phone. Where's your wife? In New York? Well, call her up and say hello."

Seaver hesitated, and Muhammad said, "I'll place the call. What's your number?"

Seaver gave Muhammad the phone number, and Muhammad reached the mobile operator and placed the call, and when Nancy Seaver picked up the phone, she heard a deep voice boom, "This is the baddest cat in the world, and I'm with your husband and five hookers."

Nancy Seaver laughed. Her husband had told her he was having dinner with the champ.

Later, we returned to my hotel room, and after a few questions about his physical condition, Muhammad took off his suit jacket and his shirt and began shadow-boxing in front of a full-length mirror. For fifteen straight minutes, he shadow-boxed, letting out "Whoosh, whoosh," the punches whistling, a dazzling display of footwork and stamina and sheer unbelievable speed, all the time telling Seaver his life story, his religious beliefs and his future plans.

"I never saw anything like that in my life," said Seaver afterward.

Neither had anyone else.

A few weeks later in the fall of 1969, Muhammad appeared as a guest on a sports-talk show, a show in which I served each week as sub-host and willing straight man for Joe Namath. For each show, we had one sports guest and one non-sports guest, and that week Muhammad was joined by George Segal, the actor.

After the interview with Muhammad, Joe and I began chatting with Segal, and the subject of nudity came up. Segal had just finished filming a nude or semi-nude scene with Barbra Streisand in *The Owl and the Pussycat.* As the conversation about nudity began Muhammad visibly stiffened. "What's the matter?" Joe said. "How you feel about that, Muhammad?"

Muhammad's reaction was immediate. He was affronted and insulted. He was a minister, and he did not know that the show was going to deal with such blasphemy, and he was about to walk off the stage rather than join in, or even tolerate, such talk.

"Aw, c'mon," Joe said.

Muhammad sat uncomfortably through the remainder of the show, punctuating his distaste with winces and grimaces. It made for a very exciting show, and when it was over, Joe and I both sort of apologized to Muhammad for embarrassing him. "I gotta act like that," Muhammad explained. "You know, the FBI might be listening, or the CIA, or somebody like that."

He is now twenty-nine years old. He has been a professional fighter for a full decade, and he has fought thirty-one times, and he has never been beaten.

On March 8, he faces Joe Frazier, who has also never been beaten, who is younger, who is considerably more single-minded. Logic is on Frazier's side. Reason is on Frazier's side.

But logic and reason have never been Muhammad Ali's strong suits. They were never Cassius Clay's either. His game always will be emotion and charm and vitality and showmanship.

Eight weeks before the night of the Frazier fight, the telephone rang in my bedroom late one night. I picked it up. "Hello," I said.

"The *champion* of the world," said the caller. "I'm back from the dead."

I hope so. The man-child should be the heavyweight champion of the world. It is the only role he was born to play.

70.20
9.00
$74.00

31.00   LEFT
22.00   PAY
25.00   JEFF
78.00

4. PR FR PAIR SOCKS

25.00

1 2 1
16.50
4.95
4.95
$26.40

1   1
27.00
1.50
1.75
30.2?

2.00

3.00

4.00

91.90

8.00
25.00
22.00
41.00